THE MOUNTAIN ENCYCLOPEDIA

THE MOUNTAIN

Frederic V. Hartemann and

ENCYCLOPEDIA

An A–Z
Compendium
of More Than
2,300
Terms, Concepts,
Ideas, and
People

Robert Hauptman

Illustrated with drawings, art, maps, and more than four hundred color photographs by Ansel Adams, Jonathan Adams, Pat Ament, Frédéric and Emanuel André, Kevin Barton, Albert Bierstadt, Nelson Chenkin, Frederic Edwin Church, Jeremy Frimer, Max Giraud, Gary Goldenberg, Fred Hartemann, Judy Hedding, Russ Heinl, Nasrollah Kasraian, Andy Kerry, Reinhold Messner, Rudolf Prott, Frank Sanders, Debbie Santa Maria, John Shively, Ido and Herma Spaan, Jeff Stahler, Pierre Tairraz, Jim White, Gregory Yanagihara, Gary Yates, Steve Zinsli, and many others

With a Foreword by Jamling Tenzing Norgay

The Scarecrow Press, Inc.

Lanham, Maryland · Toronto · Oxford

2005

SCARECROW PRESS, INC.

Published in the United States of America
by Scarecrow Press, Inc.
A wholly owned subsidinary of The Rowman & Littlefield Publishing Group, Inc.
4501 Forbes Boulevard, Suite 200, Lanham, Maryland 20706
www.scarecrowpress.com

PO Box 317
Oxford
OX2 9RU, UK

A paperback edition of *The Mountain Encyclopedia* is available from Taylor Trade Publishing.

British Library Cataloguing-in-Publication Information Available

Library of Congress Cataloging-in-Publication Data

Hartemann, Frederic, 1960-
  The mountain encyclopedia : an a-z compendium of more than 2,300 terms, concepts,
ideas, and people / Frederic V. Hartemann and Robert Hauptman.
      p. cm.
  Includes bibliographical references (p.   ).
  ISBN 0-8108-5056-7 (hardcover : alk. paper)
  1. Mountains—Encyclopedias. I. Hauptman, Robert. II. Title.
GB500.5.H37 2005
551.43'2'03—dc22

                           2004008539

I have given my whole life to the mountains.
LIONEL TERRAY

This book is for Debbie and Bernard, and for Terry and Kira

CONTENTS

BLACK AND WHITE FIGURES: CAPTIONS AND CREDITS

Photos

Drawings

SIDEBARS AND TABLES

FOREWORD

Beginning with the first ascent of Mont Blanc by Balmat and Paccard in 1786, continuing with the epochal conquest of the Matterhorn by Whymper in 1865, and culminating with the first climb of the world's highest peak, Mt. Everest, by Sir Edmund Hillary and my father, Tenzing Norgay, half a century ago, mountaineering has long been one of the most inspiring endeavors in human activities. Beyond the sheer joy of climbing, the amazing beauty of the landscape, the depth of challenge presented by these formidable "hills," as the Victorians called them, the tender colors of dawn and the terrible roar of avalanches, mountains represent a unique realm, full of animal and plant life, that has inspired religions, the arts, legends, and science. Mountains mirror human life and provide a path to enlightenment, through physical and mental challenges, through the fragile beauty of a butterfly in the morning winds and the grandiose fury of a thunderstorm on a high ridge; this books attempts, successfully, to give the reader a taste of the mountains, one of the last outposts where Nature reigns supreme.

The vastness of the mountain landscape, both literal and allegoric, is aptly presented in this wonderful book: from the science of volcanoes to the music of the mountains; from the techniques of ice climbing to the poetry of a moonrise over a high ridge; from the snow leopard to satellite cartography; from haunting tragedies to sheer triumph; innumerable aspects of the high realm are presented in detail, along with beautiful color photographs and maps. Sidebars add a very educative and entertaining dimension to the book.

Therefore, it is most opportune that fifty years after the first ascent of Everest, the goddess of all mountains, *The Mountain Encyclopedia* will be published, a fitting tribute to the magical realm where I followed my father's soul.

JAMLING TENZING NORGAY
Kathmandu, May 29, 2003

PREFACE

Encyclopedic compilations exist for virtually all disciplines and topics. Surprisingly, there is no general, comprehensive English-language reference work available on the mountain and the terminology used to clarify its features and influences, despite the innumerable volumes given over to descriptions and extraordinary illustrations of individual examples. This lacuna is remedied with the publication of *The Mountain Encyclopedia*, which is intended to serve two purposes. First, it is an alphabetically arranged overview of all things connected to mountains; if a person encounters a term, concept, or peak not included or explicated in a dictionary or general encyclopedia, then he or she can turn to these pages for a definition or explanation. Second, despite the arrangement, one can read straight through, from cover to cover, and emerge with a thorough understanding of the etiology, evolution, and demise of mountains as well as their influence on plants, animals, and human beings.

The earth's diverse geological development has resulted in thousands of separate peaks, ranges, chains, and systems, and because these are so important in human history, many of them have been named. It would be impossible to mention each one in a concise overview and so the authors have included only the most important ones in the body; the appendix does offer a fairly comprehensive list. Huxley's *Standard Encyclopedia of the World's Mountains*, *The Columbia Gazetteer*, or the index to any good world atlas as well as many excellent websites (included in appendix H, Websites) may provide additional examples and their locations. The same may be said for explorers, surveyors, mountaineers, rock climbers, skiers, and snowboarders. There are so many of these well-known people that it would be inappropriate to attempt to squeeze all of them into this volume. Instead only the most influential are noted here. Others may be sought in biographical dictionaries, histories of particular regions or sports, accounts, and memoirs, some of which are included in the present volume's bibliography. (See especially Huxley's *Standard Encyclopedia* for about one hundred capsule biographies, Unsworth's *Encyclopaedia of Mountaineering* for almost four hundred important early climbers, and Child's *Climbing*. Also useful is the website www.simpkin57.freeserve.co.uk/mountain_lakes_books/whoswho/whoswhodetails.html.) Finally, there are so many species of animals, birds, flowers, trees, and other life-forms that only a limited number of the most important are favored with individual entries.

Most terms are defined where they fall in the alphabetical listing; in some cases, though, a cross-reference leads either to a more appropriate term or an additional brief though comprehensive essay. There are a few of these detailed overviews (for example, on climbing, clothing, ethics, mountain building, or weather), and they exist because the concept under discussion is too complex for concise definition or explanation. Thus, although the rock or ice climbing and mountaineering entries briefly clarify these endeavors, the overview presented under climbing sets them in a general context.

Finally, we would like to point out that many entries and factual data derive directly from the authors' experience: studying, reading, traveling, logging, skiing, hiking, bouldering, rock and ice climbing, mountaineering, and observing and participating in nature. Indeed, we have traveled extensively to document this book, including trips to numerous national parks, both in the United States and Canada; to exotic locales, such as Hawaii, the Coast Range of British Columbia, and New Zealand; and to closer regions, including the Cascade and Wind River Ranges. For more than two years, we have traveled by foot, on float planes, or by helicopter for the purpose of bringing information, photographs, or even film clips to our documentation; in addition, we have used previously gathered materials and contacted a number of friends and mountain enthusiasts to try to provide as wide and deep a view of our subject as possible. As for the rest, information was confirmed or discovered through general or purposeful reading, viewing, or consulting of the material noted in the reference list. Credit is given in the text whenever required.

ACKNOWLEDGMENTS

We would like to present our heartfelt thanks to the many people who helped us with this project: first and foremost, our editors, Kim Tabor and Lynn Weber; Marc-Antoine Hartemann (M-A. H.) for some seventy-five entries and for acting as our contact point in Europe; Jonathan Adams, Kay Anderson, Frédéric and Emanuel André, Kevin Barton, Niklas Bergendal, Hartmut Bielefeldt, Nelson Chenkin, Jeremy Frimer, Roman Garba, Max Giraud, Gary Goldenberg, Judy Hedding (Phoenix Guide), Russ Heinl, Chiam Chye Heng, Nasrollah Kasraian, Graham Jones, Andy Kerry, Dean Lofquist, Manvel Melikian, Reinhold Messner, Ricardo Montayo, Carsten Nebel, Rudolf Prott, Frank Sanders (Devils Tower Lodge), Frank Sauer, Jan Schmidt, John Shively, Ido and Herma Spaan, Fred Spicker, Debbie Santa Maria, Josef Stranner, Pierre and Marie Tairraz, Tao, Surat Toimastov, Jim White, Rudolf Willing, Gregory Yanagihara, Gary Yates, and Steve Zinsli for their superb photographs; Laura Lindblad, Marie Madgwick, and Jeff Stahler (Cincinnati *Post*) for the drawings; Randy Hankins (Black Diamond) for the many images he provided; John Rutter (*National Geographic* magazine) for his kind words and the Everest map; Patrick Zook for his helpful remarks; Fran Loft and Elaine Perkins for their kindness at the American Alpine Club (AAC) library; Joan O'Driscoll and Debbie Josephson of St. Cloud State University's (SCSU) Interlibrary Loan Office for acquiring an avalanche of books; Mary Schrode (SCSU) for image digitization; Plamen Miltenoff (SCSU) for CD reproduction; Lloyd Athearn (AAC), Greg Glade, Pat Ament, and Chuck Nelson (SCSU) for reading the manuscript and making many valuable suggestions; Stephen Brown (Proteus Workshop) for image digitization; Kate Long and Margaret Ecclestone (Alpine Club) for their help with the engravings by Edward Whymper; Dianna Delling (*Outside* magazine); Alain Carbon (IGN); Leonie Rubiano-Moncada (*National Geographic* magazine); Rhea Stewart (Maxx Images, Inc.); Sylvia Inwood (Detroit Institute of Art); Ruth Ennemoser; Ed Viesturs; Lynn Hill; Sir Christian Bonington; Maekus Hauser; Alexandra Kappler (The Huntington Library Art Collections); Sandra Wiskari-Lukowski (Metropolitan Museum of Art); Karen Christenson (Portland Art Museum); Shane Winser and Justin Hobson (Royal Geographical Society); Barbara Goldstein Wood (National Gallery of Art); Tony Mohr; Heidi Müller; Francine Lauber; Matthias Fredriksson; Jessica Poblete and Anais Maroon (Corbis); Kin Plett (*Outside* magazine); Maura Peters (United Media); Claire Gosson (Canada Natural Resources); Mark Burrows (Peakware); Debra Hornsby (Banff Mountain Film Festival); last but not least, Jamling Tenzing Norgay for writing the foreword and Norbu Tenzing Norgay for helping us coordinate the foreword.

In addition, we have benefited from the direct or indirect (web) help from many organizations, including AbleStock; the Argentina Government Tourist Information; Canada Natural Resources; Corbis; Google; the Institut Géographique National (IGN); NASA; the Office du Tourisme La Grave-La Meije; Peakware; the USGS, and U.S. National Parks.

EXPLANATORY NOTE

The entry words in the alphabetical list are **bolded**. When a term mentioned in the text has its *own* entry in the alphabetical list and is particulary relevant, it too is often bolded. Foreign terms commonly used in English are cross-referenced to their English equivalents. The foreign word follows the English and these abbreviations indicate the source: C=Chinese, F=French, G=German, H=Hawaiian, I=Italian, Ic=Icelandic, N=Nepali, S=Spanish, Sc=Scottish, T=Tibetan, W=Welsh. Fl., in lieu of birth and death dates, indicates that a person flourished in his or her activity at about this time. Authors' names, noted in the text parenthetically for scholarly ascription, along with titles for additional information, and in the sidebars are included in the reference list at the end of the volume. The photographs were chosen based on one of three criteria: importance of the mountain; necessity to illustrate a feature (gully, butte) or a device (piton); or some special quality (beauty, danger, historical importance, uniqueness). Photographs are reproduced with the permission of their creators and are acknowledged below each image. Snowboarding jargon is limited to the most important terms. Finally, even today, there is some discrepancy in the recorded altitudes of the world's mountains; different sources may offer slightly different elevations. Nevertheless, whenever possible, we have striven to provide consistent altitudes throughout; these are the most common in the literature. (The altitudes noted on a few historical black and white photographs are inaccurate.)

INTRODUCTION

Why do we love mountains so? Maybe one should imagine a world without them to realize how close to our hearts and minds the high peaks have come to be. . . . In any event, I thought it would be appropriate to give a brief essay describing my first personal contact with the mountains, in hope of further motivating the reader to go out and enjoy the wonderful (and eventful!) realm of the mountains.

For each of us, the transition from daily routine to extraordinary achievements yields a wonderful sense of accomplishment; this is particularly true of physical endeavors, when our rational thoughts give way to the "zone," often experienced by professional athletes; when being and survival become our dominant mode of perception; when our evolved minds regress to the delightful feeling of simply besting ourselves, in a physical, immediate manner. This does not necessarily imply record-breaking performance, or Olympic feats; it just corresponds to our very own sense of physical achievement, no matter how insignificant for the *Guinness Book of World Records*, *Who Wants to Be a Millionaire?*, or the Hall of Fame: for my father, who was diagnosed with Parkinson's disease long ago, at the young age of forty-two, walking two blocks along the busy sidewalks of Paris to bring back home two baguettes, a "baba au rhum" (my Dad's favorite), and a "religieuse au chocolat" (my Mom's favorite) was his own Annapurna, to paraphrase Maurice Herzog.

Within my own modest climbing abilities, my most difficult climb was arguably the Col Est du Pelvoux, a notorious 2,000-foot, 55- to 65-degree, sustained ice couloir in the southern French Alps, in the Oisans Range, across the exquisitely beautiful, almost Himalayan, 4,102-meter (13,458 ft) Barre des Écrins. There, I discovered the true spiritual depth and strength of climbing, as the enterprise also proved to be my closest encounter with my own mortality, and a genuine near-miss situation developed.

As a graduate student in physics at the University of Paris, on the Orsay campus, my time was unequally divided between climbing and studying relativity and quantum mechanics; interlopers included girls, movies, friends and food, and my family. Each Sunday, when the Parisian weather proved dry enough, we would hit the climbs of Fontainebleau, scrambling up the highly technical, but small (10- to 30-foot) boulders strewn over sand, fifty miles southeast of the city.

What I loved most about these training climbs was the camaraderie and the actual, practical intelligence involved: some of these boulders were only 10 feet high, but the key to a successful climb (what we called "topping"), was a particular move, a subtle shift of balance, a tentative extension toward an often-guessed or intuited, rather than known, anchor point. Often, a group of fellow students would gather under a particularly hard boulder, and we would all offer words of advice to the lone climber, trying to resolve the nonlinear dynamics and discover the poetry of an especially challenging move, with the "graduates" trying to summarize their own experience in a few helpful tips, while we novices (I always felt I belonged in that category) were thinking out loud our own strategies to conquer each vertical inch of the challenging object, each hoping that the current climber would demonstrate the validity, or lack thereof, of our reasoning. In most cases, a simple jump off the boulder, with a prior careful evaluation of the sand below, would be the logical response to a privately unsolvable problem.

Sometimes, for extremely difficult climbs, a veritable group of disciples would assemble under a short cliff, where a twenty-five-year-old "sage," with international following like a rock-and-roll star, was seeking the epiphany of the rock; it reminded me without fail of the Greek philosophers and their students: a problem, concrete and immediate (the boulder), was presented to our group; solutions were proposed, both by the climber and by the assembly, sitting and discussing the problem at hand in the warm sand; solutions were tried, in real time, by the philosopher; each inch gained upward moved our group closer to the technical truth of this particular rock. We quickly found that climbing challenges, just like scientific theories, and possibly democracies, are forever layered in ever-increasing, ever-encompassing, strata of knowledge: no matter how good you are, or think you are, there is always another challenge. I believe this to be the true essence of science, athleticism, and life in general; furthermore, this very nature of our human condition is precisely what makes it a boundless, exciting, extraordinary, and ultimately blessed condition: each of us has her own challenges; each of us can better himself, always.

As for the easier boulders involved, part of the training was to top them quickly, with a minimum exertion of energy, climbing with our feet (not our arms!), and running in the sand to the next rock face. We all knew that the pure technical level reached at Fontainebleau had to be lowered by one to three grades (i.e., from 5.11 to 5.10 or even 5.8) when climbing in the Alps, with heavy mountaineering boots and thousands of feet of "air" beneath them! In any event, it was a wonderful distraction from our technical studies (I found, and keep finding through my reading of the climbing literature, that a large number of technically, intellectually, philosophically, and/or scientifically inclined people tend to form the bulk of the recreational, or-not-so with the current "extreme" sport fashion, climbing originals [i.e., in the early days of REI]; reciprocally, a number of pure climbers, such as Reinhold Messner, Edmund Hillary, Maurice Herzog, George Leigh Mallory, or Edward Whymper, have often written essays of a deep philosophical nature).

It was also a demanding sport, involving technique and focus. When applied in its natural high-mountain arena, climbing requires one to carefully control one's own fears: there is an element of balance between our atavistic reaction to danger, heights, void; the overwhelming presence of the elements; and the technical, as well as psychological factoring of the environment in terms of a more reasoned assessment of the situation at hand. I have often found this private conquest of one's own fears to be a deeply satisfying aspect of climbing: three deliberate, measured steps on a narrow, steep snow ridge, with careful attention paid to the overhanging cornices and the slow dynamics of background clouds lying in the distance over the Swiss Alps, have proven to be the very best, most alive time I ever spent with my brother Olivier, who was leading our two-man *cordée* (team) on the sensational ridge spanning the void between the Aiguille de Bionassay and the Dôme du Goûter! I will always remember walking above the clouds at sunrise, in the frigid blue sky, with the perspective of Mont Blanc in the north, along the Arête de Bionassay, after seven hours and over 4,000 vertical feet of technical climbing spent fighting the ice slowly cascading down the northwest face, deep in the darkness of a predawn summer day. Each step on that ridge was a small intellectual victory, where we considered only our immediate, local environment, with a simple move forward, abstracting the immense, light blue and green, glistening, seductive void of the surrounding ice slopes, 70 degrees down to France, and 50 degrees on the Italian side; the ridge was no wider than 10 inches at places, and over a mile long!

Back to Mare Frigoris, my very near miss—but first, a difficult situation in Switzerland. One year, I decided that after my final exams I would spend an extended period of time climbing; my reasoning was that I would gain both further physical conditioning and acclimatization by hiking around and summitting various peaks in the Alps, and by doing so for at least three weeks uninterrupted. My first outing that year, in early June, and following a successful traverse of Mont Blanc (at 4,807 m, or 15,771 ft, the highest point in western Europe) with my brother Olivier and the Chamonix guide Serge Trezamini, two years earlier, was to climb the

Lenzspitze, a 14,000-footer east of Zermatt, high above the ski resort of Saas-Fee, where the towering masses of the Dom (14,911 ft) and nearby Taschhorn frame an exceptional landscape of angular ridges, steep ice couloirs, and cascading glaciers. My companion students Laurent Terray (no direct relation with Lionel) and Alain Magneville and I drove from Paris to Saas-Fee for twelve hours straight; the crossing of the border into Switzerland was fast and easy, as I recall, and the weather looked good.

We were climbing between exams, and our time was limited; therefore, after an uneventful night spent sleeping on the concrete steps of a ski-lift station (French students could hardly afford the very dear housing prices in Swiss hotels in a ski resort area), we immediately set out to climb to the refuge high above Saas-Fee. Paris lies approximately 100 feet above sea level, while Saas-Fee's altitude is 6,000 feet; the refuge is another 5,900 feet above Saas-Fee. We climbed nearly 12,000 feet in thirty-six hours: not good. Reaching the hut was a major accomplishment for at least two reasons: first and foremost, the sheer elevation of the hut, with no acclimatization whatsoever; second, the carrying of a 45-pound pack over 5,900 vertical feet, within six hours. I remember that a number of sections along the trail were either obstructed by deep snow or so steep that a steel cable was running down the path; this did not afford much protection when climbing unroped, with a heavy pack, no excess red cells, little sleep, and physics exam weariness, not to mention the usual state of "girl trouble" that seemed to be highly pervasive for our group in those days!

Well, we made it up the hill, and reached the refuge; as all things Swiss, the place was incredibly clean . . . and locked! This happened last century, so I feel almost okay in admitting that we used our ice axes to get the lock open; as it turned out, this was but a minor infraction along the way. We spent the evening fighting insidious headaches, eating crushed food, drinking vast quantities of fluids, and discussing the climb. The Lenzspitze has a beautiful, classic, 55-degree northeast ice slope, followed by an equally esthetic traverse leading back to the hut; we had traveled over 500 miles, quite a bit for western Europe, to experience the pristine snow on this wide, protected couloir, which we had first learned

about "au Vieux Campeur" (at the Old Camper's), by reading the available Alpine literature. The northeast face of the Lenzspitze had looked mighty impressive then; the flaming red upper slopes, burning in the gorgeous sunset, now loomed high above us, an awe-inspiring challenge.

The next morning, well before sunrise, we all had a bit of lukewarm tea and got ready for the climb. The hut sits on a fairly narrow ridge overlooking Saas-Fee; the western side delineates a rough, heckled glacier, with a foreboding icefall plunging toward the rising sun, in the direction of the Weissmies. Our objective lay straight ahead, a mile to the west of the refuge. I roped up with Laurent and Alain, and we proceeded across the level glacier toward the prominent Lenzspitze "rimaye" (*bergschrund*). Most crevasses were buried under the deep, late spring snows, and ice bridges were pretty good; within two hours, we reached the bottom of the route. I remember spending some time with them looking for a snow bridge across the rimaye, which was four to eight feet wide, translucent and blue-green, and well over 100 feet deep. At 5 A.M., near sunrise, when we reached the bottom of the slope, ice and snow flurries were already ominously coming down the icy slope every few minutes. This looked very bad to me; in addition, high altitude was clouding my concentration, and my energy level had not recovered from the previous day's 5,900-vertical-foot, 45-pound-backpack sherpa-ing. I decided that I should not attempt the 2,000-foot, 55-degree ice slope, especially in view of the fact that I could dangerously slow down the efforts of my climbing partners on this avalanche-prone couloir: any delay at the base of the Lenzspitze slope was translating into increased snow, ice, and stonefall danger for my comrades, as its southwest orientation made it particularly vulnerable to early heating from the sun, destabilizing the couloir by heating the delicate ice crystals.

However, the decision to turn back and return to the refuge was equally difficult: I was to cross the same rough, "blind" (snow-covered) glacier, at a later time of day when the snow bridges would be softer and much more unsafe, alone, as this was quite early in the season, and we had not met a soul on our way up. "Alone" is key here, as anyone familiar with glacier travel will understand: when traveling on this crevasse-ridden terrain, roping up is of paramount importance, as it both protects one from unforeseen, shallow falls into ice gaps, and prevents accidents in the deep, tortured terrain characterizing icefalls, overhanging séracs, and rimayes. However, in my experience, the most important role played by roping up on a glacier is the fact that party members can identify the whereabouts of any climber at all times; in particular, if one were to fall in a crevasse, the rest of the team would be immediately notified. This proves to be a critical factor in numerous climbing accidents, where a team member can freeze to death anonymously in a crevasse, simply because the other team members are unaware of her condition. In fact, as will be amply demonstrated in our accounts, one of the leading causes of accident and death on the mountain is the separation of the team members, as exemplified by the incredible odyssey of Beck Weathers during the 1996 Rob Hall expedition on Everest, or by the impossible adventure of Joe Simpson, as related in *Touching the Void*. This became quite clear to me as I bade farewell to my climbing companions, who were now negotiating an ephemeral snow bridge across the fateful *bergschrund*: as I proceeded east, I felt as lonely as if I had been walking on the moon; very soon, I started worrying about hidden crevasses, and decided to systematically probe each and every suspicious undulation of the terrain with my ice ax. I was painfully aware that my crossing this tortured, early-season glacier alone implied the very real possibility of dying a very slow death, deep in a crevasse, slowly freezing as my companions felt the elation of victory on their way back to the refuge, 200 feet above, in the glory of the setting sun!

This cautious frame of mind took some care to maintain because of the sheer beauty of the sun rising over the Weissmies, coloring the glacier in deep, wonderful hues of blue, pink, red, orange, and vermilion; furthermore, each color transition corresponded to an increased and welcomed warmth provided by the slanted sun rays, making my glacier traverse both an intensely scary, lonely experience, and one of the most fabulous spectacles I have ever had the joy and privilege to behold and experience. If I so much as slipped into a crevasse, my death could be early, colorful, lonely, and ex-

tremely slow, as long as I didn't first shatter my neck bouncing on the green ice of a Swiss crevasse, 12,000 feet above my stamping ground; on the other hand, my very solitude enhanced my experience to a near epiphany. It took me well over six hours to get back to the refuge, as I witnessed the advance of the mountain shadows from Austria to France, across Western Europe, along with momentous historical milestones!

I settled back down in my sleeping bag, as the sun's warmth proved feeble in comparison with the deep cold of an early June day; I then located the emergency radio, just in case. Hours passed, and the orange light of late afternoon flooded the refuge. I was expecting Laurent and Alain anytime now. So far, I had simply been waiting for the normal, reasonable amount of time required to perform the climb of the Lenzspitze and the traverse back down to elapse; since my friends started around 5:30 A.M., I expected a twelve-hour delay to be appropriate. Well before sunset, which was to occur near 9 P.M., I started to wonder about my friends' whereabouts. After an hour or so, around 8 P.M., I used the emergency radio for the first time; I was a bit shy, as I had no idea whom I would contact, and which language (German or French) they would use; furthermore, I had no real emergency to declare, just an uneasy feeling about Laurent and Alain being late. The first words I heard were definitely German, but the Saas-Fee police officer quickly switched into Valaisan French, and after a brief heads-up instructed me to go up across the glacier to the bottom of the slope to verify that my friends had not fallen down the Lenzspitze slope! This was quite a shock to me because there was no way I was going to wander alone on this glacier again, especially under the oblique light of sunset, and because I deeply feared that there was a distinct possibility that I would have to approach the slope to identify the mangled bodies of my friends after a 2,000-foot fall on a 55-degree ice slope! Still, after some instructions from the police officer, I very reluctantly set out to cross the glacier alone again.

I moved very carefully on the very soft snow, and used my morning footprints as a guide; all the time, the Lenzspitze *bergschrund* was hidden from my view due to the slight uphill slope of the glacier, and I knew full well that if my friends had fallen, their bodies would most likely had been swallowed by the crevasse, or would have flown right over the rimaye, to the upper glacier slopes. As I slowly moved upward in the setting sun, my field of vision opened up toward the *bergschrund*, and I became very fearful of what I might see: what would I do faced with the tattered bodies of my very good friends? Would I even muster enough energy to climb back down to the refuge and alert the Swiss authorities? So there I was, moving up on that wretched glacier, hoping that I would see nothing at the bottom of the big slope facing east at the upper end of the ice. In the dim light of sunset, I reached the *bergschrund*, and saw nothing but the usual avalanche debris. Relieved, I now faced the prospect of crossing the very glacier I had scaled alone that morning, this time in the twilight of an early June sunset; crevasses were as open as they would be this time of year, and snow bridges were destroyed. Somehow, I got down fast; I guess that the urgency of the situation gave me wings. When I reached the refuge, it was dark and cold; my friends were up in the mountain, somewhere. After reporting to the police officer, who instructed me to wait until dawn, I spent a miserable, very lonely night. I was to lead a mountain rescue effort at dawn, but I had to make the decision (legal and financial, as was clearly explained to me) to trigger the search.

I did not sleep; I hoped and wished that my friends would show up, tired, exhausted, but okay. When I lapsed into drowsiness, the harrowing wind would wake me, scratching at the window, muttering an SOS that echoed deep within my sleepy mind; startled awake, I remembered with saddening clarity the precarious situation of my friends, up and deep on the mountain, in that same howling wind, our tenuous connection through the difficult night. Their return did not happen; at dawn, I was still alone and called back on the emergency radio. A helicopter would be launched, as long as I took the legal and financial responsibility of making the call. Since my friends would be, at best and if alive, incapable of getting back down on their own after a night above 13,000 feet, with temperatures dropping to 10 or 20 degrees Fahrenheit, the call was easier than I thought. I waited for the helicopter, hoping against hope that my friends would show up. The helicopter arrived after half an hour; as

soon as they landed, the pilot asked me to board the aircraft to help them locate my friends; at the very same time, two indistinct points appeared in the morning mist, up on the glacier. The points were definitely moving down slope; however, they were also moving transversely over an extremely wide berth, and it seemed unlikely to us that these points corresponded to human beings.

Time stopped. We all looked up in the haze, trying to make out the exact movements of these shapeless forms; sometimes they would vanish behind the deep blue glaze of a small sérac. The early, flaming sun rays were also playing tricks on our eyes, illuminating the glacial mist with vermilion flares, deep purple ghosts wavering on the ice. Our shadows had a clear purpose, however: unlike the dawn's early phantoms, these shapes were going down, straight down, if you averaged out the fancy meandering imposed by the glacial flow and the restless fatigue of a high-altitude, impromptu bivouac.

I rushed up in the fog, catching Laurent, whose frostbitten face looked harrowed and stunned; he had used most of his considerable strength to get back to the refuge, where he knew that he could surrender to fatigue, at least for a few precious hours of sleep. He did not know how far behind Alain was. We guided him into the relative warmth of the hut, when a second ghost appeared. This time, Alain was wavering across the ice, thin and nearly disembodied, jaws tightened, every step down reflected in a considerable lateral motion, balance an elusive instinct chemically wired to guide Alain's inner ear. He collapsed near the refuge, and a Swiss Zermatt guide helped me direct him toward a low wood bench, by the refuge.

We had avoided the worst; however, I had to think fast, as the helicopter pilot was getting ready to take the rescue team down. I knew full well that my friends would require at least a full day to recover from their ordeal; furthermore, at the altitude of the refuge, it was not clear how much longer this process would take. In fact, I was quite worried that between the adverse effects of the bivouac at high altitude, including some fairly severe frostbite, and their general fatigue, my friends would simply not be capable of negotiating the steep, iced, cable-ridden footpath down to Saas-Fee, especially carrying the heavy backpacks that we had hauled up. I asked the helicopter pilot to take them down; I was to climb down on my own, and catch up with them in Saas-Fee later. He told me that was okay, but I was to go down with them, being the only person in our party capable of signing the various insurance release documents: my friends, considered quite lucky to have survived, were incapable of carrying on any conversation beyond two or three words. Various heavy accents did not help either!

The pilot was to drop us down first, and then fly back up to pick up the other members of the rescue party. Our aircraft was a small French-built Alouette helicopter, capable of carrying three people, plus the pilot. I boarded the cabin, sitting next to the pilot; during the whole episode, he had kept the helicopter running, and he took off as I latched my safety belt. The aircraft gently rotated toward the Weissmies in the east; then, the horizon flipped right, and we started falling toward the valley, faster, closer to the arduous slopes I had climbed a mere two days ago. The early sun promptly disappeared behind the jagged ridge to the east, and, as I was fighting the nauseating feeling triggered by my ruffled inner ears and welling up deep in my stomach, we turned west again, the foreboding mass of the Dom towering above us, its chaotic glacier flowing by. We landed with the hard precision characterizing experienced, Alpine piloting. I got out first, and helped my staggering friends; I also got our gear on the concrete. As I was pulling the last backpack out, the pilot had a clipboard with the insurance paperwork ready; I knew we were deep in the Valais, but talk about Swiss efficiency! I signed the form, and the pilot signed off: he was high above Saas-Fee within seconds. This had been my very first time in a helicopter, and quite a physical experience. I was a bit disoriented, both horizontally and vertically, and my stomach wasn't happy either; however, this paled in comparison with the state of my friends, frostbitten, fairly severely wind- and sunburned, tired beyond simple exhaustion, dehydrated, and incapable of swallowing solid food, at least for now.

It was 8 A.M., and our situation was unclear. Sunday morning, everything was closed; furthermore, the skiing season was long over, and tourists did not frequent the Swiss Alps for recreational reasons

until the end of the month, July and August being favorites for this crowd, as well as the European families in search of good, healthy fun along the steep, scenic paths of the Valaisan Alps. Making things worse, I did not know how to drive, so it was up to either Laurent or Alain to get us down; the road to the Rhône valley was steep, curvy, and narrow. Swiss engineers were the best: they could build roads that would make the highways in the Rockies, the "Old Priest Road" in the California Sierras near Yosemite, or French roads anywhere look like spacious freeways, with slow inclines and a deep respect for one's inner ear and digestive tract. I suspect that many paths around the world easily compare with these engineering feats, but unlike our Swiss expressway, I do not believe that these are designed for anything but climbers and yak; they certainly are not covered with macadam, and do not appear on topographical maps as continuous lines!

We decided that a few hours of sleep were needed for all of us, especially for Alain and Laurent; I dozed off for half an hour, then went around the village looking for a bakery to buy food and possibly drinks. Word of our rescue had gone around quickly, as I found when accosted by an old lady, the guardian of the refuge. She knew we had spent a couple of nights up there, and decided it was time to collect her duties; to her credit, she first briefly inquired about the status of my friends: apparently, had they been dead, she would have waived their dues! I did not argue with her: she was the widow of a famous Swiss guide, and the refuge was, apparently, one of her main sources of money. I paid $100 for one of the very, very worst nights of my life. I did ask her about the fact that the refuge was nominally closed when we used it, and she explained that the winter refuge was open; what she did not know was that we had used our ice axes to force the padlock left on the door to the summer refuge (I assume that she became aware of this fact a few weeks later, after her slow hike up to 12,000 feet).

We did receive a hefty bill from the Swiss rescue services: approximately $1,000 each. Fortunately, Laurent and I had insurance from the CAF (Club Alpin Français); Alain was not registered at the time, and, in his weakened state, we had him swear that he would apply immediately upon his return in Paris. In the meantime, we told the Swiss authorities that he had lost his ID, and registered him under the thinly veiled pseudonym of Alain Sartres! He never received a bill.

I found a small store open and bought almond croissants, as they like in Valais, water, and Orangina with what little money I had left. My friends, upon awakening, had what they deemed the best meal of their young lives; they promptly dozed off again. I walked around the village some more, people accosting me and asking questions about our climb, the mountains, and my friends; some were a bit puzzled about such an early attempt of the Lenzspitze. Our lack of information about the general climbing conditions in the area was becoming painfully clear, and I learned a crucial lesson: snow, ice, altitude, weather, conditioning, and acclimatization mattered. My friends very nearly lost their lives because of our cavalier attitudes and general ignorance.

Later in the day, the sun revived Laurent and Alain; they were ready to leave this foreboding place at once! Laurent started driving down, and we quickly reached the sun-drenched Rhône Valley and its many villages among beautiful vineyards under the towering Alps. Glaciers gleamed in the distance, and the frozen snows of altitude faded near the horizon. Lake Geneva was in front of us, a silvery surface glittering under the afternoon sun, where Rousseau and Voltaire had argued; where physicists were smashing atoms and discovering the subtleties of the electroweak interaction at the great ring of CERN, where some of us hoped to build a career after graduation; where the United Nations tried to resolve pressing international matters in the idyllic landscape framed by the Alps and the Jura.

At the border with France, our luck ran out: the dismal appearance of my friends, after a bivouac at high altitude, the smell of fear and sweat, and our rambling explanations convinced the Swiss border patrol that a full search of our car was in order; this included the spare tire, as well as places in the car unknown to most mankind, including serious mechanics; these guys were also nasty. The only drugs we had were adrenaline and a number of endorphins, all naturally generated, courtesy of our vari-

ous states of exhaustion, general tiredness, high-altitude fatigue, sleeplessness, and overall agitation. Reluctantly, the Swiss border patrol let us go, after a solid hour's search. Thirty yards down the road, on the French side, the *douaniers* were laughing their heads off! We sailed through, immediately after they asked us, very slowly, very deliberately: "Anything-to-de-cla-re?" and roared with laughter, again!

Our drive back to Paris was fairly uneventful until we reached Mâcon, in Burgundy: the car, an old BMW that belonged to Alain, who was now driving, began swerving across the *route nationale* (equivalent to a state road); we had elected to avoid the turnpike because my friends were extremely tired by now. Earlier on, we had to ask Alain to stop for a while, a couple of times, as he was visibly starting to doze off behind the wheel. I felt pretty bad about my inability to drive, as I was, by far, in the best shape of us three! The swerving continued; in fact, it increased, but Alain, after three espressos, was very awake. This went on for another fifty miles or so; then, the car suddenly jerked off to the left. Alain was struggling with the steering wheel, and I looked toward the back of the car: the right rear tire had blown off! Alain got the car under control and parked it on the breakdown lane: after escaping a lonely, frigid death high up the mountains, Alain's lack of attention to the maintenance of his aging car had almost cost our lives! That was too much, and we had a high-level, impromptu session of scream therapy! Within a half hour, composures were reestablished, though ego bruising was prevalent among our crew; we resumed our course toward Paris.

The exact facts about my friends' desperate night, in the harrowing winds of high altitude, were also revealed during this long, painful, slow drive back to Paris. The climb of the ice slope had been considerably lengthened by the extreme softness of the snow after a few hours of sun: each step up required a painful struggle, and the crampons were all but useless; the ice axes were barely affording any safety, as they dug through dull, melting snow covering what turned out to be a deadly sheet of black ice! Ice screws were nearly useless for protection, as the black ice was near impenetrable, and the surface snow an inconsequential, unstable layer of mush. My friends summitted the great Lenzspitze face near sundown, and immediately started along the heavily corniced summit ridge, trying to reach a reasonable bivouac before night. The ridge turned out to be much more technically challenging than described in the literature; this might have been partially due to the snow conditions, and to my friends' fatigue after their struggle on the 2,000-foot, 50-degree slope in deteriorating conditions. It took them hours to cover a quarter mile on the narrow ridge, having to climb around numerous "gendarmes" and precarious rock spires; they must have strayed from the main line in the dimming twilight, as they had to surmount technical steps in the 5.8 range, in the increasingly hostile wind. They reached the next intermediate 13,000-foot summit at 10 P.M., toward the Nadelhorn, and had to decide whether to bivouac on the ridge or try to climb down, away from the normal route, directly across the east face of the peak, down to the glacier. This face, a mixed battleground of steep rock gullies and overhanging séracs, a maze of short couloirs and zigzagging buttresses, was considered extremely dangerous and exposed as a day climb; in the dark of night, with failing flashlights, it would have been suicide for my exhausted friends!

In the cold, howling wind, without any bivouac gear, Laurent and Alain opted to go down, fast. Laurent, by far the more experienced climber, would lead and set belays; Alain would follow. They went at it until 2 A.M., climbing down extremely steep and precarious iced gullies, outlining horrendous precipices, blindly following the east face of the mountain, under the Nadelhorn, without any path. More than once, they dead-ended over insurmountable, overhanging ice faces and had to climb back up, in the dark of night, to try another way toward the glacier. The average slope of this face exceeds 60 degrees; it was therefore impossible for them to find any reasonable platform where they could have waited a couple of hours for the first guiding light of an early June day. They kept going until Alain weakened to the point where he was dangerously slowing down Laurent's progress; at that fateful moment, Laurent decided to unrope and keep climbing down the treacherous terrain without any protection. Alain, alone and frightened, resolved to follow Laurent down the steep gully; this spelled disaster: exhausted and disoriented, he stepped over

the strap of his crampons, and started sliding down on the ice, dislodging rocks as he gained momentum.

Laurent heard the gathering avalanche and looked up; realizing what was happening, he dug his ice ax deep into the frozen snow and prepared to help Alain, who was now tumbling down the couloir, out of control. Unroped, the probability of Laurent arresting Alain's fall was very slim; furthermore, it was a one-shot deal. Astoundingly, it worked, and Alain suffered minor bruises, although he was, understandably, very badly shaken. They roped back up, and continued down, trying to keep moving to maintain a small level of warmth; for Alain, this was imperative, as the bruises and cuts and his general state of shock threatened to cramp up his muscles. He was, according to Laurent, shaking and shivering nearly uncontrollably for the next five hours. Further minor miracles occurred, and they reached the upper reaches of the glacier in the pale gray light delineating the earth's shadow at the time before dawn when the turbulent air rushes between night and day, and the cold is deepest. They staggered toward camp, and reached the refuge at the very time we were ready to take off for a rescue operation. In retrospect, it is amazing that they were able to drive us back 500 miles within another sixteen hours.

In case you wonder, we all passed our exams with flying colors!

Later on that very summer, Laurent, myself, my brother Olivier, and a couple of friends from the university decided to go to Chamonix for what we thought would be three weeks of sustained climbing on the wonderful granite spires of the formidable Mont Blanc range, the highest in Western Europe. Continued bad weather and a high avalanche risk due to the foehn, that southern wind bringing tiny specks of reddish Saharan sand across the Mediterranean and coloring the upper glacial snowfields to produce the deepest reds and most vibrant crimsons on the western slopes at sunset, forced us to change our plans. Alain was already in the Oisans range, at his folks' ski chalet in Puy-St.-Vincent, so we decided to go south, to look for better weather and solid climbs. This turned out to be a fateful decision.

The road from Chamonix to the Oisans range takes one through the Vanoise region, with its pristine flower fields and low-altitude alps; further up, large glaciers shimmer under the crisp, cold skies of the high realm. Most notable along the way are Mt. Pourri, literally the rotten mountain, so-called because of its infamous unstable ridges, and the elegant Grande Casse, near the ski resorts of Val d'Isère and Tignes; two high passes mark the way south: the Iseran Pass, well over 9,000 feet, and the Galibier Pass, near 9,000 feet. The view to the south from the Galibier is breathtaking: due south, the distinctive summit ridge of the Barre des Écrins dominates the horizon; slightly to the west, but incredibly close, are the summits of the 3,983-meter (13,068 ft) Meije, connected by a complex, intricate system of ridges, buttresses, and suspended glaciers. The very summit ridge of the Meije is extremely steep and jagged, and the Doigt de Dieu, the Finger of God, marks the most abrupt point of the crest; the finger itself is a mighty overhang, a terrible place to be caught by a storm, as lightning repeatedly strikes the chiseled rocks, and no fast way down exists on this extremely exposed ridge. The south face is a 2,500-foot wall of rock terminating on an extremely isolated glacier in one of the most desolate valleys in Europe.

A few more pleasant miles on a warm road take us past Briançon, an old city with a beautiful fort built by Vauban in the seventeenth century, to Vallouise and Puy-St.-Vincent. The area is quite different in character from Chamonix: more southern and laidback, with a larger climber-to-tourist ratio; hitchhiking is a safe and efficient way to travel in the valley, as people are used to climbers with big summit dreams and small pockets.

We hook up with Alain, and spend a nice evening at his parents' chalet; as there are too many of us, we find a local inn that caters to climbers and their particular budgetary constraints: the place is pretty, very clean, and we share bunk beds like in a refuge. That night, we discuss our climbing plans: Laurent is very excited by the Col Est du Pelvoux, a difficult technical ice climb, approximately 2,000 feet of sustained 60- to 65-degree hard ice. The others are less than enthusiastic, but I find myself tempted by the elegant route, although I am concerned by the fact that the lower part of the climb, while relatively easy, is exposed to rock and icefalls from the west fork of the couloir. Laurent reminds me that

we would not climb the west fork, as it terminates under a suspended glacier, making the ascent extremely difficult; instead, we would opt for the east fork, which is more sustained, but slightly easier: the maximum slope reaches a strong 65 degrees, whereas some pitches on the hanging glacier reach 75 to 80 degrees! Laurent and I agree that if we were to attempt this route, we would leave extremely early, around 1 A.M., to minimize the rock and icefall danger, as the night freeze would help maintain the precarious balance of embedded stones and séracs; this implied that we would bivouac on the main glacier under the couloir to be ready to go as quickly as possible. The irony behind our careful plans would soon reveal itself.

The next day, I found myself on the terminal moraine of the Glacier Noir, the Black Glacier, at the end of a warm afternoon, my backpack filled up with technical equipment: crampons, two ice axes, carabiners, rope, loops, ice screws, and other climbing paraphernalia. The Glacier Noir is, indeed, black: it is almost entirely covered with moraines, rocks, stones, debris, and sand; this is in sharp contrast with the Glacier Blanc (the White Glacier), which stands on the north side of the Barre des Écrins, immaculate snowfields lazily undulating between the high ridges, before tumbling toward the icefall. A number of marmots followed our slow progress up along the path, hoping for some food, either now, through our good will, or later by rummaging through our camp, while we slept!

One of the most striking features of the Glacier Noir is the ominous, nearly continuous wall of the north faces, spanning over two miles above 12,000 feet, from the Pelvoux to the triple summit of the Ailefroide. The north faces of the Glacier Noir compare favorably with the legendary faces nord d'Argentières: couloirs of la Verte, Couturier and Cordier; the impossibly vertical, 3,500-foot ice and mixed wall of the Droites; the classic Courtes; and the pure lines of the north face routes on the Aiguille du Triolet. The sheer desolation of the Glacier Noir cirque is hard to describe: it truly is a deep feeling that the climber must rationalize in order to mentally prepare for a successful ascent on one of the many challenging routes, zigzagging on the steep walls, under the awesome sentinel that is the south pillar of the Barre des Écrins, an 8,000-foot climb cresting near 13,500 feet in the rarefied air of high altitude. On the Glacier Noir, retreat is typically a difficult proposition: the precipitous nature of most of the routes makes a climb down an almost impossible task; the desolation of the site and its remoteness result in a challenging trek to the closest village, Ailefroide, via unfrequented glaciers and isolated valleys. Therefore, most of the routes require a high level of commitment from the climbers. Locking the mouth of the glacial cirque, directly across from the south pillar of the Barre, the Pelvoux stands, a mute vigil, its complex rock walls riddled with vertical ice couloirs and hanging glaciers, under the huge séracs of the summit ice field. Walking into the Glacier Noir cirque feels a lot like entering a sacred place, where Nature rules as a powerful, capricious god.

We quickly found that the best bivouac site for us was a somewhat flat, sandy area near a large boulder affording some protection against the biting wind. The sporadic rumbling of avalanches kept reminding us of the danger of our climb: we had to start as early as possible to take advantage of the relative protection offered by the night freeze; we agreed to leave between midnight and 1 A.M. We didn't sleep much that night: adrenaline was already building in our blood, and the anticipation of a difficult climb in such an extraordinary sanctuary was nearly overwhelming. Stars were illuminating the night, and the ghostly appearance of the north faces under the pale, wavering light was burning an indelible picture in my memory. The night was relatively cold, and the wind helped cement stones and debris in the ice, high above our bivouac.

At 11:30 P.M., we were starting our short trek toward the lower slopes of the couloir; the ragged appearance of the glacier, strewn with boulders and huge chunks of ice, was far from reassuring. We also noted well-defined gullies, approximately two feet wide and up to six feet deep, where the debris falling from high above was obviously channeled during the avalanches. We quickly devised a strategy: we would avoid these gullies as much as possible, and would proceed very fast when crossing one of them. As the terrain was not terribly steep, we were not roped up, which made for a brisk pace. Most of the crevasses were fairly obvious, and we found good snow bridges on the glacier. We felt that luck was with us; all the descriptions of the climbs that we had read were very clear: the avalanche and rockfall danger was almost nil after the *bergschrund*, and we were now moving quickly on the dangerous lower part of the climb. Over the next hour, we did experience three or four major falls, but they were well channeled through one of the gullies, and save for the deafening roar and rush of cold air accompanying these avalanches, no problems were encountered up to that point. We were happy that our climb would take us to the other side of the mountain, as it was difficult to imagine how bad this area would become under the hot sun of the day.

During our second hour of climbing, we started to encounter increasingly steep terrain and were forced to negotiate a few short, steep ice walls. With the front-point crampons and the ice axes, this proved relatively easy, as we had trained in the winter on frozen waterfalls; we decided to rope up after topping a 15-foot wall, where a fall would have been problematic, to say the least. After a few more twists and turns on the lower glacier, the rimaye appeared over us.

We looked around. We were already surprisingly high above the Glacier Noir, and the gigantic south pillar of the Barre des Écrins took its full perspective: only very strong, highly qualified climbers should attempt this precipitous route, with a height of over a mile and a half! The ominous look of the north faces was subtly accentuated by the pale starlight as we prepared for the more technical part of our climb; at least, we thought, the avalanche danger was over! We roped up, double-checked our crampons and harnesses: the rope would be our only safety in this new world of nearly vertical ice, gleaming under the night sky. We were alone.

The serious night and our immediate contact with the mineral world helped us focus on our task: first cross the rimaye, then climb, as efficiently as possible, the 2,000-foot ice slope, to the point where the crest meets the sky, high above. The *bergschrund* looked deeper and wider after each step we took. It was going to be a very serious challenge. The center of the crevasse was over 10 feet wide, and the upper lip was over 4 feet above the rimaye: impassable. The right-hand side looked bad too, as it essentially merged into a sheer rock spur, with no place to go; we were left with the left-hand side of the *bergschrund, a sinistra,* as the Romans said. There, the width of the crevasse was manageable, of the order of 4 feet, and the slope started 2 to 3 feet above the gaping hole; however, the ice was immediately extremely steep on this side of the couloir: 75 degrees for the first 50 feet, progressively easing down to the announced 65-degree ice further up. We were definitely going to jump-start this climb! To compound the problem, the ice proved to be extremely hard at our point of attack: after crossing the gap, we found that our ice axes and the front points of our crampons would bite by less than a quarter inch with a reasonable effort; any further front pointing would have resulted in such a taxing exercise that we would have been totally exhausted after two or three pitches. We traded safety for energy, and started moving up on the curving wall, like tentative spiders. Fifty feet above the rimaye, I looked down between my legs: the lower glacier cascaded down toward the moraine, the slope evanescing into the crevasse with a frighteningly elegant curve; this was the big league!

Laurent was heading our *cordée* and climbing fairly fast, still adjusting to the very steep, hard ice. He was setting an anchor point with an ice screw every 30 feet, and installed a strong belay at the end of our first pitch. I was relieved to be able to start moving up, as keeping a steady position on the slope proved quite difficult: the only way to relax the calf muscles was to pitch each ice ax at arm's length, and to rely on the short rope connecting the ax to the harness to support my weight; in this fashion, I could pull away from the slope and shift my weight from my legs to the anchor points of the ice axes. Believe me, this requires a fair amount of trust in your equipment and technique when practiced at night, high above the Glacier Noir, on steep ice! In addition, the ice axes complement the anchor provided by ice screws at a belay.

One of the most difficult tasks for me, as the second climber, was to dislodge the ice screws set by the lead climber, Laurent. The ice being so hard made it difficult to set those screws in the first place; the ice would then refreeze over the metal, forcing me to hammer at the screws to remove them. Again, this is a non-trivial enterprise, when performed under the conditions we were in. When

I fought hard to get the ice screws, I sometimes accidentally pushed myself away from the slope, dangling on the rope belayed by Laurent.

On the positive side, the rock and icefalls had indeed stopped after we had crossed the *bergschrund*, and we were quickly gaining altitude as we sharpened our technique. The sun was still below the horizon, but streams of purple and green already illuminated the eastern sky, overwhelming the fragile stars; the dawn wind started to pick up, dancing between the walls of our ice couloir. Far below, the glacier groaned and strained, pushing its way under unknown tons of rocks, under the eternal pull of gravity.

That's when we first noticed a stream of small ice particles gliding down the slope; not much bigger than grains of sand, they fell almost gently, like very cold snow. We were, however, somewhat preoccupied by this telltale sign of a possible avalanche, and tried to divine the exact provenance of the ice droplets. Furthermore, the couloir was extremely exposed, and the two vertical rock pillars delineating the ice slope offered little or no protection. We kept on going, keeping close attention to the now constant stream of ice dust.

For a while, nothing more happened; we climbed, and the routine of establishing belays, using the ice axes and crampons, and inching up on the great slope became more and more like an automatism. Under these circumstances, it is of paramount importance to keep one's mind alert, as the combined effects of the altitude, physical effort, emotional stress, and the monotony of the task tend to induce a sensory state somewhat akin to the "zoning" experienced by athletes, but which can prove dangerous for climbers who need to keep monitoring their surroundings for signs of trouble, including bad weather, avalanches, or hidden crevasses.

An hour or so later, as the summit ridge of the Barre des Écrins was beginning to shimmer into a deep red hue under the ultraviolet sky, we noticed that the sweeping ice droplets had grown in size, and were accompanied by tiny chunks of rock. The mineral rain was also more steady, an unmistakably ominous sign. We were now quite puzzled: the climbing guide books had been absolutely, unanimously clear about the fact that the eastern spur of the couloir, although quite steep and sustained, was not exposed to avalanches: one could "relax" after the initial climb under the *bergschrund* and focus on the technical aspects of the ascent. What, then, were those constant, miniature slides? Had we mistakenly started to climb on the dangerous west fork of the couloir? After quickly checking our bearings, the answer was a clear no! The situation was both mysterious and frightening, as we still had a huge climb ahead of us, and the air was rapidly warming up in the first glancing rays of the sun!

Then came the bullets: larger pieces of rock and ice started to pour down on us, ricocheting on the hard ice, spinning up and whizzing by with incredible speed. The noise was terrifying, as the small pebbles sounded exactly like stray bullets in a war movie; their trajectories were completely unpredictable, as they would slam hard on the ice and rebound in a totally different direction at 250 miles per hour! We were now in a desperate situation, as the couloir exploded with the fury of ten thousand guns, randomly shooting deadly projectiles! We had no choice but to keep climbing, trying to dodge the horrendous stones, hoping to stay alive in the murderous rain.

Our helmets were constantly drumming under the ice pellets, and we could hardly communicate, precariously inching up on the 65-degree ice. But I heard Laurent yelling, "There comes a huge one! Lookout!" By the time I looked up, a mere fraction of a second, the 200-pound chunk of rock had bounced on the ice again, and traversed 100 feet of void, now rushing by Laurent and heading straight for me. All I could do to avoid a certain death was to slam my body against the ice, letting myself hang from my ice axes, and hoping that my backpack was not protruding far enough to intercept the furious rock. Given the sheer momentum of the falling body, any contact would mean that I would be hurled down to my death, the shock transmitted by the rope taking Laurent along. If it touched my helmet, I would be decapitated; if it met my backpack, it would fling me off the slope, like a spider on a wall.

Silence.

The tingling of adrenaline was all over my body; I realized that I still was alive. Fear had not had time to engulf me. Then it came, wave after wave of nausea, tremors dancing along my limbs, teeth chattering, a dearticulated puppet hanging on an awesome ice slope, in the Glacier Noir's sanctuary of death! I wanted to go down now, away, quickly, badly. At the same time I could not move; the dire reality of our situation was slowly percolating through my shocked brain: we were completely helpless, another stone could come at any time and take us, another story on TV, two more young climbers buried on the mountains. . . .

And we still did not know why or how this happened: we were supposed to be on the "safe" part of the climb! That's when we first heard the Spaniards, high above us: "Piedra! Piedra!" Immediately, we looked up: more thunder, more fear, more stones hurling down at us! Again, we trusted our anchors, and let ourselves hang on the slope, waiting, waiting, waiting excruciatingly.

Remember to breathe, I told myself, gather yourself! "Laurent, I can't climb anymore—just go!" was all I could say. I simply gave up, accepting my fate: I had gambled and lost, this climb was too much for me, and I was going to pay the ultimate price. At this fateful time, Laurent demonstrated the most astonishing psychological insight: he transformed my fear into anger; he sublimed my terror into sheer survival instinct. He made me murderously mad at the party above us: they had triggered the ice and rockfalls! We knew that at the very end of the couloir, a slightly unstable, mixed passage of ice and rock was the last hurdle on the climb; what happened was suddenly, painfully clear: the avalanches were man-made!

Our strategy was exceedingly simple: we were going to race up the 65-degree ice to catch up with the bastards and make them pay dearly; we had ice axes, plenty of adrenalin, and barely cared anymore! We started with astonishing speed, cursing at the top of our lungs in the rarefied air. Our goal was extremely pointed: their blood on the pristine ice, their fear to exorcise ours.

It worked: the trembling in my calves was all but gone; my lungs were burning the sharp air; I was climbing so fast that the rope had enormous slack. Belays were barely respected, and we maneuvered the rope with exquisite efficiency, borne from the deadly poison of extreme fear transmuted into agonizing wrath. The Spaniards got the message: a veritable race on steep ice ensued. In a matter of minutes, it seems, we hit the rock band near the top of the couloir; seconds later, we crested the Col Est du Pelvoux. In front of us lay the desolate Glacier de Sialouze; we could see forever, and no humans were in sight. It was 2 P.M., several hours later; we were alive and unhurt. Fear, and fear alone had saved us all.

The Col Est, so fierce looking on the Glacier Noir side, is a simple accident of terrain between the mighty Pelvoux and the 3,915-meter, 12,845-foot Pic sans Nom, the Peak with No Name. Further along the ridge to the Ailefroide, the prodigious Coup de Sabre, literally, the Saber's Slash, and numerous secondary summits mark the seal of Nature, the uncontested ruler of this realm.

Going down, gathering our physical and psychological strengths, life seems more than precious; miraculous, indeed. Our weak, tiny bodies feel nearly immaterial against a vast, mineral background of such incredible beauty. In my mind's eye, the fantastically wider space of our solar system appears, its gargantuan geology spanning eons unknown, yet a speck in the galaxy, an atom in the universe. We are spiritual creatures in creation. Laurent and I descend back into the realm of Man, each isolated in the silence of a beautiful high-altitude afternoon; each obstacle along our way, a large crevasse, a short rock wall, a laughing waterfall, accepted as our rite of passage back into the land of the living.

A panaché in Ailefroide brings us back to more immediate considerations: our waitress seems amazingly pretty; the old guide smoking his pipe to our left, a genuine sage, surely a great philosopher; the young couple over the bridge, and their wonderfully healthy little baby, a clear sign that life will go on forever. A panaché is a two-thirds mix of beer with a one-third part of fruit syrup—most of the time mint syrup. It proves a potent brew for our overexercised bodies and minds: we have been awake for the best part of forty-eight hours, we have survived Man and Nature, and we have probably burned over fifteen thousand calories. When Laurent decides to go to the bathroom, after our second panache, he finds himself incapable of rising from his comfortable chair in the early evening light; as for me, my apparent paralysis seems almost wonderful, and will prove felicitous.

We chat for a while, mostly praising the waitress's great, but declining (it's amazing how fast humans adapt to normal circumstances) beauty, when we both fall silent: to our right, a group of young men order "cerveza" with strong Spanish accents. . . .

Laurent went on to a number of successful climbs in Peru, and I believe he now works for the Centre National de la Recherche Scientifique (CNRS) in France; I am currently a physicist at the Lawrence Livermore National Laboratory (LLNL), in the United States. I have now summitted Mt. Whitney five times; climbed forty of the fifty highpoints in the United States, including Mt. Rainier in Washington, Mt. Elbert in Colorado, and Mauna Kea in Hawaii; and reached the altitude of 17,500 feet in Mexico. Neither of us has been accused of any serious crime.

FRED HARTEMANN

ABBREVIATIONS AND ACRONYMS

AAC	American Alpine Club	IGN	Institut Géographique National
AMS	acute mountain sickness	LLNL	Lawrence Livermore National Laboratory
B.A.S.E.	building, antenna, span, earth [jump]	NASA	National Aeronautics and Space Administration
BMC	British Mountaineering Council		
CAF	Club Alpin Français	NOLS	National Outdoor Leadership School
CERN	Conseil Européen pour la Recherche Nucléaire	NSIDC	National Snow and Ice Data Center
CNRS	Centre National de la Recherche Scientifique	REI	Recreational Equipment, Inc.
		RMI	Rainier Mountaineering, Inc.
CTMA	China-Tiber Mountaineering Association	RURP	Realized Ultimate Reality Piton
		SCSU	St. Cloud State University
EMS	Eastern Mountain Sports	UIAA	Union Internationale des Associations d'Alpinisme
FIS	Fédération Internationale de Ski		
GPS	global positioning system	USGS	U.S. Geological Survey
HACE	high altitude cerebral edema	USSA	United States Ski and Snowboard Association
HAPE	high altitude pulmonary edema		

A

A *cheval* (French, "on horseback") In mountaineering, sitting astride an extremely narrow ridge and pulling oneself along.

A *la Conquête de l'Inutile* (Conquistadors of the Useless) This classic mountaineering book was written by **Lionel Terray**, one of the protagonists of the first climb of **Annapurna**, and a participant in the successful first climb of **Makalu**. It is a beautiful and inspiring volume that has been influential in many climbing and intellectual circles. (See also **10 Great Mountain Adventure Books** sidebar.)

A *la Conquête des Cîmes*   A French documentary film shot in 1925 by René Moreau; it depicts a climb of **Mont Blanc**. Unfortunately, the only known print is not complete and lasts only about 40 minutes. (M-A. H.)

Aa   (H) Rough, angular, cindery **lava**. (See also **pahoehoe**.)

Aamodt, Kjetil André   (1971–   ) He won seven Olympic medals, the most of any Alpine skier.

Ablation   Reduction of a land mass, mountain, or **glacier** by **erosion**, **weathering**, or evaporation.

Abodes of the Gods   The **high mountains** have often been considered the homes of the gods and thus sacred sites. **Mt. Olympus** in **Greece** exemplifies this belief.

Abominable snowman   See **yeti**.

Abraham, Ashley Perry   (1876–1951) Born: Keswick, England. Bibliography: *Rock Climbing in Skye* (1908), *Rock Climbing in North Wales* (1906) (with G. D. Abraham), *Camera on the Crags* (1975), by Alan Hankinson.

Abraham, George Dixon   (1872–1965) Born: Keswick, England. Bibliography: *The Complete Mountaineer* (1907), *British Mountain Climbs* (1909), *Mountain Adventures at Home and Abroad* (1910), *Swiss Mountain Climbs* (1911), *On Alpine Heights and British Crags* (1916), *First Steps to Climbing* (1923), *Rock Climbing in North Wales* (1906) (with A. P. Abraham), *Camera on the Crags* (1975), by Alan Hankinson.

Abruzzi, Luigi Amedeo Giuseppe Maria Ferdinando Francesco, Duke d' (Duca) (1873–1933) Born: Italy. Grandson of King Victor Emmanuel II of Italy. An avid climber who organized enormous expeditions, including a foray into the Arctic in 1899 that reached a record 86°43′ northern latitude, and did some first ascents, for example, **Mt. St. Elias** and **Ruwenzori**. One of the main ridges on **K2** is named after Abruzzi. Bibliography: *The Ascent of Mount St. Elias (Alaska) by H.R.H. Prince Luigi Amedeo di Savoia, Duke of the Abruzzi* (1900) by F. de Filippi, *Ruwenzori* (1908) by F. de Filippi, *Karakoram and Western Himalaya 1909* (1912) by F. de Filippi.

Abseil   See **rappel**.

Access Fund, The   Supports climbing by helping to keep areas open and protect the environment (www.accessfund.org).

Accidents   **Mountains** pose a **danger** to everyone who comes within their purview. **Avalanches** inundate towns built in the **valleys**; volcanic eruptions destroy and kill; **rockfalls** and especially **mudslides** bring down houses and harm those caught in their wake; and flash floods carry away everything in their paths. But naturally, when one thinks of mountain accidents, it is the climber who comes to mind. There are three primary causes for climbing mishaps. First, one may make a bad decision. For example, when conditions or one's strength are deteriorating and a climber is only a few hundred feet from the summit, it is often very difficult psychologically to turn around. **Lynn Hill**, the great rock climber, once threaded the **rope** through her **harness**, but forgot to tie a **knot**; she fell 75 ft (Hill). Marty Hoey cut the leg straps on her harness and failed to double the belt back through the buckle; it pulled off and she fell to her death on **Everest**. The second cause is the **weather**; it can catch people unawares. If an unexpected **thunderstorm** finds someone on the **Mt. Whitney ridge**, getting struck by **lightning** is a very real possibility. The obvious signs accompanying a gathering storm include rapid changes in atmospheric pressure, wind di-

rection and strength, cloud cover, and temperature; more pronounced and immediate warning signs include a buzzing or hissing sound produced by the "leaders" of the thunderbolt, somewhat similar to the buzzing of a bee (*les abeilles*, in French), **Saint Elmo's Fire**, and the extremely sharp sound produced by thunder in the immediate proximity. In such circumstances, leaving high ground as quickly as possible, avoiding ridges, caves, and **spires**, is the only course of action. Third, occasionally and through no real fault of the climber, an unexpected occurrence causes harm. One may stumble on a precipice, take a false step on black ice, get hit by falling debris or another climber, succumb to heatstroke, or have a heart attack. A major disas-

Mountain Fatalities in the 14 Highest Peaks

Peak	Height		Climbs	Deaths	Mortality Rate
Annapurna	8,078 m	26,505 ft	109 climbs	55	50.5% mortality
Nanga Parbat	8,125 m	26,658 ft	186 climbs	61	32.8% mortality
K2	8,611 m	28,253 ft	164 climbs	49	29.9% mortality
Manaslu	8,156 m	26,758 ft	190 climbs	51	26.9% mortality
Kanchenjunga	8,579 m	28,146 ft	153 climbs	38	24.8% mortality
Dhaulagiri	8,172 m	26,811 ft	298 climbs	53	17.8% mortality
Everest	8,850 m	29,035 ft	1,173 climbs	165	14.1% mortality
Makalu	8,470 m	27,790 ft	156 climbs	19	12.2% mortality
Shisha Pangma	8,013 m	26,289 ft	167 climbs	19	11.4% mortality
Gasherbrum I	8,068 m	26,470 ft	164 climbs	17	10.4% mortality
Broad Peak	8,047 m	26,400 ft	217 climbs	18	8.3% mortality
Lhotse	8,516 m	27,939 ft	129 climbs	8	6.2% mortality
Gasherbrum II	8,035 m	26,360 ft	468 climbs	15	3.2% mortality
Cho Oyu	8,153 m	26,750 ft	1,090 climbs	23	2.1% mortality

This data reveals that the most dangerous mountain, Annapurna, is also the least climbed; similarly, the least dangerous, Cho Oyu, is second only to Everest in the number of climbs. In fact, there is an almost direct correlation between low mortality and high number of climbs, except for Everest, whose special status as the world's highest peak offsets the dangers it presents in the mind of climbers. Some peaks that are relatively safe are also climbed relatively less often due to their remoteness, or to the current political situation between India and Pakistan. Finally, it is somewhat ironic to note that Annapurna, where an astonishing one out of two climbers perishes, was the first 8,000-meter peak climbed, in 1950 by Herzog and Lachenal; it certainly reinforces the value of their extraordinary achievement.

Note: this data is compiled through December 31, 1999, from the book *Climbing the World's 14 Highest Mountains*

ter occurred on **Nanga Parbat** in 1934, when three climbers and seven **Sherpas** died during a retreat (Unsworth). Recent major accidents include thirteen deaths on **K2** in 1986, many deaths on **Everest** in 1996 (recounted in Krakauer), **Anatoli Boukreev**'s and **Alex Lowe**'s deaths in **Himalayan avalanches**, and the horrific concatenating events in 2002 on **Mt. Hood**, in which three climbers died in the *bergschrund* and a rescue helicopter crashed on the mountain. Total numbers of deaths for **mountains** such as Everest, **Denali**, or **Washington** are often quite high. Accidents also occur when people are at rest. Very high up on Everest, as a climber changed butane cylinders on a stove, something ignited. The ensuing fire burned the facial hair on the tent's occupants and "consumed" an oxygen mask, and smoke inundated the tent (Ullman, *Americans*). Mountaineers refer to all of these under two headings: objective (uncontrollable) and subjective (controllable) dangers. (See also **safety**, the **Mountain Fatalities in the 14 Highest Peaks** sidebar, and *Accidents in North American Mountaineering*, a yearly compilation, for detailed accounts.)

Acclimation (Acclimatization) Getting used to the thinner atmosphere that one encounters as the **altitude** increases. Failure to acclimate may result in **acute mountain sickness** (AMS) or even death. During this complex physiological process, the body produces an increased amount of red blood cells to compensate for the lower partial pressure of **oxygen** encountered at higher altitudes. A typical strategy for acclimation is well encapsulated by the admonition "climb high, sleep low." The ideal amount of time for acclimation is approximately three weeks, but can vary greatly with individuals and altitude. Athletes sometimes use this process to prepare for an important competition by training at altitude; the optimum in that case is a three-week stay between 2,000 and 3,000 m, 7,000 ft to 10,000 ft. Related to this process, the practice of "blood doping," now forbidden by most athletic committees, consisted of having an athlete train at altitude and acclimate, then have his oxygen-rich blood drawn and stored; a self-transfusion shortly

before the competition concluded the procedure. For climbs in the continental United States and in the Alps, where the highest mountains are only about 14,000 ft high, one or two days may suffice for most people to acclimate well enough and climb comfortably, although the medically documented case of an athletic man in his early forties skiing in Colorado at altitudes varying between 9,000 ft and 11,000 ft provides a tragic exception to this rule. He died of cerebral and pulmonary edema over a period of less than three days after complaining to his wife about violent headaches, shortness of breath, and dizziness; he had flown in from sea level to spend the weekend (Houston/Hackett). This terrible death could have been avoided if the couple had heeded the man's symptoms and gone to lower altitude as quickly as possible: knowing those symptoms and recognizing them when they occur can literally save one's life. Collomb, writing in 1958, claims that this acclimation period "is about ten days," a rather conservative estimate. For altitudes above 20,000 ft, much longer periods are mandatory. On **Denali**, 6,194 m, 20,320 ft, where the atmospheric pressure is further diminished by the proximity of the mountain to the North Pole (see **altitude**), two or more weeks are required if one is to avoid AMS, and in the higher elevations found in the **Himalayas,** four to twelve weeks are allocated for **expeditions**.

Acid rain Occurs when pollutants, such as those produced by coal-burning power plants, raise the acidity level of rain; it can be extremely harmful to the natural environment by destroying trees and poisoning water and farmlands.

Aconcagua, Cerro 6,959 m, 22,831 ft. Also known as the "Sentinel of Stone," its original name in Quechua language. Aconcagua was conquered in 1897 by Swiss **guide Matthias Zurbriggen**. Located near the Argentinean–Chilean border, this is the world's highest mountain outside of the Himalayas, the South American **highpoint**. Although it is not a volcano, it is of volcanic origin. The summit ridge, between the north, or main peak, and the south peak, 6,930 m, 22,736 ft, is called the Cresta Guanaco. The normal route is located in the south and circles to the west side of the mountain, then ascends the northwest ridge; it is reached by a three-week-long trek through the lower **Andes**. It is a surprisingly easy climb, if one adapts quickly to high altitude: a strong climber, **Vern Tejas**, hauled a mountain bike up to the summit and proceeded to go down the mountain on this most unlikely equipage! (See also the **Seven Summits** sidebar, and color photos.)

Acropolis   This was the center of ancient Greek cities. The Acropolis in Athens, located high on a hill, is the most famous example. At first, it contained bureaucratic buildings and then temples.

Acute mountain sickness (AMS)   (Formerly, altitude sickness) *Bergkrankheit* (G), *mal de montagne* (F), *puna* (S), *soroche* (S). People who reside below 10,000 ft do not have the natural acclimation to the thinner **oxygen** that one finds in the higher mountains. Humans who are born and raised at 12,000 ft, in **La Paz**, for example, or at 16,000 ft, in some Himalayan villages, have a different physiology (one that produces more red blood cells), which allows them to function unhindered at higher elevations; furthermore, on average, they are shorter and more squat than people born at lower altitudes, thus providing a more favorable surface-to-volume ratio to minimize heat exchange, allowing them to better cope with the extremely cold winter seasons characteristically occurring in the high regions of the globe. When they move permanently to a sea-level community, they can still return to the heights with impunity, whereas an indigenous New Yorker or Parisian may get extremely sick on a visit to La Paz. For some still unexplained reason, different **flatlanders** react differently to **altitude** gain. Many suffer no physiological effects; others may get a headache, cough, stomach cramps, nausea, or become dizzy or mentally impaired. Still others get violently ill; moreover, the same individual may enjoy a headache-free climb of **Mt. Whitney** one year, only to return to a miserable, or even failed, attempt the next climbing season. However, at altitudes above 7,000 m, 23,000 ft, any human will become extremely weakened in this so-called **death zone**: there the body simply cannot replenish nutrients and energy, and even lying in a tent with supplemental oxygen will slowly, but steadily, result in

a deterioration of all major body functions, ultimately leading to death. In view of this, all Himalayan climbers strive for a quick summit push, after an extensive acclimation period; failure to proceed in this manner has resulted in countless deaths, including the very dramatic passing of New Zealander **Rob Hall** and American **Scott Fischer**, both world-class climbers stranded on the high summit ridge of Everest during the 1996 disaster (Krakauer). Minor retinal hemorrhaging and swelling of the limbs are not unusual but recede and disappear upon return to one's accustomed elevation. High altitude pulmonary edema (HAPE) or high altitude cerebral edema (HACE), in which water invades the lungs or the brain, are the worst possible results of altitude gain, and if not immediately remedied by going down, cause death. Since children and the obese are especially susceptible to altitude sickness, they should be carefully monitored. Charles S. Houston (in Wilkerson) affirms this by observing that susceptibility decreases as one ages. In addition to supplemental oxygen, there are a variety of prescription medications that have been used to prevent or alleviate symptoms including acetazolamide (Diamox), an alkaline diuretic, and dexamethasone (Decadron), a steroid. Ellsworth and his colleagues, in an excellent randomized study (on **Mt. Rainier**), have shown that the latter drug is a more effective preventative (although one must be wary of side effects). Nifedipine (Adalat and Procardia), a pressure reducer, relieves the symptoms of HAPE. All of these are potent pharmaceuticals and should be used only under a doctor's supervision. In countries such as **Bolivia**, the indigenous people take *soroche* pills, which consist of Micoren, caffeine, and aspirin. In order to acclimate, climbers who are above 15,000 ft try to ascend slowly (1,000 ft per day), and when possible, reach a highpoint and then retreat for the night: "climb high, sleep low" is more than a witty maxim. Some **expeditions** carry an expensive, inflatable device such as a **Gamow bag**, which resembles a sealed sleeping bag. Inflating the device increases the pressure; the effect on the patient is similar to an actual descent of thousands of feet. But this is a temporary, emergency measure. A person suffering from AMS, HAPE, or HACE will not recover until he or she descends. Houston (in Wilkerson) insists that precautions will preclude these problems: "Almost no one should get altitude sickness." This would undoubtedly come as a major surprise to the many experienced and acclimated people who get violently ill and even die. Peter Hackett's concise *Mountain Sickness* is, as is his coauthored chapter on high-altitude medicine in Auerbach, extremely helpful. (See also **medicine**.)

Adams, Ansel Easton (1902–1984) A celebrated nature photographer who produced some of the most famous mountain images, for example, "Moon over Half Dome." He particularly loved the **Sierra Nevada**. He was a master of folio reproduction, specializing in black-and-white images. (For some examples of Adams's wonderful work, see the black-and-white photos.)

Adams, Mt. 3,742 m, 12,276 ft. The second-highest peak in **Washington** is a massive, heavily glaciated, dormant strato-volcano. Because it is harder to reach than **Mt. Rainier**, it is much less often climbed, although its normal route is considerably easier.

Adirondacks A major range in the northern Appalachian system.

Afanassieff, Jean (1953–) Born: Paris, France. One of the strongest French climbers of the generation following the pioneers of **Annapurna**. Main achievements in the **Alps**: the Croz spur in the **Grandes Jorasses**, the Couzy spur in the **Droites**, the Cordier channel in the **Aiguille Verte**, the Poire and the Sentinelle Rouge in **Mont Blanc**. Expeditions: first ascent of Mont Ross in the Kerguelen Islands; two expeditions on Fitzroy; one in **Bolivia**; four on **Everest**, where he was one of the first Frenchmen to summit; three in **Pakistan**, including **Nanga Parbat**, **Broad Peak**, and **K2**; one on **Makalu**.

Afghanistan Lowest point, Amu Darya 258 m, 846 ft; highest point, **Nowshak** 7,530 m, 24,704 ft. The western end of the **Hindu Kush** mountain range runs through Afghanistan; major summits include: Lunkho 6,902 m, 22,644 ft; Shah Fuladi 5,143 m, 16,873 ft; Kūh-E-Fūlādi 4,951 m, 16,243 ft; Kāfar Jar Ghar 3,808 m, 12,493 ft. Un-

fortunately, this war-torn country has been geopolitically unstable for most of the past half century, thus barring mountain climbers and other hiking enthusiasts from enjoying its great geographical diversity and impressive mountains.

Africa One of the seven **continents**, and the second largest, it has a land area of 30,365,000 square km, 11,724,000 square miles; the highest point is **Kilimanjaro**. The continent is mostly equatorial or tropical, in terms of climate, and very rich in unique plant and animal life. The **Great Rift Valley** is one of its most important geological features; it is lined by a series of impressive volcanoes and peaks, including Kilimanjaro, **Mt. Kenya**, and **Ruwenzori**.

Agassiz, Jean Louis (1807–1873) A Swiss American naturalist and geologist. A number of peaks in North America bear his name; for example, Mt. Agassiz 4,235 m, 13,893 ft, in the **California Sierras** and Agassiz Peak 3,766 m, 12,356 ft, near the Arizona highpoint. (See also **Humphreys Peak**.)

Agriculture Even on extensive high **plateaus** (in **Tibet**, for example), the **weather**, growing season, and soil quality are likely to differ radically from **valley** conditions; thus, different farming techniques are necessary. **Mountain slopes** are more extreme; people cultivate these for two reasons: either they run out of room in the valleys where they live, or they choose to reside in the mountains, for example, for protection against enemies. Where arable land is at a premium, even very steep slopes are extensively terraced and a surprisingly broad variety of edible **plants** are grown. The steeper the slope, the more this becomes subsistence farming, since even if the indigenous farmers could afford tractors and combines, it is difficult or impossible to get large, modern equipment to roll along a 40-degree incline. In Norway, hay is grown on slopes so steep that it is difficult to even stand up; the bundles are pulled to the top on a steel cable. High **Alpine** meadows are often less precipitous and may be used for summer pasturage for cows and sheep.

Ahluwalia, Hari Pal Singh Born: India. A member of the team that reached the summit of

Everest in 1965. Bibliography: *Higher Than Everest* (1973), *Faces of Everest* (1978), *Eternal Himalaya* (1982), including *Views in Himalaya* by George Francis White.

Aid (Formerly, artificial) In **rock climbing**, this indicates that something artificial (**rope**, **sling**, **nut**, **piton**) has been used not merely as **protection** against the possibility of a fall but to help one move past a difficult point. (See also **free**.)

Aiguille This French term for needle is used in the names of innumerable **Alpine peaks**, especially in the **Mont Blanc chain**.

Aiguille, Mt. See **Mont Aiguille**.

Aiguille Blanche de Peuterey 4,112 m, 13,490 ft. This is the 41st highest of the 60 major 4,000-meter peaks in the **Alps**; it is also one of the most esthetically pleasing summits in the **Mont Blanc Range**; it is also a very difficult climb, with no easy route up to the summit: the Aiguille Blanche is a mighty **satellite** of **Mont Blanc**. Generally, alpinists follow the climb of the overhanging

The Grand Mulets (S. G. Wehrli/National Geographic)

glacier of the Aiguille Blanche, on the Italian side, by an ascent to the summit of Mont Blanc, followed by a **traverse** back down to the **Chamonix** Valley, on the French side of the **massif**. The Aiguille Blanche de Peuterey was first climbed in 1885 by H. Seymour King, Emile Rey, Ambrosio Supersaxo, and Aloys Anthamatten.

Aiguille d'Argentière 3,900 m, 12,795 ft. This important peak in the **Mont Blanc Range** presents numerous challenges to the alpinist, ranging from the easy normal route to the highly esthetic north face, a massive series of hanging **glaciers** connected by 55-degree ice slopes often swept by **avalanches**. Because of its character and topology, the North Face evolves rapidly from year to year, depending upon the snowfall in winter: in the 1950s, the face presented an almost continuous 55- to 65-degree ice slope, some 600 m, 2,000 ft, tall; at the time of this writing (2003), the slope is interrupted by a series of gigantic **séracs**, as tall as 60 m, 200 ft. A very large rimaye marks the boundary between the Glacier de Saleina and the North Face itself. It was first climbed by **Edward Whymper**, A. Reilly, **Michel Croz**, M. Payot, and H. Charlet on July 15, 1864. (See also www.mountainarea.com/argentiere/aiguille.html and color photos.)

Aiguille de Bionassay 4,052 m, 13,293 ft. This is the 53rd highest of the 60 major 4,000-meter peaks in the **Alps**. One of the most famous **satellites** of **Mont Blanc**, it is also one of the most elegant Northwest faces in the Alps: a rugged 600-meter, 2,000-foot, 45 to 60 degree slope, interrupted by near-vertical **séracs**, towering above the **Chamonix** Valley. The summit itself is a very narrow **ridge**, over 65 degrees in slope on the French side, more than 50 degrees on the Italian side, and riddled with overhanging **cornices**. A luminous, extremely narrow, half-mile-long ridge takes the summiter across the Col des Italiens, onto the **Dôme du Gôuter**; from that point, one can either climb to Mont Blanc along the Arête des Bosses, or descend back into the valley via the normal route. The first climb of Aiguille de Bionassay was performed in 1865 by Edward N. Buxton, F. C. Grove, R. S. McDonald, Michel Payot, and Jean-Pierre Cachat. (See also color photos.)

Aiguille de Rochefort 4,001 m, 13,126 ft. This is the 59th highest of the 60 major 4,000-meter peaks in the **Alps**. It was first climbed in 1873 by J. Eccles and Alphonse and Michel Payot. It is located on the main ridge connecting the **Dent du Géant** to the **Grandes Jorasses**, and offers magnificent views of the **Mont Blanc Range**.

Aiguille du Fou 3,501 m, 11,486 ft. By most standards, this is a modest summit in terms of altitude; however, it offers some of the most exciting pure rock climbing in the **Chamonix** area; in particular, the south face, which was only opened in 1963 by T. Frost, J. Harlin, G. Hemming, and S. Fulton, presents an exceedingly difficult and sustained route, rated ED (see **rating systems**): although only 300 m, 1,000 ft, in height, it takes 15–25 hours for exceptional climbers to complete.

Aiguille du Géant See **Dent du Géant**

Aiguille du Goûter 3,835 m, 12,582 ft. This is an important **satellite** of **Mont Blanc**, especially in view of the fact that the main **refuge** on the **normal route** is located at the top of the Aiguille du Goûter; some 200–300 climbers routinely sleep there during the busy summer months, some, with reservations, in the bunk beds; others, unannounced, anywhere warm and flat! Unfortunately, such situations are now common all over the **Alps**, and rapidly expanding to other locales, including the base camps of **Aconcagua**, **Everest**, and **Denali**.

Aiguille du Jardin 4,035 m, 13,238 ft. This is the 51st highest of the 60 major 4,000-meter peaks in the **Alps**. It was first ascended in 1904 by E. Fontaine, Jean Ravanel, and Léon Tournier; as such, it was the penultimate major peak above 4,000 meters to be climbed in the Alps.

Aiguille du Midi 3,842 m, 12,605 ft. Perhaps one of the most famous French Alpine peaks after **Mont Blanc**. A series of cable cars or **gondolas** (*téléphériques*), a bridge, and an elevator take one from the **Chamonix**, as well as the Italian valley floor, to the summit. This is the highest *téléphérique* in the Alps and an astonishing **engineering** marvel. (See also color photos.)

Aiguille du Plan 3,673 m, 12,051 ft. This is a major summit of the **Aiguilles de Chamonix**, which posed critical difficulties to 19th-century climbers, alongside with the nearby Grands Charmoz and the Grépon. Its sheer verticality, and the pure granitic nature of its rock, both typical of climbing on the Aiguilles, created some of the most competitive climbing challenges for the gentlemen of the British Alpine Club and their continental counterparts. The first **Dulfer**, named after its inventor, was implemented in the Aiguilles, and the *glacier* suspendu route is now a classic; other very interesting routes include the Arête Ryan.

Aiguille du Tour 3,542 m, 11,621 ft. This is one of the best climbs in the **Alps** for the novice: while the high-altitude ambiance is provided aplenty by the proximity of the Chardonnet, the **Aiguille Verte**, and **Mont Blanc**, the direct route is a simple enterprise taking the climber from the Refuge **Albert I**, to the Glacier du Tour, on to the Glacier du Trient, on the Swiss side, and up a short scramble to the vertiginous summit. The Arête de la Table de Roc, on the other hand, is a classic, direct, climb: a brief (approximately 200-meter, 600-foot) ascent up the 45-degree couloir by the same name is followed by a wonderfully aerial scramble on the arête itself; soon, the Table de Roc appears, accompanied by the most exciting part of the climb, an **exposed traverse** along a slanted granite **slab**, which **overhangs** the very steep French side of the aiguille. (See also color photos.)

Aiguille du Triolet 3,870 m, 12,697 ft. The north face of this peak is a difficult challenge, with an average slope exceeding 65 degrees and a very continuous, hard-ice **headwall** towering above the Glacier d'Argentière.

Aiguille Noire de Peuterey 3,773 m, 12,379 ft. The west face of this **satellite** of the **Aiguille Blanche de Peuterey** presents 650 m, or 2,150 ft, of sustained TD rock climbing (see also **rating systems**).

Aiguille Verte 4,122 m, 13,524 ft. This is the 39th highest of the 60 major 4,000-meter peaks in the **Alps**. One of the best-known peaks in the **Mont Blanc Range**, it played an important role in the history of alpinism, and was first climbed in 1865 by **Edward Whymper**, **Christian Almer**, and Franz Biner by the couloir that now bears Whymper's name. From the **Chamonix** Valley, the Aiguille Verte, also known as "La Verte" by the locals, is a prominent presence, with the exquisite **spires** of Les **Drus** in the foreground; the summit is a small hanging **glacier**, which takes magnificent green hues, after which the mountain is called: in French, *verte* means green. The Cordier and Couturier couloirs are classic ice climbs on the Argentière side of the mountain, with slopes in excess of 60 degrees. A lenticular cloud capping the Aiguille Verte often announces bad weather in the Mont Blanc range; this specific meteorological phenomenon is known as *le capuchon de la Verte* (the Verte's hood), and indicates strong winds in the upper atmosphere, a harbinger of violent storms. Indeed, the weather can change with exceeding rapidity on this high peak, and numerous parties have been stranded near the summit after a difficult climb; one of the main problems with the mountain is that its easiest **descent** route, the Whymper couloir, is in fact a steep (50-degree) gully, often swept by rock and ice falls; in bad weather, retreat is nearly impossible, especially when hoarfrost ices up the couloir. The only reasonable rock descent route is via the Aiguille du Moine, and it is a long, treacherous ridge, especially in a storm; as a result, the fatality rate on the Aiguille Verte remains too high. (See also color photos.)

Aiguilles de Chamonix An extraordinary array of sheer granite **spires**, rising almost vertically over the **Chamonix** Valley and including many famous peaks, such as the Grands Charmoz, the Grépon, the **Aiguille du Plan**, the Dent du Requin, and the highest peak of the group, the **Aiguille du Midi**. On the Chamonix side, there are no easy routes up the Aiguilles, which are quite vertiginous and offer superb climbing on excellent rock; some mixed routes can also be found, including the very difficult hanging glacier on the Aiguille du Plan. Early in the history of **Alpinism**, the Aiguilles played an important role, as they helped push the envelope in terms of difficult rock climbing, and numerous standard climbing techniques, including the **Dulfer**, chimney climbing, and overhangs were pioneered there. Their relatively low altitude and

the very short approach from Chamonix make them enduring favorites among climbers. (See also color photos.)

Aiguilles de Trélatête 3,920 m, 12,861 ft. These are the southernmost major summits of the **Mont Blanc Range**; there are four distinct peaks, the highest being the South summit. The first ascent was performed on July 12, 1864, by A. Reilly, **Edward Whymper**, **Michel Croz**, M. Payot, and H. Charlet. The Aiguilles are heavily glaciated, and the main summit is an ice cap, cascading into an overhanging glacier on the north face. The traverse is a highly recommended, relatively easy, classic snow and ice course with superb views of the powerful Italian side of **Mont Blanc** and the **Aiguille de Bionassay**, over the Col Infranchissable (The Un-crossable Pass; see also color photos).

Ailefroide 3,954 m, 12,972 ft. In the heart of the **Dauphiné Alps**, near the splendid **Barre des Écrins**, lies the austere Ailefroide, first climbed by **Coolidge**. The north face rises extremely steeply from the Glacier Noir, and comprises a few small hanging **glaciers**; the crest comprises three distinct **summits**: the Ailefroide Occidentale, which is the highest; the Ailefroide Centrale; and the Ailefroide Orientale, 3,848 m, 12,625 ft. A steep ridge, the Arête de Coste-Rouge, comparable in scope for the climber to the Arête des Hirondelles at the **Grandes Jorasses**, is found on the west side of the mountain. To the east, the jagged Coup de Sabre, 3,914 m, 12,841 ft., and the mighty **Pelvoux** complete the north faces above the Glacier Noir, forming a formidable **cirque** analogous to that of the Glacier d'Argentières in the **Mont Blanc Range**.

Ainslie, Charles (1820–1863) Born: England. A member of the party that performed the first ascent of **Mont Blanc** without a guide, in 1855. Bibliography: *The Annals of Mont Blanc* (1898) by C. E. Mathews.

Alabama Lowest point, Gulf of Mexico, 0 m; highest point, Cheaha Mountain, 734 m, 2,407 ft (the 35th highest of the 50 state highpoints).

Alaska Lowest point, Pacific Ocean, 0 m; highest point Mt. McKinley, or **Denali**, 6,194 m, 20,320 ft (the highest of the 50 state highpoints). The largest state in the **United States** (1,530,700 sq km, 591,004 sq miles), it is replete with extraordinary ranges (39) and peaks including Denali; **St. Elias** 5,489 m, 18,009 ft; **Foraker** 5,303 m, 17,400 ft; **Blackburn** 5,037 m, 16, 526 ft; **Bona** 5,006 m, 16,424 ft; **Sanford** 4,941 m, 16,211 ft; **Hunter** 4,445 m, 14,583 ft; **Wrangell** 4,318 m, 14,167 f; **Hayes** 4,189 m, 13,743 ft; Marcus Baker 4,017 m, 13,179 ft; Silverthrone 4,015 m, 13,173 ft; and Moose's Tooth. There are also many thousands of glaciers here. Alaska is an incredible wildlife preserve, where bears of all ilk, including grizzlies, polar, and brown bears; wolves, foxes, and wolverines; large sea mammals including seals, orcas (so-called "killer whales"), humpback and sperm whales; and other wonderful animals, such as the Alaskan sockeye salmon and the golden eagle, roam the majestic land, swim the powerful seas and rivers, and fly the ultramarine, subarctic skies, where the **aurora borealis** dances under the midnight sun.

Alaska Range This 400-mile long Alaskan **range** is home to **Denali** and some of the world's worst weather, directly channeled by frequent, angry, arctic fronts.

Albania Lowest point, Adriatic Sea 0 m; highest point, Maja e Korabit (Golem Korab) 2,753 m, 9,032 ft.

Albert I (1875–1934) King of Belgium commencing in 1909; he had been given the nickname of *roi chevalier* (knight king) because of his important activities with the allies during World War I, both in the diplomatic sphere as well as on the battlefield. He died falling off a rock during a climb at Marche-les-dames, near Namur. The place is known as the Rocher d'Albert Premier (Rock of Albert the First) and is approached by the Rue du Roi Chevalier (Street of the Knight King). The Belgian Alpine Club funded the construction of a refuge in the **Mont Blanc Range** that is the starting point for climbs of the **Aiguille du Tour** and the Chardonnet; this refuge is named after the king: Refuge Albert Premier. (M-A. H.)

Alberta Lowest point 173 m, 568 ft, along Slave Lake; highest point, Mt. Columbia, 3,747 m, 12,293 ft. One of the 13 Canadian provinces and territories, it is home to some major and extremely beautiful ranges of the **Canadian Rockies**. Important peaks can be found in Alberta, including North Twin 3,733 m, 12,247 ft; Mt. Alberta 3,620 m, 11,877 ft; **Mt. Assiniboine** 3,618 m, 11,870 ft; Mt. Forbes 3,612 m, 11,850 ft; South Twin 3,581 m, 11,749 ft; Mt. Temple 3,547 m, 11,637 ft; Mt. Brazeau 3,525 m, 11,565 ft; Snow Dome 3,520 m, 11,549 ft; Mt. Lyell 3,998 m, 13,177 ft; Hungabee Mountain 3,492 m, 11,457 ft; **Mt. Athabasca** 3,491 m, 11,453 ft; Mt. King Edward 3,490 m, 11,450 ft; and Mt. Kitchener 3,490 m, 11,450 ft.

Alcohol In the early days of mountaineering, climbers carried lots of wine and other alcoholic beverages with them. We now know that drinking alcohol at higher elevations is physiologically detrimental. (It should never be given to someone suffering from **acute mountain sickness**.) Nevertheless, mountaineers, **Sherpas**, and **porters** may still drink these beverages at **base camp**, which can be set as high as 18,000 feet in some locations.

Alder A **deciduous tree** of many species; mountain and sitka alder, for example, both grow at **altitude**.

Aletsch Glacier Located in the **Bernese Alps**, this is the largest **glacier** in the **Alps**, some 22 km, 14 miles, long.

Aletschhorn 4,195 m, 13,763 ft. This is the 32nd highest of the 60 major 4,000-meter peaks in the **Alps**. It was first climbed in 1859 by Francis Fox Tuckett, J. J. Bennen, Victor Tairraz, and Peter Bohren. It is a magnificent summit, the second highest in the **Bernese Alps**.

Algeria Lowest point, Chott Melrhir −40 m, −131 ft; highest point, Tahat 3,003 m, 9,852 ft.

Allain, Pierre (1904–2000) A famous French climber, who perfected **friction climbing** and the extremely difficult moves on the boulders of **Fontainebleau**. Applying these new techniques in the **Alps**, in August 1935, Allain and Raymond Leininger performed the **first ascent** of the north face of the Petit **Dru**, one of the first sixth-degree alpine climbs. (See also **rating systems**.)

Allalinhorn 4,027 m, 13,211 ft. This is the 53rd highest of the 60 major 4,000-meter peaks in the **Alps**. It was first ascended in 1856 by Johann

Almer's Leap, by Edward Whymper (Alpine Club)

Josef Imseng, Franz-Josef Andenmatten, and E. L. Ames. Compared to the giants of the **Valaisan Alps**, the Allalinhorn may be considered as a secondary summit; nevertheless, it is a beautiful mountain, and a pleasurable climb.

Allegheny Mountains A range of the Appalachians in **Pennsylvania** and **West Virginia**.

Allison, Stacy (1958–) Allison was the first American woman to reach Everest's summit (1988) (Child).

Almer, Christian (1826–1898) Early, extraordinary **guide** who made **first ascents** of the **Aiguille Verte** (1865), the **Mönch** (1857), the **Eiger** (1858), the Croz and Whymper summits of the **Grandes Jorasses** (1864), the Fiescherhorn (1862), and the **Barre des Écrins** (1864). He is responsible for the famous, and controversial, jump **Almer's Leap** on the summit ridge of the Barre des Écrins. (See also **10 Best Guides** sidebar.)

Almer's Leap The fabled, controversial jump **Christian Almer** is purported to have taken during the first ascent of the **Barre des Écrins**, in 1864. The story was widely disseminated by **Edward Whymper**, who, as an engraver, illustrated it in a most dramatic fashion (see photos). It was acrimoniously disputed by another prominent member of the Alpine Club, **William Coolidge**, an American-born climber who had opened many new routes in the **Alps**, with increasing degrees of difficulty: for example the Arête de Coste-Rouge on the **Ailefroide**.

Alp A high meadow.

Alpaca A South American animal similar to the **llama** and **vicuña**.

Alpamayo 5,947 m, 19,511 ft. Arguably, the most beautiful Peruvian peak: the **fluted** snow and ice under the summit ridges appear to deli-

cately float and shimmer under the low sunrays. It is a difficult climb, because the normal route uses a narrow and extremely **corniced** ridge. It was first ascended in 1951 by a French–Belgian team including René and André Mailleux and Jacques Jongen, although they mistakenly reached a point that was not the actual summit. A German team summitted in 1957. (See also the **10 Most Beautiful Mountains** sidebar.)

Alpenglow Colorful (orange, gold, yellow) effect observed on (snowy) **mountains** at sunrise and sunset (Smith). (See also color photos.)

***Alpensinfonie, Eine**/An Alpine Symphony* Op. 64. Composed between 1911 and 1915 by Richard Strauss (1864–1949). This is one of Strauss's last symphonic works and is far less popular than his *Thus Spake Zarathustra*. It is descriptive music complete with sunrise, reaching the summit, thunderstorm on the way back, and safe return, all within 50 minutes. Each of the 22 movements, linked in a continuous flow, has a title giving a pretty clear idea of what is happening ("Sunrise," "The Ascent," "On the Glacier," "Dangerous Mo-

Eine Alpensinfonie, Richard Strauss

ments," "On the Summit," "Mists Rise," "Thunder and Tempest"). It begins and ends with a "Night" movement. The large orchestra contains up to 137 musicians. The storm is one of the noisiest movements ever conceived. (M-A. H.)

Alpenstock A cumbersome staff that hikers carried in the past. For mountaineers, it has been replaced by the **ice ax**.

Alphubel 4,206 m, 13,799 ft. This is the 30th highest of the 60 major 4,000-meter peaks in the **Alps**. Located in the **Valaisan Alps** of **Switzerland**, within the Allalin group, it was first ascended in 1860 by Leslie Stephen, T. W. Hinchliff, **Melchior Anderegg**, and Peter Perren. (See also color photos.)

Alpine Club See **clubs**.

Alpine life zone The area above the **treeline** anywhere in the world where vegetation grows (it may also be known as the high-Andean or afro-alpine zone). It varies from less than one kilometer on the Arctic **tundra** to five kilometers in the **Himalayas**.

Alpine style Attempting to reach a summit by using a small group of climbers, small quantities of equipment, and doing so quickly in one push. (See also **siege style**.)

Alpinism The term used to describe climbing in the **Alps**, and by extension mountain climbing in general.

Alps The main **mountain system** in **Europe**. It has a variety of branches (**Bernese**, Bernina, Central, **Dolomites**, Eastern, **Mont Blanc**, Pennine, **Dinaric**, Julian, etc.) and is especially impressive in **France** and **Switzerland**, but also stretches through **Austria**, **Germany**, and **Italy**, as well as some other lands. The Alps count some 60 major peaks above 4,000 m (13,123 ft). *Hochgebirge* (G) or *hautes montagnes* (F) designate the **high mountains** and *mittelgebirge* (G) or *moyennes montagnes* (F) indicate the **medium mountains**. Among the books one might consult is *The Alps* (National Geographic) with countless photographs. (See also color photos.)

Altai A mountain system in Central **Asia**.

Altimeter In **mountaineering**, initially, a small analogue device, now often digital and contained within a specialized wristwatch, that indicates the **altitude** in meters or **feet** based on changes in barometric pressure, or electronic data from the **Global Positioning System** (**GPS**).

Altiplano The plateau area (high plains) in the **Andes** of **Argentina**, **Bolivia**, and **Peru**.

Advancing across the Glacier for an Attack (Comando Supremo, Italian Army/National Geographic)

Altitude   Generally, height above mean sea level. There are several distinct approaches to determining the altitude of a specific geographical point. First, one can obtain elevation by triangulation, a geometrical process whereby the distances and relative azimuthal angles of various reference points are used to calculate the altitude of the landmark under investigation; this is the oldest method, and it has been used since Greek geometry. Later on, it was noticed that the atmospheric pressure decreases exponentially with altitude; this is the basic principle of operation of so-called barometric **altimeters**; the major concomitant problem with such devices is that one cannot differentiate simply between variations in the ambient atmospheric pressure, such as the decrease accompanying a storm, and altitude itself. That being said, it is clear that for fixed positions, such as a camp at night, any variation must be of meteorological origin. To date, the most accurate method for determining altitude relies on the **Global Positioning System** (GPS): a series of satellites, in geosynchronous orbits, regularly beam a reference signal, synchronized with extreme precision to a reference atomic clock; the time of flight of the speed-of-light signal from each satellite over the horizon allows a computerized receiver to calculate its three-dimensional position with respect to the reference beacons, with a precision limited only by the wavelength of the signal, currently in the gigahertz range (fraction of a foot). The only potential setbacks include the canopy in a dense forest, which attenuates and scatters the satellites' signals; major peaks, which act as obstacles to the radio frequency signals; and weather conditions, with water vapor as one of the strongest absorbers of the reference signal. Finally, we note that **Everest** was recently fitted with special retro-reflectors, designed to bounce a probe signal emitted by a satellite; using a technique similar to GPS, and involving the speed-of-light time of the flight signal, the altitude of the highest peak on earth was determined with unprecedented accuracy and raised from the conventional 8,848 m found in older atlases, to the current value of 8,850 m, or 29,035 ft. With this new and extremely accurate measurement method, it was also confirmed that Everest and the other major summits of the **Himalayas** continue growing at a pace of a few centimeters, or inches, per year, as a result of the ongoing collision between the Indian subcontinental plate and the Asian **tectonic plate**. Altitude plays a seminal role in climbing because the higher one goes the thinner the air becomes. At 15,000 ft, the lungs get only about half as much oxygen as at sea level. Thus, one must breathe considerably faster. At 26,000 ft the body simply cannot keep up, and after a short time in the **death zone** one perishes. It is important to note that, because of the rotation of the earth, the barometric pressure at a given altitude is significantly higher near the equator than near the poles: the atmosphere bulges out near the equator under the centrifugal force. As a result, climbing **Denali**, at 20,320 ft, feels like climbing a much higher Himalayan peak, near 24,000 ft! Finally, one should keep in mind that for some mountains, for example the Mexican volcanoes, the altitudes quoted by various sources can differ by significant amounts: **Orizaba** registers at 18,700 ft on Mexican military topographic maps, while other sources indicate 18,402 ft (www.peakware .com/encyclopedia/peaks/orizaba.htm).

Altitude, effects of   Even moderate increases in altitude can have a potent effect on human physiology. At 8,000 to 10,000 feet, respiration becomes more difficult and **acute mountain sickness** can ensue; as one goes higher, the effect is more pronounced. As altitude increases other things happen: the diversity of animal and plant life as well as temperature decrease; helicopters become less efficient, eventually losing the ability to stay aloft; wind and storms increase in ferocity; snow accumulates and glaciers form; and at a mere 6,000 feet normal plasma television sets do not function as well as at sea level, because their gas expands, which causes them to hum. (See also **death zone** and **radiation**.)

Altitude sickness   See **acute mountain sickness**.

Altitude 3200   A French play by Julien Luchaire, adapted for the screen by the author in 1937. The film was directed by Jean Benoît-Levy and

Marie Epstein and released in 1938. Seven young men spend summer vacations in a refuge at 3,200 meters. Six young women look for shelter in the same place. Tensions ensue. This work was a big success for obvious reasons. It gave opportunities for stage managers to test inexperienced actors. No print seems to exist. (M-A. H.)

Altitudes A symphony (Op. 53) written on a commission offered to **Jean Martinon** by the Chicago Symphony Orchestra for its 75th season. Written in 1964–1965, it had its premiere in 1965, the composer conducting. Martinon was then in the middle of his five years' tenure as the orchestra's conductor. Writing about the symphony, the composer said: "In listening to my symphony 'Altitudes,' please do not think that it's a narrative composition. There are no descriptions of blue glaciers, threatening masses of shifting ice or aerial crossing over scalloped peaks etched against the sky. No dangerous descent or mountain songs. . . . In my mind, 'Altitudes' implies diverse heights that man, with muscle and stamina, can attain by his own strength and perseverance. . . . Perhaps it is a metaphysical position, a spiritual ascent toward an immeasurable infinity." (M-A. H.)

Altyn Tagh A range in China along which runs along a major and tectonically active **fault**.

Alung Gangri 7,315 m, 24,000 ft. This major peak is located within the **Himalayas** in **Tibet**.

Alverstone Peak 4,439 m, 14,564 ft. Located in **Canada's Saint Elias Mountains**, in the **Yukon**. This is a major peak straddling the boundary between the **Wrangell–St. Elias** and **Kluane-Logan National Parks**.

Ama Dablam 6,856 m, 22,494 ft. A splendid, highly recognizable mountain in Nepal, in the Everest region. Ama Dablam towers high above the Tengboche monastery in the **Khumbu** area. It was first ascended in 1961 by Mike Gill, Barry Bishop, Mike Ward, and Wally Romanes. (See also color photos.)

Amateur This term is applied to a mountaineer who climbs for pleasure, even if he or she is a superb climber with many **first ascents**. (See also **professional**.)

Amateur d'Abîmes, L'/The Chasm Seeker What the title refers to is a young man spending his two-week vacation in the Chamonix Valley at the end of the 1930s. With two friends, he attempts—and succeeds—in a few climbs and tells of his experiences and of his knowledge of Alpinism. Better known for his drawings, author **Samivel**'s (1907–1992) first novel was written in 1938. Ranging from witty recollection to philosophical comments or fantasy, the work is an informative account of then-current climbing techniques, but it also deals with more general ideas on mountains, their protection, and tourism. (M-A. H.)

Ament, Patrick Oliver (1946–) An outstanding Colorado rock climber, poet, and the author of 30 books on climbing including the invaluable *History of Free Climbing in America*. Bibliography: *Swaramandal* (1973), *Master of Rock* (1977), biography of John Gill, *Rock Wise* (1978), *High Endeavors* (1991), *Climbing Everest* (2001). His biography of Gill, viewed now as a classic, introduced the climbing world to a more spiritual side of climbing and to a new consciousness of difficulty. Ament did the first 5.11 climbs in **Colorado** and **Yosemite** in 1965, 1966, and 1967.

American Alpine Club Founded in 1902 and located in Golden, **Colorado**, the AAC has more than seven thousand members and is the premier American organization for those interested in climbing and conservation of the mountain environment. **John Muir** was once its president. It has a strong publication program and its superb **library** is open to both members and nonmembers (www.americanalpineclub.org). (See also **clubs**.)

American Mountaineering Center Here, in Golden, **Colorado**, one will find the headquarters of the **American Alpine Club,** a museum, and other organizations, as well as much very useful information related to climbing and trekking (www.mountaincenter.org).

American Samoa Lowest point, Pacific Ocean 0 m; highest point, Lata 966 m, 3,169 ft.

Amne Machin 6,282 m, 20,610 ft. The peak was first climbed in 1981 by Galen Rowell, Harold Knutsen, and Kim Scmitz. It was one of two peaks erroneously estimated at above 30,000 ft by the American botanical explorer

Joseph Rock, in 1929; the other peak is **Minya Konka**.

Amphibian These are cold-blooded creatures such as frogs and toads that generally prefer watery environments and warmer temperatures. Some, like the newt, olm, or salamander, do inhabit mountainous areas (Burnie). (See also **reptile** for additional elucidation.)

Anabatic wind See **winds**.

Anchor To attach oneself (or an object) to a solid point (a **face**, a **rock**, a **picket**) in order to create a **belay** point. (Also used as a noun.)

Anchor point For **belays**, **rappels**, or even to set up **protection**, anchor points are extremely important in technical climbing: the safety of the roped party depends upon the reliability of these protection points. For highly technical, extremely difficult climbing, be it on rock or ice, it is recommended to set up an anchor every 10 ft, which would yield a **pendulum** of 20 ft in case of a fall (*dérapage*, in French). For ice, this would consist of an **ice screw**, or, possibly, an **ice ax**, the second technique generally being used to reinforce the anchor on a belay; for rock, a variety of hardware is available, ranging from **pitons** to **hexcentrics**, **friends**, or **slings**.

Ancohuma 6,388 m, 20,958 ft. This is the 23rd highest peak in the **Andes**, and the 14th of 20 premier climbing peaks in that range; it was first climbed in 1919 by Rudolf Dienst and Adolf Schulze. This is the third highest major peak in **Bolivia**, although it must be noted that for a while there was some confusion on the exact order between **Sajama**, **Illimani**, and Ancohuma.

Anderegg, Melchior (1828–1912) Born: Zaun, Switzerland. One of the greatest of the early guides who climbed with **Leslie Stephen** and **Horace** and **Lucy Walker**. First ascents: **Rimpfischhorn** (1859), **Mont Blanc** by the Bosses Ridge (1859), **Alphubel** (1860), **Dent d'Hérens** (1863), Parrotspitze, or Pointe **Parrot** of **Monte Rosa** (1863), **Zinalrothorn** (1864), **Obergabelhorn** (1865), Mont Blanc by the Brenva Face (1865), Walker summit of the **Grandes Jorasses** (1868), Mont Mallet (1871). Bibliography: *The Early Alpine Guides* (1949) by R. W. Clark. (See also the **10 Best Guides** sidebar.)

Anderson, Robert Mads (1958–) The only person to solo the **seven summits**, as recounted in his extraordinary volume, *Summits*. (He missed the top of **Everest** by 100 meters.) (See also the **Seven Summits** sidebar.)

Andes The major South American **mountain system**. The Andes comprise the longest **range** in the world and run some 4,500 miles from north to south along the western coast of the continent through Chile, Argentina, Bolivia, Peru, Ecuador, Colombia, Venezuela, and Panama. Many of the peaks (some of which are **volcanoes**) are more than 20,000 ft high, and **Aconcagua**, at almost 23,000 ft, is the highest mountain in the world outside of the **Himalayas**. (See also color photos.)

Andinismo Analogous to **Alpinism**, this is the term that describes climbing in the **Andes**.

Andorra Lowest point, Riu Runer 840 m, 2,756 ft; highest point, Coma Pedrosa 2,946 m, 9,665 ft. This tiny principality is located in the heart of the **Pyrénées**, between **France** and **Spain**; a number of interesting hikes and short climbs can be reached from Andorra.

Andromeda, Mt. 3,450 m, 11,319 ft. A superb summit near the **Columbia Ice Field**, in the **Canadian Rockies**. (See also color photos.)

Anemone A **flower** in the shape of a star that comes in many colors including white, yellow, or blue. Fourteen (of 120) species can be found in the **Rocky Mountains** (Nicholls).

Aneto, Pico de 3,404 m, 11,168 ft. The highest peak in the **Pyrénées**, it is located in **Spain**. It was first ascended in 1842 by Albert de Franqueville, Platon Chihacher, and other anonymous climbers.

Angola Lowest point, Atlantic Ocean 0 m; highest point, Morro de Moco 2,620 m, 8,596 ft.

Anguilla Lowest point, Caribbean Sea 0 m; highest point, Crocus Hill 65 m, 213 ft.

Animal Many lowland creatures (including **mammals**, **birds**, **fish**, **reptiles**, **insects**, arthropods, etc.) occasionally wander, fly, swim, or crawl into mountainous regions. Sometimes they survive and even prosper; at other times they perish. A limited group of animals make their home in the mountains, and some thrive there. Temperature, climate, and sustenance vary dramatically depending both on whether the mountain is temperate or tropical and on its altitude. Different animals inhabit different mountainous regions. Those that thrive above 10,000 or 12,000 ft produce more red blood corpuscles (just as their human counterparts do). Many of the most important mammals and birds are noted separately in their respective alphabetical locations. (For a magnificent overview of mountain creatures, see Burnie and Wilson's *Animal*; Costello offers three chapters on animals and birds in *The Mountain World*; and Thapar's *Land of the Tiger* presents an outstanding overview of India's mountain animals.)

Animals, protection against Animals pose one of the many dangers that humans face in a mountain environment. A broad array of small and larger creatures can harm or kill, if one is unprepared or careless. In Africa and/or Asia, one may very infrequently encounter tigers, snow leopards, or elephants, although generally they do not pose a threat. Primates, especially mountain gorillas, can be dangerous; never look directly at one of these large creatures since eye contact is considered an aggressive gesture. In many areas of the United States, coyotes, cats, and bears can be real problems. One should be wary even of mustangs, moose, elk, or bighorn sheep. These are all large creatures that can inflict painful or fatal wounds. Most dangerous are mothers with young; very hungry creatures; and those that have become inured to humans, show no fear, and then are frightened into action. (A moose killed a person on the Anchorage campus of the University of Alaska, and cats have killed even in populated areas.) It is a good idea to avoid solitary mountain travel, although that is not always feasible. When encountering medium-sized animals such as mountain lions, one should make oneself as large as possible (using a coat or a pack), create a lot of noise by shouting or growling, and attempt to frighten the animal into retreat. (One of the authors once cowed a large, attacking dog he met high above the sea along the Welsh coast by growling and barking at it.) Carry a bear bell and ring it in suspect territory; this warns bears that someone is invading their domain, and they will attempt to avoid

contact. Bears are extremely fast and excellent tree climbers, so running or climbing on the part of a human will be counterproductive. With black bears, one may play dead—which is a nerve-wracking procedure. Note that this does not work with brown bears. In grizzly bear territory, one might carry some form of pepper spray especially formulated to ward off bears—and learn how to use it. (See French's informative chapter on "Bear Attacks" in Auerbach.) Less probable are instances of aggression by wolves, wolverines, and a variety of poisonous snakes and insects. (Carry a snakebite kit.) It is an excellent idea to avoid contact with all wild animals. They may be frightened, malicious, or ill, but appear to be friendly or curious. Remember that all mammals are potential vectors of rabies, and in some species such as raccoons or bats in some geographical areas, this horrific ailment is endemic. Being prepared both physically and informationally will help to avert a tragedy.

Anker, Conrad (1963–) An expert mountaineer and the person who located **George Mallory**'s body, as recounted in his *Lost Explorer*.

Annapurna, Premier 8000 A beautiful, inspiring classic film that tells the harrowing account of the first climb of an 8,000-meter peak, in 1950, by a French party lead by **Maurice Herzog**, who also authored the book. In fact, Herzog had the other members of the expedition, sponsored by the Club Alpin Français, sign a contract giving him exclusive rights for a period of five years after the climb. More recently, a controversial book raised some disturbing questions about the leadership of that expedition, and some of the fateful decisions made during the summit bid, which resulted in severe **frostbite** for both Herzog and **Lachenal**, who summitted, and temporary **snow blindness** for **Rébuffat** and **Terray**. (See also **10 Great Mountain Adventure Books** sidebar.)

Annapurna I (Also Morshiadi; "Goddess of the Harvests," in Sanskrit) 8,091 m, 26,545 ft. One of the great **Himalayan mountains**, it was the first 8,000-meter (26,247 ft) peak to be climbed; it is the tenth highest mountain in the world. Indeed, in 1950, a French party led by **Maurice Herzog**, and including great climbers like **Lionel Terray**, **Gaston Rébuffat**, and **Louis Lachenal**, made it to the summit after extraordinary adventures and sufferings, related in the book ***Annapurna, Premier 8,000***. Since the first climb by Herzog and Lachenal, on June 3, 1950, the mountain had been climbed only 106 times as of the end of 1999; during that period 55 fatalities occurred on the mountain, making it by far the most dangerous of the 14 great 8,000-meter peaks (See also the **14 8,000-Meter Peaks** and **Mountain Fatalities in the 14 Highest Peaks** sidebars as well as color photos.)

Annapurna II 7,932 m, 26,040 ft. This major peak is located within the **Himalayas** in **Nepal**. It was first ascended in 1960, by Ang Nyima, **Chris Bonington**, and R. H. Grant.

Annapurna III 7,555 m, 24,786 ft. This major peak is located within the **Himalayas** in **Nepal**. It was first ascended in 1985 by John Beament.

Annapurna Sanctuary This area is located north of Pokhara, in **Nepal**, deep within the Annapurna **Himal**; in addition to the **Annapurnas**, other major peaks are located in the vicinity, including **Machupuchare**, Hiunchuli, and Fang; further to the west is the **Dhaulagiri** Himal. The **gorge** of the Modi Khola runs from the sanctuary down to the Kali-Gandaki River.

Antarctica Lowest point, Southern Ocean 0 m; highest point, **Vinson** Massif 4,897 m, 16,066 ft. One of the seven continents; it is extremely cold, dry, and windy here and there are no indigenous peoples, only representatives from various countries who maintain research facilities. The mountains are high, snow covered, and lovely. Antarctica is a gigantic land of extreme cold (the lowest temperature recorded on earth is −88.3°C, −127°F, at the Vostok Russian station, 3,500 m, 11,483 ft) and ice: the average layer of ice exceeds one mile in thickness, as it is estimated at 2,000 m, 6,500 ft. Titanic glaciers slowly make their way to the Southern Ocean, sculpting and eroding the rock beneath. Large active volcanoes, like Erebus, are also part of this surreal landscape, from which man is prominently absent; life, however, flourishes along the shores of the continent: penguins of all ilk; sea birds; sea mammals, including whales and numerous species of seals; an abundance of fish; and plankton find their home here in this most inhospitable land. In Antarctica, one also finds very large dry valleys, where no precipitation has been recorded for periods extending over many years: the extreme cold tends to sublimate all humidity, creating unique ecosystems where highly adapted, microscopic forms of life thrive, including algae living at the bottom of lakes forever sealed under a layer of ice. Antarctica is also a land of vast mountain ranges, emerging from the permanent ice sheath and rising above enormous glaciers that end up in majestic ice floes and icebergs carved by the Southern Ocean, as well as gigantic ice shelves: Ross, Ronne, Amery, and Shackleton being the most prominent. Among the major ranges and peaks are: the Hawkes Mountains, culminating at Mt. Hawkes, 3,660 m, 12,008 ft; the Queen Alexandra Range, including Mt. Kirkpatrick, 4,528 m, 14,856 ft, and Mt. Markham, 4,351 m, 14,275 ft; the Queen Maud Mountains, with Mt. Fridtjof Nansen, 4,069 m, 13,350 ft, and Mt. Wade, 4,084 m, 13,399 ft, towering above the Shackleton Glacier; the Executive Committee Range, culminating at Mt. Sidley, 4,181 m, 13,717 ft; **Mt. Erebus**, 3,794 m, 12,447 ft, and Mt. Sabine, 3,719 m, 12,201 ft, both located within Victoria Land; the Mühlig-Hoffman Mountains, and Habermehl Peak, 3,300 m, 10,827 ft; the Humboldt and Wohlthat Mountains, culminating at 4,300 m, 14,108 ft; Mt. Jackson, 4,191 m, 13,750 ft, on the Antarctic Peninsula; finally, the Ellsworth Mountains, including the Sentinel Range, where Mt. Vinson, Mt. Tyree 4,865 m, 15,961 ft, Mt. Shinn 4,801 m, 15,751 ft, Mt. Gardner 4,688 m, 15,381 ft, and Mt. Epperly 4,600 m, 15,092 ft dominate a desolate, barren, frozen landscape.

Anticline Rock beds that decline away from each other. (See also **syncline**.)

Antigua and Barbuda Lowest point, Caribbean Sea 0 m; highest point, Boggy Peak 402 m, 1,319 ft.

Ape These large primates (gibbons and gorillas) often wander in the mountains. (See also **mountain gorilla**.)

Apennines An Italian range.

Api 7,132 m, 23,399 ft. This major peak is located within the **Himalayas** in **Nepal**. It was first ascended in 1960, by K. Hirabayashi and Gyltsen Norbu.

Appalachian Mountain Club People who care about hiking, climbing, and other outdoor activities in the Appalachians and elsewhere join this

Boston club (the oldest such organization in the United States); since 1876, it has published books, sponsored research, and educated people (www.outdoors.org).

Appalachian Trail　A 2,168-mile trail through the wilderness from Springer Mountain, Georgia, to **Mt. Katahdin**, Maine. Thousands of people walk along parts of this during the warmer months and some few hundred through-hikers cover the entire trail between March and August or September. (See also **Brian Robinson** and Irwin's *Blind Courage*.)

Appalachians　A major **mountain system**, and the oldest in **North America**, they run some 1,500 miles along the eastern seaboard of the United States. **Ranges** include the **Adirondacks**, Berkshires, Blue Ridge, **Catskills**, Great Smokies, Green, Taconic, and **White**. The highest summit, Mt. Mitchell, in North Carolina, is only 2,037 m, or 6,684 ft.

Approach　The drive, ride, hike, trek, or walk to the beginning of any type of climb. Sometimes approaches can be quite challenging in themselves: for example, one may need to walk on a steep glacier, cross numerous snow bridges, and negotiate a difficult rimaye before the climb proper begins. In another instance, mixed climbing may be required before reaching the **crux** of an ascent, where **friction** climbing and **chaussons d'escalade** are now required; finally, many locations worldwide cannot be reached easily, and somewhat "dicey" means of transportation are necessary, including uncooperative mounts and locals, or dangerous flights on **float planes**, or hair-raising, off-road drives up what basically amounts to a dry mountain creek.

Aprés-ski　After **skiing**, when people eat, drink, dance, and talk; also, comfortable shoes worn after skiing.

Arapiles, Mt.　Greg Child notes that the Australian sandstone here offers "one of the finest free climbing areas in the world."

Ararat, Mt.　5,165 m, 16,945 ft. A peak in **Turkey** upon which Noah's ark is purported to have landed. (See also color photos.)

Mount Ararat (H. F. Reid/National Geographic)

Arch   A rock formation resembling an arch that has been hollowed out by **erosion**.

Arctic Circle   Located at a latitude of 66°30′ North, it corresponds to the southern limit of the region where, for at least one day each year, the Sun does not set (summer **solstice**) or rise (winter solstice).

Arête   (F) See **ridge**.

Argentina   Lowest point, Salinas Chicas −40 m, −131 ft (located on Peninsula Valdes); highest point, Cerro **Aconcagua** 6,959 m, 22,831 ft. Numerous other high summits of the **Andes** can be found in Argentina, including: Nevado Ojos del Salado, 6,880 m, 22,572 ft; **Cerro Bonete** 6,410 m, 22,020 ft; **Monte Pissis** 6,779 m, 22,240 ft; **Mercedario** 6,770 m, 22,211 ft; **Llullaillaco** 6,723 m, 22,057 ft; **Tupungato** 6,550 m, 21,489 ft; La Ramada 6,410 m, 21,020 ft; Plata 6,315 m, 20,718 ft; Sierra de Famatina 6,250 m, 20,505 ft; Cordillera de Colanguill 6,122 m, 20,085 ft; Nevado Lavadero 6,122 m, 20,085 ft; Alma Negra 6,290 m, 20,636 ft; Marmolejo 6,100 m, 20,013 ft; Volcano Antofalla 6,409 m, 21,027 ft; Cima Kelo 6,015 m, 19,734 ft; Pico Polaco 6,001 m, 19,688 ft; Cerro Rojo 5,911 m, 19,393 ft; Cerro El Potro 5,830 m, 19,127 ft; Vallecitos 5,770 m, 18,930 ft; Cerro Negro 5,500 m, 18,044 ft; El Clavillo 5,500 m, 18,044 ft; Cerro Cuerno 5,462 m, 17,920 ft; Tolosa 5,432 m, 17,821 ft; Wanda Peak 5,400 m, 17,716 ft; Cerro de los Horcones 5,395 m, 17,700 ft; Cerro Alto Río Blanco 5,350 m, 17,552 ft; Volcano Maipo 5,290 m, 17,356 ft; Cerro Sosneado 5,189 m, 17,024 ft; Almacenes 5,100 m, 16,732 ft; Volcano Domuyo 4,709 m, 15,449 ft; Volcano Lanin 3,776 m, 12,388 ft; Cerro San Lorenzo 3,700 m, 12,139 ft; and **Cerro Fitzroy** 3,375 m, 11,073 ft.

Arizona   Lowest point Colorado River, near Yuma, 21 m, 70 ft; highest point, **Humphreys Peak** 3,851 m, 12,633 ft (the 12th highest of the 50 state highpoints).

Arkansas   Lowest point, Ouachita River, 17m, 55 ft; highest point, **Magazine Mountain**, 839 m, 2,753 ft (the 34th highest of the 50 state highpoints). (See also color photos.)

Arlberg   An area in the province of Tyrol in western **Austria** famous for its downhill **ski** resorts, which include St. Anton, Lech, and Zurs. It is possible to ski from one of these towns to another and then take a lift up and return to the original point of departure. The Arlberg method of the mid-1950s used an exaggerated upper body rotation to force one's skis to turn (Barnes).

Armenia   Lowest point, Debed River 400 m, 1,312 ft; highest point, Aragats Lerr 4,095 m, 13,435 ft.

Arrest   In climbing, the act of halting a fall, slide, or tumble. (See also **self-arrest** for the method.)

Arroyo   A gulch through which water cascades after a storm but which spends much of the year dry.

Art   Although mountains have sometimes petrified those who live in their shadows, they have also inspired the creative. Visual artists depict peaks in paintings and prints; the musical offer compositions, for example, Mussorgsky's *Night on Bald Mountain*; and directors make movies. (See also **movies and mountains, music and mountains, petroglyph, photography,** and **painters** as well as the **10 Best Hollywood Mountain Movies** and the **10 Recommended Mountain and Climbing Documentaries** sidebars.)

Aruba   Lowest point, Caribbean Sea 0 m; highest point, Mt. Jamanota 188 m, 617 ft.

Ascender   (Also jumar, originally a brand name.) A device that contains a spring-loaded unit with angled serrations that grip the **rope**; the ascender slides upward unimpeded, but when pulled upon, it holds. An ascender (sometimes used as a pair) allows a climber to move (or jumar) up a **fixed rope** easily and safely. In escaping from a **crevasse** after a fall, one's full weight may be placed upon the ascenders, for example, by putting both feet into attached toe loops.

Ascent   In **climbing,** upward movement.

Asgard, Mt.   2,011 m, 6,598 ft. Located on Baffin Island, in the **Nunavut** Territory of **Canada,** this is an extremely impressive, monolithic mountain, with sheer vertical granite faces all around and a square top. The rise of the cliffs is 400 m, 1,300 ft; the weather can be extremely fierce, as the mountain is situated a few miles north of the **Arctic Circle**. (See also the **10 Awesome Monoliths** sidebar.)

Ash   A **deciduous tree** with a short growing season especially at higher elevations. Its hard wood is turned into baseball bats.

Ash   Tiny particles produced by a volcanic eruption. In large enough numbers they can block sunlight and thus alter the climate of an affected area. These particles can be carried around the world, as recently seen after the 1991 eruption of **Pinatubo**. Ash buried and preserved **Pompeii** and Herculaneum.

Ashmore and Cartier Islands   Lowest point, Indian Ocean 0 m; highest point, unnamed location 3 m, 10 ft.

Asia   It is the largest of the seven **continents**: with a land area of 44,614,000 sq km, 17,226,000 sq miles, it covers more than 30 percent of all landmass on the globe. It is home to many of the world's great ranges, for example, the **Himalayas** and the **Karakoram**. Both the world's highest and lowest points are located within Asia: **Everest** and the **Dead Sea**.

Aspen   A **Colorado** ski resort; also a tree.

Assiniboine, Mt.   3,618 m, 11,870 ft. A very beautiful mountain in **Canada**; it is often compared to the **Matterhorn**. Assiniboine was first climbed in 1901 by James Outram, C. Bohren, and C. Hasler. (See also color photos.)

Associations   See **clubs**.

Aster   A flower often found in Chinese mountains.

Asterix chez les Helvètes/Asterix in Switzerland   A comic book written by René Goscinny (1926–1977) and drawn by Albert Uderzo (1927–), published in 1970. The two fearless Gaulois, Asterix and Obelix, are heading for Helvetia in search of an edelweiss. Roman spies are on their tracks and try to sabotage their mission.

Athabasca, Mt.   3,491 m, 11,453 ft. A superb summit near the **Columbia Ice Field**, in the **Canadian Rockies**. Athabasca was first climbed in 1898 by J. Norman Collie and Herman Wooley. (See also color photos.)

Athabasca Glacier   Located near **Banff, Alberta, Canada**, this large **glacier** flows down from the **Columbia Ice Field**, which feeds many other glaciers as well. The Athabasca Glacier is some four miles long and, as many other ice caps in these days of global warming, shrinking.

Mount Assiniboine (Walter D. Wilcox/National Geographic)

Athans, Pete   (1957–) He has summitted **Everest** seven times; he is the only non-Sherpa to accomplish this.

Athos, Mt.   (Holy Mountain) 2,033 m, 6,670 ft. An area in Greece upon whose precipitous slopes 20 monasteries have been constructed home to a semiautonomous community of monks. Women and even female animals are not allowed to enter these precincts. (See also **Metéora**.)

Atkins, Henry Martin   (1818–1842) Born: England. He made the 24th ascent of **Mont Blanc**. Bibliography: *Ascent to the Summit of Mont Blanc on the 22nd and 23rd of August, 1837* (1838), *Annals of Mont Blanc* (1898) by C. E. Mathews.

Atlantic Peak   4,879 m, 16,008 ft. This is the sixth highest peak in **Canada**.

Atlantis   A mythical continent; some people believe that it is based on Thira, an Aegean island that was destroyed by a **volcano**.

Atlas   A compilation of maps in a large volume. Atlases also contain charts, geographical, economical, and political data, and photographs.

Maps in an atlas most generally use a grid indicating **latitude** and **longitude**. In the 16th century, the cartographer Gerardus Mercator, inventor of the projection method bearing his name, initiated the custom of using the figure of the Titan Atlas, holding the globe on his shoulders; the name derives from this usage.

Atlas Mountains A 1,000-mile range in Morocco, Algeria, and Tunisia.

Atmosphere The earth is surrounded by various gaseous spheres differing in size and constitution. The atmosphere contains the precise proportions of elemental materials, notably oxygen and nitrogen, necessary to sustain life. As one moves higher above the earth's surface, there is less oxygen, thus making it more difficult for the body to function. Very few people can sustain life for more than a few hours above 25,000 ft, which is the area known as the **death zone**.

Atna Peaks 4,225 m, 13,860 ft; 4,145 m, 13,600 ft. These very precipitous and heavily glaciated mountains are located in the **Wrangell–St. Elias National Park**, near **Mt. Blackburn**, in **Alaska**.

Attitude toward mountains Human perception of the mountain environment has changed dramatically during the past five thousand years. We have feared and worshipped the heights; considered mountains to be barriers to travel; and finally discovered their intrinsic beauty and therefore visited and scrambled on, over, and across them. (See Price for some prescient and detailed remarks on this topic.)

Augusta, Mt. 4,288 m, 14,069 ft. A high peak located in the **Yukon** Territory in **Canada**, and straddling the boundary between the **Wrangell–St. Elias** and **Kluane-Logan National Parks**.

Auldjo, John Richardson (1805–1886) Born: Ireland. He made the 19th ascent of **Mont Blanc**. Bibliography: *Narrative of an Ascent to the Summit of Mont Blanc, on the 8th and 9th of August, 1827* (1828), *Annals of Mont Blanc* (1898) by C. E. Mathews.

Aurora borealis Near the poles, the earth's magnetic field is stronger, and its field lines can capture high-energy, charged particles from the solar wind; in turn, these particles can ionize the upper atmosphere, which then glows at the characteristic transition lines of the various elements thus excited, producing a ghostly, wonderfully colored pattern of lights slowly evolving over a few hours. The light produced is relatively weak, and major stars can be seen through the aurora; nevertheless, it is a splendid and awesome spectacle that can often be seen at **latitudes** higher than 60 degrees; at lower latitudes, it becomes exceedingly rare, but at the peak of the 11-year solar cycle, auroras can sometimes be viewed from latitudes as low as 45 degrees.

Ausangate 6,384 m, 20,944 ft. This is the 24th highest peak in the **Andes**, and the 15th of 20 premier climbing peaks in that range; it was first climbed in 1953 by Fritz März, **Heinrich Harrer**, and Jürgen Wellenkamp. The peak is located in **Peru**.

Australasia The geographic entity grouping **Australia** with the major islands in the southwestern Pacific Ocean, including **New Zealand**, New Guinea, Java, Borneo, and Sumatra, into the seventh continent, rather than Australia itself. For the climber, this distinction is important because the highpoint of Australasia is **Carstensz Pyramid**, 5,039 m, 16,532 ft, located on the island of New Guinea, rather than the much more pedestrian **Mt. Kosciusko**, 2,229 m, 7,313 ft, in Australia. It has now become customary for those on the quest for the **Seven Summits** to ascend both Kosciusko and Carstensz, leaving the ultimate decision on the exact definition of a continent to the geographers.

Australia Lowest point, Lake Eyre −15 m, −49 ft; highest point, **Mt. Kosciusko** 2,229 m, 7,313 ft. This gigantic country, the sixth largest (7,617,930 sq km, 2,941,283 sq miles), is sometimes considered as the seventh **continent**; as such, its highest point, Mt. Kosciusko, is the easiest of the **Seven Summits**, the highpoints of the seven continents. However, **Australasia** is also sometimes regarded as the seventh continent; in that case, the much more challenging **Carstensz Pyramid**, 5,039 m, 16,532 ft, becomes an important peak to climb; its location and altitude make it rather hard to reach. Australia is also home to **Ayers Rock**, known to the aborigines as Uluru, 867 m, 2,844 ft, the biggest monolith in the world, located near the geographical center of the land down under and in the vicinity of the Olgas, a unique group of large rocks emerging from the desolate landscape of the Great Australian Desert. In the northwest, one can find some of the oldest terrain on earth, containing rock layers over three billion years old, in the Connemara region. Other peculiarities of this amazing land include the Great Barrier Reef; amazing flora and fauna, for example kangaroos, wombats and the eucalyptus tree; and the unusual meteorological phenomenon observed in the Cape York Peninsula of a single cloud, hundreds of miles long, rolling as a wave over the northern Australian landscape. (See also color photos.)

Australian Alps A range in eastern Australia; the highpoint is **Mt. Kosciusko.**

Austria Lowest point, Neusiedler See 115 m, 377 ft; highest point, **Grossglockner** 3,798 m, 12,461 ft. This is one of the most important alpine countries, and it contains numerous lovely mountains, including the **Grossvenediger**, the Piz Buin, and the Silvretta group.

Autour d'un Film de Montagne A 20-minute documentary, directed by Alain Pol in 1943, concerning the shooting of Daquin's ***Premier de Cordée***. Strangely, this very rare movie is far more spectacular than the feature film with which it deals. It shows the stunning scenery and the incredible risks the crew took. The documentary shows how leading man Roger Pigaut got hurt and was replaced on the spot by André Le Gall. (M-A. H.)

Avalanche A 1978 American film directed by Corey Allen, also responsible for *The Erotic Adventures of Pinocchio*. More notably, it was produced by exploitation phenomenon Roger Corman. Mixing disaster films with mountains was a new experience. (*Avalanche Express*, 1977, deals more with spying.) Due to the low budget the photography is rather crude and the avalanche scene looks like "mutant powder sugar on the loose." Rock Hudson, Mia Farrow, and Robert Forster all appear. It was made at a resort near Durango, Colorado. (M-A. H.)

Avalanche *Lawine* (G), *valanga* (I). A downward, gravitationally enhanced movement of material on a mountain **slope** or couloir. **Rock** and mud avalanches (also called **landslides** and **lahars**) occur with some frequency and can have a devastating effect on anything caught in their paths, but when the term is mentioned, most people think of plummeting **snow** (or **ice**). Snow avalanches can be inconsequential or extraordinarily massive. If there is nothing in their path, they are harmless, sometimes loud, and a superb manifestation of nature's enormous power. They occur with increasing frequency as one moves into the upper, steeper terrain of the **high mountains**, especially above the **timberline**. Generally, avalanches occur only when the slope is angled between 25 and 50 degrees, 35–40 being optimum; if the angle is too low, snow will not flow, and if it is too high, it will not have accumulated in appreciable amounts. Sometimes surface snow releases in small quantities and gathers additional material as it descends; this is called a loose snow avalanche. A slab avalanche (usually wider than it is long) occurs when an entire deep-seated layer of snow has failed to adhere and conjoin with the frozen surface upon which it has collected. Avalanches depend on many factors including the constituency of the snow, the surface to which it adheres, wind and temperature alterations, and triggering mechanisms such as a snowboarder or a sonic boom. Under the right conditions, in the **Alps**, Alaskan and Canadian mountains, **Andes**, and **Himalayas**, avalanches can occur almost continually, which is psychologically disconcerting as well as dangerous for mountaineers who are huddled in a small tent. As a large avalanche descends, it destroys and carries off everything in its path. It can level a forest, chalets, and even small villages situated in the **foothills** or **valleys**. Avalanches can approach speeds of 300 miles per hour. **Hermann Buhl** noted that the avalanches he observed on **Nanga Parbat** could be "a mile and a half wide and 600 or 700 feet high." As early as 1618, it was reported that an avalanche killed approximately 2,430 souls in the city of Pleurs; this was the largest loss of life recorded in the history of the Alps (Fleming). As people seek out less frequented areas for extreme sports, the chance that one will be caught in an avalanche increases. During the winter of 2001–2002, 35 Americans were killed by avalanches in these areas; by mid-February of the 2002–2003 season, 15 Americans and 16 Canadians had been killed, 14 in just two avalanches in British Columbia (Egan). The American Avalanche Institute maintains a website at avalanchecourse.com, as does the National Avalanche Center at www.avalanche.org. (See also **avalanche protection**, **avalanche rescue,** and **avalanche survival**.)

Avalanche, Mt. 4,212 m, 13,820 ft. A high peak located in the **Yukon** Territory in **Canada**.

Avalanche protection Because avalanches can be so harmful (when they hit a village or large building, many lives can be lost simultaneously— 20 in one Icelandic example), people who live under their threat have come up with many ways to protect against their inevitable arrival. Series of structures, fences, or barricades may be erected, sometimes thousands of feet above the threatened area. These impede, deflect, or halt the progress of cascading snow. Concrete extrusions may cover high roads built on a mountain slope; the falling snow will thus pass over that section of highway. Where potential avalanches are an immediate danger, for example, in high country frequented by skiers or snowboarders, empowered officials may purposely set them off with explosives. These stimulated avalanches can be precisely controlled, and electronic detection systems are now used or in the offing in some locations. These are either penetrometers, that is, probes that measure snow resistance or sensors that relay rumblings back to a computerized system that will analyze the sounds (Eisenberg). See the chapter on avalanches by Williams et al. in Auerbach.

Avalanche rescue When someone is carried off by and buried in a massive avalanche (and this happens thousands of times a year in the Alps), he or she is trapped below the surface, often by large, hard blocks of snow. It is difficult or impossible to move and help must come from outside. Surprisingly, although the person may be severely hurt, death is neither immediate nor inevitable. An air pocket provides oxygen for a few minutes and sometimes much longer, and so if fellow skiers or climbers can quickly locate the victim, he or she will probably survive. When situated above or below a descending avalanche, one must visually follow the victim's path and mentally mark where he or she may be buried. Digging at this point can result in a successful rescue; searchers may use long poles to probe the ground for a victim; sensitive **dogs** can smell the correct location to dig; avalanche cords, which flow out along the surface, indicate where a person is located; and some people now carry transceivers, which emit a signal that indicates precisely where the victim is buried. One of the most recent advances in avalanche survival is the AvaLung II, a piece of equipment that resembles a swimmer's life vest, except that this device provides extra time by increasing the oxygen available to the victim. Inflatable balloons that lift one above the cascading snow are also available (Egan). Despite all of this, many people do lose their lives, 39 in one horrific 1970 example, according to McClung and Schaerer, and as many as 35 in a single season in the United States. Interestingly, 25 percent of avalanche deaths are due not to asphyxiation but rather to collisions with objects (McClung and Schaerer).

Avalanche survival When caught in an avalanche, many things can be done to increase one's chances of survival. McClung offers some excellent and detailed advice including the following: move to the periphery; attract attention; keep breathing passages clear of snow; catch onto a passing object; "swim, kick, fight"; get to the surface; create an air pocket; dig; call out. That victims fail in these efforts is shown by the following horrific statistic: Between 1985–1986 and 2001–2002, 2,395 people lost their lives in avalanches around the world.

Ayers Rock (Uluru) 867 m, 2,844 ft; 348 m, 1,142 ft above the plain. With a circumference of five miles, this is the largest **rock** in the world. It is set on a broad plain in central Australia and is a sacred site for the Aboriginal population. Nevertheless, and analogous to the situation at **Devil's Tower**, it is photographed and climbed by tens of thousands of visitors every year.

Azema, Marc Antonin Born: France. Bibliography: *The Conquest of Fitzroy* (1957).

Azerbaijan Lowest point, Caspian Sea −28 m, −92 ft; highest point, Bazarduzu Dagi 4,485 m, 14,715 ft.

Aztec The civilization that flourished in and dominated ancient **Mexico** until the conquistadors arrived from **Spain**, in the 15th century; their language was Nahuatl, and is still reflected in the names of some of the mighty Mexican peaks.

B

Bacher, John (1957–) An extraordinary climber who dominated **free** climbing in **Yosemite** from about 1975 through the 1990s; he was one of the world's great free climbers and free soloists. See Boga's *Climbers* for a profile.

Backpack A unit that easily and quickly can be strapped on the back in order to carry the necessary materials required for a walk, **hike**, or **rock** or **mountaineering** climb. (See also **climbing equipment** and color photos.)

Badile, Piz 3,308 m, 10,853 ft. A mountain in **Switzerland**. (See also the **6 + 1 Great Alpine North Faces** sidebar and color photos.)

Badrinath 7,138 m, 23,420 ft. This major peak is located within the **Himalayas** in **India**.

Bahamas, The Lowest point, Atlantic Ocean 0 m; highest point, Mt. Alvernia, on Cat Island 63 m, 207 ft.

Bahrain Lowest point, Persian Gulf 0 m; highest point, Jabal ad Dukhan 122 m, 400 ft.

Baïkal, Lake Located in the mountainous southern part of East Siberia, in the republic of Buryatia and the Russian province of Irkutsk, it is the oldest freshwater lake on earth, at 20–25 million years. Lake Baïkal is also the deepest lake in the world, with a maximum depth of 1,620 m, 5,315 ft. The lake is very large: 31,500 sq km, 12,200 sq miles, with a length of 636 km, 395 miles, and an average width of 48 km, 30 miles. Finally, it contains the largest volume of fresh water, approximately one-fifth of the fresh water on the earth's surface, or 23,000 cubic km, 5,500 cubic miles.

Baker, Ernest Albert Born: England. Bibliography: *Moors, Crags and Caves of the High Peak and the Neighbourhood* (1903), *The Voice of the Moun-* *tains* (1905), with Francis E. Ross, *The Highlands with Rope and Rucksack* (1923), *On Foot in the Highlands* (1932), *The British Highlands with Rope and Rucksack* (1933).

Baker, Mt. 3,285 m, 10,778 ft. An imposing volcanic peak in northern **Washington**. A number of interesting routes go up the mountain, ranging from relatively simple navigation on a crevassed glacier, to the difficult ascent of the **headwall**, after the long Ptarmigan Ridge **approach**. Baker is also a heavily glaciated mountain, which receives record snowfall year after year (up to 50 m, or 150 ft); in fact, the glaciers on Baker are substantially more extensive than those found on **Mt. Rainier**. This is partially due to the fact that Baker stands less than 20 miles (32 km) from the Pacific coastline. The mountain was named after the first lieutenant on the boat under the captainship of George Vancouver. (See also **snow**.)

Baker Island Lowest point, Pacific Ocean 0 m; highest point, unnamed location 8 m, 26 ft.

Balaclava Now usually called a face mask.

Balcony See **cornice**.

Ball, John (1818–1889) Born: Ireland. The first president of the Alpine Club from 1858 to 1860. In 1857 he made the ascent of Pelmo, the first major mountain to be climbed in the **Dolomites**. Bibliography: *Ball's Alpine Guides*; *The Western Alps* (1863), *The Central Alps* (1864), *The Eastern Alps* (1868); editor of *Peaks, Passes and Glaciers*, Vol. 1 (1859).

Ball up The term that indicates that soft, wet **snow** is sticking to the bottom of one's boots or **crampons** thus making them inefficient or useless, which can be extremely dangerous. One can tap the crampons with an **ice ax** to dislodge the snow, but care must be taken not to detach the crampons, especially the step-in variety. Some people insert stiff plastic or rubber units on the underside of the crampons, which discourages balling up. When this condition is severe, it may be safer to remove the crampons. (See also color photos.)

Balmat, Auguste (1808–1862) **Guide** and beloved friend of many early Alpine climbers. He summitted **Mont Blanc** 12 times.

Balmat, Jacques (1762–1834) Born: Chamonix, France. A crystal and chamois hunter who, with **Michel-Gabriel Paccard**, made the first ascent of **Mont Blanc** on August 8, 1786. A few years later he made an ascent with **Marie Paradis**, who became the first woman to reach the summit. Bibliography: *The Annals of Mont Blanc* (1898) by C. E. Mathews.

Balti One of a number of Himalayan and Kashmiri people, including the Pahari Ladakhi, Champa, Kanet, and Dart peoples; sometimes, more specifically, the native inhabitants of the Baltoro area of **Pakistan**, and their dialect.

Baltoro Glacier Located in **Pakistan**'s **Karakoram**, and fed by peaks including **K2**, **Gasherbrum**, **Masherbrum**, and **Broad Peak**, this is the largest **glacier** outside the polar areas and Alaska.

Baltoro Kangri 7,300 m, 23,950 ft. This major peak is located within the **Himalayas** in Kashmir.

Band An obviously different strip or section of **rock** on a face. For example, the Yellow Band on the north face of **Everest**.

Bandolier (Not used in America) In **rock climbing**, the physical **sling** worn across the shoulder on which **gear** is carried. (See also **rack**.)

Banff The gateway to the national park by the same name, it is also a beautiful ski resort, and a very touristy town. Many hikes and climbs in the **Canadian Rockies** are accessible from Banff.

Banff Mountain Film Festival One of the premier events of its kind, it attracts famous climbers, authors, and mountain aficionados. (See also color photos.)

Banff National Park A wonderful national park in the **Canadian Rockies**; it abounds with very beautiful mountains and sites, including the pristine **Lake Louise**, the magnificent **Columbia Ice Field**, and **Mts. Athabasca** and **Andromeda**.

Bangladesh Lowest point, Indian Ocean 0 m; highest point, Keokradong 1,230 m, 4,035 ft.

Banks, Michael Edward Borg (1922–) Born: England. A British marine and mountaineer who performed the first ascent of **Rakaposhi** in 1958, with Tom Patey. Bibliography: *Commando Climber* (1955), autobiography, *High Arctic* (1957), *Rakaposhi* (1959), *Greenland* (1975), *Mountaineering for Beginners* (1977).

Baquet, Maurice (1911–) French cellist, actor, showman, writer, and climber. His athletic abilities made him a first choice in sport movies such as *Le Grand Élan* (1939), **Premier de Cordée** (1944), and *Le Voyage en Ballon* (1960), and swashbucklers like *Mandrin* (1962). He opened the south face of the **Aiguille du Midi** with **Gaston Rébuffat** in 1956 and was third in climbing the north face of the Col du Plan. He played Bach atop **Mont Blanc**. (M-A. H.)

Barbados Lowest point, Atlantic Ocean 0 m; highest point, Mt. Hillaby 336 m, 1,102 ft.

Barber, Henry (1953–) A brilliant rock climber and mountaineer who led the first 5.12 in **Yosemite**, in 1975. He made a stunning solo of the 2,000-foot Steck-Salathé in Yosemite in two and one-half hours, in 1973 (Ament, personal comment).

Barre des Écrins See **Écrins, Barre des**.

Barry, John (1944–) Born: England. One of Britain's best winter climbers. Bibliography: *Cold Climbs* (1983) with Ken Wilson and Dave Alcock, *The Great Climbing Adventure* (1985), *Safety in Mountains, Snow and Ice Climbing* (1987), *K2 Savage Mountain, Savage Summer* (1987), *Alpine Climbing* (1988), *Climbing School* (1988), *Rock Climbing* (1988).

Bartholomew, Orland (1899–1957) In 1929, Bartholomew became the first person to ascend **Mt. Whitney** in winter. He accomplished this during a 14-week period of ski **mountaineering** in the **Sierras** ("Recognition").

Baruntse 7,168 m, 23,517 ft. This major peak is located within the **Himalayas** in **Nepal**. It was first ascended in 1954, by Colin Todd and

Geoff Harrow of the **Hillary** New Zealand Expedition via the South Ridge. (See also color photos.)

Basalt The most abundant volcanic **rock**, dark, sometimes black and dense. It may solidify in columnar form, for example, on **Devil's Tower**.

Base In **skiing**, the amount of **snow** that has accumulated and solidified, upon which the new powder falls. A base of five inches, for example, is inadequate, whereas a base of 48 inches provides an excellent skiing surface.

Base camp In expeditionary **mountaineering**, the camp set up at the lowest point of the climb; in the **Himalayas**, this may be as high as 18,000 feet. The coordinator and other members remain here in large, comfortable, and well-stocked tents, as the climbers attempt to set up and stock higher camps (as many as seven) at increasing altitudes, until a summit bid can be made. At popular climbing sites (on **Denali** or **Everest**, for example), the base camp area bristles with innumerable, colorful tents.

B.A.S.E. jumping (sometimes BASE) An acronym for a comparatively new sport in which people jump off a building, antenna, span (bridge), or earth (cliff).

Basin A depression, sometimes filled with **water**.

Bass, Dick (1937–) In 1985, Bass became the first person to do the **seven summits**. (See the riveting account in *Seven Summits*.)

Bassas da India Lowest point, Indian Ocean 0 m; highest point, unnamed location 2.4 m, 8 ft.

Bat The only flying **mammal**, bats feed on blood, insects, and fruit, but the species likely to be encountered at higher elevations are probably insectivores. During the day, bats rest in caves and mines. The eastern pipistrelle and the big brown can be seen in mountainous regions, while the big free-tailed enjoys "crevices in cliffs" (Collins).

Bates, Robert (Bob) (1901–) Accompanied **Washburn** on **Lucania** and **Houston** on two **K2** expeditions. (See Roberts's *Escape from Lucania*.)

Batholiths A large quantity of intrusive **igneous rock**; there are many in the western United States and Canada.

Batholith (Laura Lindblad)

Battle Flame (1959) This very low-budget movie by R. G. Springfield, set during the Korean War, is notable for its bizarre use of "stock shots." Many parts of the movie, whether battle scenes, platoons progressing, or ships sailing away, come from other films. The movie is rather slow and unexciting and the transitions from location to studio are rather awkward, but there are nice mountains in the stock-shots and lots of snow even in the studio. (M-A. H.)

Battle of the Bulge, The A 1965 American film directed by Ken Annakin; it depicts the last counterattack by the Nazis on the French–Belgian border, during the winter of 1944–1945. The Ardennes, where the fight took place, are smaller mountains, but the topography as well as climatic conditions made this battle rather unusual for the Allied Forces. (M-A. H.)

Batura 7,785 m, 25,541 ft. This major peak is located within the **Karakoram** Range in **Pakistan**; it was first climbed in 1976 Hubert Bleicher and Herbert Oberhofer.

Bauer, Paul (1896–) Born: Germany. He led the 1929 and 1931 German expeditions to **Kangchenjunga**. Bibliography: *Himalayan Campaign* (1937), *Himalayan Quest* (1938), *Kangchenjunga Challenge* (1955), *The Siege of Nanga Parbat, 1856–1953* (1956).

Bear A large and sometimes aggressive **mammal** weighing as much as 2,200 pounds. Three species can be found in the mountains. The black (weighing up to 660 pounds, but usually less) is ubiquitous in the eastern and western United States. The brown (to 2,200 pounds) is widely dispersed in Montana, Wyoming, the Yukon, and northern Europe and Asia, and is perhaps the most dangerous of the mountain bears. The grizzly (a subspecies of the brown) can be found in the western states. The bearlike giant panda, despite its prescribed diet, also inhabits mountainous terrain (Burnie). Bears are omnivorous and famous for picking berries, stealing honey from hives and food from humans, and catching salmon. They are smart, powerful, extremely fast, and good tree climbers, and they have an extraordinary sense of smell. Bears are now frequently inured to humans, and thus less afraid than they may have been hundreds of years ago. Some hibernate. All bears, but especially mothers with cubs, are extremely dangerous, and should be avoided in the wilderness or **high mountains**. One can carry a warning bell and bear-deterrent as a precaution.

Bear, Mt. 4,521 m, 14,831 ft. Located in the **Wrangell–St. Elias National Park**, in **Alaska**.

Beardtongue There are almost three hundred species of this **flower** (Nicholls), which grows on stalks and comes in many colors; petals sometimes resemble an extended tongue.

Beartooth Highway An amazing engineering feat, this road, which crosses from the northeast entrance of **Yellowstone** to the city of Red Lodge, **Montana**, climbs up a high pass, well over 10,000 ft, and affords wonderful vistas of the rugged Absaroka Mountains and the **Beartooth Range**. **Granite Peak**, Montana's highpoint, is located nearby. (See also **10 Mountain Roads** sidebar.)

Beartooth Range A powerful range in southern **Montana**, near **Yellowstone**. The highpoint of Montana, **Granite Peak**, is located within this range.

Beaver A **mammal** that cuts trees down in order to dam flowing water; this creates ponds and small lakes.

A Park Bear in Yellowstone (Haynes/National Geographic)

Beckey, Fred (1921–) An influential American mountaineer with many first ascents to his credit including the first winter climb of **Mt. Robson**; he was the second person to reach **Mt. Waddington**'s summit. Beckey is the author of *Mountains of North America* (Child).

Bedrock Rock that underlies the earth's surface; when visible, it is an **outcrop**.

Beech A widely dispersed **deciduous tree**, hardy though prone to disease.

Belarus Lowest point, Nyoman River 90 m, 295 ft; highest point, Dzyarzhynskaya Hara 346 m, 1,135 ft.

Belay *Assurance* (F), *Sicherheit* (G), *sicurezza* (I). A term used to indicate some form of control in order to protect a moving climber. A self-belay might entail connecting one's **harness** via a **rope** to a **piton, cam,** or **picket**. The climber could then sit, lean, or stand without fear of falling, or he or she could pay out the rope and lower down the **slope** or **wall**. In tandem **climbing**, a person might attach to a piton or **nut** and then play out the rope as the second person worked up or down. A belay device, such as a **figure eight**, through which the rope is threaded, creates friction on the rope and thereby gives the belayer a potent advantage; thus, a small woman can easily hold a heavy man, even though he may swing freely or **pendulum** with full weight on the rope.

Belgium Lowest point, North Sea 0 m; highest point, Signal de Botrange 694 m, 2,277 ft. From this small nation, known as the "flat country," as sung wonderfully by Jacques Brel, hail some important climbers, including King **Albert I**. Some fine rock climbing is found in the cliff areas near Luxembourg.

Belize Lowest point, Caribbean Sea 0 m; highest point, Victoria Peak 1,160 m, 3,806 ft.

Bell, Gertrude (1868–1926) Excellent mountaineer (and British intelligence agent).

Bell, James Horst Brunnerman (1896–1976) Born: Scotland. Bibliography: *British Hills and Mountains* (1940), *A Progress in Mountaineering* (1950).

Bella Coola This small harbor is located on the rugged coast of **British Columbia**, in **Canada**. Bella Coola is surrounded by remote, beautiful mountains and misty **fjords**; Tweedsmuir Provincial Park and the Coast Ranges are highlights of the area. A road leading to Williams Lake, some 400 km away, was recently opened; along that road is the tiny town of Tatla Lake, which is the starting point for some climbs in the **Mt. Waddington** area; there are more bears than people in this pristine wilderness.

Belt An area characterized by something, for example, a **deciduous** belt.

Ben (Sc) Mountain.

Ben Nevis 1,343 m, 4,406 ft. Located in Scotland, this is the highest peak in Great Britain.

Benchmark A mark placed by a surveyor indicating **altitude**. In the **United States**, it takes the form of a metallic disk cemented into a rock surface usually, though not always, at the highest point on the mountain. (See also color photos.)

Benin Lowest point, Atlantic Ocean 0 m; highest point, Mont Sokbaro 658 m, 2,159 ft.

Berg-Ejvind och Hans Hustru/The Outlaw and His Wife/You and I A 1918 Swedish movie by Victor Sjöström (1879–1960), who stars with his then mistress Edith Erastoff (1887–1945). A stranger arrives to work on a farm, and the boss's daughter falls in love with him; when it turns out he is an escaped convict, they run away in the mountains. The movie was one of the first to use landscapes as part of the dramatization, thus having a lasting influence. In fact, it did for mountains what Sjöström's *Terje Vigen* (1916) had done for the sea: backgrounds were no longer just scenery; they enhanced the conflicts, induced relationships, and put the stress on depth of focus more than any movie up to that time. The photography was by Julius Jaenzon (1885–1961), who had an uncanny capacity to catch the light despite the poor technical equipment at his disposal. Aside from its great aesthetic value, the film is also a rough drama, strikingly realistic, and still considered one of the finest silent pictures ever made. (M.-A. H.)

Bergschrund (*'schrund*) (G), *rimaye* (F). This word is used to describe a large **crevasse** that opens at the point where a glacier and either the upper snow or the rock of the mountain meet.

Bergsymphonie/Mountain Symphony First of the 13 tone poems by Hungarian composer Franz

Liszt (1811–1886), sketched as early as 1833 but composed mostly in 1849–1850; it was inspired by a Victor Hugo poem, "Ce Qu'on Entend sur la Montagne" ("What One Hears on the Mountain"). What one hears is the soft melody of nature as well as the harsh cries of suffering humanity. (M-A. H.)

Berhault, Patrick, (fl. 1980s–1990s) One of the top rock climbers in France in the 1980s and 1990s. Mountaineering achievements: in 1978, first winter ascent on the Plaques route in the **Ailefroide**; in 1981, with **Jean-Marc Boivin**, in series, south side of the Fou, American direct in one day; in 1991, complete traverse of the Mont Blanc massif; in 1992, with Fred Vimal, series in one day, super integral of Peuterey; in 1995, first solo ascent on the Hughetto-Rugeri way, north side of the Corno Stella; in 1996, first winter ascent of the Fourastier route in the Rateau. He also participated in numerous expeditions: **Shisha Pangma**, Chinese route; first complete west to east traverse of the spurs; opening of new rock climbs in the Hoggar. Technical rock climbing: several 8a's and 8b's.

Bermuda Lowest point, Atlantic Ocean 0 m; highest point, Town Hill 76 m, 249 ft.

Bernese Alps Located near Bern, in **Switzerland**, this range counts numerous high peaks, including the **Finsteraarhorn**, the **Jungfrau**, the **Eiger**, and the **Mönch**. The largest **glacier** in the **Alps**, the **Aletsch Glacier**, is located in the Bernese Alps, or Bernese Oberland.

Bernina, Piz 4,049 m, 13,284 ft. This is the 54th highest of the 60 major 4,000-meter peaks in the **Alps**, and the highest peak in the Swiss region of **Engadine**. The Bernina is a truly superb, heavily glaciated mountain. The weather is generally nice and dry in Engadine, highly favorable for excellent alpine climbs. The Bernina was first climbed in 1850 by Johann Coaz and Jon and Lorenz Ragut Tscharner. (See also color photos.)

Beta Information concerning a rock climb.

Between Heaven and Hell (1956) This war movie directed by Richard Fleischer deals with the spoiled son of a rich Southerner who finds himself fighting in the Pacific during World War II. The movie is set on a mountainous island, woods surround the soldiers, traps are found in the vegetation, and enemies are everywhere. The incredibly long tracking shot following a character as he climbs down the hill is quite famous. (M-A. H.)

Bhutan Lowest point, Drangme Chhu 97 m, 318 ft; highest point, **Kula Kangri** 7,554 m, 24,783 ft. For mountaineers and trekkers alike, this small country may be the famed Shangri-La: beautiful mountain villages, spectacular summits, and relatively easy high-altitude treks can be found there, as well as some extremely serious, unclimbed peaks. (See color photos.)

Bierstadt, Albert (1830–1902) A 19th-century painter, famous for his mountain landscapes; he was a founding member of the Hudson River School; he was born in **Germany** and immigrated to the **United States**. A number of North American peaks bear his name, including one in **Colorado**'s **Front Range**. (See also **Mt. Bierstadt**, **Frederic Edwin Church**, and color photos.)

Bierstadt, Mt. 4,286 m, 14,060 ft, one of the 54 14,000-foot peaks in **Colorado**. It is named after the painter.

Big Wall See **climbing**.

Bigfoot See **yeti**.

Bighorn sheep A **bovid** found in the **Rocky Mountains**; it is an agile climber and sometimes seems to defy gravity as it moves up and down on **cliff** faces.

Birch A **deciduous tree** whose peeling bark varies dramatically according to species. Yellow and white can be found in mountainous areas.

Bird A warm-blooded, feathered, and winged creature, of which there are thousands of species. Most fly. Sometimes, those associated with lower elevations are found at **altitude**, for example, the **flamingo**. See individual species throughout this volume.

Bishop, Barry Chapman (1932–1994) American mountaineer with **first ascents** of **Ama Dablam** and **Denali's** West Buttress. He was a member of the 1963 American **Everest expedition**.

Bishorn 4,159 m, 13,645 ft. This is the 36th highest of the 60 major 4,000-meter peaks in the **Alps**. It was first climbed in 1884, by G. S. Barnes, R. Chessyre-Walker, Joseph Imboden, and J. M. Chanton. It is located in the **Valaisan Alps**, in the **Weisshorn** group.

Bison Also called buffalo; the correct name is the American bison. This magnificent animal once roamed the plains and traveled in herds totaling many millions of individuals. Hunting decimated its numbers and, in the wild, it is now limited to preserves in national parks.

Bivouac (bivy) *Bivacco* (I), *Biwak* (G) When **climbing**, a planned or forced halt during which one curls up as best one can, on the surface or in a **snow cave**, and waits until inclement **weather** or darkness abates.

Bivouac (bivy) bag A compact, waterproof enclosure, similar to a sleeping bag, used by climbers in an emergency to protect against cold and wetness when a tent is unavailable or unusable.

Black Canyon of the Gunnison At 2,000 feet, this Colorado **canyon** is the fifth deepest **gorge** in the United States (Ament, personal comment). Its difficult faces, composed of rocks that are among the oldest in North America, are popular with those who enjoy big wall **climbing**.

Black Diamond Founded by **Yvon Chouinard**, this company produces superb climbing equipment. Its catalog is a work of art.

Black Hills A mountainous area in **South Dakota** that has an austere beauty. **Mt. Rushmore** is located here.

Black ice See **ice**.

Black Narcissus A 1947 English film, starring Deborah Kerr and David Farrar, written, produced, and directed by Michael Powell (1905–1990) and Emeric Pressburger (1902–1988) and based on a novel by Rumer Godden. It tells of the attempted settlement of a monastery by English nuns in Tibet. A great achievement by Powell and Pressburger. The stupendous Technicolor photography of Jack Cardiff won both Golden Globe and Academy Awards, and the art direction of Alfred Junge also garnered an Academy Award. The film is full of gorgeous landscapes and breathtakingly high scenes. It was entirely shot near London, with special effects by veteran W. Percy Day (1878–1965). Some people say that the film is more realistic than many documentaries shot on location. (M-A. H.)

Blackburn, Mt. 4,996 m, 16,390 ft. One of the highest peaks in the **Wrangell–St. Elias Na-**tional Park**, in **Alaska**. This is a heavily glaciated and corniced mountain that can be accessed from McCarthy, which is reached by traveling more than 60 miles on a dirt road. The area is magnificent, with abundant wildlife and superb peaks and glaciers.

Blind Husbands (1919) An American movie written and directed by Erich von Stroheim. During an Austrian vacation, an American couple faces an attempted seduction of the wife by a local military officer. Stroheim of course plays the nasty officer, with shaven head and monocle, suavity concealing lustful ideas and cowardliness. Climbing reveals the real personalities of the characters, when the suspecting husband and the potential lover find themselves alone on top of a peak. Stroheim's original title was *The Pinnacle*. (M-A. H.)

Blizzard A severe **storm** accompanied by lots of **snow**, **wind**, and low temperatures. It may lead to extremely hazardous conditions, such as a **whiteout**.

Blodig, Karl (1859–1956) The first person to climb all of the 4,000-meter Alpine mountains. He wrote *The High Mountains of the Alps*, which "is one of the best-selling mountaineering books of all time" (Ardito).

Blowdown Trees that are knocked over by the force of the wind. On **Mt. Elbert**, the authors observed thousands of such downed trees, the result of severe winds (or perhaps the final run-out of an **avalanche**). In 1999, in **Minnesota's** Boundary Waters, ten million trees were blown over in a severe windstorm.

Bluebird This small bluish bird, once so common, has been less visible during the past decade or so. The mountain bluebird can be found at higher altitudes.

Bluff Steep and broad **cliff**.

Blum, Arlene (1945–) Leader of the all-woman team that in 1978 put the first Americans on the summit of **Annapurna**. (See *Annapurna, A Woman's Place*.)

Boar Indigenous to Europe, wild boar, with long tusks, now also inhabit parts of the United States. They wander in the mountains.

Boardman, Peter (1950–1982) Born: Bramhall, England. A foremost British mountaineer in the

1970s and early 1980s, he reached the summit of **Everest** on the British southwest face expedition of 1975. The Boardman-Tasker Mountaineering Literature Award is named, in part, in his honor. Bibliography: *The Shining Mountain* (1978), *Sacred Summits* (1982), *Kongur, China's Elusive Summit* (1982) by **Chris Bonington**, *Everest the Unclimbed Ridge* (1983), by Chris Bonington and Charles Clarke.

Bobcat See **cat**.

Boivin, Jean-Marc (1951–1990) One of the top French climbers in the 1970s and 1980s; his expeditions include: Peru, 1978; Pakistan, **K2**, 1979; Pakistan, top and hang glider flight; Argentina, Chile, Venezuela, Greenland, Patagonia, and **Everest**, in 1988, when he performed the first hang glider flight from the top of Everest. Boivin also performed a series combining climbs, extreme skiing, and hang gliding, or ***enchaînements***: in 1980, the **Matterhorn**; in 1981, Fou-Dru (with **Patrick Berhault**); in 1985, Vertes–**Droites**–Courtes–Linceuil in one day. He also **soloed** a number of extreme climbs: in 1973, Cordier in the Verte; in 1976, Lagarde-Ségogne in the Plan; in 1978, Bonatti-Zapelli in the pillar of Angle. Finally, in extreme skiing, he performed a number of firsts: in 1977, first run down the Frendo; in 1978, first run down **Huascarán**; in 1980, first run down the east side of the Matterhorn; in 1985, first run down the Y-shaped channel in the Verte; in 1989, first run down the Nant-Blanc.

Bolivia Lowest point, Río Paraguay 90 m, 295 ft; highest point, Nevado **Sajama** 6,520 m, 21,423 ft. Another important mountain country, where the mighty **Andes** are divided in a number of major **cordilleras**, including the Cordillera Real and the Cordillera Occidental. Other major summits include: **Tocorpurri** 6,755 m, 22,162 ft; Sajama 6,520 m, 21,423 ft; **Illimani** 6,462 m, 21,200 ft; **Ancohuma** 6,388 m, 20,958 ft; **Illampu** 6,362 m, 20,872 ft; Nevado Parinacota 6,320 m, 20,767 ft; Chearocko 6,127 m, 20,101 ft; Huayna Potosi 6,094 m, 19,993 ft; Chachacomani 6,074 m, 19,927 ft; Sairecabur 5,978 m, 19,613 ft; Licancabur 5,930 m, 19,455 ft; and Condoriri 5,648 m, 18,530 ft. (See also color photos.)

Bollard A natural or constructed piece of **rock** or **ice** or chunk of **snow** that is used as an **anchor** point for a **belay** or **rappel**.

Bolt Similar to a **piton**, a bolt is screwed or glued into a drilled hole in the rock face in order to provide an **anchor** point for climbing **protection** or **aid**.

Bomb A small or larger piece of **lava** that takes on its form as it solidifies in flight.

Bona, Mt. 5,005 m, 16,421 ft. One of the highest peaks in the **Wrangell–St. Elias National Park**, in **Alaska**, it offers excellent climbing in a remote and pristine area. The weather can be quite dangerous, since brutal storms from the Gulf of Alaska can reach the Wrangell Range with fierce intensity.

Bonatti, Walter (1930–) Born: Bergamo, Italy. An Italian climber, guide, and author. Unsworth insists that his Alpine climbs are unequalled (*Encyclopaedia*). His **first ascents** include east face of the Grand Capucin (with L. Ghigo), 1951; SW Pillar of the Dru (solo), 1955; Eckpfeiler Buttress (with T. Gobbi), 1957; Pilastro Rosso (with A. Oggioni), 1959; **Mont Blanc** Route Major (first solo ascent), 1959; **Matterhorn** North Face Direct (winter solo), 1965. He was a member of the Italian expedition that made the first ascent of **K2** in 1954, although he was not in the summit party. In 1958 he made the first ascent of **Gasherbrum IV** with C. Mauri. Bibliography: *The Ascent of K2* (1955) by Ardito Desio, *On the Heights* (1964), *The Great Days* (1974), *Magic of Mont Blanc* (1985). Also see his *Mountains of My Life*. (See also the **10 Best All-Around Mountaineers** sidebar.)

Bone In **snowboarding**, to straighten the legs.

Bong A wide, aluminum **piton** invented by **Chouinard** and **Frost**. Bongs were used in wider **cracks** in **Yosemite** until **nuts** and **cams** replaced them (Ament, personal comment).

Bonington, Sir Christian John Storey (1934–) A well-known British climber, author, and photographer who holds numerous **first ascents**, for example, the Central Pillar of Fréney and **Nuptse**. He was also the leader of, or a participant in, innumerable successful expeditions, including: **Nuptse**, 1961; south face of **Annapurna**, 1970; southwest face of **Everest**, 1975;

Changabang, 1974; the **Ogre**, 1977; **Kongur**, 1981; Everest, 1985, when he summitted. Chris Bonington's climbing resume is extremely impressive. Bibliography: *I Chose to Climb* (1966), autobiography, *Annapurna South Face* (1971), *The Next Horizon* (1973), autobiography, *Everest South-West Face* (1973), *Changabang* (1975) with Martin Boysen and others, *Everest the Hard Way* (1976), *Quest for Adventure* (1981), *Kongur, China's Elusive Summit* (1982), *Everest the Unclimbed Ridge* (1983) with Charles Clarke, *The Everest Years, A Climber's Life* (1986), autobiography, *The Climbers* (1992), *High Achiever* (1999) biography by Jim Curran, *Tibet's Secret Mountain: The Triumph of Sepu Kangri* (2000) with Charles Clarke, *Chris Bonington's Everest* (2002) (www.bonington.com).

Bonney, Thomas George (1833–1923) Born: England. A geologist and mountaineer, he was also president of the Alpine Club in 1881–1883. Bibliography: *Outline Sketches in the High Alps of Dauphine* (1865), *The Alpine Regions of Switzerland and the Neighbouring Countries* (1868), *The Building of the Alps* (1912), *Memories of a Long Life* (1921).

Book dealers Most new and used bookstores carry material related to mountains, and **equipment retailers** such as Recreational Equipment, Inc. also offer pertinent volumes. Some concerns may have large stocks on climbing, geology, biology, ornithology, and many other topics. Only a few dealers specialize in mountains or mountaineering, for example, Top of the World Books in Williston, Vermont, www.topworldbooks.com, or Chessler Books in Evergreen, Colorado, at www.chesslerbooks.com. See also Alpenbooks in Washington State, which deals in all outdoor activities (www.alpenbooks.com).

Boots See **clothing**.

Bora See **winds**.

Borah Peak 3,859 m, 12,662 ft. The highest point of **Idaho**, it is a relatively easy, but vertiginous climb. The peak is named after a former governor of Idaho.

Bosnia and Herzegovina Lowest point, Adriatic Sea 0 m; highest point, Maglic 2,386 m, 7,828 ft. The southern tip of the **Dinaric Alps** runs through this very small country (51,130 sq km, 19,741 sq miles).

Hobnailed Boots (F. R. Martin/National Geographic)

Botswana Lowest point, junction of the Limpopo and Shashe Rivers 513 m, 1,683 ft; highest point, Tsodilo Hills 1,489 m, 4,885 ft.

Boukreev, Anatoli (1957–1999) A superb, extremely strong, and accomplished Russian climber, he guided numerous expeditions in the Himalayas, and became a participant in the 1996 **Everest** disaster, where he helped a number of climbers huddled on the South Col in a fierce storm find their way to camp. His climbing accomplishments are extremely impressive; they include: in 1980, Pik Kommunizma, 7,495 m, and **Pik Lenin**, 7,134 m; between 1981 and 1993, over 30 7,000-meter ascents and 200 other climbs in the **Tien Shan**, **Pamir**, and **Caucasus** Ranges; in 1989, April 15, **Kangchenjunga**, 8,556 m, new route, April 30–May 2, Kangchenjunga, new route, and first traverse of the four 8,000-meter summits of Kangchenjunga **Massif** (from Ylung-Khang to South Summit); in 1990, February, Pik Pobeda, 7,400 m, first winter ascent, April, **Denali**, 6,193 m, first ascent with clients on Cassin Ridge, May, Denali, first solo speed ascent West Rib 10.5 hrs, Aug., **Khan Tengri**, 7,005 m, first solo speed ascent, Aug., Pik Pobeda, 7,400 m, first solo speed ascent; in 1991, Oct. 7, Mt. Everest, 8,850 m, South Col route first Russian–American expedition, May 10, **Dhaulagiri**, 8,167 m, West Wall new route; in 1993, July 1–3, **K2**, Chogori, 8,611 m, German International Expedition; in 1994, April 29, **Makalu**, 8,460 m, guided ascent of First Summit Tower, May 15, Makalu, 8,463 m, speed ascent 46 hours; in 1995, May 17, Mt. Everest, North Ridge route, Oct. 8, Dhaulagiri, 8,167 m, 17 hrs. 15 min. record speed ascent, Dec 8, **Manaslu**, 8,163 m, winter ascent; in 1996, Oct. 9, **Shisha Pangma**, 8,008 m, north summit, solo ascent, Sept. 25, **Cho Oyu**, 8,201 m north side, solo ascent, May 10, Mt. Everest, South Col route, May 17, **Lhotse**, 8,516 m, speed solo ascent 21 hrs. 16 min.; in 1997, July 14, **Gasherbrum II**, 8,035 m, solo speed ascent, Camp ABC (5,800 m) to summit 9 hrs. 30 min., July 7, **Broad Peak**, 8,047 m, solo ascent, May 23, Lhotse, April 23, Everest. This last series represents a record four 8,000-meter peaks in 80 days! Tragically, Boukreev died in an avalanche on Annapurna. By 1999, he had climbed 10 of the 14 8,000-meter peaks. See his book on the 1996 Everest tragedy, *The Climb: Tragic Ambitions on Everest* by Anatoli Boukreev and G. Weston Dewalt.

Boulder A piece of **rock** at least eight inches in diameter, but sometimes much larger. It is also a city in **Colorado** well-known for rock **climbing**.

Bouldering Attempting to traverse or ascend a **boulder**, a sport that may require great skill. (See also **climbing** and www.Johngill.net.)

Three Boulderers (ca. 1991): Royal Robbins, John Gill, Chris Jones (Pat Ament)

Boundary Peak   4,006 m, 13,143 ft. The highest point in **Nevada**, it is located within the **White Mountain** Range, near the **California** border. The area is dry, remote, and rugged; wild **mustangs** roam the lower slopes of the mountain.

Bouvet Island   Lowest point, Southern Ocean 0 m; highest point, unnamed location 780 m, 2,559 ft.

Bovids   Of the 140 species of bovids, only a few inhabit mountainous terrain: the **bighorn sheep**, **bison**, buffalo, bushbuck, **chamois**, **ibex**, klipspringer, **mountain goat**, and **yak**, among others (Burnie and Wilson).

Boysen, Jan Anders Martin   (1941–) Born: England. One of the leading British mountaineers of the 1960s and 1970s. Bibliography: *Annapurna South Face* (1971) by Chris Bonington, *Changabang* (1975) with C. J. S. Bonington and others, *Trango, the Nameless Tower* (1978) by Jim Curran.

Brazil   Lowest point, Atlantic Ocean 0 m; highest point, Pico da Neblina 3,014 m, 9,888 ft. Most of this fifth largest country in the world (8,456,510 sq km, 3,265,242 sq miles) is occupied by the Amazon basin, a low-lying land of equatorial rain forests and attendant jungles; however, the western end of the country lies in the foothills of the **Andes** and is a spectacular landscape of enormous waterfalls, deep canyons, and river gorges, containing numerous endangered species and some of the most exotic plant life, including extremely rare orchids.

Break trail   The first person to move along any surface covered with **snow** (on foot or on skis) must work harder than those who follow. If the new snow coverage is minimal or is overlaid with a hard **crust**, then it can be fairly easy to break trail, but if there is considerable new, soft accumulation or drifting, then the leader can be worn out very quickly. Struggling through knee- or thigh-deep snow at 20,000 feet is an exhausting task. For this reason, trail breakers will sometimes alternate **leads**.

Breashears, David   (1956–) A bold, leading American rock climber and, later, mountaineer with four **Everest** summits to his credit. He is also an excellent photographer and cinematographer, responsible for the Imax Everest film. (See also the **10 Recommended Mountain and Climbing Documentaries** sidebar.)

Breccia   A coarse, sedimentary or volcanic rock.

Breche (F)   A high, narrow **notch** or saddle.

Breithorn   4,165 m, 13,665 ft. This is the 33rd highest of the 60 major 4,000-meter peaks of the **Alps**. It was first climbed in 1813 by Henri Maynard, Joseph-Marie Couttet, Jean Gras, and Jean-Baptiste and Jean-Jacques Erin. A beautiful peak, presenting a steep north face, it was ascended early in the 19th century, as its normal route is a relatively straightforward enterprise; the peak is located near **Monte Rosa**, in the heart of the **Valaisan Alps**. (See also color photos.)

Brenner Pass   An important pass that links the Tyrolean areas of **Austria** and **Italy** via the Europabrücke.

Bridge   In **rock climbing**, to **stem** or extend one's legs in opposite directions especially in a **chimney**. (See also **engineering**.)

British Columbia   Lowest point, Pacific Ocean 0 m; highest point, **Mt. Fairweather** 4,663 m, 15,299 ft. One of the 13 Canadian provinces and territories, known for its superb mountain ranges, including the Coast Ranges featuring **Mt. Waddington**, at 4,019 m, 13,186 ft, the highest point entirely within British Columbia, and **Mt. Tiedemann** 3,848 m, 12,625 ft and the **Canadian Rockies**, including the Purcell and **Bugaboo** Ranges, the **Columbia Ice Field**, and **Mt. Robson**, the highest peak in the Canadian Rockies. Its coast has been carved by glaciers and includes numerous fjords and inlets, including the Butte Inlet, and the fjords around **Bella Coola** and Prince George. Other important peaks in British Columbia include Mt. Root (on the **Alaska**–B.C. boundary) 3,901 m, 12,799 ft; in the Coast Ranges, Combatant Mountain 3,756 m, 12,323 ft, Asperity 3,716 m, 12,192 ft, Serra Peaks 3,642 m, 11,949 ft, and Monarch Mountain 3,459 m, 11,348 ft; in the Canadian Rockies, Mt. Clemenceau 3,642 m, 11,949 ft, Mt. Goodsir 3,581 m, 11,749 ft, and Snow Dome 3,520 m, 11,549 ft; in the Selkirk Mountains, Mt. Sir Sandford 3,522 m, 11,555 ft; in the Cariboo Mountains, Mt. Sir Wilfrid Laurier 3,520 m, 11,549 ft; and in the Purcell Mountains, Mt. Farnham 3,481 m, 11,421 ft.

British Indian Ocean Territory Lowest point, Indian Ocean 0 m; highest point, unnamed location on Diego Garcia 15 m, 49 ft.

British Mountaineering Council (BMC) (1944) An organization that advises and oversees mountaineering interests in Great Britain; hundreds of individual clubs are involved.

British Virgin Islands Lowest point, Caribbean Sea 0 m; highest point, Mt. Sage 521 m, 1,709 ft.

Broad Peak (Also Falchen Kangri, K3) 8,047 m, 26,400 ft. A major peak in **Pakistan**, it is the 12th highest peak in the world. Broad Peak was first climbed on June 9, 1957, by an Austrian team comprising **Kurt Diemberger, Hermann Buhl**, Marcus Schmuck, and Fritz Wintersteller. As of the end of 1999, Broad Peak had been climbed 218 times; 18 climbers died either attempting the summit or descending. (See also the **14 8,000-Meter Peaks** sidebar.)

Brooks Range A **range** that runs across northern **Alaska**.

Broome, Edward Alfred (1846–1920) Although not well known today, Broome was, according to Unsworth, "One of the most remarkable climbers of his day." His first ascents include the Schalligrat on the **Weisshorn** (*Encyclopaedia*).

Brown, Joe (1930–) Born: Ardwick, Manchester, England. A great and influential British rock climber and mountaineer; he summitted **Kangchenjunga** in 1955 (Unsworth, *Encyclopaedia*); this was the **first ascent**. Bibliography: *Kanchenjunga: The Untrodden Peak* (1956), by Charles Evans; *The Hard Years* (1967); *Portrait of a Mountaineer* (1971), by Don Whillans with Alick Ormerod.

Brown, Katie (1981–) During the 1990s, she was a gifted superstar sport climber, at a young age.

Brown, Thomas Graham (1882–1965) Born: England. A pioneer of several important routes on the Brenva Face of **Mont Blanc**. Bibliography: *Brenva* (1944).

Bruce, Hon. Charles Granville (1866–1939) Born: England. A soldier, mountaineer, and Himalayan explorer. Leader of the 1922 and 1924 **Everest** expeditions. Alpine Club president, 1923–1925. Bibliography: *Twenty Years in the Hi-malaya* (1910), *Kulu and Lahoul* (1914), *The Assault on Mount Everest 1922* (1923), *Himalayan Wanderer* (1934).

Brunei Lowest point, South China Sea 0 m; highest point, Bukit Pagon 1,850 m, 6,070 ft.

Buddhism The prevailing religion in the mountainous areas of **Nepal**; Hinduism is favored in the urban areas.

Buffalo See **bison**.

Bugaboos Extraordinary monoliths in the Purcell Range of **British Columbia**. (See also color photos.)

Buhl, Hermann (1924–1957) A superb Austrian rock climber who virtually invented the idea of oxygenless, self-contained **ascents** of high peaks. In 1953, he soloed the last 4,000 feet and four miles on **Nanga Parbat** without supplementary **oxygen**; this is perhaps the first climb of an 8,000-meter peak without this aid. Roth calls this "one of the greatest mountaineering feats ever performed." On June 9, 1957, Buhl was a member of the team that first ascended **Broad Peak.** He died eighteen days later on **Chogolisa**, when he walked off the edge of a **cornice** while descending with **Kurt Diemberger.** He holds **first ascents** of two 8,000-meter mountains; see the Diemberger entry. (His *Lonely Challenge*—the American title of *Nanga Parbat Pilgrimage*—is a riveting memoir.) Bibliography: *Nanga Parbat Pilgrimage* (1956), *Summits and Secrets* (1971) by Kurt Diemberger, *Hermann Buhl: Climbing Without Compromise* (2001) by Horst Hofler and **Reinhold Messner**.

Bulgaria Lowest point, Black Sea 0 m; highest point, Musala 2,925 m, 9,596 ft.

Buoux An important **rock climbing** center in southern France.

Burgener, Alexander (1846–1910) Born: Eisten in Saas, Switzerland. A great climber and Alpine guide; he holds many **first ascents** including the Grépon, which he did with **Mummery**. First ascents: **Lenzspitze**, 1870, Portjengrat, 1871, Grand Dru, 1878, Zmutt Ridge of the **Matterhorn**, 1879, Traverse of the Col du Lion, 1880, Grands Charmoz, 1880, Charpoua Face of the **Aiguille Verte**, 1881, Grépon, 1881, **Mont Maudit** by the Frontier Ridge, 1887,

Taschhörn by the Teufelsgrat, 1887. Bibliography: *My Climbs in the Alps and Caucasus* (1895) by A. Mummery, *The Early Alpine Guides* by R. W. Clark (1949).

Burgess shale A mountainous area in western Canada where many **fossils** are found.

Burke, Mick (1940–1975) A British mountaineer who was known for smoking at high elevations on **Annapurna** and **Everest,** where he disappeared. Bibliography: *Everest the Hard Way* (1976), by **Chris Bonington**.

Burkina Faso Lowest point, Mouhoun (Black Volta) River 200 m, 656 ft; highest point, Tena Kourou 749 m, 2,457 ft.

Burma See **Myanmar**.

Burn See **fire**.

Burundi Lowest point, **Lake Tanganyika** 772 m, 2,533 ft; highest point, Mt. Heha 2,670 m, 8,760 ft.

Butte An isolated, steeply sided extrusion, taller than wide; it exists because a larger mass has been eroded. Similar to though smaller than **mesas,** buttes are often extremely picturesque.

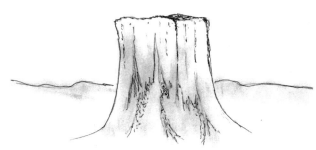

Butte (Laura Lindblad)

Buttercup A well-known and widely dispersed yellow **flower**. **Himalayan** species of this family vary in color (purple, for example) and grow to almost 16,000 ft (Polunin).

Buttress A large part of a mountain that projects outward, as in the West Buttress on **Denali**.

Byne, Eric (1911–1969) Born: England. He was an important contributor to the early guidebooks for the gritstone outcrops of the Peak District and Derbyshire. Bibliography: *High Peak* (1966), with Geoffrey Sutton.

C

Cable car See **gondola**.

Cagoule (F) (Not used in the United States.) Originally, a hood; a jacket that protects against cold and wetness.

Cairn *Chorten* (T), *homme de pierre* (F), *Steinhügel*, *Steinmann* (G), *vartha* (Ic). A small or sometimes quite large pile of **rocks** that has been set in place in order to commemorate an event, mark a location or summit, or indicate the correct route. For example, an enormous cairn is situated at Concordia, the **K2** base camp, and a series of cairns leads climbers to the top of **Mt. Washington** or along Froze-to-Death Plateau on **Montana**'s **Granite Peak**.

Cairngorm 1,245 m, 4,084 ft. A mountain in Scotland.

Calanques, Les Inlets in sea **cliffs** near Marseille, **France**. Here, the **limestone** cliffs can reach up to 400 m, 1,300 ft; most climbs are near vertical, with some **overhangs**, and the deep-blue waters of the Mediterranean below. (See also color photos.)

Caldera This Spanish word for **crater** is used to indicate a depression that is much larger than the original volcanic **vent**. It is created when a **volcano** collapses or explodes. **Crater Lake**, despite the misnomer, and **Haleakala** are examples.

Caldwell, Tommy (1979–) From about 2000 to 2003, he was one of the foremost rock climbers in the world. He did a **free** 5.13 ascent on Diamond Wall; this is the most difficult climbing ever done at ca. 14,000 ft (Pat Ament, personal comment). See Greg Child's *Over the Edge*.

California Lowest point, Badwater, Death Valley, −86 m, −282 ft; highest point, **Mt. Whitney**, 4,417 m, 14,494 ft (the second highest of the 50 state highpoints). The third largest state in the Unites States contains the highest point within the lower 48 contiguous states, Mt. Whitney, a towering **granite spire** on its eastern side, and a very large, gently sloping **plateau** on its western flank. California also contains the lowest point in the United States: Badwater, located in **Death Valley**. Extreme runners take advantage of the relative proximity of Mt. Whitney and Badwater for a 100-mile run from the lowest to the highest points within the 48 contiguous states; a grueling experience! The main mountain ranges of California include the **Sierra Nevada**, often referred to as "the Sierras"; the southernmost part of the **Cascades**, which extends as far north as **British Columbia**; the Coast Ranges; the **Trinity Alps**; the **White Mountain** Range, which forms the eastern side of **Owens Valley**; and the ranges framing the Los Angeles Basin, which include numerous peaks above 10,000 ft.

Calving When a piece of a **glacier** breaks off as an independent mass and floats away in a body of water.

Cam In **rock climbing**, a device that may be placed in an inset of rock; a spring-loaded variety that opens and holds after being inserted into a **crack** affords protection and can be extracted with ease. It is used when **nuts** may not hold the climber's weight. (See also **friend**.)

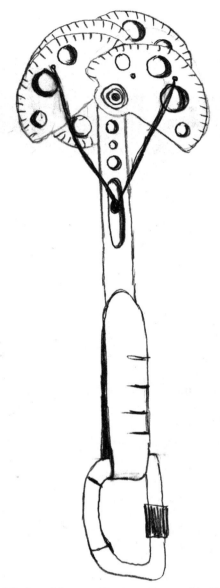

Cam with Carabiner at Bottom (Laura Lindblad)

Camber A ski's horizontal curve, which one can see by placing it on a flat surface.

Cambodia Lowest point, Gulf of Thailand 0 m; highest point, Phnum Aoral 1,810 m, 5,938 ft.

Camel A large, awkward-looking **mammal** that prefers a desert environment. Camels are used as pack **animals** and sometimes carry loads along **mountainous** trails. **Alpacas**, **llamas**, and **vicuñas** are all members of the camel family.

Cameroon Lowest point, Atlantic Ocean 0 m; highest point, Fako 4,095 m, 13,435 ft. The high-point, also known as Mt. Cameroon, is a large,

active strato-volcano, which last erupted in 1999. From the main active vent, located at an altitude of about 1,400 m, a voluminous **aa** flow of alkalic basalt extended for up to 7 km and blocked an important road.

Camp Especially in the **Andes** and **Himalayas**, a point at which tents are set up for the duration of an **expedition**. There are often several of these locations at progressively higher elevations. The lowest is called base camp, there may then be an advanced base camp; and then numbers are used, for example, camp one, camp two, etc. Climbers, **porters**, and **Sherpas** spend weeks stocking the tents, and when the expedition ends, the last climbers bring the highest material down to the lower camps. If things go badly, tents, **oxygen** cylinders, sleeping bags, and **food** may all be abandoned at various points on the mountain. According to Lloyd Ahearn (personal comment), camps are now used most frequently on commercial climbs of 8,000-meter peaks.

Camp 4 A campsite in **Yosemite** where climbers gathered; it was recently declared a historical site.

Canada Lowest point, Atlantic and Pacific Oceans 0 m; highest point, **Mt. Logan** 5,959 m, 19,551 ft. This vast country (9,330,970 sq km, 3,602,707 sq miles, the second largest in the world) is a wonderful place for the mountain lover: it contains a multitude of splendid ranges, including the **Canadian Rockies**, the Coast Ranges of **British Columbia**, and the **Wrangell–Saint Elias Mountains**, in the west, while the eastern provinces of Newfoundland and Québec contain older mountains sculpted during the last **Ice Age** and numerous **fjords**. The new territory of **Nunavut** also contains spectacular mountains carved by enormous ice fields; in particular, the physiognomy of Baffin Island is rather similar to that of Greenland, and a number of spectacular granitic spires and cliffs can be found in the north. As mentioned above, the west coast of Canada is lined with very large mountains, including **Mt. Waddington**, **Mt. Fairweather**, **Mt. St. Elias**, and Mt. Logan, all within a short distance from the seashore; as a result, numerous misty fjords can be found there, as well as active glaciers; for example, world-famous **Glacier Bay** is shared between **Alaska** and **British Columbia**. (See also color photos and maps.)

Canada goose   A large bird that inhabits mountain lakes and migrates in flocks. Its loud honking sound is extraordinary.

Canadian Rockies   The northern section of the **Rocky Mountains** is slightly lower in elevation than its U.S. counterpart, but the presence of numerous, and sometimes massive, glaciers gives it a very Alpine appearance. Many famous mountains and sites can be found in this beautiful range, including **Lake Louise**, **Banff** and **Jasper National Parks**, **Mt. Assiniboine**, the **Bugaboos**, and Mt. Columbia. The highest peak is the mighty **Mt**. **Robson**.

Canary Islands   These volcanic islands belong to **Spain**; the highest point is Teide Peak on Tenerife, at 3,718 m, 12,198 ft.

Canyon   Narrow, deep, horizontal or gently sloped **valley** between two steep lithic extrusions, often created by water erosion.

Canyoneering   A sport in which one descends steep and narrow canyons by downclimbing, rappelling, and swimming. It is especially popular in the southwestern part of the United States (www.canyoneeringusa.com/utah).

Cape Verde   Lowest point, Atlantic Ocean 0 m; highest point, Mt. Fogo 2,829 m, 9,281 ft (a volcano on Fogo Island).

Capstone   An extrusion of **rock** at the head of a **gully**.

Carabiner   (Biner) *Mousqueton* (F). Small device with a hinged, spring-loaded gate that is used to attach or control climbing **ropes**. They come in many shapes and sizes; either the gates swing freely under pressure or they lock, sometimes automatically. Carabiners, ropes, **pitons,** and **ice screws** or various types and sizes of **nuts** and **cams** all may come in handy as one moves upward. One can bully one's way up a slope in sneakers, but an **ice ax** and **crampons** help to assure that one will get back down without the aid of medical personnel. Dual axes are mandatory for vertical **ice** climbing. Other items that warrant mention include a **rack, wands, pickets, ascenders, compass** or **global position-**

ing system unit, and a cell phone or walkie-talkie. (See also **climbing shoes, skiing equipment**, and color photos.)

Carabiners and Figure Eight (Laura Lindblad)

Careful   A 1991 Canadian movie directed by Guy Maddin. This story of incestuous love and various others strange things is set in a little Swiss village where loud sounds are forbidden in order to avoid avalanches. Shot in the usual contrived style of the director, with homage to silent expressionist movies. (M-A. H.)

Caribou   A large **deer**-like, antlered **animal** that roams the northern **tundra** often in herds. When domesticated, caribou are called reindeer.

Carpathians   A 900-mile **range** in central **Europe**.

Carrel, Jean-Antoine   (1829–1890) An outstanding Italian **guide**; he did the first ascent of **Mont Blanc** from the Italian side. He later accompanied **Whymper** to the **Andes**, where he ascended **Chimborazo** and **Cotopaxi**. (See also **10 Best Guides** sidebar.)

Carstensz Pyramid   (Also Puncak/Pik Jaya) 5,039 m, 16,532 ft. A mountain in Indonesian New Guinea, now considered by most to be the seventh continental summit, rather than **Kosciusko**. The peak, located deep within the rain forests of New Guinea, was first ascended in 1962 by **Heinrich Harrer**, with Temple, Kippaz, and Huizenga. (See also the **Seven Summits** entry and sidebar.)

Cartography   See **maps**.

Carve   In **skiing** and **snowboarding**, to make large, symmetrical turns on a wide slope.

Cascades   A 700-mile-long **chain** in the northwestern **United States** and **Canada**. Its well-known volcanic **peaks** include **Mts. St. Helens**, **Rainier, Adams**, **Hood**, **Baker**, and **Shasta** (www.virtualcascades.com).

Cassin, Riccardo   (1909–) Born: Italy. A superb climber and mountaineer, his first ascents include the northeast face of the **Piz Badile** (1937), the Walker Spur of the **Grandes Jorasses** (1938), and the South Buttress of **Denali** (1961), later called the Cassin Ridge in his honor. Bibliography: *50 Years of Alpinism* (1981). (See also the **10 Best All-Around Mountaineers** sidebar.)

Castle Peak   4,348 m, 14,265 ft. This beautiful mountain, located within the **Elk Range**, is the

Major Peaks of the Cascade Range (Marie Madgwick)

12th highest peak in **Colorado**. (See also color photos.)

Castor   4,226 m, 13,864 ft. This is the 23rd highest of the 60 major 4,000-meter peaks of the **Alps**. It was first climbed in 1861 by William Mathews, F. W. Jacomb, and **Michel Croz**. This is the twin peak of **Pollux**. (See also color photos.)

Cat   A **mammal** that varies dramatically in size depending on species. Those that inhabit mountainous areas include the Indian tiger, the snow leopard, and the American mountain lion. The tiger is an aggressive predator that occasionally takes human prey; these marauders are hunted down and killed (see Corbett's *Man-Eaters of Kumaon*). The snow leopard travels above 16,000 ft (tracks have been spotted above 19,000) and is now an endangered species (see Matthiessen's *The Snow Leopard* and the superb film *Silent Roar*). The Andean cat is a very small creature about which little is known; it roams in the high Andes (Burnie and Wilson). The American bobcat weighs under 35 pounds, but the mountain lion, which ranges from the western United States through most of South America, has an average weight of 125 pounds but can be as heavy as 260. These are very dangerous animals, and during the past decade they have killed a number of hikers. The strong impression that cats made on American settlers is reflected in the plethora of names allocated to the same species (catamount, cougar, mountain lion, panther, and puma). Cats were virtually exterminated in the eastern United States almost 100 years ago, but today they may be making a comeback. In the western states, urban expansion is curtailing their habitat, and they can be found in suburban backyards and on city streets.

Catalogs   Manufacturers produce often stunning catalogs of their products. In some cases these include not only photographs of the equipment but also exquisite reproductions of mountains as well as essays by climbers. **Black Diamond,** Mountain Hardwear, and Patagonia have especially lovely catalogs.

Catenary, Mt.   4,097 m, 13,442 ft. One of the high peaks in **Canada**.

Catskills   A range of the **Appalachian** system found in **New York** State.

Caucasus A 550-mile mountain **system** in western Russia; it is here that **Elbrus**, the highest mountain in Europe, is located.

Cave An open area within a mountain (formed in limestone or basalt) to which there is often some form of ingress. Caves can be small and autonomous or enormous (e.g., Carlsbad Caverns) or interconnected over hundreds of miles (e.g., Mammoth Cave). Caves are even found in bedrock underneath glaciers. They have played an important role in the physical and cultural development of human beings. They have served as a place of refuge for early peoples, who sometimes embellished the walls with artistic images, for example, at Altimira in Spain or Lascaux in France. They were also used to store and protect artifacts such as tablets, manuscripts, and books: the Dead Sea Scrolls were found in a cave in Qumran, Israel. (See also **snow cave**.)

Cave temple A shrine built in a **cave**, especially those high on **cliff** sides, for example, at Maichishan in China (Sullivan), which are embellished with large sculptures and contain wall paintings and statues related to **Buddhism**. (See also **pueblo**.)

Cayman Islands Lowest point, Caribbean Sea 0 m; highest point, The Bluff 43 m, 141 ft.

Cedar An aromatic, coniferous **tree** that can be found in the mountains.

Central African Republic Lowest point, Oubangui River 335 m, 1,099 ft; highest point, Mont Ngaoui 1,420 m, 4,659 ft.

Cerro The Spanish word for **hill**.

Cerro Bonete 6,410 m, 22,020 ft. This is the 18th highest peak in the **Andes**; it was first climbed in 1913 by Walther Penck, solo. The peak is located in **Argentina** and was used as an observatory for detecting cosmic rays.

Cerro Fitzroy 3,375 m, 11,073 ft. An important mountain in **Argentina**, characterized by its sheer, vertical **granite** spires, and the hoarfrost, which forms an ice "mushroom" capping the summit. (See also color photos and **10 Awesome Monoliths** sidebar.)

Cerro Torre 3,133 m, 10,280 ft. An Andean peak in **Argentina** that some consider the most beautiful mountain in the world. It is located in the same range as **Fitzroy**, in **Patagonia**.

Chad Lowest point, Djourab Depression 160 m, 525 ft; highest point, Emi Koussi 3,415 m, 11,204 ft.

Chain A series either of **ridges** that run parallel to each other or of disconnected, stand-alone volcanic peaks. For example, the **Cascades** are a chain of **volcanoes**, although they are often referred to as a **range**. Collomb claims that a chain is shorter than and part of a larger range and cites the **Mont Blanc** chain, which is part of the **Alps**.

Chairlift A device that transports skiers to the tops of mountains. It is easy to ride, quick, and efficient but not as comfortable as a **gondola**. There are single, double, triple, and quadruple chairs; some even carry six skiers simultaneously. It is generally preferable to the earlier types of **ski lifts**.

Chalet A small or larger building with wide eaves modeled after Swiss Alpine farmhouses, often situated near a **ski area**.

Chalk Soft **rock** that is difficult to climb. In crumbled form, it is carried by rock climbers and is used to keep the hands free of perspiration. Those who hold that its use is unethical call it "courage in a bag" (Child).

The First Chairlift (Courtesy of Sun Valley Resort)

Challenge, The/*Der Berg Ruft!* Films shot in two or more languages were common at the beginning of the 1930s. Yet this fairly late coproduction (1938) consists more of a reuse of the mountain footage from the German version directed by **Luis Trenker** in the English film credited to Milton Rosmer. The cast, except for Trenker as **Jean-Antoine Carrel**, and the studio scenes are entirely different. The script, which describes the **Whymper**/Carrel rivalry to climb the **Matterhorn**, is virtually the same, though the German version credits a novel by Carl Haensel and the English version does not. Both versions have the stunning, almost silent fall of the Whymper party during the descent. (M-A. H.)

Chamlang 7,319 m, 24,012 ft. This beautiful Nepali mountain was first climbed on May 3, 1962, by Soh Anma, from Japan, and Pasang Phutar, from India. (See also color photos.)

Chamois A small, goat-like creature that inhabits mountainous areas; in the past, it was a popular prey for hunters in the **Alps**.

Chamonix (Cham). A small city in southeastern France; it is one of the world's premier **mountaineering** centers, giving access to the **Mont Blanc massif**. (See also **Courmayeur**.)

Changabang 6,864 m, 22,520 ft. Located in the Garwhal Himalaya, **India**, in the **Nanda Devi** group; it was first climbed by **Chris Bonington** in 1974.

Chang-tzu 7,553 m, 24,780 ft. This major peak is located within the **Himalayas** in **Tibet**.

Chaparral This type of high-desert vegetation is also often encountered in dry mountain regions, for example in the High **Sierra** area of eastern **California** and western **Nevada**. Sage bushes and small pine trees, as well as abundant tumbleweed and fragrant plants, characterize chaparral. The bushes are sometimes as tall as a man, and the going can be quite rough if one is hiking off-trail; the typical altitude span of chaparral is 4,000–12,000 ft (approximately 1,000–3,500 m). This vegetation is also reminiscent of the *maquis* of **Corsica**, and the Mediterranean vegetation found in the **Southern Alps**.

Charlet, Armand (1900–1975) A great French **guide**.

Chamois Hunter (Th. Horschelt/National Geographic)

Chamois Hunters (Th. Horschelt/National Geographic)

Chat   A smallish **bird**; in East and Central Africa, the red-tailed prefers rocky outcrops, the stone-chat roams above 3,000 ft, and the robin chat above 5,000 ft (Williams).

Chatter   Fast and continuous vertical movement (vibration) of a snowboard or skis when traveling swiftly over a very hard surface.

Chausson d'escalade   A highly specific type of climbing shoe, designed to maximize **friction** by incorporating a highly adhesive sole, somewhat similar in its composition to the Formula 1 racing tires used in competition. This type of climbing paraphernalia was invented by the French climber **Pierre Allain**, who trained extensively on the highly difficult **boulders** of the **Fontainebleau** area and pioneered some of the hardest climbs in the **Alps**, including a direct route on the **Drus**, using friction climbing.

Cherry   A **deciduous tree** of many species that can be found in mountainous regions.

Chestnut   A **deciduous tree;** the Ozark can be found in "rocky uplands and **ravines**" (Leopold, McComb, and Muller).

Chickadee   A small, widely dispersed bird, especially the black-capped; its familiar call ending in a series of "dees" is often heard in or near forested areas. The mountain chickadee prefers higher forests (Udvardy).

Chile   Lowest point, Pacific Ocean 0 m; highest point, Cerro **Aconcagua** 6,959 m, 22,831 ft. Major ranges of the **Andes** run along this very elongated country, which also contains one of the driest areas on earth, the Atacama Desert. Tectonic activity is very intense in the subduction zone between the Pacific plate and the South American plate, and large earthquakes are quite frequent; they sometimes produce tidal waves, or tsunami, that can travel as far as the Hawaiian Islands. The main cordillera of the Andes runs along the border with Argentina, and it is there that some of the highest peaks of **South America** lie: besides **Aconcagua**, Nevado **Ojos del Salado** 6,880 m, 22,572 ft; Volcano **Llullaillaco** 6,723 m, 22,057 ft; Volcano Lascar 5,592 m, 18,346 ft; Cerro San Valentín 4,058 m, 13,314 ft; and Cerro San Lorenzo 3,700 m, 12,139 ft.

Chimborazo   6,310 m, 20,702 ft. This is the 32nd highest peak in the **Andes**, and the 18th of 20 premier climbing peaks in that range; it was first ascended in 1880 by **Edward Whymper** and Jean-Antoine and Louis **Carrel**, and became the highest peak ever scaled at that time. This is the highest peak in **Ecuador**, and, as early as 1802, **Alexander von Humboldt** reached 5,759 m, 18,893 ft on its slopes. Chimborazo is a **volcano**, and its altitude has long been controversial; it was once considered the highest peak on the planet, and it is listed at 6,287 m in **Toni Hiebeler**'s *Montagnes de notre Terre* and by the CIA and Peakware while the *Encyclopedia Britannica* and Apex indicates 6,310 m. Ironically, if one takes into account the bulging of the earth due to the centrifugal force near the equator, Chimborazo is, indeed, higher than any other peak. **Frederic Edwin Church** produced a lovely painting of the mountain in 1864. (See also color photos.)

Chimney *Camino* (I), *cheminée* (F), *Kamin* (G). A narrow, vertical incision in a rock face that provides an easy means of ascent for the entire body, e.g., House's Chimney on K2. (See also **crack**.)

China Lowest point, Turpan Pendi −154 m, −505 ft; highest point, Mt. Everest 8,850 m, 29,035 ft (1999 est.). This enormous country, the third largest in the world (9,326,410 sq km, 3,600,947 sq miles), borders some of the highest mountains in the world, including **Everest**, **K2**, **Makalu**, **Cho Oyu**, **Shisha Pangma**, **Hidden Peak**, **Broad Peak**, and **Gasherbrum II**. Only Shisha Pangma lies entirely within **Tibet**, currently an autonomous province of China.

Chinchilla A small rodent whose home is in the **Andes**. Its fur is turned into clothing.

Chinook See **winds**.

Cho Aui 7,350 m, 24,114 ft. This major peak is located in the **Himalayas** in **Tibet**; it was first climbed in 1996 by a team comprising two French, two Japanese, and three Sherpa climbers.

Cho Oyu 8,201 m, 26,906 ft. This, the sixth highest mountain in the world, is in **Nepal** and **China**. Cho Oyu was first climbed on October 19, 1954, by H. Tichy and S. Jochler, from Austria, and Pasang Dawa Lama, from India. As of the end of 1999, Cho Oyu had been climbed 1,090 times, with only 23 fatalities, either attempting or descending from the summit; it is one of the safest 8,000-meter peaks. (See also the **14 8,000-Meter Peaks** sidebar.)

Chock See **nut**.

Chockstone *Block coincé* (F). A piece of **rock** that has become lodged in a confined open area such as a **chimney**.

Chogolisa 7,665 m, 25,148 ft. A major peak in the **Masherbrum** Range of **Karakoram**, it was first climbed in 1975 by F. Pressl and G. Ammerer.

Chogori The **Balti** name of **K2**.

Cholotse 6,440 m, 21,129 ft. A magnificent peak in **Nepal**. (See also color photos.)

Chomolhari 7,315 m, 23,999 ft. This beautiful mountain is located in **Bhutan**; it was first as-

cended in 1937, by Spencer Chapman and Sherpa porter Pasang Dawa Lama.

Chomolongma (Chomolungma) An orthographic variation of the Tibetan name (Qomolangma) of **Mt. Everest**.

Chopicalqui 6,354 m, 20,846 ft. This is the 26th highest peak in the **Andes**, and the 17th of 20 premier climbing peaks in that range; it was first ascended in 1932 by Philipp Borchers, Erwin Hein, Hermann Hoerlin, and Erwin Schneider. The peak is located in **Peru**.

Chorten (stupas) Small shrines designed to house sacred relics. They are found throughout the **Himalayas**, including in **Bhutan**. Numerous designs exist, including simple square structures and elaborate pyramids. (See also color photos.)

Chough This crow-like bird can be found in the **Himalayas** where the alpine and the redbilled soar at 16,500 ft and 15,000 ft respectively (Ali).

Chouinard, Yvon (1938–) An excellent climber and the founder of Chouinard Equipment, now **Black Diamond** and **Patagonia**. Chouinard altered, redesigned, and perfected much of the climbing equipment used today.

Christie In **skiing**, a type of turn with skidding on both right or both left edges; there are many variations. See Barnes for detailed discussion of this complex subject.

Christmas Island Lowest point, Indian Ocean 0 m; highest point, Murray Hill 361 m, 1,184 ft.

Church, Frederic Edwin (1826–1900) A 19th-century painter, famous for his mountain landscapes; he was a member of the Hudson River School. (See also **Albert Bierstadt**, and color photos.)

Churchill, Mt. 4,767 m, 15,638 ft. Located in the vicinity of **Mt. Bona**, this is one of the higher peaks in the **Wrangell–St. Elias National Park** in **Alaska**.

Chute A narrow, steep **chimney** or slope. (See also **gully**.)

Cima Grande 2,999 m, 9,839 ft. An Italian peak.

Cinder A small piece of volcanic rock.

Cinto, Monte 2,710 m, 8,891 ft, the highest point in **Corsica**. (See also color photos.)

Cirque (Less usual and in Scotland, *coire* or *corrie*) *Cwm* (W; prn: kum or koom). (As in the **West-**

ern Cwm on **Everest**.) A large area enclosed by encircling mountains. Also, a substantial depression produced by a **glacier** that may be filled with water. (See also **tarn**.)

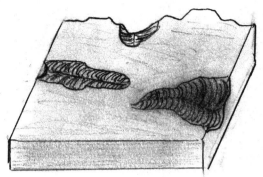

Cirque (Laura Lindblad)

Clark, Helen (1950–) The current prime minister of New Zealand and a serious climber.

Clark, Ronald William (1916–) Born: England. An important writer and mountaineering historian. Bibliography: *The Splendid Hills* (1948), *The Early Alpine Guides* (1949), *The Victorian Mountaineers* (1953), *Come Climbing with Me* (1955), *Great Moments in Mountaineering* (1956), *Six Great Mountaineers* (1956), *A Picture History of Mountaineering* (1956), *Mountaineering in Britain* (1957) with E. C. Pyatt, *The True Book About Mountaineering* (1957), *Instructions to Young Ramblers* (1958), *An Eccentric in the Alps* (1959), *The Day the Rope Broke* (1965), *The Alps* (1973), *Men, Myths and Mountains* (1977).

Clark, William (1770–1838) Second in command of the **Lewis and Clark Expedition**, he was an American frontiersman and a superb explorer.

Clarke, Charles (1944–) Born: England. He joined the 1975 British Everest Expedition as physician. Bibliography: *Mountain Medicine and Physiology* (1975), *Everest* (1978), *Everest the Unclimbed Ridge* (1983) with **Chris Bonington**, *Lightweight Expeditions to the Great Ranges* (1984) with Audrey Salkeld.

Classification systems See **rating systems**.

Clastic rock Composed of pieces of **rock** that already existed. (See also **pyroclastic**.)

Clean In **rock climbing**, to remove **gear** that has been placed in a **crack** while following a **pitch**. Also, to remove vegetation for finger or hand placements.

Clean climbing Climbing without damaging anything by, for example, not using **pitons** or **bolts**.

Cleare, John (1936–) A climber, with **first ascents** including the West Face Direct of the **Aiguille du Plan**; photographer; and author of some extremely beautiful books. (See **ranges** for a remark on these volumes.) Bibliography: *Sea Cliff Climbing in Britain* (1973), with R. G. Collomb, *Mountains* (1975), *Collins Guide to Mountains and Mountaineering* (1979), *Mountaineering* (1980). (See also the **10 Best Mountain Photographers and Cinematographers** sidebar.)

Clémenceau Ice Field A large conglomerate of slow-flowing **glaciers** covering a large area in the **Canadian Rockies**. (See also **Columbia Ice Field**.)

Cliff A steep rock face or precipice.

Cliff dwelling Living quarters built directly into and often out of the stone surfaces on the sides of mountains. The White House in Canyon de Chelly is a good example. (See also **Mesa Verde National Park**, **pueblo**, **cave temple**, and color photos.)

Cliffhanger A 1993 American action film by the Finnish director Rennie Harlin (who also made *Die Hard 2*), starring Sylvester Stallone. Villains look for three suitcases of money lost in the Rocky Mountains. The general idea for popcorn movies is to offer speedy action and loud sound so that no one will notice the ultimate lack of credibility. General audiences enjoyed this film, but climbers dismissed it: a Black Diamond Buckle breaks and Stallone survives a climb in a T-shirt and a bath in ice water! (M-A. H.)

Climate The general and usual **weather** of an area.

Climbers, numbers of Mt. Washington, Mt. Hood, and Mt. Fuji are among the most frequently climbed peaks. Some ten thousand people attempt Hood each year. In 2003, about 17,000 hikers climbed **Mt. Whitney**, and between 1921 and 2003, 6,782 people managed to get above base camp on Everest. By 2004, a total of 160 people had reached the highpoints on all seven continents, the so-called **seven summits**.

The White House, Canyon de Chelly (Ansel Adams/Corbis)

Megalithic Terraces of the Hanging Gardens of Ollantaytambo (O. F. Cook/National Geographic)

Climbing Is divided into three distinct types. Although they require different skills and very different equipment, they all have the same goal: to reach the top of a geophysical extrusion. (A small number of people also climb human-made objects.) The first is called *rock* (or *technical*) climbing, and it is here that a person clings to a perpendicular face and tries to move upward. *Bouldering* is the term used for attempts on smaller extrusions, for example, rocks that extend upward only 10 to 20 or 30 feet. Most technical work is done on faces that are a few hundred feet high. Big **wall** climbing allows one to reach the top of sheer faces that extend upward for many thousands of feet, for example, **Half**

Dome; this requires that one sleep hanging off the side of the wall, sometimes for a week or more. *Traditional* is the term used to designate climbs using **gear** or **protection**, for example, various devices that are placed in cracks. *Sport* climbing is done on faces that already have **pitons** or **bolts** attached or on **climbing walls**. The second form is a variation on the first. In *ice* climbing, one attempts to ascend on something other than pure rock. Frequently, a stone surface covered with ice is sought; sometimes a frozen waterfall is the objective; and when one is in the proximity of a **glacier**, its sides can present a formidable challenge. A very popular form of climbing is called **mountaineering**. This is because the transition from **hiking** to mountaineering is subtle and in its most basic form requires very little specialized equipment or skill. Any fit person can climb the Middle **Teton** on a warm summer day, for example, by simply hiking up. That this is extremely dangerous to attempt in **winter** without the appropriate warm and waterproof **clothing, helmet, crampons, ice ax,** and specialized knowledge seems to matter very little to the adolescents who, in shorts and T-shirts or halter tops, waltz up the steep, slippery snow or the rock-infested couloir. Mountaineers climb on forested, rocky, or **scree**-covered slopes, **lava**-encrusted **volcanoes**, snow and **ice fields, glaciers**, and exposed, narrow **ridges**. On a pleasant day, one may meet hundreds of fellow climbers on some popular **peak** in the **Rocky Mountains** or **Alps. Alpine-style** climbs are done quickly in a day or two; **expeditionary** climbs, sometimes with hundreds of members and porters, take many weeks, and in the **Himalayas** they may drag on for three months. *Mixed* climbing combines these different styles. For example, to attempt **Everest** or **K2** one must be adept at mountaineering but also be able to climb both rock and ice. The boundaries in all forms of climbing are continually expanding. What was impossible 20 years ago is now commonly achieved. It took humanity 25,000 years to reach the summit of Everest; now many climbers manage this feat each year. A 5.13 rock climb was once the apex of the sport; recently,

Members of the Alpine Club of Canada Ascending Mount Vice-President (Rev. George Kinney/National Geographic)

Chris Sharma managed a 5.15. (See **rating systems**.) There are two reasons for this: first, extremely dedicated people continually hone their skills while attempting increasingly difficult tasks; occasionally, they succeed and set a precedent for those who follow. Second, better, more sophisticated equipment allows climbers to do things that truly were impossible in the past. Another taxonomy trisects climbing into rock (traditional, sport, big wall, bouldering), snow and ice (mountaineering/glaciers, waterfalls, mixed), and Alpine (aspects of rock and ice). (See the various books by Cox and Fulsaas, Barry, Fyffe and Peter, and Salkeld, for excellent practical advice. Barry's *Climbing School* is perhaps the single best concise source for information on the practical aspects of climbing and mountaineering. It offers one- or two-page [and sometimes longer] illustrated commentaries on everything from equipment and navigation to first aid and scrambling. This superb volume concludes with a series of illustrated overviews of the world's great climbing and mountaineering areas.)

Climbing accounts Many hundreds of rock climbers, mountaineers, and interested authors have written accounts of their exploits. Alpine and Himalayan mountaineers are especially enamored of these recitations, some of which are among the world's most exciting and powerful memoirs. Few people could read Krakauer's *Into Thin Air* or Joe Simpson's *Touching the Void* without being moved to tears. It is an unpleasant truth, though, that the literature of climbing is littered with dead bodies.

Climbing equipment Many companies, for example, **Black Diamond**, Marmot, and Petzl, produce excellent general and specialized climbing equipment, which can be divided into four

Guglea Edmondo de Amicis (National Geographic)

Chilikoot Pass—Yukoners Approaching Summit, 1897 (E. S. Curtis/National Geographic)

broad categories: **clothing**, packs and haul bags, protection against the weather, and the highly specialized devices that advanced rock, ice, and mountain climbing require. Clothing is covered in its own entry. *Packs and haul bags:* In order to conveniently transport the requisite equipment along steep and precipitous trails, up and down snow or ice slopes, or on rock faces, something other than a suitcase is required. Various forms of knapsacks, backpacks, and pack boards have been used for carrying things for hundreds of years. In the early days, climbers employed simple canvas bags or sacks with shoulder straps. In 1952, Kelty manufactured the first external frame pack, and this caught on with hikers and climbers. Later they switched to the internal frame pack, which is more stable and conforms more easily to the shape of and holds the weight closer to the body. New innovations were added, and now nylon packs are extremely complex with many pockets, sections, straps, zippers, and detachable

units, but at the same time light enough to avoid adding an additional burden to the climber, since he or she may also have to haul along an **ice ax**, **crampons**, **skis**, snowshoes, and/or shovel all conveniently attached to the outside of the pack. Many manufacturers produce an astonishingly diverse assortment of packs, which range in price from $30 for a simple book bag on straps to almost $500 for an enormous and complex **expedition** pack. Haul bags are large, heavy, waterproof units that are filled with equipment and food and hauled up by a big wall climber (on **Half Dome**, for example) after he or she reaches a **stance**. *Protection against the weather:* Clothing, naturally, affords protection against heat, cold, and wind, but here we have in mind **tents** and sleeping bags. The former, like packs, are extremely diverse in size, style, quality, and cost. The primitive and heavy canvas tents of the past have given way to ripstop nylon units with built-in floors, some of which are self-supporting, that is, they do not have to be staked to the ground, ice, or snow. (These can tip over in heavy winds and when untenanted, may fly away.) A simple and inexpensive two-person tent provides shelter in a downpour, but would tear apart or collapse in an Alpine blizzard. Specialized mountain tents or those designed to withstand the rigors of winter are aerodynamic, compact, light, and extremely expensive (up to $700). Larger all-season tents that can sleep 10 to 15 people can run $5,000. Sleeping bags provide a means for the body to retain warmth, especially at night when the temperature drops and one is stationary and thus generating less heat. The more insulation they contain, the more effective they are. Those used in summer temperatures in the mountains (for example, to 20 degrees Fahrenheit) may be filled with down or synthetic fibers and cost between $30 and $100. An excellent winter bag that would keep one comfortable at 30 or 40 degrees below zero can cost almost $800. *Specialized devices:* Rock, ice, and mountain climbers have developed a formidable array of devices to both help as well as to protect against disaster. A **harness** is the sine qua non for all of these endeavors. One may also need **carabiners, rope, protection** such as **nuts** and **cams,** ice axes, crampons, a **rack, wands, pickets, ascenders, compass, lights,** or a **GPS** unit, (See also **climbing shoes** and **skiing equipment**.)

Climbing shoes   *Espadrilles* (F), *Kletterschühe* (G). **Rock** climbers wear very specialized, diminutive shoes, similar to ballet slippers. Serious rock specialists often choose shoes that are a few sizes smaller than their feet; they pinch and are very uncomfortable, but the tight fit allows for less flexibility and thus more precise control on small holds. (See also **clothing**.)

Climbing wall   A series of small extrusions, incisions, or holds put up on a gym or retail outlet's wall, or on its own portable structure that can be raised after transportation to a site. Some artificial walls are 50-foot towers built for the express purpose of indoor or sport climbing.

Climbsearch   This is a specialized search engine for locating websites that deal with **climbing** and **mountaineering**. There are separate directories for many areas including climbers, **bouldering**, magazines, and organizations (http://climbsearch.port5.com).

Clingmans Dome   2,025 m, 6,643 ft. The highest point in **Tennessee**, and one of the highest mountains in the **Appalachians**.

Clip (in)   To thread a **rope** through an anchored **carabiner**.

Clipperton Island   Lowest point, Pacific Ocean 0 m; highest point, Rocher Clipperton 29 m, 95 ft.

Clothing   Hundreds of companies manufacture clothing appropriate for use in the mountains. Some, like North Face, Patagonia, and REI, specialize in garments that are especially warm, lightweight, and waterproof. A taxonomy of clothing would include **climbing shoes**, boots, overboots, and **gaiters**; undergarments; pants, shirts, sweaters, and vests; outerwear; hoods, hats, and face masks; gloves; and glasses and goggles. *Boots, overboots:* Early leather **mountaineering** boots were no different than stiff work or hiking boots; as such they were most inadequate. Feet got wet and cold, and climbers lost toes due to frostbite. As climbers attacked ice and glaciated peaks, nails (clinkers, tricouni) or other metallic accoutrements were added to the soles in order to decrease slippage; these boots, naturally, were awkward when used on rock. Insulated, leather boots followed and various methods of waterproofing were employed, but keeping one's feet dry and warm remained a major problem. Late in the 20th century, perhaps inspired by the high plastic ski boot, a number of companies (e.g., Asolo and Koflach) began to produce plastic mountaineering boots. These enormous units consist of an outer, completely waterproof plastic shell with laces (rather than buckles); the most recent models have little pulleys to facilitate lacing. An inner, removable, insulated bootie keeps the feet warm and dry. These boots are mandatory for serious mountaineering and cost about $300. An $800 model comes with built-in gaiters. Occasional climbers often wear sophisticated leather or synthetic hiking boots, but these are no substitute for plastic mountaineering boots for serious attempts on high peaks, especially if one requires **crampons.** In the **Himalayas**, **Andes**, and other extremely cold environments, it is necessary to add overboots; these resemble small sleeping bags shaped to fit over the boot and add additional **protection** against the cold, which can drop to 60 or more real degrees below zero Fahrenheit. *Undergarments:* The socks and underwear that one places next to the skin used to be made of cotton, which is comfortable, but retains moisture; it was inimical to maintaining body heat. Modern synthetics are now used to make all of these garments, which wick natural and external moisture away from the body; they are expensive but worth the investment, since they help one stay dry and warm even in extreme conditions. *Pants, shirts, sweaters, and vests:* Many people continue to wear cotton shorts, jeans, socks, and shirts for hiking, climbing, and mountaineering, but this is a major blunder. Cotton retains moisture, fails to maintain body heat, and produces friction and skin injuries. Wool is preferable, but synthetic materials (such as Polartec) do not retain moisture as easily as cotton, continue to provide insulation when wet, and dry quickly. These garments are now layered depending on changes in temperature: As it gets colder, another shirt, sweater, or vest is added. *Outerwear:* Early climbers wore everyday clothing. Indeed, the British were notorious for strolling up **Everest** in their Oxford tweeds and scarves. All climbers suffered dramatically from the cold and wetness. Improvements in both attitude and fabrication have added comfort and saved lives. Highly insulated and bulky outer pants and coats are now the most important items in the armamentarium of clothes that one requires to flourish in a harsh mountain environment. The pants ensconce the boot and run to the chest, while the coat covers the upper torso from the neck and continues down to the thighs. Some of these suits are designed to withstand temperatures of 50 degrees below zero Fahrenheit and even more extreme wind chills. One-piece units also exist, and these offer certain advantages (e.g., one can never misplace the coat and there are no cold gaps in the waist area), but they are also inconvenient and sometimes provide too much warmth. Outerwear is often, though not always, protected by a water-proofing process (such as Gore-Tex). The cost of these suits ranges from $500 to $1,200. These same suits can be used for other outdoor activity, for example, **skiing** or **snowboarding**, but they are probably too efficient. Less bulky and less expensive products are more appropriate. *Hoods, hats, and face masks:* An astonishingly high percentage of body heat is lost at the extremities. Additionally, when body temperature begins to drop, the brain directs the remaining heat to the torso and vital organs. Thus, the hands and feet begin to cool and they are the first areas to suffer frostbite. It is therefore obvious that protecting the extremities is crucial. A hood (generally attached to the coat) to completely ensconce the head is a mandatory accessory, since it adds a secondary layer above the hat and, additionally, covers exposed areas (cheeks, chin, and mouth). A balaclava or face mask, now extremely effective when made of two layers of Polartec, will keep the entire face, including the nose, warm at 60 below zero. Some models contain tubes that recirculate hot breath back toward the upper torso. *Gloves:* Gloves are made of a diversity of materials and come in innumerable styles depending on their purpose. Those without fingers are called mittens or mitts. As with clothing, in extreme cold, they are layered with thin, soft liners; felt insulators; and external, often waterproof, overgloves that also protect against the ground (in snowboarding) and rope burn (in **rappelling**). Although it is difficult or even impossible to do certain necessary tasks (in rock climbing or mountaineering) while wearing gloves, it is mandatory to keep the hands covered and warm when it is well below zero. At extreme temperatures, the hands quickly lose heat and frostbite may set in. Some mountaineers tape their metallic **ice axes** in order to insulate against the transmitted cold. At 67 degrees below zero Fahrenheit, skin freezes upon contact with the air; touching anything with bare hands is severely counterindicated. Gloves are so important in extreme conditions that despite the added weight, it is advisable to carry an extra pair in case of wetness or loss. **Maurice Herzog** lost his gloves on **Annapurna** and suffered horrible pain and bodily loss. (See also **Beck Weathers**.) *Glasses and goggles:* In skiing, goggles protect against glare, radiation, and most importantly, stinging snowflakes, which, when falling or floating, make it impossible to keep the eyes open at speed without some protection. In the **high mountains** and especially in snow country and on glaciers, eye protection is more important than any other item of clothing. On a warm day, it would be possible, though unpleasant, to scurry down a snow slope in stockings, but without glacier glasses or goggles to offset the glare, one would quickly become snow-blind. In high snow country, it is an excellent idea to carry two pair of dark glasses.

Cloud *Nuage* (F), *nube* (I), *Wolke* (G). Small water and/or ice particles that are visible in the sky. Clouds vary in form from thin wisps to fluffy or lowering masses and in color from bright white to dark gray. Cloud taxonomy is complex but cirrus, cumulus, nimbus, and stratus are the basic constituents that form the various permutations. Thunderheads are large, dark cumulonimbus masses that augur a storm. Lenticular clouds, almond-shaped and sometimes dark, are an important signal in the **high mountains**, especially the **Himalayas**, that a storm is approaching. (See Smith for details.)

Clubs There are hundreds of groups in many countries that are devoted to either the protection and preservation of the mountain environment or climbing, skiing, and other endeavors. A partial list would include the Alpine Club (1857), Alpine Club of Canada, **American Alpine Club**, **Appalachian Mountain Club**, Club Alpin Français (CAF) (1874), Deutscher Alpenverein, The Mazamas, The Mountaineers, Outward Bound, and the Sierra Club. See Barry for a limited country-by-country listing of organizations and their addresses. The **Union Internationale des Associations d'Alpinisme** maintains a website that links to more than 100 clubs (www.uiaa.ch).

Clyde, Norman (1885–1972) An American mountaineer, who performed numerous **first ascents** in the California **Sierras**, and western **United States**. A 4,223-m, 13,920-ft peak located in the **Palisades** bears his name.

Coal A combustible mineral, the existence of which derives from the decomposition of organic matter; it is burnt in order to produce heat and electricity. (See also **mining**.)

Coast Ranges Along the **California** coast, on the west side of the Central Valley (which is bounded on the east by the **Sierra Nevada**) lie the north and south branches of the coastal ranges.

Cocos (Keeling) Islands Lowest point, Indian Ocean 0 m; highest point, unnamed location 5 m, 16 ft.

Col See **pass**.

Colima 4,450 m, 14,600 ft. The most active and dangerous Mexican **volcano**.

Collie, John Norman (1859–1942) Born: Alderley Edge, near Manchester, England. An outstanding British climber and mountaineer with many **first ascents** in the **Alps** and Canada including the Dent du Requin, **Athabasca**, and Diadem. Collie was also an eminent scientist; he discovered the noble gas neon and was one of the first to make practical use of X-rays (Unsworth, *Encyclopaedia*). His best-known British first climbs include the crossing of the Thearlaich-Dubh Gap; the ascent of Sgurr Coire an Lochan, the last summit to be attained in Britain; and the ascent of Tower Ridge on **Ben Nevis**. Collie was also famous for cutting, with an **ice ax**, the controversial Collie Step during his ascent of Moss Ghyll, Scafell, in 1892. In the Alps he climbed with **Mummery**. Here his firsts include the southwest face of the Plan, the Grépon **traverse**, and the first guideless ascent of the Old Brenva Route. He also achieved first ascents in the Rockies and Lofoten Islands. Sgurr Thormaid (Norman's Peak), on Skye, is named after him. Bibliography: *Climbing on the Himalaya and other Mountain Ranges* (1902).

Colombia Lowest point, Pacific Ocean 0 m; highest point, **Nevado del Huila** 5,750 m, 18,864 ft. Another major Andean country, it contains many peaks and superb cordilleras. (See also color photos.)

Colorado Lowest point, Arikaree River, near **Kansas**, 1,012 m, 3,320 ft; highest point, **Mt. Elbert**, 4,399 m, 14,433 ft (third highest of the 50 state **highpoints**). A magnificent state containing 54 14,000-foot mountains, and a multitude of beautiful summits. It is a mecca for climbers, mountaineers, and skiers. The main ranges are the **Sawatch, Elk, Sneffels, San Miguel, Needle Mountains, Front, Ten Mile, Mosquito, Sangre de Cristo,** and **San Juan**. (For the complete list of Colorado's 14,000-foot peaks, see appendix D.)

Columbia Glacier   Located within the Chugach National Forest near Valdez, **Alaska**, it is among the largest **tidewater glaciers** in North America, with a length of 66 km, 42 miles, and a width of 6 km, 4 miles at its terminus. It is the last Alaskan tidewater **glacier** still filling the entire length of its **fjord**.

Columbia Ice Field   A very large ice field near **Banff, Alberta, Canada**.

Columbine   A variously colored and diversely structured **flower**.

Columna, La   See **Pico Bolivar** and **Venezuela**.

Come off (the **rock,** face, or **wall**)   In rock climbing, to fall off while on **belay**.

Comici, Emilio (1901–1940)   An important and excellent Italian rock climber with a **first ascent** of the **Cima Grande** north face. (See also the **6 + 1 Great Alpine North Faces** sidebar.)

Communication   In rock climbing, a system of succinct commands has been developed to help climbers communicate accurately with each other. These naturally differ from country to country. In the United States, simple phrases such as "on belay," "climbing," "climb on," "off belay" allow sometimes widely separated or out-of-sight people to know what is going on above or below despite other noisy climbers or howling winds and pounding rain.

Comoros   Lowest point, Indian Ocean 0 m; highest point, Le Kartala 2,360 m, 7,742 ft. This tiny group of islands (2,230 sq km, 861 sq miles) contains major ancient volcanic lava chimneys, which rise sharply above the ocean, well above 7,000 ft.

Compagnie des Guides de Chamonix   See **guiding services**.

Compagnoni, Achille (1914–) Born: Italy. The first, together with **Lino Lacedelli**, to ascend **K2**, in 1954. Bibliography: *Ascent of K2* (1955) by Ardito Desio. (See also the **10 Best Two-Man Teams** sidebar.)

Compass   A device that balances a pointer of magnetized material on a spindle inside a sealed chamber filled with air or liquid. The pointer spins, stops, and points to the magnetic north pole. It offers a simple way of orienting geographically, and until the recent advent of **global positioning systems**, a person traveling in the mountains would usually carry a compass. Although the first devices were enormous (Marco Polo's was mounted on a wheeled cart pulled by animals), modern units can be held in the palm of one's hand.

Competition climbing   Ascending real or **climbing walls** in order to win prizes.

Conditioning   As in any activity, the more the body (and mind) is honed to the task, the easier it is to succeed. Rock climbers practice hanging their entire weight from one finger so that when this is required they can do it; mountaineers train by running and exercising so that they can carry on for exceptionally long periods of time under horrific conditions. The extraordinary endurance of the highly trained may appear almost impossible: **Lionel Terray**, with little food and 50 pounds on his back, once climbed and descended more than 17,000 ft in one day. But physical conditioning is not enough. Germane knowledge as well as the necessary skills required for the endeavor are mandatory if one is to accomplish more than mere fumbling up a cliff, stumbling up a mountain, or crashing one's way down a slope on skis, snowboard, or bicycle. Since most of these sports are quite dangerous, these fumblings and stumblings can result in severe injury or death. On Mt. St. Helens, the ascending authors encountered a single **crampon** on the lower trail. Some time thereafter, a harried descender asked if we had seen it. Five hours later, as we descended, there he was again, literally stumbling his way toward the summit!

Condor   The **California** condor is an enormous, endangered bird that flies as high as 25,000 ft. The Andean is at home throughout all of western **South America**.

Conebill   A bird of many species; the giant may reach 16,000 ft in the **Andes** (Fjeldså and Krabbe).

Conglomerate A **sedimentary rock** that is made up of pieces of other rock.

Congo, Democratic Republic of the Lowest point, Atlantic Ocean 0 m; highest point, Pic Marguerite on Mont Ngaliema (**Mt. Stanley**) 5,109 m, 16,763 ft. This African country is home to one of the highest peaks in the whole continent, and to an amazing variety of wildlife, including specialized animals and plants living in the higher elevations. This country was formerly known as Zaire.

Congo, Republic of the Lowest point, Atlantic Ocean 0 m; highest point, Mt. Berongou 903 m, 2,963 ft.

Conifer (Coniferous) A taxonomic designation that generally indicates those **trees** that do not lose their foliage (needles) during the winter. (There are some exceptions, including the tamarack and bald cypress.) Their wood is softer than that found in their **deciduous** cousins.

Connecticut Lowest point, Long Island Sound 0 m; highest point, Mt. Frissell 725 m, 2,380 ft (36th highest of the 50 state highpoints). The highpoint is actually located on the slope of the hill, at the **Massachusetts** border.

Conquest of Everest, The A British documentary film by George Lowe, depicting the 1953 Hillary/Norgay ascent. Gorgeously shot in Technicolor, neatly crafted, and well explained, this film is not only a document but a very well-made cinematic work as well. Mountain fans will get a fair amount of information, never-seen-before sights, and reports on the technique of the day. Film fans will get their share of extraordinary scenery, suspense, and human interest. Unlike **Victoire sur l'Annapurna** though, the quiet pace of the expedition as well as the general conditions encountered (precise preparation, good weather, etc.) result in a less dramatic production. (M-A. H.)

Conservation The attempt to protect the earth and conserve its resources, especially oil, gas, and other nonrenewable treasures. Conservationists care about the earth, its mountains, and their inhabitants as well as the human impact. During the past few decades many people have become concerned and involved, but there are pragmatic, economic, and individual forces that counter conservationist attitudes, ethics, and policies—even among those people such as climbers and mountaineers who respect the mountain environment.

Constans/The Constancy Factor A 1980 Polish film written and directed by Krzysztof Zanussi; this is an attempt of an amateur climber to join a party in the Himalayas, where his father died. Since he refuses to play the game and abjures corruption, his attempt fails. (M-A. H.)

Continent Extensive primarily granitic landmass of which there are seven: **Africa**, **Antarctica**, **Asia**, **Australia**, **Europe**, **North America**, and **South America**. They are all mountainous to a greater or lesser extent.

Continental divide The imaginary line that bisects a continent on either side of which water flows to antithetical sides of the landmass. In **North America** it can be found in the **Rocky Mountains:** depending on where it falls, rainwater flows toward the Gulf of Mexico and the Atlantic or toward the Pacific Ocean.

Continental Divide Trail A 3,100-mile-long trail through the central western U.S. states. (See also **Brian Robinson**.)

Continental drift Alfred Wegener's theory that the continents were once a single landmass; split apart, the pieces moved away from each other. (See also **tectonic plates**.)

Contour interval The elevation difference between **contour lines**.

Contour line The same elevation along a specific course is represented on **maps** by a contour line; these lines run roughly parallel to each other. Thus, it is possible to look at a topographic **map** and envision the represented landscape with its changes in elevation.

Control Perhaps the key term in downhill **skiing**. One is constantly adjured to ski in control, which means one should be able to turn or stop when necessary. Extreme skiing often precludes this, since it is difficult to stop on a 60- or 70-degree slope without falling over and tumbling downward.

Conway, William Martin, Lord Conway of Allington (1856–1937) "He organized the first major climbing expedition to the Himalaya" (Greg Glade, personal comment). Born: England.

Bibliography: *Zermatt Pocket-Book* (1881), *Climbing and Exploration in the Karakoram Himalayas* (1894), *The Alps from End to End* (1895), *The First Crossing of Spitsbergen* (1897), *With Ski and Sledge over Arctic Glaciers* (1898), *The Bolivian Andes* (1901), *Aconcagua and Tierra del Fuego* (1902), *The Alps* (1904), *No Man's Land* (1906), *Mountain Memories: A Pilgrimage of Romance* (1920), *Episode in a Varied Life, by Lord Conway of Allington* (1932).

Cook, Mt. (Aoraki, Maori for "cloud-piercer") 3,764 m, 12,349 ft. The highest mountain in **New Zealand**, it recently lost some 30 feet in altitude in a rock avalanche. (See also color photos.)

Cook Islands Lowest point, Pacific Ocean 0 m; highest point, Te Manga 652 m, 2,139 ft.

Cook Peak 4,194 m, 13,761 ft. A high mountain located in the **Yukon** Territory in Canada. Like its homologue in **New Zealand**, this is a heavily glaciated peak standing near the ocean, where powerful storms rage over the winter months. The peak is actually straddling the boundary between the **Wrangell–St. Elias** and **Kluane-Logan National Parks**.

Coolidge, William Augustus Breevort (1850–1926) Born: New York. A superb climber, mountaineer, and Alpine historian; he is given credit for more than 1,700 climbs. His **first ascents** include **Piz Badile** and the **Ailefroide**. Bibliography: *Swiss Travel and Swiss Guide Books* (1889), *Climbs in the Alps Made in the Years 1865 to 1900* (1900), *Walks and Excursions in the Valley of Grindlewald* (1900), *The Alps in Nature and History* (1908), *Alpine Studies* (1912), *The Alpine Career (1868–1914) of Frederick Gardner Described by His Friend W. A. B. Coolidge* (1920).

Coot A water **bird**. In the **Andes**, the giant breeds as high as 16,500 ft and the horned travels even higher (Fjeldså and Krabbe).

Copper Canyon Located in northern **Mexico**, it is even larger than its U.S. counterpart, the **Grand Canyon**.

Coral Sea Islands Lowest point, Pacific Ocean 0 m; highest point, unnamed location on Cato Island 6 m, 20 ft.

Cordée See **rope**.

Cordillera In Spanish (rope or belt), "any mountain **chain**"; in English, a cluster of **ranges**, generally the major ranges of a large area (Reider); extensive agglomeration of ranges or "the main mountain axis of a continent" (Gary).

Cordillera Blanca This is the highest range in **Peru**; it culminates at Nevado **Huascarán**, but also contains other magnificent summits, including **Alpamayo**, **Chopicalqui**, and **Huandoy**.

Cordillera Huayhuash A Peruvian **cordillera**.

Cordillera Oriental A **cordillera** in **Bolivia** divided into six sections.

Cordillera Real A **cordillera** in **Bolivia**.

Cordillera Vilcabamba A Peruvian **cordillera**.

Cordillera Vilcanota A Peruvian **cordillera**.

Corduroy In **skiing**, the ridged surface that **grooming** equipment produces (Barnes).

Corner A point where two rock faces meet at right angles. An outside corner resembles the outside corner of a building; an inside corner is similar to an interior corner in a room.

Cornice (Sometimes, balcony) *Corniche* (F), *Überhang* (G). **Ice** or blown **snow** that has partially solidified and cantilevered out over the edge of a ridge or summit. It is sometimes difficult to tell where the surface ends and a cornice begins, so it can pose a great risk to climbers, since it may break off under weight. The summit of **Mt. St. Helens**, for example, which is a four-foot-wide ridge, may extend another few feet into the crater on a cornice.

Coropuna 6,613 m, 21,696 ft. This is the 10th highest peak in the **Andes**, and the eighth of 20 premier climbing peaks in that range; it was first climbed in 1911 by Hiram Bingham and H. L. Tucker. The peak is located in **Peru**, the third highest in that country.

Corrie See **cirque**.

Corsica A magnificent, mountainous island off the French and Italian Rivieras, it contains numerous splendid peaks, including **Monte Cinto**, Monte Rotondo, and l'Incudine. The calanques of Porto and Piana are magnificent; the Col de la Bavella is also a superb mountain site. Corsica's beautiful, mild winter weather and hot summers support a unique flora, including the *maquis*, a fragrant, **chaparral**-like vegetation. (See *Corsica Mountains* by Robin G. Collomb.)

Cortina d'Ampezzo An Italian center for skiing and climbing in the **Dolomites**.

Costa Rica Lowest point, Pacific Ocean 0 m; highest point, Cerro Chirripo 3,810 m, 12,500 ft.

Côte d'Ivoire Lowest point, Gulf of Guinea 0 m; highest point, Mont Nimba 1,752 m, 5,748 ft.

Cotopaxi 5,897 m, 19,347 ft. Located in **Ecuador**, this is the highest active volcano in the world. First climbed in 1872 by Dr. Wilhelm Reiss and A. M. Escobar. (See also color photos.)

Cougar See **cat**.

Couloir See **gully**.

Courmayeur The Italian city that like its French counterpart, **Chamonix**, functions as a center for **climbing** in the **Mont Blanc** area. A tunnel that cuts through the massif connects the two cities.

Couttet, François (1825–1890) Early guide; he ascended **Mont Blanc** 27 times.

Couzy, Jean (1923–1958) Terray calls Couzy "one of the greatest mountaineers of all time." They both performed the first ascent of **Makalu** in 1956.

Coyote Indigenous to much of the United States and Canada, this wily doglike **mammal**, after years of extirpation, is making a comeback, especially in the eastern mountains. Coyotes may wander into urban areas.

Crack *Fissure* (F), *fessura* (I), *Riss* (G). In **rock climbing**, a narrow or larger cleft or **crevice** in the rock face varying in depth into which one's fingers, hands, body, or **protection** can be inserted. (See also **chimney**.)

Crag Steep, rough, jagged **rock,** as of a **cliff**.

Craig Mountain 4,050 m, 13,288 ft. A high peak located in the **Yukon** Territory in **Canada**.

Cramponing There are different ways to use **crampons,** and they are referred to with French terms: *pied marche* (walk), *pied en canard* (duck walk), *pied à plat* (flat foot). (See Cox and Fulsaas.)

Crampons *Raniponi* (I), *Steigeisen* (G). Devices that consist of a hardened metal frame with 10 razor-sharp points oriented downward and two forward. They are strapped or locked onto **mountaineering** boots. Crampons allow one to walk safely on steep, hard **snow** or **ice** or to climb vertical ice, for example, a frozen waterfall. Similar devices are thousands of years old, and primitive climbing models existed in the 19th century, but they did not become popular until the second half of the 20th. For the most part, they make **step cutting** superfluous.

Crater A round depression that develops at the apex as a volcano spews out material or collapses. Ritchie incisively observes that in most examples, the interior upper rim is a crag above a talus-covered, vegetationless slope. (See also **caldera**.)

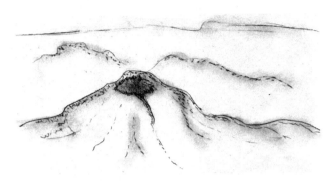

Crater (Laura Lindblad)

Crater In rock **climbing**, to fall off a face while off **belay**, i.e., while unprotected.

Crater Lake An extraordinary and beautiful lake in the **caldera** of **Oregon**'s Mt. Mazama, a gigantic ancient **volcano**.

Crevasse *Crepaccio* (I), *grieta* (S), *Schrund* (G). An intrusion in the surface of a **glacier**. Crevasses can be minuscule or dramatically large and deep. During the spring they are covered with accumulations of **snow** called snow bridges; as the temperature consistently increases, the bridges get thinner and may collapse under the weight of a climber. The ***Bergschrund*** on **Mt. Hood** is narrow in March, but by late August it so big that, as Zumwalt observes, it can hold several freight trains.

Crevice A narrow opening in a rock face.

Crimp In **rock climbing**, to pull oneself up on the tips of the fingers.

Croatia Lowest point, Adriatic Sea 0 m; highest point, Dinara 1,830 m, 6,004 ft.

Crocus A hardy flower whose stem comes up through the snow and then blossoms.

Croft, Peter (1958–) More than simply a great climber, Croft set the standard in terms of integrity in climbing. His **free solo** and incredible speed **ascents** of **El Capitan** placed him at the forefront of world rock climbing. On July 6, 1990, he and Dave Shultz climbed both the Nose of El Capitan and the **Salathé Wall** (6,000 ft of

Crossing a Crevasse (S. G. Wehrli/National Geographic)

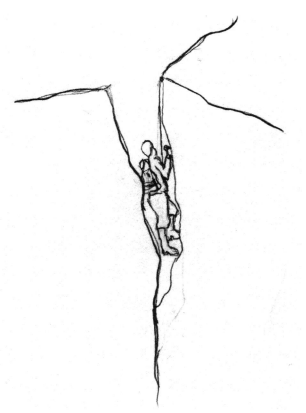

Crevasse Escape (Laura Lindblad)

vertical granite) in 20 hours (Pat Ament, personal comment).

Crow The American crow is a common bird in all environments. It is black, caws loudly and repeatedly, and may be mistaken for a **raven**. It prefers lower elevations, according to Johnsgard.

Crowley, Edward Alexander (Aleister) (1875–1947) Born: Scotland. A fairly controversial figure, who dabbled in the occult, he also was a mountaineer and led expeditions to **K2** in 1902 and **Kangchenjunga** in 1905. Bibliography: *The Spirit of Solitude* (1929), later retitled *The Confessions of Aleister Crowley, The Great Beast* (1951), biography by John Symonds.

Croz, Michel (1830–1865) A superb guide; born in Le Tour, near **Chamonix**. He worked alongside his friend and fellow guide **Christian Almer**, although they spoke different languages. He was killed in the **Whymper** debacle on the **Matterhorn**. His many first ascents include: **Castor** (1861), **Aiguille d'Argentière** (1864), Barre des Écrins (1864), the Whymper and Croz summits of the **Grandes Jorasses** (1864), and the Matterhorn (1865). (See also the **10 Best Guides** sidebar.)

Crust Either the outer shell of the earth formed from cooled molten **lava** or the hardened or frozen surface that forms on **snow**. In spring and summer, frozen crust is usually hard in the early morning hours, but as the heat of the day increases, it softens so that one may break through and sink in deeply at every step.

Crux The most difficult part of a **rock climb**.

Cryosphere Those areas of the world that contain **snow** or **ice**.

Cuba Lowest point, Caribbean Sea 0 m; highest point, Pico Turquino 2,005 m, 6,758 ft.

Cudahy, Mike Born: England. Ultra long-distance runner who, in 1984, set a new Pennine Way record of 2 days, 21 hours, 54 minutes. Bibliography: *Studmarks on the Summits* (1985) by Bill Smith, *Wild Trails to Far Horizons* (1989).

Cuesta A **ridge** with a gentle slope on one side and a steep one on the other.

Culture The way of life that a group of people develops and cultivates. The culture of people who live in the mountains may differ dramatically from similar or related groups who reside in nearby valleys. Substantial variations in **climate**, arable land, vegetation, and **animal** life as the **altitude** increases will have a dramatic influence on culture even though language and **religion** remain constant.

Cunningham, John (1927–1980) Born: Scotland. A leading Scottish climber in the 1950s. Bibliography: *Guide to Winter Climbs: Cairngorms and Creag Meaghaidh* (1973), *Creagh Dhu Climber—The Life and Times of John Cunningham* (1999) biography by Jeff Connor.

Curran, James (1943–) Born: England. Bibliography: *Trango, the Nameless Tower* (1978), *K2: Triumph and Tragedy* (1987), *K2: The Story of the Savage Mountain* (1995), *High Achiever* (1999) biography of **Chris Bonington**.

Cwm (prn: kum or koom) A Welsh term for **cirque**; for example the **Western Cwm** on **Everest**.

Cyprus Lowest point, Mediterranean Sea 0 m; highest point, Olympus 1,951 m, 6,401 ft.

Czech Republic Lowest point, Elbe River 115 m, 377 ft; highest point, Snezka 1,602 m, 5,256 ft.

D

Daisy A ubiquitous flower of many species; in the **Himalayas,** various *Saussurea* are found as high as 18,400 ft (Polunin and Stainton).

Daisy chain In **rock climbing**, a **sling** that is sewn in such a way that it produces a series of small loops. It offers quick, adjustable connection points.

Dall sheep One of the major mammals found in the **mountains** of **Alaska** and the **Yukon**, Dall sheep inhabit relatively dry, open alpine **ranges**, and the contiguous steep and rugged terrain, which offers fast escape routes from predators (these include grizzly **bears** and **wolves**). Indeed, Dall sheep are extremely impressive climbers, and can run over long distances on seemingly impassable, precipitous terrain. The males are called rams, while females are known as ewes; during the winter months, when food is very scarce, they feed on frozen grass, and even **lichen** and **moss**.

Damavand 5,670 m, 18,603 ft. The highest point in **Iran** was first climbed in 1837 by W. T. Thomson. (See also **Volcanic Seven Summits** sidebar and color photos.)

Danger In climbing, one speaks of objective dangers (e.g., falling rock or lightning) that one cannot control and those such as running out of water or dropping one's ice ax that a thoughtful and careful person can eliminate. These are called subjective dangers.

Dauphiné Alps A large **massif** in the French **Alps**, primarily comprising the **Meije–Écrins** complex, but also secondary ranges. Major summits include: **Barre des Ecrins** 4,102 m, 13,458 ft; **La Meije**, 3,983 m, 13,068 ft; the **Ailefroide** 3,954 m, 12,972 ft; Mont **Pelvoux** 3,943 m,

12,936 ft; the Pic Sans Nom 3,915 m, 12,845 ft; the Pic Gaspard 3,880 m, 12,730 ft; the Pic Coolidge 3,756 m, 12,323 ft; the Grande Ruine 3,754 m, 12,317 ft; the Rateau 3,754 m, 12,317 ft; the Montagne des Agneaux 3,660 m, 12,008 ft; Les Bans 3,651 m, 11,979 ft; the Sommet des Rouies 3,634 m, 11,923 ft; the Aiguille du Plat 3,602 m, 11,818 ft; the Pic d'Olan 3,577 m, 11,735 ft; the Pic Bonvoisin 3,560 m, 11,680 ft; the Aiguilles d'Arves (highest point) 3,514 m, 11,529 ft; Les Grandes Rousses 3,473 m, 11,395 ft; the Roche de la Muzelle 3,459 m, 11,349 ft; and, finally, the Sirac 3,438 m, 11,280 ft, which is the southernmost major peak of the French Alps.

de Beer, Sir Gavin Rylands (1899–1972) Born: England. An authority on the history of travel in the Swiss Alps. Bibliography: *Early Travelers in the Alps* (1930), *Alps and Men* (1932), *Travelers in Switzerland* (1949), *Speaking of Switzerland* (1952), *Alps and Elephants* (1955).

de Filippi, Filippo (1869–1938) Born: Italy. A surgeon, scholar, mountain traveler, and official recorder of the Duke of **Abruzzi**'s expeditions. Bibliography: *The Ascent of Mount St. Elias (Alaska) by H.R.H. Prince Luigi Amedeo di Savoia* (1900), *Ruwenzori* (1908), *Karakoram and the Western Himalaya 1909* (1912), *The Italian Expedition to the Himalaya, Karakoram and Eastern Turkestan (1913–1914)* (1932).

de Lepiney, Jacques and Tom (fl. 1920s) Born: France. The brothers made many significant first ascents in the **Mont Blanc** range in the 1920s including: **Aiguille du Plan**, north face, Pointe de Lepiney. Bibliography: *Climbs on Mont Blanc* (1930).

de Saussure, Horace Bénédict (1740–1799) Born: France. He was a naturalist living in Geneva, who became fascinated with the local mountains, especially the **Mont Blanc** Range. In 1762 he offered a substantial reward for the first person to climb Mont Blanc. It was finally climbed 24 years later by **Jacques Balmat** and **Michel Paccard**. De Saussure made the second ascent on August 3, 1787.

Dead Sea −408m, −1,339 ft. This is the deepest depression on earth; the weather is fiercely hot, and the sea is constantly evaporating, thus increasing the concentration of salt in the water. An austere desert, where rocky cliffs and small mountains rise under torrid skies, surrounds the Dead Sea.

Deadman Anything that can be placed under **snow** to act as an **anchor**. A **picket** is manufactured for this purpose, but in an emergency a pack can be filled with snow and then buried.

Death Attempting to reach the top of a low cliff or high mountain is an inherently dangerous pursuit. At least 216 people have died on **Everest**, 116 on **Washington**, 85 on **Denali**, 67 on **Rainier**, and 45 on **K2**. (See also **Mountain Fatalities in the 14 Highest Peaks** sidebar.)

Death Valley The hottest place in the **United States**, it is also the lowest point in the country and in **North America**, −86 m, −282 ft, at Badwater. (See also color photos.)

Death zone The area above 8,000 m, 26,240 ft where the body cannot regenerate. Because the air is so thin, most people begin to slowly die here, and very few humans have spent more than a few hours between 26,000 and 29,000 feet. A number of astonishing **bivouacs** high on **Everest** and **K2** have been successful. (7,000 m, 23,000 ft, are sometimes cited as the onset of the death zone.)

Debris Small **rocks** or mud. **Avalanche** debris is the material that an avalanche carries along and leaves at its terminus.

Deciduous A taxonomic designation for **trees** that lose their leaves during the winter. Their wood is harder than that found in **conifers**.

Deer White-tailed deer, **caribou**, **elk**, moose, and mule deer are all members of this large, antlered family. They vary in size from 3½ to 7½ ft at the shoulder; moose can weigh up to 1,400 pounds. All species, including moose, can be found at higher elevations. The musk is especially at home on high, rocky slopes, up to almost 12,000 ft (Burnie and Wilson).

Defile A narrow mountain **pass**.

Degree Unit used to measure angles, **latitude** and **longitude,** and **temperature**. It is often used to indicate the steepness of a slope, generally ice or snow: for example, 90 degrees is vertical; 35 degrees is optimal for **avalanches**; and climbing up to approximately 45 degrees on snow is relatively easy, while it is much harder on ice. Classic couloirs average 50 to 65 degrees; extremely difficult and long Alpine north faces, such as **Les Droites**, can average well over 70 degrees, with **gullies** at 80–85 degrees. On frozen waterfalls, one can find sustained vertical ice climbs.

Degree of difficulty See **rating systems**.

Dehydration Loss of fluid in the body. A person dehydrates if he or she does not drink enough liquid. Additionally, with **altitude** gain, one naturally dehydrates more quickly than one would at sea level.

Delaware Lowest point, Atlantic Ocean 0 m; highest point, Ebright Azimuth 135 m, 442 ft (49th highest of the 50 state highpoints). The only state with a lower highpoint is **Florida**.

Denali ("The Great One") 6,194 m, 20,320 ft. Also called Mt. McKinley, this is the highest peak in **North America**; it also has the largest change in elevation from base to summit (17,000 ft) of all the world's mountains. An awe-inspiring mountain that stands a few hundred miles south of the **Arctic Circle**, it creates own weather. It was first summitted by Walter Harper in 1913 and is now climbed frequently, especially along its West Buttress; the Cassin Ridge is a another more difficult route. The **massif** of which Denali is a part contains some of the biggest **glaciers** in the world. There is an extensive library of many hundreds of books on Denali; a good place to start is Becky's *Mount McKinley* (www.nps.gov/dena). (See also the **Seven Summits** sidebar and color photos.)

Denmark Lowest point, Lammefjord −7 m, −23 ft; highest point, Ejer Bavnehoj 173 m, 568 ft.

Dent See **tooth**.

Dent, Clinton Thomas (1850–1912) Born: England. An important mountaineer in the late 18th century. First ascent of the Aiguille du **Dru** with J. Walker Hartley, Alexander Burgener, and Kaspar Maurer in 1878. Bibliography: *Above the Snow Line* (1885), *Mountaineering* (1892).

Dent Blanche 4,356 m, 14,291 ft. This is the 13th highest of the 60 major 4,000-meter peaks in the **Alps**. A superb, steep peak in **Valais**, it was first ascended in 1862 by T. S. Kennedy, William Wigram, Jean-Baptiste Croz, and Johann Kronig. (See also color photos.)

Dent d'Hérens 4,171 m, 13,684 ft. This is the 32nd highest of the 60 major 4,000-meter peaks of the **Alps**. It was first ascended in 1863 by W. E. Hall, F. Crawford Grove, R. S. McDonald, W. Woodmass, **Melchior Anderegg**, Peter Perren, and Jean-Pierre Cachat. Because of the close presence of the mighty **Matterhorn**, the Dent d'Hérens does not always get the respect it deserves: it is, by all accounts, a formidable peak, with serrated ridges and steep faces, and a difficult climb. (See also color photos.)

Dent du Géant 4,013 m, 13,166 ft. This is the 57th highest of the 60 major 4,000-meter peaks in the **Alps**. The first ascents occurred in 1882: the north summit, 4,009 m, 13,153 ft, was reached by Alessandro, Alfonso, Corradino, and Gaudenzio Sella, and B., D., and **J.-J. Maquignaz**, while the main summit was climbed by W. W. Graham, Auguste Cupelin, and Alphonse Payot. The Dent du Géant is a highly recognizable summit, which protrudes at a slight overhang over the ridge connecting it to the Col du Géant, high above **Courmayeur**. It is a short, but difficult ascent on good rock.

Der Blaue Licht/The Blue Light A German film cowritten, coproduced, and codirected in 1932 by Leni Riefenstahl (1902–2003); it was shot in the Dolomites and the Tessin, and set in 1866: on full moon nights, the Monte Cristallo gleams with a blue light, urging youngsters to climb it at night and meet their deaths. It also depicts the Junta (Riefenstahl), a young girl said to be a sorceress. The photography by Hans Schneeberger and Heinz von Jaworsky is most glorious and the locations are stunning. (M-A. H.)

Der Dämon des Himalaya A 1935 German film codirected by Professor Günter Oskar Dyrenfurth and Andrew Marton. This partial documentary uses real Himalayan footage that the two directors shot during expeditions in the early 1930s. The film deals with the mask of the demon Kali Mata, a spirit guarding the Himalayas and a subsequent curse troubling a love affair. The studio work in Berlin, the storm scene shot on the Jungfrau, and Swiss composer Arthur Honegger's score (recorded by the Berlin Philharmonic) all make this a most interesting production. (M-A.H.)

Der Ewige Traum/*Der König des Mont Blanc*/*Le Rêve Éternel*/*Le Roi du Mont Blanc* There are two titles for each version of this 1934 German–French coproduction directed by **Arnold Fanck** after a novel by Karl Ziak (*Paccard wider Balmat* [Paccard against Balmat]). The plot deals with a legend stating that gold is to be found on the heights of Mont Blanc. Poor Chamonix inhabitant **Jacques Balmat** tries his luck. If we believe what Alexandre Dumas notes in his *Impressions de Voyage: En Suisse*, Balmat and **Paccard** were never foes and neither climbed Mont Blanc for greedy reasons. Yet in the final pages of his book, Dumas reports that Balmat died trying to find gold in the mountains, but this was in the 1830s. This might be the basis for the novel. The movie, shot in two languages, has a large part of the cast playing in both through dubbing, which is quite unusual for that time. Sound mars the documentary possibilities of the movie—live sound, editing, and mixing were still very difficult in the early talkies, and the result is awkward—and some expressionist gimmicks (e.g., flaming letters appearing at the climax) seem out of place but the result is very honest. (M-A. H.)

Descent Coming down the mountain, generally using the simplest possible route: it is well-known among climbers that the technical level of difficulty increases upon descent because one cannot see the holds and general route as well as when one is ascending; however, in many cases, the descent may involve a series of **rappels**, if no simple alternative route is available. Unfortunately, many accidents do happen during descent, where the psychological relaxation, and sometimes elation, of having summitted and fatigue conspire to lower the attention and concentration of the climber. Furthermore, in the aforementioned case of multiple rappels, one must pay extreme attention to the setting of the **anchor point**, doubling up of the rope, figuring out the position and distance of the next platform, and making absolutely sure that a brake is available to properly slow down the rappel: numerous fatalities have occurred when climbers missed a ledge upon rappelling down, or failed to slow down, simply continuing past the end of the rope. Sometimes, the descent takes an entirely different route (see **traverse**), and it is usually much faster than the **ascent**, especially if one rappels down, as explained above. **Down climbing** a difficult rock face is often extremely treacherous or impossible. In **mountaineering**, a change in **weather** or **snow** or **ice** conditions can make the descent a slow and laborious affair.

Desert Mountains can border and transect deserts and are in turn sometimes located within a desert environment. Mountains influence **weather** patterns and when precipitation diminishes a desert may result. This is the case on the eastern side of the **Sierras. Antarctica**, replete with **snow** and **ice**-encrusted **mountains,** is also a desert. And part of **Nepal** and northern **India** comprise the Himalayan desert, barren and dry, although snow covered in places. See Nina Rao's beautifully illustrated *Himalayan Desert* for further discussion.

Desio, Ardito (1897–2001) Born: Palmanova, Italy. The leader of the first successful expedition to **K2** in 1954. Bibliography: *Ascent of K2* (1955).

Desmaison, René (1930–) This French mountaineer is well known for his winter climbs. He did the **first ascent** of **Jannu** in 1962, a winter climb of the Walker Spur of the **Grandes Jorasses**, and many Alpine climbs. Bibliography: *Total Alpinism* (1982).

Destivelle, Catherine (1960–) A superb rock climber and mountaineer, she was the first female to climb 8a, 8a+ (see **rating systems**) and was considered the best female climber between 1985 and 1988. Her major climbing and mountaineering achievements include: the first female solo ascent on the Bonatti pillar in the **Drus**, in four hours; opening of a new west side in the Drus in 11 days; Walker Spur in the **Grandes Jorasses** in

three days; Bonatti route on the north side of the **Matterhorn** in four hours; expedition to the **Great Trango Tower**; second ascent of the Loretan/Troillet route on **Shisha Pangma** with Erik Decamp; and in the Ellsworth massif, **Antarctica**, opening of a 1,700-m (5,100 ft) high virgin mountainside with Erik Decamp. (See also **10 Best Female Climbers** sidebar.)

Detritus Accumulation of **rock** fragments. (See also **debris** and **talus**.)

Devil's Postpile National Monument A volcanic configuration in **California** that consists of extraordinary, 60-foot-high, contiguous, fluted columns of basalt.

Devil's Tower A sheer, 865-foot symmetrical monolith in **Wyoming**, much beloved by climbers. This **volcanic plug** is sacred to Native Americans, who request that people refrain from **climbing**, at least during the month of June. It was the first national monument. (See also **10 Awesome Monoliths** sidebar and color photos.)

Dhaulagiri I 8,167 m, 26,794 ft. The seventh highest **mountain** in the world, it is located entirely within **Nepal**. It was first climbed on May 13, 1960, by an international team led by Max Eiselin that included P. Diener, E. Forrer, A. Schelbert, Nawang Dorje Sherpa, and Nima Dorje Sherpa. The second ascent occurred 10 years later; the mountain had been climbed 298 times, as of the end of 1999, 53 deaths occurring either on attempts or after summitting. (See also the **14 8,000-Meter Peaks** sidebar.)

Dibona, Angelo (1879–1956) Ardito claims that Dibona "was one of the best **guides** of all time." He climbed in the **Dolomites** and in **France**.

Dictionaries and encyclopedias Other than the present work, there is no English-language A–Z volume that offers a comprehensive overview of the mountain, including entries on botanical, geological, zoological, and innumerable other subjects, but there are some allied tools. Unsworth's *Encyclopaedia of Mountaineering* is a formidable and useful compilation limited to climbing terminology and related matters; the same may be said of Collomb's concise *Dictionary of Mountaineering*. Greg Child's excellent *Climbing: The Complete Reference* is a more recent volume. Barnes's *Complete Encyclopedia of Skiing* is quirky, and includes some surprising entries, but clarifies the esoterica of skiing. In French, we have Jouty and Odier's recent *Dictionnaire de la Montagne*, an extraordinary accomplishment, wonderfully illustrated, but found in only six libraries around the world. Gautrat's French *Dictionnaire de la Montagne* is similar but much older. In German, Kwiatkowski's *Schlag nach* offers sometimes detailed entries on terms associated with climbing, hiking, skiing, and the mountain environment. Rudolf Weiss has compiled a *Mountaineering Dictionary* (there is also a German version entitled *Wörterbuch Alpiner Begriffe*), which is divided into four linguistic sections (English, French, German, Italian). Each of the included terms is then presented in the other three languages. In Spanish there are two germane titles: Zorilla's recent enormous *Enciclopedia de la montaña* and Faus's *Diccionario de la montaña*, which contains 600 pages of terminology (including words in Basque, Catalan, and dialects) and even some trees and animals, but almost no people and no individually listed peaks; he does present extremely detailed essays on climbing in, for example, the **Himalayas** (14 pages) and the **Pyrénées** (20 pages).

Die Geier-Wally A novel written in 1873 by Wilhelmine von Hillern (1836–1916): in Tyrol, around 1830, a girl named Wally is in love with a boy named Joseph. Their parents, on the other hand, are enemies. The vulture to which the titles refers belongs to Wally and is a symbol of her being ostracized by the village. This work was quite popular and in 1892 was turned into an Italian opera: *La Wally*, composed by Alfredo Catalani (1852–1893). The first version of the work had an eerie ending, the characters disappearing in the mist, while in a second one, Wally jumps off a precipice in a snowstorm. There are two movie versions: one in 1921 (seemingly lost) and one in 1940. (M-A. H.)

Die Lawine/The Avalanche An Austrian film shot in 1923; this an average drama of a man forced to marry a girl bearing his child on the very day he was to wed a rich fiancée. A few years later, the rich woman comes into his life again and he is torn between her and his wife. It is set amid snowy mountains. The avalanche scene is incredibly short and unspectacular. Yet, the movie has a nice ski chase. (M-A. H.)

Die Weisse Hölle vom Piz Palü/White Hell of Piz Palu A 1929 German film directed by **Arnold Fanck**, starring Gustav Diessel, Leni Riefenstahl, and Ernst Petersen; it was released toward the end of the silent film era, and might be considered the ultimate mountain film. It was shot almost entirely on location, abjuring, for the most part, the use of stunt actors; its plot is as simple as can be: a party tries to climb the northern side of **Piz Palu**, but fails. With no acrobatic nonsense or subplots dealing with rivalry or love affairs, the film concentrates on the climb from beginning to end, with the exception of the five-minute prologue in which Diessel loses his beloved in a fall. He then turns into this well-known character: the man haunted by his past. It should be noted that codirector for this movie was Georg Wilhelm Pabst, one of Germany's most important filmmakers. Everything seems right in place and though the presentation might be too slow for those who prefer action, the result is really gripping. The standard technique for silent movies (short focals and slow emulsions) enhances the impression of hugeness; the black-and-white photography can be stunning (in daylight with the shining snow or during night scenes with magnesium torches). (M-A. H.)

Diédre (F) See **dihedral**.

Diemberger, Kurt (1932–) A well-known Austrian climber and mountaineer and the only person other than **Hermann Buhl** to have made **first ascents** of two **8,000-meter peaks** (**Broad Peak** and **Dhaulagiri I**). Bibliography: *Nanga Parbat Pilgrimage* (1956) by Hermann Buhl, *The Ascent of Dhaulagiri* (1961) by Max Eiselin, *Summits and Secrets* (1971), *The Endless Knot* (1991), autobiography, *Spirits of the Air* (1994), *K2—Challenging the Sky* (1997).

Dihedral *Diédre* (F). In **rock climbing**, an inside or open **corner**.

Dike A raised length of **rock** that transects the surrounding, eroded rock.

Dinaric Alps A southern spur of the main range, located within **Bosnia and Herzegovina**.

Dingle, Graeme (1945–) Born: New Zealand. Bibliography: *Two against the Alps* (1972), *Wall of*

Shadows (1976), *First across the Roof of the World* (1982), with **Peter Hillary**.

Diorite   An igneous rock.

Direct   See **route**.

Disease, protection against   In preparing for an exciting **mountain** adventure in **Kenya, Argentina**, or **Nepal**, it is easy to overlook the necessity for protection against a host of horrible ailments and infections. It is often mandatory to take shots, and also to begin a regimen of ongoing tablet consumption to ward off cholera, tuberculosis, yellow fever, or malaria. Water, even the pristine-looking glacial water found in **Switzerland** or **Alaska**, may contain parasites that can cause discomfort or dysentery and other maladies; it should always be filtered, boiled, or treated with iodine tablets. Food, especially fresh fruit and vegetables, should be completely cooked or washed with bottled water. See www.cdc.gov/travel and www.istm.org for help and advisories.

Distaghil (Disteghil) Sar   7,885 m, 25,869 ft. This major peak is located in the **Karakoram**; it was first ascended in 1960 by G. Starker and D. Marchart, both members of the expedition led by Wolfgang Stefan.

Divide   "Ridge separating two adjacent drainage basins" (Hamblin and Christiansen). (See also **continental divide**.)

Djebel   (Also jebel) In Arabic, a hill or mountain. Often used in place names, for example, Djebel Musa.

Djibouti   Lowest point, Lac Assal −155 m, −509 ft; highest point, Moussa Ali 2,028 m, 6,654 ft. For such a small country (23,180 sq km, 8,950 sq miles), Djibouti contains both very low areas and relatively high mountains; the weather there is terribly hot, with temperatures often reaching well in excess of 50°C, or 122°F.

Dogs   People like their dogs (replete with little packs) to accompany them on long hikes, mountaineering assaults, and glacier excursions. This book's authors have seen dogs, in all seasons, on trails, slopes, and 14,000-foot summits (**Wheeler Peak** or Bierstadt, for example). Three outstanding canines deserve mention. Tschingel (d. 1879) accompanied **William Augustus Breevort Coolidge** on 66 Alpine climbs. Diente, Roger Edrinn's dog, somehow managed to reach the

summits of all 54 of Colorado's 14,000-foot peaks. And Orient led Bill Irwin, a blind hiker, along the entire **Appalachian Trail** (as recounted in *Blind Courage*). Additionally, dogs such as St. Bernards are used for general rescue work in the mountains, and others are trained to locate avalanche victims.

Dolomites   An Italian **range** in the South Tirol that contains some colorful and extraordinarily beautiful, steep, and jagged configurations including "The Rose Garden." The limestone offers some excellent climbing opportunities. The name Dolomites came from the French naturalist Dieudonné Dolomieu (www.dolomiti.it/eng).

Dolphin, Arthur Rhodes   (1925–1953) Born: near Bradford, Yorkshire, England. A foremost climber in the 1940s who made the first ascent of Kipling Groove on Gimmer Crag in 1948. He was killed after falling on relatively easy snow slopes while descending, having soloed the **Dent du Géant**. Bibliography: *Lakeland's Greatest Pioneers, 100 Years of Rock Climbing* (1983), by Bill Birkett, *100 Years of Rock Climbing in the Lake District* (*Fell and Rock Journal*, 1986) edited by A. G. Cram.

Dolpo   An arid region of **Nepal**, ideal for trekking and climbing 20,000-foot peaks.

Dom   4,545 m, 14,911 ft. This is the sixth highest of the 60 major 4,000-meter peaks in the Alps. A superb mountain in the heart of the **Valais** of **Switzerland**, the Dom was first ascended in 1858 by J. L. Davies, Johann Zumtaugwald, Johann Kronig, and Hieronymus Brantschen. The vast face of the Dom towers above the ski resort village of Saas-Fee, and a mighty ridge connects it to its neighbor, the **Taschhörn**, another giant of the **Valaisan Alps**. (See also color photos.)

Dôme   (F) A summit that is round.

Dôme de Rochefort   4,015 m, 13,172 ft. This is the 56th highest of the 60 major 4,000-meter peaks in the **Alps**. It was first ascended in 1881 by J. Eccles and Alphonse and Michel Payot. The summit is located east of the **Grandes Jorasses**, and offers superb views of the **Mont Blanc Range**, including the delicate Arêtes de Rochefort.

Dôme du Goûter   4,304 m, 14,120 ft. Generally, this is not considered as an independent summit;

rather, it is a **satellite** of **Mont Blanc**. If the Dôme were treated as a separate entity, it would be the 19th highest summit in the **Alps**. (See also color photos.)

Dominica Lowest point, Caribbean Sea 0 m; highest point, Morne Diablatins 1,447 m, 4,747 ft.

Dominican Republic Lowest point, Lago Enriquillo −46 m, −151 ft; highest point, Pico Duarte 3,175 m, 10,417 ft. This very small country (48,730 sq km, 18,815 sq miles) presents another example of a wide range of altitudes, with an amplitude exceeding 10,500 ft and a correspondingly wide variety of plant and animal life.

Donner party A group of pioneers who were trapped by a fierce storm at what is now called Donner Pass in **California**. Some of the party resorted to cannibalism.

Dormant The state in which a **volcano** exists when not producing an **eruption**.

Douglas fir A **tree** that can be found at **altitude**, especially in the western United States and Canada. It is a false **hemlock** and can grow to 260 feet. The bark is furrowed and **bears** sometimes scrape it to get at the sap (www.bcadventure.com).

Dove A pigeonlike **bird**; in East Africa, the pink-breasted prefers higher altitudes and in the **Andes,** the golden-spotted ground-dove reaches 16,500 ft (Fjeldså and Krabbe).

Down climb In **rock climbing**, to return down the face the way one came up or via another route; it is often much more difficult than the **ascent**. (See also **descent**.)

Downhill skiing   (also Alpine) The type of **skiing** done by most people at commercial **ski areas**. After being hauled to the top of a mountain on a lift, the skier shoots down the **slope**. Downhill is also a racing event, less controlled by **gates** than **slalom**, so the speeds are much greater.

Droites, Les 4,000 m, 13,123 ft. This is the 60th highest of the 60 major 4,000-meter peaks in the Alps. A magnificent and spectacular summit in the **Mont Blanc Range**, it is one of the most difficult north faces in the Alps; it is extremely sustained, and over 800 m, 2,600 ft tall, with an average slope well in excess of 75 degrees, and vertical mixed terrain over the last 200 m, 650 ft. It was first climbed in 1876, from the Talèfre

Glacier, by Thomas Middlemore, J. Oakley Maund, Henry Cordier, Johann Jaum, and Andreas Maurer. (See also color photos and the **6 + 1 Great Alpine North Faces** sidebar.)

Drumlin A hill that has been smoothed by a **glacier**.

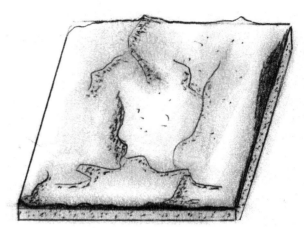

Drumlin (Laura Lindblad)

Drus, Les Two amazing **granite** spires, **satellites** of the **Aiguille Verte**; some of the most difficult rock and mixed climbing in the **Alps** can be found there, and many exceptional climbers have opened new routes on the Drus, including **Walter Bonatti**, **Pierre Allain**, and **Catherine Destivelle**. (See also color photos.)

Duck A small waterfowl that comes in innumerable species (canvasback, harlequin, mallard, ring-necked, ad infinitum); it can be found in virtually all habitats wherever lakes and rivers are located. In the **Himalayas**, the tufted has been spotted as high as 17,500 ft (Ali) and in the **Andes** the crested and the comb can be found above 13,200 ft (Fjeldså and Krabbe).

Dufourspitze 4,634 m, 15,203 ft. This is the second highest peak in the **Alps**, and the main summit of **Monte Rosa**, located between **Switzerland** and **Italy**. The Dufourspitze was first climbed in 1855 by the **Grenville** brothers, Christopher Smyth, **Charles Hudson** (who perished in 1865, during the **Matterhorn** first ascent and subsequent tragedy), John Birbeck, E. J. Stephenson, Matthäus and **Johann Zumtaugwald**, and Ulrich Lauener. (See also color photos.)

Dulfer, Hans (1893–1915) Dulfer "was one of the best climbers of all time," according to Ardito. In 1913, he did 173 climbs with 23 **first ascents**. In technical rock climbing, a specific move is now called a Dulfer; it involves the **friction climbing** of a **dihedral**. He also created the Dulfersitz **rappel** technique.

Dunagiri 7,066 m, 23,184 ft. This major peak is located within the **Himalayas** in **India**.

Durrance, Richard Henry (Dick) (1914–2004) Forwarded the sport of skiing on two fronts. First, he won 17 United States titles and, second, he was instrumental in developing the Sun Valley, Aspen, and Alta ski areas. He also was the producer of some 46 films on skiing ("Dick").

Dürrenhorn 4,034 m, 13,235 ft. This is the 52nd highest of the 60 major 4,000-meter peaks in the Alps. It was first ascended in 1879, by **A. F. Mummery**, William Penhall, **Alexander Burgener**, and F. Imseng. The Dürrenhorn is located within the **Mischabels**, in the **Valaisan Alps**.

Duvet (F) (Not used in the United States.) Originally, comforter; sleeping bag.

Dwarf primrose This frequently red or pink **flower** with variously shaped petals grows in replete clusters.

Dynamic See **rope**.

Dyno In **rock climbing,** a move in which one makes a dynamic movement, e.g., a jump, to a hold that cannot be reached by stretching.

Dyrenfurth, Gunter Oscar Born: Switzerland. The leader of the 1930 international **Kangchenjunga** expedition. Bibliography: *To the Third Pole* (1955).

Eagle A large, majestic bird that soars in the **high mountains**. Species include the bald, which feeds on fish and so water is a necessary concomitant to its presence, the golden, Philippine, and wedge-tailed. In **Ethiopia** and **Kenya**, Verreaux's favors **crags** and **cliffs** and the tawny enjoys the Ethiopian mountains (Williams).

Earthquake Wave movement below or along the earth's surface at a **fault** caused by shifts in **tectonic plates**. Earthquakes vary in potency from mild (1) to extremely destructive (8.5+) on the **Richter** scale. Individual examples are not included in this listing. One of the missions of the **U.S. Geological Survey** is to study earthquakes, especially potential warning signs. (See also color photos.)

Easter daisy These common **flowers** have a yellow center surrounded by many purple, red, white, or yellow petals. Nicholls points out that they bloom at Easter time.

Eastern Mountain Sports (EMS) See **equipment retailers**.

Eckenstein, Oscar Johannes Ludwig (1859–1921) Born: England. Bibliography: *The Alpine Portfolio* (1889), with August Lorria, *The Karakorams and Kashmir* (1896).

École Nationale de Ski et d'Alpinisme The school one must attend in order to become a licensed ski instructor in **France**.

Ecology The study of the interactions of all inhabitants of a given environment.

Écrins, La Barre des 4,102 m, 13,455 ft. This is the 38th highest of the 60 major 4,000-meter peaks in the **Alps**. An exceptionally beautiful mountain in France, La Barre des Écrins is the undisputed monarch of the **Dauphiné Alps**. It

is also the place where the famed, and controversial, **Almer's Leap** occurred during the first ascent, by a party led by **Edward Whymper** in 1864, and including **Michel Croz**, **Christian Almer**, A. W. Moore, and **Horace Walker**. The normal route starts from the Pré de Madame Carles, and goes up the **Glacier** Blanc, via the refuge of the same name, under the Dôme de Neige des Écrins, to the Brèche Laury, and up the delicate, abrupt ridge, to the summit. The south face, on the other hand, is a formidable enterprise: over 1,800 m (6,000 ft) high, it rises nearly vertically from the Glacier Noir; numerous variations can be followed, with difficult pitches, and incredible vistas of the north faces of the Glacier Noir, including the **Pelvoux**, Le Coup de Sabre, and the **Ailefroide**. (See also color photos.)

Ecuador Lowest point, Pacific Ocean 0 m; highest point, Chimborazo 6,310 m, 20,702 ft. With a well-deserved name, as it lies right on the equator, this small country contains some of the highest volcanoes in the world, including its highpoint. Most of these are active or dormant, a reflection of the intense tectonic activity in the area.

Edelweiss Perhaps the most famous mountain flower, and symbolic of the **Alps**; it is white, looks like a star, and can be found in **Europe** and **Asia** especially at higher **altitudes**.

Edema See **acute mountain sickness**.

Edge In **rock climbing**, a small hold, or to place the edge of the foot here. Also, the long, bottom lip of a ski or snowboard (often made of sharpened metal), upon which one places angular pressure in order to dig into the **snow** or **ice**.

Edging In **rock climbing**, relying on just the edge of one's shoes.

Edlinger, Patrick A remarkable French pure rock climber, his achievements include the following: in 1982, the first 8a's in the Biou of the Four Puros and in the Verdon; in 1982, first visual 7c; in 1983, 8a, *Ça glisse au pays des merveilles* ("Sliding in Wonderland"); and several victories in World Cup climbing competitions (http://profiles.bleau.info/patrick.edlinger/).

Edwards, John Menlove (1910–1958) Born: Crossens, Lancashire, England. Bibliography: *Samson: The Life and Writings of Menlove Edwards* (1960), edited by Wilfrid Noyce and Geoffrey Sutton, *Menlove* (1985), a biography by Jim Perrin.

Egypt Lowest point, Qattara Depression −133 m, −436 ft; highest point, Mt. Catherine 2,629 m, 8,625 ft. This ancient land of the pharaohs contains astonishing landmarks, including the Giza pyramids; but it is also the land of the Blue and White Nile Rivers and the cataracts of Aswan.

Eiger 3,970 m, 13,025 ft. A very difficult peak to climb in **Switzerland**. It lives up to its name (ogre in English): the north face is one of the world's most dangerous climbs with its horrific storms and continual barrage of falling rock, ice, and snow. Between 1935 and 1977, 43 people lost their lives here. It is an extremely difficult mixed climb, which seems to have little effect on people; on a 1962 climb, high up on the wall, **Chris Bonington** met two climbers who did not know how to **rappel**! One had been climbing for less than a year (Roth). This is obviously an invitation to disaster. The Eiger was first ascended in 1858 by Charles Barrington, **Christian Almer**, and a few other anonymous climbers. The climb of the north face, the famous Eigerwand, has marked some of the most adventurous and intensely competitive climbing endeavors in history; some of this epic story is recounted in the remarkable book *The White Spider*, written by one of the protagonists, **Heinrich Harrer**. (See also **north face** and the **6 + 1 Great Alpine North Faces** sidebar [www.fdrs.ch/eiger-live/english/index-eiger.html].)

Eiger Sanction, The An American film directed by Clint Eastwood and released in 1975; it is based on a novel by Trevanian. Eastwood plays a college art teacher who doubles as a part-time assassin for the American government. He is supposed to kill an unidentified enemy agent during a climb of the **Eiger** (Eastwood actually did the climb). The awkward script is forwarded with style by Eastwood but it does not match his usual standards. The director had problems with the production after shooting, the endless sexual innuendoes are representative of the mid-1970s, and the female characters are leftovers from a James Bond movie. Nevertheless, the U.S. training of the hero in Arizona as well as the forty-minute ascent of the Eiger are quite spectacular. There are no stunts or studio work here, thanks to Norman Dyhrenfurth, the climbing expedition leader. The photography for the sequence by **John Cleare** and others is excellent. (See also the **10 Best Hollywood Mountain Movies** sidebar.) (M-A. H.)

Eight thousand–meter peaks (Eight thousanders). There are 14 8,000-meter (26,247 ft) peaks in the world, nine in the **Himalayas**, five in the **Karakoram**. To climb all 14 peaks, one must ascend almost 116 vertical km

14 8,000-Meter Peaks

1. Everest 8,850 m, 29,9035 ft (1953)
2. K2 8,611 m, 28,251 ft (1954)
3. Kangchenjunga 8,586 m, 28,169 ft (1955)
4. Lhotse 8,516 m, 27,939 ft (1956)
5. Makalu 8,463 m, 27,766 ft (1955)
6. Cho Oyu 8,201 m, 26,906 ft (1954)
7. Dhaulagiri 8,167 m, 26,794 ft (1960)
8. Manaslu 8,163 m, 26,781 ft (1956)
9. Nanga Parbat 8,126 m, 26,660 ft (1953)
10. Annapurna 8,091 m, 26,545 ft (1950)
11. Gasherbrum I (Hidden Peak) 8,068 m, 26,469 ft (1958)
12. Broad Peak 8,047 m, 26,400 ft (1957)
13. Shisha Pangma 8,046 m, 26,398 ft (1964)
14. Gasherbrum II 8,035 m, 26,361 ft (1956)

Year in parentheses indicates year first climbed.

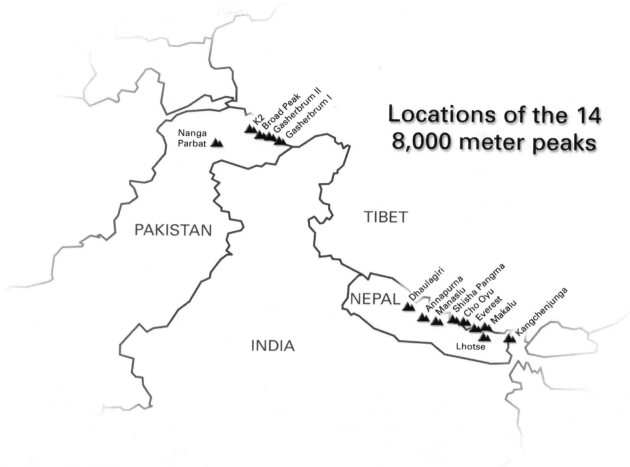

Locations of the 14 8,000 meter peaks

K2
Broad Peak
Gasherbrum II
Gasherbrum I
Nanga Parbat
PAKISTAN
TIBET
NEPAL
INDIA
Dhaulagiri
Annapurna
Manaslu
Shisha Pangma
Cho Oyu
Everest
Makalu
Kangchenjunga
Lhotse

Location of the 14 8,000-meter peaks (Marie Madgwick)

(115,969 m, 380,476 ft), or a little over 72 miles, one way! The average height of the 8,000-meter peaks is 8,283.5 m, 27,177 ft; the actual peak closest to that value is **Cho Oyu**, at 8,201 m. (See also the **14 8,000-Meter Peaks** sidebar.)

Eiselin, Max Born: Germany. Led the first ascent of **Dhaulagiri** Bibliography: *The Ascent of Dhaulagiri* (1961).

Eisriesen Located in **caves** near Salzburg, Austria, these are large **ice** formations that take on the shapes of various recognizable entities such as **bears**.

Ejecta Solid material that is spewed out during a volcanic **eruption**.

El Capitan (El Cap) 2,307 m, 7,568 ft. A large mass of granite nearly a mile wide in **Yosemite**. Its 3,000-foot wall is extremely popular with rock climbers.

El Salvador Lowest point, Pacific Ocean 0 m; highest point, Cerro El Pital 2,730 m, 8,957 ft.

Elbert, Mt. 4,399 m, 14,433 ft. The highest **peak** in the **Rocky Mountains** and the second highest in the continental **United States**, after **Mt. Whitney**; because it is located in **Colorado**, where one will find 54 14,000-foot peaks and because it is an easy if tedious climb, it does not get the respect it deserves. Indeed, sometime after World War II, a jeep managed to drive to the summit. (See appendix G.)

Elbrus, Mt. 5,642 m, 18,510 ft. Located in western Russia, this is the highest mountain in **Europe**; it was first ascended in 1874, by **A. W. Moore**, F. Gardiner, **F. Crawford Grove**, **Horace Walker**, and Pete Knubel. (See also the **Seven Summits** sidebar and color photos.)

Elbruz, Mt.   See **Elbrus, Mt.**

Elburz   A **range** in **Iran**.

Eldorado Canyon   One of the world's great rock climbing areas; it is located six miles south of Boulder, Colorado.

Elk   The North American elk is a fairly large, antlered deer family member that wanders high in the **mountains**.

Elk Range   One of **Colorado**'s main **ranges**; its major summits include: **Castle Peak**; the **Maroon Bells**; Capitol Peak 4,307 m, 14,130 ft; Snowmass Mountain 4,295 m, 14,092 ft; and Pyramid Peak 4,273 m, 14,018 ft, one of the hardest of Colorado's 14,000-foot peaks. (For the complete list of Colorado's 14,000-foot peaks, see appendix D.)

Ellingwood, Albert   (fl. early 20th century) One of America's premier rock climbers, he pioneered such standard-setting climbs as Ellingwood Ledge (1914), Lizard Head (1920), and The Bishop (1924) (Pat Ament, personal comment).

Elm   A deciduous tree; the rock elm can be found on ridges and outcrops (Leopold, McComb, and Muller).

Enchaînement   (F) Climbing a series of sometimes extremely difficult peaks in succession, without returning to a camp. But also the unusual sport of quickly climbing the series, ferried by helicopter to the base of the first, then from its summit to the base of the second, and so on. (See also **Christophe Profit**.)

Encyclopedias   See **Dictionaries and encyclopedias**.

The Endurance   Although this book, written by Alfred Lansing, is not strictly about mountains, it does make our list of the **10 Best Mountain Books**, because it centers around man's instinct for survival in the hostile, dangerous, barren environment of the polar ocean, as instinct that is also found in the high peaks. In addition, the crossing of the mountains and glaciers of **South Georgia Island** by **Shackleton** and two of his companions, after months of incredible suffering and privation, provides an apt and very moving closing chapter to the amazing story of the *Endurance* and her crew, stranded for nearly two years in the icy netherworld of the southern subpolar regions.

Engadine   A small, beautiful and sunny region in southern **Switzerland**, where the peaks of the Rhaetian Alps, including **Piz Bernina**, rise within a pristine Alpine landscape.

Engel, Claire-Elaine   (fl. mid-1900s) Born: France. Bibliography: *They Came to the Hills* (1952), *A History of Mountaineering in the Alps* (1959), *Mont Blanc* (1965), *Mountaineering in the Alps* (1971).

Engineering   Until fairly recently, mountains were considered inconveniences, impediments to fruitful activity or transport; they were acceptable as the **abodes of the gods** but hardly fit for human occupation, agriculture, or visits. Indeed, as holy sites, it would have been imprudent for mortals to trespass on high. Few Paleolithic hunters,

Nose of El Capitan (Pat Ament)

Road Construction and Tunneling (National Geographic)

Sumerian merchants, or Viking seafarers ventured into the upper areas of the **Alps**, **Himalayas**, or other ranges. When necessary, because other viable options were lacking or because height offered physical advantage, some peoples built agricultural terraces, cities, pueblos, fortresses, or castles on plateaus or the sides of mountains in **Israel**, the **Andes**, **Tibet**, **Asia**, **Europe**, and **New Mexico**. But it is only during the past few hundred years that real progress has been made in conquering the heights. The Romans rolled their roads through the Alps, but these were rather unsophisticated feats that took advantage of natural passes. Modern engineering has made mountain travel convenient: it has blasted tunnels through solid rock, bridged chasms, covered exposed passages, laid rail track across ranges, and otherwise eliminated every exigency. These often astonish-

ing engineering triumphs could not be carried out until steel production, blasting powder, and other recent innovations came along. Hand-produced work of the distant past may be similar but it exists on a much smaller scale. A rope footbridge in the Himalayas is qualitatively different from the Europabrücke, which allows automobile passage from Italy to Austria so swiftly that many people do not even realize that they are crossing an Alpine pass. Roads that wind their way up, around, and then down through passes are engineering feats of the highest order comparable to the construction of hundred-story skyscrapers or mile-long suspension bridges.

England   See **United Kingdom**.

The Epic of Everest   A 1924 English documentary, directed by Captain Joel B. L. Noel, concerning the ill-fated Mallory Everest expedition. This 90-minute movie depicts both the preparation as well as the actual attempt. The techniques and equipment are rather old-fashioned, but this enhances the historical interest. Although the camera does not leave base camp, one is able to glimpse Mallory disappearing behind the summit crest. (M-A. H.)

Equatorial Guinea   Lowest point, Atlantic Ocean 0 m; highest point, Pico Basile 3,008 m, 9,869 ft.

10 Mountain Roads

1. Beartooth Highway (Montana)
2. Col de l'Iseran (France)
3. Khyber Pass (Afghanistan)
4. L'Alpe d'Huez (France)
5. Mauna Kea Observatory (Hawaii)
6. Mount Evans Byway (Colorado)
7. Mount Washington (New Hampshire)
8. Pan-American Highway from Patagonia to Alaska
9. Pikes Peak (Colorado)
10. White Mountain Peak (California)

Equinox The two days of the year when the day and night are equal in length, each 12 hours long. In the Northern Hemisphere, the vernal equinox, or first day of **spring**, is on March 21; the autumnal equinox, on September 22, marks the beginning of the **fall**. The seasons are reversed in the Southern Hemisphere.

Equipment The most esoteric (protective) equipment is manufactured for miners, glaciologists, and other professionals who work in or on mountains; for example, vulcanologists may require full asbestos bodysuits to protect against the searing heat they encounter on the edge of a crater spewing out lava, and miners need headlamps and boots. (See also **climbing equipment** and **skiing equipment**.)

Equipment retailers General sporting goods stores carry many of the things required for the various types of **climbing** or **skiing**, but specialized and often expensive **climbing equipment** is handled by specialty shops. The first, founded in 1938 and the largest retail cooperative in the United States, is Recreational Equipment, Inc. (REI), a company that pays dividends to its members. It has branches in 60 cities including Berkeley, Denver, and Seattle. The flagship stores are enormous and remind one of the original Macy's except that REI only sells equipment and clothing related to outdoor pursuits. Eastern Mountain Sports (EMS) is similar, although its stores are smaller. There are additionally hundreds of excellent independent retailers scattered around the country, for example, Climb High, in Shelburne, Vermont, or Midwest Mountaineering in Minneapolis.

Erebus, Mt. 3,794 m, 12,448 ft. A large and active **volcano** located in **Antarctica**. It was first

Camp 7,000 Feet Up Mount Erebus (National Geographic)

ascended in 1908 by a climbing party including T. W. E. David.

Eriksen, Stein (1927–) Influential, mid-20th-century downhill skier, he won a gold medal in giant slalom at the 1952 Olympics.

Eritrea Lowest point, near Kulul within the Denakil Depression −75 m, −246 ft; highest point, Soira 3,018 m, 9,902 ft. The arid land where the French poet Arthur Raimbaud died is home to some of the most inhospitable, austere, and beautiful high-plateau landscapes on earth.

Erosion The process through which **wind**, **water**, **ice**, and temperature alteration wear away exposed surfaces, and move the material to other locations. (See also **weathering**.)

Erratic A **boulder** carried by a **glacier** from one geological area to another, so that it ends up in a location where its fellow rocks are compositionally different. (See also color photos.)

Eruption The often explosive release of **lava**, gas, and other materials from a **volcano**; the taxonomy of eruptions includes Strombolian, Icelandic, and Vulcanian. (See Ritchie and Gates for details.)

Escarpment (Also scarp) Long **cliff** or steep **slope** topped by a flat area.

Esker A long ridge of glacial material created by a stream.

Estonia Lowest point, Baltic Sea 0 m; highest point, Suur Munamagi 318 m, 1,043 ft.

Ethics For millennia, humans have used and frequently abused nature and its resources without compunction or fear of retribution. As we have harmed, sullied, depleted, disfigured, polluted, and destroyed the environment, we have come to realize that things must change. In the United States, **John Muir** and Theodore Roosevelt, inter alia, effected early alterations that brought about preservation and protection of the natural environment in the form of **national parks**. Other countries followed our lead. During the second half of the 20th century many individuals, organizations, corporations, and elected officials began to ameliorate the untenable attitude that had evolved toward pristine natural areas. Unregulated, unenforceable ethical standards began to evolve, and these now help to guide people in their use of natural areas and resources. The goal is to protect the land, forests, lakes, rivers, oceans, mountains, flora, and fauna from unnecessary depredation. Laura and Guy Waterman, in various books, but especially *Wilderness Ethics*, analyze our commitment and failures and alert us to the many ways in which we alter nature by participating in it: too many people, loud sounds (of radios), bright colors (of clothing and tents), use of technologies (cell phones, GPS devices, snowmobiles**),** and rescue services all degrade the pristine experiences of those who wish to abjure civilization by visiting areas that supposedly preserve a natural, unsullied habitat. This is an extreme perspective, but one with which many people will sympathize. Forest rangers, department of natural resources personnel, and other empowered officials enforce governmental laws (e.g., **The Wilderness Act** of 1964) and regulations

Natural Bridge, Virginia (National Geographic)

when personal ethical commitment fails. Hikers, climbers, kayakers, and other users of the natural environment (but also loggers, miners, and drillers) are expected to leave the area the way they found it. "**Leave No Trace**" is more than just a catchy phrase: it insists that those who enter the wilderness make no alterations. Thus, one must carry out all rubbish, bury natural wastes, leave streams unsullied, stay on trails, use removable wedges rather than **pitons** (so that the rock face is not marred) when rock climbing, and generally act in such a way that our progeny will find the mountains in the same natural state that we have. There are very few lovers of the wild (including hunters, recreational snowmobilers, and all-terrain vehicle riders) who would want to see these areas reduced to agglomerations of urban tenements, suburban malls, or garbage dumps. And so most people now cooperate. Ironically, the very people who should be most respectful, caring, and protective of the mountain environment (which they do adulate) do cause some harm. Large expeditionary forces climbing in the **Andes** and the **Himalayas** have arrived with many tons of equipment, hauled their stuff on the backs of thousands of mules, yaks, or humans across damageable terrain, littered, burned, polluted, and harmed. Most egregiously, they have left vast quantities of trash high up on mountains like **Everest** or **K2**: uneaten **food**, excrement, torn tents, thousands of **oxygen** cylinders, and the bodies of unburied climbers litter the landscape. So unseemly is this that a number of cleaning **expeditions** have attempted to haul off some of the rubbish. In fact, to celebrate the 50th anniversary of **Hillary's** Everest triumph, a joint Nepalese–Indian army team planned to climb Everest in 2003 in order to clear away some of the trash. Mountain depredation generally has become such a problem that the University of **Montana** now offers "Sheer Decency: Ethics of Climbing and Mountaineering," a short course designed to sensitize students to the crucial ethical issues. As the earth's population continues to increase, more people will visit the remaining natural areas. If they fail to comport themselves in an ethical fashion, either the environment will be destroyed or the law will become so draconian that it will be preferable to stay home and participate in nature vicariously by observing it on the Discovery Channel.

Ethiopia   Lowest point, Denakil −125 m, −410 ft; highest point, Ras Dashen Terara 4,620 m, 15,157 ft.

Etna, Mt.   3,350 m, 10,990 ft. A famous active Sicilian **volcano**. The first recorded ascent occurred sometime between 490 and 430 B.C.E. During the recent **eruption** of Mt. Etna, NASA recorded its smoke plume on a satellite photo. (See also color photos.)

Étrier   A large, sewn piece of webbing with loops or steps used as a ladder in **aid climbing**.

Europa Island   Lowest point, Indian Ocean 0 m; highest point, unnamed location 24 m, 79 ft.

Europe   The second smallest of the seven **continents**, with a land area of 10,400,000 sq km, 4,000,000 square miles, it contains a number of important **ranges**, including: the **Alps**, the **Pyrénées**, the **Apennines**, the **Caucasus**, the **Carpathians**, the Pennine mountains of the **United Kingdom**, and the mountains of **Norway** and **Sweden**.

Evans, Mt.   4,347 m, 14,264 ft. One of the giants of **Colorado**'s **Front Range**; a road leads to its summit!

Evans, Sir Robert Charles   (1912–1995) Born: England. He acted as deputy leader of the 1953 **Everest** expedition, and he was one of the first to reach the south summit of the mountain. Bibliography: *Eye On Everest* (1955), *Kangchenjunga: The Untrodden Peak* (1956), *On Climbing* (1956).

Everest, Mt.   (Also **Chomolungma** or **Qomolangma**: "Goddess mother of the snows" [T]; **Sagarmatha** [N]) 8,850 m, 29,035 ft. Located on the **Nepal–China** border, this is the world's highest mountain. It was first climbed on May 29, 1953, by **Sir Edmund Hillary** and **Tenzing Norgay Sherpa**. Its exact altitude fluctuates, as the summit bedrock is covered by a variable layer of hard snow, which is thickest in September and thinnest in May, after the high winter winds have blown off most of the fresh snow. These variable conditions change the altitude of the summit by 4.5 m, 15 ft. Its **summit** is the goal of many serious mountaineers, and it is attempted by hundreds of sometimes-successful climbers each spring. Some 2,000

Everest Escalator (Jeff Stahler, reprinted by permission of Newspaper Enterprise Association, Inc.)

people have reached the top, but at least 186 have died in the attempt (56 of whom have been **Sherpas**). It is an extremely difficult climb, even with supplemental **oxygen**, but **K2** is harder.

(See also the **Most Difficult Seven Summits** and the **14 8,000-Meter Peaks** sidebars.)

Everest, Mt. (father/son)   A number of fathers and sons have reached the summit of **Everest**. These include **Sir Edmund Hillary** (1953) and **Peter Hillary** (1990); Barry Bishop (1963) and Brent Bishop (1994); **Tenzing Norgay** (1953) and **Jamling Tenzing Norgay** (1996); Jean-Noel Roche and Bertrand Roche (1990, together); Sherman Bull and Brad Bull (2001, together); John Roskelley and Jess Roskelley (2003, together); and Yuichiro Miura and Gota Miura (2003, together) (Greg Glade, personal comment).

Everest, Sir George   (1790–1866) The surveyor general of India for whom **Mt. Everest** is named. Bibliography: *The Great Arc* by John Keay.

Everest 1996   This is the famous disaster that saw the Mountain Madness-guided team headed

12 Everest Facts

1. Fastest climbers: Marc Batard, from France, Base Camp to summit in 22½ hours (September 26, 1988), without supplemental oxygen; Babu Chhiri Sherpa, from Nepal, 16 hours, 56 minutes (May 21, 2000); Lakpa Gelu Sherpa, from Nepal, 10 hours, 56 minutes, 46 seconds (May 26, 2003); Pemba Dorjee, a Sherpa, 8 hours, 10 minutes (May 2004)
2. First blind climber: Erik Weihenmayer, from the United States (June 13, 2002)
3. First climb without supplemental oxygen: Reinhold Messner, from Italy, and Peter Habeler, from Austria (May 8, 1978)
4. First climbers: Sir Edmund Hillary, from New Zealand, and Tenzing Norgay Sherpa, from Nepal (May 29, 1953)
5. First female climber: Junko Tabei, from Japan (May 16, 1975)
6. First paraglider flight: Jean-Marc Boivin, from France (September 26, 1988)
7. First ski descent: Pierre Tardivel, from France (September 1992), from below the summit; Davo Karnicar (October 2000) from the top
8. First solo climb: Reinhold Messner, from Italy (August 20, 1980), without supplemental oxygen
9. Most climbs: Apa Sherpa, from Nepal, climbed Everest 11 times between May 10, 1990, and May 24, 2000, all without supplemental oxygen; at the time of this writing, he had summitted an amazing 14 times!
10. Oldest climber: Yuichiro Miura, a 70-year old man from Japan (May 24, 2003)
11. Sea to summit: Tim Macartney Snape, from Australia (May 11, 1990); he began trekking from the Bay of Bengal, all the way to Base Camp, and up the South Col route, using no supplemental oxygen
12. Youngest climber: Mingkipa, a 15-year-old Nepalese Sherpa girl (May 25, 2003); she climbed with her two sisters, aged 24 and 30

A very useful source for Everest facts is www.mnteverest.com/history.html.

by **Scott Fischer**, and the guided party led by **Rob Hall**, climb to the summit of **Everest** only to be caught on Friday, May 10, 1996, by a fierce storm upon **descent**, ultimately causing the death of eight people, including Fischer and Hall. Much has been written about this tragic episode of modern mountaineering, which has been thoroughly documented by the various protagonists: see, for example, *Above the Clouds*, by **A. Boukreev** (2001); *The Climb*, by A. Boukreev and G. W. DeWalt (1997); *High Exposure*, by **D. Breashears** (1999); *Everest: Mountain Without Mercy*, by B. Coburn (1997); *The Death Zone*, by M. Dickinson (1998); *Climbing High*, by L. Gammelgaard (1999); *Sheer Will*, by M. Groom (1997); *Doctor on Everest*, by K. Kamler (2000); *Into Thin Air*, by **J. Krakauer** (1997); *Ultimate High*, by **G. Kropp** and D. Lagercrantz (1997); *Touching My Father's Soul*, by **J. T. Norgay** (2001); *Just for the Love of It*, by C. O'Dowd (1999); *Everest-Free to Decide*, by C. O'Dowd and I. Woodall (1997); *Dark Shadows Falling*, by **J. Simpson** (1997); *Ascent and Dissent: The SA Everest Expedition—The Inside Story*, by K. Vernon (1997); and *Left for Dead,* by **B. Weathers** and S. Michaud (2000).

Exfoliation   The process through which pieces of a large **rock** are stripped away by **wind**, water, **ice**, or **temperature** change. **Yosemite** granite is the most prominent example of ice exfoliation.

Expedition   (Expeditionary) A **mountaineering** climb that may require vast quantities of equipment, **porters**, **Sherpas** or other **guides**, medical personnel, scientists, and many team members. Some expeditions have involved as many as 1,000 people and might last three months. Applying siege tactics, the peak is attacked by groups of people who set up many camps along the way. In Alpine style, fewer climbers attempt to reach the summit quickly without outfitting many higher camps. (See also **climbing**.)

Exposed   (Exposure) This term designates extremely precipitous gradients on very narrow ridges, faces, or other terrain. Here, a minor error by an unbelayed climber can lead to disaster, since a fall may be fatal. It also indicates extreme height with a direct drop, one that may produce vertigo.

Exposure   See **exposed**.

Exum, Glenn   (1911–2000) An excellent American climber and guide; in 1931, Exum, friend and colleague of **Paul Petzoldt**, made the famous first ascent of the ridge on the Grand Teton that bears his name and is now the **normal route**. See *Glenn Exum: Never a Bad Word or a Twisted Rope*, by Charlie Craighead.

Exum Ridge   See **Grand Teton**.

F

Face See **wall**.

Fairweather, Mt. 4,663 m, 15,299 ft. Located in **Canada**'s Fairweather Mountains, this is a dormant **volcano**, and the highest peak in **British Columbia**. It was first ascended in 1931 by Allen Carpé and Terris Moore. The name of the mountain was chosen by its discoverer, Captain James Cook, in 1778. As the **Fairweather Range** experiences some of the worst weather on the planet, with over 100 annual inches of precipitation, the name must have been given with some humor.

Fairweather Range This range, which is the southern extension of the **Wrangell–Saint Elias Mountains,** straddles the border between **Alaska** and **British Columbia**. The highest peak is **Mt. Fairweather.**

Fakie In **snowboarding**, riding backward.

Falcon See **hawk**.

Falkland Islands (Islas Malvinas) Lowest point, Atlantic Ocean 0 m; highest point, Mt. Usborne 705 m, 2,313 ft.

Fall In climbing, when someone, usually inadvertently, releases from a face and plummets downward against the mountain or out into the void or when someone goes down on a **slope** or into a **crevasse**. It is possible to lessen the length of a fall through **belays**. Falls can be brief or extensive, harmless or fatal. In 1964, Jan Mostowski plummeted down off the Eiger north face. His free fall covered more than 1,000 feet; he ended up in a snowbank with just a sprained knee (Roth)! In skiing, when a person loses **control** and ends up sitting, lying, or tumbling on the slope.

Fall See **waterfall**.

Fall The season beginning on the autumnal **equinox**. It is generally a difficult season for mountaineering, as the crevasses on glaciers are wide open in many regions; the shorter days are also less favorable for long climbs.

Fall line In **skiing,** the natural, direct (steepest) line down a **slope**.

False summit There are many peaks where the true summit is only a few meters above other pinnacles, and it becomes difficult to locate the actual highpoint: see for example **Nanga Parbat** and **Mt. Logan**. In other cases, the ridge leading to the summit has a number of local highpoints, such as the south summit on **Everest**; the climber thinks he or she is approaching the true summit, only to be disappointed to find that more ridges and higher points lie past the false summit. This is sometimes reflected by the name given to the features, such as Disappointment Cleaver on **Mt. Rainier**.

Fanck, Arnold (1889–1974) As a child, Fanck suffered from tuberculosis and was sent to a sanatorium near Davos, Switzerland. The treatment included spending hours in the cold, even in winter, and ice-skating without coats. Later on, Fanck blessed this rather drastic cure. First of all, it healed his illness (except for lasting asthma). And, more important, it let him discover the Alps. Trained as a geologist, interested as early as 1913 in filming his excursions (in this case, Monte Rosa), he began producing and directing semi-fictionalized documentaries from 1919 onward. His movies were great successes and included *Im Kampf mit der Berge* (1921) with music by Paul Hindemith, *Der Berg der Schicksals/* Peak of Fate (1924), *Die Heilige Berg/*The Holy Mountain (1926), *Der Weisse Hölle der Piz Palu/*White Hell of Piz Palu (1929), *Sturm über der Mont Blanc/*Storm over Mont Blanc (1930), and *Der Ewige Traum* (1934). This last movie, co-produced with Jewish French associate Gregor Rabinovitch, had Nazi propaganda chief Goebbels asking the director, "Couldn't you choose a German mountain?" Fanck resented stunt actors and directed a few non-mountain films. (M-A.H.)

Farming   See **agriculture**.

Faroe Islands   Lowest point, Atlantic Ocean 0 m; highest point, Slaettaratindur 882 m, 2,894 ft.

Fault   A fracture and displacement that occurs in **lithic crust** or mass, for example, the San Andreas Fault. Faults come in many forms: normal, overthrust, slip-strike, and reverse. (See also **earthquake** and **graben**.)

Fédération Internationale de Ski (FIS)   Founded in 1924, this organization has 101 national ski association members.

Feet   Mountains are measured in feet or meters. One meter is equal to 3.2808 feet; one foot is equal to .3048 meters. Thus, a 4,000-meter peak is 13,123 feet high. (See also **meter**.)

Feldspar   The most abundant mineral.

Fifi hook   A hook used in big wall **climbing**. It is set on a small ledge or flake for an anchor or to support body weight.

Figure eight   A small **belay** device shaped like a numeral eight that has been distorted; it creates friction as a rope slips through during a rappel. (See also color photos.)

Fiji   Lowest point, Pacific Ocean 0 m; highest point, Tomanivi 1,324 m, 4,344 ft.

Film   There exists a replete armamentarium of creative and documentary films concerning various aspects of the mountain. Hollywood has given us *Across the Great Divide, Alive,* **Cliffhanger**, **The Eiger Sanction**, **K2**, *The Mountain, The Treasure of the Sierra Madre,* and *Vertical Limit,* among others, and **mountaineering** cinematographer **David Breashears** has produced the Imax *Everest.* (See also **movies and mountains, movies and mountains, [documentaries]** and **movies and mountains [west-**

erns], as well as individual entries and the **10 Best Hollywood Mountain Movies** and **11 Recommended Mountain and Climbing Documentaries** sidebars.)

Film festivals   Periodically, various locales or organizations offer collections of new climbing films to the public for viewing, for example, the **Banff Mountain Film Festival**, Mountain Film Festival in Telluride, Colorado, the Taos Mountain Film Festival, and the **Vancouver** International Mountain Film Festival. After the Banff showings, its films travel around the world and are presented, for example, on college or university campuses, by a representative of the festival.

Finch   A smallish, widely dispersed bird of innumerable species. In the **Andes** these creatures reach astonishing altitudes: the plumbeous sierra-finch, for example, can be found at 17,400 ft (Fjeldså and Krabbe).

Finch, George Ingle   (1888–1969) Born: England. He was the scientist in charge of the **oxygen** equipment on the British **Everest** expedition of 1922. He was also president of the Alpine Club, 1959–1961. Bibliography: *The Making of a*

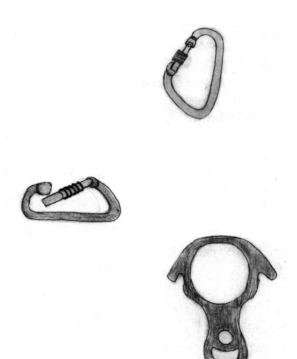

Carabiners and Figure Eight (Laura Lindblad)

11 Recommended Mountain and Climbing Documentaries

1. *Above All Else: The Everest Dream*
2. *Alpine Search and Rescue*
3. *Victoire sur l'Annapurna* (Ichac)
4. *Below the Volcano: Mt. St. Helens*
5. *Conquest of Everest*
6. *Everest: IMAX* (Breashears)
7. *Everest: The Death Zone*
8. *First Ascent*
9. *Everest: Mountain of Dreams, Mountain of Doom*
10. *National Geographic: Surviving Everest*
11. *Touching the Void*

Mountaineer (1924), *Climbing Mount Everest* (1930).

Finland   Lowest point, Baltic Sea 0 m; highest point, Haltiatunturi 1,328 m, 4,357 ft.

Finsteraarhorn   4,274 m, 14,022 ft. This is the 20th highest of the 60 major 4,000-meter peaks of the **Alps**. It was first climbed in 1812 by Arnold Abbül, Josef Bortis, Alois Volker and three **chamois** hunters. It is the highest peak in the **Bernese Alps**, a magnificent, heavily glaciated mountain with a superb summit ridge; the first ascent was an important accomplishment because it is technically more challenging than the old normal route of **Mont Blanc**.

Fir   A **conifer** such as balsam or Douglas that grows (the latter to 250 feet tall) at higher elevations.

Fire   (Sometimes called a burn) Combustion. Mountains offer trees, grasses, animals, and other naturally occurring entities as well as constructed structures (houses, huts) to the ravaging effects of fire. Fires begin in many ways. **Lightning** is responsible for much natural destruction in the wild. A tree is struck and burns and the fire spreads. Sometimes very large trees, such as **redwoods** or **sequoias,** can ignite, endure a great deal of damage, but nevertheless survive. Accidental burns can occur because campers, smokers, and others fail to extinguish their fires. Occasionally a controlled burn, a fire purposely started by park rangers, forest managers, road maintenance workers, or farmers, will get out of hand and destroy tens of thousands of acres. The *slash-and-burn* method of clearing agricultural land, employed by farmers for thousands of years, is still used in some parts of the world, the Amazon and Indonesia, for example. This technique is extremely detrimental to the natural environment, destroying everything in the fire's path. In some areas, Alaska, for example, there are often so many simultaneous fires that they are impossible to control; firefighters just let them burn themselves out. Extensive burning causes pollution and may have an effect on the **weather**.

10 Best Hollywood Mountain Movies

1. *Alive*
2. *Cliffhanger*
3. *K2*
4. *Seven Years in Tibet*
5. *Spencer's Mountain*
6. *The Eiger Sanction*
7. *Vertical Limit*
8. *The White Tower*
9. *The Razor's Edge (1984)*
10. *The Mountain*

Caveat: The authors are aware that some people find Hollywood's version of climbing to be offensive; nevertheless, we include this list for its entertainment value.

Fire towers   Structures built at first of wood and later of metal on the tops of mountains. They were peopled with lookouts in order to spot **fires**. In the late 20th century, they were replaced by spotter planes. Although some of these towers have been dismantled (for example on the highpoints of Kentucky and Mississippi), many still exist around the United States and in other countries.

Hikers and climbers often trudge to the top of these roughly 50-foot structures in order to get a better view of the surrounding country (www .firelookout.org and www.firelookout.com).

Firn   See **ice**.

Firsoff, Valdemar Axel (1888–1969) Born: Scotland. Bibliography: *The Tatra Mountains* (1942), *The Cairngorms on Foot and Ski* (1949), *Arran with Camera and Sketchbook* (1951).

First ascent   The first time that either a **peak** or a **route** is successfully climbed. Surprisingly, there are still many thousands of peaks and routes awaiting first ascents (in **Bhutan, Nepal, Tibet**, and other countries; see appendix F).

First Blood   An 1982 American film directed by Canadian-born Ted Kotcheff, after a novel by David Morell. It depicts a Vietnam veteran starting a war of his own when he has to fight back the hostile inhabitants of a village. Shot in British Columbia, this action film also deals with the relationship between man and nature. John Rambo, taught by his military experience to use his surroundings to battle the enemy, deals with all possible weapons that nature provides. The usual dramatization of such conflicts has the hero easily beating the police forces that had lost contact with the soil. Mountain locations offer a wider scope and strategic possibilities, if not much realism in climbing. (M-A. H.)

Firth   See **fjord**.

Fischer, Scott (1956–1996) A gifted American **mountaineer** and **guide** who formed the guiding company Mountain Madness; he died tragically on **Everest** in 1996. (See also **Everest 1996**.)

Fish   Fish (and other water-dependent creatures) are scarce in mountainous environments. Salmon move upward but do not reach the higher altitudes; trout, darters, and catfish can be found in flowing water and lakes, but decrease in numbers as the altitude and cold increase. Shad and sturgeon can also be seen at altitude.

Fissure   A fracture that has opened in **rock**.

Fitzgerald, Edward Arthur (1871–1931) In 1897, Fitzgerald led the first ascent of **Aconcagua**. Born: England. Bibliography: *Climbs in the New Zealand Alps* (1896), *The Highest Andes* (1899).

Five sacred mountains   For the Chinese, the eastern mountains are holy, the western are not; they designate five (and sometimes nine) sacred mountains: Mt. Taishan, Hengshan (in Hunan), Songshan, Huashan, and Hengshan (in Shanxi). (See also **religion**.)

Fixed rope   In **mountaineering**, a **rope** set in place for a short time or a season (or sometimes, through happenstance, permanently), which one can grasp or to which one can attach an **ascender**. It allows a climber to move up and down the difficult stretch more efficiently, and is especially helpful when the same part of the **route** has to be repeatedly negotiated with supplies. It also facilitates a fast **descent** when bad **weather** comes in. A fixed rope can cover thousands of vertical feet. If left in place after the season ends, a rope may be used the following year. Naturally, after a while it begins to disintegrate, because of abrasion or the effects of sunlight, and thus becomes extremely hazardous.

Fjord   (Also fiord; firth is preferred in Scotland) A coastal, steep-sided, narrow, and deep glacial **valley** that seawater has filled. These extremely picturesque inlets can be found in western **Norway, Alaska, Iceland**, and elsewhere. (See also **tidewater glacier**.)

Flake   *Feuillet* (F). In **rock climbing**, a small or larger natural extrusion that pulls away from the face; it can be grasped by hands, fingers, or fingertips.

Flamingo   A large, tropical wading bird with reddish or pinkish plumage, long legs, a long flexible neck, and a bill turned downward; the Puna, also called James's, astonishingly, can be found soaring in the **Andes** (rather than over some tropical paradise), above 13,200 ft (Fjeldså and Krabbe).

Flash   In **rock climbing**, to succeed on a route on the first attempt without practicing or falling. Prior knowledge is acceptable. (See also **onsight** and **redpoint**.)

Flatlander   Anyone who does not live in the mountains or in a generally mountainous region. In Vermont, Bostonians are called flatlanders, but not the Vermonters who live in Brattleboro or Burlington despite the low elevations of these urban Vermont areas. It also designates someone not especially adept at climbing.

Float plane A widely used means of transportation in places lacking infrastructure, and rich in lakes and other bodies of water; for example, **Canada** and **Alaska**. (See also color photos.)

Florida Lowest point, Atlantic Ocean 0 m; highest point Britton Hill, 105 m, 345 ft (the 50th highest of the 50 state highpoints).

Flowers Even at extreme altitude, flowers manage to take root and flourish. Alpine fields are sometimes covered by a colorful sea of flowers: for example, on the Garnet Canyon approach to the **Tetons**, the trail traverses an enormous open slope covered with hundreds of thousands of yellow flowers. Countless species are found in the **high mountains**, almost 600 in the Rockies alone (Costello); the most important have separate entries in this volume. Graham Nicholls's profusely illustrated *Alpine Plants of North America* is invaluable.

Fluke A small manufactured device that can be buried in **snow** in order to create an **anchor** point; it is similar to a **picket** except that the latter is long and narrow, whereas a fluke is flat and rectangular. (See also **deadman**.)

Flute This term pertains to the unusual aspect presented by snow or ice exposed to near-zenithal sun, in the **Andes**, the **Himalayas**, and **Karakoram**. Under the nearly vertical sun rays, the ice or snow mountain slopes acquires a different texture, whereby extremely steep and deep, wavy ridges are sculpted by the heat of noontime. Closely related are the snow **penitentes** found on **glaciers** at tropical and equatorial **latitudes**.

Flycatcher A bird of many species. Hammond's can be found at 10,000 ft.

Fog *Brouillard* (F), *Nebel* (G), *nebbia* (I). Suspended water particles (clouds) in the lower atmosphere. Fog obscures visibility.

Föhn (Foehn) See **winds**.

Folded Strata (National Geographic)

Fold A bend in **rock**.

Folded mountain belt Extensive deformation of the **lithic crust** resulting in mountain formation of, for example, the **Alps**, **Appalachians**, **Himalayas**, and **Rockies**.

Fontainebleau An area near Paris, France, where many **boulders** present complex climbing problems; there, the rock is a soft agglomerate that easily dissolves into sand and presents unusual adhesive and abrasive properties, highly favorable for **friction** climbing. Indeed, some of the highest-level **bouldering** can be found in the Fontainebleau forest, which is divided into a number of small boulder groups, often used as climbing circuits, where one attempts a series of *enchaînements*; some climbers even run in the sand between boulders. The largest rocks are found near the Rocher de La Dame Jeane and measure up to 15–20 m, 50–60 ft—guaranteed **exposure**! Because most of the climbs rely heavily on friction climbing, a technique mastered there by **Pierre Allain**, Fontainebleau is a very busy climbing place on sunny weekends, while it becomes completely empty at the first sign of rain, since humidity negatively affects the adhesive character of the rock. For climbers using this technique in high mountains, there is always a risk that the conditions will not be favorable for friction climbing; furthermore, the **approach** may be on difficult terrain, mixed, or icy, and require the proper shoes for **crampons**, thus forcing the climber to switch between different types of shoes. Finally, if the weather changes suddenly, one can find oneself in a very perilous situation, mid-climb on a very difficult cliff, with no easy **descent** or escape route; therefore, it is extremely important to ascertain the weather conditions before engaging in a long friction climb.

Food The material that all organic entities require for sustenance and survival. In a very real sense, even the nutrients in soil are food for grasses, **flowers**, and **trees**. Thus, because mountain ecology and environments differ from those at lower elevations, the **animal** and plant life indigenous in mountainous areas differ, sometimes dramatically, from what one will find in the valleys. People who live in the mountains acquire their food through hunting, fishing, trapping, gathering, and agricultural cultivation. Those who visit in order to hike, trek, or climb must carry their foodstuffs with them. In the case of large and extended expeditions, this requires the transportation of tons of raw and prepared products. Ironically, for mountaineers who reside at lower elevations, extreme ascents often result in a loss of appetite. It is thus necessary to force oneself to eat at least a little real food every day. In fact, as the elevation increases, most of the body functions, including overall metabolism, tend to slow down; above the so-called **death zone**, this trend becomes dramatic: many climbers on their final push to summit **Everest** have been known to go without sleep and minimum food for extended periods of time, sometimes up to 36 hours; in such cases, superb conditioning can be the difference between life and death.

Foothill A **hill** that is located just below a higher **mountain**.

Foraker, Mt. (Sultana) 5,303 m, 17,400 ft. This powerful mountain, located in the **Alaska Range** was first climbed in 1934 by Charles Hutson, T. Graham Brown, and C. Waterston. It is the third highest peak in the **United States**.

Forbes, James David (1809–1868) Born: Scotland. Bibliography: *Travels through the Alps of Savoy and Other Parts of the Pennine Chain with Observations on the Phenomena of Glaciers* (1843), *Norway and Its Glaciers Visited in 1851* (1853).

Ford To cross a river on foot, horseback, or in a four-wheel drive vehicle. (See also color photos.)

Forget-me-not A purplish, clustered **flower**.

Fossil Preserved remnants of organic material, for example, bones, shells, or casts. Sometimes one discovers sea fossils at higher altitudes, for example, in **Texas**'s Guadalupe Mountains. This occurs because an ancient sea once covered the area. Both the Alps and the Himalayas are quite rich in fossils, which have been found at astonishingly high elevations, confirming the upthrust theory of mountain formation.

Fourteenthousanders Those mountains over 14,000 feet high. **Colorado** has 54 (sometimes listed as 56) such peaks divided among 10 ranges (see appendix D); second in the continental **United States** is **California**, with 13 peaks above that mark; last but not least, **Washington** State counts a single fourteenthousander, the mighty **Mt. Rainier**.

Fourthousanders Those mountains over 4,000 feet (in the northeastern United States) or 4,000 meters high. In the Alps, one generally considers that the major peaks are those above the 4,000-meter mark (see appendix B); however, there are extremely notable exceptions, for example the **Eiger**, 3,970 m, 13,025 ft, in the **Bernese Alps**, the **Meije**, 3,983 m, 13,068 ft, the **Pelvoux**, 3,943 m, 12,936 ft, and the **Ailefroide**, 3,954 m, 12,972 ft, in the **Dauphiné**. Each of these mountains is important because it played a major role in the history of **Alpinism**, because it is esthetically superb, and because it is still an extremely worthy goal for many climbers; this purports to illustrate the degree of arbitrariness attached to such definitions based on a single parameter, such as altitude.

Fowler, Mick (1956–) Born: London, England. A superb mountaineer and technical ice climber, he is also well known for the long drives he took from London to the Northwest Highlands of Scotland for winter climbing over the weekends. In 1987, he performed the first ascent, together with Victor Saunders, of the Golden Pillar of Spantik (7,028 m). Bibliography: *Elusive Summits* (1990), by Victor Saunders, *Vertical Pleasure* (1995).

Fox The red is indigenous in many parts of the world. Its range moves upward depending on location.

France Lowest point, the depression of the Rhône River delta −2 m, −7 ft; highest point, **Mont Blanc** 4,807 m, 15,770 ft. France is an important European country that comprises five major mountain ranges: the **Alps**, the **Pyrénées**, the Jura, the Massif Central, and the Vosges. Within the French Alps, the mighty **Mont Blanc Range** counts 14 of the 15 major Alpine summits higher than 4,000 meters, the **Barre des Écrins** in **Dauphiné** being the other one. Geologically, France can be divided into three major areas: the ancient remains of the Hercynian massif, including the Mont d'Arrées in Brittany and parts of the Massif Cen-

tral; large plains to the north; and younger mountains produced by recent folding in the south and southwest, including the Alps and the Pyrénées. In addition the Pleistocene glaciation era has played an important direct role in eroding the terrain at altitudes above roughly 1,000 m; at lower elevation, periglacial phenomena, including the freeze–thaw cycle, have produced the very fine particulate of limon, also called loess, which results in extremely fertile land. National parks include the Massif des Ecrins and the Gavarnie area of the Pyrénées. A number of foremost climbers also hail from France, including famous guides such as Ravanel, **Balmat**, and **Croz**; the team that conquered the first 8,000-meter peak, with **Herzog**, **Lachenal**, **Terray**, and **Rébuffat**; and more modern Alpinists, such as **Desmaison**, **Edlinger**, **Profit**, and **Destivelle**, to name a few. (See also color map and photos.)

Franco, Jean Born: Italy. He led the expeditions that made the first ascents of **Makalu** and **Jannu**. Bibliography: *Makalu* (1957), *At Grips with Jannu* (1967), with **Lionel Terray**.

Francolin A game **bird** of many species, some of which can be found in the hills and higher in East Africa (Williams).

Free A rock climb that is done without any **aid**, that is, without upward movement aided by artificial support from **pitons** or **nuts**, and using those **anchor** points but only on **belay** or as protection against a **fall**.

Free-solo A rock climb that is done without any rope and no **protection**. This type of climbing is extremely dangerous, since falling even 25 or 30 feet can be harmful or fatal; some free-solos are done hundreds or thousands of feet above the ground.

Freeze–thaw cycle When **water** penetrates into small open spaces or clefts in rocks, it may freeze and thus cause the opening to expand. This is called frost or ice wedging. The **ice** thaws when the temperature rises. As this sequence occurs again and again, the cracks are enlarged. Eventually the rock may split apart. (See also color photo.)

Fremont Peak 4,190 m, 13,745 ft. The second highest peak in the **Wind River Range**, and the third highest in **Wyoming**, it is a mighty moutain that was first ascended in 1842 by John C. Fremont. (See also color photos.)

French Guiana Lowest point, Atlantic Ocean 0 m; highest point, Bellevue de l'Inini 851 m, 2,792 ft.

French Polynesia Lowest point, Pacific Ocean 0 m; highest point, Mont Orohena 2,241 m, 7,352 ft.

French Southern and Antarctic Lands Lowest point, Indian Ocean 0 m; highest point, Mont Ross on Îles Kerguelen 1,850 m, 6,070 ft. (See also **Jean Afanassieff**.)

Freshfield, William Douglas (1845–1934) Born: England. According to Unsworth, Freshfield was "one of the greatest of all mountain explorers." His first ascents include Cima di Brenta and La Tour Ronde; he also was a productive author (*Encyclopaedia*). As a mountain explorer, he traveled extensively, especially in the **Caucasus** and around **Kangchenjunga**. He was president of the Alpine Club from 1893 to 1895. Bibliography: *Across Country from Thonon to Trent* (1865), *Travels in the Central Caucasus and Bashan* (1869), *Italian Alps* (1875), *The Exploration of the Caucasus* (1896), *Round Kangchenjunga* (1903), *Hannibal Once More* (1914), *Unto the Hills* (1914), *The Life of Horace-Benedict de Saussure* (1920), *Quips for Cranks and Other Trifles* (1923), *Below the Snow Line* (1923).

Friction In **rock climbing**, using the naturally adhesive qualities of the sole of one's shoe and the rock to adhere or move upward, especially on slabs; technique plays an important part in this. In modern climbing, specialized shoes, called **chaussons (d'escalade)**, are specifically designed to maximize friction: the sole is made of a rubberlike compound, somewhat similar to the material used for Formula 1 racing tires. The French climber **Pierre Allain**, who trained extensively in **Fontainebleau** and opened an extremely challenging route on the **Drus** using this technique, perfected it. Friction climbing is now used extensively around the world, from the granite faces of **Yosemite**, to the gigantic spires of the **Great Trango Tower** of the **Karakoram**, and the pure **monoliths** of Baffin Island.

Friend The trademarked name of a specific type of aluminum, spring-loaded **cam**, designed to easily go into a **crack**, wedge, and serve as an **anchor** or **protection** point, then easily be removed. It revolutionized climbing, eliminating the need for **pitons**.

Frison-Roche, Roger (1906–1999) Chamonix guide and author of *Les Montagnes de la Terre* (1964), the single most comprehensive, detailed overview of the world's mountains and their etiology, ecology, inhabitants, and influence. For some inexplicable reason, this enormous two-volume set has never been translated into English. Frison-Roche also wrote a number of novels set in the **Alps**, including the wonderful *Premier de Cordée*, which was later adapted as a movie. (See also the **10 Great Mountain Adventure Books** sidebar, as well as the information on the website www.alpinisme.com/fr/histoire/rfrSomm/index.htm.)

Front Range This is the phrase applied to the easternmost **range** of the **Rocky Mountains**; it appears suddenly and obtrusively when traveling westward across the plains and offers a magnificent sight of soaring peaks reaching into the western skies. The mighty Front Range serves as a background to the cityscapes of **Denver** and Boulder, as well as a wonderful mountaineering and winter recreation area to their inhabitants. Main summits include: Grays Peak 4,349 m, 14,270 ft; Torreys Peak 4,348 m, 14,267 ft; **Mt. Evans** 4,347 m, 14,264 ft; **Longs Peak**; **Pikes Peak**; and **Mt. Bierstadt**. (For the complete list of Colorado's 14,000-foot peaks, see appendix D.)

Front-point In **mountaineering** or ice climbing, to move up (or infrequently down and thus backward) on steep, hard snow or ice on the two front, razor sharp prongs of 12-point **crampons**.

Frost Ice crystals that appear on any surface (Smith).

Frost, Tom (fl. early 1960s–1990s) The best **aid** climber in the early 1960s in **Yosemite**, teaming with **Royal Robbins** and **Chuck Pratt** for many **first ascents** on El Capitan. He was also an important photographer and designer of equipment, with **Yvon Chouinard** (Pat Ament, personal comment).

Frost wedging See **freeze–thaw cycle**.

Frostbite When the body is unable to produce enough heat, whatever is available is shunted to the core in order to protect vital organs; thus, the extremities (toes, fingers, nose, and ears) receive less heat and begin to freeze. If this situation is not remedied, then frostbite sets in. A mild case is painful, but curable. If the tissue remains frozen for an extended period, severe frostbite may result in gangrene, which necessitates amputation of the frozen parts. Robert McFarlane's recent *Mountains of the Mind* sheds some personal light on how one reacts to its onset. The vasodilator Ronicol (a brand of nicotinyl alcohol that is no longer available) has been shown to reduce symptoms in the field (Roth), but this is anecdotal. McCauley et al. claim that "no anticoagulant or vasodilation treatment has proved useful in controlled clinical trials." The chapter by McCauley et al. on frostbite in Auerbach is extremely helpful. There are many myths concerning treatment in the field, for example, rubbing and direct heat can be harmful. **Maurice Herzog**'s account in **Annapurna, Premier 8,000** is the *locus classicus*. (See also **clothing**, especially the "hoods, hats, and face masks" section, and Syme's position paper.)

Führerbuch (G), *livret* (F). Carried by a mid-19th century mountain guide, this was a small book in which his employer (the climber) wrote a brief comment. It was shown to potential customers to convince them that the guide was competent. It later became a form of certification (Clark). Greg Glade (personal communication) indicates that this system was also used to certify porters in early Himalayan expeditions.

Fuji-san (Also Fujiyama, Mt. Fuji) 3,776 m, 12,388 ft. A dormant **volcano** located on Honshu. Its image is the de facto national symbol of Japan. It is considered a sacred site (by practitioners of Shinto), but unlike holy mountains in other parts of the world, it is a mecca for thousands of people who attempt its summit every year (as a reverential act), despite the fact that is not such an easy climb. On summer days, as many as 5,000 people climb Fuji, which produces enormous quantities of trash and sewage. Fuji is an extremely symmetrical mountain, the upper reaches of which are often covered with snow that cascades downward in tentacles. (See also **religion**, the **10 Most Beautiful Mountains** sidebar, and color photos.)

Fumarole A small **vent** in a volcanic area from which hot gases or steam emanate; sometimes the term *fumarole* is used, by extension, to describe the smoke emitted by the vent.

Funicular A sometimes oddly shaped, trainlike device that runs on rails and transports people on mountains, especially in Europe but also in other parts of the world. The French use the term *funiculaire*. Frequently, as one car is pulled up on a cable or device located between the tracks, a balancing car moves down; they meet at the halfway point (www.funimag.com).

Gabbro A dark, coarse, granular, **igneous** type of rock that is good for climbing.

Gabon Lowest point, Atlantic Ocean 0 m; highest point, Mont Iboundji 1,575 m, 5,167 ft.

Gaiters Protective devices that cover the top of the boots, the shins, and sometimes the legs. They stop **snow** from entering the boots and may provide extra warmth. Gaiters come in three styles: a thin, short model made out of nylon; a heavier, larger type; and insulated expedition gaiters, which extend from below the boot to above the knee. Specialized boots, which can cost up to $800, are manufactured with permanently attached gaiters. (See also **clothing**, especially "boots, overboots.")

Galápagos Islands A group of many large and smaller volcanic mountainous islands off the coast of **Ecuador**. It was here that Darwin discovered species diversification, which led him to the theory of evolution.

Gambia Lowest point, Atlantic Ocean 0 m; highest point, unnamed location 53 m, 174 ft.

Gamow bag A hermetically sealed bag shaped like a large sleeping bag that can be pressurized by means of an external pump, thus providing a higher partial pressure of **oxygen** than that reigning in the local environment and temporarily alleviating the effects of high altitude for the patient in the bag. (See also **acute mountain sickness**.)

Ganesh Himal 7,429 m, 24,373 ft. This major peak is located in **Nepal**, and was first climbed in 1955 by Raymond Lambert, Claude Kogan, and E. Gauchat.

Gannett Peak 4,207 m, 13,804 ft. The **Wyoming highpoint**. A climb of Gannett requires a 50-mile round trip, the longest of all the U.S. highpoints. Gannett Peak is located deep within the **Wind River Range**, one of the most remote wilderness areas in **Wyoming**, which contains a number of peaks above 13,000 ft that are fairly heavily glaciated on their northern sides. It was first ascended in 1922 by A. Tate and F. Stahlnaker. (See also appendix G and color photos.)

Gap A narrow **pass,** generally set between steep **cliffs**, for example, Cadaver Gap on the normal route of **Mt. Rainier**. A deep cleft in a **ridge** or mountain.

Gardening In rock climbing, cleaning a route of rubble and vegetation.

Garhwal A **range** in India that includes the mighty **Nanda Devi**.

Gasherbrum I (Also Hidden Peak, K5) 8,068 m, 26,469 ft. A splendid mountain in the **Karakoram**, between **Pakistan** and **China**, and one of the 14 peaks above 8,000 meters (26,247 ft), it is the 11th highest peak in the world. It was first climbed on July 5, 1958, by Andrew Kauffman and **Pete Schoening**, from the United States. As of the end of 1999, the peak had been scaled 164 times; 17 climbers lost their life either attempting the summit or descending from the mountain. (See also the **14 8,000-Meter Peaks** sidebar and color photos.)

Gasherbrum II (Also K4) 8,035 m, 26,361 ft. Another giant of the **Karakoram**, located between **Pakistan** and **China**; it is the 14th highest peak in the world. It was first climbed on July 7, 1956, by an Austrian team including Fritz Moravec, Sepp Larch, and Hans Willenpart. As of the end of 1999, Gasherbrum II had been climbed 468 times; 15 climbers died either attempting the mountain or after summitting. (See also the **14 8,000-Meter Peaks** sidebar.)

Gasherbrum III 7,946 m, 26,069 ft. A fine mountain on the border between **Pakistan** and **China**; it was first climbed in 1975 by **Wanda Rutkiewicz**.

Gasherbrum IV 7,932 m, 26,023 ft. A mountain in Pakistan and China. It was first ascended in 1958, by **Walter Bonatti** and Carlo Mauri. If it were a bit higher, it would be an 8,000 meter peak, and one of the more difficult ones (Greg Glade, personal comment).

Gate In **skiing**, a pole or poles placed on the **slope** to control the speed and direction of a skier, especially in **slalom** racing.

Gauri Sankar 7,145 m, 23,440 ft. This major peak is located within the **Himalayas** at the border between **Nepal** and **Tibet**. It was first ascended in 1979, by **John Roskelley** and Dorje.

Gaza Strip Lowest point, Mediterranean Sea 0 m; highest point, Abu 'Awdah (Joz Abu 'Auda) 105 m, 344 ft.

Géant, Aiguille du See **Dent du Géant**.

Gear (Also hardware, ironmongery, or **protection**.) In **rock climbing**, the various pieces of **equipment** (carried on a **rack**) used to attach oneself to cracks in rock. Generically, gear can apply to a mountaineer's equipment.

***Geheimnis Tibet**/Secret Tibet* A 1939 German documentary by Hans Albert Lettow on the Ernst Schäfer expedition; Dr. Schäfer, a zoologist, along with other scientists, was one of the first to bring back reports from the then unknown Tibet. The film shows the usual problems with logistics as well as the daredevil aspects of this kind of expedition, along with shots of mountains and accounts of Tibet's everyday life and ceremonies. But this documentary was also a propaganda work. The Nazis searched for a race pure of any miscegenation and looked for it in unexplored places. The film lingers on swastikas, and the narrator's voice adds many innuendoes. After completion and German release, it was dubbed in various languages and shown in occupied countries. (M-A. H.)

Geiger, Hermann (1913–1966) Born: Switzerland. An airplane pilot who specialized in mountain rescue. Bibliography: *Alpine Pilot* (1956), *Geiger and the Alps* (ca. 1958).

Gems See **precious stones**.

Gendarme *Torre* (I), *Türm* (G). A tower of rock on a **ridge**. (See also **tooth** and **pinnacle**.)

Geneva, Lake A large body of fresh water located between **Switzerland** and **France**. The Rhône River flows through the lake, from which the peaks of the **Mont Blanc Range** can be seen in the south, while other smaller peaks frame the east and south sides of the lake.

Geneva Spur Located along the **normal route** of **Everest**, on the Nepali, or Khumbu, side of the mountain, on the steep slope between the **Western Cwm** and the **South Col**.

Gentian A diverse flower. Some **Himalayan** species flourish above 18,000 ft; Polunin and Stainton note that *Gentiana urnula* has been found above 20,000 ft.

Geode A piece of rock that contains colorful crystals inside.

Geography The study of the earth's surface and its influence, topography of specific areas, and culture. (See Gerrard.)

Geology The study of the physical earth. (For terminology, see www.webref.org/geology/geology.htm.)

Geomorphology The study of the precise forms that the earth's surface takes, for example, **buttes** and **moraines**.

Georgia (Asia) Lowest point, Black Sea 0 m; highest point, Mt'a Mqinvartsveri (Gora Kazbek) 5,048 m, 16,562 ft.

Georgia (U.S.) Lowest point, Atlantic Ocean 0 m; highest point, Brasstown Bald 1,458 m, 4,784 ft (25th highest of the 50 state highpoints).

Geo-Situ A company that manufactures pewter replicas of **benchmarks**; they take various forms including paperweights and earrings (www.geositu.com).

Geothermal activity The roiling of heat within the earth that results in emitted **lava** from **volcanoes**, and hot water and steam from geysers and **vents**.

Geranium A flower that can be found above 10,000 ft. (See Costello.)

Germany Lowest point, Freepsum Lake −2 m, −7 ft; highest point, **Zugspitze** 2,962 m, 9,718 ft.

Gervasutti, Giusto (1909–1946) Born: Italy. A superb Italian climber, with **first ascents** of the east face of Tacul and the Right-Hand Pillar of Freney, according to Unsworth's *Encyclopaedia*. Bibliography: *Gervasutti's Climbs* (1957).

Gesner, Konrad (1516–1565) A Swiss renaissance man, knowledgeable in zoology, botany, and medicine, he loved mountains and wrote the *Descriptio Montis Fracti sive Montis Pilati*, one of the first accounts of a mountaineering climb.

Geyser From the Icelandic word *geysir*, "to rush forth"; a geyser is a specific type of hot spring that intermittently produces jets of steam and water. In general, geysers are associated with ongoing or recent volcanic activity, as they are produced by the heating of underground waters by **magma**. Geysers often offer a spectacular display, discharging a steaming jet of boiling water as high as 500 m, 1,640 ft, although 20–50 m is more typical; one example is Old Faithful in **Yellowstone National Park**. The water and steam ejected by geysers contains numerous dissolved chemicals, which produce colorful displays near the geyser vent; thermophile algae also contribute to these beautiful variations in hue. (See also color photos.)

Ghana Lowest point, Atlantic Ocean 0 m; highest point, Mt. Afadjato 880 m, 2,887 ft.

Ghats A **range** in India, divided into eastern and western branches.

Gibraltar Lowest point, Mediterranean Sea 0 m; highest point, Rock of Gibraltar 426 m, 1,398 ft.

Gill, John (fl. mid-1950s–1960s) A superb **free rock** climber who is widely believed to be the greatest boulderer in the world. In 1961, he did the first 5.12 in America (see **rating systems**), long before such a standard had arrived anywhere else. His humility and excellent writings have made him an international icon (Pat Ament, personal communication).

Gillman, Peter (1940–) Born: England. Bibliography: *Eiger Direct* (1966) with **Dougal Haston**, *Fitness on Foot (Climbing and Walking for Pleasure)* (1978), *In Balance* (1989), *Everest: The Best Writing and Pictures from Seventy Years of Human Endeavour* (1993), *The Wildest Dream: Mallory, His Life and Conflicting Passion* (2001) with

Leni Gillman, *Everest: Eighty Years of Triumph and Tragedy* (2001).

Giordani, Pointe 4,322 m, 14,179 ft. This is the 16th highest of the 60 major 4,000-meter peaks in the **Alps**. An important satellite of **Monte Rosa**, it was conquered in 1872 by Giuseppe Gugliermina and Giuseppe Farinetti.

Girardelli, Marc (fl. late 1980s) An exceptional ski racer from Austria; he won five World Cup titles.

Girdlestone, Rev. Arthur Gilbert (1842–1908) Born: England. Bibliography: *The High Alps without Guides* (1870).

Glacial drift (Also called drift, **till**) Material (clay, sand, rocks) deposited by a **glacier**.

Glacial preservation In August 2004, a melting Italian glacier revealed the mummified remains of some World War I Austrian soldiers. (See also **Iceman**.)

Glacial silt The minerals and rocks carried by **glaciers** from the mountains whence they originate all the way to the terminus, forming **moraines** along the way. During the entire process, rocks are ground into finer pieces and particles, finally forming the sand-like silt.

Glaciation A glacier's extension and growth over and alteration of a landmass. (See Smith.)

Glacier *Ghiacciaio* (I), *Gletscher* (G). A glacier is born when the previous winter's **snow** is so extensive that it does not melt, but stays frozen;

Flowing Glaciers (Laura Lindblad)

this **ice** then forms the foundation for the following winter's accumulation. Over the years, this mass increases. Some glaciers are fairly small, while others are extremely large and may extend over hundreds of cubic miles. **Valley** glaciers are confined to the mountain and the valley below; continental glaciers cover much of **Greenland** and **Antarctica**; and hanging glaciers cascade off a steep **slope** or **cliff** and appear to hang in the air. On high **peaks**, one will find many glaciers moving downward in different directions. During the past century, the world's glaciers have been shrinking and receding, and it is thought that in a few years, the glaciers on top of **Kilimanjaro** and other equatorial peaks will disappear. Glaciers move very slowly over terrain, grind the surface of the mountain down, and leave rocky **detritus** (**moraines**) in their wake; they also transport natural and other material along with them. For example, thousands of years after **the Iceman** was buried in a storm, he reappeared in an Alpine glacier. Occasionally, enormous quanti-

ties of glacial material break off above inhabited areas and cascade down into the valley, destroying property and lives; for example, in September 2002, a mass of ice hundreds of feet high destroyed much of Karmadon in the **Caucasus** mountains and 95 people were declared missing ("Devastated"). Seven hundred feet beneath the Svartisen Glacier in northern **Norway**, scientists have eked out tunnels and living quarters. Here they are learning some surprising things: glaciers, it turns out, are not merely passive respondents to changes in the climate; instead, they cause them (McNeil). Costello offers the following catalogue: **Washington** has 800 glaciers, **Montana** 106, **Wyoming** 80, **California** 80, and **Oregon** 38. (A useful website can be found at http://nsidc.org/glaciers/glossary.) (See also **iceberg, piedmont glacier, tidewater glacier**, and color photos.)

Glacier Bay An amazing series of **fjords** and gigantic **glaciers** born in the high snowy peaks of the **Saint Elias Mountains** and running directly into the ocean, where they break and

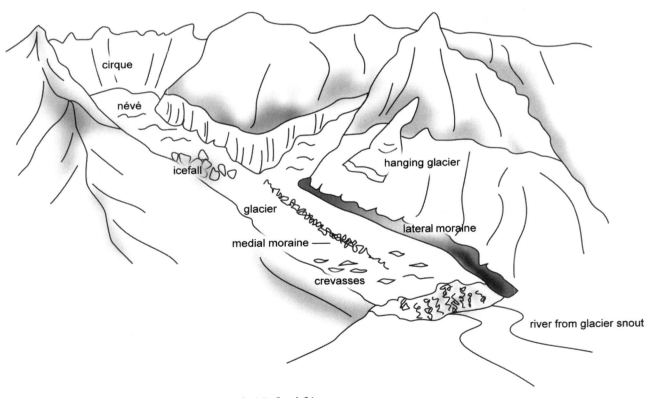

Glacier and Surrounding Landscape (Marie Madgwick)

White Glacier (National Geographic)

calve numerous **icebergs**. It is located near the northern terminus of the **Inside Passage**. (See also color photos.)

Glacier Express A mountain train that runs from **Zermatt** to **St. Moritz, Switzerland,** across 291 bridges and through 91 tunnels.

Glacier Peak 3,213 m, 10,541 ft. A remote, glaciated peak in **Washington**'s **Cascades**, first climbed in 1898 by Thomas Gerdine with a **U.S. Geological Survey** team.

Glissade To slide on **snow** or **ice** on one's feet or in a sitting position, which is safer, since here an ice ax can control velocity with some precision. Climbers often use this method, even on steep slopes, since it speeds up the descent. Indeed, on well-traveled mountains, people utilize the same route over and over again and eventually it comes to resemble a miniature bobsled run. Glissading can be quite dangerous if one loses **control**.

Global positioning system (GPS) A system using satellite signals that small handheld devices can pick up. It indicates geographic location with extreme accuracy, and is thus invaluable for **navigation** in the mountains. The small units can now be purchased for as little as 100 dollars.

Glorioso Islands Lowest point, Indian Ocean 0 m; highest point, unnamed location 12 m, 39 ft.

Godwin Austen See **K2**.

Godwin-Austen, Col. Henry Haversham (1834–1923) Born: England. In 1886, K2 was named after this geographer and surveyor; eventually the name reverted to its original survey designation. Bibliography: *When Men and Mountains Meet* (1977) by John Keay.

Gold A **mineral**; the **ore** is sometimes mined in mountainous regions. It is valuable for its esthetic and utilitarian applications, for example, it is a superb electrical conductor. The discovery of gold has set off frantic incursions of thousands of people to or through specific mountainous areas; examples include the **California** Gold Rush of 1849 and a similar eruption in the Klondike in 1898.

Gold Rush, The An American film by Charlie Chaplin (1889–1977), released in 1925 and set near Chilkoot Pass. The "undaunted lone prospector" (Chaplin, playing the "little man") finds himself chased by a bear, falls down, and ends up in a hut balanced on the edge of a high cliff. Filming began on location, only to be completely redone in the studio, as shown in the 1980 documentary *Unknown Chaplin*. Some location shots survive, notably at the very beginning. In 1942, Chaplin reedited the film, cut the titles and two short scenes, and added music and commentary. (M-A. H.)

Goldfinch A small bird; the American is bright yellow seasonally. It is ubiquitous in the United States and southern Canada and can be observed at altitude.

Gondola (Also called cable car) *Seilbahn* (G), *Téléphérique* (F). An enclosed unit that is pulled up a mountain on an overhead cable. There are two basic types. The first is a large cabin (tram) that may hold 100 people. As it moves up or across (sometimes hundreds or even thousands of feet above the ground), its counterbalancing sister moves down or back. Thus, a total of 200 people can be carried in both directions simultaneously. The second type is much smaller and holds only one to five skiers. The advantage is that there may be 100 or more cabins on a single cable depending on its length. Although skis must be removed, skiers prefer gondolas to **chairlifts** because they are warmer and more comfortable. (See also **ski lift** and color photos.)

Gongga Shan 7,596 m, 24,921 ft. This major peak is located in the Daxue Shan Range of **Tibet**. It was first ascended in 1980, by a Chinese military expedition.

Gorge (Also ravine). A narrow **valley** with steep sides through which a river may run.

GPS See **global positioning system**.

Grab In **snowboarding**, to hold onto the board's edge with one or both hands.

Graben A **fault** depression in the lithic **crust** bounded by horsts that are raised on either side.

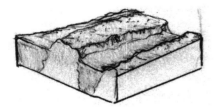

Horst/Graben (Laura Lindblad)

Graduated length method In **skiing**, one begins the sport on very short skis and slowly works one's way up to longer models. It facilitates the learning process.

Graham, Bob (1889–1966) Born: England. He was the first to complete, in 1932, the long-distance traverse of the Lakeland fells now bearing his name. See *The Bob Graham Round—A Brief History*. Bibliography: *42 Peaks—The Story of the Bob Graham Round* (1982) by Roger Smith, *Studmarks on the Summits* (1985) by Bill Smith.

Gran Paradiso 4,061 m, 13,323 ft. This is the 45th highest of the 60 major 4,000-meter peaks in the **Alps**. It was first ascended in 1860 by J. J. Cornwell, W. Dundas, Michel Payot, and Jean Tairraz. A beautiful, massive mountain in the Graian Alps of **Italy**, it is also often considered the easiest of the Alpine 4,000-meter peaks. The Gran Paradiso is also the highest peak entirely within Italy. (See also color photos.)

Grand Canyon A canyon in the western **United States** through which the Colorado River runs. It is 1–18 miles across, up to a mile deep, and 277 miles long. It is one of the only places in the world where all five climatic zones are represented in one location. The Grand

The Devil's Corkscrew on the Bright Angel Trail (Kolb Brothers/National Geographic)

The Grand Canyon from the Fossil Rocks (Kolb Brothers/ National Geographic)

Canyon is one of nature's most extraordinary and beautiful creations, a living laboratory for geologists and naturalists.

Grand Combin 4,314 m, 14,153 ft. This is the 18th highest of the 60 major 4,000-meter peaks in the **Alps**. Located on the west end of the **Valaisan Alps**, it was first climbed in 1857 by Benjamin and Maurice Felley and Jouvence Bruchez. (See also color photos.)

Grand Teton 4,197 m, 13,770 ft. This is a superb peak, within a powerful group of mountains, in a grandiose location. It was first scaled in 1898 by the Rev. W. Owen, F. Spaulding, J. Shive, and F. Peterson. It is the second highest peak in **Wyoming**, only shorter than **Gannett Peak** by 10 m, 34 ft; **Fremont Peak**, at 4,190 m, 13,745 ft, is number three in Wyoming, by only 7 m, 25 ft. The modern **normal route** was opened in 1931 by **Glenn Exum**, and bears his name; it is a relatively difficult, technical rock climb, and it is extremely vertiginous. (See also color photos.)

Grandala In the **Himalayas,** this bird manages to reach almost 18,000 ft. (See Ali.)

Grande course A (major) classic climb in the **Alps**.

Grande Rocheuse, La 4,102 m, 13,458 ft. This is the 39th highest of the 60 major 4,000-meter peaks of the **Alps**. It was first climbed in 1865 by R. Fowler, **Michel Croz**, and Michel Balmat. This is a **satellite** of the **Aiguille Verte**, in the **Mont Blanc Range**.

Grandes Jorasses, Les 4,208 m, 13,805 ft. This is the 27th highest of the 60 major 4,000-meter peaks in the **Alps**. The highest peak, the Pointe Walker, was first climbed in 1868 by **Horace Walker**, **Melchior Anderegg**, Johann Jaun, and J. Grange; the Pointe Croz, 4,110 m, 13,484 ft, was opened four years earlier, in 1864, by **Edward Whymper**, **Michel Croz**, **Christian Almer**, and Franz Biner. It is a magnificent, powerful mountain in the **Mont Blanc Range** of France, and one of the classic and extremely difficult climbs in the Alps along either the Croz or Walker Spur. Indeed, the north face of the Grandes Jorasses was long considered an impossible climb: approximately a mile wide, over 1,200 m, or 4,000 ft, high, and reaching inclinations well in excess of 65 degrees on average, while being continuously vertical over 90-m, 295-ft-long pitches, it presents superb challenges on unpredictable mixed terrain; the first winter climb of the Walker Spur, by **Walter Bonatti** and Cosimo Zappelli in 1963, was one of the greatest achievements in the annals of alpinism. The Arête des Hirondelles is also a wonderful climb, similar to the Arête de Coste Rouge on the **Ailefroide**, and the east face of the Jorasses, although shorter than its northern counterpart, remains one of the most difficult climbs in the Mont Blanc Range. The Linceuil is located on the north face of the mountain; it is a 65- to 70-degree snow and ice slope that has long been considered one of the most sustained and exposed ice climbs in the Mont Blanc Range. (See also the **6 + 1 Great Alpine North Faces** sidebar and color photos.)

Granite A coarse, hard, **igneous rock** that comprises many of the earth's mountains. It appears in many colors including gray, black, and red and is used in building. It offers excellent rock climbing opportunities, because it is not brittle and therefore does not break off in one's hands.

Granite Peak   3,901 m, 12,799 ft. The highest point in **Montana**, it is a place of severe, austere, but haunting beauty, which is often exposed to furious storms coming from the north or the west. The climb to the summit involves a steep scramble on precipitous rock, for the last few hundred feet of the ascent.

Grapnel   A climbing tool invented by **Edward Whymper**, it is a cross between an **ice ax** and a specialized hook.

Grass: A Nation's Battle for Life   An American documentary shot in 1924 by Merian C. Cooper, Ernest B. Schoedsack, and Marguerite Harrison. Cooper, then freelancing for the Polish army after being a pilot during World War I, met the newsreel photographer Schoedsack in 1920. Attracted by adventure and exoticism, they decided to team up and make movies related to these genres. They eventually were responsible for two classics: *The Most Dangerous Game* (1932) and *King Kong* (1933). (See **Skull Island**.) Their first effort was supported by Harrison, a journalist, ex-spy, and adventure buff. The three followed the Bakhtiari tribe in the Iranian Mountains searching for grass to feed their herds. Even if some parts were reenacted to enhance the spectacular aspect of the film, the genuine sight of thousands of people climbing mountains and passing through valleys was stunning, and the film was a great success when it was released by Paramount in 1925.

Gravel   Coarse fragments that comprise larger rocks such as **boulders**.

Great Britain   See **United Kingdom**.

Great Rift Valley   An enormous area in East Africa that is home to many famous **volcanoes** and countless animal species.

Great Trango Tower   (Trango Tower) 6,286 m, 20,623 ft. A spectacular summit in the Karakoram range of Pakistan. 2,000-m, 6,000-ft, vertical cliffs can be found in the Trango area; recently, one of these gigantic monolithic spires was first climbed, then **B.A.S.E.-jumped** from! The Great Trango Tower was first ascended in 1977 by **Galen Rowell**, **John Roskelley**, Kim Schmitz, and Dennis Hennek. (See also color photos.)

Greece   Lowest point, Mediterranean Sea 0 m; highest point, **Mt. Olympus** 2,917 m, 9,570 ft. Greece is a very mountainous country, containing numerous areas where amazing landscapes can be found.

Green, William Spotswood   (1847–1919) Born: Ireland. One of the first Alpinists to climb in the high peaks of **Canada** and **New Zealand**. Bibliography: *The High Alps of New Zealand* (1883), *Among the Selkirk Glaciers* (1890).

Greenbank, Anthony   Born: England. Bibliography: *Instructions in Rock Climbing* (1963), *Climbing, Canoeing, Skiing and Caving* (1964), *Instructions in Rock Climbing* (1967), *A Book of Survival* (1967), *Climbing Mountains* (1973), *Climbing Rocks* (1973), *Enjoy Your Rock Climbing* (1976), *Climbing for Young People* (1977), *Walking, Hiking and Backpacking* (1977).

Greenland   Lowest point, Atlantic Ocean 0 m; highest point, Gunnbjorn 3,700 m, 12,139 ft. This incomparable land of mountains, sea, and ice is the largest island on earth. Grandiose **fjords**, gigantic **ice fields**, **aurora borealis**, and the midnight sun are staples of this faraway land. Greenland is a superb location for the amateur of extreme cold weather, offering solitude and beauty as well.

Gregory, Alfred   (1913–) Born: England. He was the official photographer of the successful 1953 British **Everest** expedition. Bibliography: *The Picture of Everest* (1954).

Grenada   Lowest point, Caribbean Sea 0 m; highest point, Mt. Saint Catherine 840 m, 2,756 ft.

Grenville, Edmund J.   (fl. mid-1800s). An active Alpinist in the Victorian era, he was part of the first ascents of the **Strahlhorn** (1854) and the **Dufourspitze** (1855).

Griffin, A. Harry   (1903–) Born: England. A prolific writer about his beloved Lake District, he was also a rock climber, scrambler, walker, and historian. Bibliography: *Inside the Real Lakeland* (1961), *In Mountain Lakeland* (1963), *Pageant of Lakeland* (1966), *The Roof of England* (1968), *Still the Real Lakeland* (1970), *Long Days in the Hills* (1974), *A Lakeland Notebook* (1975), *A Year in the Fells* (1976), *Freeman of the Hills* (1978), *Discovering Lakeland (A Motorist's Guide), Adventuring in Lakeland* (1980), *A Lake-*

land Mountain Diary (1990), *The Coniston Tigers* (1999).

Grizzly   See **bear** and color photos.

Grohmann, Paul   (1838–1908) An excellent mountaineer who climbed in the **Dolomites**. He did the **first ascent** of the **Marmolata**.

Groom   In **skiing**, to smooth the snow on slopes because of ski ruts, icy patches, or new snow accumulation. This is done at most commercial ski areas in the United States. In the high or backcountry, where people seek deep powder, it is abjured.

Grossglockner   3,798 m, 12,461 ft. The highest peak in **Austria**, it is surrounded by beautiful mountains, including the **Grossvenediger**, the second highest peak in Austria. It was first climbed in 1800 by Count von Salm, the Prince Bishop of Gurk, and their party of 60!

Gross-Grünhorn   4,044 m, 13,267 ft. This is the 49th highest of the 60 major 4,000-meter peaks in the **Alps**. It was first climbed in 1865 by Edmund von Fellenberg, Peter Egger, Peter Michel, and Peter Jnäbnit. It is located in the **Bernese Alps**, in the Fiescherhorn **massif**.

Grossvenediger   3,674 m, 12,054 ft. This is the second highest peak in **Austria**; it was first climbed in 1841 by Forester Rohregger and party.

Grouse   A ground and forest **bird**, the grouse dances, drums, hoots, or struts. Species include the blue, ruffed, sage, and sharp-tailed.

Grove, Florence Crawford   (1838–1902) Born: England. President of the Alpine Club, 1884–1886. Despite the fact that he was one of the best British climbers of his day, he vehemently opposed guideless climbing during the 1870s. Bibliography: *The Frosty Caucasus* (1875).

Guadalupe Peak   2,667 m, 8,749 ft. The high-point in **Texas**, some 50 miles from El Paso, it rises steeply from the desert floor, projecting the mighty cliffs of El Capitan over the arid landscape; Carlsbad Caverns National Park is nearby. The peak was probably first scaled by Native Americans.

Guadeloupe   Lowest point, Caribbean Sea 0 m; highest point, Soufrière 1,467 m, 4,813 ft.

Guam   Lowest point, Pacific Ocean 0 m; highest point, Mt. Lamlam 406 m, 1,332 ft.

Guatemala   Lowest point, Pacific Ocean 0 m; highest point, Volcan Tajumulco 4,211 m, 13,816 ft. Many **volcanoes** are located in this Central American country including Fuego and Pacaya.

Guernsey   Lowest point, Atlantic Ocean 0 m; highest point, unnamed location on Sark 114 m, 374 ft.

Guide   During the early years of Alpine mountaineering, many skillful and courageous local men provided **guiding services** to people who wished to investigate or climb in the French and Swiss **Alps**. **Christian Almer, Melchior Anderegg, Jean-Antoine Carrel, Michel Croz**, and **Ulrich Lauener** are among the most famous of these pioneers. In most areas the guides were independent contractors (not affiliated with a service), who worked with those climbers they liked, and they often guided the same people year after year. In **Chamonix**, though, the Compagnie des Guides de Chamonix controlled a climber's choice of guides, all of whom rotated through an inflexible sequence. Thus, if an English mountaineer wanted an English-speaking guide and the next person in the rotation only spoke French, the climber was out of luck. This system was helpful to the incompetent guides (who were thus assured of work) but harmful to everyone else (Clark). Independent guiding continued to flourish in the Alps and later developed in other parts of the world. Today one can hire a guide to hike, trek, or climb anywhere on earth. But there are still some locations where independents are barred from operating, for example, in national parks such as **Mt. Rainier** or **Denali**. Guides offer a number of services: They may know the **route**, so that one does not become entangled in navigational problems or get lost; they teach, lead, help, carry, and stimulate; they provide protection and rescues in contingencies; and they help with logistics. Interestingly, some guides provide professional services even in areas they have never visited. For example, Terray led his Dutch clients on climbs in the **Andes** that were new to him too. (See also **Führerbuch** and the **10 Best Guides** sidebar.)

Guidebooks   Overviews of various countries, locations, mountains, climbs, or routes; they help to orient rock climbers and mountaineers. The most precise offer detailed descriptions of an entire

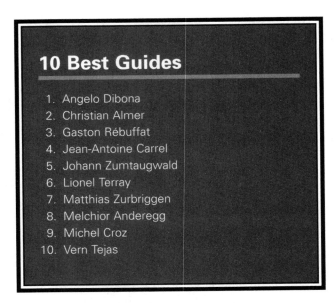

10 Best Guides

1. Angelo Dibona
2. Christian Almer
3. Gaston Rébuffat
4. Jean-Antoine Carrel
5. Johann Zumtaugwald
6. Lionel Terray
7. Matthias Zurbriggen
8. Melchior Anderegg
9. Michel Croz
10. Vern Tejas

climb, including **anchor**, **belay**, and **rappel** locations. Famous guidebooks include the Guide *Vallot*, for the **Mont Blanc Range**, and numerous publications by The Mountaineers for both U.S. and foreign ranges, for example, *Climber's Guide to the Teton Range*, by Reynold Jackson, *The High Sierra*, and *Mexico's Volcanoes: A Climbing Guide*; the last two books are authored by **R. J. Secor**.

Guiding services   There are now innumerable companies around the world that provide guides for **trekking** and short climbs as well as for **expeditions** to the highest peaks. As early as 1823, local residents offered to guide people around **Chamonix** in the French **Alps**. The first organized service was provided by the Compagnie des Guides de Chamonix. In order to become a recognized guide here one had to be born in the Chamonix Valley and go through a rigorous training program. Indeed, many of the guides came from the same families. In the United States, Lou Whittaker founded Rainier Mountaineering, Inc. (RMI) in 1968. In the past, this was the only official service allowed on **Mt. Rainier**. The American Alpine Institute, in Bellingham, Washington, and Alpine Ascents International provide guides for climbs in many parts of the world. Exum Mountain Guides helps people reach summits in the **Tetons**. Yamnuska is located in western Canada.

Guinea   Lowest point, Atlantic Ocean 0 m; highest point, Mont Nimba 1,752 m, 5,748 ft.

Guinea-Bissau   Lowest point, Atlantic Ocean 0 m; highest point, unnamed location in the northeast corner of the country 300 m, 984 ft.

Gully   *Burrone* (I), *couloir* (F; prn: coolwaar), *Schlucht* (G). A steep defile or gorge between two **slopes**. Although there is no connotative difference in the meanings of the English and French terms, couloir (which is now also considered an English word) is the favored locution. Collomb holds that Alpine couloirs "are more open" and steeper than British gullies. They often are covered with ice, snow, or stonefall.

Gurla Mandata   7,694 m, 25,242 ft. This major peak is located in the Nalakankar **Himal** in **Tibet**; it was first climbed by a large expedition in 1985.

Guyana   Lowest point, Atlantic Ocean 0 m; highest point, Mt. Roraima 2,835 m, 9,301 ft.

Gyachung Kang   7,952 m, 26,089 ft. This major peak is located within the **Himalayas** in **Nepal**. It was first ascended in 1964, by Y. Kato, K. Sakaizawa, and Pasang Phutar.

H

Habeler, Peter (1942–) In 1978, he accompanied **Reinhold Messner** on the first ascent of **Everest** without supplemental oxygen. Bibliography: *Everest, Impossible Victory* (1979).

Hackett, Bill (fl. 1940s–1980s) The first person to attempt the **Seven Summits**, he managed to reach five, along with many other conquests.

Hail *Grandine* (I), *grêle* (F), *Hagel* (G). Falling **ice** particles. (See also **rain**, **sleet**, and **snow**.)

Haiti Lowest point, Caribbean Sea 0 m; highest point, Chaîne de la Selle 2,680 m, 8,793 ft.

Haleakala 3,055 m, 10,023 ft This massive **shield volcano** located on the island of Maui, in **Hawaii**, contains a very large **caldera**.

Haleakala National Park Along with **Hawaii Volcanoes National Park**, this is a magnificent natural preservation area located in the state of **Hawaii**.

Half Dome A large and imposing rock configuration in **Yosemite**. It is a favorite big wall climb and photographic image.

Halfpipe In **snowboarding**, a construction consisting of two parallel snow banks intercepted by a valley. They vary in height, width, and length, but 2 by 15 by 100 meters is recommended. Boarders move down one bank and up the other performing twists, rotations, and somersaults. A quarter-pipe is similar but consists of just one wall.

Hall, Rob (1960–1996) Born: New Zealand. He was the leader of one of the teams involved in the **Everest 1996** tragedy. His passing, high on the summit ridge of Everest, after being patched through to his pregnant wife, in New Zealand; remains one of the most poignant, lamentable, sad moments of climbing history. Hall was a superb all-around mountaineer, and he was the ninth person to complete the **Seven Summits**; following is the chronology of his successful quest: first summit, **Vinson, Antarctica** (1989); **Denali, North America** (1990); **Elbrus, Europe** (1990); **Kilimanjaro, Africa** (1990); **Kosciuszko, Australia** (1990); **Everest, Asia** (1990); **Aconcagua, South America** (1990); **Carstensz Pyramid, Australasia** (1994).

Hanging glacier See **glacier**, **hanging valley**.

Hanging valley A tributary, elongated depression located above the main valley.

Hankinson, Alan (1926–) Born: England. Bibliography: *The First Tigers* (1972), *Camera on the Crags* (1975), *Changabang* (1975), with **C. J. S. Bonington** et al., *The Mountain Men* (1977), *A Century on the Crags* (1988), *Coleridge Walks the Fells—A Lakeland Journey Retraced* (1991), *Geoffrey Winthrop Young* (1995).

Hannibal In 218 B.C.E., this Carthaginian general somehow managed to cross the **Alps** with his elephants.

Haramosh Peak 7,490 m, 24,573 ft. This major peak is located within the **Karakoram** Range in **Pakistan**. It was first ascended in 1958, by an Austrian expedition.

Harding, Warren (1924–2002) An important **rock** climber responsible for the **first ascent** of the **Nose** on **El Capitan** (1958). (See also **Lynn Hill**.)

Hardware See **climbing equipment**, **equipment**, **gear**.

Hare Similar to though larger than a cottontail (rabbit); the arctic and the white-tailed jackrabbits inhabit rocky and mountainous slopes (Collins).

Hargreaves, Alison (1962–1995) Born: England. One of the premier mountaineers of the late 20th century. She was killed on **K2**. Bibliography: *A Hard Day's Summer* (1994), *One and Two Halves to K2* (1996) by James Ballard, *Regions of the Heart: The Triumph and Tragedy of Alison Hargreaves* (1999) by David Rose and Ed Douglas.

Harness   A device made of narrow strips of strong webbing sewn together; it is worn around the waist and legs. To it is attached the **rope** that protects in case of a fall in climbing. A sit harness allows one to end up in a sitting position rather than upside down. More **protection** is afforded by an additional chest harness. Before harnesses existed, the rope was tied directly around the waist, but in a long fall this resulted in horrible damage to the body. Wearing a harness and using it correctly are two very different things. See **accidents** for further elucidation.

Harney Peak   2,207 m, 7,242 ft. The highest point in **South Dakota**, it is also the highest point in the continental United States east of the **Rockies**. A nice, short hike leads up to the summit; **Mt. Rushmore** is nearby, as well as Jewel Cave.

Harrer, Heinrich   (1912–) A pioneering Austrian climber; he was a member of the first team to climb the **Eiger**'s **north face** (1938). He was interned in India at the start of World War II but escaped and journeyed to **Lhasa**. Bibliography: *Seven Years in Tibet* (1953), *The White Spider* (1959), *I Come from the Stone Age* (1964), *Return to Tibet* (1984). His *Seven Years in Tibet* and *The White Spider* are classic accounts. (See also the **10 Great Mountain Adventure Books** and **10 Best Hollywood Mountain Movies** sidebars.)

Haston, Dougal   (1940–1977) A great Scottish climber and **guide**; he did some difficult winter climbs, including the **first ascent** of the **Eiger** Direct and the **north face** of the **Aiguille d'Argentière**. He and **Doug Scott** made the first British ascent of **Everest**, which also was the first ascent of the difficult southwest face. Bibliography: *Eiger Direct* (1966) with Peter Gillman, *In High Places* (1973), *The Eiger* (1974), *Dougal Haston—The Philosophy of Risk* (2002), by Jeff Connor (biography).

Haul bag   A large, waterproof bag that contains **gear** and **food**; it is pulled up after a **pitch** is completed in big wall climbing.

Haute Route, La   It is possible to walk or ski from **Chamonix** to **Zermatt** along a magnifi-

cent route that runs along the **high mountains** and through a series of **passes**. There are sleeping accommodations in **refuges** or inns along the way, and the trip takes about 10 days.

Hawaii   Lowest point, Pacific Ocean, 0 m; highest point, **Mauna Kea** 4,205 m, 13,796 ft (sixth highest of the 50 state highpoints). An antithesis to **Alaska**, both of which lie along the **Ring of Fire**. Here one will find ongoing and spectacular volcanic activity at Hawaii **Volcanoes National Park**. **Volcanoes** include Kilauea, **Mauna Kea**, and **Mauna Loa**. (See also color photos.)

Hawaii Volcanoes National Park   A wonderful area in Hawaii, on the largest island, where one can experience active volcanoes. (See also **national parks**).

Hawk   Hawk taxonomy is complex because species of this bird are sometimes quite dissimilar, but they all soar and hunt for live prey, sometimes swooping down at speeds approaching 200 miles an hour. Examples include the Cooper's, harrier, kestrel, peregrine falcon, sharp-shinned, red-tailed, and Swainson's. In the **Himalayas**, the kestrel can fly as high as 18,000 feet (Ali); in East Africa, the kestral and the peregrine can be found near cliffs (Williams); and in the **Andes** the puna hawk soars at 16,500 ft.

Hayes, Mt.   4,189 m, 13,743 ft. This peak is located within the **Alaska** Range and was first ascended in 1941 by **Bradford Washburn** and his party.

Headlamp   A small, battery-powered light worn on the forehead by miners and climbers. They are now extremely compact and produce powerful and long-lasting illumination. (See also color photos.)

Headland   A high projection over water, especially the sea.

Headwall   Where the steep part of any lithic extrusion begins. Also, the steep part of a snow or ice face, above the *bergschrund*.

Heard and McDonald Islands   Lowest point, Southern Ocean 0 m; highest point, Big Ben 2,745 m, 9,006 ft.

Heatstroke   The condition that occurs when the body is unable to cool itself. If not treated, it can be fatal. It is the antithesis of **hypothermia**.

Heckmair, Anderl   (1906–2005) Born: Germany. A prominent climber before World War II, he is best known for leading the first ascent of the

North Wall of the **Eiger** in 1938. Bibliography: *My Life as a Mountaineer* (1975), *My Life* (2002).

Heimaey In 1973, the eruption of this Icelandic **volcano** produced vast quantities of **tephra** and **lava** that inundated its island and destroyed many houses. The Icelanders fought back in many unusual ways, returned, rebuilt, and now live there once again. (See Ritchie and Gates for a detailed account.)

Hekla 1,491 m, 4,892 ft. Perhaps the most famous of all Icelandic **volcanoes**. It has erupted more than 150 times during the last 900 years.

Helicopter For mountain rescue, especially in remote areas where landing strips or lakes are scarce (see **float planes**), helicopters have revolutionized the difficult work involved in helping stranded and otherwise incapacitated alpinists in dangerous predicaments. See, for example, the remarkable job performed by Lieutenant Colonel Madan K. C. (Kathri Chhetri) in coming to the rescue of Makalu Gau and **Beck Weathers**, after the 1996 **Everest** debacle using a Squirrel helicopter, as related in the excellent book *Left for Dead*, by Weathers with Stephen Michaud. The pilot achieved not one, but two near-perfect landings more than 6,000 m, 19,000 ft, above the **Khumbu Icefall**, a record altitude, where the rarefied atmosphere and the strong thermal disturbances due to the sun tremendously increase the difficulty in properly maneuvering any aircraft, and where the crevasses make for a dangerous landing. The French-made Puma helicopter is the highest-flying rotary-wing aircraft and is often used for mountain rescue missions.

Helmet The use of a lightweight helmet in order to protect the head in rock and ice climbing and mountaineering has become more widespread during the past few decades. Even 50 years ago, helmets were not used, and many climbers were seriously hurt or killed, especially on rockfall-prone mountains. On the north face of the Eiger, a large stone hit Claudio Corti on the head and knocked him off his hold; he tumbled down a gully until the belay rope stopped his fall, but he was seriously hurt (Roth). The unhelmeted authors of this volume once refused to continue up the final, steep couloir on the Middle **Teton** because of the **stonefall**, a continual shower of falling, rolling **debris**. Those who participate in **mountain biking** use a slightly different type of head protection. (See also color photos.)

Hemlock A **conifer** that resembles **spruce**. Mountain hemlock flourishes on ridges and slopes; it does well at altitude despite the severe weather. Some species of this tree reach 200 ft tall.

Herford, Siegfried Wedgwood (1891–1916) Born: England. One of the best early **rock** climbers, whose short climbing days began around 1910 and ended during World War I, in the trenches at Ypres in 1916. He was a member of the first party to climb Central Buttress on Scafell Crag in 1914. Bibliography: *Siegfried Herford—An Edwardian Rock Climber* (2000) by Keith Treacher.

Hermit A religious ascetic who often repairs to a mountain **cave** or hut to live out his or her life in contemplative seclusion. Hermits are found in many religious traditions. When ascetics band together and live in mountain monasteries (**Mt. Athos**, for example) or **lamaseries** (Thangboche), they are no longer hermits.

Heron A **bird** one associates with water; surprisingly, in the **Andes**, the night heron breeds as high as 15,800 ft (Fjeldså and Krabbe).

Herrligkoffer, Karl (1917–1991) Born: Germany. He led the successful 1953 expedition to **Nanga Parbat**, when **Hermann Buhl** soloed the summit, performing the first ascent of the mountain. Bibliography: *Nanga Parbat* (1954).

Herzog, Maurice (1919–) Born: France. The leader of the first team to reach the summit of an **8,000-meter peak**. After summitting **Annapurna**, on June 3, 1950, Herzog suffered severe **frostbite** and subsequently lost parts of his extremities. *Annapurna, Premier 8,000*, his riveting memoir, continues to outsell all other climbing accounts. Later, Herzog was mayor of **Chamonix**. Bibliography: *True Summit*, by David Roberts (2000).

Hexcentric (Hex). In rock climbing, a type of **nut**, hexagonal in shape, used for **protection**.

Hidden Peak See **Gasherbrum I**.

Hiebeler, Toni (1930–1984) Born: Germany. The leader of the party that made the first ascent of the **Eiger** North Wall in winter. Bibliography:

North Face in Winter (1961), *The Alps, Montagnes de Notre Terre.*

High altitude cerebral edema (HACE) See **acute mountain sickness.**

High altitude pulmonary edema (HAPE) See **acute mountain sickness.**

High mountains *Hautes montagnes* (F), *Hochgebirge* (G). The higher **ranges**, for example, the High **Sierras** or the **Alps.** (See also **middle mountains.**)

Highpoint The highest natural point in a given location, for example, a state, province, country, or continent. The desire to reach highpoints is increasing, but there were climbers attempting the complete cycle of U.S. state highpoints as early as 1930; thus far, 131 people have managed to reach the highpoints in all 50 states. (See also **Seven Summits**, Holmes, Winger, **Zumwalt**, and http://highpointers.org/index.html.)

Hike *Randonnée* (F), *wandern* (G). To walk, often on trails that run up, along, and across mountains. The difference between a hike or **trek** and **mountaineering** is a matter of degree. In Great Britain it is sometimes called **hill walking**, and in Germany this type of rambling is extremely popular.

Hill *Cerro* (S). A large extrusion on the earth's surface that is not as high as a mountain. It may be composed of soil rather than rock; in addition, the slope of a hill is generally gentle, below 30 degrees. The difference between a hill and a mountain is sometimes obvious, as in the case of the Alabama Hills near Lone Pine, **California**, dwarfed by the High **Sierras** (see color photos). However, in places like **Tibet**, there are hills that are higher than the **Matterhorn.**

Hill, Lynn (1961–) Born: America. One of the world's finest rock climbers; she was the first person to **free** climb the Nose on **El Capitan** (1993). Ament calls her 1994, 23-hour climb of the Nose, "one of the greatest free-climbing achievements anywhere in the world and in the history of climbing." See her *Climbing Free* (2002), and Boga's *Climbers* for a profile. (See also color photos.)

Hill station A settlement in the mountains to which government officials in India repair, when the heat becomes too intense at lower elevations.

Hill walking The British term for hiking and easy climbing.

Hillary, Peter The son of **Sir Edmund Hillary**, he climbed **Everest** twice, in 1990 and 2002; together, they wrote *Two Generations.* They are the first father and son to reach the summit of Everest, as well as the South Pole by land.

Hillary, Sir Edmund (1919–) Born: New Zealand. The first person, along with **Tenzing Norgay**, to reach the summit of **Mt. Everest** (1953). A New Zealander, Hillary was honored by Queen Elizabeth II of England with a knighthood. Perhaps the most revered climber in the world, Hillary has devoted his life to helping the **Sherpa** community in **Nepal**. In 2003, we celebrated the 50th anniversary, or Golden Jubilee, of the **first ascent** of Everest. Bibliography: *High Adventure* (1955), *Challenge of the Unknown* (1958), *No Latitude for Error* (1961), *High in the Thin Cold Air* (1962), with Desmond Doig, *Schoolhouse in the Clouds* (1964), *Nothing Venture, Nothing Win* (1975), autobiography, *From the Ocean to the Sky* (1979), *View from the Summit* (2003).

Hillary Step On **Everest**, the last difficulty of the **South Col** route, a 30-foot wall on a heavily corniced ridge; its intrinsic difficulty is considerably magnified by the extreme altitude. On the first ascent of Everest, **Hillary** led that short pitch.

Himal Groups of mountains. (See also **Himalayas.**)

Himalayan goral A small, 60-pound **bovid** that lives in the **Himalayan** region.

Himalayas (Often called the Himalaya, especially in Great Britain). Located along the **Nepal–Tibet** border, "the abode of the snows," it is a 1,500-mile **chain**, the most impressive collocation of mountains on earth. Here one will find 9 of the 10 highest peaks including **Everest, Kangchenjunga, Lhotse,** and **Makalu.** The Himalayas are divided into three sections: the Siwalik, the Lesser Himalaya, and the Great. Groups of mountains are called *himals* (Unsworth, *Encyclopaedia*). Cameron's *Mountains of the Gods* is a superb and profusely illustrated overview of these mountains and

The Crest of Siniolchum (Vittorio Sella/National Geographic)

their people. (See also the **14 8,000-Meter Peaks** sidebar and color photos.)

Himalchuli   7,864 m, 25,801 ft. This major peak is located within the **Himalayas** in **Nepal**.

Hinchliff, Thomas Woodbine   (1825–1882) Born: England. He initiated **Edward Whymper** to mountaineering, by taking him on his first Alpine climb, the Riffelhorn, in 1860. He was president of the Alpine Club 1875–1877. Bibliography: *Summer Months among the Alps* (1857).

Hindu Kush   A **range** that runs for 500 miles primarily in Afghanistan. See Newby's *Short Walk in the Hindu Kush* for a classic account.

Hinter-Fiescherhorn   4,025m, 13,205 ft. This is the 54th of the 60 major 4,000-meter peaks in the **Alps**. It was first ascended in 1864 by Edmund von Fellenberg, Peter Jnäbnit, Ulrich Kaufmann, and Peter Baumann. The peak is located in the **Bernese Alps**.

Hmong   An ethnic group of people who inhabit mountainous areas in **China**, **Laos**, **Thailand**, and other countries.

Hogback   See **ridge**.

Hoggar   (Ahaggar). A **range** in the Sahara Desert in southern **Algeria**.

Hohberghorn   4,219 m, 13,841 ft. This is the 25th highest of the 60 major 4,000-meter peaks in the **Alps**. It is part of the **Mischabels**, in the **Valaisan Alps**. It was first climbed in 1869 by R. B. Heathcote, Franz Biner, Peter Perren, and Peter Taugwalder fils.

Holmes, Don W.   He is the author of the book *Highpoints of the United States: A Guide to the Fifty State Summits*.

Holy mountains   See **religion**.

Holy See   (Vatican City). Lowest point, unnamed location 19 m, 62 ft; highest point, unnamed location 75 m, 246 ft.

Honduras   Lowest point, Caribbean Sea 0 m; highest point, Cerro Las Minas 2,870 m, 9,416 ft.

Honeysuckle   Species of this flowering shrub grow at various altitudes; in the Himalayas, *Lonicera spinosa* manages to reach 16,500 ft in Tibet (Polunin and Stainton).

Hong Kong   Lowest point, South China Sea 0 m; highest point, Tai Mo Shan 958 m, 3,143 ft.

Hood, Mt.   3,426 m, 11,239 ft. A glaciated **volcano** in the **Cascades**; it is the highest point in **Oregon** and though dormant, it does have active **fumaroles**. (See the appendix G and the **10 Most Beautiful Mountains** sidebar.) Should it erupt it would cause major damage to nearby populated areas. It was first climbed in 1857 by H. L. Pittock, L. Chittenden, W. Cornell, and the Rev. T. A. Wood. While the **normal route**, on the southern flank of the mountain through the "Pearly Gates," is one of the most climbed anywhere in the world, the north face of Mt. Hood presents a difficult challenge to the climber, compounded by the rotten quality of the rock, characteristic of most volcanoes. Due to its proximity to the Pacific Ocean, like most Cascade volcanoes, the weather can change extremely quickly and drastically on Mt. Hood; unfortunately, this, and the fact that it is often climbed by totally

Eliot Glacier, Mount Hood (U.S. Forest Service/National Geographic)

inexperienced and unprepared "accidental climbers," has led to far too many fatalities on this mountain. (See also color photos.)

Hoodoo   Colorful, eroded, bizarrely shaped spires that can be seen in dry, wind-eroded areas, including the western United States. "Thor's Hammer" in Bryce Canyon National Park is an example. (See also color photos.)

Hoodoo (Laura Lindblad)

Hooker, Sir Joseph Dalton   (1817–1911) Born: England. The first person to almost completely encircle Kangchenjunga (Greg Glade, personal comment). Bibliography: *Himalayan Journals* (1854), *Journal of a Tour in Morocco and the Great Atlas* (1878) with **John Ball**.

Horn   A small or large rock extrusion, often used to drape a **sling** over for **protection** or **rappelling**; or a peak shaped like a horn.

Hornbein, Thomas Frederick   (1930–) Born: America. A pioneer of difficult, short rock climbs in the mid-20th century, he was the first to **traverse** Everest, up by the West Ridge and down the normal route, in 1963, with **Willi Unsoeld**. Bibliography: *Everest: The West Ridge* (1966), *Fatal Mountaineer* (2002) by Robert Roper.

Hörnli Ridge   See **Matterhorn**.

Horst   See **graben**.

Hotels   See **lodges**.

Houston, Charles Snead   (1913–) Born: United States. A medical doctor, with a specialty in high altitude matters, and a mountaineer; he was coleader of the 1938 and the famous 1953 **K2 expeditions**. Bibliography: *Going High* (1980).

Howard, William   (1793–1834) Born: United States. On July 12, 1819, Howard made the ninth ascent of **Mont Blanc** with Dr. Jeremiah van Rensselaer; it was the first ascent by Americans. Bibliography: *A Narrative of a Journey to the Summit of Mont Blanc, 1819* (1821).

Howard-Bury, Charles Kenneth   (1883–1963) Born: England. The leader of the 1921 British **Mt. Everest** expedition. Bibliography: *Mt. Everest: The Reconnaissance, 1921* (1922).

Howland Island   Lowest point, Pacific Ocean 0 m; highest point, unnamed location 3 m, 10 ft.

Huandoy   6,395 m, 20,980 ft. This is the 21st highest peak in the **Andes**, and the 12th (tied) of 20 premier climbing peaks in that range; it was first climbed in 1932 by Erwin Hein and Erwin Schneider. It is located in **Peru**; although it has the same altitude as **Huantsan**, its **normal route** is considerably easier.

Huantsan   6,395 m, 20,980 ft. This is the 22nd highest peak in the **Andes**, and the 12th (tied) of 20 premier climbing peaks in that range; it

Big Bad Lands—Sandstone Caps on Clay Columns (National Geographic)

was first ascended in 1952 by H. Egener, M. T. De Booy, and **Lionel Terray**. The peak is located in **Peru**; although it has the same altitude as **Huandoy**, its **normal route** is considerably harder.

Huascarán, Nevado 6,768 m, 22,204 ft. This is the fifth highest peak in the **Andes**; it was first climbed in 1932 by Franz Bernard, Phillip Borchers, Erwin Hein, Hermann Hoerlin, and Erwin Schneider. It is the highest major peak in **Peru**, located within the **Cordillera Blanca**. It is a splendid mountain, with some extremely difficult routes. (See also color photos.)

Huayhuash, Cordillera Located in **Peru**, this major range contains beautiful peaks, including **Jirishanca** and **Yerupajá Grande**.

Hubbard Glacier This enormous 80-mile (128 km) long **glacier** lies within the equally large **Wrangell–St. Elias National Park**; the termi-

nus of this **tidewater glacier** is located in Disappointment Bay. Its movements are on such a scale that it can alter the topography of the surrounding areas. For example, in the mid-1980s, nearby Russell Fjord was temporarily closed by the Hubbard Glacier. It is one of the world's largest non-polar glaciers.

Hubbard Peak 4,577 m, 15,017 ft. Located in **Canada**'s **Saint Elias Mountains**, in the **Yukon**. This is a heavily glaciated mountain standing in the vicinity of **Alverstone Peak**, near the ocean, where powerful storms rage during the winter months. It straddles the boundary between the **Wrangell–St. Elias** and **Kluane-Logan National Parks**.

Hudson, Charles (1828–1865) Born: England. One of the best amateur mountaineers of the Victorian era, he made the first guideless ascent of **Mont Blanc**. He accompanied **Edward**

Whymper on the first ascent of the **Matterhorn** but was killed on the descent. Other first ascents: **Monte Rosa**; **Dufourspitze**, 1855; **Mont Blanc du Tacul**, 1855. Bibliography: *Where There's a Will There's a Way* (1856), with Edward Shirley Kennedy, *Annals of Mont Blanc* (1898) by C. E. Mathews.

Humble, Benjamin Hutchinson 1903–1977) Born: Scotland. Bibliography: *Tramping in Skye* (1933), *The Songs of Skye* (1934), *Songs for Climbers* (1938), *On Scottish Hills* (1946), *The Cuillin of Skye* (1952).

Humboldt, Alexander von (1769–1859) Born: Berlin. He was a great German naturalist and explorer, and a major figure in the classical period of physical geography and biogeography, which are now part of the earth sciences and ecology. The Humboldt Current off the west coast of South America is named after him. In 1802, while in **Ecuador**, he climbed **Chimborazo** to an astonishing 5,759 m, 18,893 ft (he did not reach the summit).

Hummingbird The ruby-throated is "one of the smallest warm-blooded animals in the world," according to Johnsgard; it flaps its wings so quickly that it can hover. The broad-tailed's habitat lies at 7,500 ft or higher (Johnsgard) and mountain hummingbirds hibernate at night to protect against the cold in the **Andes** (Burnie and Wilson), where the giant can be seen as high as 14,800 ft (Fjeldså and Krabbe).

Humphreys Peak 3,851 m, 12,633 ft. The highest point in **Arizona**. It is located near Flagstaff, some 50 miles south of the **Grand Canyon**; **Meteor Crater** is close by.

Hungary Lowest point, Tisza River 78 m, 256 ft; highest point, Kekes 1,014 m, 3,327 ft.

Hunt, John (1910–1999) Born: England. The leader of the first successful expedition to **Everest** in 1953. Bibliography: *The Ascent of Everest* (1953), *Our Everest Adventure* (1954), *The Red Snows: An Account of the British Caucasus Expedition 1958* (1960), with Christopher Brasher, *Life Is Meeting* (1978), *My Favourite Mountaineering Stories* (1978).

Hunter, Mt. 4,442 m, 14,573 ft. This beautiful mountain, located in the **Alaska Range**, was first climbed in 1954 by **Heinrich Harrer**, Fred Beckey, and Henry Meybohm.

Hunza A high valley area in the **Karakoram** in **Pakistan**. It has been claimed (and disputed) that the inhabitants live very long lives.

Hut See **refuge**.

Hyena All hyena species will travel in mountainous environments; hyenas hunt alone or in packs (Burnie and Wilson).

Hyoheki/The Precipice A Japanese novel by Yasushi Inoue (1907–1991) published in 1957. On January 1, 1956, while climbing Maehodaka (1,429 m., 4,688 ft) in the Hotaka Mountains, Otohiko Kosaka falls while his friend Kyôta Uozu watches helplessly. Was it an accident, a suicide, or a murder, or could the nylon rope—which they were using for the first time—have been defective? The author explores the accident's influence on the lives of various characters. As early as 1958, the book was turned into a movie by Yasuzo Masumura. (M-A. H.)

Hypothermia Reduction of body heat, which results first in shivering and eventually, with a loss of 10 degrees, in death. It can take as little as three hours for this to occur. (See also **medicine**.)

Hypoxia Lack of oxygen. People suffering from hypoxia are weaker and more susceptible to additional physical problems, for example, **frostbite**. Hypoxia is enhanced by other maladies that occur at **altitude** such as cold, exhaustion, and **dehydration** (Wilkerson).

Hyrax A rabbit-like creature found primarily in Africa; it enjoys scurrying on steep slopes (Burnie and Wilson).

I

Ibex   This bovid has enormous horns and roams to 22,000 ft; it is found in parts of Africa, Asia, and Europe.

Ice   *Hielo* (S), *glace* (F). Frozen **water**. When **snow** recrystallizes and becomes granular ice, it is called **névé** or firn; a large, permanent agglomeration of ice is called a **glacier,** which, when covering the top of a mountain is an ice cap. This latter term is also applied to the ice surrounding the poles. Extensive glacial ice or an ice cap may be called an ice field. An ice sheet is a glacier that is not restricted to valleys. Ice can take slightly different forms and these have various names, for example, graupel (snow pellets or soft hail), **hail** (ice pellets), hoarfrost (feathery frost), and rime (rough frost). (See Smith for detailed distinctions.) Black ice is very hard, or a thin glaze of frozen rain that makes rock climbing extremely difficult (see **verglas**). Black ice is generally a sign of extremely steep terrain, when minerals and small rocks are embedded within the ice that has gone through many **freeze-thaw cycles**; in intense cold, it becomes extremely hard, and sometimes impossible to climb, as the **ice ax** simply bounces off the surface, with hardly a chip.

Ice age   A period during which some or much of the earth is covered by **glaciers**.

Ice ax   *Piccoza* (I), *Pickel* (G), *piolet* (F). A specialized and required tool used in some forms of **climbing**. Ice axes vary in length, size, and shape depending on their specific purpose. Those used in **mountaineering** are longer and contain sharp, dual heads (adze and pick) that can be used for cutting, penetration, or self-arrest. Smaller, curved models (sometimes with hammer heads) help an ice climber hold onto a vertical ice wall; they usually contain wrist loops, which protect against loss or offer support to a resting climber. All axes have a shaft that ends in a point called a spike. In mountaineering, specific terms are sometimes used to describe the position of the ax in relation to the body; the French word for ice ax, *piolet,* is followed by one of six possible locutions: *canne, ramasse, ancre, panne, poignard,* or *traction*. (See also color photos.)

Ice cap   A massive quantity of unmelting ice. Unlike a **glacier**, it does not flow downward. Both **Antarctica** and **Greenland** are covered by ice caps.

Ice climbing   Moving up frozen waterfalls, glacial faces, and other generally perpendicular **ice** using **crampons** and **ice axes**. (See also **climbing** and color photos.)

Ice climbing festival   People climb **ice** individually or in pairs in quarries and on waterfalls or **glaciers**, but they also sometimes gather together in large groups at a specific location to climb, discuss, and attend illustrated lectures. Of the many festivals held, those in Canmore, **Alberta**, **Canada**; Ouray, **Colorado**; and Valdez, **Alaska**, are especially noteworthy.

Ice field   Flat, glacial **ice** such as is found in the **Columbia Ice Field** (Child).

Ice screw   In **climbing**, a small, threaded hollow tube (resembling a **piton**) that can be screwed into **ice** in order to afford **protection**.

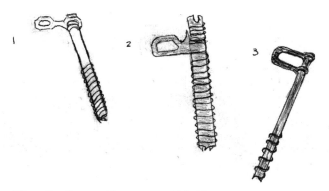

Three Ice Screws (Laura Lindblad)

Ice sheet   A thin layer of ice. (See also **ice**.)

Ice shelf   A glacier that flows into the sea and extends for some distance in the ocean, for example the Ross Ice Shelf in Antarctica. (See also **ice**.)

Ice worm   Reminiscent of the snow flea, this small creature (up to one inch in length) lives below the surface, but can sometimes be found on top of coastal glaciers from Washington to Alaska. Ice worms survive by eating algae plus anything that may blow across the ice.

Iceberg   (A peculiar term combining the English "ice" and the German word for mountain.) A large chunk of a **glacier** that breaks off and floats out into a body of water, especially the ocean.

Icefall   A precipitous and chaotic area of a **glacier**, where **crevasses** open and close and enormous blocks of **ice** can come tumbling down. Ice falls, such as the Khumbu on Mt. Everest, are extremely dangerous.

Iceland   Lowest point, Atlantic Ocean 0 m; highest point, Hvannadalshnukur 2,119 m, 6,952 ft. The name "Land of fire and ice" is well-deserved by Iceland: this lovely island is replete with active **volcanoes**, extensive **glaciers**, and superb **fjords**.

Iceman, the   A frozen, Bronze Age man, "Otzi," found in the Alps in 1991. The *Ultimate Guide: Ice Man Video* points out that at 5,300 years, he is the oldest human to have survived with organs intact. Maintained in a freezer locker in Bolzano, Italy, the mummy has been thawed once for a brief period. Through careful detective work, scholars have concluded that an arrowhead lodged in his shoulder caused his death, which means that he was murdered. (See also **glacier** and **glacier preservation**.)

Ichac, Marcel   (1906–1994) A French movie director; he is probably the most important sport filmmaker in France. Among his achievements are *Karakoram* (1936), *A l'Assaut des Aiguilles du Diable* (1942), *Victoire sur l'Annapurna* (1950), and *Nouveaux Horizons* (1953), the first French short in Cinemascope. He also produced one of the most awarded shorts (its honors include the Academy Award): *La Rivière du Hibou/An Occurrence at Owl Creek Bridge* (Robert Enrico, 1962). Ichac's movies, though sometimes technically maladroit due to a lack of money as well as difficulties during shooting, have always been able to convey the sense of grandeur and the towering power of mountains. (M-A. H.)

Idaho   Lowest point Snake River, on the **Washington** border, 216 m, 710 ft; highest point, **Borah Peak** 3,859 m, 12,662 ft (11th highest of the 50 state highpoints). A beautiful, rugged state, with numerous high mountain ranges, including the Bitterroot, Sawtooth, Pioneer, Beaverhead, and Continental Divide.

Igloo   The traditional dwelling of the Inuit peoples. In some situations, mountaineers cut blocks of **snow** and construct igloos in order to protect themselves from the cold and wind in extreme weather. Snow blocks are also used to build walls in order to protect tents against high winds.

Igneous   (Relating to fire) A type of rock created by the solidification of **magma**. Plutonic rock is formed well below and volcanic rock near or on the earth's surface; **granite**, **gabbro**, and **basalt** are examples. (See also **metamorphic** and **sedimentary**.)

***Il Tempo si è Fermato**/Time Stood Still*   A 1958 Italian film by writer-director Ermanno Olmi (1931–). The movie deals with two antithetical characters, an old fellow from the country and a young man from the city. They find themselves in the Venerocolo Valley, watching over a dam under construction. This is one of the best examples of the clever use of an unfriendly natural environment to enhance the differences between personalities. Their loneliness at almost 10,000 ft, the tension, and their various attempts to get along are made more relevant, pressing, and immediate by the stunning snow-covered mountain (Monte Adamello, 3,554 m, 11,660 ft). The physical and psychological climax occurs in a snowstorm. (M-A. H.)

Illampu 6,362 m, 20,872 ft. This is the 25th highest peak in the **Andes**, and the 16th of 20 premier climbing peaks in that range; it was first ascended in 1928 by Hans Pfann, Alfred Horeschowsky, Hugo Hörtnagel, and Erwin Hein. The peak is located in **Bolivia**.

Illimani 6,462 m, 21,200 ft. This is the 17th highest peak in the **Andes**, and the 11th of 20 premier climbing peaks in that range; it was first climbed in 1898 by William M. Conway, A. Maquignaz, and another alpine guide. This is the second highest major peak in **Bolivia**, an extinct volcano located near **La Paz**. (See also color photos.)

Illinois Lowest point, Mississippi River, on the **Kentucky** border 85 m, 279 ft; highest point, Charles Mound 376 m, 1,235 ft (45th highest of the 50 state highpoints).

Impressions de Voyage/Impressions of a Journey Alexandre Dumas (1802–1870), of *Three Musketeers* and *Monte-Cristo* fame, traveled a lot. To escape political unrest, debts, and other such inconveniences, he journeyed in Switzerland, Italy, Spain, Algeria, Tunisia, and Russia and published accounts of his wanderings (*En Suisse, En Russie*). Of course, he encountered mountains. He climbed in Switzerland, went to the top of **Etna** and **Stromboli**, and passed by the **Caucasus** (he didn't climb there because this trip was made in 1858 and he was rather plump by then). During these trips, he also cooked, encountered people (in *En Suisse*, **Jacques Balmat** tells him of the first climb of **Mont Blanc**), heard stories, told some, invented a few, and reminded the reader that he was one of France's greatest authors. (M-A. H.)

Inca A group of people in **South America** who created a great empire that encompassed many mountainous countries including **Bolivia**, **Chile**, **Ecuador**, and **Peru**. The Incas were conquered by the Spanish invaders. Their various cities were connected by roadways—the Inca Trail. (See also **Machu Picchu**.)

Inderbinen, Ulrich (1900–2004) Inderbinen spent 70 of his 103 years acting as a **guide** for climbers in Switzerland. He reached the **Matterhorn's** summit at least 370 times. He continued to guide until he was 95 years old ("Ulrich").

India Lowest point, Indian Ocean 0 m; highest point, **Kangchenjunga** 8,579 m, 28,146 ft. **Nanda Devi**, at 7,816 m, 25,643 ft, is no longer the highest point of this country, since **Sikkim** was annexed by India.

Indian paintbrush A distinctive, often bright red **flower**, sometimes called scarlet paintbrush, it can be found in **Texas**, **Colorado**, and the Southwest. Some species are parasitic.

Indiana Lowest point, Ohio River 98 m, 320 ft; highest point, Hoosier Hill 383 m, 1,257 ft (44th highest of the 50 state highpoints).

Indonesia Lowest point, Indian Ocean 0 m; highest point, **Carstenz Pyramid** (Puncak Jaya) 5,030 m, 16,502 ft. Located deep within impenetrable jungle and rain forest, Carstensz Pyramid is often considered to have one of the hardest approaches of the **Seven Summits**. (See also color photos.)

Insect These small creatures can be found in mountainous habitats in great numbers and diversity. Extreme cold and vast quantities of **snow** and **ice** do not deter even butterflies from ascending to heights where they cannot long survive. Ants and hornets can be found at altitude. The fungus gnat, rove beetle (Burnie and Wilson), caddis fly, and snow flea do well in mountainous environments. Spiders (technically arachnids) also do not let the heights deter them from prospering. Insects provide sustenance for smaller **mammals** and **birds** that also thrive at higher elevations. (See also **mosquito**.)

Inside Passage An extraordinary systems of straits and inlets, leading from **Vancouver** all the way to **Glacier Bay**. Numerous **fjords** and magnificent **glaciers** can be seen from the cruise ships running the Inside Passage; fantastic snowy peaks abound, as well as wonderful marine wildlife: orcas, whales, seals, sea lions, and all manner of birds and fish.

Institut Géographique National (IGN) The French equivalent of the **U.S. Geological Survey**, it produces superb, highly accurate topographical maps. (See also color maps.)

Instruction   One can take a class, join a tour, or hire a tutor or guide in order to learn how to ski, snowboard, or climb. One can also consult a host of useful books. See especially **Ament** (*How*), Cox and Fulsaas, **Chouinard**, and Fyffe and Peter for climbing.

Insurance   Because mountain **rescue** can be extremely expensive, many organizations and clubs provide some degree of insurance coverage for their members. For those people venturing above 20,000 ft, additional coverage is required. Uninsured climbers in many parts of the world are responsible for the costs of a rescue; in the United States, federal employees frequently perform the rescue and do not charge (although that may change). Private rescue groups also help and do not require payment.

International Federation of Mountain Guides Associations   Some 35 member groups from many countries comprise this organization (www.ivbv.info).

International Mountain Society   Located in Bern, Switzerland, this organization is devoted to research, development, and publication concerning mountains.

International Year of the Mountains   The United Nations designated 2002 the Year of the Mountains to help protect and celebrate one fifth of the earth's land (www.unesco.org/mab/IYM.htm).

Intrusion   **Igneous rock** that has intruded itself into other rock. The long, vertical **basalt** column on the Middle **Teton** is a blatant example. (See also color photos.)

Iowa   Lowest point, Mississippi River and Des Moines River 146 m, 480 ft; highest point, Hawkeye Point 509 m, 1,670 ft (42nd highest of the 50 state highpoints).

Iran   Lowest point, Caspian Sea −28 m, −92 ft; highest point, Qolleh-ye **Damavand** 5,670 m, 18,603 ft. This ancient land is home to numerous mountain ranges, including the Elburz Mountains, and the Kūh-E Bozqūsh in the north. In the central desert area, the Ddasht-E Kavīr depression is a noteworthy feature. Important summits include Zard Kūh 4,545 m, 14,910 ft; Kūh-E Gereh 3,975 m, 13,041 ft; near the ancient city of Persepolis, Kūh-E Harmā 3,202 m, 10,505 ft, and to the east, Kūh-E Seh Konj 3,995 m, 13,107 ft; finally, near the Pakistan border, Kūh-E Bazma 3,491 m, 11,453 ft. The region is quite active tectonically, and major earthquakes occur regularly in the northern part of Iran, where large dormant volcanoes, including Damavand, dominate the landscape. (See also color photos.)

Iraq   Lowest point, Persian Gulf 0 m; highest point, Haji Ibrahim 3,600 m, 11,811 ft.

Ireland   Lowest point, Atlantic Ocean 0 m; highest point, Carrauntoohil 1,041 m, 3,415 ft.

Ironmongery   (Colloquial) See **gear**.

Irvine, Andrew "Sandy" Comyn   (1902–1924) Born: Birkenhead, England. In 1924, he and **George Mallory** disappeared on **Everest**; they were last seen high on the north ridge of the mountain and had clearly broken the altitude record reached by any human at that time. He was a superb, inventive, and resourceful climber, who was mentored and appreciated by Mallory. Bibliography: *The Fight for Everest: 1924* (1925), by E. F. Norton, *The Irvine Diaries* (1979), by Herbert Carr, *The Mystery of Mallory and Irvine* (1986), by Tom Holzel and Audrey Salkeld, *The Ghosts of Everest* (1999), by Jochen Hemmleb, Larry A. Johnson, and Eric R. Simonson, *Fearless on Everest* (2000), by Julie Summers. (See also www.pbs.org/wgbh/nova/everest/lost/mystery/.)

Irving, Robert Lock Graham   (1877–1969) Born: England. Bibliography: *The Romance of Mountaineering* (1935), *The Alps* (1938), *The Mountain Way* (1938), *Ten Great Mountains* (1940), *The Mountains Shall Bring Peace* (1947), *A History of British Mountaineering* (1955).

Island   A small or large extruding mass of rock that rises from the ocean floor. If fairly level with the ocean surface, an island is not considered a mountain, but if it rises well above the surface, it is; some islands are volcanic in origin. Thus, it is possible to think of Manhattan as a small mountain. (See also **Mauna Kea**.)

Ismail Samani, Pik   (Formerly Pik Kommunizma) 7,495 m, 24,590 ft. This major peak is located within the **Pamirs** in **Tajikistan**. It was first ascended in 1933 by Evgenii Abalakov, **solo**.

Israel   Lowest point, **Dead Sea** −408 m, −1,339 ft; highest point, Har Meron 1,208 m, 3,963 ft.

Istoro Nal   7,388 m, 24,240 ft. This major peak is located within the **Hindu Kush** in **Pakistan**.

Italy   Lowest point, Mediterranean Sea 0 m; highest point, **Mont Blanc de Courmayeur** 4,748 m, 15,577 ft, on the border with **France**. The highest peak shared between **Switzerland** and Italy is **Monte Rosa** (**Dufourspitze**), 4,634 m, 15,203 ft; the highest peak entirely within Italy is the **Gran Paradiso**, 4,061 m, 13,323 ft (the **Mont Blanc** de Courmayeur is a **satellite** of Mont Blanc; for more information about the question of Italy's highpoint, see the excellent discussion on www.peakbagger.com/peak/italyhi.htm). Italy counts numerous mountain ranges, including the **Apennines** and large volcanoes: **Mt. Etna** 3,350 m, 10,990 ft, the highest active volcano in **Europe**, and **Vesuvius** 1,281 m, 4,202 ft, which destroyed the Roman cities of **Pompeii** and Herculaneum in 79 B.C.E.

Iztaccíhuatl   (also Ixtaccíhuatl) (Aztec for "sleeping woman") 5,295 m, 17,373 ft. One of the three major Mexican **volcanoes** that climbers relish. The mountain has three distinct summits: la cabeza (the head), el cuello (the neck) and el seno (the breast); thus explaining its name. Legend has it that Iztaccíhuatl and **Popocatépetl** were once lovers, but were turned into mountains after displeasing the Aztec gods. Iztaccíhuatl was turned into a dead mountain, while Popocatépetl was condemned to eternal life, a terrible curse: forever he must gaze upon the extinct form of his beloved soul mate. Popocatépetl's anguish is to blame for the frequent tremors rattling the region. The mountain is located along the Neo-Volcánica **Cordillera**, which also includes Popocatépetl and **Nevado Toluca**. The first recorded climb occurred in 1889, by James de Salis. (See also **Orizaba**.)

J

Jam In rock climbing, to place a hand or other extremity inside a crack and wedge it in order to gain support, or to move upward using alternating jams.

Jamaica Lowest point, Caribbean Sea 0 m; highest point, Blue Mountain Peak 2,256 m, 7,402 ft.

Jan Mayen Lowest point, Norwegian Sea 0 m; highest point, Haakon VII Toppen/Beerenberg 2,277 m, 7,470 ft.

Jannu 7,710 m, 25,295 ft. A magnificent Himalayan summit, located in the **Kangchenjunga** Himal. It was first climbed in 1962 by Robert Paragot, Paul Kellar, **René Desmaison**, and Gyalzen Mitchu Sherpa. (See also color photos.)

Japan Lowest point, Hachiro-gata −4 m, −13 ft; highest point, **Fuji-san** 3,776 m, 12,388 ft. Japan is comprised of five main islands: Honshu, Kyushu, Shikoku, Hokkaido, and Ryukyu. It is a very mountainous land, with cold winters, especially in the beautiful pristine northern island of Hokkaido. Geographically, Japan is an island chain that lies along a fault line where **tectonic plates** collide, thus ensuring much volcanic activity, as well as devastating earthquakes and tsunamis.

Japanese Alps The major mountain **range** in **Japan**.

Jarvis Island Lowest point, Pacific Ocean 0 m; highest point, unnamed location 7 m, 23 ft.

Jasper Smaller than its southern counterpart, **Banff**, Jasper is a small town and the gateway to **Jasper National Park** in **Alberta**, **Canada**.

Jasper National Park The northern component of the **Banff–Jasper National Parks** complex, its southern limit coincides with the **Columbia Ice Field**. Magnificent peaks of the **Canadian Rockies** abound, as well as wildlife and grand vistas.

Jay The gray (also called the Canada) and the more common blue and Steller's can be found at higher elevations. Their loud screeches are disconcerting.

Jeremiah Johnson A 1972 American film directed by Sidney Pollack, starring Robert Redford, after a novel by Vardis Fischer. "His name was Jeremiah Johnson. They say he wanted to be a mountain man. The story goes that he was a man of the proper wit and adventurous mind, suited for the mountains" states the off-screen voice at the beginning of the movie. Johnson hardly climbs anything, but he does travel in snow-packed mountains, meeting strange hunters, Indians he cannot understand, a shocked boy who remains silent for the whole movie, and an Indian girl he marries. The photography by Duke Callaghan is glorious. (M-A. H.)

Jersey Lowest point, Atlantic Ocean 0 m; highest point, unnamed location 143 m, 469 ft.

Jet stream The system of high-altitude air currents found in the upper atmosphere; these currents, responsible for the difference of time that a plane takes to fly eastward and westward, can reach astonishing speeds, as high as 500 km/h, or 350 mph. The highest summits in the world are often tall enough to be directly subjected to these extremely fierce and dangerous winds. On Everest, many climbers note that the jet stream can be heard from the Khumbu Glacier, and sounds like an express train, roaring continuously.

Jirishanca 6,126 m, 20,098 ft. An important summit of the Cordillera **Huayhuash** in **Peru**; this is the 56th highest peak in the Andes, and the 20th of 20 premier climbing peaks in that range. It was first ascended in 1957 by T. Egger and S. Jungmeier.

Joch (G) See **pass**.

John Muir Trail A ca. 200-mile trail that is often contiguous with the **Pacific Crest Trail**; it connects **Yosemite National Park** and **Mt. Whitney**. For more detailed information, one can consult the following website: www.pcta.org/about_trail/muir/over.asp. (See also **John Muri**.)

Johnston Atoll Lowest point, Pacific Ocean 0 m; highest point, Summit Peak 5 m, 16 ft.

Jones, Owen Glynne (1867–1899) Born: Paddington, London. Bibliography: *Rock Climbing in the English Lake District* (1897).

Jongsong Peak 7,483 m, 24,550 ft. This major peak is located within the **Himalayas** in **Nepal**.

Jordan Lowest point, Dead Sea −408 m, −1,339 ft; highest point, Jabal Ram 1,734 m, 5,689 ft. Jordan shares the Dead Sea with Israel, and is the home of the world-famous ruins of **Petra**. (See also color photos.)

Joshua Tree National Park Located in southern **California**, this botanically interesting park is beloved by rock climbers for the many challenging climbs it offers.

Journals See **periodicals**.

Juan de Nova Island Lowest point, Indian Ocean 0 m; highest point, unnamed location 10 m, 33 ft.

Jughandle (Jug) In rock climbing, a large, easily grasped hold.

Jumar See **ascender**.

Jungfrau 4,158 m, 13,641 ft. This is the 35th highest of the 60 major 4,000-meter peaks of the **Alps**. It was first ascended in 1811 by Hieronymus Meyer, and the **chamois** hunters Alois Volker and Josef Bortis. The Jungfrau is a truly beautiful peak, the third highest in the **Bernese Alps**. Its name means "Virgin" in German; a train travels part way up toward the summit.

Juniper A widely dispersed coniferous **tree** that can sometimes be found on cliffs.

K

K2 A 1992 American–British–Japanese film directed by Franc Roddam (*Quadrophenia*) dealing with a party attempting to climb **K2**. Screenwriters do not believe that climbing one of the most dangerous mountains on earth is dramatic enough to sustain attention; they usually add villains, explosives, and lust to their films. *K2* is different: it describes a summit attempt, and was shot in part on location. The characters do interact dramatically though. Mountain fans might be saddened, since dreadful falls and snowstorms are kept to a minimum, and the result is quite believable. The summitting was actually shot in **British Columbia**. (M-A. H.)

K2 (Also **Godwin Austen**, Chogori) 8,611 m, 28,251 ft. Located in **Pakistan**'s **Karakoram**, K2 is the world's second highest mountain. K2 was first climbed on July 31, 1954, by **Achille Compagnoni** and **Lino Lacedelli**, from Italy. As of the end of 1999, K2 had only been climbed 164 times; 49 climbers perished on the mountain, either attempting it or after summitting. It is considered the most difficult of the **8,000-meter peaks** to climb; it is also a truly magnificent peak, grand on a scale only found in the **Himalayas** and **Karakoram**. Unfortunately, the ongoing dispute over **Kashmir** between **India** and **Pakistan** means that soldiers are patrolling the high ridges in the area and that actual battle fire occurs from time to time, in this otherwise pristine high mountain region. (See also the **14 8,000-Meter Peaks** sidebar.)

Kabru 7,338 m, 24,074 ft. This major peak is located within the **Himalayas** in **Nepal**. It was first ascended in 1965, by a Swiss expedition.

Kain, Conrad (1883–1934) An Austrian-Canadian **guide** whose **first ascents** include **Robson** and the Bugaboo Spire (Unsworth, *Encyclopaedia*).

Kamchatka Peninsula Located in far eastern Russia, the Kamchatka Peninsula lies between the Sea of Okhotsk on the west and the Pacific Ocean and Bering Sea to the east. It is about 1,200 km, 750 miles, long from north to south and approximately 480 km, 300 miles, across at its widest. Two major mountain ranges, the Sredinny and Vostochny, extend along the peninsula and rise to 4,750 m, 15,584 ft, at the Klyuchevskaya volcano. Kamchatka counts 127 volcanoes, 22 of them still active, and a number of geysers and hot springs can be found there. The majority of the active volcanoes lie along a fault line on the eastern flank of the Vostochny Range.

Kamet 7,756 m, 25,446 ft. This major peak is located within the **Himalayas** on the border between **India** and **Tibet**. It was first ascended in 1931, by **Frank Smythe**, **Eric Shipton**, R. L. Holdsworth, and Lewa Sherpa.

Kamm (G) A jagged snow or rock ridge.

Kangbachen 7,858 m, 25,781 ft. This major peak is located in the **Kangchenjunga** Himal in **Nepal**; it was first ascended in 1959 by an English expedition.

Kangchenjunga (Also Kanchenjunga, Kanchanfanga) 8,579 m, 28,146 ft. Found in **Nepal**, this is the third highest mountain in the world; it is considered a sacred site (and so respectful climbers do not actually step on the top). The first ascent of Kangchenjunga occurred on May 25, 1955; an English team, comprised of G. Band

Kangchenjunga (Vittorio Sella/National Geographic)

and J. Brown, made the summit on that day. As of the end of 1999, the peak had been climbed 153 times; 38 climbers had died, either attempting the summit or descending from the mountain. (See also the **14 8,000-Meter Peaks** sidebar and color photos.)

Kangto 7,090 m, 23,260 ft Located within the **Himalayas** in **Tibet**.

Kanjut Sar 7,760 m, 25,459 ft. This major peak is located within the **Karakoram** Range in **Pakistan**.

Kansas Lowest point, Verdigris River, on the **Oklahoma** border 207 m, 679 ft; highest point, Mt. Sunflower 1,231 m, 4,039 ft (28th highest of the 50 state highpoints).

Karakoram A French documentary by **Marcel Ichac** about the 1936 Henry de Segogne expedition to climb **Gasherbrum I** (Hidden Peak; 8,068 m). Ichac's first effort in filming high-mountain journeys describes this unlucky at-

tempt. It was, along with **Geheimnis Tibet**, among the first opportunities to have a close look at the Himalayas. (M-A. H.)

Karakoram(s) A 250-mile **range** in **Pakistan** divided into the Greater and the Lesser; it is here that **K2**, the world's second highest mountain, is located. Some of the largest **glaciers** in the world can be found in the Karakorams, including the **Baltoro**.

Karisimbi 4,507 m, 14,787 ft. A large **volcano** and the highest point in **Rwanda**.

Karlowicz, Mieczyslaw (1876–1909) A Polish composer born in Wiszniew (now Vishnevo, Belarus); he was educated in Heidelberg, Prague, Dresden, and Warsaw. He wrote songs, piano pieces, and six tone poems of a dark atmosphere in the manner of the early Richard Strauss. Toward the end of his life, he developed a strong attraction to the **Tatras** Mountains, the natural border between Poland and Slovakia. He was a member of a local society, published accounts of his excursions in papers, wrote guides, and was among the pioneers of mountain photography in Poland. He died during a climb, killed by an avalanche. (M-A.H.)

Karst An area of dolomite or **limestone** that has been eroded and therefore contains sinkholes and **caves**.

Katabatic wind See **winds**.

Katahdin, Mt. 1,605 m, 5,267 ft. An impressive, if relatively small, mountain and the highest peak in **Maine**. **Zumwalt** calls it the most difficult climb of all of the eastern U.S. **highpoints**. A large **cairn** has been erected on the summit, in order to allow the peak to reach the mile-high mark, at 1,609 m, or 5,280 ft. The Knife-Edge route to the summit is a precipitous **ridge**, and the east face of the mountain presents an impressive sight, especially in winter.

Katmai, Mt. In 1912, this **Alaskan volcano** erupted in what Ritchie calls "one of the most famous events in volcanology." Katmai spewed out vast quantities of ash and then collapsed, creating a large **caldera**.

Kauk, Ron (fl. mid-1970s–late 1990s) He was rivaled only by **John Bacher** as the star **free** climber in **Yosemite**.

Kazakhstan Lowest point, Vpadina Kaundy −132 m, −433 ft; highest point, Khan Tangiri Shyngy (Pik Khan-Tengri) 7,005 m, 22,982 ft.

Keay, John Born: England. Bibliography: *The Gilgit Game—The Explorers of the Western Himalayas, 1886–95* (1979), *When Men and Mountains Meet—The Explorers of the Western Himalayas, 1820–75* (1977), *The Great Arc* (2000).

Keenlyside, Francis Born: England. Bibliography: *Peaks and Pioneers: The Story of Mountaineering* (1975).

Kelseya An unusual plant that forms a green mosslike mat on steep rock surfaces, from which the small, purplish flowers propagate.

Kenai Fjords National Park A superb Alaskan park, located a few hours from Anchorage. Here, the landscape is dominated by a superabundance of **ice fields** and **glaciers** that slowly sculpt majestic **fjords**, and then flow directly into the sea. Highlights include the mighty Harding Ice Field (775 sq km, 300 sq miles), and Exit Glacier, a re-

treating mass of ice near Seward, whose ancient fjord is now Resurrection Bay; numerous beautiful waterfalls, small coves, and deep fjords; and wildlife ranging from mighty orcas and bears, to seals and horned puffins. Flora is also extensive in the summer months, and includes such lovely flowers as Nookta lupines and dwarf dogwood; the woods are very dense at low elevations, but quickly give way to alpine and arctic vegetation, followed by the icy world of **nunataks**.

Kennedy Peak 4,238 m, 13,905 ft. A high peak located in the **Yukon** Territory in Canada.

Kentucky Lowest point, Mississippi River, Tennessee border 78 m, 257 ft; highest point, Black Mountain 1,263 m, 4,145 ft (27th highest of the 50 state highpoints).

Kenya Lowest point, Indian Ocean 0 m; highest point, **Mt. Kenya** 5,199 m, 17,058 ft.

Kenya, Mt. 5,199 m, 17,058 ft. An impressive mountain in **Kenya**, it is the second highest **peak** in Africa and much harder to climb than **Kilimanjaro**.

Khan Tengri 7,005 m, 22,982 ft. Located on the border between **Kyrgyzstan**, **Kazakhstan**, and **China**, this mighty peak of the **Tien Shan** Range was first ascended in 1931 by an expedition led by M. T. Pogrebetsky. It is the highest peak in Kazakhstan.

Khiangyang Kish 7,852 m, 25,761 ft. This major peak in the **Karakoram** was first ascended in 1971 by A. Zawada, A. Heinrich, J. Stryczynski, and R. Szafirski.

Khumbu Icefall A highly crevassed section just above base camp on **Everest's** southern route on the Nepalese side, in which enormous blocks of **ice** constantly threaten to come crashing down. It is extremely dangerous and many lives have been lost here. The danger is further compounded by the constant microtectonic activity related to the continuing **upthrust** of the **Himalayas**, which results in a multitude of small (2–3 on the **Richter scale**) earthquakes, making the icefall even more unstable.

Khyber Pass A famous **pass** between Afghanistan and Pakistan. It runs for 33 miles and narrows to a mere 10 feet.

Kidd, William Winston (Billy) (1943–) When he won medals in Alpine skiing at the 1964

Olympics, he became the first American male to manage this feat.

Kilauea 1,247 m, 4,090 ft. An active **volcano** located in **Hawaii Volcanoes National Park**. Because its ongoing eruptions are not dangerously explosive, it is visited by countless specialists, and also tourists, who are able to observe the **lava** flows at close hand. The Kilauea **caldera** once contained an active lava lake, one of only two in the world, the second one being located in the **Nyiragongo** volcano in the **Great Rift Valley** area of East Africa.

Kilimanjaro, Mt. (Also Kibo) 5,895 m, 19,340 ft. Located on the border between **Tanzania** and **Kenya**, this is the highest mountain in Africa; it is also the largest lone-standing **volcano** in the world. A climb of this peak begins in tropical rain forests and ends on **glaciers** (which are currently receding). (See also the **Seven Summits** sidebar.)

Killdeer A plover that favors though does not require water. Its screeching call is haunting; it may scurry away or feign injury to protect its young.

Killy, Jean-Claude (1943–) French skier; he won three gold medals in the 1968 Winter **Olympics**. He currently holds an important position within the Olympic Committee.

Kinabalu 4,101 m, 13,455 ft. A mountain on the island of Borneo and the highest in **Malaysia**.

King Peak 5,173 m, 16,973 ft. This is the fourth highest peak in **Canada**. It is a heavily glaciated, remote mountain standing near **Mt. Logan**, in the **Kluane-Logan National Park**.

Kingman Reef Lowest point, Pacific Ocean 0 m; highest point, unnamed location 1 m, 3 ft.

Kings Peak 4,123 m, 13,528 ft. The highpoint of **Utah** is also a wonderful peak, rising high above the Uinta Mountains. A 13-mile-long trail leads to the peak, which can be climbed in a long day.

Kiribati Lowest point, Pacific Ocean 0 m; highest point, unnamed location on Banaba 81 m, 266 ft.

Kirkus, Colin (1910–1942) Born: Liverpool, England. One of the very best rock climbers of the 1930s, especially in Wales. Bibliography: *Let's Go Climbing* (1941), *Hands of a Climber* (1993) a biography by Steve Dean.

Klammer, Franz (1953–) An exceptionally exciting, Austrian downhill skier. He won a gold medal in the 1976 Innsbruck Winter Olympics.

Klipspringer A very small, ca 25 pound antelope; it inhabits areas along the eastern coast of Africa.

Kluane-Logan National Park Located in Canada's **Yukon** Territory, this vast area is adjacent to **Alaska's Wrangell–St. Elias National Park**, and contains some of the world's largest nonpolar **glaciers**, as well as **Mt. Logan**,and **Mt. Saint Elias**, the second highest mountains in North America, respectively. Most of the park is accessible only by air, and the mountains are very remote and rarely climbed. Weather conditions near the St. Elias coastal range can be extremely icy and snowy, while the interior, lying in its **rain shadow**, is comparatively dry. Like its sister park, Wrangell–St. Elias, it is a haven for abundant wildlife, including **Dall sheep**, **bears**, **foxes**, and **eagles**.

Klucker, Christian (1853–1928) Born: Austria. One of the greatest of all the alpine **guides**, who made many first ascents, especially with Ludwig Norman-Neruda in 1890. Bibliography: *Adventures of an Alpine Guide* (1932) published posthumously, *The Climbs of Norman-Neruda* (1899) by Ludwig Norman-Neruda.

Knife edge An especially narrow, steep, and therefore dangerous **ridge**, for example, the Knife Edge on **Mt. Katahdin**.

Knot In **climbing**, since one's life may depend on a **rope** tied to a **belay** point or another climber, knots are extremely important. The figure-eight, along with a backup knot, is used to connect the rope to a **harness** or **carabiner**. A **Prusik** allows one to move a smaller rope up along a larger one, but then to put weight on the former without pulling it downwards. Thus, a person can hoist herself up a vertical rope. This method has been replaced by the use of **ascenders**. Other important knots include the clove hitch and double fisherman's. See Clem et al. on "Ropes and Knot Tying," a chapter in Auerbach.

Koch, Stephen (1970–) He attempted to snowboard down **Everest** during the summer of 2003; had he succeeded, he would have become the first person to snowboard or ski the **Seven Summits** (Calhoun emended).

Kongur (Kungur) 7,719 m, 25,324 ft. This major peak is located within the **Muztagh Ata** Range in **China**. It was first ascended in 1981, by **Michael Ward** and party.

Kor, Layton (fl. early to mid-1960s) Kor dominated American rock climbing, especially in his fast **aid** and many **first ascents** in **Colorado**. At six-foot-seven, he was a formidable figure. His autobiography is entitled *Beyond the Vertical*. (Pat Ament, personal comment.)

Korea, North Lowest point, Sea of Japan 0 m; highest point, Paektu-san 2,744 m, 9,003 ft.

Korea, South Lowest point, Sea of Japan 0 m; highest point, Halla-san 1,950 m, 6,398 ft.

Korzhenevski Peak 7,105 m, 23,310 ft. This mountain is located within the **Pamirs** in **Tajikistan**.

Kosciusko, Mt. 2,228 m, 7,310 ft. The highest peak in Australia, and one of the **Seven Summits**. (See also **Carstensz Pyramid** and the **Seven Summits** sidebar.)

Kosciuzko See **Kosciusko**.

Krakatoa (Krakatau) 813 m, 2,667 ft. In 1883, this Indonesian **volcano** exploded and destroyed its island in one of the most powerful eruptions known; 36,000 people were killed and the world's weather was affected. (See Winchester's *Krakatoa*.)

Krakauer, Jon An adventurer, climber, and best-selling author; his books include Into Thin Air, *Into the Wild*, and *Eiger Dreams*.

Kraus, Hans (fl. early 1940s–mid 1950s) His bold, 1941 lead of "High Exposure," in the **Shawangunks**, was a significant rock first ascent.

Kropp, Göran (1966–2002) In 1996, Kropp rode a bicycle from Sweden to **Nepal** and back. During his stay in Asia, he climbed **Everest** unsupported, lugging a 150-pound pack to **base camp**. He was killed in a rock climbing accident. (See his account in *Ultimate High*, and *Jag Klarede Det/*I Made It; a Swedish film version is also avail-

able.) His climbing resume includes the following: in 1988, **Pik Lenin** (7,134 m); in 1989, Illiniza Sur (5,266 m), **Cotopaxi** (5,897 m, solo), **Chimborazo** (6,310 m), **Illimani** (6,402 m, solo), Huayana Potosi (6,088 m, solo, new route), **Illampu** (6,362 m); in 1990, **Mustagh Tower** (7,273 m); in 1991, **Pik Pobeda** (7,134 m, solo); in 1992, **Cho Oyu** (8,201 m); in 1993, **K2** (8,611 m); in 1994, **Broad Peak** (8,047 m, solo, 17 hours); in 1996, Mt. Everest (8,850 m) without supplemental oxygen); in 1997, **Shisha Pangma** (8,046 m); in 1999, Mt. Everest.

Kugy, Julius (1858–1944) Born: Austria. To quote the excellent, informative website www.simpkins57.freeserve.co.uk/mountain_lakes _books/whoswho/whoswhodetails.html, he was "A climber who, because of his love, knowledge and experience of the **Julian Alps**, was revered by the people of that area." Bibliography: *Alpine Pilgrimage* (1934), *Son of the Mountains: The Life of an Alpine Guide* (Anton Oitzinger) (1938).

Kukuczka, Jerzy (1948–1989) The second person (after **Reinhold Messner**) to reach the summits of all 14 **8,000-meter peaks**. Bibliography: *My Vertical World*. His climbing resume is very impressive: 1979, **Lhotse**; 1980, **Mt. Everest**; 1981, **Makalu** (solo); 1982, **Broad Peak**; 1983, **Gasherbrum I** and **Gasherbrum II**; 1984, Broad Peak; 1985, **Dhaulagiri, Cho Oyu, Nanga Parbat**, and **Kangchenjunga** (!); 1986, **K2** and **Manaslu**; 1987, **Annapurna** and **Shisha Pangma**. He was lost on the south face of Lhotse on October 24, 1989, at an altitude of 8,200 m.

Kula Kangri 7,554 m, 24,783 ft. This major peak is located within the **Himalayas** in **Bhutan**, where it is the highest point.

Kun Lun A range in **Tibet**.

Kuwait Lowest point, Persian Gulf 0 m; highest point, unnamed location 306 m, 1,004 ft.

Kyrgyzstan Lowest point, Kara-Darya 132 m, 433 ft; highest point, Jengish Chokusu (**Pik Podeba** or Pobedy) 7,439 m, 24,406 ft.

L

La Tibetan word meaning pass; for example, Lo La on **Everest**.

La Grande Guerra/The Great War An Italian film directed by Mario Monicelli in 1959. This is both a realistic account of World War I in the Alps (with stunts, explosions, numerous extras, and much bloodshed) and a black comedy involving the unlikely pair formed by loudmouth Vittorio Gassman and shy Alberto Sordi as well as voluptuous Silvana Mangano. (M-A. H.)

La Paz The capital of Bolivia lies at elevations between 3,250 m and 4,100 m, or 10,650 ft and 13,250 ft; it is the highest capital city in the world. This often leads to cases of **acute mountain sickness** for the occasional visitor that can range from mild to severe. The **Cordillera Real** serves as an impressive background landscape, and is dominated by **Illimani**.

Labrador See **Newfoundland and Labrador**.

Laccolith Solidified **magma**, that is, **igneous** rock, that remains underground and causes the surface to bulge.

Lacedelli, Lino (1925–) Born: Italy. The first, with **Achille Compagnoni**, to ascend **K2**, in 1954. Bibliography: *The Ascent of K2* (1955) by Ardito Desio.

Lachenal, Louis (1921–1955) A Frenchman who was one of the main protagonists in the epochal **first ascent** of **Annapurna**, he summitted the 8,091-m (26,545 ft) peak together with **Maurice Herzog** on June 3, 1950. His climbing companions affectionately called him "Biscante." He was a very strong, dedicated climber who passed away in the prime of his life doing what he loved most: climbing the high peaks.

Lachmatter, Franz (1878–1933) An outstanding Swiss **guide** (Ardito).

Lagginhorn 4,010 m, 13,156 ft. This is the 58th highest of the 60 major 4,000-meter peaks in the **Alps**. It was first ascended in 1856 by Johann Imseng, Franz-Josef Andenmatten, E. L. Ames, and six other anonymous alpinists. The peak is located in the **Weissmies massif** of the **Valaisan Alps** in **Switzerland**.

Lahar A powerful landslide of volcanic ash and melted glacial ice—that is, mud—that inundates and destroys anything in its path.

Lake A body of usually fresh water contained within a prescribed area. Mountain lakes are often found in **cirques** and are sometimes called **tarns**. At times, the **crater** of a **volcano** fills with water. An artificial lake is formed when a river is dammed between two natural elevated extrusions.

Lake Baika See Baikal, Lake

Lake Geneva See Geneva Lake

Lake Louise A pristinely beautiful and much-visited mountain lake near **Banff** in Canada.

Lake Tanganyika This is the second largest lake in East Africa. It is the longest freshwater lake in the world: 660 km, 410 miles. It is also the second deepest lake in the world, after Lake **Baïkal** in **Russia**: 1,436 m, 4,710 ft. It is quite elongated, with a width ranging from 16 to 72 km, 10 to 45 miles; its area is approximately 32,900 sq km, 12,700 sq miles. Lake Tanganyika forms a natural border between Tanzania and Congo; it is located at the southern end of the western **Great Rift Valley**; the mountainous land rises steeply from its shores.

Lake Titicaca A large lake located along the border of **Bolivia** and **Peru**; its surface lies at an elevation of 3,812 m, 12,507 ft. Some indigenous peoples build reed islands, which they inhabit.

Lamasery   A monastery built high up in the Himalayas and inhabited by Buddhist monks (lamas). Thangboche in **Nepal** is located at almost 4,000 m, 13,000 ft; it is here that mountaineering expeditions are often blessed. Without these ceremonies and the rituals performed at **base camp**, **Sherpas** and other local people (porters) would not help the climbers. (See also **puja**.)

Landslide   The movement of any substance (rock, mud) except snow downward along a **slope**. A landslide can roll along at more than 200 mph. (See also **avalanche**, **lahar**, and **stonefall**.)

Langley, Mt.   The southernmost 14,000-footer in the **California Sierras**. Its first recorded climb was performed in 1864 by William Bellows.

Laos   Lowest point, Mekong River 70 m, 230 ft; highest point, Phou Bia 2,817 m, 9,242 ft.

Lassen Peak   3,187 m, 10,457 ft. One of only two active **volcanoes** in the continental **United States**, it is located at the southern end of the **Cascades**, in a **national park**. (See also color photos; Mt. Lassen.)

Latitude   A measure of the angle from a given location to the equator; it can vary from 0 degrees at the equator to 90 degrees at the poles. The labels *north* and *south* refer to the two hemispheres. (Compare **longitude**.)

***L'Atlantide*/Atlantis**   This novel by once famous French writer Pierre Benoît (1886–1962) locates the remains of Atlantis in the **Hoggar** Mountains. Its queen, Antinea, captures explorers and holds them captive in her palace. It won the Grand Prize of the Académie Française in 1919. No less than five cinema versions exist; the first one in France was made in 1921. A French–German–English version by Georg-Wilhelm Pabst with Brigitte Helm (of *Metropolis* fame) appeared in 1932. The 1947 American version, *Siren of the Atlantis*, by Greg Tallas, stars Maria Montez, "the queen of Technicolor," but is in black and white for it reuses parts of an earlier film (both were produced by Seymour Neybenzhl). Edgar G. Ulmer directed a 1961 French–Italian updated version. Eventually, a French TV version shot in En-

glish for theatrical release was added in 1992 starring Victoria Mohoney. (M-A. H.)

Latvia   Lowest point, Baltic Sea 0 m; highest point, Gaizinkalns 312 m, 1,024 ft.

Lauener, Ulrich   (1821–1900) **Guide** who holds the first ascent of **Monte Rosa**.

Lauteraarhorn   4,042 m, 13,261 ft. This is the 50th highest of the 60 major 4,000-meter peaks in the **Alps**. It was first ascended in 1842 by Edouard Desor, Arnold Escher von der Linth, C. Gerard, and five guides. It is located in the **Bernese Alps** of **Switzerland**.

Lava   When **magma** flows out of a volcano onto the surface, it is called lava.

Lava dome   Lava piled up near a **vent**.

Lava flow   Solidified lava that has moved away from its source; also, a large volume of molten lava moving on the surface.

Lava tube   An open area inside (under the surface) of a **lava flow**. An external opening is called a **skylight**. One can walk through these tubes or tunnels in **Hawaii Volcanoes National Park**.

Layback   See **lieback**.

Le Blond, Elizabeth Alice Frances   (1861–1934) Born: England. According to www.simpkins57.freeserve.co.uk/mountain_lakes_books/whoswho/whoswhodetails.html, "Founder and first president of the Ladies Alpine Club in 1907. She also published under her other married names of Mrs. Fred Burnaby or Mrs. Main." Bibliography: *The High Alps in Winter* (1883) by Mrs. Fred Burnaby, *High Life and Towers of Silence* (1886) by Mrs. Fred Burnaby, *My Home in the Alps* (1892) by Mrs. Main, *Hints on Snow Photography* (1894) by Mrs. Main, *True Tales of Mountain Adventure for Non-climbers Young and Old* (1902), *Adventures on the Roof of the World* (1904), *Mountaineering in the Land of the Midnight Sun* (1908), *Day In, Day Out* (1928) autobiography.

Lead   In **climbing**, to go first. On rock or vertical ice, the lead climber places the **protection**; in a group of two, which is most usual, the follower removes it. The follower may have to wait in one spot for an hour or more, until the leader reaches a point of adequate safety or the end of the **rope**. In **mountaineering**, the leader must **break trail** in deep snow or cut steps in the ice (although the latter does not occur very often today). Because leading can be extremely de-energizing, climbers frequently alternate leads. On the question of the optimum number of climbers on a rope, it should be noted that roped parties larger than two or three climbers are inherently much slower and less secure, especially on an exposed area: for example crossing a couloir or traversing under **séracs**. Sometimes one encounters parties of up to eight inexperienced climbers roped to a single **guide**; this practice can be quite dangerous, as the guide cannot physically arrest the fall of more than two people; for other climbers in the area, such parties should be avoided, as they also tend to create ice, snow, or rockfall. (See also **pitch**.)

"Leave No Trace" A wilderness philosophy or ethic that advocates leaving the visited area exactly as it was found (www.lnt.org). (See also **ethics**.)

Lebanon Lowest point, Mediterranean Sea 0 m; highest point, Qurnat as Sawda' 3,088 m, 10,131 ft.

Ledge *Band* (G), *cengia* (I), *vire* (F). A flat rocky extrusion on a **slope** or the face of a mountain. Ledges vary in width from a few feet to mere inches. They provide a resting or sleeping place for rock climbers.

Lenin, Pik 7,134 m, 23,405 ft. This major peak is located within the **Pamirs**, at the border between **Tajikistan** and **Kyrgyzstan**. It was first ascended in 1928, by Karl Wien, Eugene Allwein, and Erwin Schneider.

Lenticular cloud This very specific type of cloud is generally an ominous sign, forewarning of an impending storm, as it reflects the high winds at altitude and the shear present in the atmosphere. **Mt. Shasta** is famous for the frequency of lenticular clouds near its summit; in the **Alps**, the **Aiguille Verte** is often capped by such a cloud.

Lenzspitze 4,294 m, 14,087 ft. This is the 19th highest of the 60 major 4,000-meter peaks in the **Alps**. This elegant mountain in the **Mischabels** of the **Valaisan Alps** was first climbed in 1870, by Clinton T. Dent and Alexander and Franz Burgener. The east face is a superb snow and ice slope, rising some 600 m, 2,000 ft, at an average slope of 55 degrees; the summit ridge connects to the **Nadelhorn**. (See also color photos.)

Les Étoiles de Midi/Stars at Noon A 1958 French film by **Marcel Ichac**; it is a reenactment of various factual accounts and is hailed by mountain fans as extremely faithful to the originals. Ichac is known for his documentaries, and the cast mixes actual actors like Roger Blin (1907–1984) with famous climbers such as **Lionel Terray**, **René Desmaison**, and Michel Vaucher and ski champion René Collet. The last half hour pictures the realistic ascent of the Grand Capucin. *Les Étoiles du Midi* won the Grand Prix du Cinéma Français and was a nominee for the Golden Bear in the Berlin Film Festival. The title refers to the high-altitude dark sky that allows one to see stars at noon. (M-A. H.)

Lesotho Lowest point, junction of the Orange and Makhaleng Rivers 1,400 m, 4,593 ft; highest point, Thabana Ntlenyana 3,482 m, 11,424 ft.

Lewis, Meriwether (1774–1809) The leader of the famous **Lewis and Clark Expedition** to the Pacific Northwest (1804–1806); he served as personal secretary to President Thomas Jefferson. He died mysteriously while on the Natchez Trace in the South.

Lewis and Clark Expedition (1804–1806) Perhaps one of the most ambitious and difficult expeditions ever completed, it allowed for the mapping of an enormous swath of land in what is now the northwest United States. One of the incentives of the expedition, which was planned by Thomas Jefferson, was the recent Louisiana Purchase; Jefferson was also extremely interested in finding an all-water route from the East Coast to the Pacific Ocean. Numerous interactions with Indian tribes also resulted in first contact between very different cultures; most of these initial encounters were friendly.

Lhasa (The Forbidden City) The capital of **Tibet**, currently an autonomous region of **China**, located at 3,650 m, 11,975 ft. Its name is a romanization of La-sa, where one recognizes the Tibetan word **la**, which means **pass**. The city has long been an important spiritual center for **Buddhists**, and a large temple, called Gtsuglag-lag-khang, can be found there; it is recognized as the holiest in Tibet. Other important landmarks,

The Gateway to Lhasa, and the Potola (John Claude White/National Geographic)

including the **Potala** palace can be found in Lhasa. (See also **La Paz**.)

Lhotse   (Also Khumbu Lhotse, Lotzu, Lo-Tzu Feng) 8,516 m, 27,939 ft. A splendid mountain in **Nepal** (on the Tibetan border) and the fourth highest peak in the world, it stands across the **South Col** of **Everest**; its west face is a powerful, steep, broad ice and rock slope, reaching severe inclinations under the summit. It was first climbed on May 18, 1956, by Luchsinger and Reiss, from **Switzerland**; as of the end of 1999, Lhotse had been climbed by 129 alpinists, with a total of eight fatalities (two after successfully summitting). (See also the **14 8,000-Meter Peaks** sidebar and color photos.)

Lhotse Middle   8,430 m, 27,657 ft. This peak, located near **Everest**, was often cited as the highest unclimbed summit in the world until it was climbed by Russians in 2001. It is a satellite of **Lhotse**.

Liberia   Lowest point, Atlantic Ocean 0 m; highest point, Mt. Wuteve 1,380 m, 4,528 ft.

Libraries   Major research collections often have strong holdings concerning mountains generally, but they will be scattered according to the classification system used to arrange their materials.

One of the best special collections is located at the **American Alpine Club**'s library in Golden, **Colorado**. Here one will find more than 17,000 volumes, rare books, partial or complete runs of 200 periodicals, 3,000 maps, and videotapes, as well as John Boyle's Himalayan collection, artifacts such as historical ice axes, and material belonging to **Anatoli Boukreev** all in one convenient location. Another superb collection is located at the Alpine Club Library in London. Mountain monasteries such as St. Catherine at **Mt. Sinai** may contain collections of ancient manuscripts and books. (See also **cave**.)

Libya   Lowest point, Sabkhat Ghuzayyil −47 m, −154 ft; highest point, Bikku Bitti 2,267 m, 7,438 ft.

Lichen   Fungal/algal symbiotic vegetation that adheres to and grows on rocks and trees. Lichens are green, gray, yellow, or brown, and can be extremely beautiful. (See also **moss**.)

Lieback   (In Great Britain, layback) In rock climbing, to hold one's body away from the face, the arms pulling outward, while the feet push inward. (Also used as a noun.)

Liechtenstein   Lowest point, Ruggeller Riet 430 m, 1,411 ft; highest point, Grauspitz 2,599 m,

8,527 ft. This tiny country is located between Switzerland and Austria; while it produces its own stamps, it does not mint money and Swiss francs are the de facto currency.

Life in the mountains See **culture, mountain people**.

Lightning An electrical discharge usually accompanying a **thunderstorm**; lightning comes in different forms (ball, heat, sheet, etc.) and can be extremely harmful. It strikes combustibles such as trees and thus causes forest fires. It can also hit people, especially when they are on high, exposed ridges or peaks. See the chapter by Cooper et al. on lightning injuries in Auerbach. (See also **weather**.)

Lights Hikers and mountaineers who stay away from civilization for long periods of time require powerful hand-held flashlights, headlamps, and many batteries, as well as gas-powered table lamps that offer ongoing lighting. New halogen and LED units provide extraordinary illumination, upon which one's life may very well depend. These devices are available at hardware stores and **equipment retailers** such as REI or EMS. What may elude some people is the recent addition of laser flares. Given the possibility of an accident requiring rescue, these new, powerful flares could help rangers or volunteers locate a person at night on a glacier or in the wilderness. Greatland Laser sells rescue flares that can last for 72 hours and can be seen from 20 miles away.

Lily A large family of **flowers**; the glacier lily may come up through the snow, and the mariposa takes hold on slopes.

Limestone A **sedimentary rock** (often replete with fossils) that comprises many mountains; it is softer than **granite** but still can provide a good climbing surface, for example, in the **Dolomites**.

Limon See loess.

Linceuil, Le See **Grandes Jorasses**.

Literature Mountains play an important role in some fiction, drama, and poetry. Outstanding examples include *First on the Rope* (Roger Frison-Roche), *The Magic Mountain* (Thomas Mann), and *The White Tower* (James Ramsey Ullman). (See also **climbing accounts**.)

10 Great Mountain Adventure Books

1. *Conquistadors of the Useless* (Lionel Terray)
2. *Annapurna: First Conquest of an 8,000 Meter Peak* (Maurice Herzog)
3. *Into Thin Air* (Jon Krakauer)
4. *Nanga Parbat Pilgrimage* (Hermann Buhl)
5. *Premier de Cordée* (Roger Frison-Roche)
6. *The Endurance* (Alfred Lansing)
7. *The Long Walk* (Slavomir Rawicz)
8. *The White Spider* (Heinrich Harrer)
9. *The White Tower* (James Ramsey Ulmann)
10. *Touching the Void* (Joe Simpson)

Lithic Relating to stone or rock.

Lithuania Lowest point, Baltic Sea 0 m; highest point, Juozapines/Kalnas 292 m, 958 ft.

Livesey, Peter (1943–) Born: England. A prominent British rock climber of the 1970s. Bibliography: *Rockclimbing* (1978).

Llama An unusual, **camel**-like animal indigenous to **South America**. It is the packhorse of the **Andes**. (See also **alpaca** and **vicuña**.)

Llullaillaco, Volcano 6,723 m, 22,057 ft. This is the sixth highest peak in the **Andes** and the highest **volcano** on earth; it was probably first climbed during pre-Colombian times, by natives. The peak is located in **Argentina**.

Lodges On or near U.S. mountains, the government or commercial entrepreneurs have built living facilities. There is nothing special about the hotels and condominiums one finds at the typical ski area; indeed, in some cases, they are offensive eyesores and may even block the mountain from view. But there are a number of extraordinary structures, especially the lodges built in or near **national parks**, that warrant mention. On **Rainier**, one finds the Paradise Inn (1916), the largest log structure in the world. On **Hood** is Timberline Lodge (1937), a similar, a esthetically situated facility. In **Hawaii Volcanoes National Park**, Volcano House (1846) is ideally located for viewing. Glacier Park Lodge (1913) accommodates visitors to Glacier National Park. In **California**'s **Yosemite National Park**, the Ahwahnee lodge serves much the same functions, while **Yellowstone National Park** counts two main facilities: the Mammoth Hot Springs Lodge and Cabins, and the **Old Faithful** Lodge and Snow Lodge. At the **Grand Canyon**, the luxurious El Tovar Hotel has served people since 1905. And on Mt. Greylock, the **Massachusetts** highpoint, one is surprised by Bascomb Lodge, a lovely stone structure; like some of its sister lodges, it was built during the Depression by the Civilian Conservation Corps. (See Zimmermann's *Complete Guide* for more information and www .nps.gov/.)

Loess A sedimentary deposit of silty grains that are loosely cemented by calcium carbonate. It is usually traversed by vertical capillaries that permit the sediment to fracture and form vertical bluffs. (*Encyclopedia Britannica*)

Lofoten Islands This small island group is located in the Norwegian Sea, off the coast of northern Norway, and lies entirely within the Arctic Circle; however, the warm North Atlantic Current helps temper the weather to some extent. The archipelago comprises five main islands and countless rocky islets and reefs, called skerries. The Vesterålsfjorden separates the islands from the mainland; it is a wide and deep fjord. Geologically, the Lofoten Islands are composed of plutonic rocks, including gneiss and **granite**; the origin of the group corresponds to the eroded summits of an underwater mountain range. The highest peak is located on Austvågøya Island; Higravstind is 1,161 m, 3,809 ft, high. (See also color photos.)

Logan, Mt. 5,959 m, 19,551 ft. The highest mountain in **Canada** and the second highest in **North America**; it is also the largest mountain in the world in terms of sheer bulk: the summit plateau, lying well above 5,000 m, 16,500 ft, is many square miles in area and its summit ridge measures approximately 16 km, 10 miles, while the entire mountain is over 32 km, or 20 miles in length. The first ascent was completed on June 25, 1925, by a large expedition under the leadership of McCarthy and Lambert; the summitting party included: A. H. McCarthy, H. F. Lambert, A. Carpè, W. W. Foster, N. Read, and A. Taylor. The mountain is named after Sir William Logan, who founded the Geological Survey of Canada. (See also **Denali** and color photos.)

Logging It is necessary to cut trees, if we are to continue to produce building materials, paper, and other wood-based products, but logging has an especially detrimental effect on mountains, both esthetically and ecologically. Roads that are cut through virgin timber lots or second- or third-growth areas desecrate the land and lead to erosion; large machinery tears up the ground; helicopters produce noise; by-products that are left (stumps, branches, litter) take decades to turn into soil; burning produces pollution; clearcutting results in eyesores; and even replanted areas look displeasing for many years. Logging can be done in a caring way, without destroying the environment. It should be prohibited in the world's **national parks** and pristine areas as well as where specific species are threatened or take hundreds of years to mature. **Redwood** and **sequoia** belong in the forests and on the slopes not in a bedroom or on a deck.

The Long Walk This book is probably one of the most moving, real-life accounts ever written: in 1941, the author, Slavomir Rawicz, and a small group of fellow prisoners escaped from a Soviet labor camp. Their harrowing trek out of Siberia, through China, the Gobi Desert, Tibet, and over the Himalayas to British India is a wonderful statement about man's enduring desire for freedom. (See **10 Great Mountain Adventure Books** sidebar.)

Longitude This is an angular measure of the distance from a reference meridian, set in Greenwich, **England**. It varies from 180 degrees west to 180 degrees east. (Compare **latitude**.)

Longs Peak 4,345 m, 14,255 ft. This highly recognizable mountain, with a 2,000-ft, sheer **granite** face is located in **Colorado**'s **Front Range**. The first recorded climb was in 1868 by a team led by John Wesley Powell, and including William Byers, but the peak was almost certainly climbed earlier by native Ute and/or Arapaho.

Longstaff, Tom George (1875–1964) Born: England. President of the Alpine Club, 1947–1949, he was one of the greatest Himalayan climbers and explorers early in the 20th century. He traveled through the **Alps**, the Rockies, the **Caucasus**, the Arctic, and the **Himalayas**. In 1907, he performed the first ascent of **Trisul** (7,120m), establishing the world record in altitude at that time (See the **A Brief Chronology of Altitude Records** sidebar). Bibliography: *This My Voyage* (1949), autobiography.

Loon A ducklike bird whose haunting call can be heard from its home on mountain lakes.

Lost Valley, The An American–British film, shot in Austria by Australian-born James Clavell, and based on a novel by J. B. Pick. During the Thirty Years War, which began in 1618, a student (Omar Sharif) finds a forgotten valley, sheltered from war and plague, and tries to protect it from invasion with the help of mercenaries and their chief (Michael Caine). The movie deals with the opposition between mind (Sharif) and force (Caine). Mountains—in the Tyrol—stand here for the walls of a castle. They offer protection and refuge, and the characters climb only to prevent attacks and fight back intruding enemies. (M-A. H.)

Louisiana Lowest point, Lake Ponchartrain −2.4 m, −8 ft; highest point, Driskell Mountain 163 m, 535 ft (48th highest of the 50 state highpoints).

Lowe, Alex (1958–1999) Prior to his tragic death in a Himalayan avalanche, Lowe was considered to be the finest all-around climber in the world, a superb rock and ice climber and mountaineer. He climbed the Nose of **El Capitan** in 10 hours and conquered **Everest** twice. Jenni Lowe, **Conrad Anker**, and **Jon Krakauer** are raising money for a climbing school in Nepal modeled after Exum Mountain Guides. **Sherpas** will receive technical climbing training and a trust will be established to assist the families of fallen Sherpa climbers.

Lowe, George W. (fl. 1950s–1960s) He was a prominent American climber, especially in Utah, and participated in the 1953 **Everest** expedition. Bibliography: *Because It Is There* (1959).

Lowe, Greg (fl. mid-1960s–late 1980s) From 1965 to 1970, he was one of America's best and boldest rock climbers. He was also an important **equipment** innovator. His brother Jeff was a great mountaineer who soloed a new route on the **Eiger** (Pat Ament, personal comment).

Lucania, Mt. 5,226 m, 17,147 ft. This is the third highest peak in **Canada**; it is located in the **St. Elias Mountains**, in the **Yukon**. It was first climbed in 1937 by **Bradford Washburn** and **Robert Bates**, along with **Mt. Steele**. This epic climb is recounted in detail in *Escape from Lucania*.

Ludwigshöhe 4,341 m, 14,242 ft. This is the 14th highest of the 60 major 4,000-meter peaks in the **Alps**. A satellite of **Monte Rosa**, in the **Valaisan Alps**, conquered in 1898, by G. F. and G. B. Gugliermina, **Matthias Zurbriggen**, and Clemens Imseng.

Luge A small one-person sled, upon which one careens downhill supine and backwards, that is, with the head at the rear of the sled; luging is now an **Olympic** sport.

Lunge In rock climbing, a quick move.

Lunn, Sir Arnold Henry Moore (1883–1974) Born: England. Bibliography: *Oxford Mountaineering Essays* (1912), *Skiing* (1913), *The Englishman in the Alps* (1913), *The Alps* (1914), *Cross-Country Skiing* (1920), *Skiing for Beginners* (1924), *The Mountains of Youth* (1925), *Alpine Skiing at All Heights and Seasons* (1926), *A History of Skiing* (1927), *Switzerland* (1928), *The Complete Ski-Runner* (1930), *Come What May* (1940) autobiography, *And the Floods Came* (1942), *Mountain Jubilee* (1943), *Switzerland and the English* (1944), *Switzerland in English Prose and Poetry* (1947), *Mountains of Memory* (1948), *The Cradle of Switzerland* (1952), *The Story of Skiing* (1952), *Zermatt and the Valais* (1955), *Memory to Memory* (1956), *A Century of Mountaineering, 1857–1957* (1957), *And Yet So New* (1958), *The Bernese Oberland* (1958), *The Swiss and Their Mountains* (1963), *Matterhorn Centenary* (1965), *Unkilled for So Long* (1968) autobiography.

Lupine A widely dispersed and easily recognizable blue, white, but frequently purple **flower**, whose stalks may reach 24 inches and contain many clusters. Of the ca. 200 species some 50 can be seen in the Rockies (Nicholls).

Luxembourg   Lowest point, Moselle River 133 m, 436 ft; highest point, Burgplatz 559 m, 1,834 ft.

Lyell, Mt.   3,998 m, 13,177 ft. This is the highest peak within **Yosemite National Park**; it was first climbed in 1871 by John Tileston.

Lyell, Sir Charles   (1797–1875) The British scientist whose work lay the foundation for modern **geology**.

Lyskamm   4,527 m, 14,852 ft. This is the seventh highest of the 60 major 4,000-meter peaks in the **Alps**. A beautiful mountain in Italy and **Switzerland**, located in the **Monte Rosa** Range, it is characterized by a heavily glaciated north face and a long summit ridge. Eight British climbers and six Swiss guides first climbed it in 1861. (See also color photos.)

M

Macau   Lowest point, South China Sea 0 m; highest point, Coloane Alto 174 m, 571 ft.

MacAulay Peak   4,690 m, 15,388 ft. Located in **Canada**'s **Saint Elias Mountains**, in the **Yukon**, it is close to **Mt. Slaggard**, in the **Kluane-Logan National Park**. These mountains are very remote and accessible only by plane; the weather can be dangerous, since the whole range is exposed to fast-moving storms from the Gulf of Alaska.

Macauly Peak   See **MacAulay Peak**.

Macedonia, The Former Yugoslav Republic of   Lowest point, Vardar River 50 m, 164 ft; highest point, Golem Korab (Maja e Korabit) 2,753 m, 9,032 ft.

Machu Picchu   A small, Incan city built on top of a **mesa**, high in the Peruvian **Andes**. Since its discovery, it has been considered a holy site, but it was probably only a secular retreat for the emperor. (See also color photos.)

Machupuchare   (Machapuchare; "Fish Tail," in Nepali) 6,997 m, 22,955 ft. A holy mountain in **Nepal**. This incomparable mountain, often cited as one of the most beautiful in the world, is located within the **Annapurna Himal** and the **Annapurna Sanctuary**, it overlooks the **Modi Khola**. There is no official record of a first climb, as, out of respect for the local religious belief that the summit should remain unclimbed, climbing parties stop a few meters under the summit. (See also color photos and the **10 Most Beautiful Mountains** sidebar.)

MacInnes, Hamish   (1920–) Born: Scotland. According to the excellent website www.simp kins57.freeserve.co.uk/mountain_lakes_books/ whoswho/whoswhodetails.html, "One of the most influential mountaineers of the 50s, 60s, and 70s. He has climbed difficult new routes, especially in winter, made a major contribution to mountain rescue, both as a leader of the Glencoe team and as a developer of new, improved rescue techniques, and has been responsible for the development of advanced ice climbing equipment." Main achievements: First winter ascent of Raven's Gully, Buachaille Etive Mor (1953) with **Chris Bonington**, Zero Gully, **Ben Nevis** (1957) with Tom Patey and A. G. Nichol. The first British ascent of the Bonatti Pillar of the **Dru** (1958), with Bonington, Whillans, and others. A member of the two **Everest** southwest face expeditions of 1973. Bibliography: *Climbing* (1963), *Call-out* (1973), *International Mountain Rescue Handbook* (1972), *Climb to the Lost World* (1974), *Look behind the Ranges* (1979), *High Drama* (1980), *Beyond the Ranges* (1984), *Sweep Search* (1985).

***Maciste Alpino**/Maciste Mountain Infantryman*   A 1915 Italian war movie directed by Romano Borgnetto; it takes place in the Alps. (M-A. H.)

Madagascar   Lowest point, Indian Ocean 0 m; highest point, Maromokotro 2,876 m, 9,436 ft.

Maeder, Herbert   (1930–) Born: Switzerland. Bibliography: *The Mountains of Switzerland* (1968), *The Lure of the Mountains* (1975).

Magazine Mountain   839 m, 2,753 ft. The highest point in **Arkansas**, it is a surprisingly beautiful summit, surrounded by cliffs and nice views of the **Ozarks**.

Magazines   See **periodicals**.

Magma   Hot, liquefied rock found below the earth's surface. (See also **lava** and **volcano**.)

Magnetic pole   Currently located near the true North and South Poles, these are the areas where the magnetic field lines of the earth converge; thus, a magnetic compass will align with the field lines and point toward the magnetic pole. It is important to note, however, that there is a slow drift of the magnetic poles over the years; this is generally indicated on topographic maps, where the magnetic declination is recorded at a given time, as well as the approximate angular drift rate. The current position of the north magnetic pole is approximately 79 degrees north **latitude** and 71 degrees west **longitude**. Over a long period of time, the earth's magnetic field actually flips, as recorded by inspecting layers of magnetic rocks of various geological ages.

Magnolia   A **deciduous tree** used as an ornamental in the southern United States. The mountain magnolia can be seen on slopes (Leopold, McComb, and Muller).

Magnone, Guido   Born: Italy. He made the first ascents of the north face of the **Dru**, **Fitzroy**, and **Makalu**. Bibliography: *The West Face* (1955).

Mahre, Phillip (Phil)   (1957–) When he won the 1981 overall World Cup **skiing** championship, he was the first American to achieve this honor. He also won the gold medal in **slalom** at the 1984 Winter Olympics.

Mahre, Steve   (1957–) **Phil Mahre**'s twin; he won the silver in **slalom** at the 1984 **Winter Olympics**.

Maine   Lowest point, Atlantic Ocean, 0 m; highest point, **Mt. Katahdin**, 1,605 m, 5,267 ft (22nd highest of the 50 state highpoints). This is the largest state in New England, a densely wooded, rugged landscape of lakes, forests, and lonely peaks. The winters can be extremely cold, particularly in the northern part of the state. The highpoint, Mt. Katahdin, is the centerpiece of Baxter State Park.

Makalu   (Also Makalufeng; "The Great Black One" in Nepali) 8,463 m, 27,766 ft. Located between **Nepal** and **Tibet**, this is the fifth highest mountain in the world. Makalu was first climbed on May 15th, 1955 by **Terray** and **Couzy**, from **France**. As of the end of 1999, the summit of Makalu had been reached by 156 climbers; 11 people died attempting it, while 8 others perished during **descent**. (See also

the **14 8,000-Meter Peaks** sidebar and color photos.)

Makalu II   7,657 m, 25,120 ft. This major peak is located within the **Himalayas** in **Nepal**. It was first ascended in 1954, by **Lionel Terray** and **J. Franco**.

Malaspina Glacier   Located in **Alaska**, within the **Wrangell–St. Elias National Park**, this is the largest **piedmont glacier** in North America: at over 3,900 sq km (1,500 sq miles), the ice mass is bigger that the entire state of Rhode Island. It results from the confluence of other large glaciers flowing from **Mt. Saint Elias** and the surrounding high peaks. It is located very near the ocean, and since the whole region is exposed to the full force of the storms that rage in the Gulf of Alaska during the winter months, it receives extraordinary amounts of snow every year, producing the powerful glaciers that feed Malaspina. It carries such large quantities of **glacial silt** that trees have been known to grow to maturity, moving along with the ice, only to be uprooted at the terminus, or when the glacier retreats.

Malawi   Lowest point, junction of the Shire River and international boundary with Mozambique 37 m, 121 ft; highest point, Sapitwa 3,002 m, 9,849 ft.

Malaysia   Lowest point, Indian Ocean 0 m; highest point, Gunung **Kinabalu** 4,101 m, 13,455 ft.

Maldives   Lowest point, Indian Ocean 0 m; highest point, unnamed location on Wilingili Island in the Addu Atoll 2.4 m, 8 ft.

Mali   Lowest point, Senegal River 23 m, 75 ft; highest point, Hombori Tondo 1,155 m, 3,789 ft.

Mallory, George Herbert Leigh   (1886–1924) Born: England. In 1924, on his third visit to **Everest**, Mallory and **Andrew Irvine** made a final summit push. They disappeared into the clouds and were never seen again. No one knows whether these early climbers actually reached Everest's summit. It was Mallory, who, when asked why he wished to climb a mountain, famously responded, "because it is there." In 1999, Mallory's body was finally located, lying face-down with a broken ankle, obvious evidence of a serious fall, probably while descending, according to Pat Ament (personal comment). Hemmleb's *Ghosts of*

Everest recounts the discovery. Bibliography: *The Fight for Everest: 1924* (1925) by E. F. Norton, *George Leigh Mallory, A Memoir* (1927) by David Pye, *George Mallory* (1969) by David Robertson, *The Mystery of Mallory and Irvine* (1986) by Tom Holzel and Audrey Salkeld, *Mallory of Everest* (1990), by Dudley Green. (See also **Sir Edmund Hillary** and the very informative website www.pbs.org/wgbh/nova/everest/lost/mystery/.)

Malta Lowest point, Mediterranean Sea 0 m; highest point, Ta'Dmejrek 253 m (near Dingli), 830 ft.

Mammal A category of warm-blooded, milk-producing creatures; mammals are extremely diverse in form and can be found in most environments: bats fly and whales cannot survive outside of water. Only a limited percentage of the world's mammals make their way up to higher elevations. Many of these are noted in this alphabetical listing. (See http://web4.si.edu/mna/)

Mammoth Hot Springs See **Yellowstone National Park**.

Man, Isle of Lowest point, Irish Sea 0 m; highest point, Snaefell 621 m, 2,037 ft.

Mana 7,272 m, 23,858 ft. This major peak is located within the **Himalayas** in **India**.

Manaslu (Also Kutang) 8,163 m, 26,781 ft. A mountain located entirely within **Nepal** and the eighth highest in the world. Manaslu was first conquered on May 9, 1956, by Timanishi, from Japan, and Gyalzen Norbu Sherpa, from Nepal. At the end of the 20th century, 190 climbers had reached the summit of Manaslu; 51 perished, either attempting the mountain or upon **descent**. (See also the **14 8,000-Meter-Peaks** sidebar.)

Manfred A dramatic poem written in 1817 by George Gordon Lord Byron (1788–1824). Tired of life, searching desperately for meaning, Manfred abjures human contact and wanders in the Alps. The appeal that this romantic theme had is shown by the fact that two great composers were inspired by it: Robert Schumann (1810–1856) wrote incidental music and Russian Peter Ilyitch Tchaikovsky (1840–1893) composed a one-hour symphony. (M-A. H.)

Manitoba Lowest point, Hudson Bay 0 m; highest point, Baldy Mountain, 832 m, 2,730 ft. The second highest point in Manitoba is an unnamed point in the Porcupine Hills, 823 m, 2,700 ft.

Mansfield, Mt. 1,339 m, 4,393 ft. The highest point in **Vermont**, it has a very alpine feel for such a relatively low mountain, and is located in lovely surroundings; the view of Lake Champlain is magnificent in good weather.

Mantle In geology, the section of the earth that lies between the crust and core. In rock climbing, to push downward with raised hands and thereby pull oneself up onto a **ledge**.

Map A graphic representation of a physical area. Cartographers have been mapping the world for thousands of years. Individuals and governments have done extensive work on mountainous regions, but even today there are some esoteric areas that are not fully mapped. Individual topographic maps (topos), which indicate elevation via contour lines, exist for the entire United States, Europe, Canada, Mexico, and numerous other countries; most of these can be purchased from the government, for example, the USGS (**U.S. Geological Survey**) or the IGN (**Institut Géographique National**, in **France**), or at **equipment retailers**; specialized map retailers are also extremely useful for hard-to-get editions. Delorme gathers a state's topos, binds them, and sells these atlases at a reasonable price. (See also examples of various maps in the color section.)

Maple A widely dispersed **deciduous** tree of diverse species, which can be found at higher elevations. The sugar maple produces sap that is turned into maple syrup.

Maquignaz, Jean-Joseph (1829–1890) Born: Breuil, Italy. A superb guide, he was with **J.-A. Carrel** on the Italian Ridge of the **Matterhorn** in 1865 when **Whymper** and his party were on their first ascent of the Hornlï Ridge. He was part of the team that performed the first climb of the **Dent du Géant**, in 1882. With his brother Jean-Pierre he led **Tyndall** on the first traverse of the mountain in 1868. In 1882, he performed the first winter traverse with **Vittorio Sella**. Bibliography: *The Early Alpine Guides* (1949) by R. W. Clark.

Marble A **metamorphic** rock; it is used for building and, as calcium carbonate, is added to baby food, cereal, paint, plastics, and other products. Marmorean is the adjective describing a marble-like object or substance. (See also **Vermont Marble Museum**.)

Marcy, Mt. 1,639 m, 5,344 ft. The highest point in **New York** state, it is a lovely, relatively long hike to a distinctive summit, including a beautiful **granite dome**.

Margherita Peak See Mt. Stanley.

Marmolata 3,342 m, 10,965 ft. The highest mountain in Italy's **Dolomites**, and a splendid, mighty **limestone** cliff.

Marmot Considerably larger than a woodchuck, which it resembles, this mammal is ubiquitous in the higher mountains of the western United States and in the **Alps**. It has become so inured to humans that campers must hang their food, even above **timberline**, an area that **bears** generally avoid. It hibernates during the colder months.

Maroon Bells Along with the Maroon Peak (4,314 m, 14,156 ft) and North Maroon Peak (4,271 m, 14,014 ft), part of a magnificent group of three sister mountains in the **Elk Range** of **Colorado**. North Maroon is one of the hardest of Colorado's 14,000-foot peaks (See also color photos.)

Mars See **mountains on other worlds**.

Marshall Islands Lowest point, Pacific Ocean 0 m; highest point, unnamed location on Likiep 10 m, 33 ft.

Martinique Lowest point, Caribbean Sea 0 m; highest point, Montagne Pelée 1,397 m, 4,583 ft. La Montagne Pelée, a dormant volcano, is an extremely dangerous mountain, which destroyed the town of St. Pierre with a *nuée ardente*, in 1902; the cloud of incandescent ash accompanying a **lahar** avalanche swept down on the city, at the foot of Mt. Pelée, killing all but two of a population of about 30,000 persons.

Martinon, Jean (1910–1976) A French composer and conductor, he also was a frequent and able climber. He was with **Maurice Baquet** when the latter played Bach on top of **Mont Blanc**. His fourth symphony is entitled *Altitudes*. (M-A. H.)

Maryland Lowest point, Atlantic Ocean 0 m; highest point, Backbone Mountain 1,024 m, 3,360 ft (32nd highest of the 50 state highpoints).

Masada A small enclave built on top of a **mesa** with 1,400-foot precipices in Israel. It is here that a group of almost 1,000 Jews held out against Roman soldiers. Eventually, virtually all of the people committed mass suicide rather than allow themselves to be captured by the Romans, who were constructing an enormous rampart in order to reach the top. A **gondola** now whisks one to the summit in a few minutes.

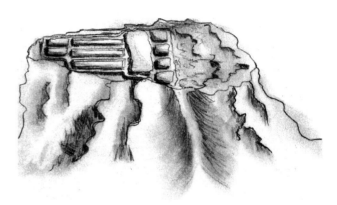

Masada (Laura Lindblad)

Masherbrum 7,821 m, 25,659 ft. Located in the **Karakoram**, near **K2**, this powerful peak was first ascended in 1960 by George Bell and **Willi Unsoeld**.

Massachusetts Lowest point, Atlantic Ocean 0 m; highest point, Mt. Greylock 1,064 m, 3,491 ft (31st highest of the 50 state highpoints). A road leads to the highpoint, marked by an intricately decorated tower.

Massif (F) An enormous mountain mass containing an outstanding peak, as in the **Mont Blanc** massif.

Massive, Mt. 4,395 m, 14,421 ft. The second highest of **Colorado**'s 54 14,000-foot summits, it is located in the **Sawatch Range**.

Mathews, Charles Edward (1834–1905) Born: England. One of the original members of the Alpine Club and its president in 1878–1880. Bibliography: *Annals of Mont Blanc* (1898).

Matterhorn (Also Cervin, Cervino) 4,477 m, 14,688 ft. This is the 10th highest of the 60 major

The Matterhorn (14,782 feet) (S. G. Wehrli/National Geographic)

rain, with slopes in excess of 65 degrees in avalanche-swept **gullies**, and is one of the most difficult north faces in the Alps (see the **6 + 1 Great Alpine North Faces** sidebar); the east face is also quite steep, up to 55–60 degrees; nevertheless, it has been descended by extreme skiers. (See also the **10 Most Beautiful Mountains** sidebar and color photos.)

Matterhorn (Laura Lindblad)

4,000-meter peaks in the **Alps**. Perhaps the world's most famous image of a mountain, this impressive peak is located in **Switzerland**. Two well-known climbing routes take one along either the Hörnli or Zmutt ridges. The Matterhorn was conquered, after a series of highly competitive trials between **Edward Whymper** and **J.-A. Carrel**, in 1865 by Whymper, **Charles Hudson**, D. Hadow, Francis Douglas, **Michel Croz**, and Peter Taugwalder father and son. During the **descent**, a rope broke, failing to arrest the fall of Hadow, who was tired, inexperienced, and had slipped on treacherous terrain; he then provoked the fatal fall of Hudson, Douglas, and Croz. This terrible tragedy is known as the 1865 Matterhorn Disaster, one of the first highly publicized mountain **accidents**. Besides the classic routes mentioned above, the north face of the Matterhorn presents some extremely difficult climbing on mixed ter-

Mauna Kea 4,205 m, 13,796 ft. A dormant shield **volcano** on **Hawaii's** Big Island, it is the highest point in the state and the location of an astronomical **observatory**. The summit of this enormous mountain, the highest in the world when measured from the ocean floor, is a complex system of **craters** and **vents**, and the landscape is reminiscent of the moon's surface (See also color photos and appendix G.)

Mauna Loa 4,170 m, 13,680 ft. An extremely active shield **volcano** located in **Hawaii**. The summit comprises a large **caldera** and numerous secondary **vents**.

Mauritania Lowest point, Sebkha de Ndrhamcha −3 m, −10 ft; highest point, Kediet Ijill 910 m, 2,986 ft.

Mauritius Lowest point, Indian Ocean 0 m; highest point, Mont Piton 828 m, 2,717 ft.

Mayotte Lowest point, Indian Ocean 0 m; highest point, Benara 660 m, 2,165 ft.

Mazamas, The See **clubs**.

Mazeaud, Pierre (1929–) Born: Grenoble, France. He was minister of sports in France, under President Valéry Giscard d'Estaing. Bibliography: *On the Heights* (1964), by **Walter Bonatti**, *The Great Days* (1974), by Walter Bonatti, *Naked before the Mountain* (1974).

McArthur, Mt. 4,344 m, 14,253 ft. A high peak located in the **Yukon** Territory in Canada, it is a heavily glaciated, remote mountain standing near **Mt. Logan**, in the **Kluane-Logan National Park**.

McKinley, Mt. See **Denali**.

Meade, Charles Francis (1881–1975) Born: England. Bibliography: *Approach to the Hills* (1940), *High Mountains* (1954).

Meadow An open, fairly flat, grassy area high up in the mountains. Alpine meadows are especially picturesque, especially when herds of domestic cows or sheep are present.

Meadowlark A meadow songbird, yellow in coloration with a black V-shaped mark on its breast. The different species are ubiquitous in the United States, southern Canada, and Mexico. The western can be found at altitudes as high as 7,000 ft.

Medicine With the exception of **acute mountain sickness** (and the more severe problems that can ensue), **hypoxia**, **frostbite**, and **snow blindness**, medical considerations and treatments in a mountain environment are no different than they would be in the lowlands. Naturally though, the equipment and personnel located in a Los Angeles or Paris hospital are not available in the **Sierras** or the **Alps**. Nevertheless, whatever can occur below can also manifest itself at **altitude**. Thus, inadvertent organ failure, heart attack, stroke, and illness as well as accidental sprains, tears, fractures, wounds, concussions, severe sunburn, **hypothermia**, and shock are all real possibilities, especially since so many people now hike and climb and some of them are ill-prepared for the rigors and dangers of both **rock climbing** and **mountaineering**. The naive sometimes rely on luck or pharmaceuticals, but both of these may prove wanting. A knowledge of first aid is extremely helpful, but basic first aid may not alleviate even a simple problem like heatstroke if there is no cooling water nearby. William Forgey's *Wilderness Medicine* contains some useful information related to the mountain environment. The fourth edition of Paul S. Auerbach's replete *Wilderness Medicine* is a ca. 2,000-page compilation; its 79 chapters cover medical as well as related topics such as rescue, bear attacks, and navigation. An expert referred to it as the "bible." Specialized texts such as Darvill's *Mountaineering Medicine*, Wilkerson's *Medicine for Mountaineering*, or Hultgrens's *High Altitude Medicine* (which is the most esoteric, replete, and definitive of these volumes) offer valuable theoretical data as well as practical advice on how to solve specific problems. The International Society for Mountain Medicine maintains a website at www.ismmed.org. (See also **accidents**, **acute mountain sickness**, and **safety**.)

Medium mountains *Mittelgebirge* (G), *moyennes montagnes* (F). We do not use this term in English, but the French and Germans refer to lower **ranges** using their respective locutions. (See also **high mountains**.)

Meije (La Meije) 3,983 m, 13,068 ft. A splendid mountain in the **Dauphiné Alps** of France, it long remained one of the unsolved problems of the Alps, and was finally conquered by Gaspard in 1877. The south face is a nearly vertical granite cliff, some 800 m, 2,600 ft high, and the ridges connecting the main peak to Le Doigt de Dieu (God's finger) and the Râteau are extremely precipitous and heavily **corniced**, especially after storms. The picturesque village of La Grave sits under La Meije and Le Rateau (www.lagrave-lameije.com/). (See also color photos.)

Melungtse (Jobo Garu) (Menlungste) 7,181 m, 23,559 ft. This major peak was summitted in 1992; it is located within the Rolwaling **Himal**, at the border between **Nepal** and **Tibet**.

Men in War A 1957 American film directed by Anthony Mann, set during the Korean War, which was fought in a rather mountainous region, requiring filmmakers to find new ways to deal with their settings. (During the two world wars only some battles in Italy took place in the mountains—see ***La Grande Guerra*** and ***Maciste Alpino***.) *Men in War* cleverly exploits the landscape; the geography is used not only for dramatization but also as a source of traps and attacks, and it forces the soldiers into new strategies to handle the situation. This interaction between location and action is a trademark of director Mann, whose films are known for their strategic use of topography. (M-A. H.)

Mendenhall, Ruth Dyar   (1912–1989) Ament indicates that she was "one of the most able female rock climbers during the 1940s."

Mer de Glace   (F), *Eismeer* (G), sea of ice. The French term designates a specific **glacier** in **Chamonix**. The Mer de Glace is a wonderful downhill ski run in the winter, when the **crevasses** are mostly sealed by fresh snow accumulation; one starts from the **Aiguille du Midi**, to end up down in the Chamonix Valley, some 2,600 m, 8,500 ft, below. The run is approximately 15 km, 10 miles, long. In the summer, the Mer de Glace is a striking, huge glacier, making its way down from the Col du Géant, down to the Montenvers, where a cog-train ferries tourists and climbers alike. The surrounding peaks are magnificent, and include the **Aiguille**

Verte and the **Drus**, the **Grandes Jorasses**, and, almost directly above the Montenvers, the Grands Charmoz and Le Grépon. Amazingly, caves, tunnels, running water, and lakes have all been found under this glacier. (See also color photos.)

Mercedario   6,770 m, 22,211 ft. This is the fourth highest peak in the **Andes**; it was first climbed in 1934 by a Polish expedition. The peak is located in **Argentina**.

Merrick, Hugh   (1898–1980) Born: England. Bibliography: *Rambles in the Alps* (1951), *The Perpetual Hills* (1964), *The Alps in Colour* (1970).

Mesa   An isolated, steeply sided extrusion larger than a **butte**, but not as big as a **plateau**; a mesa has a flat top that resists the **erosion** that has worn away a larger mass.

Mesa Verde National Park   An area in **Colorado** where the indigenous people built and inhabited **cliff dwellings** between 600 and 1300 C.E.

Mer de Glace (S. G Wehrli/National Geographic)

Mesquite A fragrant bush that is part of the **chaparral**.

Messiaen, Olivier (1908–1992) Born in Grenoble, in the middle of the **Dauphiné Alps**, Messiaen is one of the most important composers of the 20th century—Bernstein and Ozawa were his champions in the United States. This religious artist described himself as a "Frenchman from the mountains." Many of his works were written in a house he had bought in Petitchet, not far from Les **Écrins**. He often went into the Alpine countryside to collect nature sounds and bird songs, a major source of inspiration for him. One of his piano pieces is "Le Chocard des Alpes," and his personal notes often emphasize the influence of mountains on his works. He specifically stated that in his 1964 piece "Et Exspecto Ressurectionem Mortum" he "wanted the execution of Et Exspecto in the open air of La Grave, facing the glacier of La **Meije**, in those powerful and solemn landscapes which are my real fatherland." (M-A. H.)

Messner, Reinhold (1944–) Although he is a good rock climber, Messner is perhaps the best and strongest mountaineer in the history of climbing. In 1978, he and **Peter Habeler** did the first climb of **Everest** without supplemental **oxygen** or high altitude **porters**; in 1980, he did a solo climb of Everest without pre-established camps or caches. He was the first person to reach the summits of all 14 of the world's 8,000-meter peaks and this was done without supplemental oxygen. Messner's climbing resume is unmatched: from 1950 to 1964, about 500 climbs in the eastern Alps, mainly in the **Dolomites**. In 1965, Ortler north face (Direttissima), first ascent. In 1966, Walker Spur, **Grandes Jorasses**; Rocchetta Alta di Bosconero north face, second ascent. In 1970, **Nanga Parbat** (8,126 m) Rupal Side, first ascent. In 1997, journey to Kham (eastern Tibet); **Karakoram** expedition; documentary on the Ol Doinyo Lengai in Africa (holy mountain of the Masai). In 1998, journey to the Altai Mountains (Mongolia) and to Puna de Atacama (Andes). In 1999, documentary on San Francisco Peaks, **Arizona** (holy mountain of the Navajos). In 2000–2003, retraced **Shackleton**'s historic steps across **South Georgia Island**;

Nanga Parbat expedition; **Fuji-san** (documentary about the holy mountain); Dharamsala and Himalayan foothills/India; Gunung Agung/Bali (documentary about the holy mountain); in the "International Year of the Mountains" visit of mountain people in Ecuador and ascent of **Cotopaxi** (5,897 m), Ecuador. Two history books written (on Everest and Nanga Parbat); trips to Mt. Everest, Nanga Parbat, and Franz Joseph Land in the Arctic. During a 1970 climb of Nanga Parbat, Messner's brother Günther was caught in an **avalanche** and died. Recently, some of the expedition members have questioned Messner's account and accused him of disregarding Günther's welfare. Messner plans to return to Nanga Parbat in 2005, locate the body, and prove that he is correct (Rhoads). Bibliography: *The Seventh Grade* (1974), *The Challenge* (1977), *The Big Walls* (1978), *Everest: Expedition to the Ultimate* (1979), *Solo Nanga Parbat* (1980), *K2 Mountain of Mountains* (1981), with Alessandro Gogna, *High Ambition* (1982) a biography by Ronald Faux, *All 14 Eight-Thousanders* (1988), *The Crystal Horizon* (1989), *Free Spirit* (1991), *Antarctica: Both Heaven and Hell* (1991), *To the Top of the World* (1992), *Annapurna* (2000), *My Quest for the Yeti* (2000), *Hermann Buhl: Climbing without Compromise* (2000), with Horst Hofler, *Moving Mountains: Lessons on Life and Leadership* (2001), *The Second Death of George Mallory* (2001). (See also **Ed Viesturs** and the **14 8,000-Meter Peaks** and **10 Best All-Around Mountaineers** sidebars and color photos.) (www.reinhold-messner.de).

Metamorphic The term used to describe **rocks** that derive from other rocks through temperature, pressure, and chemical influences (Hamblin and Christiansen). For example, **shale** becomes slate and **sandstone** becomes quartzite (Vogel). (See also **igneous**, **marble**, and **sedimentary**.)

Meteor Crater Also known as Barringer Crater, for its discoverer; it is located a few miles from Flagstaff, Arizona. It is an amazing sight.

Metéora Similar to those on **Mt. Athos**, this is a group of monasteries built on precipitous peaks in **Greece**. In the distant past, it was necessary to use a rope to gain access.

Meters The standard unit of length in the metric system, the meter is now defined by taking the length of a path traveled by light in a vacuum during a time interval of 1/299,792,458 of a second, which is the duration of 9,192,631,770 periods of radiation corresponding to the transition between two hyperfine levels of the ground state of the cesium-133 atom. The official conversion factors are: 1 foot equals 0.3048 meters; 1 mile equals 1,609.344 meters. Therefore, an 8,000-meter peak is 26,246.719 feet high; a 14,000-foot peak is 4,267.2 meters high. (See also **feet**.)

Mexico   Lowest point, Laguna Salada −10 m, −33 ft; highest point, Volcan Pico de **Orizaba** 5,700 m, 18,701 ft. Mexico is famous for its high, active volcanoes: besides Orizaba, also known as Citlaltepetl, **Popocatépetl** 5,451 m, 17,887 ft, and **Iztaccíhuatl** 5,286 m, 17,343 ft, dominate the Mexican plateau.

Michigan   Lowest point, Lake Erie 174 m, 571 ft; highest point, Mt. Arvon 603 m, 1,979 ft (38th highest of the 50 state highpoints).

Microbes The microbial life that exists in **cracks** and clefts in rock is extremely abundant; some estimates indicate that it is considerably larger than earth's surface life.

Micronesia, Federated States of   Lowest point, Pacific Ocean 0 m; highest point, Totolom 791 m, 2,595 ft.

Middendorf, John   (fl. 1980s) A **Yosemite** rock climber. In 1985, he did the difficult Autobahn on **Half Dome**.

Middle Mountains   See **medium mountains**.

Middle Palisade   4,279 m, 14,040 ft. Located in the **Palisades** region of the **Sierra Nevada** in **California**, it was first ascended in 1930 by **Norman Clyde**.

Midway Islands   Lowest point, Pacific Ocean 0 m; highest point, unnamed location 13 m, 43 ft.

Miller, Warren   (1925–   ) For more than half a century Miller has been making exciting films of skiers careening down or off mountains. A recent example is *Journey* with Bode Miller.

Miner   A lark-like **bird**; many species, including the common, creamy-rumped, and puna, reach 16,500 ft in the **Andes** (Fjeldså and Krabbe).

Minerals   There are more than 3,000 minerals but only some 20 of these are the basic constituents of rock (Vogel); they are divided into a number of categories: felsic minerals such as feldspar, **quartz**, and mica are the sources of **granite**; mafic minerals such as olivine are found in **basalt**; and a third group consists of clay. **Dolomite**, garnet, iron, and lead are all minerals. (See also Sorrell's *Minerals of the World* for a replete overview, **precious stones**, and color photos.)

Mining   The various processes through which useful materials are extracted from the earth. There are three types that have a sometimes deleterious effect on mountains: underground, wherein tunnels are sunk and propagated in order to mine diamonds or **salt**, for example; open pit, in which an enormous hole is constructed and continually enlarged—to extract copper; and strip, through which the earth is carried off, which diminishes the surface, a system used to locate **coal**. **Precious metals**, semi-**precious stones**, **minerals**, and combustibles are all mined; a brief list would include gold, iron, lead, manganese, silver, sulfur, tungsten, and zinc. Rock is quarried, although the effect may be the same: destruction of the undergirdings or surface of mountains. (See also **mountaintop removal**.)

Minnesota   Lowest point, Lake Superior 183 m, 600 ft; highest point, Eagle Mountain 701 m, 2,301 ft (37th highest of the 50 state highpoints). A nice highpoint, located near the picturesque 10,000 Islands boundary between the United States and Canada.

Minya Konka   (Also Ganga Shan, Ninya Konka) 7,556 m, 24,790 ft. This peak, visible from Chengdu, in China, was first climbed in 1932 by Terris Moore and Richard Burdsall. It was one of two peaks erroneously estimated at above 30,000 ft by the American botanical explorer Joseph Rock, in 1929; the other is **Amne Machin**.

Mischabels   A powerful **massif** in the heart of **Valais**, comprising such peaks as the **Dom**, **Taschhörn**, **Nadelhorn**, **Lenzspitze**, **Stecknadelhorn**, **Hohberghorn**, and the **Dürrenhorn**, all above 4,000 m.

Mississippi   Lowest point, Gulf of Mexico 0 m; highest point, Woodall Mountain 246 m, 806 ft (47th highest of the 50 state highpoints).

Missouri   Lowest point, St. Francis River, Arkansas border 70 m, 230 ft; highest point Taum Sauk

Mountain 540 m, 1,772 ft (41st highest of the 50 state highpoints).

Mistral   See **winds**.

Mitchell, Mt.   2,037 m, 6,684 ft. The highest point in **North Carolina** and the **Appalachians**.

Mixed climbing   See **climbing**.

Modi Khola   This is the river (*khola* in Nepali) that originates from the **Annapurna Sanctuary**; it goes through one of the wildest and deepest **gorges** in the world.

Moffat, Gwen   (1924–) Born: England. A mountain **guide** and rescuer, who is now a fiction author. Bibliography: *Space below My Feet* (1961) Vol 1 of autobiography, *Two Star Red* (1964), *On My Home Ground* (1968) Vol 2 of autobiography, *Survival Count* (1972) Vol 3 of autobiography.

Moffat, Jeffrey   (fl. early 1980s–early 1990s) One of England's greatest **free** climbers, dominating during the 1980s.

Moguls   Bumps created on a **slope** by a continual parade of skiers cutting into the snow along the same lines. As they increase in size, moguls may present problems for skiers.

Mohs scale   The 1–10 scale used to measure the hardness of minerals. Talc at 1 is the softest and diamond at 10 the hardest.

Moldova   Lowest point, Nistru River 2 m, 7 ft; highest point, Dealul Balanesti 430 m, 1,411 ft.

Monaco   Lowest point, Mediterranean Sea 0 m; highest point, Mont Agel 140 m, 459 ft. This tiny principality is almost entirely built on rocks and cliffs over the Riviera.

Monadnock   A large, isolated rock extrusion. (The term derives from **New Hampshire**'s Mt. Monadnock.)

Mönch   4,099 m, 13,448 ft. This is the 40th highest of the 60 major 4,000-meter peaks in the **Alps** and a frequently climbed mountain in the **Bernese Alps** of **Switzerland**. The first ascent of the Mönch occurred in 1857; the first climbers were S. Parges, **Christian Almer**, and Ulrich and Christian Kaufmann.

Mongolia   Lowest point, Hoh Nuur 518 m, 1,699 ft; highest point, Tavan Bogd Uul 4,374 m, 14,350 ft.

Monkey   A primate of innumerable species, most of which are arboreal. The South American emperor tamarin (long-tailed and moustached) can be found at higher elevations. Similarly, so can the baboon and the golden (Burnie). (See also **ape**.)

Monolith   A narrow, vertical piece of stone extruding from the earth's surface. If it is wide, it is a **butte** or a **mesa**. Sometimes smaller versions are set in place by humans; these may be called obelisks or columns. (See also the **10 Awesome Monoliths** sidebar.)

Monsoon   A **wind** that blows from the southwest from early spring through early fall (and then reverses during the rest of the year) across the Indian Ocean and onto the subcontinent and surrounding areas. In lower elevations the monsoon brings torrential rain and winds; higher up, vast quantities of snow and extreme cold are hazards for climbers.

Mont Aiguille   2,085 m, 6,842 ft. Some men climbed this steep, unusual French peak, located near Grenoble, in 1492, a year made famous by the discovery of America by Christopher Colombus. They were following the orders of King Charles VII of France, who commanded his chamberlain to ascend Mt. Inaccessible, as it was known then. Astoundingly, he succeeded, thus achieving one of the very first climbs ever detailed in the historical record. (See also **Rotario of Asti**, and the superb book by Fergus Fleming describing the conquest of the Alps, *Killing Dragons*.)

10 Awesome Monoliths

1. Asgard (Baffin Island)
2. Bugaboos (British Columbia)
3. Cirque of the Towers (Wyoming)
4. Devil's Tower (Wyoming)
5. Fitzroy, Cerro Torre, Torres del Paine (Argentina)
6. Half Dome and Quarter Dome (California)
7. Spider Rock (Arizona)
8. The Drus (France)
9. Trango Towers (Pakistan)
10. Uluru/Ayers Rock (Australia)

Mont Blanc 4,807 m, 15,770 ft. The highest peak in the **Alps** and in Western Europe; it is located near the border between **France** and **Italy**; however, the summit is entirely within France (see **Mont Blanc de Courmayeur**) and figures prominently in mountaineering history. It was first climbed in 1786 by **Jacques Balmat** and **Michel Paccard**. Despite its relative difficulty, mostly due to altitude on the normal route, it is one of the most-climbed summits in the Alps. Other routes can be extremely challenging, for example the voie Major on the Pilier du Fréney, one of the longest and most sustained technical routes in the Alps, sometimes compared, in its amplitude, to Himalayan climbs. The normal route is located on the French side of the mountain, and ascends the south face of the **Aiguille du Goûter**, an easy scramble, but somewhat dangerous, because of rockfall; the Refuge du Goûter is used as a comfortable, if crowded, stop on the way up the mountain. On summit day, most summer climbers start very early, around midnight or 1 A.M., in order to guarantee the best snow and ice conditions on the **Dôme du Goûter** and further up, on the final ridge, the Arête des Bosses, a relatively vertiginous ridge, especially on the Italian side of the mountain. The major difficulty on the climb stems from the rarefied air of high altitude; a **guide** can be very useful, and is recommended for inexperienced climbers, who may have difficulties with route-finding, weather, snow, and ice conditions, and the intimidating aspect of the final ridge; minimal knowledge in ice and snow climbing, including **self-arrest** techniques, are mandatory. (See also color photos and maps.)

Mont Blanc de Courmayeur 4,748 m, 15,577 ft. A minor **satellite** of **Mont Blanc**, located approximately 500 m from the main summit, it is the highest point in **Italy**; however, the highest point is often considered to be the **Dufourspitze**, 4,634 m, 15,203 ft, the second highest peak in the **Alps** and Western Europe, and a major summit, shared by Italy and **Switzerland**.

The Summit of Mont Blanc and the Janssen Observatory (S. G. Wehrli/National Geographic)

The famous voie Major, one of the longest and most sustained climbs in the Alps, on the Pilier du Fréney, ends at the Mont Blanc de Courmayeur; the crossing to the summit of Mont Blanc does not present any technical difficulties.

Mont Blanc du Tacul 4,248 m, 13,937 ft. This is the 21st highest of the 60 major 4,000-meter peaks of the **Alps**. It was first ascended in 1851 by E. T. Ramsey and six guides. A powerful **satellite** of **Mont Blanc**, this is an easy climb from the Col du Midi, or from **Mont Maudit**, upon performing the **Mont Blanc** traverse; however, the Couloir Gervasutti is a difficult ice climb near the Triangle du Tacul, and the Aiguilles du Diables also present formidable problems in mixed terrain. (See also color photos.)

Mont Blanc Range, history of Many consider Alpinism to have been invented in 1760 when **Horace Bénédict de Saussure**, a naturalist from Geneva, offered a large reward to anyone who could find the way up **Mont Blanc**. On July 24, 1760, he visited "Chamouny" and climbed up to the Brevent. In 1786, the first ascent of Mont Blanc was performed by **Jacques Balmat**, a local crystal hunter, who teamed up with **Michel-Gabriel Paccard**, a Chamonix doctor. On August 2, 1786, the two men left Chamonix and camped at the summit of "Montagne de la Côte." Around 4:00 A.M. they left for the Grand Plateau, and at 6:23 P.M., they reached the summit. Their ascent was followed by telescope from Chamonix. The next year, on August 1, at the age of 47, de Saussure, accompanied by 18 guides, reached the summit of Mont Blanc after a bivouac at the Grand Plateau. In 1808, the first female ascent of Mont Blanc was performed by a local Chamonix woman, **Marie Paradis**. In 1818 A. Malczewski and Jean Michel, with five other guides, performed the first ascent of the **Aiguille du Midi**, on August 4. In 1820, the first disaster occurred: a group of five guides left for Mont Blanc; just under the Grand Plateau an avalanche swept them into a crevasse. Only two survived; the other three bodies were discovered 41 years later at the bottom of the Bossons Glacier. In 1823, the Compagnie des Guides de Chamonix was established. In 1857, the Alpine Club was founded in London. Mont Blanc and the Aiguille de Midi were still the only peaks conquered; the golden age of Alpine climbing was about to begin. In 1864, a British engraver, **Edward Whymper**, and a trainee guide, **Michel Croz**, accomplished three first ascents in one week: the Col du Triolet, the Aiguille de Trè-latête, and the **Aiguille d'Argentière**. In 1865, two important first ascents occurred: the **Grandes Jorasses**, on June 24, by E. Whymper, C. M. Croz, C. **Almer**, and F. Biner; on June 29, the **Aiguille Verte**, by E. Whymper, C. Almer, and F. Biner. In 1871, the **Aiguille du Plan**, was first climbed by J. Eccles and M. and A. Payot. In 1876, **Les Droites** were climbed on August 7, by H. Cordier, T. Middlemore, J. Oakley, J. Jaun, and A. Maurer. In 1879, the first ascent of the Petit Dru was performed on August 29, by Jean Charlet-Straton, Prosper Payot, and Frederic Folliguet. By 1880, approximately one century after the first ascent of Mont Blanc, over 3,000 people made the attempt. In 1881 came the first ascent of the Aiguille du Grépon, on August 5, by **A. Mummery**, A. Bergener, and B. Venetz. In 1882, the **Dent du Géant** was climbed on July 28, by the **Maquignaz** brothers. In 1887, first ascent of the Grands Charmoz, on September 10, by A. Mummery, A. Bergener, and B. Venetz. This was followed by: in 1897, first ascent of Les Courtes, on August 17, by O. Schuster and A. Swaine. In 1898, first ascent of the Aiguille de Blatière, on August 7, via the Spencer couloir, by S. Spencer, C. Jossi, and H. Almer. In 1898, first ascent of the **Aiguille du Triolet**, on September 3, by J. B. Guyot, J. Brocherel, and A. Rey. In 1901, first ascent of **Mont Maudit**, on July 31, by P. Cassan and P. Kornacker. In 1904, the Charpoua refuge opened. In 1938, the Walker Spur route on the Grandes Jorasses was done on August 6 by **R. Cassin**, L. Esposito, and U. Tizzoni; the first winter traverse of the **Drus** was performed by Armand Charlet and Camille Devouassoux. In 1952, the south face of the Drus was opened by André Contamine and Michel Bastien. On August 22, 1955, the Bonatti Pillar on the Drus was soloed by **Walter Bonatti**. In 1957, the first winter ascent of the west face of the Drus, by **Jean Couzy** and **René Desmaison**. In 1961, the Central Pillar of the Fréney on August 29, by **C. Bonnington** and **R. Robbins**. In 1962 the American Direct route on the Drus, on July 26 by G. Hemmings and R. Robbins. In 1963, first solo of the west face of the Drus, René Desmaison. In 1964, the first winter ascent of the north face of the Drus was performed by Georges Payot, Yvon Masino, and Gérard Devouassoux. The next milestones induced: In 1967, first ascent of the route des Guides on the north face of the Drus, by **Yannick Seigneur**, Claude Jager, Michel Feuillerade, and Jean-Paul Paris. In 1973, first ascent of the North Grand Couloir on the Drus, by Claude Jager and Walter Cecchinel. In 1975, first ascent of Col du Dru, by Emmanuel Schmutz and Claude Tuccinardi; also, the first descent of the south face of the Drus on skis, by **Jean-Marc Boivin**. In 1979, first ascent of the route "C'est arrivé demain," by Patrick Bérault and Claude and Yves Rémy. In 1981, *enchaînement* Fou-American Direct, by Jean-Marc Boivin and Patrick Bérault. In 1982, first solo ascent of the American Direct on the Dru, by **Christophe Profit** and first ascent of the French Direct on the Drus by Christophe Profit, Michel Bruel, Hervé Sachetat, and Hubert Giot. Between 1980 and 1989, numerous first *enchaînements*, by Eric Escoffier, Rémy Escoffier, Daniel Lacroix, Christophe Profit, and Michel Fauquet. In 1983, the American Direct was free-climbed on the Drus, by Thierry Renault, Pascal Etienne, Christophe Profit, and Eric Escoffier; the first winter ascent of the Lesueur route on the north face of the Drus was performed by Thierry Renault and Andy Parkin. In 1984, a new route was opened on the Grand Pillier d'Angle, on August 8: the direct route of the Divine Providence. In 1986, first descent on snowboard of the Dru by Bruno Gouvy. In 1989, first winter solo ascent of the Bonatti Pillar on the Dru by Alain Ghersen. In 1990, first *enchaînement* of the American Direct, Walker Spur, and Intégrale de Peuterey, by Alain Ghersen. In 1991, first ascent of the route "Destivelle" on the west face of the Grand Dru, by **Catherine Destivelle**. In 1992, first solo of the French Direct on the Dru, by Francois Marsigny. For more detail, see the excellent website www.chamonix.net/english/mountaineering/hist ofalpinism1.htm.

Mont Blanc Tunnel   An 11.5-km, 7-mile-long tunnel that connects **France** and **Italy**. In the 1960s, it was one of the longest tunnels in the world.

Mont Brouillard   4,069 m, 13,339 ft. This is the 43rd highest of the 60 major 4,000-meter peaks of the **Alps**. It was first ascended in 1906 by Karl Blodig, Oskar Eckenstein, and Alexis Brocherel; as such, it was the last major peak above 4,000 meters to be climbed in the Alps. This summit is located on the Italian side of **Mont Blanc**, near its Brenva face.

Mont Maudit   4,465m, 14,648 ft. This is the 11th highest of the 60 major 4,000-meter peaks in the **Alps** and the second-highest peak in the **Mont Blanc Range**. It was first climbed in 1878 by W. E. Davidson, H. S. King, Johann Jaun, and Johann von Bergen. It is a powerful satellite of **Mont Blanc** and presents difficult climbs on its Italian flank; it is also often climbed during the classic traverse of Mont Blanc, where one ascends the **Mont Blanc du Tacul** and the **Aiguille du Midi** after summitting **Mont Blanc**. (See also color photos.)

Mont Saint-Michel   A large rock in **France**, surrounded by water, upon which an abbey was built. For the amateur of medieval architecture, it is a true marvel.

Montana   Lowest point, Kootenai River, Idaho border 549 m, 1,800 ft; highest point, **Granite Peak** 3,901 m, 12,799 ft (10th highest of the 50 state highpoints).

Montane (zone)   The area below the **Alpine life zone** where vegetation grows.

Monte Pissis   6,779 m, 22,240 ft. This is the third highest peak in the **Andes**; it was first climbed in 1937 by Osiecki and A. Szczepanski. The peak is located in **Argentina**.

Monte Rosa   4,634 m, 15,203 ft. This is the second highest major peak in the **Alps**; it is a complex mountain, located between **Switzerland** and **Italy**, comprising five main summits: the **Dufourspitze**, the Pointe **Nordend**, the Pointe **Zumstein**, the **Signalkuppe**, and the Pointe Parrot. Monte Rosa is heavily glaciated and surrounded by other giants, including **Lyskamm**, **Castor** and **Pollux**, and the **Breithorn**, as well as the **Mischabels**, a few miles to the north. The normal route to the **Dufourspitze** is fairly simple, if long, but on the Italian side of the mountain, the east face has a number of very challenging routes, including one of the highest continuous couloirs in the Alps, over 2,000 m, or 6,500 ft high. (See also color photos.)

Montserrat Lowest point, Caribbean Sea 0 m; highest point, Chances Peak (in the Soufrière Hills) 914 m, 2,999 ft. This is an extremely active and dangerous volcanic area; recently a large number of people had to be evacuated for fear of major, catastrophic eruptions.

Monument Valley Located in southern **Utah**, near the **Arizona** boundary, this prodigious landscape sculpted over eons by **erosion** offers excellent rock climbing and a wealth of intriguing geological formations. (See color photos.)

Moore, Adolphus Warburton (1841–1887) Born: England. Bibliography: *The Alps in 1864* (1867).

Moraine Rocky **debris** or **till** left in the wake of a **glacier**, often in the form of a **ridge**. Lateral moraine is located to the sides, medial in the center (where two glaciers meet), and terminal at the farthest point the glacier has reached.

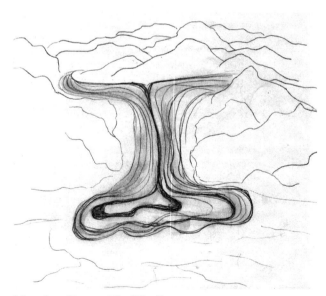

Moraine (Laura Lindblad)

Morin, Nea E. (1905–1986) Born: England. A leader in the development of women's climbing. Bibliography: *A Woman's Reach* (1968).

Morocco Lowest point, Sebkha Tah −55 m, −180 ft; highest point, Jebel Toubkal 4,165 m, 13,665 ft. The **Atlas** Mountains reach high elevations in Morocco, and are often covered with some snow throughout the year; they are part of a rugged, yet beautiful land, full of opportunities for trekkers and rock climbers. (See also color photos.)

Mosquito A small **insect** that can be found at fairly high altitudes if the air is calm. The female of the species is the one that bites animals and humans to suck their blood. Unfortunately, mosquitoes are known to transmit such serious diseases as yellow fever, malaria, filariasis, and dengue fever. Mosquitoes seem to be attracted to host animals by moisture, lactic acid, carbon dioxide, body heat, and movement. In certain damp regions of the world, such as Alaska and Labrador in the summer, gigantic swarms of mosquitoes can make the life of the hiker, trekker, or climber utterly miserable.

Mosquito Range One of **Colorado**'s main **ranges**; its major summits include: Mt. Lincoln 4,354 m, 14,286 ft; Mt. Bross 4,319 m, 14,172 ft; Mt. Democrat 4,312 m, 14,148 ft; and Mt. Sherman 4,278 m, 14,036 ft. (For the complete list of Colorado's 14,000-foot peaks, see the appendix D.)

Moss A small, green, sometimes rupestrine plant that grows in soft clumps in various environments. At altitude, where moss enhances the beauty of the rock rubble, it or **lichen** may be the only visible life form.

Moulin A hole or pothole in a **glacier**.

Mount Evans Byway This road (Colorado Route 5) is the highest paved road in North America. It reaches almost to the top of **Mt. Evans** 4,347 m, 14,264 ft.

Mount Rainier National Park Located in **Washington** State, this park encompasses 235,625 acres and elevations range from 491 m, 1,610 ft to 4,392 m, 14,410 ft above sea level. **Mt. Rainier** is an active volcano encased in over 35 square miles of snow and ice.

Mountain *Berg* (G), *montagne* (F), *montagne* (I), *montaña* (S). A large, lithic extrusion above the earth's surface, commencing on land or under the sea, and characterized by a minimum height (between 1,000 and 3,000 ft, depending on the commentator), change in vegetation and climate as one moves upward, and pronounced local relief, that is, there is a visible alteration from a lower to a higher elevation. Thus, a small hill in the **Himalayas**, even though its terrestrial elevation is 20,000 feet, is not a distinct mountain, although it is part of a mountain **range**. Large mountains rise incrementally and often contain pastures, forested areas, lakes, and other natural manifestations. Surprisingly, three of the best introductions to mountains—their etiology, dispersion, ecology, and influence—can be found in some older volumes: Lane's *Story of Mountains*, Thomas's *Lowell Thomas's Book of the High Mountains*, and the Milnes *Mountains*. Also useful is Price's *Mountains and Man*. (See also **mountain building**.)

Mountain biking A comparatively new sport in which riders and their wide-tired bicycles travel to the top of a mountain, sometimes on a **ski lift** (during the off-seasons), and then race down the slope or ski trails constructed for this purpose. It can be a very messy sport, since falls often result in contact with mud; it can also be extremely dangerous.

Mountain building Mountain development resembles the life cycle of a living being: mountains are born, grow, evolve, diminish, and die. These changes usually take place in geological time—over hundreds of millions of years—but not always. The etiology is bifurcate, that is, there are two very different ways in which mountains come into being. (1) When two **tectonic plates** collide they force the overlying material to **fold** or fracture; this upward movement results in the birth of a mountain. The movement goes on for extended periods, and thus the mountain continues to rise. (The **Himalayas** are a young **system** with jagged peaks

10 Extraordinary Mountains

1. Everest: The highest peak on earth
2. K2: The second highest, and one of the most difficult
3. Aconcagua: The highest in the Western Hemisphere
4. Denali: Highest in North America, some of the fiercest weather on earth
5. Kilimanjaro: Highest in Africa and an awesome volcano
6. Mont Blanc: Highest in the Alps; its first ascent in 1786 marks the beginning of Alpinism
7. The Matterhorn: A superb alpine peak; its tragic first ascent in 1865 is a key point in the history of mountain climbing
8. Rainier: The King of the Cascades is also an extremely dangerous peak because of a potential eruption
9. Fuji-san: A beautifully symmetric peak first climbed in 633 and now a hyper-popular pilgrimage
10. Washington: Most deaths in the United States

10 Most Beautiful Mountains

(This is highly subjective, so here are the authors' favorites)
1. Alpamayo
2. Barre des Écrins
3. Cerro Torre
4. Devil's Tower
5. Fuji-san
6. Hood
7. K2
8. Machupuchare
9. Matterhorn
10. Waddington

10 Amazing Mountain Feats

1. Aaron Ralston: The amputee climber
2. Doug Scott crawled off the Ogre with broken legs
3. Left for Dead (see **Beck Weathers**)
4. Messner's 14 8,000-meter peaks
5. One-hundred-year-old Japanese man climbs Fuji-ssan
6. Seven Summits: Dick Bass
7. *The Long Walk* (see **Slavomir Rawicz**)
8. The voyage of the *Endurance* (see **Ernest Shackleton**)
9. Touching the Void (see **Joe Simpson**)
10. Vern Tejas's first solo winter ascent of Denali

Cities Associated with Mountains

1. Anchorage (Alaska)
2. Calgary (Alberta)
3. Chengdu (China)
4. Denver (Colorado)
5. Geneva (Switzerland)
6. Innsbruck (Austria)
7. La Paz (Bolivia)
8. Lhasa (Tibet)
9. Los Angeles (California)
10. Mexico City (Mexico)
11. Quito (Ecuador)
12. Salt Lake City (Utah)
13. Seattle (Washington)
14. Turin (Italy)
15. Vancouver (British Columbia)

that are still growing.) But at the same time, water, wind, and ice erode the surface and diminish its size. These two opposing forces may counterbalance each other for some time, but eventually the tectonic plates' action ceases and the mountain reaches its apex. From then on, erosive forces work away until nothing but little **hills**, **mesas**, or **buttes** remain where once mighty peaks soared. Finally, even these remnants disappear. (The **Appalachians** are a very old system with rounded surfaces; they are one-fifth as high as the Himalayas.) See Ollier and Pain's *The Origin of Mountains* for an iconoclastically different perspective. (2) Volcanic birth and development is very different, because it can occur in human time. **Volcanoes** appear because geothermal activity forces material to pour out onto the earth's surface, either on land or on the sea floor. This occasionally occurs so

10 Mountain Resort Sites

1. Aspen, Vail, and Snowmass (Colorado)
2. Banff and Jasper (Alberta)
3. Chamonix (France)
4. Lake Tahoe (California)
5. Portillo (Chile)
6. Saint Moritz (Switzerland)
7. Sapporo (Japan)
8. Sun Valley (Idaho)
9. Whistler (British Columbia)
10. Zermatt (Switzerland)

Mountains by Numbers

6 Great Alpine North Faces
7 Summits
13 Provinces and Territories, Highpoints
14 8,000-Meter Peaks
15 14,000-Foot Peaks in California
50 States, Highpoints
54 14,000-Foot Peaks in Colorado
60 4,000-Meter Peaks in the Alps
67 4,000-Foot Peaks in New England

quickly that a new volcano is born and grows hundreds of feet in just a few weeks. Recently, this happened at least twice: **Paricutín** in Mexico and **Surtsey** off the coast of **Iceland** both appeared and grew to mammoth proportions during the course of just a few months. Eruptions of older volcanoes produce vast quantities of **lava**, which can add to the volcanoes' mass and height, but powerful eruptions often blow their tops off, which is precisely what occurred at **Mt. St. Helens** late in the 20th century. It lost hundreds of feet. (See also **volcano** for the various types.)

Mountain goat A gregarious creature that travels across mountainous terrain and glaciers in the American West in small or larger herds (60 or more individuals). It avoids human contact. (See also color photos.)

Mountain gorilla A large, endangered, African **ape** that roams up to 13,200 ft (Burnie and Wilson).

Mountain imagery Although in the distant past **mountains** were often forbidding and distasteful to those who lived in their proximity, they are now objects of desire. Thus, pictorial or textual images of mountains are used to entertain, attract, inspire, control, and seduce in advertising, recruitment, fiction, cinema, and so on.

Mountain lion See **cat**.

Mountain people Perhaps 10 percent of the world's population live in the mountains and of these there are two types. First, are those who inhabit high **altitudes** inadvertently, but do not differ from their ethnic relatives below. For example, an ethnic Swiss whose ancestors have lived near the **Matterhorn** for generations is similar to his or her counterpart who resides in Zurich. The second type includes the indigenous mountain peoples or tribes. The Quechua or Aymara who have spent thousands of years at high altitude in **Bolivia** and **Peru** are physically and physiologically different than people who live along the Gulf of Mexico. People who live in different environments will differ from each other, sometimes dramatically—from physical size, knowledge, and skills to the ways in which they dress and interact. Culture reflects the environment. **Roger Frison-Roche** insists that mountain people are also different

psychologically; he claims that they are silent, cheerful, grave, courageous, patient, enduring, and perseverant (*Montagnes*). It may be misleading and even dangerous to ascribe characteristics to such geographically dispersed peoples, but those who reside in the mountains are often shorter, stockier, and produce more red corpuscles; they live isolated lives and are therefore self-reliant, quiet, even dour, and conservative; they are extremely strong and can carry loads at high elevations for many hours, day after day. Amazingly, they may become fatigued at sea level according to Casewit. Mountain peoples who are renowned for their fighting prowess, climbing skills, individuality, or long lives include, respectively, the Gurkha, **Sherpa**, Basque, and **Hunza**. Writing in 1986, Michael Tobias claimed that the total population of mountain peoples is decreasing, due especially to migration. Additional changes have been wrought upon these peoples because of the inundations and depredations of the **tourist** industry, which brings in travelers, trekkers, and climbers in ever-increasing numbers. This is good for emerging economies, but wreaks havoc with traditional ways of life, which, in part, help to support hundreds of millions of people through farming, logging, mining, and even tourism. See Cameron for capsule overviews of Himalayan ethnic groups including the Naga, Newars, Sherpas, Tajik, and Uzbek among many others and *American Mountain People* for a profusely illustrated volume on Americans who live in very different mountain environments. Thesiger's *Last Nomad* offers some superb portraits of mountain people.

Mountain Rescue Association An association of American volunteer rescue groups (www.mra.org).

Mountain sickness See **acute mountain sickness**.

Mountain Voices A website that offers comments on many aspects of mountain life (e.g., agriculture, family, water) by the people who live there. Ten countries including **Peru** and **India** are represented (www.mountainvoices.org).

Mountain wind See **winds**.

Mountaineering *Alpinisme* (F), *alpinismo* (I), *Bergsteigen* (G). A type of climbing in which a person ascends rocky, snowy, or icy slopes or

Table 1. Important High Altitude Research Stations of the World

Name and Location	Altitude (feet/meters)
United States	
Mount Evans, Colorado	14,264 (4,350)
Summit Hut, White Mountain, California	14,246 (4,354)
Pikes Peak, Colorado	14,110 (4,304)
Mount Wrangell, Alaska	14,000 (4,270)
Mauna Kea Summit, Hawaii	13,800 (4,209)
Barcroft Laboratory, White Mountain, California	12,470 (3,803)
Climax, Colorado	11,190 (3,413)
Echo Lake Research Station, Colorado	10,700 (3,264)
Leadville, Colorado	10,500 (3,203)
Crooked Creek, White Mountain, California	10,150 (3,096)
Kole Kole, Hawaii	10,020 (3,056)
Mauna Kea Observatory, Hawaii	9,800 (2,989)
South America	
Cesar Tejos, Chile	20,000 (6,100)
Laboratorio Física, Cósmica Chacaltaya, near La Paz Bolivia	17,060 (5,203)
Ticlio, Peru	15,400 (4,700)
Institute of Andean Biology, Morococha, Peru	14,900 (4,545)
Instituto de Biología, Mina Aguilar de la Altura, Argentina	14,763 (4,503)
Cerro de Pasco, Peru	14,200 (4,331)
Infernillo, Chile	14,170 (4,322)
La Oroya, Peru	12,230 (3,730)
University of La Paz, Bolivia	11,800 (3,600)
Instituto Geofísico de Huancayo, Peru	10,990 (3,352)
Eva Perón, Argentina	10,170 (3,102)
Europe	
Capanna Margherita, Monte Rosa, Italy	14,953 (4,559)
Observatoire Vallot, Mont Blanc, France	14,281 (4,356)
L'Aiguille du Midi, Mont Blanc, France	11,810 (3,602)
Laboratorio Testa, Grigia, Val d'Aosta, Italy	11,417 (3,482)
Jungfraujoch High Altitude Research Station, Berner Oberland, Switzerland	11,397 (3,476)
Sonnblick, Austria	10,190 (3,108)
Grossglockner, Austria	9,840 (3,000)
Cal d'Olen (Instituto Angelo Mosso), Italy	9,512 (2,900)
Instituto Angelo Mosso, Monte Rosa, Italy	9,396 (2,866)
Obergurgl, Austria	6,560 (2,000)
Other areas	
Italian Research Laboratory, Lobuche, Nepal	16,175 (4,930)
Himalayan Rescue Association, Nepal	14,000 (4,270)
Everest View Hotel, Nepal	12,700 (3,874)
Mount Fuji, Japan	12,370 (3,773)
Gulmarg Laboratory, India	9,900 (3,020)

SOURCE: Hultgren, with permission of Hultgren Publications.

glaciers that can be steep, but usually not vertical. Mountaineering on high or difficult terrain may require rock or ice climbing skills. (See also Cox and Fulsaas's *Mountaineering: The Freedom of the Hills* for a replete overview; Barry's *Alpine Climbing* is also extremely helpful.)

Mountaineering history Although people have traveled, hunted, worshipped, sacrificed, farmed, and even lived in the mountains (sometimes at relatively high altitudes) for millennia, it is only during the last few hundred years that mountaineering—climbing for its own sake—has become an active pursuit or sport. What follows here is a mere footnote to the replete documented history that exists in thousands of diaries, periodical articles, accounts, and monographic studies. In the distant past, those who lived in the proximity of mountains, especially the domineering ranges, peaks, and active volcanoes that soar to 10, 15, 20, or 25 thousand feet, were intimidated and fearful of the heights: very real dangers (animals, avalanches, cold, crevasses, lava, storms, wind) lurked above, and the summits or interiors of volcanoes were the **abodes of the gods**. Unless there was a good reason for trespassing, most people kept to the valleys or lower **Alpine meadows**. In the late 18 century, European scientists, explorers, and adventurers began to make forays into the higher

12 Great Historical Mountaineers

1. Albert Mummery
2. Edward Whymper
3. Giusto Gervasutti
4. Horace Walker
5. Jean-Antoine Carrel
6. Melchior Anderreg
7. Michel Croz
8. Tom Longstaff
9. William Coolidge
10. Eric Shipton
11. Harold Tilman

areas. A small group of people became obsessed with reaching the summits of specific peaks. Horace Benedict **de Saussure** offered a reward to the first person to stand on the top of **Mont Blanc**, and in 1786, **Jacques Balmat** and **Michel-Gabriel Paccard** managed this feat, thus opening the floodgates to hundreds of amateur climbers and professional guides whose goal was to be the first to stand on the summits of the thousands of high peaks located first in Europe, then in the Americas and Asia, and finally in Africa, Australia, and Antarctica. During "The Golden Age of Mountaineering" (1854–1865 or later), almost 200 **first ascents** were achieved in the **Alps**. Many outstanding climbers pursued these summits, sometimes fanatically. **Whymper** spent many years climbing in the Alps and in 1865 finally reached the summit of the **Matterhorn**. **Coolidge**, among other early, dedicated climbers, also spent his spare time in the Alps and achieved many first ascents. Some of these same Alpine pioneers then began to stray farther from home and visited the **Andes**, the **Caucasus**, and other systems and ranges. As peaks succumbed and first ascents became less available, climbers sought out new and more difficult routes and winter climbs so that new possibilities remained open to the adventurous. Indeed, even today, there are many available mountains, routes, and seasonal variations that allow one to claim something unprecedented in mountaineering history. Climbs in the Alps could usually be done in a day or two, but once climbers traveled to the higher systems, it be-

20 Great Modern Mountaineers

1. Alex Lowe
2. Anatoli Boukreev
3. David Breashears
4. Doug Scott
5. Ed Viesturs
6. Eric Weihenmayer
7. Hermann Buhl
8. Jean Couzy
9. Jerry Kukuczka
10. Jim Whittaker
11. Kurt Diemberger
12. Lionel Terray
13. Maurice Herzog
14. Peter Habeler
15. Reinhold Messner
16. Sir Chris Bonington
17. Sir Edmund Hillary
18. Tom Hornbein
19. Walter Bonatti
20. Wojcieck Kurtyka

10 Best All-Around Mountaineers

1. Alex Lowe
2. Sir Chris Bonington
3. Edward Whymper
4. Hermann Buhl
5. Jerry Kukuczka
6. Lionel Terray
7. Reinhold Messner
8. Ricardo Cassin
9. Walter Bonatti
10. William Coolidge

came necessary to mount complicated **expeditions**, some of which roll along for many months. There are two very different reasons why an extended expedition is necessary. Even in 2003, in the Andes or Himalayas, traveling by foot or pack train, it can take a week or two to reach **base camp**. And once at the mountain, it takes long periods to acclimate as well as to equip the higher camps for a summit bid. **Alpine-style** climbs can reduce the time spent here, but the highest peaks and their undependable weather defy these tactics. Whymper and other Alpine pioneers attempted and sometimes conquered many peaks in various parts of the world. Eventually local **guides** and climbers (in the Andes and the Himalayas, for example) also began to climb. Early expeditions to the Himalayas investigated, explored, attempted, and summitted many mountains, but it was not until 1950 that **Herzog** conquered the first 8,000-meter peak (**Annapurna**); in 1953, after innumerable expeditions had tried, **Hillary** and **Norgay** finally reached the summit of **Everest**. During the subsequent half century, many more people have become interested in mountaineering and now all of the world's mountainous areas (including Antarctica) have been visited frequently and the various peaks surmounted. Two negative results of the increased interest in this sometimes dangerous sport are that in their quest to succeed, people sometimes take unnecessary risks and are hurt or killed; additionally, the mountains' surfaces may be scarred and the environment is often left littered with trash. (See also **periodicals,** as well as Ardito,

Salkeld, Ullman [*Age*], and Unsworth [*Hold*], for detailed overviews.)

Mountaineers, The   A **club**, and a prolific publisher of books pertaining to mountains and climbing (www.mountaineersbooks.org).

Mountains and nations   A few of the world's major mountains are associated with specific Western nations, because the mountaineers who attempted to reach their summits consistently, though not exclusively, came from that country. Examples include **Everest** and Great Britain, **Nanga Parbat** and Germany, and **K2** and the United States.

Mountains in paintings   Images of mountains have inspired artists in diverse cultures. (See **painters** for a fuller treatment.)

Mountains on other worlds   Io, Mars, the moon, and Venus all have mountainous terrain. (See also **Olympus Mons**.)

Mountaintop removal   A technique that removes the tops of mountains in order to mine **coal**. It destroys the natural beauty of the mountain and pollutes waterways, and is thus disliked by the environmentally conscious. It is illegal in some areas. (See also **mining**.)

Movies and mountains   Listing all the films in which a mountain appears since the Lumière brothers took Edison's motion picture into the open is an almost impossible task. Snow-capped peaks provide grandeur in many films. The first panorama shots were used in the late 1890s; by 1916 or so, thanks to lighter equipment, real location shooting was employed. Swedish movies of 1917–1920, like ***Berg-Ejvind och Hans Hustru***, conveying a then unknown sense of nature, had great influence. Because climbing was of interest to a larger part of the population and mountains were picturesque (see, for example, ***Altitude 3200***), **Arnold Fanck** was able to produce scripts dealing only with climbing matters and still have a large audience. Documentaries like The Epic of Everest also helped. When talkies arrived, studios became the rage, and mountain films faded a little. The sound equipment was very heavy, and a location film with live recording was very difficult to make. European movies, relying more on realism than their American counterparts, sometimes tried to maintain the custom (for political reasons, as in Germany).

A Brief Chronology of Altitude Records

It is now well established that during pre-Columbian times, Inca priests climbed to the summits of high peaks in the Andes to perform ritual sacrifices; for example, desiccated mummies have been found in the Andes at elevations approaching 20,000 feet: "Juanita" was discovered near the summit of Mt. Ampato, 6,288 m, 20,630 ft, in Peru. In this sidebar, however, we restrict ourselves to the historical record, as well as to actual summitting; for example, Alexander von Humboldt reaching an altitude of 5,759 m, 18,893 ft, on Chimborazo in 1802, or the extreme heights attained by Mallory and Irvine on Everest in 1924 are not included here. (see www.pbs.org/wgbh/nova/peru/mummies/high1.html)

In 633, a Japanese monk climbs Mt. Fuji, 3,776 m, 12,388 ft. This represents the first recorded climb on a snowcapped peak.

In 1786, Jacques Balmat and Michel-Gabriel Paccard ascend Mont Blanc, 4,807 m, 15,770 ft, in France.

In 1837, W. T. Thomson ascends Damavand, 5,670 m, 18,603 ft, in Iran.

In 1848, Reynolds and Maynard ascend Orizaba, 5,700 m, 18,700 ft, in Mexico.

In 1872, Wilheim Reiss and Angel Escobar ascend Cotopaxi 5,897 m, 19,347 ft, in Ecuador.

In 1880, Edward Whymper and Jean-Antoine and Louis Carrel ascend Chimborazo, 6,267 m, 20,561 ft, in Ecuador.

In 1897, Matthias Zurbriggen solos Aconcagua 6,959 m, 22,831 ft, in Argentina.

In 1907, Tom Longstaff, and Brocherel and Karbir Burathoki ascend Trisul 7,120 m, 23,359 ft, in India.

In 1928, Karl Wien, Eugene Allwein, and Erwin Schneider ascend Pik Lenin, 7,134 m, 23,405 ft, in Tajikistan and Kyrgyzstan.

In 1931, Frank Smythe, Eric Shipton, R. L. Holdsworth, and Lewa Sherpa ascend Kamet, 7,756 m, 25,446 ft, in India and Tibet.

In 1936, Noel Odell and Harold Tilman ascend Nanda Devi, 7,816 m, 25,643 ft, in India.

In 1950, Maurice Herzog and Louis Lachenal ascend Annapurna 8,091 m, 26,545 ft, in Nepal.

In 1953, Sir Edmund Hillary and Tenzing Norgay Sherpa ascend Everest 8,850 m, 29,035 ft, in Nepal and Tibet, thus ending the quest to reach higher elevations on the planet; climbers now turn to more and more difficult routes using less and less technical help.

This is a schematic representation of the chronology of the highest elevations reached, as described in this sidebar: starting with Mont Blanc in 1786, each triangle represents a new altitude record, as a function of time. The curve culminates on top of Everest, in 1953. One notices a few plateaus, during which altitude records remain almost constant, followed by rapid progression toward a new plateau; these "jumps" are generally related with new techniques and technologies aiding the climbers, as well as the opening of new mountain ranges: for example, the period 1872–1897 corresponds to very active climbing in the Andes.

After World War II, though, location shooting came back. Sound tapes were now available, and movies were fighting television, so large-scale entertainment was needed. It also became almost mandatory for mountain films to be shot in color (The White Tower, Les Étoiles de midi). From the 1960s onward, extraordinary scenery lost its appeal, lacking the sociological insights that were then trendy. Like westerns, mountain films had to be revived by mixing them with another genre (spying or disaster). Recently, with the stress on environmental issues and the craze for nature, some high-octane, popcorn movies dealing with the spectacular aspects of mountains have appeared (**Cliffhanger**, **Vertical Limit**). The separate entries in this volume offer a broad, though limited of necessity, spectrum of mountain films. Aside from the few films entirely devoted to climbing, mountains are widely used for dramatic purposes. Most of the time, they present difficulties that the hero has to overcome (in westerns, for example, or in the spectacular wide-screen movies of the 1950s such as *Around the World in Eighty Days*). Mountains can also be found in historical films in which only the accuracy of the occasion is considered and not that of the climb (**Hannibal** or Napoleon crossing the **Alps** could hardly be located at sea level; the Indian tribe pictured in *Drum Beat* actually lived in Arizona). Philosophically, mountains are considered in movies—as in literature—as pure places, free from devastating human passions: in *La Roué* (1921–1922), even though the mountains are dangerous, they are seen as a harbor against the unhappy life in the plains; in *Lost Horizon* (1937), the Himalayas (and **Mont Blanc**, in shots taken from Fanck's movies) protect the ideal city of Shangri-La from outside attacks, that is, lust, envy, and hatred. *Heidi*, set in Switzerland, exists in a multitude of versions (1920, 1937, 1952, 1965, 2001) and is replete with cute people and equally cute marmots. In *The Ten Commandments* (1956) climbing is a test that leads to knowledge. In a far more profane way, *La Montaña Sacrada*/The Holy Mountain (1973) pictures climbing as a journey through life. In American cinema, mountains and villages are often seen as indications of a potential Thoreau-like paradise

(*Wild Girl*, 1932) even if some movies explored more of the savage side of natural life (*Child Bride*, 1938; *Deliverance*, 1972). Of course, mountains are also the usual refuge of menacing characters, whether vampires (*Nosferatu*, 1922, *Dracula*, 1931), mad scientists (*Frankenstein*, 1931, but also camp master Ed Wood's *Bride of the Monster*, 1955), Nazis (*Where Eagles Dare*, 1969), or simply lunatics (*The Shining*, 1980, with Jack Nicholson running amok), not to mention the ubiquitous yetis. The mountains are also where one can lead the old so they can die (both versions of *Narayama Bushiko*/The Ballad of Narayama, 1958 and 1982), where man has to go beyond his limits to survive (cannibalism in *Alive*, 1993), where the wrath of God may at any moment crush the villain under tons of snow (Vincent Price in *Dangerous Mission*, 1954, a 3-D movie in which the avalanche flows out into the audience). As for narrative ideas, the mountain environment is an excellent place where characters can be left alone without help either for laughs (*Meyer aus Berlin*/Meyer of Berlin, 1919, squeezes a husband, wife, and lover into a hut; *Love Is News*, 1937, brings together two hostile characters surrounded by wilderness) or dramatic effect (*La Nuit Blanche*, 1948, has a man trapped in a hut with the girl he holds responsible for the death of his son). Remote locations also can enhance the loneliness of characters, hence the tension in *Andesu No Hanayome*/Bride of the Andes, 1966 or *La Trace*, 1983. Mountains are still the best way to symbolize a frontier (which was frantically used in Europe after World War II: *Die Letze Chance*/The Last Chance, 1945, is a Swiss movie dealing with American soldiers trying to help refugees get into Switzerland; *Le Dessous des Cartes*/Under the Cards, 1947, depicts a character involved with contraband; in *Fuga in Francia*/Flight into France, 1948, a fascist tries to escape justice by joining a group of workers on their illegal way to France. Film noir used mountains to create maximum contrast with the usual urban setting (*Conflict*, 1945, with Bogart murdering his wife on a mountain road; *Nightfall*, 1957, in which the villain is killed by a snowplowgh). Towering mountains are also seen as forces of nature, placing human problems in perspective (*Die Heilige und Ihr Narr*/The

Saint and Her Fool, 1928, or *Kanchzenjungha*, 1962, by Indian director Satyajit Ray). When in comedies they provide comic relief (*Die Verliebte Firma*/The Company's in Love, 1931, or *Un Oiseau Rare*/A Rare Bird, 1935). Even if some movies tried to induce higher standards (parts of *Kid Boots*, 1927, Eddie Cantor's first film or the end of *On a Volé la Cuisse de Jupiter*/Jupiter's Tight, 1979), the characters always find themselves hanging onto something and yelling (except in silent films). In the 1960s, mountains provided high-class locations for equally high-class comedies (*Charade*, 1963, *The Pink Panther*, 1964). Eventually, even American cartoons got into the game: *Mulan*, 1998; *Alpine Climbers*, 1938 (Mickey Mouse, Donald Duck, and Goofy); *Northwest Hounded Police*, 1947 (Droopy); *Alpine for You*, 1951 (Popeye); *The Abominable Snow Rabbit* 1960 (Bugs Bunny, Daffy Duck); *A Scent of the Matterhorn*, 1961 (Pepe Le Pew); and the Roadrunner series. And some mountain films have even been produced using Imax-3D technology. (M-A. H.) (See also movies and mountains [documentaries], movies and mountains [westerns].)

Movies and mountains (documentaries)
Mountaineers (and rock climbers) sometimes carry a movie camera (8, 16, 35, or 70 mm, and now digital devices) or bring along a cinematographer to document the climb. The first ascent of **Annapurna**, in 1950, was filmed by **Marcel Ichac**. Other movies include *Alaskan Reminiscences: 60 Years of Adventure with Bradford and Barbara Washburn*; *Americans on Everest*; *Everest: The Death Zone*; and *Touching the Void*, a hybrid made after the fact with actors as well as the original participants.

Movies and mountains (westerns) "Go west, young man, and grow up with the country." Horace Greeley's advice had generations of settlers hitting the Rocky Mountains before they knew how to cross them. After all, these mountains were part of the "wild west" to be conquered. It is almost easier to list movie westerns without mountains than those with them. Excluding the very special case of **Jeremiah Johnson**, mountains are just part of the dangers the valiant pioneers have to fight, alongside wild animals, rebellious Indians, and blowing sand. Climbing is infrequent; only falling off precipices occurs with any regularity.

The first westerns were shot in **New Jersey** (*The Great Train Robbery*, 1903) or in France, whether in the Bois de Vincennes not far from Paris or near the Mediterranean (*Le Railway de la Mort*, 1913), and, of course, do not display any mountains. At that time, studios were more convenient than locations, and only after 1910 did outdoor shooting become the rule. The shift from the East Coast to **California** in 1913 (*The Squaw Man*, shot near Lake Arrowhead, is supposed to be the first movie made in Hollywood) offered large areas free of buildings and roads. Westerns lost their popularity during the 1960s and subsequently only a few have been made, and those usually change the rules (*McCabe and Mrs. Miller*, 1971) or convey greater realism (*Ulzana's Raid*, 1972). In this respect, the evolution of westerns is parallel to that of mountain films. The use of mountains in westerns changes dramatically from director to director and each one has his trademark (mountains are challenges for Raoul Walsh, shelters for Delmer Daves, and strategic locations for Anthony Mann). Hollywood made use of much of the continent: from **Alaska** (all movies dealing with the 1898 gold rush such as *Trail of '98*, 1928, *Road to Utopia*, 1945, *North to Alaska*, 1960, and five versions of *The Spoilers*, 1914, 1923, 1930, 1942, and 1955) to Canada's **Alberta** (*River of No Return*, 1954, and *Buffalo Bill and the Indians*, 1976) and Hudson Bay (*North of Hudson Bay*, 1923, and *Hudson's Bay*, 1941); from the Mojave Desert (*The Wind*, 1928, and *Man of the West*, 1958) to **Montana** (*Cattle Queen of Montana*, 1954, *The Last Wagon*, 1956, and *Heaven's Gate*, 1980) to **Colorado** (*Devil's Doorway*, 1950, and *The Naked Spur*, 1953); and frequently **Arizona** (*The Outlaw*, 1943, *The Baron of Arizona*, 1950, *Broken Arrow*, 1950, *Johnny Guitar*, 1954, *Gunfight at O.K. Corral*, 1957, *The Man Who Loved Cat Dancing*, 1973, *Posse*, 1975, and *The Quick and the Dead*, 1995) as well as **Utah** (*The Big Trail*, 1930, *Westward the Women*, 1951, *Rio Conchos*, 1964, and parts of *The Outlaw Josey Wales*, 1976). Utah also represented the Mohawk Valley in *Drums along the Mohawk* (1939). **Wyoming** was used in *The Big Sky* (1952), **Idaho** in *Northwest Passage* (1940) and *Pale Rider* (1985), **Oregon** in *Canyon Passage* (1946), and **South Dakota** in *Tomahawk* (1951) and *Dances with Wolves* (1990).

Of course, there is also Monument Valley, nicknamed "John Ford's country," because the director shot numerous movies there (*Stagecoach*, 1939, *My Darling Clementine*, 1946, his "cavalry trilogy"—*Fort Apache*, 1948, *She Wore a Yellow Ribbon*, 1949, and *Rio Grande*, 1950—as well as *Wagon Master*, 1950, and *Cheyenne Autumn*, 1964). Ford was also keen on the Mojave Desert, where, in 1948 for *3 Godfathers*, he reused the same locations as he did in *Hell Bent* (1918). If most of his movies were shot in neighboring locations, *The Searchers* (1956) takes us from California to Utah, Colorado, and Alberta, even though the movie supposedly opens in **Texas**. The **Alabama Hills**, located in Lone Pine, California, are the setting for innumerable films. European westerns also use mountains as backgrounds or for dramatic effect, for example, *Il Grande Silenzio*/The Big Silence (1968). (M-A. H.) (See also **movies and mountains**.)

Mozambique   Lowest point, Indian Ocean 0 m; highest point, Monte Binga 2,436 m, 7,992 ft.

Mramornaja Stena   6,400 m, 20,997 ft. This remote peak of the **Tien Shan** Range is located in **Kazakhstan** and was first climbed in 1953 by V. Shipilov.

Mt.   For peaks whose names begin with this locution, look under the second term, for example, for Mt. Washington, see **Washington, Mt.**

Mudslide   (Also mudflow) A roiling cascade of liquefied earth (mud) downwards along a **slope**. It can be devastatingly harmful, because, like an **avalanche**, it carries houses and people along with it or buries habitations and people in the valley below. (See also **lahar**.)

Muir, John   (1838–1914) A Scottish naturalist who emigrated to the United States, Muir was also a conservationist, founder of the Sierra Club, second president of the **American Alpine Club**, and a rock climber; he was especially fond of the **Yosemite** area and influenced Theodore Roosevelt, who preserved **Yellowstone**, the first **national park**. His **solo** ascents of Cathedral Peak (1869) and Mt. Ritter (1872) marked the beginnings of American rock climbing (Pat Ament, personal comment). Bibliography: *The Mountains of California* (1894), *My First Summer in the Sierra* (1911), *The Yosemite* (1912), *Travels in Alaska* (1915), *Steep Trails* (ca.

1918), *Yosemite and the Sierra Nevada* (1948). (See also **John Muri Trail**.)

Mummery, Albert Frederick   (1855–1895) Born: Dover, England. An extraordinary British rock climber and mountaineer, who made important first ascents in the **Mont Blanc Range** and is considered by many to be the father of modern **Alpinism**. His first ascents include: the **Zmutt Nose** of the **Matterhorn**, 1879, with Alexander Burgener, J. Petrus, and A. Gentinetta; north summit of the Grands Charmoz, 1880, with A. Burgener and Benedikt Venetz; the Grépon by the Nantillons Face, 1881, with A. Burgener and B. Venetz. Despite his considerable achievements he was refused membership at the Alpine Club for several years, probably on class grounds. He died during an expedition to **Nanga Parbat**, with Hastings and Collie: Mummery and two Gurkhas disappeared high on the mountain in 1895. Bibliography: *My Climbs in the Alps and Caucasus* (1895), *Tiger in the Snow* (1967), by W. Unsworth.

Munday, Phyllis   (1894–1990) A great climber with 30 **first ascents**; she was the first woman to summit **Mt. Robson**.

Munich School   During the late 1920s and 1930s, a new philosophy of climbing evolved. Since some of those involved lived in Munich, it has become known by this city's name. According to **Willi Unsoeld**, these people abjured traditional methods; tended to be aggressive, precipitous, or even careless; adopted new equipment (pitons, carabiners); and attempted the most difficult climbs, especially the Alpine **north faces**.

Munro, Sir Hugh T.   (1856–1919) Born: London, England. Bibliography: *Munro's Tables* (altitudes of Scottish peaks) were first published in 1891 in the September issue of the *Scottish Mountaineering Club Journal*. They were revised and republished in 1921 and enlarged and republished in 1933. A new edition was published in book form in 1953. There have been many revisions and reprintings since. The first metric edition was published in 1974. (www.simpkins57 .freeserve.co.uk/mountain_lakes_books/whoswho/ whoswhodetails.html.)

Murray, William Hutchison   (1913–1996) Born: Liverpool, England. Bibliography: *Moun-

taineering in Scotland (1947), *The Scottish Himalayan Expedition* (1951), *Undiscovered Scotland* (1951), *The Story of Everest* (1953), *The Craft of Climbing* (1964), *The Evidence of Things Not Seen* (2002), autobiography.

Mushroom   The reproductive organ of an underground mycelium; mushrooms appear after rainstorms at various altitudes. Some are extremely toxic, but others are considered delicacies and are eaten by many peoples. Different species are not included in this listing.

Music and mountains   Before the Romantic era, mountains were considered annoyances that disrupted the harmony of nature; they were not mentioned in works of art, except for the fantastic landscapes found in some paintings, where cliffs and menacing peaks dwelled in the background. Only in the early 1800s did they appear in literature, and it is little wonder that descriptive music before that time abjured them. Musical description of mountains developed slowly and then faded after World War I, when music became more abstract and less related to nature. In 1802, Beethoven (1770–1827) composed an oratorio, *Christus am Ölberge*/Christ on the Mount of Olives, but it was mere coincidence. The more figurative genre of opera was where the trend began. The second scene of Act II of Carl Maria von Weber's (1786–1826) *Freischutz* (1821), which is located in the frightening *wolfsschlucht* (wolves' gorge), marks the intrusion of wild nature into music. More delicately, *La Muette de Portici*/Masaniello, by Daniel François Esprit Auber (1782–1871), was the rage of 1828. Set in Naples in 1647, during the Spanish oppression, it climaxes as Vesuvius erupts. *Der Vampyr* by Heinrich August Marschner (1795–1861) appeared in the same year, and there followed countless works by the end of the century. One notes the importance of mountains as a revealer of characters' relationships: in his *Tetralogy* (1848–1876), Richard Wagner (1813–1883) locates the lesser people under the surface of the earth while the gods and heroes are usually found on high. Since very few operas are written without a literary basis, some of the intrusions are almost compulsory: being asked by the Paris Opéra to add the mandatory ballet to his 1859 *Faust*, Charles Gounod (1818–1893) included a scene on the

Harz Mountains in which the music does not reflect the heights. Dealing with the same theme, Arrigo Boito (1842–1918), abjured the scene in his *Mefistofele* (1874). By the end of the century, opera became more realistic, which led to less interest in nature. In an attempt to import this new Italian style called *verismo* into Germany, Eugen d'Albert (1864–1932) composed the rather successful *Tiefland* (1903). Based on a Spanish play, it portrays a shepherd in the **Pyrénées**, freeing a woman from the evil influence of an urban villain. In 1913, Giacomo Puccini (1858–1924), fulfilled a commission for the Metropolitan Opera: *La Fanciulla del West*, set in the California Sierras. Apart from the few specific entries in this encyclopedia, little nonrepresentational music exists. There is the "Tatra-Album Opus 12" (1883–1884), a piano composition by Polish pianist and composer Ignacy-Jan Paderewski (1860–1941); it bears the enlightening subtitle (*Tänze und Lieder des Polnischen Volkes aus Zakopene*/Dances and Songs of the Polish People of Zakopene). The *Symphonie Cevenole* by Vincent d'Indy (1851–1931), composed in 1886, is also known as *Symphonie sur un Chant Montagnard Français*/Symphony on a French Mountain Air. Joseph Canteloube (1879–1957) spent a large part of his life composing his *Chants d'Auvergne*/Songs of the Auvergne, and Camille Saint-Saëns (1835–1921) wrote a "Rhapsodie d'Auvergne" for piano. It should also to be noted that important composers like Hungarians Béla Bartók (1881–1945) and Zoltán Kodály (1883–1867) spent years transcribing folk songs and recording them on wax cylinders both in the mountains and the plains. The Pole Karol Szymanowski (1882–1937) would stay in mountain villages in order to listen to the local music, and Russian Aram Khatchaturian (1903–1978) used folksongs in most of his works. Many European composers confessed their love for the calm one finds at altitude: Swiss Arthur Honegger (1892–1955) and Germans Paul Hindemith (1895–1963) and Ernst Krenek (1900–1991). Gustav Mahler (1860–1911) greeted conductor Bruno Walter (1876–1962), visiting him in the mountains, saying: "Don't look up there, it's all in my new symphony." Indeed, the opening of Mahler's *Third Symphony* might very well be the best depiction of mountains in music. Conductors Otto Klemperer (1885–1973) and Wilhelm Furtwängler (1886–1954) were once photographed in climbing attire and French pianist François-René Duchâble (1952–) is often pictured on recordings facing mountains or climbing them. Swiss musicologist Aloys Mooser recalled how, trapped by a storm in a little hut near the Col du Géant, he met conductor Arturo Toscanini (1867–1957) and began talking about Mussorgsky's *Boris Godunov*. Toscanini climbed **Mont Blanc** and **Monte Rosa**, and in 1905 wrote to a friend that: "We gave up the Grivola because of the storm. I'm going back there today. Sunday, I do the Herbetet which will end my climbing this year for the Matterhorn is out of the question due to weather." As late as 1950, during his American tour with the NBC Symphony Orchestra, Toscanini was seen atop Mt. Baldy with some of the musicians. (Candid footage shows that he used the chairlift.) (M-A. H.) (See also **music and mountains [popular]**.)

Music and mountains (popular) Popular songs sometimes include or feature mountains, but they invariably play a less significant role than the people (often lovers) who inhabit or visit them. "Over The Mountain," "Mountain of Love," and John Denver's "Rocky Mountain High" are blatant examples. Mountain people often create folk music played on banjos, dulcimers, fiddles, zithers, and other instruments indigenous to a specific area such as the **Appalachians**, for example, or bluegrass. (See also **music and mountains**.)

Mustang In this context, a wild horse. There are many of these creatures, usually traveling in herds, in the western part of the United States. They are plains animals but they do move upward into canyons and along slopes at higher elevations. For example, the authors have seen surprisingly large horses as high as 10,000 ft on Nevada's **Boundary Peak**. They are skittish, sometimes aggressive, and not used to human beings.

Mustard Many species of this **flower** family do well in the high Himalayas, up to 18,000 ft (Polunin).

Mutia Escarpment A towering rift set somewhere in Africa; behind it stands the elephants' burial ground. It happens to be the kingdom of Tarzan (Lord Greystoke). Invented by MGM writers for the 1932 movie, the Mutia Escarpment varies in shape, height, or topography in the sequels and is a convenient place to lose a few native porters, resist attacks of hostile tribes (it is taboo), and enhance suspense when the heroes are on the edge and villains attempt to push them off. (M-A. H.)

Muztagh In Pakistan, a designation for a series of peaks. The term means "ice mountain."

Muztagh Ata (K-5) 7,546 m, 24,757 ft. This major peak is located within the Muztagh Ata Range in **China**. It was first ascended in 1956, by three members of the Sino-Russian expedition led by E. A. Beletsky.

Muztagh Tower 7,276 m, 23,871 ft. Located in the **Karakoram**, this extremely impressive peak was first scaled in 1956 by John Hartog, **Joe Brown**, Tom Patey, and Ian McNaught Davis.

Myanmar Lowest point, Andaman Sea 0 m; highest point, Hkakabo Razi 5,881 m, 19,295 ft.

Mythology (Myths) The beliefs and belief systems of different groups of people, often explained and clarified through stories and tales. Mountains may play a seminal role in these narratives. For example, **Mt. Olympus**, for the ancient Greeks, was the **abode of the gods**, and **Mt. Sinai**, in the Judeo-Christian tradition, is the place where god gave Moses the tablets engraved with the Ten Commandments. (See also **religion**.)

Nadelhorn 4,327 m, 14,196 ft. This is the 15th highest of the 60 major 4,000-meter peaks in the **Alps**. One of the major summits of the **Mischabels**, the Nadelhorn was conquered in 1853 by Josef Zimmermann, Alois Supersaxo, Baptiste Epiney, and Franz Andenmatten.

Nails See **clothing**: *Boots*.

Namcha Barwa 7,756 m, 25,445 ft. This major peak is located within the **Himalayas** in **Tibet**.

Namibia Lowest point, Atlantic Ocean 0 m; highest point, Konigstein 2,606 m, 8,550 ft.

Nanda Devi ("Goddess of Bliss") 7,816 m, 25,643 ft. Until the annexing of **Sikkim**, it was the highest peak and a sacred site in **India**. Nanda Devi was first climbed in 1936, by **N. E. Odell** and **H. W. Tilman**. It is the 25th highest mountain in the world. (See also **religion**.)

Nanga Parbat (Also Diamir) 8,126 m, 26,660 ft. The ninth highest mountain in the world, located in **Pakistan**. Nanga Parbat was first climbed by **Hermann Buhl**, who soloed the peak on July 3, 1953. As of the end of 1999, the peak had been scaled 186 times; 61 climbers lost their lives either attempting the summit or upon **descent**. Nanga Parbat is characterized by the huge rise of its Diamir Face, and its large summit **plateau**; indeed, some climbers have been confused as to which is the actual summit of the mountain because of the long and numerous **false summits**. (See also the **14 8,000-Meter Peaks** sidebar.)

Nanga Parbat Pilgrimage This is an absolute classic, written by **Hermann Buhl**. (See also **10 Great Mountain Adventure Books** sidebar.)

National Geographic Adventure A very nice magazine, specializing in outdoor recreation, expeditions, climbing, trekking, and hiking, as well as other forms of outdoor sports, including sailing, mountain biking, and all forms of skiing.

National Geographic Society An organization, with headquarters in Washington, DC, that is devoted to exploration, discovery, and mapping. It funds scholars, researchers, and adventurers, and since 1887 has published the results of their fieldwork along with extraordinary maps and stunning photographs in the pages of *National Geographic*. It now also supports other publications and a television station. (Some of the historical photographs in this encyclopedia come from early issues of *National Geographic* [www.ngs.org].)

National parks Theodore Roosevelt, inspired by **John Muir**, established **Yellowstone** as the first national park. During the next 100 years, the United States dedicated many more parks, and other countries followed that lead. Mountains and their attributes are the main attractions in many American national parks including **Denali**, Glacier, Great Smoky Mountains, **Grand Teton**, **Hawaii Volcanoes**, Yellowstone, and **Yosemite**. See Harris for an outstanding discussion of the geology of the parks and www.nps.gov for information on hundreds of American parks, sites, and monuments.

National Snow and Ice Data Center (NSIDC) Located at the University of **Colorado**, this organization has collected data on the **cryosphere** since 1976; it also supports research projects and publications (www.nsidc .org/).

Natural line   An obvious **route** that a climber could follow.

Nauru   Lowest point, Pacific Ocean 0 m; highest point, unnamed location along plateau rim 61 m, 200 ft.

Navassa Island   Lowest point, Caribbean Sea 0 m; highest point, unnamed location on southwest side 77 m, 253 ft.

Navigation   In mountaineering, the means by which one determines how to get from one location to another. See Carleton's chapter on wilderness navigation in Auerbach. (See also **compass** and **global positioning system**.)

Naylor, Joss   Born: Cumberland, England. According to the very informative website www .simpkins57.freeserve.co.uk/mountain_lakes_ books/whoswho/whoswhodetails.html, "Outstanding long-distance fell runner of the 1970s and early 80s. In his native Lakeland hills he was supreme and virtually unbeatable." Bibliography: *Studmarks on the Summits* (1985) by Bill Smith.

Nebraska   Lowest point, Missouri River, on the Kansas border 256 m, 840 ft; highest point, Panorama Point 1,653 m, 5,424 ft (20th highest of the 50 state highpoints).

Needle Mountains   One of **Colorado**'s main **ranges**; its major summits include: Mt. Eolus 4,292 m, 14,084 ft; Windom Peak 4,293 m, 14,087 ft; Sunlight Peak, 4,285 m, 14,059 ft. (For the complete list of Colorado's 14,000-foot peaks, see appendix D.)

Nepal   Lowest point, Kanchan Kalan 70 m, 230 ft; highest point, Mt. Everest 8,850 m (1999 est.), 29,035 ft. Located between **India** and **Tibet**, it is one of the most mountainous countries in the world. Nepal counts no less than 8 of the 14 8,000-meter peaks: **Everest, Kangchenjunga, Lhotse, Makalu, Cho Oyu, Dhaulagiri, Manaslu,** and **Annapurna**. Manaslu, Dhaulagiri, and Annapurna lie entirely within Nepal; the other peaks are on the border with Tibet, except Kangchenjunga, which is on the border with **Sikkim**. In addition, some amazingly beautiful summits can be found in the **Himalayas**, including **Ama Dablam** and **Machupuchare**. (See also color photos.)

Nepal Peak   7,163 m, 23,500 ft. This major peak is located within the **Himalayas** in **Nepal**.

Nepali   The native inhabitants of **Nepal**; also, a dialect spoken in Nepal, and derived from Pahari, an Indo-Aryan language spoken throughout the **Himalayas**, under different variations.

Netherlands, The   Lowest point, Prins Alexanderpolder −7 m, −23 ft; highest point, Vaalserberg 321 m, 1,053 ft.

Netherlands Antilles   Lowest point, Caribbean Sea 0 m; highest point, Mt. Scenery 862 m, 2,828 ft.

Nevada   Lowest point, Colorado River, near Needles, **California**, 146 m, 479 ft; highest point, **Boundary Peak** 4,006 m, 13,143 ft (ninth highest of the 50 state highpoints).

Nevado   (S) Snowcapped.

Nevado del Huila   5,750 m, 18,864 ft. The highest peak in **Colombia**.

Névé   A granular snow slope on a mountain. (See also **ice**.)

Névé penetente   A tower of ice that resembles a person praying.

New Brunswick   Lowest point, Atlantic Ocean 0 m; highest point, Mt. Carleton, 817 m, 2,680 ft.

New Caledonia   Lowest point, Pacific Ocean 0 m; highest point, Mont Panie 1,628 m, 5,341 ft.

New Hampshire   Lowest point, Atlantic Ocean 0 m; highest point, **Mt. Washington** 1,917 m, 6,288 ft (18th highest of the 50 state highpoints). A beautiful, rugged state, with harsh winters, and the mighty, by East Coast standards, **Presidential Range**.

New Jersey   Lowest point, Atlantic Ocean 0 m; highest point, High Point 550 m, 1,803 ft (40th highest of the 50 state highpoints).

New Mexico   Lowest point, Pecos River, Texas, border 866 m, 2,840 ft; highest point, **Wheeler Peak** 4,011 m, 13,161 ft (eighth highest of the 50 state highpoints).

(top) **Relative elevations of some of the world's major summits.**
(Photo-mosaic by Fred Hartemann)
Blue: Australia
Red: Europe
Green: North America
Orange: South America
Brown: Africa

(bottom) **The 7 highest summits of the 7 continents; both Australia and Australasia are considered.**
(Fred Hartemann)

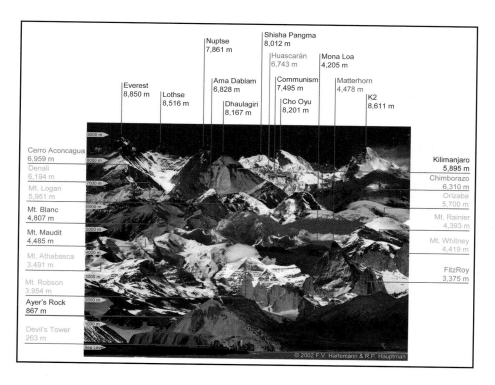

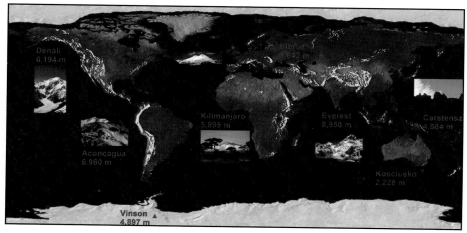

(top) The main mountain ranges of the world. (Fred Hartemann)

(bottom) The 14 8,000-meter peaks. (Fred Hartemann and Robert Hauptman)

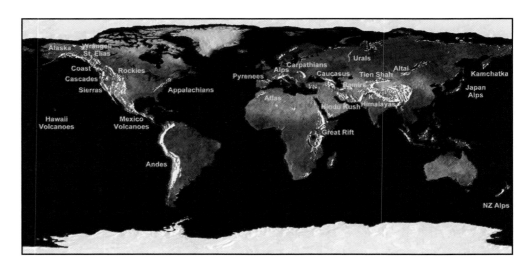

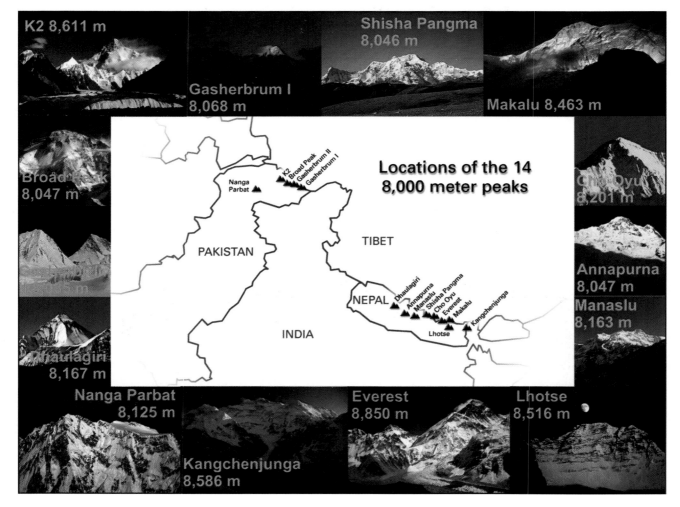

K2 8,611 m

Shisha Pangma 8,046 m

Gasherbrum I 8,068 m

Makalu 8,463 m

Broad Peak 8,047 m

Cho Oyu 8,201 m

Dhaulagiri 8,167 m

Annapurna 8,047 m

Manaslu 8,163 m

Nanga Parbat 8,125 m

Everest 8,850 m

Lhotse 8,516 m

Kangchenjunga 8,586 m

Locations of the 14 8,000 meter peaks

PAKISTAN

TIBET

NEPAL

INDIA

Nanga Parbat

K2
Broad Peak
Gasherbrum II
Gasherbrum I

Dhaulagiri
Annapurna
Manaslu
Shisha Pangma
Cho Oyu
Everest
Makalu
Lhotse
Kangchenjunga

(top) The main ranges and summits of the Alps; summits marked in red are above 4,000 meters. (Fred Hartemann)

(bottom) The main peaks of North America. (Fred Hartemann)

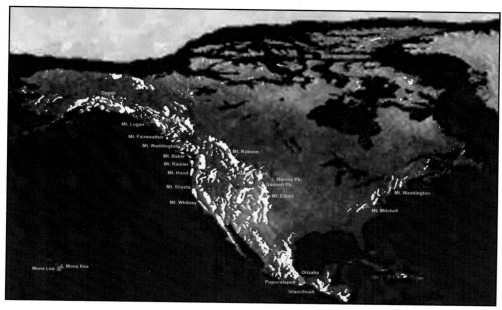

(top) Relief of Yukon.
(Geomatics Canada /
Natural Resources Canada)

(middle left) Relief of Canada.
(Geomatics Canada /
NaturalResources Canada)

(middle right) Relief of Alberta.
(Geomatics Canada /
Natural Resources Canada)

(bottom left) Relief of
British Columbia.
(Geomatics Canada /
Natural Resources Canada)

(bottom right) France relief.
(Institut Géographique National)

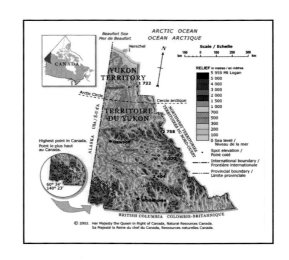

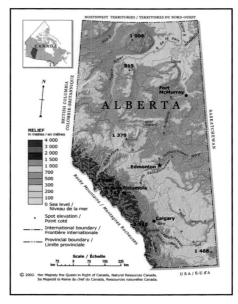

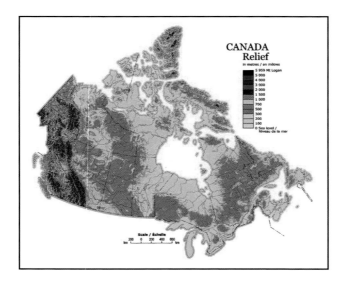

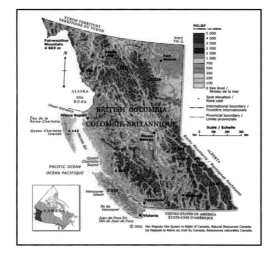

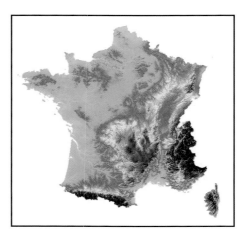

Topographical map of Mont Blanc.
(Institut Géographique National)

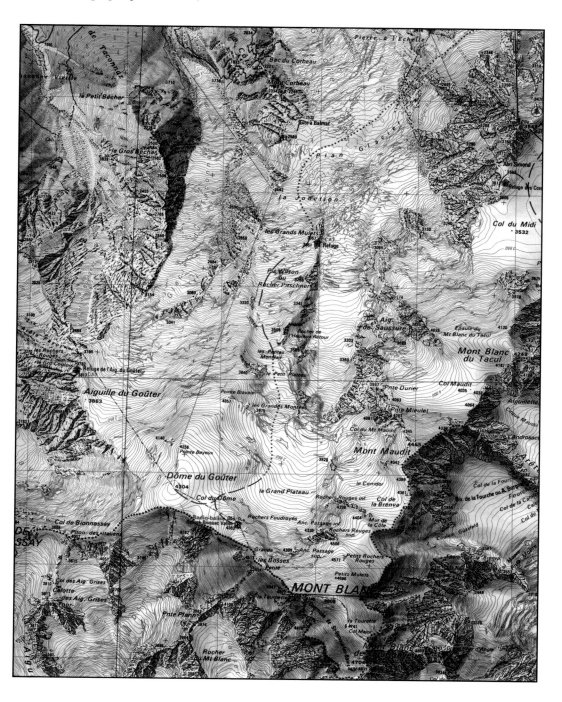

Topographical map of the
Barre des Ecrins and Glacier Noir.
(Institut Géographique National)

Topographical map
of Mt. Everest, detail.
(National Geographic Society)

Right (top to bottom): feldspar, red quartz, yellow sandstone, red sandstone, white sandstone, breccia.
Middle (top to bottom): corundum, cross-bedding, granite, hematite iron, amethyst, malachite copper.
Left (top to bottom): scoria, basalt, sandstone, grey granite, red granite, conglomerate.

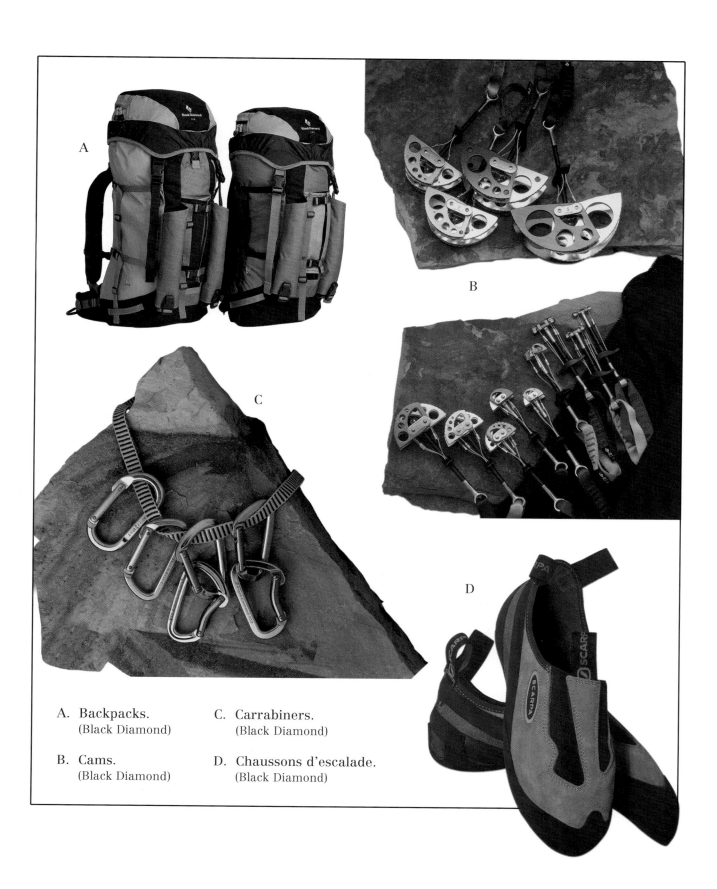

A. **Backpacks.**
   (Black Diamond)

B. **Cams.**
   (Black Diamond)

C. **Carrabiners.**
   (Black Diamond)

D. **Chaussons d'escalade.**
   (Black Diamond)

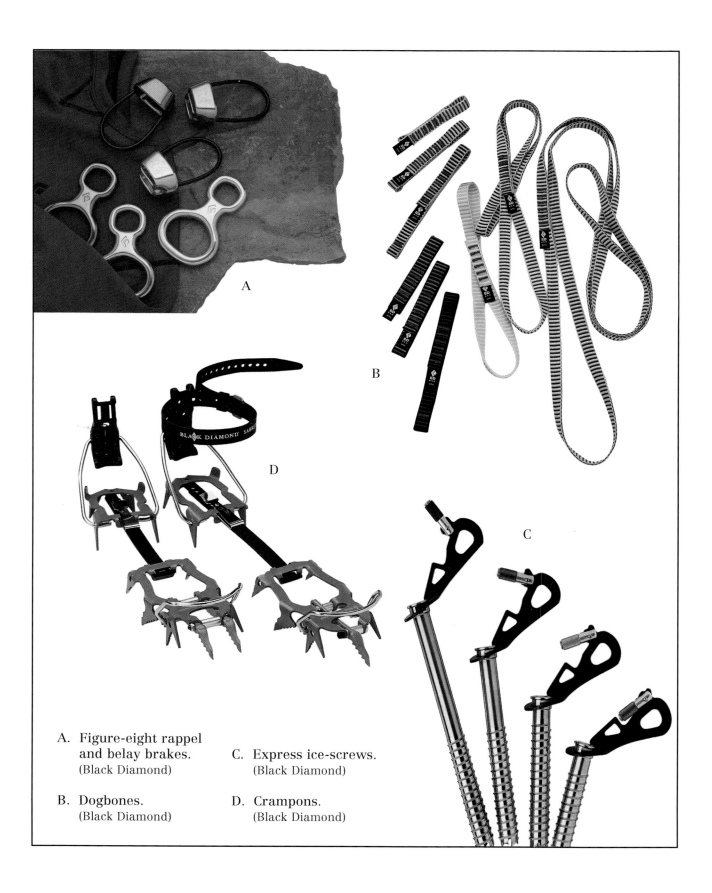

A. Figure-eight rappel and belay brakes.
(Black Diamond)

B. Dogbones.
(Black Diamond)

C. Express ice-screws.
(Black Diamond)

D. Crampons.
(Black Diamond)

A. Ice axes.
(Black Diamond)

B. Ice screws and harness.
(Black Diamond)

C. Fifi hooks.
(Black Diamond)

D. Gaiters.
(Black Diamond)

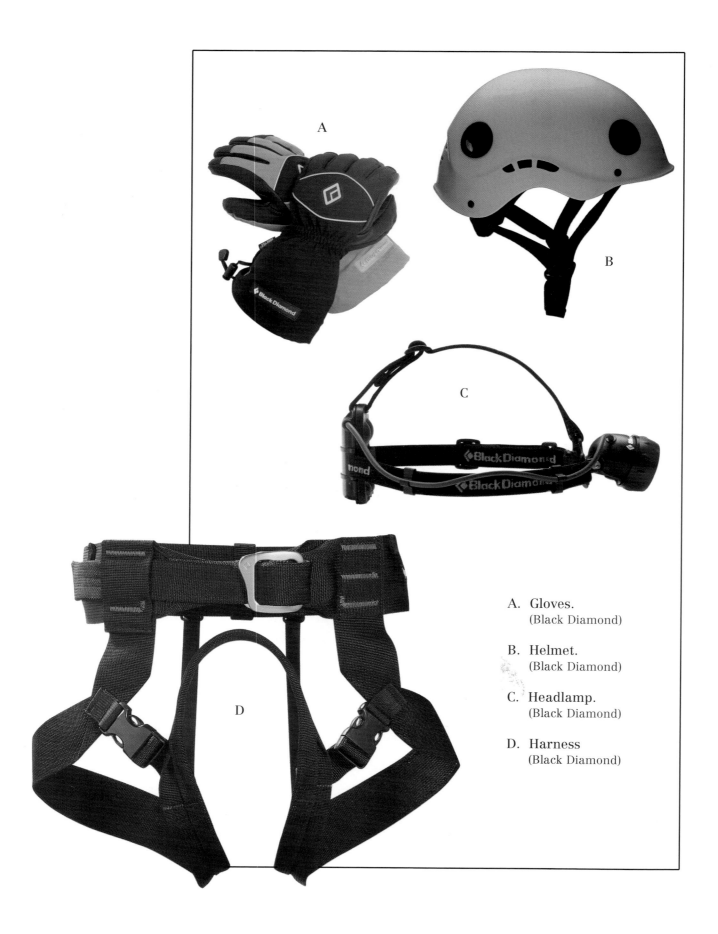

A. Gloves.
(Black Diamond)

B. Helmet.
(Black Diamond)

C. Headlamp.
(Black Diamond)

D. Harness
(Black Diamond)

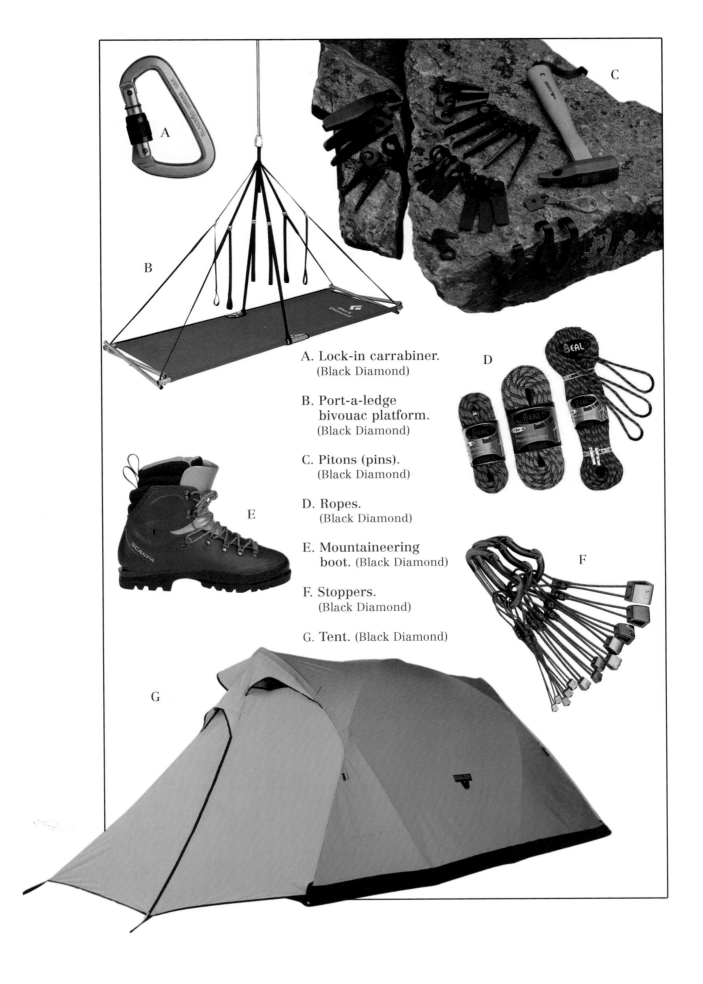

A. Lock-in carrabiner.
   (Black Diamond)

B. Port-a-ledge
   bivouac platform.
   (Black Diamond)

C. Pitons (pins).
   (Black Diamond)

D. Ropes.
   (Black Diamond)

E. Mountaineering
   boot. (Black Diamond)

F. Stoppers.
   (Black Diamond)

G. Tent. (Black Diamond)

(top left) **Io with Loki Plume on bright limb.** (NASA)

(top right) **Olympus Mons, Mars.** (NASA)

(bottom) **Lynn Hill.** (Heinz Zak)

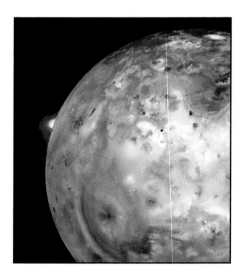

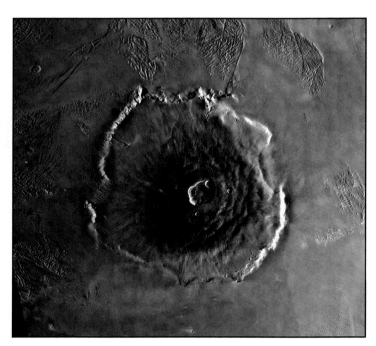

(top left) Alpine flower in the California Sierras. (Fred André)

(top right) Chaparral and high-desert vegetation, California Sierras. (Fred Hartemann)

(middle left) Cirrus cloud. (Fred Hartemann)

(middle right) Cirque Peak, summit ridge, California Sierras. (Fred Hartemann)

(bottom left) Freeze-thaw cycle, split rock, California Sierras. (Fred Hartemann)

(bottom right) Glacial cliff, California High Sierra. (Fred André)

North America
California

(top left) **Golden eagle, California Sierras.** (Corbis)

(top right) **High Sierra pine tree.** (Fred Hartemann)

(middle left) **Marmot, California Sierras.** (Emmanuel André)

(middle right) **The summit of Mt. Langley, California Sierras.** (Fred André)

(bottom left) **Sierra storm, CA.** (Fred André)

(bottom right) **Alpine flowers, California Sierras.** (Fred André)

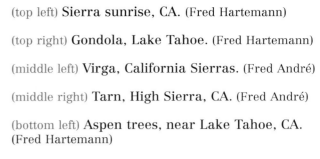

(top left) **Sierra sunrise, CA.** (Fred Hartemann)

(top right) **Gondola, Lake Tahoe.** (Fred Hartemann)

(middle left) **Virga, California Sierras.** (Fred André)

(middle right) **Tarn, High Sierra, CA.** (Fred André)

(bottom left) **Aspen trees, near Lake Tahoe, CA.** (Fred Hartemann)

(bottom right) **Alpine flowers, Lassen National Park, CA.** (Fred Hartemann)

(top right) **Forest fire, Yosemite**
(Marc-Antoine Hartemann)

(bottom right) **Wildflower, Yosemite**
National Park, CA. (Debbie Santa Maria)

(top left) **USGS benchmark, Mono Pass,**
Yosemite National Park, CA. (Debbie Santa Maria)

(middle left) **El Capitan** (Fred Hartemann)

(bottom left) **Bear protection: hanging backpack,**
Yosemite National Park, CA. (Debbie Santa Maria)

(top left) El Capitan and the Nose, Yosemite National Park, CA. (Fred Hartemann)

(top right) Erratics, Yosemite National Park, CA. (Fred Hartemann)

(middle left) Jeffrey pine, Yosemite National Park, CA. Note Robert Hauptman at the bottom of the tree, for scale. (Fred Hartemann)

(middle right) Fog, "bonsai" tree, Yosemite National Park, CA. (Fred André)

(bottom left) Lichen and moss, Yosemite National Park, CA. (Fred Hartemann)

(bottom right) Sierra pine on granite, Yosemite National Park, CA. (Fred Hartemann)

(top left) **Wild flowers, chaparral, and**
mule ears at 11,500 ft, Yosemite
National Park, CA. (Debbie Santa Maria)

(top right) **Yosemite Valley, El Capitan**
and Bridesveil Falls, Yosemite National
Park, CA. (Fred Hartemann)

(middle left) **California Coast Ranges,**
marine layer. (Fred Hartemann)

(middle right) **Badwater, Death Valley**
National Park, CA. (Fred Hartemann)

(top left) **Frozen lake, Tuolumne Meadows, Yosemite National Park, CA.** (Fred Hartemann)

(middle left) **Mt. Shasta, Cascade Range, CA.** (Fred Hartemann)

(bottom left) **Sequoia, Merced Grove, Yosemite National Park, CA.** (Fred Hartemann)

(bottom right) **Mt. Shasta, climber at sunrise on Avalanche Gully, Cascade Range, CA.** (Fred Hartemann)

(top left) **Chipmunk,**
Wind River Range, WY. (Fred André)

(top right) **Alpine flowers,**
Wind River Range, WY. (Fred Hartemann)

(middle left) **Fremont Peak,**
Wind River Range, WY. (Fred Hartemann)

(middle right) **Fremont Glacier,**
Wind River Range, WY. (Fred André)

(bottom left) **Indian Paintbrush,**
Wind River Range, WY. (Fred André)

(bottom right) **Gannett Peak,**
Wind River Range, WY. (Fred Hartemann)

(top left) **Moonlight over Seneca Lake,
Wind River Range, WY.** (Fred André)

(top right) **Setting moon,
Wind River Range, WY.** (Fred André)

(bottom) **Llama, Wind River Range, WY.**
(Debbie Santa Maria)

(top left) **Bison,
Yellowstone National park, WY.** (Fred André)

(top right) **Beartooth Highway, sunset near the
summit, WY and MT.** (Fred Hartemann)

(middle left) **Castle Geyser, Yellowstone
National Park, WY.** (Fred Hartemann)

(middle right) **Pilot and Index Peaks from the
Beartooth Highway, WY and MT.** (Fred Hartemann)

(bottom left) **First Tower, Mt. Helen, Wind
River Range, WY.** (Fred Hartemann)

(bottom right) **Canyon of the Yellowstone,
Yellowstone National Park, WY.** (Fred Hartemann)

(top left) Elk, Yellowstone National Park, WY. (Debbie Santa Maria)

(bottom left) Geyser, Yellowstone National Pak, WY. (Fred Hartemann)

(top right) Grand Canyon of the Yellowstone,
Yellowstone National Park, WY. (Fred Hartemann)

(bottom right) Lower Falls of the Yellowstone,
Yellowstone National Park, WY. (Corbis)

(top left) Thermophile algae, Grand Prismatic Springs, Yellowstone National Park, WY. (Fred Hartemann)

(top right) Yellowstone, Lower Falls, Yellowstone National Park, WY. (Fred Hartemann)

(middle) Mammoth Hot Springs, Yellowstone National Park, WY. (Fred André)

(bottom) Mammoth Hot Springs, Yellowstone National Park, WY. (Fred André)

(top) Grouse, Grand Teton National Park, WY. (Fred André)

(middle left) Alpine flower field and birch trees, Grand Teton National Park, WY. (Debbie Santa Maria)

(middle right) Grand Teton West Face, from Table Mountain, Grand Teton National Park, WY. (Fred Hartemann)

(bottom) Hale-Bopp comet over the Tetons. (Jonathan Adams)

(top left) **Mule deer, Grand Teton National Park, WY.** (Fred Hartemann)

(top right) **Mountain stream, Grand Teton National Park, WY.** (Debbie Santa Maria)

(middle left) **Indian Paintbrush, Grand Teton National Park, WY.** (Debbie Santa Maria)

(middle right) **Teton Range and Jackson Hole, Grand Teton National Park, WY.** (Fred Hartemann)

(bottom) **Teton Range and Snake River, Grand Teton National Park, WY.** (Debbie Santa Maria)

(left) Devil's Tower at sunset, Devil's Tower
National Monument, WY. (Fred Hartemann)

(top right) Devil's Tower at sunset, Devil's Tower
National Monument, WY. (Frank Sanders)

(middle right) Lake and storm clouds,
Beartooth Range, MT. (Fred Hartemann)

(bottom right) The Maroon Bells,
Colorado Rockies. (Fred Hartemann)

(top left) **Castle Peak, Colorado Rockies.** (Fred Hartemann)

(top right) **The Sawtooth Ridge, connecting Mt. Bierstadt and Mt. Evans, Colorado Rockies.** (Fred Hartemann)

(middle left) **Fording a mountain stream in Colorado.** (Robert Hauptman)

(middle right) **Colorado Front Range, seen from the summit of Mt. Bierstadt, CO.** (Fred Hartemann)

(bottom left) **Robert Hauptman free climbing on Castle Peak, CO.** (Fred Hartemann)

(bottom right) **The Rocky Mountains, Lander's Peak, by Albert Bierstadt.** (The Metropolitan Museum of Art, Rogers Fund, 1907 (07.123). Photograph © 1979 The Metropolitan Museum of Art)

(top) Cumulus clouds, Desert Southwest. (Fred Hartemann)

(middle left) Grand Canyon spring snowstorm, Grand Canyon National Park, AZ. (Fred Hartemann)

(middle right) Grand Canyon, spring snow, Grand Canyon National Park, AZ. (Fred Hartemann)

(bottom) Hoodoo, Balanced Rock, Arches National Park, UT. (Fred Hartemann)

(top) **Pueblo ruins, Grand Canyon National Park, AZ.** (Fred Hartemann)

(bottom) **The White House, Canyon de Chelly National Monument, AZ.** (Fred Hartemann)

(top) **Monument Valley, Utah.**
(Fred Hartemann)

(bottom) **Spider Rock, Canyon de Chelly National Monument, AZ.**
(Judy Hedding)

(clockwise from top)

Glacier Bay, Alaska. (Corbis)

Grey wolf. (Corbis)

Denali north face (Fred Hartemann)

Fireweed, Alaska (Debbie Santa Maria)

Denali north face (Fred Hartemann)

Denali and tundra. (Corbis)

(clockwise from top right) **Portage Glacier near Prince Williams Sound** (Debbie Santa Maria); **The road to Shangri-La, going toward Denali north face** (Fred Hartemann); **Forraker and Hunter at sunset** (Fred Hartemann); **Moose, a frequent Alaskan encounter** (Fred Hartemann); **Mt. Carpe and Alaska Range near Denali** (Fred Hartemann); **Regal Mountain, Staircase Icefall, and terminus of Root Glacier, Wrangell-St. Elias National Park** (Fred Hartemann); **Lynn canal, near Juneau and Glacier Bay National Park** (Fred Hartemann)

(top) Mt. Hood, the Pearly Gates, Cascade Range, OR. (Robert Hauptman)

(middle left) Stamps, USA 80 ¢, Mt. McKinley. (Fred Hartemann)

(middle right) Mt. McKinley, Denali National Park, AK. (AbleStock)

(bottom) Grizzly fishing salmons, Alaska. (Corbis)

(counter clockwise from top) Heather, alpine vegetation, and granite, Mt. Baker, North Cascades, WA. (Fred Hartemann); Mount Hood, Albert Bierstadt. (© 2002 Portland Art Museum, Portland, OR. Gift of Mr. Henry F. Cabell); Mt. Shuskan and morning clouds, North Cascades, WA. (Fred Hartemann); Mt. Saint Helens crater, Mt. Saint Helens National Monument, WA. (Fred Hartemann); Mt. Saint Helens from space. (NASA); Mt. Shuskan from Artist's Lake, North Cascades, WA. (Fred Hartemann)

(clockwise from top)

Mt. Rainier, Mt. Rainier National Park,
WA. (Fred Hartemann)

Mt. Baker, North Cascades, WA. (Fred Hartemann)

Smith Rock State Park, OR. (Fred Hartemann)

Colfax Peak on Mt. Baker, North Cascades, WA.
(Fred Hartemann)

The crater of Mt. Baker, North Cascades, WA.
(Fred Hartemann)

Seracs on Mt. Baker, North Cascades, WA.
(Fred Hartemann)

Dakotas

(top left) George Washington, Mt. Rushmore National Monument, SD. (Fred Hartemann)

(top right) Needles Highway, Custer State Park, SD. (Fred André)

(bottom) Mt. Rushmore National Monument, SD. (Debbie Santa Maria)

(clockwise from top)
Mt. Assiniboine,
Banff National Park, Canada. (Steve Zinsli)

Mt. Athabasca and the Columbia
Icefield, Jasper and Banff National
Parks, Canada. (Fred Hartemann)

Mt. Athabasca, Banff National Park,
Canada. (Fred Hartemann)

Lake Louise, Banff National Park,
Canada. (Steve Zinsli)

Mt. Andromeda and Mt. Athabasca,
Banff National Park,Canada. (Steve Zinsli)

Mt. Andromeda and Mt. Athabasca,
Banff National Park, Canada.
(Fred Hartemann)

(counter clockwise from top)

Refuge in the Canadian Rockies. (Steve Zinsli)

Balling-up on the Columbia Icefield, Canadian Rockies. (Fred Hartemann)

Purcell Range, Canadian Rockies. (Steve Zinsli)

Base camp in the Canadian Rockies. (Steve Zinsli)

Canadian Rockies. (Steve Zinsli)

Mountaineering skiers, near Mt. Assiniboine, Canadian Rockies. (Steve Zinsli)

(clockwise from top)

Black Tusk, Garibaldi Provincial Park, BC, Canada. (Debbie Santa Maria)

Rainbow over the Bugaboos, BC, Canada. (Steve Zinsli)

Bugaboos, Howse Tower, BC, Canada. (Gary Yates)

Mt. Robson, Robson Provincial Park, BC, Canada. (Fred Hartemann)

Float plane, Whistler, BC, Canada. (Debbie Santa Maria)

Bugaboos, Canadian Rockies, BC, Canada. (Steve Zinsli)

(clockwise from top)

Mt. Logan, East summit, Canada. (Kevin Barton/Peakware)

Mt. Lucania, Canada. (Kevin Barton)

Mt. Logan from the East, Canada. (Jeremy Frimer/Peakware)

Waterfall, BC, Canada. (Debbie Santa Maria)

Mt. Waddington, British Columbia Coast Range, Canada.
(Russ Heinl/MaXx Images Inc.)

Hiking in Robson Provincial Park, BC, Canada. (Corbis)

(top) **Orizaba, near the Sarcophago, Mexico.** (Fred André)

(bottom left) **Orizaba and Piedra Grande, Mexico.** (Fred André)

(bottom right) **Orizaba, near the summit crater, Mexico.** (Fred André)

(top) **Orizaba, as seen from the dirt
road to Piedra Grande, Mexico.**
(David de la Garza/Peakware)

(top) **Orizaba, sunrise on the Sarcophago,
Mexico.** (Gary Yates)

(top) **Popocatepetl crater, Mexico.** (Gary Yates)

(bottom) **Sarcophago sunset on Orizaba, Mexico.** (Fred André)

(top) **Cerro Aconcagua, Argentina.**
(Argentina TouristInformation/Peakware)

(middle left) **Cerro Aconcagua and El Viento Blanco
cloud cap, Argentina.** (Gregory Yanagihara/Peakware)

(middle right) **Cerro Aconcagua, aerial view,
Argentina.** (Corbis)

(bottom left) **Icefield and icebergs, Patagonia,
Argentina.** (Max Giraud)

(bottom right) **Fitz-Roy, Patagonia, Argentina.**
(Frank Sauer/Peakware)

(clockwise from top)

Cabeza de Condor and llamas, Andes, Bolivia. (Max Giraud)

Chimborazo, by Frederic Edwin Church. (Courtesy of the Huntington Library, Art Collections, and Botanical Gardens, San Marino, CA)

Condoriri, Bolivian Andes. (Max Giraud)

Nevado Sajama, Bolivia. (JanSchmidt/Peakware)

Illimani, Bolivian Andes. (Graham Jones/Peakware)

(from top to bottom)

Huayna Potosi, Andes.
(Hartmut Bielefeldt/Peakware)

Huascaran, Peruvian Andes.
(Allex/Peakware)

Cotopaxi, Andes. (Ricardo Montayo/Peakware)

Cotopaxi, 1862, by Frederic Edwin Church.
(Founders Society Purchase, Robert Tannahill
Foundation Fund, Gibbs-Williams Fund, Dexter M. Ferry,
Jr., Fund, Merrill Fund, Beatrice W. Rogers Fund, and
Richard A. Manoogian Fund; Photograph © 1985 The
Detroit Institute of Arts)

(clockwise from top)

The Andes, from space; photo-mosaic. (NASA)

Machu Picchu, Peru. (Corbis)

Salcantay, from Inca Trail, Peru. (Niklas Bergendal/Peakware)

Chacaraju, seen from Pisco, Andes. (Andy Kerry/Peakware)

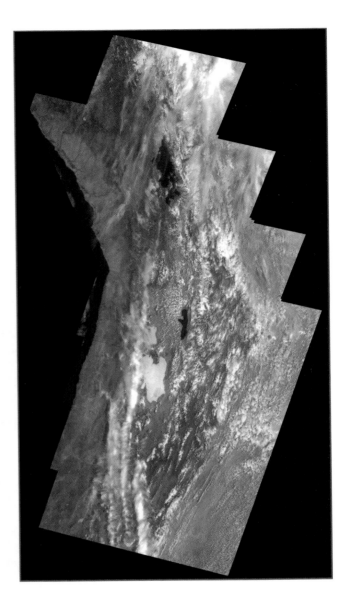

Europe
(miscellaneous)

(top) **Elbrus, Russia.**
(John Shively/
Peakware)

(middle) **Lofoten
Islands, Norway.**
(Max Giraud)

(bottom) **Midnight
sun, Lofoten Islands,
Norway.** (Max Giraud)

(top left) **Moussala, North Ridge, Rila.** (Max Giraud)

(top right) **Mont Array, Pic de Mancaperat.** (Max Giraud)

(bottom left) **Alpine Club logo (England).** (Alpine Club)

(bottom right) **Hiking over a lake, Norway.** (Max Giraud)

1857

Alpine
CLUB

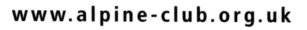

www.alpine-club.org.uk

Europe *Italy*

(top) Laurent Terray leads and Sylvie Jolie belays on the 70-degree headwall of the Ciarforon, in the Gran Paradiso Range, Italy. (Fred Hartemann)

(middle) Ciarforon and Tresenta at sunset, near the Gran Paradiso, Italy. (Fred Hartemann)

(bottom) Ciarforon, late October sunset, Italy. (Fred Hartemann)

(top left) Olivier Hartemann front-point climbing on the 70-degree headwall of the Ciarforon, Italy. Note the ice-screw and carrabiner for protection with the rope.
(Fred Hartemann)

(top right) Campanile Basso, Dolomites, Italy.
(Max Giraud)

(bottom) Trav Brenva, Dolomites, Italy.
(Max Giraud)

(top) Smoke plume off Mt. Etna, from space. (NASA)

(middle) Gran Paradiso, Italy. (Fred Hartemann)

(bottom) Mont Blanc de Courmayeur, Italy. (Max Giraud)

Switzerland/Austria/Alps

(top left) **Blue gentian, Alps.**
(Anne Minoh)

(top right) **Piz Bernina and Piz Bianco, Switzerland.**
(Josef Stranner/Peakware)

(middle) **Piz Bernina, summit ridge, Switzerland.**
(Max Giraud)

(bottom) **Combin de Corbassière; Grand Combin in the background, Switzerland.**
(Max Giraud)

(top) Dufourspitze, Monte Rosa, Switzerland. (Max Giraud)

(middle) Crevasse jump, Monte Rosa, Switzerland. (Max Giraud)

(bottom) Glacier junction, Monte Rosa, Switzerland. (Fred Hartemann)

(top) Monte Rosa and Alphubel, Switzerland.
(Fred Hartemann)

(bottom) Monte Rosa and Lyskamm, Switzerland.
(Fred Hartemann)

(counter clockwise from top)

Dom, North Face, Switzerland. (Peakware)

Dent Blanche, Switzerland. (Max Giraud)

Cornice, Alps. (Max Giraud)

Kesselwand Ferner seracs, Switzerland. (Max Giraud)

Dufourspitze, summit ridge, Switzerland. (Max Giraud)

(top) Matterhorn from Zinalrothorn, Switzerland. (Tony Simpkins/Peakware)

(middle left) Dihedral climbing, Lion Ridge, Matterhorn, Switzerland. (Max Giraud)

(middle right) Matterhorn, East Face, Switzerland. (AbleStock)

(bottom left) Matterhorn and Dent d'Hérens, Switzerland. (Max Giraud)

(bottom right) Rappel down the Hornli Ridge, Matterhorn, Switzerland. (Max Giraud)

(top left) **Gross Lekihorn, Gotthard, Switzerland.** (Max Giraud)

(top right) **Strahlhorn and Allalinhorn, Switzerland.** (Max Giraud)

(middle left) **Rosenhorn and Wetterhorn, Oberland, Switzerland.** (Max Giraud)

(middle right) **Weisshorn, Switzerland.** (Max Giraud)

(bottom) **Rimpfishhorn, Switzerland.** (Max Giraud)

(counter clockwise from top)

Petit Mont Collon and its glacier, Switzerland. (Max Giraud)

Reinhold Messner. (© Reinhold Messner)

Wildspitze, Austria. (Max Giraud)

Piz Buin, Switzerland. (Max Giraud)

Piz Palu at sunset, Bernina Range, Switzerland. (Max Giraud)

(top) North Face of the Aiguille d'Argentière at sunrise, Mont Blanc Range, France. (Fred Hartemann)

(middle left) Northwest Face of the Aiguille de Bionassay, Mont Blanc Range, France. (Fred Hartemann)

(middle right) The Italian side of the Aiguille de Bionassay and Dôme du Goûter, from the summit of the Aiguille de Tré-la-Tête, Mont Blanc Range, France. (Fred Hartemann)

(bottom) Aiguille du Tour, Mont Blanc Range, France. (Fred Hartemann)

Europe France

(clockwise from top)

The Aiguille Verte and the 80-degree North Face
of Les Droites, from the Aiguille d'Argentière,
Mont Blanc Range, France. (Fred Hartemann)

Chardonnet, Aiguille Verte, and Mont Blanc
at sunrise, France. (Fred Hartemann)

Les Courtes, Northeast Face, Mont Blanc Range,
France. (Fred Hartemann)

Les Droites and the Aiguille Verte at sunrise,
Mont Blanc Range, France. (Fred Hartemann)

Dôme and Aiguille de Rochefort, Glacier de Leschaux,
Mont Blanc Range, France. (Fred Hartemann)

(counter clockwise from top)

Grandes Jorasses, lenticular cloud, and Aiguilles de Chamonix, Mont Blanc Range, France. (Fred Hartemann); Grandes Jorasses, North Face, Arête des Hirondelles, and Linceuil, Mont Blanc Range, France. (Fred Hartemann); Grandes Jorasses, North Face at sunset, Mont Blanc Range, France. (Fred Hartemann); Grandes Jorasses. North Face, Mont Blanc Range, France. (Fred Hartemann); Glacier terminus, Glacier du Tour, Mont Blanc Range, France. (Fred Hartemann); Headwall on the Petite Aiguille Verte, Mont Blanc Range, France. (Fred Hartemann)

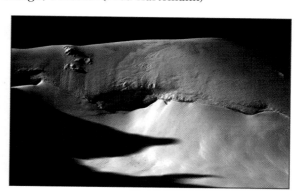

(top) Mont Maudit, seracs and rimaye, Mont Blanc Range, France. (Fred Hartemann)

(middle) Mont Blanc and Aiguilles de Chamonix, from the Grands Montets, France. (Fred André)

(bottom left) Mont Maudit, Mont Blanc Range, France. (Max Giraud)

(bottom right) Mont Blanc, from the Brévent, France. (Fred Hartemann)

(top) Mont Blanc, Mur de la Côte, France. (Max Giraud)

(middle) Mont Blanc, Mont Maudit, Mont Blanc du Tacul, France. (Fred Hartemann)

(bottom) Mont Blanc from the Aiguille de Tré-la-Tête, Mont Blanc Range, France. (Fred Hartemann)

(top left) **Mont Blanc range from Mt. Buet**
(Frederic Andre)

(top right) **Mont Blanc, seracs at the Mur
de la Côte, France.** (Max Giraud)

(bottom) **Mont Blanc, summit ridge before
sunrise, France.** (Fred Hartemann)

(top) Mt. Dolent and Aiguille du Triolet, Glacier d'Argentière, Mont Blanc Range, France. (Fred Hartemann)

(middle) A l'assault du ciel, *To the conquest of the sky*, Mont Blanc Range, France. (Pierre Tairraz)

(bottom left) Aiguille de Midi, Mont Blanc Range, France. (Pierre Tairraz)

(bottom right) Seracs and icefall, Glacier d'Argentière, Mont Blanc Range, France. (Fred Hartemann)

(top) Barre des Ecrins at sunrise, Oisans, France. (Fred Hartemann)

(middle left) Barre des Ecrins and Glacier Blanc at sunrise, Oisans, France. (Fred Hartemann)

(middle right) Barre des Ecrins and Barre Noire, Oisans, France. (Fred Hartemann)

(bottom) Barre des Ecrins from le Pic des Agneaux, Oisans, France. (Max Giraud)

(top left) Cerces-Thabor, vista on the Oisans Range, French Alps. (Max Giraud)

(top right) La Meije and Le Rateau, Oisans, France. (D. Leguen/Office du Tourisme La Grave – La Meije)

(middle left) La Meije and La Grande Ruine, Oisans, France. (Max Giraud)

(middle right) La Meije, Le Doigt de Dieu, *God's Finger*, Oisans, France.
(P. Tournaire/Office du Tourisme La Grave – La Meije)

(bottom left) Pelvoux, Coup de Sabre, and Ailefroide, Oisans, France. (Fred Hartemann)

(bottom right) Pelvoux, Pic sans Nom, and Coup de Sabre, from the Pic Coolidge, Oisans, France.
(Max Giraud)

(top) Calanque d'Envau,
Southern France. (Anne Minoh)

(middle) Croix de Belledonne,
Dauphiné Alps, France. (Max Giraud)

(bottom) Sunrise over the Pic de l'Etendard,
French Alps. (Max Giraud)

(top left) **Haute Vésubie, French Alps.** (Max Giraud)

(top right) **Dent de Llardana, Pyrénées, France and Spain.** (Max Giraud)

(bottom) **Hard going on Mt. Agul, Pyrénées, France.** (Max Giraud)

(top left) **Muraille de Banarde, Pyrénées,**
France. (Max Giraud)

(top right) **Massif des Encantats, Pyrénées,**
France. (Max Giraud)

(bottom) **Mountain goat, Pyrénées, France.** (Max Giraud)

(counter clockwise from top)

Mont Perdu, Russel Route, Pyrénées, France. (Max Giraud)

Piton des Neiges, La Réunion. (Max Giraud)

Piton des Neiges from Le Coteau Maigre, La Réunion. (Max Giraud)

Le Gros Morne, La Réunion. (Max Giraud)

Maïdo, La Réunion. (Max Giraud)

Pic du Midi de Bigorre, Pyrénées, France. (Max Giraud)

Europe Corsica

(clockwise from top)

Bocca Borba, Corsica. (Max Giraud)

Corsica, near Girolata. (Max Giraud)

Corsica, Col de la Bavella. (Max Giraud)

Monte Cinto, Corsica. (Max Giraud)

Corsica and Sardinia from space. (NASA)

Albertacce Forest, in Corsica. (Max Giraud)

(top) **Mt. Ararat.**
(Manvel Melikian/Peakware)

(middle) **Demirkazik, Turkey.**
(Max Giraud)

(bottom left) **Kizilkaya, Turkey.**
(Max Giraud)

(bottom right) **Petra, Jordan.** (Corbis)

Africa

(counter clockwise from top)

Mt. Toubkal, 4,165 m, highest point in North Africa. (Roman Garba/Peakware)

Mount Meru ash cone, from Cobra Point at sunrise, East Africa. (Chiam Chye Heng/Peakware)

Mount Kenya, Kenya. (Rudolf Willing/Peakware)

Kilimanjaro, Tanzania. (Corbis)

Hiking in the Atlas Mountains in Morocco. (Max Giraud)

Asia *Nepal/Tibet*

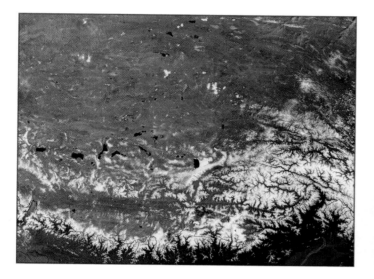

(top left) **The Himalayas, from space.** (NASA)

(top right) **Annapurna, Nepal.** (Gary Yates)

(middle left) **Ama Dablam and chorten, Nepal.** (Gary Goldenberg)

(middle right) **Ama Dablam and Chukhung Valley, Nepal.** (Max Giraud)

(bottom left) **Ama Dablam and Tramserku, Nepal.** (Max Giraud)

(bottom right) **Ama Dablam, Nepal.** (Nelson Chenkin)

(clockwise from top)

Baruntse, Nepal. (Nelson Chenkin)

Chamlang and highly unusual clouds, Nepal. (Nelson Chenkin)

Cholotse, Nepal. (Rudi Prott)

Dhaulagiri, Nepal. (Max Giraud)

Ama Dablam, Nepal. (Rudi Prott/Peakware)

(left top) **Dugla II, Nepal.** (Gary Goldenberg)

(left middle) **Dugla view, Nepal.** (Gary Goldenberg)

(left bottom) **Everest and Cho-Oyu region, from space.** (NASA)

(right top) **Mt. Everest and Khumbu Icefall, Nepal.** (Max Giraud)

(right middle) **Mt. Everest and Nuptse, Nepal.** (Gary Goldenberg)

(right bottom) **Mt. Everest and Nuptse close-up, Nepal.** (Gary Goldenberg)

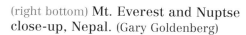

(clockwise from top)

Mt. Everest and raven, Nepal. (Max Giraud)

Gokyo yak, Nepal. (Gary Goldenberg)

Island Peak, Nepal. (Nelson Chenkin)

Tangboche monastery, Everest in the background, Nepal. (Gary Yates)

Mt. Everest, North Face, Tibet. (Corbis)

Mt. Everest and jet-stream, Nepal. (Kay Anderson/Peakware)

(counter clockwise from top)

Lhotse sunset, Nepal. (Rudi Prott)

Lamasery, Phugtal, Nepal. (Gary Goldenberg)

Kangchenjunga, Nepal and Sikkim. (Nelson Chenkin)

Jannu, Nepal. (Nelson Chenkin)

Kusum Kangru, Nepal. (Max Giraud)

(clockwise from top)

Lhotse moonlight, Nepal. (Corbis)

Lhotse and jungle, Nepal. (Corbis)

Macchupuchare, Nepal. (Max Giraud)

Makalu and frozen lake, from Komgma-La,
Nepal. (Max Giraud)

Makalu, Nepal. (Nelson Chenkin)

Macchupuchare, Nepal. (Max Giraud)

(counter clockwise from top)

Mera Peak, Nepal. (Max Giraud)

Nuptse, Nepal. (Max Giraud)

Pumori and chorten, from Kala-Patar, Nepal. (Max Giraud)

Tawache and Cholatse, Nepal. (Nelson Chenkin)

Markha Valley and fields, Ladakh. (Max Giraud)

Wanla's House, Ladakh. (Max Giraud)

(top) **Nanda Devi, India.** (Tao/Peakware)

(middle left) **Gasherbrum, Karakoram, Pakistan.** (Jim White)

(middle right) **Broad Peak, Karakoram, Pakistan** (Jim White)

(bottom left) **Layla Peak, Karakoram, Pakistan.** (Max Giraud)

(bottom right) **Layla Peak reflection, Karakoram, Pakistan.** (Andy Kerry)

Asia Pakistan

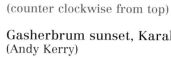(counter clockwise from top)

Gasherbrum sunset, Karakoram, Pakistan.
(Andy Kerry)

K2, Karakoram, Pakistan. (Gary Goldenberg)

Masherbrum, Karakoram, Pakistan. (Jim White)

K2, Karakoram, Pakistan. (Jim White)

K2 and the Baltoro Glacier, Karakoram, Pakistan.
(Peakware)

Hispar Pass, Karakoram, Pakistan.
(Gary Goldenberg)

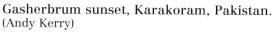

(clockwise from top)

Ogre, Karakoram, Pakistan. (Gary Goldenberg)

Porters ascending Hispar Pass, Karakoram, Pakistan.
(Gary Goldenberg)

Porters descending Hispar Pass, Karakoram, Pakistan.
(Gary Goldenberg)

Porters, Vigne Glacier, Karakoram, Pakistan.
(Gary Goldenberg)

Snow lake, Karakoram, Pakistan. (Gary Goldenberg)

Nanga Parbat, Pakistan.
(Pakistan Tourism Development Corporation/Peakware)

Trango rainbow, Karakoram, Pakistan.
(Gary Goldenberg)

Asia Bhutan/Dolpo

(counter clockwise from top)

Village near Chorta, Dolpo. (Max Giraud)

Chomolhari, Bhutan. (Gary Goldenberg)

Tsering Kang, 6,900 m, Bhutan. (Max Giraud)

Kanjiruba, Dolpo.
(Max Giraud)

Dudu Kundari, Dolpo.
(Max Giraud)

Dudu Kundari,
South Ridge, Dolpo.
(Max Giraud)

Drake, Bhutan.
(Gary Goldenberg)

Dudu Kundari,
South Ridge, Dolpo.
(Max Giraud)

(clockwise from top)

Kagmara V, 5,886 m, Dolpo.
(Max Giraud)

Jagdula Khola, Dolpo.
(Max Giraud)

Kagmara-La, 5,050 m, Dolpo.
(Max Giraud)

Kagmara-La vista, Dolpo.
(Max Giraud)

Gu Tumpa, Dolpo. (Max Giraud)

Langtang Himal, Dolpo.
(Max Giraud)

Siberian lynx. (Corbis)

Asia *Russia/The Stans/China*

(top) **Pik Engels and Marx, Tajikistan.** (Surat Toimast/Peakware)

(second from top) **Pik Engels, 6,510 m, Tajikistan.** (Surat Toimast/Peakware)

(middle left) **Siberian tiger.** (Corbis)

(middle right) **Shisha Pangma, Northeast view, China.** (Fred Spicker/Peakware)

(bottom left) **Snow leopard (Siberia).** (Corbis)

(bottom right) **Khan Tengri, Kyrgyzstan, Kazakhstan, and China.** (Hartmut Bielefeldt/Peakware)

(clockwise from top)

Snowboarding in Japan.
(Japan Tourism Bureau)

Mt. Fuji and Shinkansen, Japan.
(Japan Tourism Bureau)

Fuji-Yama, Japan. (Corbis)

Javan refuge, Indonesia. (Lim Loong Fei)

Zao skiers, Japan. (Japan Tourism Bureau)

Mt. Fuji and Lake Kawaguchi, Japan.
(Japan Tourism Bureau)

Asia *Australia/Pacific*

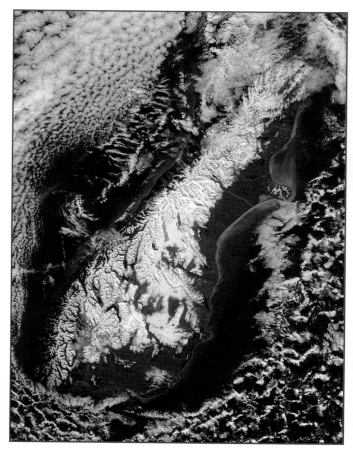

(counter clockwise from top)

Ayers Rock, Great Australian Desert. (Robert Hauptman)

Mt. Cook, New Zealand. (Max Giraud)

New Zealand, South Island from space. (NASA)

Kilauea caldera, Hawaii Volcano National Park, HI. (Fred Hartemann)

KEK Observatory, Mauna Kea, HI. (Fred Hartemann)

Chain and steps up Uluru, Great Australian Desert, Australia. (Terry Hauptman)

(clockwise from top)

Mauna Kea summit, Hawaii.
(Fred Hartemann)

Mauna Loa sunset, Hawaii Volcanoes
National Park, HI. (Fred Hartemann)

Fresh roped lava and steam vent,
Hawaii Volcanoes National Park, HI.
(Fred Hartemann)

Sulfur springs and steam vents,
Hawaii Volcanoes National Park, HI.
(Fred Hartemann)

Sea Arch, Hawaii Volcanoes National
Park, HI. (Fred Hartemann)

Mauna Ulu, Hawaii Volcanoes National
Park, HI. (Fred Hartemann)

P'u O'o vent, June 2nd, 1986,
Hawaii Volcanoes National Park, HI.
(J.D. Griggs, USGS)

New York Lowest point, Atlantic Ocean 0 m; highest point, **Mt. Marcy** 1,639 m, 5,344 ft (21st highest of the 50 state highpoints).

New Zealand Lowest point, Pacific Ocean 0 m; highest point, **Mt. Cook** 3,764 m, 12,349 ft. An island country located to the southeast of **Australia**. Like **Iceland**, it has a considerable amount of **geothermal activity**. Toward the end of the 20th century, Mt. Cook, its highest peak, lost part of its top due to a rock avalanche. New Zealand's mountains and glaciers are extremely picturesque. Indeed, an incomparable land of mountains, volcanoes, glaciers, fjords, and some of the most unusual flora and fauna on earth, New Zealand is a truly wonderful place to visit, climb, trek, or hike. The southern island is a land of fire and ice: numerous active volcanoes can be found all along the Southern Alps, which is the main mountain range on the island, culminating at Mt. Cook. New Zealand is also a country that has contributed many great climbers, including **Sir Edmund Hillary** and **Rob Hall**. (See also color photos.)

Newfoundland and Labrador Lowest point, Atlantic Ocean 0 m; highest point, Mt. Caubvik 1,652 m, 5,420 ft. The highest point entirely within the province is Cirque Mountain 1,568 m, 5,144 ft; Mt. Caubvik is on the border with **Québec**, where it is called Mt. d'Iberville. This province is very rugged and picturesque; it contains many U-shaped valleys, as the area was buried under gigantic glaciers during the last **ice age**; some **ice fields** remain in the extreme north, and a number of beautiful **fjords** can be found all along the coastlines of Labrador and Newfoundland.

Newton, Mt. 4,209 m, 13,810 ft. A high peak located in the **Yukon** Territory in Canada.

Ngorongoro An inactive **volcano** in Tanzania; its enclosed **crater** is home to many wild **animals**.

Ngoyumba Kang 7,916 m, 25,971 ft. This major peak is located in the **Himalayas** in **Tibet**; it was first climbed in 1965 by a Japanese expedition.

Nicaragua Lowest point, Pacific Ocean 0 m; highest point, Mogoton 2,438 m, 7,999 ft.

This Central American country has many active **volcanoes**.

Niger Lowest point, Niger River 200 m, 656 ft; highest point, Mont Greboun 1,944 m, 6,378 ft.

Nigeria Lowest point, Atlantic Ocean 0 m; highest point, Chappal Waddi 2,419 m, 7,936 ft.

Niue Lowest point, Pacific Ocean 0 m; highest point, unnamed location near Mutalau settlement 68 m, 223 ft.

Nojinkangsang 7,206 m, 23,642 ft. This major peak is located within the Lhagoi Kangri Shan Range in **Tibet**. It was fist climbed in 1986 by Sangzu, Gabu, and 10 other climbers from the China-Tibet Mountaineering Association (CTMA) team.

Nordend, Pointe 4,609 m, 15,121 ft. This is the third highest peak in the **Alps** and one of the five main summits of **Monte Rosa**. It was first climbed in 1861 by T. F. and Edward Buxton, J. J. Conwell, and Michel Payot. (See also color photos.)

Norfolk Island Lowest point, Pacific Ocean 0 m; highest point, Mt. Bates 319 m, 1,047 ft.

Norgay, Jamling Tenzing (1966–) The son of **Tenzing Norgay**, an excellent mountaineer, climbing leader of the Everest Imax expedition, and author of *Touching My Father's Soul*. He reached the summit of Everest in 1996; he and his father are among the few fathers and sons to both reach the summit. (See also **Everest, Mt. [Father/Son]** and the foreword.)

Norgay, Tenzing (Also Norkay or Norkey) (1914–1986) Born: Nepal. The first man, along with **Sir Edmund Hillary**, to reach the summit of **Everest** in 1953. He had been a porter on the British expeditions to the mountain in 1935, 1936, and 1938. In 1952 he was a member of the Swiss expedition and reached a height of 28,200 ft. He was a member of the **Sherpa** family, and one of the most experienced climbers in the **Himalayas**. Bibliography: *The Ascent of Everest* (1953), by John Hunt, *Man of Everest* (1955) by **J. R. Ullman** (biography), *Tiger of the Snows* (1955), by J. R. Ullman.

Normal route Generally, the simplest **route** to a summit, and also the **descent** route. Sometimes the normal route is the same as the one employed during the **first ascent**; however, there are numerous instances where this is not the case. A good example is the **Aiguille d'Argentière**: the normal route, opened in 1864 by **Whymper** and **Croz**, used the north ridge because, at the time, the current normal route using the 45-degree **headwall** of the Glacier du Milieu, was much harder technically, given the equipment available; nowadays, with a good pair of **crampons** and reasonable ice climbing training, the headwall is a simple affair. For Whymper and Croz, it would have involved many hours cutting steps above the rimaye, to reach the summit, and they employed the more difficult mixed terrain of the north ridge instead.

Norman-Neruda, Ludwig (1864–1898) Born: Austria. Bibliography: *The Climbs of Norman-Neruda* (1899), edited by May Norman-Neruda.

North America The third largest continent in terms of area (24,230,000 sq km, 9,355,000 sq miles), most of its land lies between the Arctic Circle and the Tropic of Cancer. It extends for more than 8,000 km, 5,000 miles from north to south, to within 500 miles of both the North Pole and the equator; it is also approximately 8,000 km, 5,000 miles, wide in the east–west direction. The highest peak in North America is Mt. McKinley 6,194 m, 20,320 ft, also called **Denali**; the second highest peak is Canada's highpoint, **Mt. Logan** 5,959 m, 19,551 ft; **Orizaba** 5,700 m, 18,701 ft, in Mexico, is the third highest mountain, while **Mt. Saint Elias** 5,489 m, 18,009 ft, is the fourth highest peak on the continent.

North by Northwest A 1959 American film directed by Alfred Hitchcock (1899–1980). Among the suspenseful devices used by Hitchcock during his career, "high" anxiety is one of the most enduring. His first talkie, *Blackmail* (1929), ends atop the British Museum; *Murder* (1930) has a climax involving a falling trapeze artist; his first version of *The Man Who Knew Too Much* (1934) begins in St. Moritz and ends on the roof of a house; in *Saboteur* (1942), the villain falls from the Statue of Liberty; in *To Catch a Thief* (1955), the hero forces the criminal to confess by threatening to drop her from a roof; in *Vertigo* (1958), the hero himself has high anxiety. Hitchcock was bound to discover mountains. His second film, *The Mountain Eagle* (1926) (apparently lost) is set in the Alps, and *The Lady Vanishes* (1938) has a mountainous landscape, although neither uses the mountain in the script; nor does the first *Man Who Knew Too Much. Secret Agent* (1936), on the other hand, is his first attempt to use mountains to create tension. Hitchcock's best application of mountains to enhance suspense is found in *North by Northwest*, a film in which Cary Grant and Eva Marie Saint are chased by spies on top of Mt. Rushmore. The final scene has the hero trying to catch the leading lady while almost falling. A first idea for the script, Hitchcock said, was to have Cary Grant hide in the nose of Lincoln's statue and sneeze violently. (M-A. H.)

North Carolina Lowest point, Atlantic Ocean 0 m; highest point, **Mt. Mitchell** 2,037 m, 6,684 ft (16th highest of the 50 state highpoints).

North Dakota Lowest point, Pembina, at the Canadian border 229 m, 750 ft; highest point, White Butte 1,069 m, 3,506 ft (30th highest of the 50 state highpoints).

North face *Nordwand* (G). The north faces of the big Alpine peaks (in the Northern Hemisphere) are especially treacherous and difficult. The classic climbs are listed in the **6 + 1 Great Alpine North Faces** sidebar.

North Palisade 4,340 m, 14,242 ft. Located in the **Palisades** region of the **Sierra Nevada** in **California**, it was first ascended in 1928 by **Norman Clyde**. This is the classic peak to climb in the Palisades; it is very Alpine in character, and quite strikingly beautiful.

Northern Mariana Islands Lowest point, Pacific Ocean 0 m; highest point, unnamed location on Agrihan 965 m, 3,166 ft.

Northwest Territories Lowest point, Arctic Ocean 0 m; highest point, unnamed peak, sometimes called Nirvana Peak by climbers, 2,773 m, 9,098 ft, in the Mackenzie Mountains.

The 6 + 1 Great Alpine North Faces

The first six north faces played a key role in the history of Alpinism, as they stood as the last unsolved problems in the Alps; to this day they still present tremendous challenges to climbers. The seventh north face fully deserves to be mentioned here, as it is simply a devastatingly steep, 1,000-meter tall, mixed face that remains one of the most difficult climbs anywhere.

1. Matterhorn (Franz and Toni Schmidt, 1931)
2. Cima Grande (Comici, 1933)
3. Drus (Allain and Leininger, 1935)
4. Piz Badile (Cassin et al., 1937)
5. Eiger (Harrer et al., 1938)
6. Grandes Jorasses (Cassin, Esposito, and Tizzoni, 1938)
7. Droites (Cornuau and Davaille, 1955)

This gigantic land is home to polar bears, caribou, and many birds, including migratory species.

Norton, Edward Felix (1884–1954) Born: England. He led the 1924 **Everest** expedition, during which **Mallory** and **Irvine** disappeared. Bibliography: *The Fight for Everest: 1924* (1925).

Norway Lowest point, Norwegian Sea 0 m; highest point, Galdhopiggeh 2,469 m, 8,100 ft.

Nose In **geology**, a rock formation resembling a human nose (see **The Nose**); in **snowboarding**, the board's front tip.

Nose, The The Nose is a configuration on **El Capitan**, and one of the greatest natural climbing lines in the world. (See also **Lynn Hill**.)

Noshaq See **Nowshak**.

Notch A small declivity in a ridge or mountain. (See also **pass**.)

***Notch ma Lysoj Gore*/Night on Bald Mountain** (1866) A symphonic piece by Russian composer Modest Petrovich Mussorgsky (1839–1881). Bald Mountain exists, near Kiev, and was chosen by the composer as the proper setting for a Black Sabbath gathering of witches. The original 1866–1867 version, "Saint John's Night on Bald Mountain" was not performed in the composer's lifetime and was first published in 1968. It is entirely agitated; only for use in his unfinished opera, *Sorochinsky Fair*, "where it was to depict the nightmare of a young man, did Mussorgsky add the final, calm section with distant chimes." Eventually, it was this second version that Nikolaï Andreyevitch Rimsky-Korsakov (1844–1908) re-orchestrated in 1886, and it is this recension that we listen to today. (M.-A. H)

Nova Scotia Lowest point, Bay of Fundy 0 m; highest point Cape Breton Highlands 532 m, 1,745 ft.

Nowshak 7,485 m, 24,557 ft. Located within the **Hindu Kush**, this is the highest peak in **Afghanistan**. The peak was first climbed in 1960 by Toshiaki Sakai and Goro Iwatsubo.

Noyce, Wilfrid (1917–1962) Born: England. He participated in the 1953 British **Everest expedition** and made the **first ascent** of Trivor in 1960. Bibliography: *Mountains and Men* (1947), *Scholar Mountaineers* (1950), *South Col* (1954), *Everest Is Climbed* (1954), *The Springs of Adventure* (1958), *Climbing the Fish's Tail* (1958), *Poems* (1960), *The Alps* (1961), with Karl Lukan, *To the Unknown Mountain* (1962), *They Survived* (1962), *The Climber's Fireside Book* (1964).

Nuée ardente (F) A cloud of hot gas, ash, and rock that flows along the ground; it can be extremely destructive.

Nullah On the Indian subcontinent, a **gorge** or **gully**.

Nun Kun 7,135 m, 23,410 ft. This major peak is located within the **Himalayas** in Kashmir. Kun was first ascended in 1913, by Mario Piacenza, Lorenzo Borelli, and party; Nun was first climbed in 1953 by Claude Kogan and Pierre Vittoz.

Nunatak (Inuit) A mountain or smaller extrusion around which a **glacier** flows.

Nunavut Lowest point, Arctic Ocean 0 m; highest point Barbeau Peak, 2,616 m, 8,583 ft. This newest of Canadian territories was established on April 1, 1999. It is governed by the

Inuit people and is an arctic land of cold, polar bears, sea mammals, aurora borealis, and the midnight sun.

Nunn, Paul (1943–1995) Born: England. Bibliography: *Everest the Cruel Way* (1981), by **Joe Tasker**, *At the Sharp End* (1988).

Nuptse 7,861 m, 25,790 ft. A mighty, superb **satellite** of **Everest** in **Nepal**, it rises sharply above the base camp of Everest, on the Nepalese side; it was first climbed in 1961 by Dennis Davis and Sherpa Tashi. (See also color photos.)

Nut (Also chock or wedge) In rock climbing, a metallic device varying in size and attached to a short piece of wire; it is placed (rather than hammered) in **cracks** on **walls** in order to afford **protection**.

Nutcracker This bird resembles a crow and can found in the Himalayan sky at almost 20,000 ft.

Nyainqentanglha 7,088 m, 23,255 ft. This major peak is located within the Nyainqentanglha Shan Range in **China**.

Nyiragongo 3,470 m, 11,385 ft. An active **volcano** in the **Virunga Mountains** in the east of **Africa**, it is located within the volcano region of Virunga National Park in **Congo**. The main **caldera** is 2 km, 1.3 miles wide and some 250 m, 820 ft deep. It contains one of the only two known liquid lava lakes in the world; the other one, currently dried, was located in

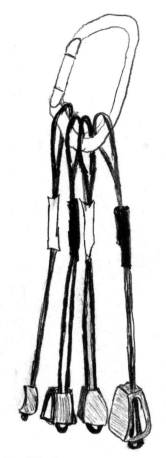

Nuts (Laura Lindblad)

Kileaua. Nyiragongo was extensively studied by French vulcanologist Haroun Tazieff; see his book, *Niracongo*.

O

Oak An extremely diverse group of **deciduous trees** divided into red and white varieties. Oaks such as scarlet, northern, pin, bear, and rock can all be found at higher elevations.

Obergabelhorn 4,063 m, 13,330 ft. This is the 44th highest of the 60 major 4,000-meter peaks in the **Alps**. It was first ascended in 1865 by **A. W. Moore**, **Horace Walker**, and **J. Anderreg**. It is located in the **Valais** region of **Switzerland**, in the **Weisshorn massif**.

Observatories There is a surprisingly diverse group of observatories located on or near mountains. The most obvious are the astronomical stations. Ancient peoples in South America and India built structures that facilitated heavenly observations. Modern optical emplacements are found, for example, on **Mauna Kea**, Mt. Wilson, and Palomar Mountain. Astronomers are able to get a clearer view of celestial bodies because their location and height eliminate some haze, pollution, weather, *gegenschein*, and other terrestrial annoyances. Radio telescopes are located in valleys and are protected by the surrounding mountains from random noise (Lutz). The second type of observatory is dedicated to meteorological matters and the prime example is the station on top of **New Hampshire**'s **Mt. Washington**, where, in 1934, the world's fiercest wind velocity was recorded: 231 miles per hour. Third are the high altitude research stations (see table 1). Fourth, are the volcano observatories (see also volcanoes.usgs.gov).

Obsidian A generally black rock of volcanic origin; it was used to make arrowheads.

Odell, Prof. Noel E. (1890–1987) Born: England. First ascent of **Nanda Devi** with **Tilman** in 1936. A member of the 1924 **Everest** expedition, he was the last to see **Mallory** and **Irvine** alive. Bibliography: *The Ascent of Nanda Devi* (1937), by H. W. Tilman, *The Fight for Everest: 1924* (1925), by E. F. Norton.

Ogre, The 7,285 m, 23,901 ft. This superb mountain is located in the **Karakoram**; it was first climbed in 1977 by **Doug Scott** and **Chris Bonington**. (See also color photos.)

Ohio Lowest point, Ohio River, Kentucky and Indiana border 139 m, 455 ft; highest point, Campbell Hill 472 m, 1,550 ft (43rd highest of the 50 state highpoints).

Oisans This very mountainous region is the heart of the **Dauphiné Alps**, and includes major peaks, such as the **Barre des Écrins**, the **Meije**, the **Pelvoux** and the **Ailefroide**. The centerpiece is the Parc Naturel Meije-Ecrins, one of the premier French national parks.

Ojos del Salado 6,880 m, 22,572 ft. This is the second highest peak in the **Andes**; it was first climbed 1937 by A. Szczpanski and J. Wojoznis. The peak is located in **Chile**.

Oklahoma Lowest point, Little River, Arkansas border 88 m, 289 ft; highest point, Black Mesa 1,516 m, 4,973 ft (23rd highest of the 50 state highpoints).

Old Faithful A popular geyser that erupts regularly, about once every hour. See also **Yellowstone National Park**.)

Old Man of the Mountain A 40-foot-high rock configuration resembling a man's head some 1,200 feet up on **New Hampshire**'s Cannon Mountain. On May 3, 2003, when the morning fog cleared, the Old Man was gone; the rocks,

Table 2. Estimated Number of Permanent High Altitude Residents and Annual High Altitude Visitors Worldwide at Altitudes above 8,000 Feet (2,439 meters), 1984–1986

Continent	Country	Permanent Residents	% Total	Visitors	% Total
Africa	Ethiopia	7,379,000	19	61,000	<1
	Kenya	6,125,000	16	541,000	1
			35		2
Asia	Afghanistan	4,778,000	12	9,000	<1
	Bhutan	426,000	1	2,000	<1
	China-Tibet	1,800,000	5	30,000	<1
	India-Sikkim	?	?	?	?
	India-Kashmir	?	?	?	?
	Nepal	4,798,000	12	181,000	<1
	USSR (now Russian Commonwealth				
	Tadzhik (now Tajikistan)	1,140,000	3	?	?
	Kirgiz (now Kyrgyzstn)	1,059,000	3	?	?
			36		<1
North America	Colorado	120,000	<1	14,370,000	39
	New Mexico	90,000	<1	5,000,000	14
	Utah	70,000	<1	10,600,000	29
	Wyoming	40,000	<1	4,750,000	13
			1		95
South America	Bolivia	2,443,000	6	127,000	<1
	Chile	1,097,000	3	394,000	<1
	Ecuador	2,902,000	8	350,000	<1
	Peru	4,069,000	11	300,000	<
			28		3
Total		38,336,000	100	36,715,000	100

SOURCE: L. Moore. Altitude-aggravated illness: Examples from pregnancy and prenatal life. *Ann. Emerg. Med.* 1987; 16:965–73.

which had been propped up with wires and glue, had finally collapsed.

Oldoinyou Lengai (Also Ol'donyo Lengai, Lengai; "Mountain of God") 2,896 m, 9,500 ft. A Tanzanian **volcano** that seems to erupt every seven years. It is the only volcano in the world that ejects a natrocarbonatite **lava** that turns white and gives the impression that the slopes are covered with **snow** (http://it.stlawu.edu/~cnya/).

Olympic Mountains Located in **Washington** state, these volcanic peaks are fairly glaciated; the prevailing weather from the Pacific Ocean is very humid and rainy: up to 3.55 m, 140 inches per year in the rainiest locations. The highest peak is **Mt. Olympus**; other summits, including Mt. Anderson and Mt. Deception, are above 2,000 m, 6,500 ft. The peculiar weather pattern gives rise to unusual vegetation, including unique, extensive rain forests, comprising enormous trees as tall as 90 m, 300 ft—Western red cedar, hemlock, Sitka spruce, Douglas fir—and an abundance of **moss** and **lichen**.

Olympics The national games of ancient Greece that were revived about 100 years ago for international competition. They take place every four years in a different location. Cities around the world bid for the privilege. The final choice of the committee honors the city and country and provides a very large revenue stream to local entrepreneurs and businesses. Many of the winter sports, including **skiing**, **snowboarding**, and **ski jumping**, take place on and around mountains.

Olympus, Mt. (Óros Ólimbos) 2,917 m, 9,750 ft. The highest mountain in Greece and home to the mythological gods.

Olympus, Mt. 2,428 m, 7,965 ft. An extinct **volcano** that is the highest peak in the **Olympic Mountains** in **Washington** state.

Olympus Mons There is no known shield **volcano** on any planet larger than Olympus Mons, which is 27 km, 88,600 ft high and located on Mars (Ritchie). (See also color photos.)

Oman Lowest point, Arabian Sea 0 m; highest point, Jabal Shams 2,980 m, 9,777 ft.

On Her Majesty's Secret Service Since stunts are a trademark of James Bond films, and mountain locations provide spectacular opportunities, it is little wonder that 007 often finds himself on the edge of a precipice: skiing in a bobsled track chased by a motorbike or falling off a Greek mountain in *For Your Eyes Only* (1981), pursued by Russians near the North Pole in *A View to a Kill* (1985), and falling off a cliff on his bike or attempting a daring bungee jump in *Goldeneye* (1995). Bond actually reached his apex in the opening sequence of *The Spy Who Loved Me* (1977): with villains chasing him, he skis off a cliff and waits until the last second to open a parachute. But only *On Her Majesty's Secret Service* (1969), shot in Mürren, Switzerland, near the **Jungfrau**, is really set in the mountains. Bond is told an ignominious villain's hideout is a crow's nest atop the Schilthorn. There are car chases on snow and highly impressive skiing—shot by Willy Bogner, who participated in several Olympic Games as a contestant. The film also has great aerial cinematography by cameraman John Jordan, who rode in a harness under a plane. Jordan, who had lost a leg shooting the previous Bond film (*You Only Live Twice*, 1967), died the following year when he fell off a plane while filming *Catch-22*. (M-A. H.)

Onsight (Sometimes, on-sight) A rock climb done with no previous information, without watching other climbers attempt the face, without preview rappelling or practice, and without falling. (See also **flash**, **pink point**, and **redpoint**.)

Ontario Lowest point, Hudson Bay 0 m; highest point Ishpatina Ridge, 693 m, 2,274 ft.

Oppenheimer, Lehmann (1868–1916) Born: Manchester, England. Bibliography: *The Heart of Lakeland* (1908).

Ordinary route This is the common route for a rock or mountain climb. (See also **normal route**.)

Ore Rock containing metal that can be profitably mined, it may be located in mountainous areas.

Oregon Lowest point, Pacific Ocean 0 m; highest point, **Mt. Hood** 3,426 m, 11,239 ft (13th highest of the 50 state highpoints). This is a lovely state, with a number of beautiful mountains, including: Mt. Jefferson 3,199 m, 10,497 ft, first climbed in 1888 by E. C. Cross and Ray L. Farmer; the Three Sisters; Mt. Bachelor; and Mt. Thielsen, a craggy remnant of a volcanic plug.

Organizations See **clubs**.

Oriole A brightly colored bird; the northern can be found at altitudes as high as 7,000 ft.

Orizaba, Pico de (Also Citlaltepetl, Aztec for "mountain of the star") 5,700 m, 18,701 ft. A beautiful, dormant volcano, Orizaba is the highest mountain in Mexico and the third highest in **North America**. Along with its sister volcanoes, **Popocatépetl** (Popo) 5,451 m, 17,887 ft and **Iztaccíhuatl** (Ixta) 5,286 m, 17,343 ft, Orizaba is visible from Mexico City on a rare clear (pollutionless) day. Because of their altitude, location, and easy slopes, these mountains are frequently visited by climbers from all over the world. It should be noted that Popo's recent eruption makes it extremely dangerous, and the Mexican government no longer allows climbing there. (See also color photos and the **10 Highest Volcanoes** sidebar.)

Orography The discipline that takes mountains as its domain.

Outcrop *Klettergarten* (G), *palestia di roccia* (I). A small stone formation that extrudes from a larger surface. According to Unsworth, a smaller lithic extrusion, away from mountainous areas (*Encyclopaedia*). (But see also **bedrock**.)

Overhang *Surplomb* (F), *strapiombo* (I), *Überhang* (G). In rock climbing, a surface that slopes at greater than 90 degrees. At ca. 180 degrees it becomes a roof.

Owens Valley This classic **rift** is located at the eastern side of **California**; it is one of the deepest valleys in North America, as its floor lies at an elevation of 3,000–4,000 ft, while both sides of the valley are surrounded by mountains reaching an altitude of 14,000 ft. It is also a rather active tectonic area, with numerous earthquakes, especially near the town of Bishop and the ski resort of Mammoth Lakes.

Owl A bird that comes in many sizes and colorations. It sits and waits for prey and then swoops down, often in the dark, in which it sees well because of its big eyes. Some species nest as high as 10,000 ft and inhabit areas up to 12,000 ft. The great horned sometimes nests on "rock ledges" (Johnsgard); in the **Andes**, the short-eared reaches 13,500 ft (Fjeldså and Krabbe).

Oxygen (Os[1]) An atmospheric gas required by most nonbotanical life forms. As the **altitude** increases the oxygen content decreases, and so above 26,000 ft (see **death zone**) many mountaineers use supplemental oxygen, which they carry in tanks. Some climbers, including **Reinhold Messner**, abjure its use, preferring to climb naturally: "Every ten or fifteen steps we collapse into the snow to rest, then crawl on again." Supplemental oxygen makes both climbing and sleeping at altitude considerably easier.

Ozarks A range that crosses parts of **Arkansas**, **Missouri**, and **Oklahoma**.

P

Paccard, Michel-Gabriel (1757–1827) Born: Chamonix, France. A doctor who, with **Jacques Balmat**, made the first ascent of **Mont Blanc** on August 8, 1786, having made three attempts on the Goûter route in 1775, 1783, and 1784. Bibliography: *The Annals of Mont Blanc* (1898) by C. E. Mathews.

Pacific Crest Trail A 2,650-mile trail that runs along the **Cascades** and **Sierras** on the west coast of the United States (www.pcta.org). (See also **Brian Robinson**.)

Pahoehoe (H) Smooth, billowy **lava**. (See also **aa**.)

Painters Even though early peoples were frightened by large peaks looming above, ascribed celestial powers to them, and avoided their summits, they nevertheless wished to visually reproduce them. Many artists have created specific or generic renderings of mountains, some of which figure importantly in the history of art. The Romantics were especially taken with this aspect of nature. Painters include Benton, **Bierstadt**, Bingham, Catlin, Cezanne, Church, Da Vinci, Friederich, Hokusei, Martin, Moran, **Roerich**, Ruskin, and Turner. (See also color photos.)

Pakistan Lowest point, Indian Ocean 0 m; highest point, **K2** 8,611 m, 28,251 ft. The mighty **Karakoram** range is located in the north of the country, which counts a total of five 8,000-meter peaks: K2, **Nanga Parbat**, **Gasherbrum I**, **Broad Peak**, and **Gasherbrum II**. All are in Pakistan except for K2, which lies along the Pakistan-China border.

Palau Lowest point, Pacific Ocean 0 m; highest point, Mt. Ngerchelchauus 242 m, 794 ft.

Palisades Extended (columnar) **cliffs**. **New Jersey**'s Palisades, which run along the Hudson River, are a famous example. (See also **The Palisades**.)

Palisades, The A mighty range in the High **Sierras** of **California**, with five peaks above 14,000 ft: **North Palisade** 4,340 m, 14,242 ft; **Middle Palisade** 4,279 m, 14,040 ft; **Mt. Sill**, 4,316 m, 14,162 ft; **Polemonium Peak** 4,292 m, 14,080 ft; and **Thunderbolt Peak** 4,268 m, 14,003 ft.

Palisades Glacier This is one of the largest **glaciers** in the **California Sierras**.

Palmyra Atoll Lowest point, Pacific Ocean 0 m; highest point, unnamed location 2 m, 7 ft.

Palu, Piz 3,905 m, 12,812 ft. An important satellite of **Piz Bernina** in the **Engadine**, it is characterized by its three distinct **buttresses**. It was first ascended in 1866 by K. E. Digby and **H. Walker**. (See also color photos.)

Pamirs A **range** in Russia. Here is where the peaks formerly named for Lenin and the revolution can be found; the highest is Pik imeni **Ismail** Samani (formerly, Pik Kommunizma) 7,495 m, 24,590 ft.

Panama Lowest point, Pacific Ocean 0 m; highest point, Volcan de Chiriqui 3,475 m, 11,401 ft.

Papua New Guinea Lowest point, Pacific Ocean 0 m; highest point, Mt. Victoria 4,073 m, 13,363 ft.

Paracel Islands Lowest point, South China Sea 0 m; highest point, unnamed location on Rocky Island 14 m, 46 ft.

Paradis, Marie (1786–1838) The first woman to climb **Mont Blanc**, in 1808.

Paraguay Lowest point, junction of Río Paraguay and Río Paraná 46 m, 151 ft; highest point, Cerro San Rafael 850 m, 2,789 ft.

Paricutín   3,170 m, 10,400 ft. A **volcano** that emerged from a Mexican farmer's field in 1943. Ritchie notes that it was "one of the most spectacular eruptions of the 20th century." (See also **Surtsey**.)

Parnassos   (Also Parnassus) 2,457 m, 8,062 ft. A mountain in Greece, which plays an important role in the country's **mythology**.

Parrot, Pointe   4,436 m, 14,554 ft. This is the 12th highest of the 60 major 4,000-meter peaks in the **Alps**. The Pointe Parrot is one of the five main summits of **Monte Rosa**. It was first climbed in 1863 by R. S. McDonald, **F. C. Grove**, M. Woodmass, **Melchior Anderegg**, and Peter Perren. (See also color photos.)

Partridge   A game **bird** that enjoys rambling along the ground. The Himalayan snow partridge can be found at 16,500 ft and the Tibetan to 18,000 ft (Ali).

Pass   (Also saddle) *Col* (F), *colle* (I), *Joch* (G), *la* (T). An often deep declivity in a **ridge** or between **summits**. It is toward a pass that road builders, travelers, and climbers head in order to cross at a convenient point; it can go on for many miles. Col (considered an English word) implies that the breach is narrow, rocky, and occurs at higher elevations. A saddle is prescribed in width and depth. The **Khyber** and **Brenner** passes are well-known examples.

Patagonia   A company making quality climbing clothing and equipment.

Patagonia   The southernmost region in **Argentina**, it combines a semi-arid **plateau** and the southern tip of the **Andes**. Many extraordinary peaks and **spires** such as **Fitzroy** and **Cerro Torre** can be found in Patagonia, as well as some **fjords** and large **glaciers**. (See also color photos.)

Patey, Thomas Walton   (1932–1970) A wonderful Scottish humorist, writer, and climber. Bibliography: *Rakaposhi* (1959) by Mike Banks, *One Man's Mountains* (1971).

Pauhunri   7,128 m, 23,385 ft. This major peak is located within the **Himalayas** at the border between **India** and **China**.

Payott, Dr. Michel   (fl. late 19th century) He is responsible for introducing skiing in **Chamonix** in 1896.

Peak   *Gipfel* or *Spitze* (G), *punta* or *cima* (I), *piz* (Romanche). In English, a mountain; in all languages, its highest and most steeply angled section.

Peakware World Mountain Encyclopedia   An excellent website that provides basic data, variously configured, on the world's major mountains and ranges (www.peakware.com) (See also the **24 Great Websites** sidebar.)

Peascod, Bill   (1920–1985) Born: Ellenborough, Cumberland. An excellent rock climber who opened a number of routes in the Lakeland area of England. Bibliography: *Journey after Dawn* (1985), autobiography.

Peck, Annie Smith   (1850–1935) Professor at various schools, including Smith College; she climbed the **Matterhorn** and in **Peru**.

Pediment   A slope at the foot of a mountain.

Peg   See **piton**.

Pele   In Hawaiian mythology, the volcano goddess; she resides in **Kilauea**. (See also **religion**.)

Pelvoux   3,946 m, 12,946 ft. In the heart of the **Dauphiné Alps**, near the splendid **Barre des Écrins**, lies the mighty Pelvoux, first climbed by A. Durand, J.-E. Matheoud, and A. Liotard in 1828. The highest peak is the Pointe Puiseux; the Pointe Durand at 3,932 m, 12,900 ft, is the second highest point on the mountain, followed by a satellite called the Petit Pelvoux, 3,753 m, 12,313 ft. One of the nicest routes on the mountain is the Coolidge Couloir, a steep snow and ice ascent; the Glacier des Violettes also offers an interesting approach, and the Col Est du Pelvoux is a difficult 60-degree ice couloir on the north side, rising directly from the Glacier Noir, and affording exceptional views of the 2,000 m, 6,000 ft, south face of the Barre des Écrins.

Pendulum   In rock climbing, to swing back and forth on a wall (purposely or inadvertently) when hanging on a rope that is anchored from above.

Penitentes   These are **gendarmes** made of **snow**, that is, **towers** of snow that are created by melting under the equatorial (zenithal) sunrays.

Pennsylvania   Lowest point, Delaware River, Delaware border 0 m; highest point Mt. Davis 979 m, 3,213 ft (33rd highest of the 50 state highpoints).

Periodicals Many thousands of scholarly journals and popular magazines are published on various aspects of mountains. All of the subdisciplines noted in this volume (for example, botany, geology, glaciology, or meteorology) produce specialized journals and thus it is impossible to mention any of these. The countless scholarly publications dealing specifically with mountains and climbing include *Accidents in North American Mountaineering* (1948–); *The Alpine Journal* (1863–); *American Alpine Journal* (1929–); *Appalachia* (1876–); *Canadian Alpine Journal* (1907–); *The Himalayan Journal* (1929–); and *Mountain Research and Development*. Magazines devoted entirely or in part to climbing include *Alp* (1985–); *Die Alpen, Les Alpes, Le Alps* (1925–) (originally a journal); *Alpinisme; Alpinisme et Randonnée* (1978–); *Alpinisimus* (1963–); *Alpinist* (2003–); *Ascent* (1967–); *Backpacker; Bergsteiger* (1929?–); *Climbing* (1970–); *High Mountain Sports* (formerly *High*) (1982–); *La Montagne et Alpinisme* (formerly *La Montagne*) (1905–); *Mountain* (1969–1992); *The Mountaineer; Off Belay* (1972–1981); *Outside; Rock and Ice* (1984–); *Sierra Club Bulletin; Summit* (1955–1996); *Vertical* (1985–); and *Vertical Roc* (2000–). Among the specialized popular publications (on skiing and other sports) are *Couloir, Powder, Skiing*, and *Warren Miller's Ski World*. These publications, especially the journals, offer a complete documented, if scattered, history of climbing by the people responsible for exploration, discoveries, attempts, and first and subsequent ascents.

Permafrost Located primarily in Siberia and **Alaska**, this is frozen ground that never unfreezes. Near **St. Moritz**, a ca. 1,500-foot wide dam has been constructed in order to hold back a **cliff** that may self-destruct because the permafrost is melting due to global warming.

Perry-Smith, Oliver (1884–1969) One of the world's great rock climbers, he moved from America to Dresden. With Rudolf Fehrmann, he set an extremely high standard for rock climbing and bold **leads** in the early 1900s (Pat Ament, personal comment).

Peru Lowest point, Pacific Ocean 0 m; highest point, **Nevado Huascarán** 6,768 m, 22,205 ft.

The famous ruins of **Machu Picchu** can be found in this beautiful country, as well as numerous extraordinary peaks, including **Alpamayo**, Huascarán, **Yerupajá Grade**, **Jirishanca**, **Coropuna**, **Huandoy**, and **Salcantay**. There are numerous mountains ranges in the Peruvian **Andes**, but the **Cordillera Blanca**, the Cordillera Occidental, and the Cordillera **Huayhuash** contain many of the highest peaks. (See also color photos.)

Petra Located in **Jordan**, this magnificent site is the crown jewel of the Nabatea Archeological Park.

Petrarch (1304–1374) Early Italian poet; the first person to write caringly about mountain climbing after ascending Mt. Ventoux, located in the Southern French Alps, in 1336; this is essentially the first recorded entry in the annals of climbing.

Petroglyph An image incised into a rock face. Along with similar colorful paintings (called pictographs), petroglyphs can be found in mountainous areas in all parts of the world. An especially rich supply is located in **New Mexico's** Petroglyph National Monument.

Petzoldt, Paul Kiesow (1908–1999) Early guide in the **Tetons**. He was a member of the first American Karakoram expedition to K2 (1938); he holds the first winter ascent of the Grand Teton. He is the founder of Outward Bound and the National Outdoor Leadership School (NOLS). (See also **Glenn Exum**.)

Pheasant A gaudy ground bird; the Himalayan monal roams at 16,500 ft (Ali).

Philippines Lowest point, Philippine Sea 0 m; highest point, Mt. Apo 2,954 m, 9,692 ft. Numerous highly active volcanoes dot the landscape of the Philippines, including **Mt. Pinatubo**, which recently erupted, destroying many villages and arable land.

Phlox Pink, white, or purple clustered flowers.

Photography Photographs of mountains are among the most powerful images that human beings have created; they awe, inspire, and seduce. The finest mountain photographers include **Ansel Adams**, **John Cleare**, **Galen Rowell**, **Vittorio Sella**, and **Bradford Washburn**. (See also **mountain imagery**.)

Picket An aluminum I-beam (ca. 1–2 ft long) that can be forced into deep snow in order to

10 Best Mountain Photographers and Cinematographers

1. Ansel Adams
2. Bradford Washburn
3. David Breashears
4. Galen Rowell
5. Gaston Rébuffat
6. John Cleare
7. Marcel Ichac
8. Pierre Tairraz
9. Vilem Heckel
10. Vittorio Sella

create an **anchor** point for a **belay**. (See also **fluke**.)

Pico Bolivar   (Also La Columna) 5,007 m, 16,427 ft. This is the highest peak in **Venezuela**; it is located near the northern tip of the **Andes**.

Piedmont glacier   An extremely broad **glacier** formed by the confluence of other, faster flowing glaciers. They differ from **ice fields** because they are not bounded by mountain ridges; instead they flow slowly along gently sloping terrain, in a broad arc, many tens of miles wide. The **Malaspina Glacier**, in **Alaska**, is an excellent example.

Pika   A small rodent (with many names, e.g., cony) whose favorite environment is the rubble on high mountain slopes.

Pikes Peak   4,300 m, 14,110 ft. Located in **Colorado's Front Range**; a road leads to the summit, one of the highest roads in the United States.

Pillar   *Pfeiler* (G), *pilastro* (I), *pilier* (F). An independent, narrow, steep rock that has a flat top. (See also **pinnacle**.)

Pilley, Dorothy   (1893–1979) Born: England. A foremost climber between World War I and World War II. Bibliography: *Climbing Days* (1935).

Pinatubo, Mt.   1,600 m, 5,248 ft. A very active and dangerous **volcano** in the **Philippines** that erupted in 1991, causing widespread damage and almost 900 deaths; the dispersed ash and toxic materials slightly altered the world's climate.

Pine   A **conifer** of innumerable species; eastern white is ubiquitous in the mountains. Jack, limber, lodgepole, mountain, ponderosa, Jeffrey, shortleaf, and other species can be found at altitude. No living entity is older than the bristlecone (found above 12,000 ft), individual examples of which have been growing in California for 4,000 years. (See also color photos.)

Pingo   An ice-covered, conical hill that emerges and continues to grow in areas covered with **permafrost**. There are about 1,450 of them in the western Arctic. (www.taiga.net/yourYukon/col171.html)

Pink and carnation   A few **Himalayan** species of this flower family may hold some altitude records: Arenaria bryophilla has been found above 20,000 ft (Polunin and Stainton).

Pinkpoint   A free climb without a fall utilizing **protection** already in place. (See also **redpoint** and **onsight**.)

Pinnacle   An independent, steep narrow rock without a flat top. (See also **gendarme** and **pillar**.) An **aiguille** or needle is larger.

Piste   (F) The groomed ski slope or trail.

Pitcairn Islands   Lowest point, Pacific Ocean 0 m; highest point, Pawala Valley Ridge 347 m, 1,138 ft.

Pitch   (Also **lead**) *Longeur de corde* (F), *lunghezza* (I). In rock and ice climbing, usually, the distance a climber can travel before the rope runs out, up to 100, 150, or more feet, or the distance between **belay stances**.

Piton   (Also pin; peg, in Great Britain) *Chiodo* (I), *Haken* (G). A small, metal spike that is pounded into a crack on a rock surface. Pitons have various names including **RURP** and **bong**, depending on size and shape. A **rope** attached or run past via a **carabiner** offers **protection** to a falling climber or **aid**. Sometimes, pitons are left in place either because they cannot be extracted or because they could be used by subsequent climbers. Pitons have generally been replaced by **nuts, cams,** and **ice screws,** which can easily be removed, thus leaving the mountain unsullied. (See also **bolt**.)

Piz See **peak**.

Placer Gold, platinum, or other minerals deposited in concentrated form in gravel or sand.

Plants An all-encompassing term for botanical entities, including bushes, **flowers**, **lichen**, **moss**, shrubs, and **trees**. Plants provide protection against **erosion** but at the same time their roots may enlarge splits in the rock thus hastening the diminution of the mountain mass. (See also color photos.)

Plate boundaries See **tectonic plates**.

Plate tectonics See **tectonic plates**.

Plateau An elevated region that is considerably larger than a **butte** or a **mesa**. Tibet is the highest plateau in the world.

Plover A small to medium-sized **bird** that manages to reach higher altitudes. In East Africa, the black-winged can be found above 7,000 ft.

Plume A spray of snow resembling a feather that springs up in the wind. (See also **spindrift**.)

Plunge step In mountaineering, aggressively forcing one's boot heel into the snow when descending a steep **slope** without **crampons**.

Plutonic See **igneous**.

Pobeda, Pik 7,439 m, 24,407 ft. The highest peak in **Kyrgyzstan**, located in the **Tien Shan Range**. This superb and heavily glaciated mountain was first ascended in 1956 by Vitali Abalakov's party.

Poland Lowest point, Raczki Elblaskie −2 m, −7 ft; highest point, Rysy 2,499 m, 8,199 ft.

Polar Relating to the Arctic and **Antarctic**, whence cold air travels to mountainous regions. The latter is an ice cap and contains many mountains. (See also the **Seven Summits** sidebar.)

Polemonium Peak 4,292 m, 14,080 ft. Located in the **Palisades** region of the **Sierra Nevada** in **California**, it was first ascended in 1933 by Lewis Clark, Ted Waller, Julie Mortimer, and Jack Riegelhuth.

Pollux 4,091 m, 13,422 ft. This is the 41st highest of the 60 major 4,000-meter peaks of the **Alps**. It was first ascended in 1857 by Jules Jacot, Peter Taugwalder father, and Josef-Maria Perren. The twin peak of **Castor**, it is located near **Monte Rosa**, in the **Valaisan Alps**.

Pompeii A city in southern Italy buried in ash in 79 C.E. by a massive eruption of **Mt. Vesuvius**. It was lost for more than 1,500 years; since its rediscovery, ongoing excavations have revealed amazing archeological, architectural, and artistic treasures.

Poplar (Also aspen) A straight growing **deciduous tree** that splits perfectly when deconstructed for use as firewood. (See also color photos.)

Popocatépetl (Alsso Popo; Aztec for "smoking mountain") 5,451 m, 17,887 ft. One of the three high Mexican **volcanoes**, which are frequently climbed because they are fairly easy. In fact, Popo was the first New World mountain climbed by Europeans: Cortes's soldiers reached the summit in 1523 when searching for sulfur. Popo is now active and off limits to mountaineers. (See also **Orizaba, Iztaccíhuatl**, and color photos.)

Poppy Some **Himalayan** varieties of this well-known yellow, orange, or blue **flower** flourish at almost 19,000 ft (Polunin).

Porcupine A small mammal covered with sharp quills. The cape porcupine (of southern Africa) can be found in the mountains (Burnie and Wilson).

Pork Chop Hill An American war movie by Lewis Milestone (*All Quiet on the Western Front*) starring Gregory Peck (who, according to the director, trimmed the film in order to eliminate pacifist issues). Set during the Korean War (see *Men in War*), this movie uses hill locations in a classic way. Having troops fighting uphill naturally enhances the graphic impression of difficulty as well as actually getting the soldiers into trouble. The various aspects the script deals with rarely come from the topography but are greatly enhanced by it, and the situation allows the audience to grasp the drama more easily. (M-A. H.)

Porter One of the three types of people who help mountaineers reach summits. (The others are **guides** and **Sherpas**.) Porters are hired by **expeditions** in the **Himalayas**, **Andes**, and a few other mountain systems to carry heavy loads to **base camp**. These sometimes unshod people haul 40, 50, 60, and even 100 pounds on their backs or heads across rivers, along precipitous trails, and up mountains for small recompense. Without them, most mountaineers would not be able to climb the higher peaks.

Porter, Charlie (fl. 1970s) A **Yosemite** rock climber and mountaineer. In 1978, he did a solo of **Denali**'s Cassini Ridge.

Portugal Lowest point, Atlantic Ocean 0 m; highest point, Ponta do Pico (Pico or Pico Alto) on Ilha do Pico in the Azores 2,351 m, 7,713 ft.

Post hole In climbing, to place one's feet and legs into deep snow as one moves up or down a slope.

Potala The Dalai Lama's former palace in **Lhasa.**

Potter, Dean (1972–) A superb rock climber; his **free-solos** and **speed** climbs of consecutive faces in **Yosemite**, during the 1990s, are legendary.

Poucher, William Arthur (1891–1988) Born: England. An excellent mountain photographer, who published a very extensive portfolio. Bibliography: *Lakeland through the Lens* (1940), *Snowdonia through the Lens* (1941), *Lakeland Holiday* (1942), *Escape to the Hills* (1943), *Snowdon Holiday* (1943), *Scotland through the Lens: Loch Tulla to Lochaber* (1943), *Highland Holiday* (1945), *Lakeland Journey* (1945), *Backbone of England* (1946), *Peak Panorama* (1946), *Camera in the Cairngorms* (1947), *Over Lakeland Fells* (1948), *Wanderings in Wales* (1949), *The Magic of Skye* (1949), *The Surrey Hills* (1949), *Lakeland Scrapbook* (1950), *Magic of the Dolomites* (1951), *Journey into Ireland* (1953), *North-West Highlands* (1954), *West Country Journey* (1957), *The Lakeland Peaks: A Pictorial Guide* (1960), *The Welsh Peaks* (1962), *Climbing with a Camera* (1963), *The Scottish Peaks* (1965), *The Peak and Pennines from Dovedale to Hadrian's Wall* (1966), *Scotland* (1980), *Lakeland Fells* (1981), *Wales* (1981), *The Lake District* (1982), *The Alps* (1983), *The Highlands of Scotland* (1983), *The Yorkshire Dales and the Peak District* (1984), *The West Country* (1984), *Skye* (1985), *Ireland* (1986), *The Magic of the Highlands* (1987), *Lakeland Panorama* (1989).

Powell, Darren (fl. late 1990s) He holds the speed record for **snowboarding** (125 miles per hour).

Pratt, Chuck (Charles) (fl. late 1950s–mid-1960s) From 1961 to 1966, Pratt was the finest off-width **crack** climber in the world, and a leading pioneer of big **routes** on **El Capitan** (Pat Ament, personal comment).

Precious metals Gold, silver, and platinum, all of which have important industrial applications. They may be mined in mountainous areas.

Precious stones (Also gems) Those **minerals** (sometimes mined in mountainous areas) that humans deem more valuable (rarer, better, clearer) than others, either because they have some practicable application (diamond) or because they are aesthetically pleasing (turquoise, opal). The economic value or cost of these naturally occurring objects is often much inflated. For example, in the past, South African mining consortia have attempted to purchase all available stones on the world's diamond markets, and thus maintain an inappropriately high price.

Precipice The top of a steep declivity or abyss; a **cliff**.

Premier de Cordée A 1941 wonderful novel by **Roger Frison-Roche**. (See also the **10 Great Mountain Adventure Books** sidebar.)

Premier de Cordée A 1944 French feature film after the novel by **Roger Frison-Roche**. This is a fairly late representative of those mountain films so popular in the 1930s. Ably cast (including **Maurice Baquet**), fine cinematography by Philippe Agostini and music by concert-composer Henri Sauguet show that those responsible cared about what they were doing. The location shots are excellent, but the production was hampered by shortages brought on by the war and the film is dramatically restrained. A documentary, ***Autour d'un Film de Montagne***, depicts the making of the film. (M-A. H.)

Presidentials A **range** in **New Hampshire**. Peaks include Mts. Adams, Jefferson, Madison, and **Washington**.

Prince Edward Island Lowest point, Atlantic Ocean 0 m; highest point Queen's County 142 m, 466 ft.

Problem A difficult move that requires a solution, especially in **bouldering**. (See also **climbing**.)

Professional A person, for example, a **guide**, who earns a living from climbing, especially mountaineering. It is possible to be both a professional and an **amateur**.

Profit, Christophe (1961–) A French climber and mountaineer whose extremely fast and spectacular ***enchaînements*** include the **Eiger north face**, the **Matterhorn** north face, and the Linceuil, in the **Grandes Jorasses**, all in less than 15 hours (Ardito)!

Project Bandaloop Mountain Dancing A group of people hang from ropes on a cliff face and dance.

Promontory A high projection over water or land. (See also **headland** and **bluff**.)

Protection (Pro) In rock or ice climbing, the **gear** that ones uses to attach to a **wall**, face, or ice so that the belayer can hold a falling person. Also, protecting oneself when climbing alone.

Prusik A specialized type of self-locking **knot** that was used as a crude **ascender** before the invention of the jumar; nowadays, it can be handy to improvise an ascender, or to tie climbing tools, such as an **ice ax**, to one's **harness**.

Ptarmigan A **bird**; the white-tailed can be found at altitude and in alpine meadows; during the winter, it alters its color to "pure white" (Udvardy and Farrand).Its range includes **Colorado**, western **Canada**, and **Alaska**.

Pueblo In **Arizona**, **New Mexico**, and **Colorado**, a type of village built into or against mountain sides or on top of **mesas** (but also at lower elevations) out of local stone or brick and inhabited by the indigenous peoples (the Anasazi) in the past. Also, similar habitation today. (See also **cave temple** and **cliff dwelling**.)

Puerto Rico Lowest point, Caribbean Sea 0 m; highest point, Cerro de Punta 1,338 m, 4,390 ft.

Puja An act of reverence through prayer, ritual, or song. It is performed by Hindu porters or climbers in the Himalayas.

Pumice Porous, glasslike substance of volcanic origin; it is a rock that floats.

Puna A high Andean plain. (See **acute mountain sickness**.)

Punta (S) See **peak**.

Pyramid 7,132 m, 23,400 ft. This major peak is located within the **Himalayas** in **Nepal**.

Pyramid Sometimes used to characterize a **peak**; for example, the summit pyramid of **K2**.

Pyramide Vincent 4,215 m, 13,838 ft. This is the 26th highest of the 60 major 4,000-meter peaks of the **Alps**. It was first climbed in 1851 by the Schlagintweit brothers and Peter Beck. The Pyramide Vincent is a powerful satellite of **Monte Rosa**.

Pyrénées A 270-mile **chain** in southern Europe that forms the French–Spanish border. It offers extremely beautiful vistas from its meandering roads and train routes. Its west end is home to the Basque people. The highest point of the Pyrénées is the Pico de **Aneto** 3,404 m, 11,168 ft.

Pyroclastic rock Fragments that are expelled during volcanic **eruptions**.

Q

Qatar Lowest point, Persian Gulf 0 m; highest point, Qurayn Abu al Bawl 103 m, 338 ft.

Qomolangma The Tibetan name of **Mt. Everest**, related to a Tibetan legend describing five goddesses (*qomo*); the most beautiful one, with an emerald face, is Qomo Langma.

Quail A game **bird**; in East Africa, the harlequin moves up as high as 8,000 or more ft (Williams).

Quarry A surface or underground pit where useful **rock** is located. As the rock, **marble** or **granite**, for example, is removed, the hole is enlarged. The 600-foot-deep granite quarry in Barre, **Vermont**, is the largest in the world. (See also **mining**.)

Quartz The **mineral** that occurs most frequently in nature; it is found in many **rocks**, for example, **granite**.

Québec Lowest point, Gulf of the Saint Laurent 0 m; highest point, Mont d'Iberville 1,652 m, 5,420 ft. The highest point entirely within **Québec** is Mt. Jacques Cartier 1,268 m, 4,160 ft, located in the northernmost part of the **Appalachians**; Mt. d'Iberville is located on the border with **Newfoundland and Labrador**, where it is called Mt. Caubvik.

Quickdraw In rock climbing, two **carabiners** attached to each other by a piece of webbing.

Quincy Adams Peak 4,092 m, 13,426 ft. A high peak located in the **Yukon** Territory in Canada.

R

Rack In rock climbing, a collection of different **protection** devices (**gear**) that is carried slung around the shoulder on a **sling** or **bandolier**, hooked to a belt, or clipped to a **harness**. A replete rack might cost $2,000 (or more), weigh 15 pounds, and include **cams**, **daisy chains**, **étriers**, **nuts**, **quickdraws**, slings, **stoppers**, and other esoteric devices. Since one's safe progress up (or down) a sheer wall depends on these pieces of protection, dropping one's rack could prove to be a fatal error. (**Pat Ament**, on **El Capitan**'s **Nose**, dropped a sling containing his big **pitons**.)

Radiation Electromagnetic energy emitted by the sun and other cosmic bodies. It is especially harmful at higher altitudes because the atmosphere is thinner and thus does not afford as much protection; sunlight reflected off snow and ice magnifies the detrimental properties. In its least potent form, radiation burns the skin and harms the eyes (both of which should be covered); large doses of radiation can be fatal.

Radiation cooling The process by which heat is radiated away from the earth, into space, in the form of infrared light. This process necessitates that the atmosphere be transparent at infrared wavelengths, which requires low water vapor pressure, or dry air, a condition that is generally satisfied at high altitude, where humidity is trapped in the form of ice crystals and where the strong winds, or even the **jet stream**, carry moisture away. Therefore, radiation cooling is generally very efficient in the high mountains, leading to a thorough refreezing of glacier surfaces, snow bridges, couloirs, and ridges.

Railroad Normal railroads have been laboriously and expensively constructed across, over, and through mountains. But there are also specialized, narrow-gauge systems in various parts of the world. Some of these may travel long distances, for example, in Switzerland or Austria. Others move over just a mile or two up a single mountain, for example, the cog railroad on **Mt. Washington**. They are propelled by locomotive power, which may be augmented by a rack and pinion system between the tracks.

Rain *Pioggia* (I), *pluie* (F), *Regen* (G). Liquid precipitation that takes place above 32 degrees Fahrenheit.

Rain shadow The area protected from most storms by a mountain range standing in the path of the predominant local winds. For example, the region east of the **Sierras** in **California** is an extremely dry desert, where **Death Valley** is located; in **British Columbia**, the terrain east of the Coast Range gets a much lower accumulation of snow in the winter; and northern **Italy** typically enjoys much sunnier weather than **France** and **Switzerland**, because it is protected by the **Alps** from the predominant storms coming from the northwest.

Rainier, Mt. 4,392 m, 14,411 ft. A famous dormant **volcano** in the **Cascades**, it is the highest point in **Washington** and the third highest mountain the continental United States. It offers many difficult routes along its 27 **glaciers** to the summit. At Paradise, at the foot of the mountain, snow falls at the rate of 15 to 20 feet per year, but higher up the mountain averages 50 to 60 feet. Americans who plan to climb in the **Himalayas**

or the **Andes** often train on Rainier. Although it has not erupted for many years, seismologists predict that a major cataclysm is in the offing, one that will have even more devastating consequences than other volcanic **eruptions**: flowing **lava** will melt the accumulated snow and glacial ice and the resulting **lahar** will destroy nearby towns; even Seattle could be devastated by mudslides or ash. Ritchie and Gates point out that the upper mountain is laced with steam **caves**, tunnels inside the glacier. (See appendix G.)

Rainier Mountaineering, Inc. (RMI) See **guiding services**.

Rakaposhi 7,788 m, 25,551 ft. This major peak is located within the **Karakoram** Range in **Pakistan**. It was first ascended in 1958, by Mike Banks and Tom Patey.

Ralston, Aron (1976–) In the spring of 2003, while on a solitary hike/climb, Ralston's arm was trapped under a falling boulder. He waited for help for five days, but eventually he was forced to free himself by amputating his arm. Astonishingly, he then rappelled and walked many miles to get back to civilization. *Between a Rock and Hard Place*, his account of the experience, appeared in late 2004.

Ramuz, Charles-Ferdinand (1878–1947) A Swiss author whose novels are set in the mountains. Ramuz's plots often deal with fantastic premises either expressed factually (in *Derborence*, 1934, a man dead for three months actually comes back to his village) or as impressions of the characters (in *La Grande Peur dans la Montagne*, 1926, a pasture is cursed). (M-A. H.)

Randonnée (F) See **skiing**.

Range A series of connected peaks that form one continuous line, for example, the **Front Range** of the **Rocky Mountains**; a series of peaks near each other that have the same etiology. Ranges often run parallel to each other, interrupted by valleys. The term is also loosely used to indicate a series of ranges, for example, the Rockies or the **Sierras**. (See also **chain** and **system**.) There are hundreds of mountain ranges in the world and many of them are noted here in their correct alphabetical location. **John Cleare**, in *The World Guide to Mountains and Mountaineering* (not to be confused with his *Mountains of the World*) offers an excellent, detailed overview of the major ranges and their associated peaks. Both of these volumes are profusely illustrated, primarily with Cleare's stunning photographs. **Roger Frison-Roche**'s comprehensive taxonomy also includes the world's ranges.

Rappel (Rap) (F), *Abseil* (G). There is no English term for this act of lowering oneself down a steep slope or cliff, usually quickly, on a supported **rope** that is controlled by the body and hands or more recently by a **belay** or rappel device such as a **figure eight**. The German term is frequently used in Great Britain. (The phrase "roping down" was used in the past.)

Rating systems In **rock climbing**, systems of ranking the difficulty of **routes** have been devised in different countries. Since these differ dramatically from each other depending on whether one is using, for example, the American, Australian, or British system, things can be very confusing. In the United States, one normally employs the Yosemite Decimal System. Here, 1 indicates walking or **hiking**; 2 crossing difficult terrain or simple **scrambling**; 3 scrambling, some rock; 4 moving upward on a steep incline or simple **climbing**; 5 is serious climbing with **belays**: 5.1 through 5.3 indicate easy routes and from 5.4 through 5.15, things get progressively more difficult. From 5.10 upward, subtle distinctions are noted through the use of the letters a–d; thus 5.13b is more treacherous than 5.13a. Since this originally was a decimal system, the difference between 5.8 and 5.9, for example, is larger than one might expect. Sometimes a plus or minus sign is added. In Europe (the UIAA system), the Roman numerals I through X (with pluses and minuses) indicate progressively more difficult climbs: I walking; II scrambling; III steep terrain, but belays are not required; IV high, steep faces, and belays are required; V vertical and difficult; VI holds are proscribed; the higher numbers mean that things get progressively more horrific. For **mountaineering** in the **Alps** and especially in France, abbreviated terms are used: F (*facile*); PD (*peu difficile*); AD (*assez difficile*); D (*difficile*); TD (*très difficile*); ED (*extrèmement difficile*). Infrequently, ABO (*abominable*) is used; it refers more to the unpleasant conditions, such as black ice in mixed terrain, or wet rock in friction climbing. Sup (*supérieur*) or inf (*inférieur*) are sometimes appended. In Italy, the numbers 1–6 are used. (See the excellent and exhaustive overview in Cox and Fulsaas.)

Ratti, Abate Achille (Pope Pius XI)   (1857–1939) Born: Italy. Like John Paul II, this pope was a mountain enthusiast. Bibliography: *Climbs on Alpine Peaks* (1923).

Raven   (The northern raven is called *gorak* in the Himalayas.) Similar to a **crow** but larger, its croaking sound differs from the latter's caw. It resides at higher elevations and has the reputation of being the smartest **bird**. Mountaineers on Denali, for example, recount tales of how ravens locate caches marked with wands, dig through the snow, break open containers, and steal the food. Johnsgard points out that ravens nest on cliffs, but when these are unavailable they build their nests in trees.

Ravenous   A 1999 British–American black comedy directed by Antonia Bird, full of blood and violence; it deals with human flesh addicts fighting at an army outpost in the northern Sierras in 1847. The tagline ("You are who you eat") tells much about prospect and style. Robert Carlyle and Guy Pearce seem to enjoy it very much. It was shot in the Slovakian part of the **Tatras** Mountains. (M-A. H.)

Ravine   A **gorge**, or a **gully**, as in Tuckerman's ravine on **Mt. Washington** in New Hampshire.

Razor's Edge, The   A novel published in 1944 by English author William Somerset Maugham (1874–1965). It depicts Larry Darrell, a member of the "lost generation" after World War I, searching for life's meaning in books and journeys. He eventually finds an answer during a retreat in Tibet but fails to convey his knowledge to his friends upon his return. The sojourn in the Himalayas is central to the plot. The title comes from his guru's main message: "The pathway to salvation is as narrow and as difficult to walk as a razor's edge." Twice turned into movies, first in 1946, starring Tyrone Power, Gene Tierney, and Anne Baxter (an all-studio film) and again in 1984, starring Bill Murray, Catharine Hicks, and

Theresa Russell (shot on location). The 1946 version was nominated for best picture and won Baxter an Academy Award. (M-A. H.)

Rébuffat, Gaston   (1921–1985) Born: Marseilles, France. Arguably one of the greatest French guides and mountaineers, he made numerous first ascents in the **Mont Blanc massif** and was a member of the successful French expedition to **Annapurna**, the first 8,000-meter summit ever climbed, in 1950. His *Starlight and Storm* is a classic; he was also an excellent mountain photographer. Bibliography: *Mont Blanc to Everest* (1956), *Starlight and Storm* (1956), *On Snow and Rock* (1963), *Between Heaven and Earth* (1965), *Men and the Matterhorn* (1967), *The Mont Blanc Massif: The 100 Finest Routes* (1975).

Recreational Equipment, Inc. (REI)   See **equipment retailers**.

Recrystallization   Change in the structure of **minerals**, whereby a melted solid refreezes into a crystal structure.

Redpoint   A **free** rock climb in which the **route** is studied beforehand and then is done while placing **protection** without falling. (See also **pinkpoint** and **onsight**.)

Redstart   A small **bird** of many species that enjoys higher elevations; the whitethroated reaches almost 15,000 ft and the güldenstädt's and black more than 17,000 ft, all in the **Himalayas** (Ali).

Redwood   A North American **conifer**, the redwood is taller than any other **tree** (to almost 300 feet).

Refuge   *Refuge* (F), *Hütte* (G), *rifugio* (I). A building (hut, cabin) placed high up on a mountain. Climbers sleep here, rise very early, attempt the summit, return to the refuge, and descend to the valley. These buildings vary in size and amenities. In the French **Alps**, they may sleep 200, contain stoves, and serve gourmet meals ferried in by helicopter. On **Orizaba** (18,700 ft), Mexico's highest peak, the drafty, noisy structure (at 14,200 ft, it is higher than most European summits), sleeps some 30 people in a single, tiered room that lacks toilet facilities. There are a few of these buildings in the United States, but here most climbers carry a tent for ascents longer than a single day. Recently, new series of huts

The Bergli Hut (9,745 feet). (G. P. Abraham/National Geographic)

(and sometimes yurts) have been set up in the western United States to accommodate hikers and now mountain bikers who travel from one to another on an extended trip. For example, the 215 miles between Durango, Colorado, and Moab, Utah, are sprinkled with six well-equipped cabins, each of which sleeps eight adventurers (www.sanjuanhuts.com). Other sometimes primitive hut systems can be found along the Long Trail in **Vermont** and the **Appalachian Trail** in **New Hampshire**. The 10th Mountain Division Hut Association maintains 29 American cabins. See www.huts.org.

Regal Mountain   4,220 m, 13,845 ft. A beautiful, heavily glaciated peak, located near **Mt. Blackburn**, in the **Wrangell–St. Elias National Park**, in **Alaska**. A broad **ice field** and the Root Glacier descend from the mountain to the west, and lead to the mighty Staircase Icefall.

Register   A small book (concealed in a protective box or tube situated on the summits of many mountains) in which climbers sign their names to indicate that they have been there.

Relief   The physical disparity between a higher and lower location. (See **topography**.)

Religion   Because of the awesome nature of high **peaks**, many religions ascribe sacred or supernatural qualities to mountains. Religious rituals are performed either directly on the mountain or in temples or **lamaseries** that have been laboriously constructed high up or on the summits

Weisshorn Hut (9,380 feet) (A. G. Wehrli/National Geographic)

*The Old "Cabane" on the East Face of the Matterhorn
(12,526 feet) (G. P. Abraham/National Geographic)*

(see, for example, **Machu Picchu**). Especially holy sites include **Mt. Ararat**, upon which Noah's ark came to rest; **Mt. Sinai**, where God gave Moses the Ten Commandments; **Machupuchare**, where climbing to the summit is forbidden; **Tibet**'s Mt. Kailas, venerated by both Hindus and Buddhists; **Ayers Rock**, Cave Rock (near Lake Tahoe), and **Devil's Tower**, which are climbed despite the objections of indigenous peoples; **Nanda Devi**; **Fuji-san**; and Pele, a volcano, whose goddess, Pele, could only be propitiated by human sacrifice. See Bernbaum's *Sacred Mountains of the World* for a stunning overview of the subject. (See also **abodes of the gods**, **superstition**, **mythology**, and **five sacred mountains**; www.holymtn.com/world.htm).

Reptile Because reptiles are cold-blooded, they are not as ubiquitous in mountain environments as are **mammals** and **birds**. Turtles may move upward, but alligators and crocodiles do not. All of these creatures prefer watery environments. Lizards and snakes can be found in the high country, if the sun warms the environment during the day so that the animal's body temperature can rise. It is improbable that any reptile could survive for long in snowy, glaciated, or extremely cold areas. Up to 10,000 ft and even higher, many snakes including the garter, milk, flat-headed, copperhead, timber rattler, and racer can be found in or near rocky areas, ledges, and outcrops (Collins). Almost 45 species are at home in the **Karakoram**. (Individual reptiles are not included in the alphabetical listing.)

Rescue To help or save someone who is lost or injured and can no longer function alone. See "Search and Rescue," a chapter by Cooper et al. in Auerbach. Mountain rescue groups, some of whose members may have medical training, often come to the aid of stranded hikers, climbers, skiers, snowboarders, and snowmobilers. Since the use of a helicopter or plane may be necessary, since this is expensive, and since the lost or injured may be required to pay, having rescue insurance is a good idea. The senior author of this volume once had to call in a helicopter unit in the French Alps. This rescue may have saved the lives of two or three climbers.

Resplendent quetzal This central American inhabitant is considered one of the most beautiful **birds** in the world (Burnie and Wilson).

Réunion, La Lowest point, Indian Ocean 0 m; highest point, Piton des Neiges 3,069 m, 10,069 ft. (See also color photos.)

Revolution Peak 6,974 m, 22,880 ft. This major peak is located within the **Pamirs** in **Tajikistan**. It was first ascended in 1954, by A. Ugarov.

Rey, Guido (1861–1935) Born: Italy. Bibliography: *The Matterhorn* (1907), *Peaks and Precipices* (1914).

Rhea A large ostrichlike **bird**. Surprisingly, it can be found as high as 14,800 ft in the Andes (Fjeldså and Krabbe).

Rhode Island Lowest point, Atlantic Ocean 0 m; highest point, Jerimoth Hill 247 m, 812 ft (46th highest of the 50 state highpoints). To reach this highpoint, one formerly had to cross private land, leading to some problems; the High-Pointer Club resolved that problem, and a new path, avoiding the private plot, now leads to this highpoint.

Rhododendron A **deciduous tree** that prefers high mountainous regions; it diminishes in size as the altitude increases. Its large **flowers** are fragrant and impressive.

Rib *Nervure* (F), *Rippe* (G). A ridge on a face that is short and steeply inclined (Collomb).

Richter scale A logarithmic system (from 1 to 10) for measuring the potency of an **earthquake**: 6.5 is powerful, but because a factor of ten exists between numbers, 7.5 is ten times as strong. It should be noted that what is measured on the Richter scale is the amplitude of the ground motion during an earthquake, not the energy liberated by the event; roughly, for every factor of 10 in the ground motion, the total energy radiated by the earthquake grows by a factor of 30.

Ridge *Arête* (F), *cresta* (I), *crib* (W), *Grat* or *Kamm* (G). A high, often narrow, sometimes rocky, snowy, or icy crest where the two ascending sides of a mountain meet; it may lead to the summit. An arête (considered an English word) is sharply crested and separates glacial valleys. A hogback is narrow, sharp, and steep. One well-known hogback can be found on **Mt. Hood**.

Ridgeway, Rick (1949–) A foremost American climber and mountaineer, he ascended **K2** without

oxygen in 1978. Bibliography: *The Boldest Dream* (1979), *The Last Step* (1980).

Rift An opening or **graben**. When **tectonic plate** movement occurs, **valleys** and **ridges** form on the ocean floor and on land; the **Great Rift Valley** in East **Africa** is an example.

Rimaye (F) See ***bergschrund***.

Rimpfischhorn 4,198 m, 13,772 ft. This is the 29th highest of the 60 major 4,000-meter peaks of the **Alps**. It was first ascended in 1859 by Leslie Stephen, R. Living, **Melchior Anderegg**, and **Johann Zumtaugwald**. The Rimpfischhorn is located in the **Valaisan Alps**, in the Allalin group.

Ring of Fire A series of **volcanoes** in the Pacific circling from **Alaska** and the Aleutians southwestward, past **Japan**, the area north of **New Zealand** (including **Hawaii**), and then back northward along the coast of **South** and **North America**. Most of the world's active volcanoes lie along this circle. (See also maps.)

River A large body of flowing fresh water (as opposed to a small brook or stream) that may carry mountain or glacial runoff to the oceans.

Road See **engineering** and **10 Mountain Roads** sidebar.

Robbins, Royal (1935–) Excellent **Yosemite National Park** climber with many **first ascents**. From 1962 to 1964, he was the leading light in California climbing and was viewed as America's great master rock climber. He did several of the earliest 5.11 routes (**See rating systems**,) in Boulder Canyon, and pioneered more big wall routes than anyone else (Pat Ament, personal comment). His books, for example, *Advanced Rockcraft*, have been extremely influential.

Ridge (Laura Lindblad)

Ring of Fire (Marie Madgwick)

Royal Robbins on Long's Peak, 1964 (Pat Ament)

powerful peak, and a very difficult multiday climb. Robson is unequalled in the Canadian Rockies; it was first ascended in 1913 by W. M. Foster, A. H. McCarthy, and Conrad Kain.

Roch, Andre (1906–2002) Born: Switzerland. A foremost climber and mountaineer in his time, he was a member of the 1952 Swiss **Everest** expedition. Bibliography: *On Rock and Ice* (1947), *Climbs of My Youth* (1949), *Everest 1952* (1953).

Roche moutonnée (F; prn: rosh mootnay). A (striated) rock **outcrop** that has been eroded by a passing **glacier**.

Rock *Felsen* or *Stein* (G), *roccia* (I), *roche* (F). An agglomeration of **minerals**. Mountains are composed of rock. (See also **igneous, metamorphic**, and **Sedimentary**.)

Rock climbing (Also called technical.) A type of climbing, in which a person ascends on extremely steep rock surfaces (from somewhat less to more than 90 degrees). (See Fyffe and Petere.)

Rock climbing, history of This sport began inadvertently. As hikers or climbers in the **Alps** trudged upward (see **mountaineering history**), they naturally encountered steeper slopes, cliffs, walls, and other impediments. If they wished to reach the highest point in their path, they were forced to attempt to surmount these barriers. The more difficult mountaineering climbs, the **Matterhorn**, for example, entailed

Roberts, David S. (1943–) Born: United States. Bibliography: *The Mountain of My Fear* (1968), *Deborah: A Wilderness Narrative* (1970), *Great Exploration Hoaxes* (1982), *Moments of Doubt* (1986), *True Summit* (2000), *Escape from Lucania* (2002).

Robertson, Rev. Archibald Aeneas (1870–1958) Born: Helensburgh, Scotland. The first to complete the Munros, in 1901. Bibliography: *The First Munroist* (1993) by Peter Drummond and Ian Mitchell.

Robin A songbird ubiquitous in all habitats.

Robinson, Brian (fl. early 21st century) The first and only person to walk the **Appalachian, Continental Divide**, and **Pacific Crest Trails** in one year.

Robson, Mt. 3,954 m, 12,972 ft. The highest **mountain** in the **Canadian Rockies**; it is a

10 Great Rock Climbing Sites

1. Buoux (France)
2. Devil's Tower (Wyoming)
3. Eldorado Canyon (Colorado)
4. Fontainebleau (France)
5. Grand Canyon du Verdon (France)
6. Joshua Tree (California)
7. Shawangunks (New York)
8. Smith Rock (Oregon)
9. The Calanques (France)
10. Yosemite (California)

20 Great Rock Climbers

1. Albert Mummery
2. Alex Lowe
3. Alexander Burgener
4. Beth Roden
5. Chris Sharma
6. David Graham
7. Dean Potter
8. Emilio Comici
9. Fritz Niessner
10. Gaston Rébuffat
11. Hans Dulfer
12. John Bachar
13. John Gill
14. Lisa Rands
15. Lynn Hill
16. Patrick Berhault
17. Patrick Edlinger
18. Peter Croft
19. Pierre Allain
20. Warren Harding

10 Best Female Climbers

1. Alison Hargreaves
2. Annie Peck
3. Arlene Blum
4. Beth Rodden
5. Catherine Destivelle
6. Colette Richard
7. Katie Brown
8. Lynn Hill
9. Robin Tunney
10. Wanda Rutkiewicz

this type of work. After a while, the steep faces were sought out for their own sake. British climbers took to rock early in the 19th century; Americans did so with a vengeance a century later and often favored the big wall climbs, of **El Capitan**, for example. The introduction of ever more sophisticated gear allowed climbers to succeed where their predecessors could only dream. But some people criticized the use of vast quantities of equipment, including pneumatic drills and permanently attached **bolts**, as an unethical **aid**. At any rate, two very different types of rock climbing have evolved: in **free** climbing, one uses gear to protect against a fall, but the climber does not rely on it for **ascent**; in **aid** climbing, one may pull on a **rope**, hang on a **cam**, or attach an **étrier** and climb up the rungs. (See Ament and Salkeld for detailed overviews.)

Rock gym   An indoor facility that provides an artificial **climbing wall**.

Rockfall   Variously sized rocks cascading downward off a cliff. (See also **stonefall**.)

Rockslide   Rocks tumbling down a slope.

Rocky Mountains   (Also Rockies) An impressive mountain **system** (the longest in the world) in the western part of **North America**. It commences in **Mexico**, bisects the **United States** running from **Arizona** through **Colorado**, where it is especially potent, and then turns northward into **Canada**. The American and **Canadian Rockies** are extremely picturesque. **Ranges** include the **Elk**, Jemez, **San Juan**, **Tetons,** Uintas, Wasatch, and Wind River, among many others. (See also **Mt. Elbert** and **Mt. Robson**.)

Rodden, Beth   (1980–) A former three-time national junior champion, Rodden is a superb rock climber; she is married to Tommy Caldwell.

Rodent   A type of **mammal** (whose teeth never stop growing) of many diverse species. Some of these (**hare, pika, shrew**) are listed in their appropriate alphabetical location.

Roerich, Nicholas   (1874–1947) Many artists paint mountains and some concentrate on mountainous environments, but few produce as many images of the world's mountains as Roerich did. This Russian painter traveled widely and lived in many diverse locations. For Roerich, the higher elevations represent a mystical and spiritual landscape. His imaginative, semi-realistic paintings are often stunningly beautiful. Many of his works are viewable at the Nicholas Roerich Museum in New York City.

Rognon (F; prn: ronyon) Rock embedded in rock of another type. A large chunk of rock extruding from a glacier's surface.

Romania Lowest point, Black Sea 0 m; highest point, Moldoveanu 2,544 m, 8,346 ft.

Romm, Michael D. Born: Russia. Bibliography: *The Ascent of Mount Stalin* (1936).

Roof See **overhang**.

Roof of the World The area of Asia's high **ranges**, including the high **plateau** of **Tibet**. This is the largest region in the world with an altitude exceeding roughly 4,500 m, 15,000 ft.

Rope (Infrequently, cord) *Corda* (I), *corde* (F), *Seil* (G). Strong, braided material (hemp in the distant past, nylon today) that is used in various continuous lengths up to 70 meters (230 feet) for **protection** and **aid** in climbing. There are two types: static rope does not stretch, whereas dynamic may stretch many feet when loaded by a falling body weighing 200 pounds. Static rope transfers its energy to the falling person, which can cause grievous harm, whereas this energy is dissipated as a dynamic rope stretches. Thus, in all applications where there is a danger of falling more than a few feet, dynamic rope must be employed. Rope length is usually measured in meters and width in millimeters: 9-, 10-, and 11-mm ropes are commonly used in all forms of climbing. In extended big wall climbs and especially in mountaineering, unless one is using a treated rope, it may get wet and ice up or freeze. These conditions make progress extremely difficult. The drag on an already heavy rope increases because of the added weight; additionally, it may no longer flow through **carabiners**, **slings**, or other devices. See Clem et al. on "Ropes and Knot Tying," a chapter in Auerbach. (See also color photos.)

Rope, a *Cordée* (F). In climbing, this synecdochic expression indicates that two or more persons are physically connected for the purpose of ascending. One might say, "Phil and I were a rope."

Rope up Preparing to climb. (See also **tie in**.)

Rose Some **Himalayan** roses manage to survive at 17,500 ft (Polunin and Stainton).

Roskelley, John (1948–) An outstanding rock climber and mountaineer, he has participated in

10 Best Two-Man Teams

1. Achille Compagnoni and Lino Lacedelli
2. Chris Bonington and Doug Scott
3. Dick Bass and Frank Wells
4. Edmund Hillary and Tenzing Norgay
5. Edward Whymper and Michel Croz
6. George Mallory and Sandy Irvine
7. Joseph Ravanel and Albert Mummery
8. Lionel Terray and Jean Couzy
9. Louis Lachenal and Maurice Herzog
10. Reinhold Messner and Peter Habeler

20 Himalayan expeditions and was the first American to reach the summit of **Makalu**. Bibliography: *Nanda Devi: The Tragic Expedition* (1987), *Stories off the Wall* (1993). (See also **Everest [father/son]**.)

Rotario of Asti A knight who climbed the approximately 3,500-m, 11,600-ft, Roche Melon in 1358, thus becoming one of the very first recorded climbers in history. His motive was religious: he placed a triptych at the top of the peak. (For more information, see *Killing Dragons*, the excellent book detailing the conquest of the Alps, by Fergus Fleming.)

Roth, Arthur (1925–) Born: United States. Bibliography: *Eiger: Wall of Death* (1982).

Rotondo, Monte 2,622 m, 8,602 ft. This is the second highest peak on the wonderfully picturesque island of **Corsica**.

Rouse, Alan (1951–1986) Born: Wallasey, Merseyside, England. During the 1970s and 1980s, he was a superb mountaineer who was especially strong in solo rock climbs. The team that made the first ascent of Mt. Kongur (7,719 m, 25,324 ft), in 1981, comprised **Chris Bonington**, **Joe Tasker**, **Peter Boardman**, and Rouse. He died tragically on **K2**. Bibliography: *Everest the Cruel Way* (1981) by Joe Tasker, *Kongur, China's Elusive Summit* (1982), by Chris Bonington, *A Mountaineer's Life* (1987), compiled by Geoff Birtles, *The Endless Knot* (1991), by **Kurt Diemberger**.

Route *Via* (I), *voie* (F), *Weg* (G). The precise way that one travels or climbs. An **ordinary route** or **normal route**, is the usual direction in which one moves and it is generally the easiest; a direct (*direttissima*, in Italian) is straight up and more difficult; and a classic is repeated because it is of historical interest or especially exciting. Proficient mountaineers and rock climbers attempt to locate and succeed on new and untried routes.

Route-finding Navigation on a short rock face or an extended mountaineering expedition that may cover 50 or more miles. Along with requisite equipment and climbing knowledge, it is the most important skill one must have in order to reach the goal and return safely. Although disasters occur for many reasons, losing one's way, especially in bad weather in the high mountains, is at the top of the list. The ability to use a map, compass, or **GPS** device and to recall landmarks are mandatory skills. Storms, whiteouts, fog, and even wind make route-finding more difficult.

Rowell, Galen (1940–2002) A climber and photographer who produced extraordinary images of the world's mountains. He died in a plane crash in 2002. He is one of the featured people in Boga's *Climbers*. (See his film, *Mountain Light*.). Bibliography: *The Vertical World of Yosemite* (1974), *In the Throne Room of the Mountain Gods* (1977), *High and Wild* (1979), *Many People Come, Looking, Looking* (1980), *Alaska* (1981), *Mountains of the Middle Kingdom* (1985), *Mountain Light* (1986). (www.mountainlight.com)

Royal Geographical Society Founded in 1830, this British organization is devoted to geographical exploration; like its U.S. cousin, the **National Geographic Society**, it publishes the results in scholarly and popular periodicals including *The Geographical Journal* and *Geographical* (www.rgs.org).

Ruapehu 2,797 m, 9,175 ft. A **volcano** on the North Island of New Zealand.

Runner See **sling**.

Runout The length of unprotected **rope** between climbers. When a runout is extensive, say 75 feet, the term indicates that true **protection** is prescribed, since a climber on a face or steep slope will fall 150 feet, 75 feet to the last piece of protection and 75 feet past it.

RURP (An acronym for Realized Ultimate Reality Piton) In climbing, a guitar-pick-sized **piton** used for **protection** when the **cracks** are very thin and shallow. Invented in the early 1960s by **Tom Frost** and **Yvon Chouinard**, it revolutionized **aid** climbing (Pat Ament, personal comment).

Rushmore, Mt. A mountain in western South Dakota upon which the faces of four American presidents have been carved.

Russia Lowest point, Caspian Sea −28 m, −92 ft; highest point, Gora Elbrus 5,633 m, 18,481 ft. Russia is the largest country in the world (17,075,400 sq km, 6,592,846 sq miles). It contains many systems, ranges, and peaks including the highest point in Europe (**Elbrus**), the **Caucasus**, and the **Urals**.

Rutkiewicz, Wanda (1943–1992) A powerful Polish climber who performed numerous first ascents in the **Himalayas** and **Karakoram**, including **Gasherbrum III**. Bibliography: Gertrude Reinisch. *Wanda Rutkiewicz: A Caravan of Dreams* (2000).

Ruttledge, Sir Hugh L. (1884–1961) Born: England. He led two British Everest expeditions, one in 1933 and another in 1936. Bibliography: *Everest 1933* (1934), *Everest: The Unfinished Adventure* (1937).

Ruwenzori ("Mountains of the Moon") A group of six glaciated peaks all higher than 4,500 m, 15,000, ft in **Uganda** and **Congo**, including **Mt. Stanley** 5,109 m, 16,763 ft.

Rwanda Lowest point, Rusizi River 950 m, 3,117 ft; highest point, Volcan **Karisimbi** 4,507 m, 14,787 ft.

S

Sacred mountains See **religion**.

Sacrifice See **religion**.

Saddle See **pass**.

Safety Those who enjoy the mountains like to climb quickly or **free** or unaided, but the only thing that really matters is to climb safely. There are eight points to keep in mind: think; cultivate humility; be prepared; be cautious; use appropriate devices correctly; protect yourself and your equipment; respect the weather; and expect the unexpected. Climb smart! Many people purposely ignore this sagacious advice and sacrifice safety. The superb climber **Yvon Chouinard,** for example, suggests 27 ways to increase one's speed. And **Lionel Terray** observes, "He who respects all the wise rules found in the climbing manuals virtually condemns himself to inaction." There is nothing inherently wrong with moving more quickly, but pushing oneself, abjuring **crampons** for a short stretch, or depending on balance rather than an **ice ax** on self-belay all may lead to disaster. Safe and careful actions also pertain to hiking, skiing, trekking, logging, mining, and other activities. (See also **accidents**.)

Sagarmatha The **Nepali** name of **Mt. Everest**, derived from **Sanskrit**, it means "Mother of the Universe," an apt name for such a mighty mountain.

Sagarmatha National Park Located in **Nepal**, this is a 1,243 sq km, 480 sq mile, conservation area, designated as a World Heritage site by UNESCO. **Everest** lies within its boundaries.

Sailer, Anton (Toni) (1935–) Austrian skier; he won three gold medals in the 1956 Winter Olympics.

Don't Leave Home without It: 10 Crucial Mountaineering Requirements

1. Clothing: hat, coat, gloves, rain gear
2. Footwear: hiking boots, chaussons d'escalade, mountaineering boots, gaiters
3. Sun management: sunblock, sunglasses
4. Food and plenty of water
5. Technical gear: harness, rope, ice ax, crampons, carabiners, skis
6. Orientation: compass, maps, altimeter, GPS, topos
7. Goodies: toilet paper, camera, bug protection
8. Camping gear: backpack, tent, sleeping bag
9. First aid
10. Stamina, skills, training, conditioning, and knowing when to turn back!

Saint Elias Mountains A major range, located between the Canadian territory of the **Yukon** and **Alaska**. Many important peaks are found there, including **Logan**, **St. Elias**, **Lucania**, **King**, **Steele**, **Vancouver**, **Churchill**, **Fairweather**, **Hubbard**, **Bear**, and **Alverstone**.

Saint Elmo's Fire The glow or corona sometimes present when atmospheric electricity permeates the environment; for example, before or during a thunderstorm. It presents a fractal appearance, with a treelike structure. Most of the time, it just indicates that static electricity is plentiful in the area; however, the buzzing sound accompanying these miniature "leaders" can also be associated with an imminent lightning strike; therefore it is strongly recommended that the climber retreat to lower ground in the presence of such atmospheric phenomena. St. Elmo's fire can appear on virtually any metallic object carried by an Alpinist; this includes an ice ax protruding from a backpack, crampons, ice screws, and other climbing paraphernalia. St. Elmo's fire is also encountered in aircraft and spacecraft, where charge accumulation due to the solar wind, also responsible for the **aurora borealis**, is a serious problem. The name is a corruption of Saint Erasmus. One of the authors once witnessed a particularly spectacular St. Elmo's fire display at the refuge of the **Aiguille du Goûter**, on **Mont Blanc's** normal route: an intense thunderstorm was raging over the Glacier de Bionassay, lightning zigzagging across the dark clouds below the refuge, illuminating them from within with an ominous brownish glow. Outside the refuge, the aluminum safety railing was aglow with St. Elmo's fire: thousands of electrical discharges, dancing along the metal tubes, buzzing in the dark, ozone filling the atmosphere with its peculiar, aseptic smell.

Saint Helena   Lowest point, Atlantic Ocean 0 m; highest point, Queen Mary's Peak on **Tristan da Cunha** 2,060 m, 6,759 ft. Most famous for being the place of the final exile and death of Napoleon, Saint Helena also includes the small island of Tristan da Cunha, one of the most remote places on earth, where whalers used to conduct long campaigns in the South Atlantic and Southern Oceans.

Saint Kitts and Nevis   Lowest point, Caribbean Sea 0 m; highest point, Mt. Liamuiga 1,156 m, 3,793 ft.

Saint Lucia   Lowest point, Caribbean Sea 0 m; highest point, Mt. Gimie 950 m, 3,117 ft.

Saint Pierre and Miquelon   Lowest point, Atlantic Ocean 0 m; highest point, Morne de la Grande Montagne 240 m, 787 ft. Located within a few miles of the Canadian island of Newfoundland, these small French islands are home to a small community of fishermen who brave the dangerous waters of the North Atlantic, along with their Canadian and American counterparts, to fish in the rich waters of the Grand Banks.

Saint Vincent and the Grenadines   Lowest point, Caribbean Sea 0 m; highest point, Soufrière 1,234 m, 4,049 ft.

Sajama   6,520 m, 21,423 ft. This is the 13th highest peak in the **Andes**, and the 10th of 20 premier climbing peaks in that range; it was first climbed in 1939 by Piero Ghiglione and Joseph Prem. This is the highest peak in **Bolivia**.

Sakhalin Island   This island, located off the Pacific coast of **Russia**, is 948 km, 589 miles, long from north to south and approximately 160 km, 100 miles, wide, with a surface area of 76,400 sq km, 29,500 sq miles. Most of the island is mountainous; the highpoint is Mt. Lopatin, 1,609 m, 5,279 ft.

Salathé, John   (1899–1992) Excellent Swiss American climber and forger of hard steel **pitons**. He was a bold pioneer of **Yosemite** rock walls including **Half Dome**, South Face, and Lost Arrow Chimney.

Salathé Wall   One of the world's great rock faces, 3,000 feet of sheer granite on the southwest side of **El Capitan**. It was pioneered in 1961 by **Royal Robbins**, **Chuck Pratt**, and **Tom Frost** (Pat Ament, personal comment).

Salcantay   6,271 m, 20,574 ft. This is the 35th highest peak in the **Andes**, and the 19th of 20 premier climbing peaks in that range; it was first ascended in 1952 by C. Kogan, B. Pierre, F. Ayres, G. Bell, G. V. Matthews, and D. Michael. This beautiful, powerful peak is located within the Cordillera Vilcabamba of the Peruvian Andes.

Salt   A **mineral** that derives from brine and is sometimes mined in mountainous areas. Salt has many uses but is especially important as a supplementary food source for many animals including humans, and has sometimes been considered as valuable as precious metals.

Samivel   (1907–1992) (b. Paul Gayet-Tancred) A French illustrator, cartoonist, and writer. He chose his pen name from a character in Dickens's *Pick-*

wick Papers. Though an all-purpose illustrator, he specialized in mountains, climbers, and the cutest marmots, but also worked on Rabelais's *Gargantua and Pantagruel* as well as *The Pied Piper of Hamelin*. He traveled to Greenland in 1948 with Paul-Emile Victor (the journey was filmed by **Marcel Ichac**), and wrote two mountain novels (**L'Amateur d'Abîmes** and *Le Fou d'Edenberg*) as well as various short stories. A lifelong mountain enthusiast, he was involved in environmental protection long before it was a popular cause. He was the first person to climb the Aiguille de la Lex Blanche (1931). (M-A. H.)

Samoa   Lowest point, Pacific Ocean 0 m; highest point, Mauga Silisili 1,857 m, 6,093 ft.

San Juan Range   One of **Colorado**'s main **ranges**; its major summits include: Uncompahgre Peak, 4,361 m, 14,309 ft, the sixth highest in Colorado; Handies Peak, 4,281 m, 14,048 ft; and Sunshine Peak, 4,267 m, 14,001 ft, barely making the list of the 54 14,000-foot peaks in Colorado. (For the complete list of Colorado's 14,000-foot peaks, see appendix D.)

San Marino   Lowest point, Torrente Ausa 55 m, 180 ft; highest point, Monte Titano 749 m, 2,457 ft.

San Miguel Range   One of **Colorado**'s main **ranges**; its major summits include: Mt. Wilson, 4,342 m, 14,246 ft; El Diente Peak, 4,315 m, 14,159 ft, one of the hardest of Colorado's 14,000-foot peaks; and Wilson Peak, 4,272 m, 14,017 ft. (For the complete list of Colorado's 14,000-foot peaks, see the appendix D.)

Sandstone   A soft **sedimentary** rock that comes in many colors.

Sanford, Mt.   4,949 m, 16,237 ft. This mighty extinct **volcano** is located near the north boundary of the **Wrangell–St. Elias National Park** in **Alaska**. It dominates the landscape when viewed from the Tok cutoff highway.

Sangre de Cristo Range   One of Colorado's main **ranges**; its major summits include: Blanca Peak, 4,372 m, 14,345 ft; Crestone Peak, 4,356 m, 14,294 ft, one of the hardest of **Colorado**'s 14,000-foot peaks; and Kit Carson Peak, 4,317 m, 14,165 ft. The range continues south into **New Mexico**; there, its highpoint is **Wheeler Peak**. (For the

complete list of Colorado's 14,000-foot peaks, see appendix D.)

Sanskrit   An important Indo-Aryan language.

Santorini   A **volcano** on Thira in Greece; its eruption in about 1470 B.C.E. destroyed the Minoans. This may have been the site of **Atlantis** (Ritchie).

Sao Tome and Principe   Lowest point, Atlantic Ocean 0 m; highest point, Pico de Sao Tome 2,024 m, 6,640 ft.

Saser (Sasir) Kangri   7,672 m, 25,170 ft. This major peak is located within the **Karakoram** Range in **India**. It was first ascended in 1973, by an Indo-Tibetan Border Police expedition.

Saskatchewan   Lowest point, Lake Athabasca 213 m, 699 ft; highest point Cypress Hill 1,392 m, 4,567 ft.

Sasquatch   See **yeti**.

Sastrugi   Undulating ridges of snow that are produced by the force of the wind.

Satellite   A lesser summit, directly in the vicinity of a major peak; generally, a satellite is located along one of the major **ridges** of a main summit: for example, **Mont Blanc de Courmayeur** is a satellite of **Mont Blanc**; the **Drus** are satellites of the **Aiguille Verte**; the mighty **Lhotse** itself is sometimes considered a satellite of **Everest**.

Saudi Arabia   Lowest point, Persian Gulf 0 m; highest point, Jabal Sawda' 3,133 m, 10,279 ft.

Saunders, Victor   (1951–) Born: Lossiemouth, Scotland. Bibliography: *Elusive Summits* (1990), *Vertical Pleasure* (1995), by Mick Fowler.

Saussure, Horace-Bénédict de   See **de Saussure**.

Sawatch Range   One of **Colorado**'s main **ranges**; its major summits include: **Mt. Elbert**, the highpoint of Colorado; **Mt. Massive**, the second highest peak in the state; Mt. Harvard, 4,395 m, 14,420 ft, the third highest peak in the state; and La Plata Peak, 4,369 m, 14,336 ft (number five). (For the complete list of Colorado's 14,000-foot peaks, see appendix D.)

Saxifrage   Some species of this **flower** thrive as high as 18,000 ft in the **Himalayas** (Polunin).

Scarp   A group of **cliffs** that exist because of faulting or **erosion**.

Schneider, Hannes (1890–1955) In skiing, founder of the **Arlberg** Technique. Schneider influenced many generations of skiers.

Schoening, Pete (1927–2004) An exceptional mountaineer with **first ascents** in the Mount Vinson Massif. He is most famous for "the belay": In 1953, on K2, he held six falling men on a hip ax belay and saved most of their lives.

Schreckhorn 4,078 m, 13,379 ft. This is the 42nd highest of the 60 major 4,000-meter peaks of the **Alps**. It was first climbed in 1861 by Leslie Stephen, Christian and Peter Michel, and Ulrich Kaufmann. This peak is located in the **Bernese Alps**.

Schuss In skiing, to go straight down the slope without braking.

Schwarzhorn 4,322 m, 14,180 ft. This is the 17th highest of the 60 major 4,000-meter peaks of the **Alps**. A major satellite of **Monte Rosa**, in the **Valaisan Alps**, the Schwarzhorn was conquered in 1873, by Marco Maglionini, Albert de Rothschild, Peter and Nikolaus Knubel, Edouard Cupelin, and three porters.

Scotland See United Kingdom.

Scott, Douglas Keith (Doug) (1941–) An important British mountaineer; his **first ascents** include new routes on **Nuptse** and **Shisha Pangma**. He broke his legs on the **descent** of the **Ogre**, but continued down with help; on the **glacier** he crawled to safety. Ardito calls this "one of the most amazing feats in **climbing** history." (See **Joe Simpson**.) He was the first English climber to summit **Everest**. Bibliography: *Big Wall Climbing* (1974), *The Shishapangma Expedition* (1984) with Alex Macintyre, *Himalayan Climber* (1992).

Scramble An easy climb, using the hands, on a slope over **boulders** or **scree**. Whymper was probably not understating his accomplishments in *Scrambles amongst the Alps*, since in the late 19th century the term probably connoted more serious climbing.

Scree *Éboulis* (F), *Geröll* (G). Small pieces of rock that are found on slopes. (See also **talus** and **till**.)

Sea cliff A rock formation that falls off steeply into the ocean or rises out of it. Sea cliffs can be found in many parts of the world including Hawaii and New Zealand, where the highest of these impressive structures are located.

Secor, R. J. A mountaineer who has climbed extensively in North America. He also authored a number of excellent **guidebooks**, some published by the Mountaineers. Bibliography: *Mexico's Volcanoes: A Climbing Guide; The High Sierra*.

Sedimentary This delineates rock that derives from the agglomeration of sediment; examples are **shale** and **sandstone**. (See also **igneous** and **metamorphic**.)

Seigneur, Yannick (1942–) An important French climber, guide, and mountaineer; his first ascents include the integral of Peuterey; the direct ascent of the north side of the Petit **Dru**; the north side of the Innominata; the west **pillar** of **Makalu**, the north face of **Huascarán**, and **Gasherbrum II** without supplemental oxygen.

Seismic The term that indicates earthquakes and the waves that they propagate; they are recorded by a seismograph.

Self-arrest In mountaineering, the act of halting a fall when sliding or tumbling down a slope. This is accomplished by first flipping onto one's stomach with the head uphill, and then pushing the **ice ax** into the snow or scraping it along the ice so that one slows down in a controlled fash-

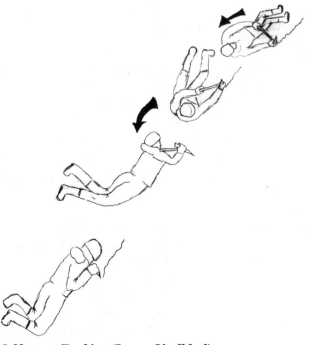

Self-arrest/Braking (Laura Lindblad)

ion. If the slope is extremely steep or the ice very hard, the procedure may not work.

Sella, Vittorio (1859–1943) A mountaineer who participated in many influential expeditions and an especially important early mountain photographer. Some of his exquisite images are collected in *Summit*. Bibliography: *Among the Alps* (1900) by Samuel Aitken, *The Splendid Hills* (1948) by **R. W. Clark**, *Karakoram and Western Himalaya 1909* (1912) by **F. de Filippi**.

Senecio Various species of this **flower** can be found at altitude in Africa (on **Mt. Kenya**), and in the Andes to 12,000 plus ft.

Senegal Lowest point, Atlantic Ocean 0 m; highest point, unnamed feature near Nepen Diakha 581 m, 1,906 ft.

Sequoia This is a North American **conifer** and the largest **tree** in the world. (See also color photos.)

Sérac A large block or **tower** of ice that sits or hangs in or at the edge of a **glacier** and that may fall off.

Serbia and Montenegro Lowest point, Adriatic Sea 0 m; highest point, Daravica 2,656 m, 8,714 ft.

Serrated Within the context of mountain climbing, this refers to a knife-edge ridge, with **fluted** snow.

Seven Brides for Seven Brothers A 1954 American musical comedy directed by Stanley Donen, written by Albert Hackett and Frances Goodrich and based on *Sobbing Women* by Stephen Vincent Benét. The songs were written by Gene De Paul (music) and Johnny Mercer (lyrics) and arranged by Saul Chaplin and Adolph Deutsch, who won the Academy Award. In Oregon in 1850, the seven strong, healthy Pontipee brothers live at a remote farm in the mountains. The oldest brother goes to the city to find food and a woman (Jane Powell). Of course, the six others are interested, since their "Pa used to say love is kind of like the measles. You only get it once." There is lots of fake snow, nice painted mountains, and a model avalanche-doomed pass. (M-A. H.)

Seven Summits The highpoints on the seven continents; depending upon the choice between **Australia** and **Australasia** as a continent, they include: **Everest**, 8,850 m, 29,035 ft, in **Asia**; **Aconcagua**, 6,959 m, 22,831 ft, in **South America**; **Denaki**, 6,194 m, 20,320 ft, in **North America**; **Kilimanjaro**, 5,895 m, 19,340 ft, in **Africa**; **Elbrus**, 5,642 m, 18,510 ft, in **Europe**; **Carstensz Pyramid**, 5,039 m, 16,532 ft, in Australasia; **Vinson**, 4,897 m, 16,066 ft, in **Antarctica**; and **Kosciusko**, 2,229 m, 7,313 ft, in Australia. Many climbers aspire to climb each one; the first to accomplish this feat was the American **Dick Bass**, who completed his quest by summitting Everest on April 30, 1985. Pat Morrow was the first to do them including Carstensz Pyramid. As of January 2004,

Seven Summits

Africa	Kilimanjaro	5,895 m	19,340 ft	(1889)
Antarctica	Vinson	4,897 m	16,066 ft	(1966)
Asia	Everest	8,850 m	29,035 ft	(1953)
Australasia	Carstensz Pyramid	5,039 m	16,532 ft	(1962)
Australia	Kosciuszko*	2,229 m	7,313 ft	(n.a.)
Europe	Elbrus	5,642 m	18,510 ft	(1874)
North America	Denali	6,194 m	20,320 ft	(1913)
South America	Aconcagua	6,959 m	22,831 ft	(1897)

* Now discredited

The Most Difficult Seven Summits

Africa: Mt. Kenya
Antarctica: Rohekniven
Asia: K2, Lhotse Middle
Australasia: Mt. Cook, Carstensz Pyramid
Europe: Shkara (Caucasus), super-couloirs on
    the Pilier du Fréney (Mont Blanc)
North America: Kitchatna Spire
South America: Torre Eger

160 people had accomplished this feat. (See also http://7summits.com/ and the **Seven Summits** sidebar.)

Seven Years in Tibet A 1997 American movie starring a German-accented Brad Pitt, based on the excellent book by **Heinrich Harrer**.

Seychelles Lowest point, Indian Ocean 0 m; highest point, Morne Seychellois 905 m, 2,969 ft.

Shackleton, Ernest H. (1874–1922) The captain of the *Endurance*, which was caught in the ice and foundered in the Antarctic. The crew had to survive the bitter weather on Elephant Island. Shackleton and a few men set out on one of the greatest adventure-rescues in history, sailing 900 miles in an open boat and then crossing some difficult mountains in order to reach a whaling station. Many months later, they returned, and every crew member was rescued!

Shale A **sedimentary** rock composed of clay, mud, or silt.

Sharma, Chris (1981–) The first person to do a 5.15 climb ("Realization," in 2001.) (See also **rating systems**.)

Shasta, Mt. 4,316 m, 14,162 ft. An enormous **volcano** located in the **Cascades** of northern **California**; it is the second highest peak in the Cascades Range, and the only 14,000-foot peak in California outside the **Sierras**. Shasta is heavily glaciated by California standards, and counts nine separate **glaciers**, including the Whitney Glacier, the longest in California.

Shawangunks (Gunks) **Quartz cliffs** near New Paltz, **New York**, where some of the best rock climbing in the United States can be found.

Sherpa The family name and now an ethnic group of some 25,000 people who live in **Nepal**. They are well acclimated to high **altitudes** and are often hired by **expeditions** to help carry loads to higher camps and to climb along with expedition members. They are distinguished from **porters**, who carry material only up to **base camp**. Sherry Ortner's *Life and Death on Mt. Everest* offers an excellent sociological overview of Sherpa life. (See also **Tenzing Norgay, Ang Rita Sherpa**, and **Appa Sherpa**)

Sherpa, Ang Rita (1948–) Called Snow Leopard; he has summitted **Everest** 10 times without supplemental oxygen.

Sherpa, Appa (fl. 1960) He has summitted **Everest** 12 times without supplemental oxygen.

Shiprock At almost 450 m, 1,400 ft, in height, this monolithic structure lies in **New Mexico**. In 1939, bolts for climbing were used there for the first time in America. Ritchie calls this volcanic neck one of the "most spectacular and famous landforms" in the United States.

Shipton, Eric Earle (1907–1977) Born: England. Probably the greatest mountain explorer of all time, he participated in many expeditions, and authored numerous books, including *Nanda Devi* and *Men against Everest*. Bibliography: *Blank on the Map* (1938), *Upon That Mountain* (1943), *Mountains of Tartary* (1951), *The True Book About Everest* (1955), *The Mount Everest Reconnaissance Expedition, 1951* (1962), *Land of Tempest: Travels in Patagonia, 1958–62* (1963), *Mountain Conquest* (1967) with Bradford Washburn, *That Untravelled World* (1969), *Tierra del Fuego—The Fatal Lodestone* (1973), *The Six Mountain-Travel Books* (1985).

Shisha Pangma (Also Xixabangma, Goisainthan) 8,046 m, 26,398 ft. A spectacular mountain in Tibet, this 8,000-meter summit is the 13th highest peak in the world, and was first climbed in 1964, on May 2nd by a Tibetan–Chinese team comprising Chen San, Cheng Tianliang, Doje, Mima Zaxi, Sodnam Doje, Wang Fuzhou, Wu Zongyue, Xu Jing, Yungdenm and Zhang Junyan.

It was the last 8,000-meter peak to be climbed, and it is the only one entirely located within the autonomous province of **Tibet**, currently part of **China**. As of the end of 1999, 167 climbers had reached its summit, with only 19 fatalities overall, making it one of the safest 8,000-meter peaks. (See also the **14 8,000-Meter Peaks** sidebar.)

Shoes Ancient, occasional mountain travelers were probably unshod; indeed in many parts of the world people may still travel in snow without any foot coverings. Depending on necessity and temperature, one may wear light shoes or sneakers, or specialized boots for (different types of) skiing, climbing, mountaineering, farming, mining, or vulcanological observation. Some are made of canvas, others of leather or plastic. Outer coverings for booted mountaineers, who may face 50-degree-below-zero environments for long periods of time, resemble fluffy sleeping bags. (See also **climbing shoes** and color photos.)

Shrew Small, omnivorous, yet insatiable ground **mammal**, similar to a mouse; the masked can be found in alpine meadows.

Sia Kangri 7,422 m, 24,350 ft. This major peak is located within the **Himalayas** in Kashmir. It was first ascended in 1934, by Gunther Dyhrenfurth and party.

Sidestep In skiing, moving sideways, usually uphill.

Siege style Attempting to reach the summit of a mountain by laying siege to it with hundreds of **porters**, **Sherpas**, and many tons of equipment. A series of **camps** are set up and only a few of the **expedition**'s participants reach the top. (See also **Alpine style**.)

Sierra Club See **clubs**.

Sierra Leone Lowest point, Atlantic Ocean 0 m; highest point, Loma Mansa (Bintimani) 1,948 m, 6,391 ft.

Sierra Madre (Spanish for Mother Range) Three **ranges** in Mexico.

Sierra Nevada (Sierras) A ca. 350-mile **range** of mountains in central **California**; it is here that one will find **Mt. Whitney**, the highest peak in the continental United States. (See also color photos.)

Sierras (Also Sierra; Spanish for saw) A **range** of mountains in **California** (see **Sierra Nevada**); also, a **range** in **Spain**.

Signalkuppe 4,556 m, 14,948 ft. This is the fifth highest peak in the **Alps** and one of five main summits of **Monte Rosa**. It was first climbed in 1842 by Giovanni Gnifetti, Giuseppe Farinetti, Christoph Ferraris, Christopher Grober, Johann and Jakob Giordani, and two porters. (See also color photos.)

Sikkim A small (7,096 sq km, 2,740 sq miles), very mountainous state of **India**; on its border with **Nepal** lies **Kangchenjunga**, the world's third-highest peak and the highpoint of India.

Silk Road The 4,000-mile route followed by traders bringing silk and spices to Europe and other products back to China. Marco Polo followed it to the east. It used the **Khyber Pass** to cross the mountains of **Pakistan**.

Sill This is **igneous** rock that is found between layers of other material.

Sill, Mt. 4,316 m, 14,162 ft. Located in the **Palisades** region of the **Sierra Nevada** in **California**, it was first ascended in 1903 by Joseph LeConte, James Moffitt, James Hutchinson, and Robert Pike. The north face is an extremely impressive wall; the summit view is considered by some to be the best in the Sierras.

Simplon Tunnel A long tunnel that connects Italy and **Switzerland**.

Simpson, Joe (fl. mid-1980s to present) A British mountaineer who broke his leg while climbing in Peru. His partner lowered him for hundreds of feet during a storm but eventually was forced to cut the rope because he was being pulled off the face. Simpson fell into a deep **crevasse**, and his partner gave him up for dead. His epic escape from the crevasse and long crawl back to camp is told in his *Touching the Void*, one of the most moving mountaineering accounts ever written (see the **10 Great Mountain Adventure Books** sidebar) and was recently reenacted in an excellent movie of the same name. Bibliography: *Touching the Void* (1988), *The Water People* (1992), a novel, *This Game of Ghosts* (1993), *Storms of Silence* (1996), *Dark Shadows Falling* (1997), *The Beckoning Silence* (2002).

Sinai, Mt.   A mountain located in the southern Egyptian desert. It is here, according to the account in Exodus, that god gave Moses the tablets containing the Ten Commandments. (There is some controversy concerning the precise location of this mountain.) Located here is the Monastery of St. Catherine, where monks are digitizing 3,300 ancient manuscripts.

Singapore   Lowest point, Singapore Strait 0 m; highest point, Bukit Timah 166 m, 545 ft.

Singhi Kangri   7,207 m, 23,645 ft. This major peak is located in the **Karakoram**; it was first climbed in 1976 by a Japanese expedition that used the north face and north ridge, from the Staghar Glacier.

Sinkhole   A hollow that exists because the roof of a cavern collapses (Hamblin and Christiansen).

Sirdar   In the **Himalayas**, the local person in charge of those hired to help an expedition carry materials to **base camp** and beyond. He may be a **Sherpa**. Women sometimes are hired as porters, but probably never serve as sirdar.

Sitzmark   A hole left on the slope by a skier who has fallen.

Skeleton   A type of sled used for racing on **snow**.

Ski area   The first commercial ski areas (or resorts) in Austria and the United States were small affairs with rope tows onto which one held in order to be pulled to the top of the hill or small mountain. Early larger areas include Bromley in Vermont, Timberline (on **Mt. Hood**) in Oregon (1938), and Sun Valley in Idaho (1936). Now there are hundreds of small, medium, and gargantuan complexes catering to the needs of millions of skiers all over the world. (There are some 80 major ski areas in the United States.) Davos and **St. Moritz** in Switzerland, St. Anton in Austria, and **Aspen** and **Vail** in the United States exemplify the massive complexes, some of which have more than a hundred diverse runs and trails served by as many as 32 **chairlifts** and cable cars or **gondolas**. As skiing has matured and become more accessible to the middle class, despite its high costs, more adventurous skiers have moved away from confining commercial areas to seek out distant high peaks and **glaciers** to

which they are sometimes ferried by snowcat or helicopter. This type of extreme skiing (or snowboarding) can be quite dangerous, since there are unknown obstacles and steep declivities. If someone is injured or caught in an **avalanche**, there may be no one around to help. (See Mergen's *Snow in America*, which has an excellent chapter on the historical aspects of ski area development.)

Ski jumping   Downhill skiers often jump off little mounds of snow, which might carry them 10 or 20 feet through the air. The sport of ski jumping requires a constructed tower and an artificial slope that ends high in the air. The skier shoots down and then out into space covering hundreds of feet before touching down. It is an **Olympic** sport. (See also **skiing**.)

Ski lift   Many types of lifts have been used to ferry skiers to the tops of hills and mountains. A rope tow is a loop of thick rope that is continuously pulled around a wheel; it is powered by a gasoline engine or electric motor. The skier grabs on and is pulled upwards. This is an unpleasant business. A J-bar is a spring-loaded steel rod in the shape of a J that one leans against; a T-bar pulls two people along; a poma lift is similar except that a disk fits between one's legs. There are also variations such as an enormous bar onto which seven people can hold as it hauls them quickly upward. Falling off any of these can be rather traumatic, since one can get hurt or be forced to walk through the woods to get back to a skiable slope or trail. Most of these are now generally avoided, since **chairlifts** and **gondolas** are so much more convenient and comfortable.

Ski plane   A widely used means of transportation in places lacking infrastructure, and rich in snow fields and other glaciated bodies and **ice fields**; for example, Canada and Alaska. Indeed, ski planes and **helicopters** are often used to ferry skiers up to where the deep powder snow is, for example in the **Bugaboos** of **British Columbia**. For an interesting story regarding a stranded ski plane, deep in the **Saint Elias Mountains**, see *Escape from Lucania*, by **David Roberts**.

Skiing   *Schifahren* (G). People have undoubtedly slipped, slid, and **glissaded** on their feet or on strapped-on boards for millennia, moving across fairly level ground; this is called cross-country (or Nordic) skiing. Commercial **downhill** (or Alpine) skiing is a comparatively recent development (from the early 1930s onward), dependent as it is on some form of continuous power and constructed devices that are capable of hauling skiers up the mountain. Additionally, even 100 years ago, the general population had neither the time nor the financial resources to indulge in such a "frivolous" endeavor. The emergence and development of a middle class, first in the United States and then in Europe and other parts of the world has allowed an increasing number of individuals and families to pursue this fairly expensive hobby. Many geographical areas are now economically dependent on the skiing industry. Indeed, Vermont derives much of its income from tourism and skiing. Downhill (first practiced in Colorado as early as 1882) and cross-country (see Cook) are the most popular forms, but there are others. In skijoring, a person is pulled along on ice by a horse, dog, or a snowmobile; telemark allows one to ski downhill under control on cross-country skis; and randonnée offers the possibility of cross-country, and then with a small adjustment to the binding, one can lock down the heel and shift to normal downhill. Recently, a number of sometimes eccentric variations have become popular; these include monoskiing, ski boarding, ski or snow biking (also called ski bobbing), ski skating, and snow blading. (See the film, *Legends of American Skiing* as well as **ski area**, **ski jumping**, **slalom**, **skiing equipment,** and **snowboarding**.)

Skiing equipment The basic equipment required for any form of skiing consists of four items: skis with appropriate bindings to hold the booted foot in place; poles (except in jumping), which help in balancing; boots to attach the feet to the skis, so that bodily movement can be transferred for turning and climbing, to protect the ankles, and to maintain body heat; and protective clothing including warm pants, jackets, gloves, and hat as well as goggles. Some people may choose to wear **helmets**. From 1900 to the mid-1950s equipment was simple and consistent: wooden skis (sometimes with metal edges), cable

bindings, and leather boots. Midcentury changes included metal skis (from Head) and step-in bindings (from Cubco). Soon thereafter, plastic and fiberglass skis (Whitestar) appeared. Eventually plastic boots replaced the earlier leather models, and by the 1990s, these high boots used in conjunction with shaped skis (wide at the head and tail and narrow in the middle) allowed novices to learn to ski well quickly and efficiently.

Skull Island The home of Kong, a mammoth gorilla worshipped by the natives. At least, that is what the 1933 movie *King Kong* by Merian C. Cooper and Ernest B. Schoedsack depicts. Such a character needs a suitable surrounding. On his island, Kong lives on a huge mountain, separated from the natives by a towering log fence. There are also giant spiders (this scene is often deleted), pterodactyls, and other strange animals. (M-A. H.)

Skyang Kangri 7,544 m, 24,750 ft. This major peak is located within the **Himalayas** in Kashmir.

Skyhook In **aid climbing,** a device hung on a small extrusion or indentation in the rock to support the climber.

Skylight When the roof of a **lava tube** falls inward, it leaves an opening that is called a skylight.

Slab *Plaque* (F), *placca* (I), *Platte* (G). Large, smooth rock surface that can approach vertical.

Slab avalanche A slab avalanche occurs when large amounts of snow have accumulated and consolidated, and the wind or refreezing of the surface has created a thin, hard slab, which suddenly gives way, releasing all the snow into a powerful, destructive slide. Slab avalanches are particularly deadly and treacherous because the climber or skier can penetrate deep into the danger zone unaware, as the hard slab does not show signs of instability, that a very large slide is about to occur.

Slack The lack of tension on the climbing **rope**. Slack may be required (and called for) when moving on a face or slope.

Slaggard, Mt. 4,742 m, 15,559 ft. The 10th highest peak in Canada, it is located in the **Saint Elias Mountains**, in the **Yukon**. It is a mighty and remote mountain and is one of the crown jewels in the **Kluane-Logan National Park**.

Slalom   In skiing, a type of race in which the participant must ski between **gates** (poles) set up along the course. It requires the ability to make swift and precise turns, and is the antithesis of **downhill skiing**, which allows the racer to fly nearly straight down the **fall line**.

Slate   A **metamorphic** rock that easily splits into layers.

Sleet   Frozen rain. See also **weather**.

Slesser, C. G. Malcolm   (1926–) Born: Scotland. Bibliography: *Red Peak* (1962), *The Andes Are Prickly* (1966).

Sling   (Also runner) In rock climbing, a sewn loop of webbing or tied rope; a sling can be placed around or hung on rocks or hooked to **carabiners** for **protection** or **aid**. It is also used to carry **gear**. (See also **bandolier**.)

Slingsby, William Cecil   (1849–1929) Born: England. One of the best climbers and mountain explorers of the late 19th and early 20th centuries, he is considered the father of British and Norwegian mountaineering. His first ascents include Barnes Peak. He explored the mountains of **Norway** extensively. Bibliography: *Norway: The Northern Playground* (1904).

Slope   The inclined portion of a mountain. When a slope becomes very steep it is called a face or **wall**. (In the plural it may mean **foothills**.)

Slovakia   Lowest point, Bodrok River 94 m, 308 ft; highest point, Gerlachovka 2,655 m, 8,711 ft.

Slovenia   Lowest point, Adriatic Sea 0 m; highest point, **Triglav** 2,864 m, 9,396 ft. The Julian **Alps** reach their highest elevations in this small, new European country.

Smear   In rock climbing, to place pressure on the full sole of the shoe so that it sticks to the rock surface through **friction**.

Smith, Albert Richard   (1816–1860) Born: England. A writer and entrepreneur who was passionate about the **Alps**, especially **Mont Blanc**. He eventually ascended the peak in 1851, although he was not in good physical shape. He made good business presenting illustrated lectures about his mountaineering experiences to the

public in England. Bibliography: *Mont Blanc* (1852), *A Boy's Ascent of Mont Blanc* (1859), *The Story of Mont Blanc* (1860), in *Boy's Own Magazine*, *Mont Blanc* (1860), with a memoir of the author by Edmund Yates, *The Story of Mont Blanc, and a Diary to China and Back* (1860).

Smith, Walter Parry Haskett   (1859–1946) Born: Trowswell, Kent, England. He was a pioneering rock climber in the Lakeland area in England; he soloed the first ascent of Napes Needle in 1886. Bibliography: *Climbing in the British Isles, Volume 1—England* (1894), *Volume 2—Wales and Ireland* (1895).

Smythe, Frank Sydney   (1900–1949) Born: England. Bibliography: *Climbs and Ski-Runs* (1929), *The Kangchenjunga Adventure* (1930), *Kamet Conquered* (1932), *An Alpine Journey* (1934), *The Spirit of the Hills* (1935), *Over Tyrolese Hills* (1936), *Camp Six* (1937), *The Mountain Scene* (1937), *The Valley of Flowers* (1938), *Peaks and Valleys* (1938), *A Camera in the Hills* (1939), *Edward Whymper* (1940), *Mountaineering Holiday* (1940), *My Alpine Album* (1940), *The Adventures of a Mountaineer* (1940), *Over Welsh Hills* (1941), *The Mountain Vision* (1941), *Alpine Ways* (1942), *British Mountaineers* (1942), *Snow on the Hills* (1946), *Again Switzerland* (1947), *The Mountain Top* (1947), *Rocky Mountains* (1948), *Swiss Winter* (1948), *Mountains in Colour* (1949), *Climbs in the Canadian Rockies* (1950).

Snake   See **reptile**.

Sneffels Range   One of **Colorado**'s main **ranges**; its major summit is Mt. Sneffels, 4,312 m, 14,150 ft. (For the complete list of Colorado's 14,000-foot peaks, see appendix D.)

Snipe   A **bird**; the common (long-billed) snipe presents "spectacular aerial displays" (Johnsgard).

Snow   *Neige* (F), *neve* (I), *Schnee* (G). Precipitation that occurs when the temperature drops below 0 degrees Centigrade, 32 degrees Fahrenheit. Snow accumulates and remains if the temperature stays below freezing. There are many different types of falling and accumulated snow, depending on temperature, water content, and other factors. The different types have different names depending on the culture, sport, or occupation involved. Here it will suffice to mention the basic terms:

powder, wet, dry, and slush—all of which are self-explanatory. Artificial snow is created on ski slopes, when the natural variety is inadequate. Many parts of the world never receive any snow; in other areas, a few inches or feet fall each year. The American record is held by **Mt. Baker** in **Washington**, where, during the 1998–1999 season, 1,140 inches (almost 100 feet) fell (Egan). Mergen's *Snow in America* has an extensive chapter on terminology. Kirk's *Snow* offers an overview of snow's influence on the environment and those who inhabit it. It also contains a useful bibliography. (See also **hail, ice, snowmaking**, and **weather**)

Snow blindness   The temporary loss of sight due to extreme glare, reflection, and/or radiation at higher altitudes, especially on **snow fields** or **glaciers**. Those who spend time here must wear very dark sun or glacier glasses or goggles. Some people wear both simultaneously. Even temporary blindness could prove fatal to a solo climber. On **Herzog**'s **Annapurna** expedition, two superb climbers did not wear their glasses and were struck by this malady. **Reinhold Messner** was partially blinded on the first successful climb of **Everest** without supplemental oxygen.

Snow bunny   In skiing, a beginner.

Snow cave   A covered hole dug in the snow; it provides protection in bad weather.

Snow cups   Small indentations caused by evaporation; they can cover a large area.

Snow field   A large area covered by snow.

Snow leopard   See **cat**. (See also color photos.)

Snow pack   Accumulated snow.

Snow plume   See **plume**.

Snowboarding   In this fairly recent development in winter sports, one's feet are attached to a single wide board, rather than the two comparatively narrow shafts used in **skiing**. The board is controlled by shifting one's weight. It is especially popular with youngsters who enjoy doing

The Great Snow Field on the Summit of Mount Vice-President (Rev. George Kinney/National Geographic)

acrobatic twists and flips in the air. It is now an official **Olympic** sport.

Snow bridge See **crevasse**.

Snowdon 1,113 m, 3,560 ft. The highest mountain in Wales, United Kingdom.

Snowdrift Loose (often fluffy, new) snow that is blown about by the wind and accumulates (like a sand dune). Under certain conditions, the snow can quickly solidify into a hard mass.

Snowfield, Mt. 4,060 m, 13,321 ft. A high peak located in the **Yukon** Territory in Canada.

Snowline On a glacier or mountain, the point above which snow accumulates and below which the previous year's snow melts.

Snowmaking The production of artificial snow at ski areas. Water is transported through large pipes set along the sides of the skiable terrain. At night, when the temperature drops, it is shot out of guns and scatters above the slope. When it hits the air, it turns into snow, which accumulates and is then spread and smoothed or **groomed** by enormous machines. In order to create the perfect snow for winter sports a chemical additive is usually included.

Snowmobile A motorized (and often noisy) device that allows one or two riders to move quickly across almost any type of snow. Used primarily for recreational purposes, but people who work in snow country may utilize them for transportation (in the Arctic) or to move around a sugarbush (the forests where trees are tapped to collect sap for the production of maple syrup). The authors once saw a snowmobile racing up and down **Mt. St. Helens**'s extremely steep summit slope.

Snowplow (Obsolete) To configure one's skis so that the points almost touch while the tails are spread apart. It helps to **control** and to slow one down. It is an unsophisticated movement. (Also used as a noun.) (See also **wedge**.)

Snowshoes In order to walk in deep snow without sinking in, sometimes up to one's chest, humans must increase the size of their feet. Primitive, large, and extremely cumbersome snowshoes were constructed from tree limbs and some type of cording. Today, they come in a plethora of sizes, are made of aluminum and synthetic materials, and sometimes have built-in **crampons**. People enjoy strapping them on and wandering around in the snow. See Cook's *Essential Guide* for basic information, as well as an overview of snowshoeing locations in the 38 states that get enough snow to warrant inclusion.

Snowy Mountains A range in **Australia**.

***Sobre a linhas das montanhas do Brazil*/On the Lines of Brazilian Mountains** The Sixth Symphony, composed in 1944, by the Brazilian Heitor Villa-Lobos (1887–1959). The melodic lines of the symphony were actually designed using the shape of certain mountains: the height and width of summits and passes provided notes and rhythm. (Villa-Lobos later did the same thing with New York's skyline.) (M-A. H.)

Solo A climb of any kind that is done alone, with self-**belaying**.

Solomon Islands Lowest point, Pacific Ocean 0 m; highest point, Mt. Makarakomburu 2,447 m, 8,028 ft.

Solstice The shortest day of the year, the winter solstice, occurs on December 22 in the Northern Hemisphere; the longest day, the summer solstice, is on June 21. The seasons are reversed in the Southern Hemisphere.

Somalia Lowest point, Indian Ocean 0 m; highest point, Shimbiris 2,416 m, 7,927 ft.

Somervell, Theodore Howard (1890–1975) Born: England. He was a mountaineer and medical missionary, and participated in the 1922 and 1924 **Everest** expeditions. Bibliography: *After Everest* (1936).

Soper, N. Jack (1934–) Born: England. Bibliography: *The Black Cliff: The History of Rock Climbing on Clogwyn du'r Arddu* (1971), with Ken Wilson and Peter Crew.

Soroche See **acute mountain sickness**.

South Africa Lowest point, Atlantic Ocean 0 m; highest point, Njesuthi 3,408 m, 11,181 ft. Famous for its diamond mines, this country is also a very beautiful land of savannahs, rich with wildlife, rugged mountains and cliffs, and an amazing coastline.

South America The fourth largest continent (17,814,000 sq km, 6,878,000 sq miles), it extends some 7,500 km, 4,700 miles, from north to south. The northernmost point is Point Gallinas, in **Colombia**, while the southernmost point is Cape Horn. The widest east–west extent in South America is approximately 5,300 km, 3,300 miles, from Cape Branco, in **Brazil**, to Punte Pariñas, in **Peru**. Cerro Aconcagua 6,959 m, 22,831 ft, in **Argentina**, is the highest point on the continent, and also the tallest mountain in the Western Hemisphere; **Ojos del Salado** 6,880 m, 22,572 ft, in **Chile**, is the second-highest major summit; **Cerro Bonete** 6,410 m, 22,020 ft, is located in Argentina and is the third highest peak in South America, while **Monte Pissis** 6,779 m, 22,240 ft, and **Mercedario** 6,770 m, 22,211 ft, both in Argentina, are numbers four and five in altitude.

South Carolina   Lowest point, Atlantic Ocean 0 m; highest point, Sassafras Mountain 1,085 m, 3,560 ft (29th highest of the 50 state highpoints).

South Col   The saddle below the summit of **Everest**; at 7,000 m, 26,300 ft, it is the highest pass in the world.

South Dakota   Lowest point, Minnesota River, on the **Minnesota** border 294 m, 966 ft; highest point, **Harney Peak** 2,207 m, 7,242 ft (15th highest of the 50 state highpoints).

South Georgia and the South Sandwich Islands   Lowest point, Atlantic Ocean 0 m; highest point, Mt. Paget (South Georgia) 2,915 m, 9,564 ft. These islands are famous because it is there that the amazing voyage of the Endurance, led by **Sir Ernest Shackleton**, began and where it ended after extraordinary hardships, including the crossing of South Georgia Island, a land of cold, ice, angry storms, high peaks, powerful **glaciers**, and sheer **sea cliffs**.

Southern Alps   The impressive range on **New Zealand**'s South Island. (See also **Mt. Cook** and color photos.) Also, the southern part of the French Alps, south of the **Dauphiné**. High peaks include l'Argentera 3,297 m, 10,817 ft, some 80 km, 50 miles north of Nice, on the Italian border.

Spain   Lowest point, Atlantic Ocean 0 m; highest point, Pico de Teide (Tenerife) on the Canary Islands 3,718 m, 12,198 ft. Most people associate Spain with the **Pyrénées**, and conclude, erro-

neously, that the highest point must be the **Pico de Aneto** 3,404 m, 11,168 ft. In fact, the Canary Islands are volcanic islands, containing a number of high peaks exceeding 3,000 m, 10,000 ft.

Sparrow   An extremely common bird whose many species, for example, the chipping, can be found in mountainous habitats.

Speed climbing   A variation on normal rock climbing or mountaineering in which one attempts to reach the top as quickly as possible.

Speleology   The discipline devoted to the investigation of **caves**.

Spencer's Mountain   A 1963 American film written for the screen and directed by Delmer Daves, after a novel by Earl Hammer, Jr., with Henry Fonda and Maureen O'Hara. This is not a mountain film, despite the title, but rather a family comedy and drama set in rural Wyoming. The scenery is excellent and the Technicolor photography by Charles Lawton, Jr., is really beautiful. The movie was shot in **Grand Teton National Park**. (M-A. H.)

Spindrift   Snow that is picked up by the wind and blown around, sometimes fiercely. There is an almost continuous plume of spindrift blowing off the summit of **Everest**, due to the fact that the mountain is high enough to be immersed within the **jet stream**.

Spire   A high, sharp-pointed peak.

Spirit   See **religion**.

Spitsbergen, West   This is the largest island of the Spitsbergen group, located in the Arctic Ocean. The islands belong to **Norway**. The Spitsbergen group (61,230 sq km, 23,641 sq miles) is the main group of the Svalbard archipelago. West Spitsbergen, with a land area of 39,044 sq km, 15,075 sq miles, is about 450 km, 280 miles, in length, and nearly 225 km, or 140 miles, at its widest. The terrain is very mountainous, with numerous **fjords**; the majority of the island is covered with extensive **glaciers**. The highest point is Mt. Newton 1,717 m, 5,633 ft; other important summits include Hornsundtind 1,431 m, 4,695 ft, and the Drygalski Crest 1,423 m, 4,669 ft.

Spitze   (G) See **peak**.

Sport climbing   See **climbing**.

Spratly Islands   Lowest point, South China Sea 0 m; highest point, unnamed location on Southwest Cay 4 m, 13 ft.

Spring   The season that begins with the vernal **equinox** and ends at the summer **solstice**. In spring, the snow cover is generally maximal at high elevations, which provides good skiing, but hard climbing, especially on mixed terrain; nevertheless, the end of spring is often chosen by expeditions in the **Himalayas**, as well as in the Alaska Range; part of the reason is the longer days, and the fact that the snow cover generally makes crossing **crevasses** easier.

Spruce   A widely dispersed **conifer**; red spruce prefers higher elevations. (See also color photos.)

Spur rock   An extrusion heading downward. (See also **rib**.)

Squirrel   A small ground and arboreal **mammal**; some species make their way up to higher elevations.

Sri Lanka   Lowest point, Indian Ocean 0 m; highest point, Pidurutalagala 2,524 m, 8,281 ft.

St. Bernard   See **dogs**.

St. Bernard Passes   Two Alpine passes: the Great connects Switzerland and Italy while the Little lies between France and Italy. There is a **refuge** at each pass for people traveling on foot (Einstein).

St. Elias, Mt.   5,489 m, 18,009 ft. An important **peak**, this is the second highest peak in **Canada** and the fourth highest in **North America**, as well as part of a large **range**, the **Saint Elias Mountains**, in the **Yukon** and **Alaska**; it was first climbed in 1897 by an expedition led by the duke of **Abruzzi**.

St. Gotthard Pass   A pass in **Switzerland**.

St. Helens, Mt.   (Also Baldy) 2,550 m, 8,366 ft. A volcano in the **Cascades**; it erupted in 1980, causing much widespread damage and at least 57 deaths. It lost 1,300 feet in height during the process. The mountain's northern flank exploded into a pyroclastic *nuée ardente*, moving at some 300 mph and consuming everything in its path; **glaciers** melted, producing giant **mudslides**, and ash fell for weeks on eastern Washington.

Peak Margherita, Mt. Stanley (16,815 feet) in the Ruwenzori Range (Vittoria Sella/National Geographic)

St. Michel d'Aiguille A small church built on top of a large rock at Le Puy, France.

St. Moritz A famous ski resort in **Switzerland**.

Stance *Punto di sosta* (I), *relais* (F), *Standplatz* (G). In rock climbing, where one stands (or sits) in order to rest or **belay**.

Stanley, Mt. (Also Pic Maguerite, Peak Margherita) 5,109 m, 16,762 ft. This is the highest peak in the **Democratic Republic of the Congo**; it was first climbed in 1906, by an expedition led by the duke of **Abruzzi**. The summit party comprised the duke, J. Petigax, C. Ollier, and J. Brocherel. The main summit has a number of important **satellites**, including: Alexandra 5,091 m, 16,703 ft; Albert 5,087 m, 16,690 ft; Savoia 4,977 m, 16,330 ft; Ellena 4,968 m, 16,300 ft; Elizabeth 4,929 m, 16,170 ft; Phillip 4,920 m, 16,140 ft; Moebius 4,916 m, 16,130 ft; and Great Tooth 4,603 m, 15,100 ft.

Static See **rope**.

Steck, Al (fl. late 1940s–early 1950s) Excellent and important pioneering American *rock* climber, and partner to **Salathé**.

Stecknadelhorn 4,242 m, 13,917 ft. This is the 22nd highest of the 60 major 4,000-meter peaks in the **Alps**. This is another major peak in the **Mischabels**, in the **Valais**. The first ascent was performed by Oscar Eckenstein and **Matthias Zurbriggen** in 1887.

Steele, Mt. 5,073 m, 16,645 ft. This is the fifth highest peak in **Canada**; it is located in the **Saint Elias Mountains**, in the **Yukon**. The second climb was done in 1937 by **Bradford Washburn** and **Robert Bates**. Their epic achievement is recounted in detail in *Escape from Lucania*.

Steele, Peter R. C. (1935–) Born: England. Bibliography: *Two and Two Halves to Bhutan* (1970), *Doctor on Everest* (1972), *Medical Care for Mountain Climbers* (1976).

Stem In rock and ice climbing or skiing, to spread one's legs or skis apart.

Stenmark, Ingemar (1956–) An exceptional Swedish skier; Stenmark won three World Cup championships as well as gold medals in both the **slalom** and giant slalom at the 1980 Olympics.

Cassin Stemming (Alpina di Giula)

Step cutting In mountaineering, before **crampons** existed, the **lead** climber used an **ice ax** to cut steps into steep, icy slopes. This was both time consuming and deenergizing. Nevertheless, even when crampons became available, many climbers refused to use them and continued cutting steps. **Sir Edmund Hillary** cut steps on **Everest** even when wearing crampons. ("I tried cramponing along the slope without cutting steps but my feet slipped uncomfortably down the slope. I went on cutting" [Hillary].) So did **Hermann Buhl** on the north wall of the Triolet. When icy conditions warrant it, step cutting can make a climb safer.

Stephen, Sir Leslie (1832–1904) Born: England. A British mountaineer with many **first ascents**, including the **Rimpfischhorn, Alphubel, Schreckhorn**, and **Zinalrothorn**.

He was one of the founders of the Alpine Club. Stephen was an extremely influential critic and the father of Virginia Woolf. Unsworth indicates that his *Playground of Europe* is a mountaineering classic (*Encyclopaedia*). Bibliography: *Men, Books, and Mountains* (1956), collected by S. O. A. Ullman.

Stone, applications for   Useful stone is quarried in various countries. From Vermont's Rock of Ages comes **granite**, which in block form is turned into building material and tombstones. **Marble** is much softer than granite; in addition to building applications, it is used by artists to produce sculptures. New York, Minnesota, Italy, and Egypt also produce excellent stone. Cut into slabs, it is used for countertops, interior facings, and flooring; quarried stone can also be crushed and turned into an abrasive. (See also **quarry**.)

Stonefall   In mountaineering, the release and falling or rolling of rock from above caused by melting snow or ice as the sun heats up the mountain. For this reason it is often wise to start down long before noon. Steep, narrow couloirs are especially dangerous, since loose rock can be set in motion by a higher climber. **Mt. Hood** is infamous for its falling rock. In late 2002, Ed Hommer, a double amputee, was killed by a falling rock on **Mt. Rainier**.

Stopper   In rock climbing, the trade name for a metallic device with an attached wire that is placed in **cracks** in order to protect against a **fall**. (See also **nut**.)

Storm   *Tempête* (F), *Sturm* (G), *tempesta* (I). A weather disturbance in which rain or snow falls; the wind may blow and thunder and lightning often are also present. **Blizzard** implies a severe storm with heavy snowfall.

Strahlhorn   4,190 m, 13,747 ft. This is the 31st highest of the 60 major 4,000-meter peaks of the **Alps**. It was first climbed in 1854 by **Edmund J. Grenville**, Christopher Smyth, Franz-Josef Andenmatten, and **Ulrich Lauener**. The Strahlhorn is located in the **Valaisan Alps**, in the Allalin group. (See also color photos.)

Stratum   (Plural: strata) A layer of rock.

Strickland Peak   4,260 m, 13,977 ft. A high peak located in the **Yukon** Territory in Canada.

Stromboli   ("Lighthouse of the Mediterranean") 926 m, 3,038 ft. An Italian volcanic island; because its reactivation is imminent, a warning system alerts people within two minutes of any change.

Stump, Terry ("Mugs")   (1949–1992) An outstanding all-around climber, he was killed in a **crevasse fall** on Denali.

Sturme über dem Mont Blanc*/Avalanche**   This is the first talking movie by **Arnold Fanck**, filmed in 1930 right after ***Die Weisse Hölle der Piz Palu. Mostly shot as a silent film, with some talking scenes added, as was customary in those days, it is far more episodic in structure than *Weisse Hölle*. The plot includes a love story between a young woman involved in astronomy and geology and the fellow in charge of the Mont Blanc meteorological station. During a stunning half hour, the hero is caught in a storm and tries to get down to the valley, while a party attempts to rescue him. (M-A. H.)

Stutfield, Hugh Edward Millington   (1858–1929) Born: England. Bibliography: *Climbs and Exploration in the Canadian Rockies* (1903) with Norman Collie.

Styles, Frank Showell   (1908–) Born: England. Bibliography: *Climber in Wales* (1948), *The Mountaineer's Weekend Book* (1950), *Mountains of the Midnight Sun* (1954), *Introduction to Mountaineering* (ca. 1954), *The Moated Mountain* (1955), *Getting to Know Mountains* (1958), *How Mountains Are Climbed* (1958), *Look at Mountains* (1962), *Modern Mountaineering* (1964), *Blue Remembered Hills* (1965), *The Foundations of Climbing* (1966), *Mallory of Everest* (1967), *On Top of the World* (1967), *Rock and Rope* (1967), *Men and Mountaineering* (1968), *The Climber's Bedside Book* (1968), *First on the Summits* (1970), *The Forbidden Frontiers* (1970), *Mountains of North Wales* (1973), *Backpacking in the Alps and Pyrenees* (1976).

Subalpine   The area below the **Alps**; the area on a mountain below the **treeline**.

Subduction   When one **tectonic plate** is forced down under a second.

Sudan   Lowest point, Red Sea 0 m; highest point, Kinyeti 3,187 m, 10,456 ft.

Summer   The warmest time of year. Summer begins at the summer **solstice**, on June 21 in the Northern Hemisphere. During the warm summer months, the snow covering **glaciers** melts; as a result, the **crevasses** and rimayes open. This is favorable in terms of being able to see otherwise hidden crevasses, but makes for harder-route finding on a difficult glacier and rimaye crossing.

Summit   *Cima* (S). The top of the mountain. Some mountaineers collect summits. (Also used as verb.)

Summit photos   Summit photos are often used to authenticate a first ascent. There have been some controversies, one of the most notable being the claim made by Dr. Frederick Cook, in 1906, that he had performed the first ascent of **Denali**. Using the so-called summit photos submitted by Dr. Cook, **Bradford Washburn** debunked that claim by showing that the photos had in fact been taken from a small Alaskan mountain. (See *The Dishonorable Dr. Cook: Debunking the Notorious Mount McKinley Hoax*, by Bradford Washburn and Peter Cherici.)

Sun   The star around which earth rotates. It produces heat, which makes all life possible. Alternating cycles of heat and cold help to erode the rock of which mountains are composed. In the high, glaciated mountains, the sun also sears the skin and harms the eyes. (See also **freeze–thaw cycle** and **snow blindness**.)

Sunbird   Some species may prefer higher altitudes: the malachite can be found above 5,000, the tacazze above 7,000, and the variable above 8,000 ft, all in East Africa (Williams). In the **Himalayas**, Mrs. Gould's manages to reach 11,000 ft, and the firetailed yellowbacked soars even higher, to 13,200 ft (Ali).

Sunrise   High in the mountains, the few hours preceding dawn are the coldest; it is then that the ice and snow refreeze on the steep *couloirs* and precipitous ridges, locking stones and rock in place in the process; **snow bridges** over **crevasses** also tend to become sturdier and more reliable. Therefore, the predawn hours are ideal to begin a technical climb on snow or ice or to cross a difficult **glacier**; in addition, an early start ensures that most of the climbing will be done under cool conditions, which helps breathing at high altitude, and will avoid late afternoon thunderstorms in those areas where such storms are prevalent. However, this time of night

is also subject to fierce winds produced by the temperature gradient at the transition from night to day. The first rays of the sun quickly warm up the environment, while a few tens of miles to the west, the mountains are still illuminated by the thousands of stars in the cold night sky. **Radiation cooling** is particularly strong high in the mountains, because the cold and ice tend to trap the humidity, yielding a pure, crystalline, and highly transparent sky, especially to infrared light, carrying heat away from the earth, into the firmament. These conditions reinforce the quick cooling that occurs during the night, and the steep temperature gradient and accompanying winds at sunrise.

Sunscreen   Because solar radiation and glare are dramatically intensified at altitude, especially in the presence of snow or ice, it is mandatory to protect exposed skin (including the scalp) with ongoing applications of sunscreen. Failure to do so will result, as it did for one of the authors of this volume, in a visit to the emergency room.

Sunset   This is a magical time in the high realm: the wonderful colors of **alpenglow** long linger on the highest peaks, while the valleys below are already plunged into the dark of night. The dry, crystalline high-altitude atmosphere is particularly conducive to **radiation cooling**, which sets in immediately after sunset and lasts thruout the night, enabling the cold to take hold of the glaciers, ridges, and couloirs, making them more stable for the climbers in the predawn hours.

Superstition   A belief that is sometimes unfounded and produces fear. Some peoples believe that the gods who inhabit the higher elevations may be offended by certain actions. Thus, inhabitants are often afraid to venture very high or must perform certain rituals to propitiate the supernatural forces.

Suriname   Lowest point, unnamed location in the coastal plain −2 m, −7 ft; highest point, Wilhelmina Gebergte 1,286 m, 4,219 ft.

Surtsey   A **volcano** off the coast of **Iceland**. In 1963, the tip of this new volcano emerged from the Atlantic Ocean; it grew at a prodigious rate and soon was a full-fledged island spewing out vast quantities of **lava**. During the 1960s, some commercial flights swooped steeply downward when crossing Surtsey. The close view of the **crater** with its erupting lava and subsequent ocean steam was an astounding sight. (See also **Paricutín**.)

Surveying The process through which topography and altitude are measured; from the resulting data, **maps** are produced. Early surveyors were also adventurers, visiting some areas for the first time. (See also **U.S. Geological Survey**.)

Survival madness *Épuisement* (F). A condition brought on by exhaustion (which is what the French term means) that sometimes strikes mountaineers; it is characterized by irrationality and/or hysteria (Roth).

Sutton, Geoffrey J. S. (1930–) Born: England. Bibliography: *Samson* (1961), with Wilfrid Noyce, *Artificial Aids in Mountaineering* (1962), *High Peak* (1966), with Eric Byne.

Svalbard Lowest point, Arctic Ocean 0 m; highest point, Newtontoppen 1,717 m, 5,633 ft.

Swallow A **bird**; many swallow species breed and range in mountainous areas. The cliff swallow nests, appropriately, on sheer rock faces. In South America, many species fly high: the Andean roves above 15,000 ft (Fjeldså and Krabbe).

Swaziland Lowest point, Great Usutu River 21 m, 69 ft; highest point, Emlembe 1,862 m, 6,109 ft.

Sweden Lowest point, Baltic Sea 0 m; highest point, Kebnekaise 2,111 m, 6,926 ft.

Swift A **bird** of many species; the black as well as the white-throated enjoy the mountains, cliffs, or rocky regions. In East Africa, the nyanza breeds in high cliffs.

Swiss Miss A 1938 American film directed by John Blystone (1892–1938), starring Stan Laurel (1890–1965) and Oliver Hardy (1892–1957). To sell mousetraps, one needs to go where the mice are; since mice love cheese and there is lots of cheese in **Switzerland**, the best place to sell mousetraps is Switzerland. Any movie with this kind of logic is bound to please mountain lovers. There is not much climbing here but one scene involves a piano, a rope bridge, the two daredevil heroes, and a gorilla. (M-A. H.)

Switchback An extreme reversal of a **trail** so that it turns back in the direction from which it comes, but on a higher or lower level. It makes climbing or descending a slope much easier and helps to eliminate **erosion**. Hikers and climbers are often adjured not to "cut" switchbacks, that is, not to cross from one switchback to another but to stick to the trail. Famous switchbacks include the infamous 96 switchbacks on the normal route of **Mt. Whitney**, as well as some "25 switchbacks from hell" on the way up to Froze-to-Death Plateau, on the normal route to **Granite Peak**, in **Montana**.

Switzerland Lowest point, Lake Maggiore 195 m, 640 ft; highest point, **Dufourspitze** 4,634 m, 15,203 ft. Despite its relatively small size (41,284 sq km, 15,940 sq miles), this is one of the most mountainous countries in the world: there, the **Alps** are divided into many high ranges, including the **Valaisan Alps**, the **Bernese Alps**, and the Rhaetian Alps. One of the most famous mountains in the world, the **Matterhorn**, is located above **Zermatt**, in the heart of Valais and along the Italian border. Switzerland counts 44 of the 60 major 4,000-meter summits in the Alps, most of them entirely within the country, while others are on the border with **Italy**. (See also color photos.)

Syncline Rock beds that dip toward each other. (See also **anticline**.)

Syria Lowest point, unnamed location near Lake Tiberias −200 m, −656 ft; highest point, Mt. Hermon 2,814 m, 9,232 ft.

System An extremely large **chain** of mountains such as the **Appalachian** system, which in turn is divided into specific **ranges**, for example, the **Catskills** or the Great Smokies. More broadly, there are two major continuous systems on earth: the contiguous Pacific group (running north–south) which includes the Brooks Range, the **Rocky Mountains**, and the **Andes**; and the Eurasian group, which travels along an east–west axis from North Africa through Europe and Asia and includes the **Alps**, the **Pamirs**, and the **Himalayas**.

T

Tabei, Junko (1939–) (Born: Japan) First woman to summit **Everest,** in 1975.

Taiga Extensive forest land in subarctic areas. (See also **tundra.**)

Tail In **snowboarding**, the board's rear tip.

Tairraz, Pierre (1933–2000) Born: France. A superb mountain photographer, especially famous for his magnificent images of the **Mont Blanc massif.** Bibliography: *The Seven Valleys* (1961), with Roger Frison-Roche, *Journey to the Heart of Mont Blanc* (1999), with Mario Colonel. (See also the **10 Best Mountain Photographers and Cinematographers** sidebar and color photos.)

Taiwan Lowest point, South China Sea 0 m; highest point, Yu Shan 3,997 m, 13,114 ft.

Tajikistan Lowest point, Syrdariya 300 m, 984 ft; highest point, Pik imeni **Ismail Samani** 7,495 m, 24,590 ft.

Talus Small pieces of rock that are found at the bottom of a cliff. (See also **scree** and **till**.)

Talus (Laura Lindblad)

Tambora The eruption of this Indonesian **volcano** in 1815 caused more than 90,000 deaths and probably altered the global climate (Ritchie and Gates).

Tanggula The southeast extension of the **Karakoram range**.

Tanzania Lowest point, Indian Ocean 0 m; highest point, **Kilimanjaro** 5,895 m, 19,340 ft. (See also color photos.)

Tarn A mountain lake sometimes in a cirque. (See also color photos.)

Tartarin sur les Alpes/Tartarin in the Alps   In 1872, the French author Alphonse Daudet (1840–1897) wrote a novel entitled *Tartarin de Tarascon* after its main character and the city he is from. Tartarin is a braggart, quick to blow his top, promising all sorts of things and failing to accomplish any since he is very much of a coward, but he would rather die than admit it; since his peers are similar, no one takes offense. In 1885, Daudet published another episode in which the hero, president of the Alpine Society of Tarascon (25 feet above sea level), has to face an opponent. He thus decides to climb a summit in the Alps to prove his ability and settles for the **Jungfrau**, "whose maiden name enhances the glory of its conquest." Before the climb, Tartarin spends his time surrounded by transparent English girls, romancing a Russian nihilist, and waiting for the clouds to stop producing rain. A rather tepid French film version was shot by Henry Vorins in 1920. (M-A. H.)

Taschhörn 4,490 m, 14,731 ft. This is the ninth of the 60 major 4,000-meter peaks in the **Alps**. One of the giants in the **Valaisan Alps**, in the **Mischabels**, it was first climbed in 1862 by J. L. Davies, J. W. Hayward, Stephan and **Johann**

Zumtaugwald, and Joseph Summermatter. A superb knife-edge ridge connects this peak to its mighty neighbor, the **Dom**.

Tasker, Joe (1948–1982) Born: Hull, England. One of the foremost mountaineers in the 1970s and early 1980s he climbed the north face of the Eiger in the winter of 1974–1975. Bibliography: *Everest the Cruel Way* (1981), *Savage Arena* (1982).

Tatras A **range** in the Slovakian **Carpathians**.

Technical climbing See **climbing**.

Tectonic plates In the 1920s, Alfred Wegener published a monograph on **continental drift**. Scholars were skeptical that the continents had once been conjoined, and it was only much later in the century when plate tectonics was hypothesized that continental drift seemed more plausible. Geologists believe that some 10 large plates undergird the earth's surface; when they shift, they cause various geological changes including earthquakes, volcanic eruptions, and the buckling that results in uplift and thus the birth or evolution of mountains. According to Hamblin and Christiansen, plates collide at convergent plate boundaries; they drift apart at divergent plate boundaries; and they pass each other with no damage at transform plate boundaries. The most important of the named plates are the Eurasian, African, North American, South American, Indian, and Pacific (http://dialspace.dial.pipex.com/town/parade/henryr/earth/plate/ and http://earth.leeds.ac.uk/dynamicearth).

Tejas, Vern (Vern) (1953–) The first person to **solo Denali** in winter (1988), and one of the strongest **guides** in the **Alaska** Range, where he has guided well over 30 ascents of Denali. Tejas has also made the first solo ascent of **Vinson Massif** and was the lead guide for Col. **Norman Vaughn**'s ascent of Mt. Vaughn in **Antarctica**; he has also successfully climbed the **Seven Summits**. Bibliography: *Dangerous Steps* (1990) by Lewis Freedman.

Telemark See **skiing**.

Téléphérique de l'Aiguille du Midi See **Aiguille du Midi**.

Temperature Variation in heat or cold. The Fahrenheit scale is used in the United States and the Celsius in most other countries to measure temperature. The Fahrenheit scale is based on the freezing and boiling points of alcohol, which is a convenient chemical to use for thermometers; the Celsius scale, on the other hand, records the freezing and boiling point of water. In both cases, the measurements are performed under normal atmospheric pressure at sea level. As a result, the zero on the Fahrenheit scale corresponds to approximately −18 degrees Celsius, while a temperature of 100 degrees Fahrenheit equals 38 degrees Celsius. The conversion equation from Celsius to Fahrenheit is $F = 9/5 \, (C) + 32$. There is no greater variation in earth's surface temperature than that which occurs in the mountain environment. During the day, in **Everest**'s **Khumbu Icefall** it might reach 100 degrees F. At night, higher up on the mountain, it can drop to −50 degrees F. **Reinhold Messner** reports that during a forced stay in his tent at Everest's **South Col** (26,300 feet), the temperature was −50 degrees C. and the wind was blowing at 125 miles per hour. Lava flowing from a volcano can reach 2,000 degrees F.

Temple, R. Philip (1939–) Born: New Zealand. Bibliography: *Nawok!* (1962), *The Sea and the Snow* (1966), *The World at Their Feet* (1969), *Mantle of the Skies* (1971), *Castles in the Air* (1973).

Ten Mile Range One of **Colorado**'s main **ranges**; its major summit is Quandary Peak, 4,347 m, 14,265 ft, an easy climb, either on foot or cross-country skiing. (For the complete list of Colorado's 14,000-foot peaks, see appendix D.)

Tennessee Lowest point, Mississippi River, Mississippi border 54 m, 178 ft; highest point, **Clingmans Dome** 2,025 m, 6,643 ft (17th highest of the 50 state highpoints).

Tent A small or larger, easily portable enclosure made out of a variety of materials (canvas, plastic, nylon) that is a necessary piece of **equipment** in overnight climbing and especially for expeditions at high altitude. Without a wind-resistant tent, it would be impossible to survive the bitter cold and fierce winds. Over the years, tents have become more refined: the traditional A-shaped units gave way to the dome, which preceded the geodesic form. For high altitude survival a small, light, aerodynamic mountain tent is best. The units described here should not be confused with the more permanent types used by nomadic peoples. These include tepees and yurts (now sometimes constructed with wheels). (See also **climbing equipment**.)

Tent Peak 7,365 m, 24,165 ft. This major peak is located within the **Himalayas** in **Nepal**.

10th Mountain Division An American army division that trained to fight in mountainous terrain during World War II. Members included **Paul Petzoldt**, founder of Outward Bound and NOLS, and Senator Bob Dole. Among the recent books devoted to its history is Peter Shelton's *Climb to Conquer*.

Tephra Any solid material ejected by a volcanic **eruption**.

Terrace A flat area on a face wider than a **ledge**.

Terray, Lionel (1921–1965) One of the great **mountaineers** of the 20th century. He climbed the Grands Charmoz when he was 12; accompa-

nied **Maurice Herzog** on the 1950 **Annapurna** expedition; and later made **first ascents** of **Makalu II** in 1954 with Jean Franco, **Makalu** in 1955 with **Jean Couzy**, Fitzroy, and **Jannu,** among others. **David Roberts** claims that Terray is "the greatest expeditionary mountaineer of all time." His *A la conquete de l'Inutile* is a classic account. Bibliography: *A la conquete de l'Inutile* (Conquistadores of the Useless) (1963), *At Grips with Jannu* (1957) with Jean Franco. (See also the **10 Best All-Around Mountaineers** and **10 Best Guides** sidebars.)

Tetons (French for breasts). A high, impressive, picturesque **range** in **Wyoming**. The main road is very close to the mountains and so even those who choose not to hike or climb can almost touch the **Grand**, Middle, or South **Teton**. The

Tetons and Snake River (Ansel Adams/Corbis)

first of these is a fairly difficult technical climb that almost any fit person can master. The normal route follows the Exum Ridge. (See also **national parks**.)

Texas   Lowest point, Stell-Lind Banco No. 128, near Rio Grande estuary −0.6 m, −2 ft; highest point, **Guadalupe Peak** 2,667 m, 8,749 ft (14th highest of the 50 state highpoints).

Thailand   Lowest point, Gulf of Thailand 0 m; highest point, Doi Inthanon 2,576 m, 9,042 ft.

Thaw   When the temperature goes above 32 degrees F, 0 degrees Centigrade, and snow or ice melts.

Thermopylae   In ancient Greece, this was a **pass** in the mountains where a famous battle was fought.

Thomas, Eustace   (1869–1960) Born: Manchester, England. He began Alpine climbing at the age of 54, after being an extraordinary long-distance hill walker, and succeeded in climbing all the major 4,000-meter summits in the **Alps**. Bibliography: *High Peak* (1966) by Eric Byne and Geoffrey Sutton, *Studmarks on the Summits* (1985) by Bill Smith.

Thompson,   Dorothy   Evelyn   (1888–1961) Born: England. Bibliography: *Climbing with Joseph Georges* (1962).

Thrush   A bird whose species vary in coloration. The hermit is extremely shy but its song is often heard. The **Himalayan** blackfaced laughing reaches almost 14,000 ft, and the chiguanco can be seen above 14,000 in the **Andes** (Fjeldså and Krabbe).

Thunderbolt Peak   4,268 m, 14,003 ft. Located in the **Palisades** region of the **Sierra Nevada** in **California**, it was first ascended in 1931 by Robert Underhill, **Norman Clyde**, Bestor Robinson, Francis Farquhar, Glen Dawson, Lewis Clark, and Jules Eichorn.

Thunderstorm   *Orage* (F). A fierce storm accompanied by heavy rain, wind, thunder, and dangerous lightning. One may occur virtually every spring and summer afternoon in the **high mountains**; thus, it is best to climb early and start down before noon: "We were caught in a terrific high thunderstorm; flash upon flash, roar upon roar, as we raced like hunted animals down the upper part of the ridge" (Buhl). (See also **weather**.)

Tibet   A mountainous country in Asia. The north side of **Everest** is in Tibet. The current political status of Tibet is that of a so-called autonomous region, within **China**. The Rowell Fund for Tibet maintains a website at www.savetibet.org. (See also **Lhasa**.)

Tibetan greybacked shrike   A bird that manages to reach about 15,000 ft in the **Himalayas** (Ali).

Tibetan snowcock   A partridge-like bird that roams the Tibetan plateau to 18,000 ft (Ali).

Tichy, Herbert   (1912–1987)   Born: Austria. He made the first ascent of **Cho Oyu** in 1954 with S. Joechler and Pasang Dawa Lama. Bibliography: *Tibetan Adventure* (1938), *Cho Oyu* (1957), *Himalaya* (1970).

Tidewater glacier   A glacier that flows directly into the sea; generally a tidewater glacier carves a **fjord** on its way down from the mountains into the ocean. At their terminus, icebergs are formed when the ice is warmed by seawater. Magnificent examples of tidewater glaciers can be viewed all along the coast of the Gulf of **Alaska**, with particularly exquisite areas near **Glacier Bay**, **Kenai Fjords**, **Wrangell–St. Elias**, and Prince William Sound, all **national parks**. The **Columbia Glacier** is the largest of the 52 tidewater glaciers found in Alaska.

Tie in   (Tie on) In climbing, to attach a **rope** to a **harness**.

Tiedemann, Mt.   3,848 m, 12,625 ft. The second highest peak in the Coast Ranges of **British Columbia**, it is a magnificent, difficult, and heavily glaciated summit in a very remote area: the shortest **approach** is some 80 km, 50 miles, long.

Tien Shan   ("Celestial mountains") A high **range** in **China**. Important summits include: **Khan Tengri** 7,010 m, 22,998 ft, on the border between **Kyrgyzstan** and China; **Mramornaja Stena** 6,400 m, 20,997 ft, in **Kazakhstan**; **Pik Pobeda** 7,439 m, 24,407 ft, on the border between Kyrgyzstan and China; and Pik Talgar 5,020 m, 16,470 ft, in Kyrgyzstan.

Tiger   See **cat** and color photos.

Till   Glacial deposits of **gravel** and rocks. (See also **glacial drift**, **scree**, and **talus**.)

Tilman, Harold William (1898–1978) Born: England. An outstanding mountain explorer; he made the **first ascent** of **Nandi Devi** with **Noel Odell**, in 1936. He is the author of innumerable books, and led the 1938 **Everest** expedition. Bibliography: *The Ascent of Nanda Devi* (1937), *Snow on the Equator* (1937), *When Men and Mountains Meet* (1946), *Mount Everest* 1938 (1948), *Two Mountains and a River* (1949), *China to Chitral* (1951), *Nepal Himalaya* (1952), *'Mischief' in Patagonia* (1957), *'Mischief' among the Penguins* (1961), *'Mischief' in Greenland* (1964), *Mostly 'Mischief'* (1966), *'Mischief' Goes South* (1968), *In 'Mischief's' Wake* (1971), *Ice with Everything* (1974), *Triumph and Tribulation* (1977), *The Seven Mountain-Travel Books* (1983).

Timberline (Treeline) The point on a mountain where trees stop growing. It varies dramatically in **altitude** depending on the peak's location. In the **Appalachians**, the timberline may be as low as 5,000 ft, whereas on some slopes in the **Sierras**, trees may be found at 11,000 ft. **Climate** and soil conditions are major influences on the timberline.

Time, geological The long period (4.5 billion years) for which the earth has existed and during which mountains are born, evolve, and die.

Time, human The short chronological period (ca. 100,000 years) during which *Homo sapiens* has flourished.

Timms, Christopher (fl. early 20th century) In 1906, Timms survived a 7,500-ft fall that ended in a crevasse (Boga).

Tinamou A ground bird of many species; the puna manages to reach 17,400 ft in the **Andes**.

Tirich Mir 7,708 m, 25,288 ft. This major peak is located within the Hindu Kush in **Pakistan**. It was first ascended in 1950, by Arne Naess, P. Kvernberg, H. Berg, and Tony Streather.

Toboggan A wooden sled without runners whose surface curves upward at the front.

Tocorpurri 6,755 m, 22,162 ft. This is the seventh highest major summit in the **Andes**; it was probably first climbed during pre-Columbian times, by natives. The peak is located on the border between **Bolivia** and **Chile**.

Togo Lowest point, Atlantic Ocean 0 m; highest point, Mont Agou 986 m, 3,235 ft.

Tokelau Lowest point, Pacific Ocean 0 m; highest point, unnamed location 5 m, 16 ft.

Toluca, Nevado de 4,632 m, 15,197 ft. A high Mexican **volcano**.

Tonga Lowest point, Pacific Ocean 0 m; highest point, unnamed location on Kao Island 1,033 m, 3,389 ft.

Tooth *Dent* (F). A rock projection resembling a (jagged) tooth. (See also **gendarme**.)

Topographic (Topo) map See **map**.

Topography The **relief** of the earth's surface or of a prescribed area; also, mapping this.

Top-rope Prior to rock or ice climbing, to attach a **rope** at the top of a low cliff or ice wall, and use it to **belay** rather than placing **nuts**, **cams**, **ice screws**, or other forms of **protection** as one moves upwards.

Tor A rocky hill or pinnacle.

Touching the Void This extraordinary, true climbing account, written by **Joe Simpson**, tells the harrowing story of an accident, high in the **Andes** in stormy weather, where one member of a two-climber party is forced to do the unthinkable: cut the rope and leave his friend behind to die. The film version stars trained actors, but the real protagonists also participate; it won the British award for best film of 2003. We prefer to refer the interested reader to this exceptional book, rather than divulge the amazing struggle that ensues. (See also **10 Great Mountain Adventure Books** and **10 Best Hollywood Mountain Movies** sidebars.)

Tourist People have visited distant lands for thousands of years. But only since the Renaissance have the adventurous sallied forth with no desire to conquer, trade, or resettle but rather to observe, learn, and interact. Tourists now visit mountainous areas in such profusion that they alter the ecological balance. (See also **mountain people**.)

Tower *Tour* (F), *Türm* (G). A vertical rock extrusion. Also a large metal structure built on top of hills and mountains as a conduit for broadcasting and telephonic microwave signals. (See also **fire towers**.)

Track In **skiing**, the warning term shouted by an approaching uphill skier. It should be used only in true emergencies, and not merely to clear the slope for an out-of-control lunatic. Also, a **trail**.

Traditional climbing   See **climbing**.

Trail   (Also track) *Trace* (F). An often obvious path through or across any wild terrain, for example, woods, jungle, slopes, or snow. A trail is either worn inadvertently by passing people or animals or created by park workers in order to afford easier passage or to protect the surrounding environment. Also, a **groomed** route through the woods, for skiing.

Transportation   All means of conveyance are used in the mountains: **camels**, elephants, horses, **llamas**, mules, **yaks**, and other **animals**; carts and wagons; cars and trucks; **chairlifts** and **gondolas**; **funiculars**; and various types of **railroads**. (See also **skipland** and **helicopter**.)

Traverse   *Quergang* and *überschreitung* (G). In skiing or climbing, to move perpendicularly or obliquely across a slope or a wall, rather than directly up or down. In mountaineering, it can be

On the Traverse of the Grépon (G. P. Abraham/ National Geographic)

more dangerous than direct upward movement, because one is unbalanced, and a mistake can easily result in a fall. In this latter endeavor it also means to go up one route, across, and down another.

Tre Cime di Lavaredo   Three monolithic **spires**, among many in the **Dolomites**, popular with rock climbers.

Tree   A **plant** with a single, erect, bark-covered stem; trees vary dramatically in width and height from smaller shrublike entities to enormous **sequoias** and **redwoods**. Some species live for many thousands of years. Both **deciduous** trees and **conifers** are indigenous to the world's mountainous zones. See especially *The Mountain World* in which David Costello discusses forests and trees.

Treeline   See **timberline**.

Trek   *Raid* (F) To walk or hike over an extended period (e.g., for one to four weeks), especially in the **Himalayas**.

A Slippery but Not Difficult Crossing (G. P. Abrahams/ National Geographic)

Trenker, Luis (1892–1990) (b. Alois Franck Trenker) Trenker was a student of architecture; during World War I, he fought in the Dolomites. In 1920, he acted as a guide for **Arnold Fanck** when he shot *Das Wunder des Schneeschus*. He then began to act in Fanck's films, beginning in 1924 with *Der Berg des Schicksals*/Mountain of Destiny. He was the production manager on the 1928 Italian–German film, *Der Kampf ums Matterhorn*/Fight for the Matterhorn, a movie he remade in 1938 as *Der Berg Ruft!*/The Challenge. (M-A. H.)

Triglav 2,864 m, 9,396 ft. This was the highest point of the former Yugoslavia, now the highpoint of **Slovenia** and the Julian Alps.

Trinidad and Tobago Lowest point, Caribbean Sea 0 m; highest point, El Cerro del Aripo 940 m, 3,084 ft.

Trinity Alps A relatively small range in northwestern **California**; its highpoint is Mt. Eddy 2,751 m, 9,025 ft; other high peaks include: Thompson Peak 2,744 m, 9,002 ft; Mt. Hilton, 2,733 m, 8,964 ft; Russian Peak 2,498 m, 8,196 ft; South Yolla Bolly Peak 2,466 m, 8,092 ft; and Preston Peak 2,228 m, 7,310 ft. The area is wild and remote, and the forests of the Trinity Alps are said to be home to sasquatch.

Tristan da Cunha See **Saint Helena**.

Trisul 7,120 m, 23,360 ft. This major peak is located within the **Himalayas** in **India**. It was first ascended in 1907, by Tom Longstaff, Brocherel Burathoki, and Karbir Burathoki.

Trisuli 7,074 m, 23,210 ft. This major peak is located within the **Himalayas** in **India**.

Tromelin Island Lowest point, Indian Ocean 0 m; highest point, unnamed location 7 m, 23 ft.

Tschingel See **dogs**.

Tsunami A massive wave, sometimes hundreds of feet high, that can inundate land areas and harm property and life. Tsunamis are usually caused by undersea disturbances or **earthquakes**, but they can also develop when a **volcano** erupts and sends ice and mud cascading down into the ocean. Although tsunamis can travel at high speed, 420 mph, the wavelength associated with the disturbance is generally quite long: a few hundred miles. The net result is a relatively slow, but steady, motion of the ocean surface, which can rise hundreds of feet above its normal height, over a period of half an hour, flooding everything in its path. When the contours of the coastline enhance the effects of the tsunami, a much more violent wave may result. The fact that a very large portion of the ocean rises with a tsunami also explains why, in islands like **Hawaii**, the north shore can be devastated by a wave resulting from an earthquake in **Chile**. Two of the largest tsunamis ever recorded were produced by the massive 9.2 Good Friday earthquake of 1964, in **Alaska** and the tragic 9.0 December 26, 2004, **earthquake epicenter**ed off the coast of **Indonesia**, which created a powerful **tsunami** that killed more than 155,000 people.

Tuck In skiing, bending the knees and lowering the body for the least air resistance.

Tuckett, Francis Fox (1834–1913) Born: England. He made the first ascent of the **Aletschhorn** in 1859. Bibliography: *A Pioneer in the High Alps* (1920), letters and diaries edited by **W. A. B. Coolidge**.

Tuff A **rock** that derives from **ash** or **cinder**.

Tullis, Julie (1939–1986) A British mountaineer who died on **K2** during a storm. Bibliography: *Clouds from Both Sides* (1986), autobiography, *The Endless Knot* (1991), by Kurt Diemberger.

Tumulus A mound in lava.

Tundra Snowy area where trees do not grow because of the cold. Arctic tundra is located near the Arctic Circle, in **Greenland** or **Alaska**, for example. **Alpine-zone** tundra is found in mountainous regions (Bliss). (See also **taiga**.)

Tunisia Lowest point, Shatt al Gharsah −17 m, −56 ft; highest point, Jabal ash Shanabi 1,544 m, 5,066 ft.

Tunnel See **engineering**.

Tupungato 6,550 m, 21,489 ft. This is the 12th highest peak in the **Andes**, and the ninth of 20 premier climbing peaks in that range; it was first climbed in 1897 by Stuart Vines and **Matthias Zurbriggen**. The peak is located in **Argentina**.

Turkey Lowest point, Mediterranean Sea 0 m; highest point, **Mt. Ararat** 5,165 m, 16,945 ft.

Turkey vulture This large black scavenger, which feeds only on carcasses, can be seen soaring (as high as 8,000 ft) in almost all habitats. Nests can be found on cliffs or in crevices (Johnsgard).

Turkmenistan Lowest point, Vpadina Akchanaya −81 m, −266 ft (note—Sarygamysh Koli is a lake in northeastern Turkmenistan whose water levels fluctuate widely; at its shallowest, its level is −110 m; it is presently at −60 m, 20 m above Vpadina Akchanaya); highest point, Ayrybaba 3,139 m, 10,299 ft.

Turks and Caicos Islands Lowest point, Caribbean Sea 0 m; highest point, Blue Hills 49 m, 161 ft.

Turning In **skiing**, it is necessary to turn not merely to conform to the direction of the slope or trail but also to control one's speed, which, because of gravity, can quickly soar to 50 or 60 miles per hour if unchecked. Turning on skis entails many subtle movements (including edging), but most important are weighting and unweighting the downhill or uphill ski and some form of body rotation. How one manages a turn depends on the particular method one is applying. Turning in **snowboarding** requires weighting the tip of the board and pushing with the back leg. Turning on a skeleton or similar device requires the use of the feet, body, and the contoured run along which the sled is speeding.

Tuvalu Lowest point, Pacific Ocean 0 m; highest point, unnamed location 5 m, 16 ft.

Tyndall, Prof. John (1820–1893) Born: England. A prolific British climber who made the first ascent of the **Weisshorn** in 1861. He was also a scientist and worked extensively on the problem of **glacier** formation, a subject that also fascinated **Jean Louis Agassiz**. Bibliography: *The Glaciers of the Alps* (1860), *Mountaineering in 1861* (1862), *Hours of Exercise in the Alps* (1871).

Tyrant A small, diversely named bird of many species. The puna ground-tyrant enjoys the thin Andean air at 16,500 ft (Fjeldså and Krabbe).

Tyrolean traverse In mountaineering, moving across a gap on a rope attached above the climber (Fyffe); also, **rappelling** horizontally or barely supporting oneself supported by a tense rope.

U

Uganda Lowest point, Lake Albert 621 m, 2,037 ft; highest point, Margherita Peak on **Mt. Stanley** 5,109 m, 16,763 ft.

Ukraine Lowest point, Black Sea 0 m; highest point, Hora Hoverla 2,061 m, 6,762 ft.

Ullman, James Ramsey (1908–1971) Born: United States. Bibliography: *High Conquest: The Story of Mountaineering* (1941), *The White Tower* (1945), *Kingdom of Adventure Everest* (1947), *Tiger of the Snows* (1955), *Americans on Everest* (1964), *Straight Up* (1968).

Ulugh Muztagh 7,723 m, 25,340 ft. This major peak is located within the Kunlun Range in **Tibet**. It was first ascended in 1985, by Hu Fengling, Zhang Baohua, Ardaxi, Mamuti, and Wu Qiangxing.

Unclimbed The question of which is the highest unclimbed peak is a very interesting one for mountaineers; it is thought to be **Bhutan**'s Gangkar Phunsum (Punsum) at 7,541 m, 24,770 ft. Other unclimbed high peaks include the southeast summit of **Makalu** 8,010 m, 26,280 ft, located some 20 km southeast of **Everest**; the east summit of **Manaslu** 7,992 m, 26,220 ft, in the Gurka Himal; and the east peak of **Nuptse** 7,804 m, 25,604 ft, in the Khumbu Himal. All these peaks are in **Nepal**. The information presented here is derived from a list compiled for Peakware by Simon Perritaz, and gathered from the UIAA (Union Internationale des Associations d'Alpinisme); for more details, see the appendix F and the excellent, highly informative website www.peakware.com/encyclopedia/unclimbed.htm.

Underwater mountains Although most mountains rise above land, some, like the Hawaiian **volcanoes**, rise from the bottom of the ocean; others barely make it to the surface; and some mountains are entirely submarine.

Union Internationale des Associations d'Alpinisme (UIAA) An organization of more than 80 member associations; its website offers links to innumerable other useful and informative sites (www.uiaa.ch).

United Arab Emirates Lowest point, Persian Gulf 0 m; highest point, Jabal Yibir 1,527 m, 5,010 ft.

United Kingdom Lowest point, Fenland −4 m, −13 ft; highest point, **Ben Nevis** 1,343 m, 4,406 ft. Despite the lack of high mountain ranges in the United Kingdom, it has played a prominent role in the history of alpinism, and many superb climbers and mountaineers hail from that country, including **Whymper** and **Bonington**.

United States Lowest point, Badwater, **Death Valley** −86 m, −282 ft; highest point, **Denali** 6,194 m, 20,320 ft. The United States of America (9,166,600 sq km, 3,539,242 sq miles) is the fourth largest country in the world, after **Russia**, **Canada**, and **China**; it contains numerous important mountain ranges, including: the **Rocky Mountains**, the **Sierras**, the **Cascades**, the Coast Ranges along the Pacific Ocean, and the **Appalachians**, all within the 48 lower states. **Alaska**, the 49th state, is in itself an incredibly rich mountain area comprising a complex system of ranges and massifs. **Hawaii**, the 50th state, features several very large **volcanoes**. (See also color photos.)

United States Geological Survey (USGS) Founded in 1879, the USGS is an arm of the government that classifies, explores, and maps the biological, hydrological, and physical makeup of the country. Its surveys and maps are invaluable (www.usgs.gov).

United States Ski and Snowboard Association (USSA) Founded in 1904, this is the governing body of **Olympic skiing** and **snowboarding** (www.ussa.org).

University Peak 4,411 m, 14,470 ft. Located near **Mt. Bona** in the **Wrangell–St. Elias National Park**, this is a beautiful mountain in a remote location.

Unsoeld, Willi (1926–1979) A great mountaineer; along with Tom Hornbein, he holds the first ascent of **Everest** by the west ridge route. In 1976, he and his daughter, **Nanda Devi**, attempted to reach the summit of the Indian mountain for which she was named. Typically, she did not survive the climb.

Unsworth, Walter (1928–) Born: England. He has published numerous important books and guidebooks and has worked extensively as a magazine editor. Bibliography: *The Young Mountaineer* (1959), *The English Outcrops* (1964), *Matterhorn Man* (1965), *Tiger in the Snow* (1967), *Because It Is There* (1968), *The Book of Rock Climbing* (1968), *North Face* (1969), *The High Fells of Lakeland* (1972), *Encyclopaedia of Mountaineering* (1975), *Walking and Climbing* (1977), *Everest: A Mountaineering History* (1981), *Peaks, Passes and Glaciers* (1981), *This Climbing Game* (1984), *Classic Walks of the World* (1985), *Savage Snows* (1986), *An Illustrated Companion into Lakeland* (1989), *Hold the Heights: The Foundations of Mountaineering* (1994).

Uplift The upward movement of the earth due to **tectonic plate** activity.

Upthrust The lifting action at the contact between two **tectonic plates**; upthrust is mainly responsible for the formation of mountains, volcanic activity being the other major geological phenomenon capable of producing large mountains.

Urals A ca. 1,500-mile **range** in **Russia**.

Uruguay Lowest point, Atlantic Ocean 0 m; highest point, Cerro Catedral 514 m, 1,686 ft.

Utah Lowest point, Beaver Dam Wash, **Arizona** border 610 m, 2,000 ft; highest point, **Kings Peak** 4,123 m, 13,528 ft (seventh highest of the 50 state highpoints). This is a very interesting state from the viewpoints of the climber and geologist alike; superb mountains and unusual rock formations and geological features abound, as reflected by the numerous **national parks** one finds in Utah, including Zion, Arches, Canyon, and Bryce Canyonland, as well as **Monument Valley**.

Uzbekistan Lowest point, Sariqarnish Kuli −12 m, −39 ft; highest point, Adelunga Toghi 4,301 m, 14,111 ft.

V

Vail A town and major ski area located in **Colorado**.

Val d'Aosta A region in Italy bounded by extraordinary mountains: **Gran Paradiso**, **Monte Rosa**, **Mont Blanc**, and the **Matterhorn**. At **Courmayeur**, one will find the duke of **Abruzzi**'s mountaineering museum.

Valais A small region of southwest **Switzerland,** where the **Valaisan Alps** are located.

Valaisan Alps A series of powerful ranges, comprising some of the highest peaks in the **Alps**: the **Monte Rosa** group, the **Mischabels**, the **Matterhorn**, and the **Weisshorn**. The **Valais** counts more 4,000-meter peaks than any other region in the Alps: 34 out of the 60 major peaks, including the second to tenth highest summits.

Valley *Vallée* (F), *Tal* (G). A low area that exists between the slopes of two parallel mountains or ranges (but also anywhere on earth where there is a depression). Some valleys are very narrow, which has not deterred humans from inhabiting them, often to their detriment, since debris falls and avalanches pose constant danger. Others are quite wide, for example, the Imperial Valley in California. The taxonomy is diverse and includes canyons, and hanging, rift, and glaciated valleys.

Vallot, Guide This is one of the most detailed and comprehensive guidebooks on any range in the world; it describes many hundred of routes in the **Mont Blanc Range**, and is constantly updated, to include new, and often extremely difficult, routes. A must for the serious climber interested in the **Massif** du **Mont Blanc**.

Vancouver, British Columbia This is a lovely city surrounded by beautiful mountains and the waters of the Pacific Ocean, in the South Georgia Straight, the beginning of the **Inside Passage**. Nearby is the world-famous ski resort of Whistler, and Garibaldi Provincial Park. (See also the **10 Mountain Resort Cities** sidebar.)

Vancouver, Mt. 4,812 m, 15,788 ft. The eighth highest peak in Canada; it is located in the **Yukon** and **Alaska**, in the **Saint Elias Mountains**. It is a heavily glaciated summit standing between **Alverstone Peak** and **Cook Peak**, near the ocean, where powerful gales rage during the winter months. It straddles the boundary between the **Wrangell–St. Elias** and **Kluane-Logan National Parks**.

Vanuatu Lowest point, Pacific Ocean 0 m; highest point, Tabwemasana 1,877 m, 6,158 ft.

Vaughan, Norman (1905–) Accompanied Admiral Byrd to Antarctica as a dog handler. A few years ago, he climbed Mt. Vaughn in the Antarctic, named in his honor. In 2005, on his 100th birthday, he plans to reclimb it.

Vegetation The botanical material of a specific location. (See also **plants**.)

Venables, Stephen (1954–) A phenomenal British mountaineer, pioneering, for example, the Kangshung face of **Everest** in 1988. Bibliography: *Painted Mountains* (1986), *Everest, Kangshung Face* (1989), *A Slender Thread* (2000).

Venezuela Lowest point, Caribbean Sea 0 m; highest point, Pico Bolivar (La Columna) 5,007 m, 16,427 ft.

Vent An opening in a **volcano** from which lava, ash, or gas is emitted.

Verdon, Grand Canyon du   This is the deepest gorge in **France**, with vertical limestone cliffs exceeding 600 m, 2,000 ft. It is located in Provence, in the southeast of France, with good weather prevailing, and offers the most challenging pure rock climbing in that country. The region is lovely and picturesque; some 50 miles to the south lies the French Riviera, while the canyon is located within the **Southern Alps**.

Verglas   (prn. vergla) A thin coating of **ice** on **rock**. It makes climbing extremely difficult.

Vermont   Lowest point, Lake Champlain 23 m, 75 ft; Highest point, **Mt. Mansfield** 1,339 m, 4,393 ft (26th highest of the 50 state highpoints). The "Green Mountain State" is a beautiful, picturesque, rural state that reflects the idyllic beauty of New England, as described by Thoreau; the winters, however, are powerful, and can ensconce the entire area under a crystalline layer of blue ice. Good skiing can be found there.

Vermont Marble Museum   Located in Proctor, near an old **quarry**, this is the largest collection of **marble**-related artifacts in the world. The extensive exhibits offer overviews of geology, quarrying, various types of marble, and the diverse products that derive from this useful stone (www.Vermont-Marble.com).

Vertical Limit   A 2000 American action film, directed by New Zealander Martin Campbell, starring Chris O'Donnell and Robin Tunney. It is set on **K2**, but it was shot in Utah and New Zealand. There are many problems with the unrealistic plot and the impossible things that the climbers are apparently able to do. Thus, purists find the film objectionable as the following summary, noted on a website, insists: "Everything shown about belaying and climbing techniques, high altitude mountaineering, helicopter usage, high altitude medicine . . . , high altitude mountaineering clothes, and the shape of K2 is wrong." Despite all of this, audiences did enjoy the film. **Ed Viesturs** makes a cameo appearance. (See also the **10 Best Hollywood Mountain Movies** sidebar.) (M-A. H.)

Vesuvius, Mt.   (Also Vesuvio) 1,281 m, 4,202 ft. An active volcano in southern Italy. An eruption in 79 C.E. buried Herculaneum and **Pompeii**.

The New Cone of Vesuvius, Shrouded in Snow-White Ashes (National Geographic)

Victoire sur l'Annapurna   A 1953 French documentary by **Marcel Ichac** concerning **Herzog**'s 1950 Himalayan expedition. Considering his love of adventure and climbing, it is no wonder that Ichac created an epic account of the first successful ascent of an 8,000-meter peak. Unlike *The Conquest of Everest*, this film enhances the difficulties of the expedition with all of the cinematic elements available at the time. The lack of accurate maps (which forced the members to alter their plans), the weather, the climbing, the snowstorm on their descent, and the difficult and painful return to civilization are all genuinely suspenseful and moving. And Ichac always knew how to present the feeling of immensity: his color photography above 6,000 meters was among the first to reach the screen. Involved as it is, the film is part of the legend of this expedition, as is Herzog's account in *Annapurna*. Neither, naturally, gives any indication of the recent controversies concerning the expedition. (M-A. H.)

Vicuña   Similar to the **llama** and **alpaca**, these **animals** roam to 16,000 ft in the **Andes**.

Vie Ferrate   (Italian for iron routes) Those 80 high **Dolomite** routes that have been equipped with excessive climbing aids including wires, ladders, and bridges (http://freespace.virgin.net/paul.benham/dolo/dolomites.htm).

Viesturs, Ed   (1959–) One of the world's premiere mountaineers; he is one of the few non-Sherpas to climb **Everest** five times, and he is currently completing climbs of the 14 **8,000-meter peaks** without supplementary **oxygen** (www.edviesturs.com). (See also **Pete Athans** and **Reinhold Messner**.)

Vietnam   Lowest point, South China Sea 0 m; highest point, Ngoc Linh 3,143 m, 10,312 ft.

Vinatzer, Hans   (fl. 1930s) According to Ardito, Vinatzer "was one of the best climbers of all time"; he sometimes climbed rock barefoot.

Vinson, Mt.   (Also Vinson Massif) 4,897 m, 16,066 ft. The highest mountain in **Antarctica**. It was first climbed in 1966 by an American expedition sponsored by the **National Geographic Society**, the National Science Foundation, and the **American Alpine Club**. (See also the **Seven Summits** sidebar.)

Violet   A common **flower** that comes in blue, white, or yellow varieties.

Virga   A meteorological phenomenon, whereby rain evaporates before reaching the ground. (See also color photos.)

Virgin Islands   Lowest point, Caribbean Sea 0 m; highest point, Crown Mountain 474 m, 1,555 ft.

Virginia   Lowest point, Atlantic Ocean 0 m; highest point, Mt. Rogers 1,746 m, 5,729 ft (19th highest of the 50 state highpoints). A lovely state, with beautiful mountain areas; the highpoint is located in an idyllic spot, with nice views along the path to the summit.

Virunga Mountains   Located near the **Great Rift Valley** of East Africa, this is where the **Nyiragongo volcano** is found. Virunga is also sometimes spelled Birunga, and the range itself may be called the Mufumbiro Mountains. The range is volcanic and extends for some 80 km, 50 miles, north of Lake Kivu in east-central Africa, along the borders of Congo, Rwanda, and Uganda. The range contains eight major volcanic peaks, the highest being **Karisimbi** 4,507m, 14,787 ft. The area has been designated as a national park.

Visser-Hooft, Jenny   (1888–1939) Born: England. Bibliography: *Among the Kara-Korum glaciers in 1925* (1926).

Volcanic activity   Steve O'Meara has theorized that there is a strong correlation between gravity, lunar influence, and tidal activity on the one hand and volcanic eruptions on the other. Despite his empirical verifications, many geologists remain skeptical, but see Junzo Kasahara's iconoclastic piece in *Science* in which he affirms the possibility.

Volcanic plug   (Or neck) A solitary **lava** extrusion that is resistant to **erosion** and thus remains standing after the surrounding material has worn away. Examples include **Devil's Tower** in **Wyoming**, **Shiprock** in **New Mexico**, and Black Tusk in the **Garibaldi** Provincial Park of **British Columbia**.

Volcano   A hole in the earth's surface through which **magma** transformed into **lava** pours; the mountain that emerges from this. Because geothermal activity manifests itself in diverse

Volcano Chronology (Marie Madgwick)

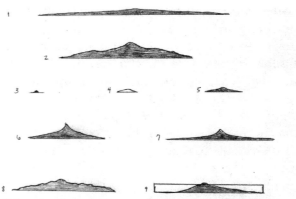

Volcanic Forms (Laura Lindblad); 1. Flood Basalt Flow, 2. Kilimajaro Shield, 3. Cinder Cone, 4. Lava Dome, 5. Vesuvius–Composite, 6. Fuji–Composite, 7 Mt. St. Helens–Composite, 8 Shasta–Composite, 9 Stromboli–Composite

ways and to varying degrees, volcanoes differ from each other in etiology, form, and size. A cinder cone consists of material that has been expelled into the air (e.g., **Paricutín**); these cones grow very quickly. A composite or strato-volcano results from an accumulation of cinder and ash layered with lava (e.g., **Fuji-san**). A

Volcanic Seven Summits

Africa: Kilimanjaro 5,895 m, 19,340 ft, in Tanzania (also the highpoint)

Antarctica: Mt. Sidley 4,181 m, 13,717 ft, in Marie Byrd Land

Asia: Damavand 5,670 m, 18,603 ft, in Iran

Australasia and Oceania: Mauna Kea 4,205 m, 13,796 ft, in Hawaii

Europe: Elbrus 5,642 m, 18,510 ft, in Russia (also the highpoint)

North America: Orizaba 5,700 m, 18,700 ft, in Mexico

South America: Nevado Ojos del Salado 6,880 m, 22,572 ft, in Chile (also the highest volcano in the world)

10 Highest Volcanoes

1. Nevado Ojos del Salado 22,572 ft, 6,880 m, Chile and Argentina
2. Monte Pissis 22,240 ft, 6,779 m, Argentina
3. Cerro Mercedario 22,211 ft, 6,770 m, Chile and Argentina
4. Volcan Llullaillaco 22,057 ft, 6,723 m, Chile and Argentina
5. Cerro Cazadero 21,844 ft, 6,658 m, Chile and Argentina
6. Nevados Tres Cruces 21,719 ft, 6,620 m, Chile and Argentina
7. Cerro de Incahuasi 21,656 ft, 6,601 m, Chile and Argentina
8. Cerro Tupungato 21,489 ft, 6,550 m, Chile and Argentina
9. Nevado Sajama 21,423 ft, 6,520 m, Bolivia
10. Cerro Bonete 21,020 ft, 6,410 m, Argentina

shield volcano derives from fluids that pour out of vents without any explosive eruption; thus, its slopes are very gradual and it resembles a flattened **dome** (e.g., *Mauna Kea*). And a **volcanic plug** or neck is all that remains of an eroded volcano (e.g., **Devils Tower**) (Ritchie and Gates). Active volcanoes (of which there are currently 1,500) either continuously or intermittently eject material; dormant volcanoes no longer erupt but could; and extinct volcanoes are completely extinguished. The world's highest volcano is Chile's **Llullaillaco**. Indonesia, Iceland, and New Zealand have many active volcanoes, and the Aleutian area in **Alaska** is the most active area on earth. (See Simkin and Siebert's *Volcanoes of the World* for a listing of all volcanoes and a complete chronology of eruptions.) Of the many germane websites, see especially that of *Volcano World* (http://volcano.und .nodak.edu/vw.html).

Volcanoes National Park See Hawaii Volcanoes National Park.

Volcanoes on other worlds Mars, Mercury, and Venus all have **volcanoes. Olympus Mons,** on Mars, "is the largest mountain in the solar system" (Vogel). (See also color photos.)

Vulture A large carrion eater that comes in many species; these **birds** soar to sometimes great heights. The Himalayan griffon vulture roams as high as 15,000 ft; the bearded vulture or lammergeyer (with a 10-ft wingspan) enjoys Himalayan altitudes to 13,000 ft (Ali) and has been seen flying above 30,000 ft! It can also be found in the Ethiopian highlands (Williams).

W

Waddington, Mt. 4,019 m, 13,186 ft. Located in **Canada**'s **British Columbia** Coast Range, Waddington is the highest summit entirely within that province, as **Fairweather** is shared with **Alaska**. It is also the 37th highest peak in Canada, and was first climbed in 1936 by Fritz Wiessner and William House. Mt. Waddington is a magnificent mountain, located only 40 km, or 25 miles, from the seashore, at Knight Inlet; as a result many strong storms from the Gulf of Alaska deposit extremely large quantities of snow, feeding large and extensive **glaciers**. The area is wild and extremely remote, inhabited by numerous bears; large remnant **ice fields**, including the Homathko Ice Field lie within the Waddington Range. The Waddington group includes a number of extremely impressive, heavily glaciated, and very isolated peaks: **Mt. Tiedemann** 3,848 m, 12,625 ft; Combatant Mountain 3,756 m, 12,323 ft; Mt. Asperity 3,716 m, 12,192 ft; Serra 3,642 m, 11,949 ft; Mt. Munday 3,367m, 11,047 ft; Spearman 3,365 m, 11,040 ft; Arabesque Peaks 3,072 m, 10,079 ft; Bravo Peak 3,105 m, 10,187 ft; Stiletto 3,397 m, 11,145 ft; Damocles 3,487 m, 11,440 ft; and Hickson 3,171 m, 10,404 ft. Large glaciers include: Franklin, Corridor, Agar, Tiedemann, Repose, and Scimitar. On the north side of Tiedemann Glacier, there is a small **refuge**, the Plummer hut. (See also color photos.)

Wadi A channel, ravine, or valley through which water runs in Near Eastern desert environments. Wadis are often dry until a rainstorm causes a large flow of water for a short period.

Wainwright, Alfred (1907–1991) Born: Blackburn, England. Bibliography: *Wainwright the Biography* (1991), by Hunter Davies.

Wake Island Lowest point, Pacific Ocean 0 m; highest point, unnamed location 6 m, 20 ft.

Walk See **hike**.

Walker, Horace (1838–1908) His first ascents include the **Barre des Écrins** (1864), the **Obergabelhorn** (1865), and **Elbrus** (1874). One of the summits of the **Grandes Jorasses** and one of the main spurs of that mountain bear his name.

Walker, James Hubert (1901) Born: Scotland. Bibliography: *Mountain Days in the Highlands and Alps* (1937), *On Hills of the North* (1948), *Walking in the Alps* (1951).

Walker, Lucy (1835–1916) A mountaineer; she was the first woman to reach the **Matterhorn**'s summit (1871).

Walker Spur See **Grandes Jorasses**.

Wall (Also face) *Face* and *morale* (F), *mural* (I), *wand* (G). In rock climbing, a steep, expansive side of a cliff or mountain. Big walls extend upwards uninterrupted for thousands of feet. (See also **headwall**.)

Wall creeper A **bird** indigenous to Europe and Asia; it can nest as high as 18,000 ft.

Wallis and Futuna Lowest point, Pacific Ocean 0 m; highest point, Mont Sinai 765 m, 2,510 ft.

Walsh, Mt. 4,505 m, 14,780 ft. This high peak is located in the general vicinity of **Mt. Lucania** and **Mt. Steele**, in the **Kluane-Logan National Park**. These mountains are very remote, and accessible only by plane; the weather can be dangerous, since the whole range is exposed to fast-moving storms from the Gulf of **Alaska**.

Wand In mountaineering, a thin bamboo or metal staff to which a small, colorful flag is attached. On an ascent, a series of wands are placed in the snow to guide climbers on their return trip.

Even a GPS-equipped climber may wish to consider their use. Wands can eliminate navigational mistakes and save lives.

Warbler There are innumerable species of this **bird** and some of them visit the mountain environment, for example, the yellow and blackpoll. In East Africa, the cinnamon bracken can sometimes be found above 12,500 ft; the brown woodland and black-collared appalls are highland birds (Williams).

Ward, Michael Phelps (1925–) Born: England. A physician by training, he was the doctor on the 1953 British **Everest** expedition. Bibliography: *The Mountaineer's Companion* (1966), *In This Short Span* (1972), *Man at High Altitude* (1974), *Mountain Medicine* (1975).

Ward's trogon An exceptionally colorful **bird** that, in the **Himalayas**, manages to reach almost 10,000 ft (Ali).

Washburn, Barbara (1914–) Wife of **Bradford Washburn**; she was the first woman to stand on the summit of **Denali**.

Washburn, Bradford (1910–) A superb mountaineer and pioneer in observing **Denali**. His early aerial photographs are stunning, and his cartographic accomplishments are unequalled. At well over 90, he continued his work at Boston's Museum of Science. He made the first or early ascents of **Mt. Lucania** and **Mt. Steele**, and pioneered the West Buttress route on **Denali**. In 2003, at the age of 93, he published *Mount McKinley's West Buttress: The First Ascent*, his log of the first climb of what is now the most popular route. This oversize book includes 79 of his extraordinary photographs. Bibliography: *The Dishonorable Dr. Cook: Debunking the Notorious Mount McKinley Hoax; The Trails and Peaks of the Presidential Range of the White Mountains* (1926), *Among the Alps with Bradford* (1927), *Bradford on Mount Washington* (1928), *Bradford on Mount Fairweather* (1930). (See also the **10 Best Mountain Photographers and Cinematographers** sidebar.)

Washington Lowest point, Pacific Ocean 0 m; highest point, **Mt. Rainier** 4,392 m, 14,411 ft (fourth highest of the 50 state highpoints). A wonderful state for mountain climbers, it counts 800 **glaciers** and numerous high peaks, including **Mt. Adams**, **Glacier Peak**, **Mt. Baker**, **Mt. Olympus**, and **Mt. St. Helens**.

Washington, Mt. 1,917 m, 6,288 ft. An impressive mountain in **New Hampshire**'s **Presidential Range**, it is also the highest point in that state. It provides hikers, climbers, and skiers with a diversity of possibilities. The latest spring skiing in the east can be found on Tuckerman's Ravine. Visitors can ascend on foot, by car, or on a cog railway (built in 1869). In 1934, the weather station at the top recorded the world's highest wind velocity, 231 mph. (See also appendix G.)

Water *Aqua* (I), *eau* (F), *Wasser* (G). Water plays a crucial role in the life of the mountain. Rain and melting snow or ice flow in rivulets that become streams and rivers that eventually replenish the evaporating oceans. Water, in the form of ice, comprises **glaciers**. Moving water and glaciers erode and thus dramatically alter the mountain's physiognomy; the most extraordinary example of the eroding power of liquid water can be seen at the Grand Canyon. Additionally, water offers sustenance to the indigenous animal and plant life that abounds in and around mountains. Finally, the mountains provide urban areas with their water supplies; surface rain water and especially glacial runoff is bottled as drinking water; in fact a number of fairly fancy waters come from various mountain ranges, including Evian (Alps), Perrier (Massif Central), San Pellegrino (Alps), and Big Bear Mountain (Southern Sierras); and in at least one instance it is used in the production of beer (Coors).

Water gap A **pass** through which water crosses; the Delaware Water Gap is a well-known example.

Waterfall As rain and melted snow move downward, the water sometimes flows over cliffs. These waterfalls can be insignificant or carry hundreds of thousands of gallons per minute over sheer walls hundreds of feet high. They are thus extremely impressive. Examples include Angel and Victoria Falls. See the World Wide Waterfalls Web, which leads to innumerable sites offering information and exquisite photographs: http://park10

.wakwak.com/~wwww/waterfall.html. (See also color photos.)

Wax When all skis were constructed out of wood, wax was a necessity: one spent some time prior to skiing applying various types of cold or hot wax depending on snow conditions and temperature, a process that helped to increase one's speed. Metal and fiberglass **downhill** skis with plastic bottoms made waxing superfluous for many recreational skiers, although some still do wax; racers continue to hone their skis in any way they can in order to improve their speeds. Cross-country skiers also continue to use wax.

Weather Weather in the mountains is like weather in the valleys: clear and cloudy, calm and stormy by turns. It is also different. There is perhaps no single, immediate element more important in the life of the mountain than the weather, which in extreme cases has a reciprocal, even symbiotic, relationship with the higher peaks. The weather controls and influences the mountain: its structure, evolution, ecology, and all of those living entities that visit or reside in, on, or near its environment. Concomitantly, the soaring **massifs** that reach up into the higher atmosphere, by their very presence, influence the production and movement of wind, clouds, precipitation, and air temperature. And naturally, volcanic eruptions change the local weather. All of these manifestations can dramatically alter global climatic conditions: A major storm in the **Himalayas** may send cold air and winds into distant areas and the eruption of an Indonesian **volcano** can cause weather-related problems for farmers thousands of miles away: Krakatoa's explosion resulted in cooler air temperatures around the globe. The mountain mass and its altitude are but two of the controlling factors; things are naturally more complex. Whiteman points out that latitude, whether a mountain is near the edge or the center of a continent, and regional circulations (winds and ocean currents) also influence weather patterns. Given the extended periods that occur within geological time, wind, precipitation, and glaciers will erode even the hardest rock surfaces (see **weathering**). These forces work slowly but in-

exorably, grinding the mountain down first to lower elevations, then to mere hills, and finally to plains, at which time the **mountain building** process may commence again. Even smaller rock or earth masses produce or attract fog and mist, so naturally large mountains create true microclimates. It is not unusual to find a clear sky surrounding **Rainier**, but a trailing cloud ensconcing the peak. **Denali**, **Everest**, and hundreds of other enormous mountains produce or enhance cloud systems, wind, and precipitation. Weather in the mountains has a dramatic effect on plant, animal, and human life. As altitude increases, precipitation, solar **radiation**, temperature, and wind alter, and these changes affect living entities, some of which can no longer survive under these different and often harsher conditions. Plant and animal species diminish in number as the altitude increases; eventually **timberline** is reached and trees and then even flowers stop propagating; glaciated peaks are generally devoid of plants. Some animal species roam quite high but if the harshness of the weather obviates other life forms (for sustenance), snow leopards or **vultures** will move downward. Humans have the advantage of being able to clothe themselves in warm materials and so can survive in the extreme weather found at altitude, at least for short periods. But even the warmest protective materials can fail and modern mountaineers continue to perish because of fierce storms, which can produce many feet of new snow during the course of a night, hundred mile an hour winds, and real temperatures as low as −50 or −60 degrees Fahrenheit. Wind chills are obviously extreme. Since skin freezes at −67°F, no part of the body can be exposed. (At −40°F. real temperature, the warmly clothed junior author of this book could feel the cold only inside his eyes.) One of the most dangerous weather phenomena for people exposed at altitude is **lightning**. Since the standing person, replete with metallic, lightning-attracting pack frame, tent poles, and ice ax is the highest point on a summit or ridge, he or she is prone to strikes, which are harmful or fatal. Every year, a surprising number of people are killed by lightning (some 200 in the United States); those who survive may still have ongoing health problems. Authors approach the weather from a variety of different angles: The most recent edition of *Mountaineering* (Cox and Fulsaas) offers pragmatic advice; Jacqueline Smith's dictionary is excellent for terminology and a list of useful websites; and C. David Whiteman's *Mountain Meteorology* is comprehensive, informative, and includes an extensive specialized glossary (see www3.bc.sympatico.ca/lightningsurvivor)

Weathering The effect that weather has on rock and other surfaces. Wind, water, and abrasive particles are responsible for alterations in mountain forms, but so too are chemicals such as those contained in **acid rain**. Chemical weathering, for example, oxidation, refers to changes in the **mineral** content of a rock (Hamblin and Christiansen). (See also **erosion**.)

Weathers, Beck (1946–) In 1996, he was one of the many climbers trapped in the open on the **descent** from **Everest**'s **summit**. He was left for dead twice, but then many hours later re-vived, arose, and reached the tents. He lost some extremities but continues in his work as a pathologist and speaks around the country. (See his account in *Left for Dead*.)

Webbing A synthetic material such as nylon that comes in various widths. It is tied in loops of differing length for various purposes (**protection**, ax attachment) in climbing.

Websites The Worldwide Web is replete with innumerable sites that offer useful data and information on mountains. Many of these are noted in various entries in this volume. The outstanding examples can be found in the **24 Great Websites** sidebar.

Webster, Ed (1956–) A climber who ascended **Everest** via the Kangshung Face without supplemental oxygen or **Sherpa** aid. (He did not reach the summit.) His exploits are recounted in *Snow in the Kingdom,* an extraordinary volume replete with black-and-white and color photographs.

Wedeln To move one's parallel skis to the left and right very quickly, so that the turns are short and swift; only an expert skier can perform this.

24 Great Websites

Adventure Photographs: www.adventurephotographs.com

All about Glaciers: http://nsidc.org/glaciers/glossary

Ancient Bristlecone Pine: www.sonic.net/bristlecone

Appalachian Mountain Club: www.outdoors.org

Cascades Volcanoes Observatory: http://vulcan.wr.usgs.gov

Climbing Dutchman: www.climbingdutchman.com

EverestNews.com: www.everestnews.com

Illustrated Glossary of Alpine Glacial Landforms: www.uwsp.edu/geo/faculty/lemke/alpine_glacial_glossary/

Mountain Forum: www.mountainforum.org

Mountain Voice: www.mountainvoices.org

Mountain Zone: www.mountainzone.com

Mountains: www.mountains.it

Mountains on the Earth: www.igf.fuw.edu.pl/hill

National Geographic: www.nationalgeographic.com

National Park Service: www.nps.gov

Peakware World Mountain Encyclopedia: www.peakware.com

Rays Web: http://raysweb.net

Sacred Places: Mountains and the Sacred: www.arthistory.sbc.edu/sacredplaces/mountains.html

Ski Mountains of the United States and Canada: http://Skimountains.com

Union Internationale des Associations d'Alpinisme: www.uiaa.ch

Virtual Cascades: http://virtualcascades.com

Virtual Wildlife Mountains: www.panda.org/kids/wildlife/mnmntain.htm

Webref.org: www.webref.org/geology

Wildflowers of the Santa Monica Mountains: www.timetotrack.com/jay

Wedge In skiing, tips close, tails apart; this term has replaced **snowplow**. (See also **nut**.)

Weihenmayer, Erik (1968–) The first blind climber to reach the summit of **Everest** (2001) and the first and only to complete the **Seven Summits**. (See his *Touch the Top of the World*.)

Weir, Thomas (1914–) Born: Glasgow, Scotland. A gifted climber, traveler, and photographer. Bibliography: *Highland Days* (1948), *The Ultimate Mountains* (1953), *Camps and Climbs in Arctic Norway* (1953), *East of Katmandu* (1955), *Focus on Mountains* (1965), *Weir's World* (1994), autobiography.

Weisshorn 4,505 m, 14,780 ft. This is the eighth highest of the 60 major 4,000-meter peaks in the **Alps**. One of the most powerful summits in the Alps of **Valais**, it was first climbed in 1861, by John Tyndall, J. J. Benin, and Ulrich Wenger. The north ridge is long and **serrated**; it is a classic climb in the Alps. (See also color photos.)

Weissmies 4,023 m, 13,199 ft. This is the 55th highest of the 60 major 4,000-meter peaks in the **Alps**. The first ascent occurred in 1855, by Peter-Josef Zurbriggen and Jokob-Christian Heusser. The mountain is located near the eastern boundary of the **Valais**, in **Switzerland**.

Welzenbach, Willo (1900–1934) Born: Germany. An excellent rock and ice climber and mountaineer; he is associated with the **Munich School** (Unsworth, *Encyclopaedia*). Bibliography: *Welzenbach's Climbs* (1981) by Eric Roberts.

West Bank Lowest point, **Dead Sea** −408 m, −1,339 ft; highest point, Tall Asur 1,022 m, 3,353 ft.

West Virginia Lowest point, Potomac River, on the **Virginia** border 73 m, 240 ft; highest point, Spruce Knob 1,482 m, 4,863 ft (24th highest of the 50 state highpoints).

Western Cwm The long **valley** that leads up toward the **South Col** on **Everest**.

Western Sahara Lowest point, Sebjet Tah −55 m, −180 ft; highest point, unnamed location 463 m, 1,519 ft.

Wheeler Peak 4,011 m, 13,161 ft. The highest point in **New Mexico**, it is a lovely mountain, with beautiful vistas.

Wheeler Peak 3,982 m, 13,063 ft. The second highest peak in **Nevada** after **Boundary Peak**, it also has a small **glacier** on its north side, which is the southernmost glacier in the **United States**.

Whillans, Donald Desbrow (1933–1985) A superb, extremely accomplished, and tough British mountaineer and rock climber, with many rock climbs and expeditions to his credit. He climbed extensively with **Joe Brown** in the 1950s and helped push the limits of **free** climbing to the highest standard in the world at the time. He holds some **first ascents**, including the Central Pillar of Fréney (Unsworth, *Encyclopaedia*). He also climbed the **Eiger** Direct in winter and made the first ascent of the south face of **Annapurna** with **Dougal Haston**. (Pat Ament, personal comment.) Bibliography: *The Hard Years* (1967), by Joe Brown, *Portrait of a Mountaineer* (1971), with Alick Ormerod.

White Mountain Peak 4,342 m, 14,246 ft. Located in the range bearing the same name, it is one of only two 14,000-foot peaks in **California**, together with **Shasta**, that is not in the **Sierras**. **Boundary Peak**, the highest point in **Nevada**, lies at the northern end of the White Mountain Range.

White Mountains A **chain** primarily in **New Hampshire** that includes the **Presidentials**. It is here that **Mt. Washington** is located.

The White Spider A superb book by **Heinrich Harrer**, it presents a personal account of the attempts to climb the notorious north wall of the **Eiger**, in 1938. As a member of the first party to climb the face, and although the book describes the grimness of the mountain environment, the author also communicates the joy he derives from climbing. (See also **10 Great Mountain Adventure Books** sidebar.)

The White Tower A 1950 American film directed by Ted Tetzlaff (1903–1995) that is based on a novel by **James Ramsey Ullman** (1908–1971) (see also **10 Great Mountain Adventure Books** sidebar). Carla Alten's father, a great climber, died during an attempt on the White Tower before World War II. After the war, Carla gathers a party to avenge her father. This is standard melodrama of the early 1950s. The climbing is only used as a way to enhance suspense and reveal the inner selves of the characters. Aside from the daring girl (Alida Valli) attempting to cure her Oedipus complex, one finds a weak and disabused French writer (Claude Rains) with a sour-tempered wife; a slow but mountain-wise Swiss guide (Oscar Homolka); an old English climber, aware of his faults (Sir Cedric Hardwicke); a bold German who turns out to be a Nazi (Lloyd Bridges); and a hard-to-convince American (Glenn Ford) who will win the heart of the leading lady. The good cast obviously enjoyed filming on location. Though set in the Swiss village of Andermatt, the film was entirely shot in the Chamonix Valley. The White Tower of the film is, in reality, the **Aiguille Verte**. The scenery, gorgeously shot in Technicolor, is extraordinary. Beware of black-and-white prints sometimes shown on TV. (M-A. H.)

Whiteout   A situation in which fog or falling or blowing **snow** is so severe that one cannot see more than a few feet in any direction.

Whitney, Mt.   4,417 m, 14,494 ft. This is the highest peak within the lower 48 contiguous states, and the highpoint in **California**. It is a towering granite **spire** on its eastern side, and a very large, gently sloping **plateau** on its western flank. The normal route begins at an altitude of approximately 8,500 ft, at Mt. Whitney Portal, a short drive from the town of Lone Pine, located in the **Owens Valley** of eastern California. It is so popular that it is now necessary to get a permit to hike or climb above 9,500 ft. (See also the appendix G.)

Whittaker, Jim   (1929–   ) The first American to reach the summit of **Everest** (1963), he was also president of **Recreational Equipment, Inc.** (and **Lou Whittaker**'s twin brother.)

Whittaker, Lou   (1929–   ) Climber and founder of Rainier Mountaineering, Inc. (and **Jim Whittaker**'s twin brother.)

Whymper, Edward   (1840–1911) Born: England. A pioneer in Alpine climbing. During the early 1860s, he visited various French and Swiss mountain areas, hired guides, and did many **first ascents** before he had to return to England at the end of each season, to work as an engraver in his father's business. Although shaken to the core after the terrible **accident**

that claimed many lives during the **descent** following the first successful climb of the **Matterhorn**, "Whymper did not stop exploring: he made two expeditions to **Greenland**, he climbed new peaks in the Andes and the Rockies with select Swiss guides—among them **Carrel**—and, his funds having been exhausted by these forays, wrote **guidebooks** to **Zermatt** and **Chamonix**." He later visited the Andes. His *Scrambles amongst the Alps* is a riveting account of his many exploits. His first ascents include: **Barre des Écrins** (1864), with A. W. Moore, **Horace Walker**, **Christian Almer**, and **Michel Croz**; **Grandes Jorasses**, Whymper and Croz summits (1864), with Almer, Croz, and F. Biner; **Aiguille d'Argentière** (1864); Grand Cornier (1865), with Almer, Croz, and Biner; **Aiguille Verte** (1865), with Almer and Biner; Matterhorn (1865), with Croz, Lord Francis Douglas, Douglas Hadow, **Charles Hudson**, and Peter Taugwalder father and son; **Chimborazo** (1880). Bibliography: *Scrambles amongst the Alps in the Years 1860–69* (1871), *Travels amongst the Great Andes of the Equator* (1891–92), *How to Use the Aneroid Barometer* (1891), *Chamonix and the Range of Mont Blanc* (1896), *The Valley of Zermatt and the Matterhorn* (1897), *A Right Royal Mountaineer* (1909), *Episodes from the Ascent of Mont Blanc* (1928), *Edward Whymper* (1940), biography by Frank Smythe, *The First Descent of the Matterhorn* (1997), by Alan Lyall. (See also the **12 Great Historical Mountaineers** sidebar.)

Wickwire, Jim   (1940–   ) In 1978, Wickwire and Louis Reichardt became the first Americans to summit **K2**. Wickwire is one of the few people to survive a **bivouac** high in the **death zone**.

Widow-bird   Finch-like in appearance, some species in East Africa range high: the Jackson's above 5,000 ft and the long-tailed above 6,000 ft (Williams).

Wiessner, Fritz Hermann Ernst   (1900–1988) A German and then extremely influential American **rock** climber and mountaineer; he holds the first ascents of **Mt. Waddington** (1936), **Devil's Tower** (1937) through a bold, unpro-

Fogbow on the Matterhorn, after the 1865 tragedy, by Edward Whymper (Alpine Club)

tected **lead** of a difficult off-width **crack**, among many others. In 1939, he almost reached the summit of **K2**.

Wilcox, Walter Dwight (1869–1949) Born: Canada. Bibliography: *Camping in the Canadian Rockies* (1896).

Wilderness Act This 1964 federal law aims to protect the wilderness for future generations. (See also **ethics**.)

Wilderness Medical Society An organization of medical professionals who care about health-related issues in the wilderness. (www.wms.org).

Williamson, Mt. 4,381 m, 14,375 ft. The second highest peak in **California**, it was first climbed in 1884 by W. L. Hunter and C. Mulholland.

Willow A deciduous tree that can be found at altitude.

Wills, Sir Alfred (1828–1912) Born: England. One of the founding members of the Alpine Club and its president, 1864–1865. Bibliography: *Wandering among the High Alps* (1856), *The Ascent of Mont Blanc* (1858), *'The Eagle's Nest' in the Valley of Sixt* (1860).

Wilson, Claude (1860–1937) A mountaineer with 360 important climbs to his credit. Unsworth calls him "One of the outstanding climbers of all time." (*Encyclopaedia*).

Wilson, Ken (1941–) Born: England. Bibliography: *The Black Cliff* (1971), with Jack Soper and Peter Crew, *Hard Rock* (1974), *Classic Rock* (1978), *The Games Climbers Play* (1978), *The Big Walks* (1980), *Classic Walks* (1982), *Cold Climbs* (1983), *Extreme Rock* (1986).

Wind *Vent* (F), *vento* (I), *wind* (G). Physical movement of the air caused by atmospheric alterations in temperature and pressure; it is measured on the Beaufort scale from 0 through 12.

Wind River Range A **range** in **Wyoming**; it is here that one will find **Gannett Peak**, the Wyoming **highpoint**. It is a mighty range, with numerous **glaciers**, and high peaks, including Fremont, 4,190 m, 13,745 ft, and Warren, 4,182 m, 13,720 ft. The Cirque of Towers is located in the south of the range; it is a beautiful, impressive site, where mighty **spires** reach into the deep blue skies of this great wilderness area, full of wildlife and unusual plants, well-adapted to the high, dry desert and cold winters.

Windbreak A wall built most frequently out of **rocks** but sometimes from blocks of cut snow in order to protect a tent. In a windy location, without a windbreak, even a superb tent may tear apart in high winds, which on certain peaks can reach 100 or more miles per hour.

Winds The winds that exist on and around **mountains** have specific names. Generically, a "mountain wind or breeze" evolves after sunset and flows down into valleys in the late night/ early morning hours; an anabatic wind moves upward in a valley while a katabatic moves down (Smith). The Alberta Clipper roars out of the Canadian **Rockies** and carries extremely cold weather to its east and south, especially to the Dakotas and **Minnesota**. During the winter months, the *föhn* periodically blows southward off the **Alps** and brings dramatically warmer temperatures; it may cause depression in the local inhabitants. This same phenomenon is called a chinook in the Rockies and a Santa Ana in California. A mistral is a cold Mediterranean occurrence that blows south between the Massif Central and the Alps, and a bora moves downward anywhere but especially in the Balkan Alps (Smith). A **monsoon** is a powerful wind that crosses the Indian subcontinent. (See also **wind**.)

Windy Mountain   4,130 m, 13,551 ft. A high peak located in the **Yukon** Territory in Canada.

Wine   Since Roman times, when Caesar's legions used to plant vineyards in the areas surrounding their fortified encampments, the ancestors of the great wine regions of **France** and **Italy**, it has been known that the **foothill** regions in the mountains were ideal and very fertile grounds to grow grapes. In the case of volcanic soil, the chemicals trapped in the highly permeable **igneous** rock act as natural fertilizers, while limestone and sandstone are also excellent locations for vineyards. In addition, the alternation of sun and shade in the valleys plays an important role in the process, as does the general prevailing weather patterns during the growing season. Mountain wines are produced in many locations, including the Alpine countries, where the Fendant is a good example. In the south of France, the Rhône Valley yields excellent wines produced on its steep hillsides such as Croze-Hermitage; Gigondas and Beaumes-de-Venise, near the Dentelles de Montmirail, at the foot of Mont Ventoux, also produce wine. The Burgundy region also uses many small, steep hillsides: Hautes Côte-de-Nuit, Aloxe-Corton, and Meursault, to name a few. In **Chile**, the foothills of the **Andes** are very fertile, and good wine is produced there. Finally, recently, in northern **California**, so-called "mountain wines" have appeared on the market; these rare wines are produced on the steep hills above the Napa and Sonoma Valleys, where unique climatic and soil conditions prevail, including misty, foggy autumn nights and very dry summers, which produce wines with unique taste and character.

Winter   The coldest season, when most snow accumulates in the mountains. In the Northern Hemisphere, it starts on the winter **solstice** on December 22, and ends at the **spring equinox**, on March 21. In the northern latitudes, above the **Arctic Circle**, the six-month polar night begins at the **fall** equinox, and reigns throughout fall and winter.

Winter ascent   This term designates a climb performed during the winter season, when conditions are at their coldest; generally, in the Northern Hemisphere, this would cover the months of November–March; however, such conditions can vary a great deal by region, and year to year. Winter ascents are generally much harder; the shorter days and large snow accumulation, especially on mixed terrain and rock, further complicate the endeavor. Therefore, first winter ascents are recorded separately from first ascents, just like solo ascents, or oxygen-free ascents in the **Himalayas**.

Wisconsin   Lowest point, Lake Michigan 176 m, 579 ft; highest point, Timms Hill 595 m, 1,951 ft (39th highest of the 50 state highpoints).

Wolf   A large, doglike **mammal**; the gray is widely distributed (even after years of harassment and destruction) across the northern United States, Canada, Europe, and Asia. It has recently been reintroduced in many areas. It may be found in the mountains.

Wolverine   A small bearlike **mammal** (weighing up to 55 pounds) now rarely found in Asia, Europe, and North America; it has the reputation of being one of the fiercest animals in the world.

Wombat   The common wombat (of Australia) is one of the few marsupials to wander into the mountains (Burnie and Wilson).

Wood Peak   4,842 m, 15,887 ft. This is the seventh highest peak in **Canada**; it is located in the **Saint Elias Mountains**, in the **Yukon**. It is heavily glaciated and extremely remote; it stands at the northern boundary of the **Kluane-Logan National Park**.

Woodpecker   A **bird** that varies dramatically in size from quite small (perhaps five inches) to enormous: the pileated is as large as a crow. Woodpeckers live in or near forested lands and peck at trees, but some feed in other ways. Williamson's sapsucker breeds at altitudes as high as 8,500 ft (Johnsgard) and the crimson-breasted pied as well as the darjeeling pied both journey above 13,000 ft in the **Himalayas** (Ali). In East Africa, the bearded and fine-banded prefer the highlands (Williams). In the **Andes**, many species can be found at altitude, for example, the Andean flicker, which reaches 16,500 ft (Fjeldså and Krabbe).

Woodrat   (Pack rat) A small **mammal**; it can be found near "caves, cliffs, and rocky outcrops" (Collins).

Workman,   William   Hunter   (1847–1937) Born: America. Publications, with Fanny Bullock Workman (1859–1925): *In the Ice-World of Himalaya* (1900), *Ice-Bound Heights of the Mustagh* (1908), *Peaks and Glaciers of Nun Kun* (1909), *The Call of the Snowy Hispar* (1910), *Two Summers in the Ice-Wilds of Eastern Karakoram* (1917).

Wrangell, Mt.   4,317 m, 14,163 ft. The only active volcano in the **Saint Elias Mountains**, this massive and heavily glaciated peak is a relatively easy climb, although access is difficult as always in this area.

Wrangell–Saint Elias Mountains   A series of **ranges** in **Alaska** and the **Yukon** that includes some **volcanoes**, many gigantic **glaciers**, and high mountains, e.g., **Alverstone** and **Atna Peaks, Mt. Augusta, Mt. Bear, Mt. Blackburn, Mt. Bona, Mt. Churchill, Cook Peak, Hubbard Peak, Regal Mountain, Mt. Sanford, Mt. Saint Elias**, Mt. Seattle, University Peak, **Mt. Vancouver**, and **Mt. Wrangell**.

Wrangell-St. Elias National Park   The largest park in the **United States**, it is bigger than the country of **Switzerland**. A powerful volcanic range lies in the northern reaches of the park, containing mighty peaks such as **Mt. Wrangell, Mt. Sanford, Mt. Blackburn**, and Mt. Drumm, 3,661 m, 12,010 ft. The highest peak in the park is **Mt. Saint Elias**, the fourth highest mountain in **North America** and the second highest peak both in the United States and **Canada** (it is located on the border). The Saint Elias coastal range is one of the highest in the world: from the Gulf of Alaska, Mt. Saint Elias rises some 5,000 m, 16,500 ft, directly over the **Malaspina Glacier**, and the surrounding peaks present an extraordinary wall to the fierce winter storms that rage in the Pacific Ocean; a superabundance of snow feeds the gigantic **glaciers** lying within the high ranges and deep **fjords**. Very high peaks also include **Mt. Bona, Mt. Churchill**, and **Mt. Bear**, and the boundary peaks along the border: **Mt. Augusta, Mt. Cook, Mt. Vancouver, Mt. Alverstone**, and **Hubbard Peak**. The Bagley **Ice Field** lies in the south of the park, as does the Columbia Glacier. Part of the enormous Logan Glacier and the 80-mile (128 km) long **Hubbard Glacier** are natural wonders found there. Wildlife is abundant and includes **bears** and **Dall sheep**. The region is remote, but offers superb climbing opportunities, far from the crowds attracted by mighty **Denali**.

Wren   A small **bird** of many species; the rock wren, according to Johnsgard, prefers various rocky terrains including **outcrops, cliffs**, and **talus** up to 12,000 ft.

Wright, Jeremiah Ernest Bamford   (1895–1975) Born: England. A professional **guide** who founded the Mountaineering Association. Bibliography: *Mountain Days in the Isle of Skye* (1934), *Technique of Mountaineering* (1955), *Rock Climbing in Britain* (1958).

Wyoming   Lowest point, Belle Fourche River, **South Dakota** border 945 m, 3,099 ft; highest point, **Gannett Peak** 4,207 m, 13,804 ft (the fifth highest of the 50 state highpoints). This is a very mountainous state, with high mountains, including the **Wind River** and **Teton** ranges.

Y

Yak An extremely hardy wild ox that roams to almost 20,000 ft in Asia; the domesticated version is used for transport in the **Himalayas**.

Yates, Simon (1963–) Born: Leicestershire, England. Bibliography: *Touching the Void* (1988), by **Joe Simpson**, *Against the Wall* (1997), *The Flame of Adventure* (2001).

Yellowstone National Park As indicated in the opening statement of its official website (www.nps.gov/yell/), "Established on March 1, 1872, Yellowstone National Park is the first and oldest national park in the world." This is a beautiful, pristine area located at the northwest corner of **Wyoming**; numerous peaks and **geysers** can be found in this highly active geothermal region. In addition, wildlife abounds in Yellowstone, including **bison**, **wolves**, **bears**, **coyotes**, **deer**, and numerous other species. The Grand Canyon of the Yellowstone River is a magnificent site, as are the Upper and Lower Falls of the Yellowstone. (See also color photos.)

Yemen Lowest point, Arabian Sea 0 m; highest point, Jabal an Nabi Shu'ayb 3,760 m, 12,336 ft.

Yerupajá Grande 6,634 m, 21,765 ft. This is the eighth highest peak in the **Andes**, and the seventh of 20 premier climbing peaks in that range; it was first climbed in 1950 by Dave Harrah and Jim Maxwell. The peak is located in the Cordillera **Huayhuash** of **Peru**, and is the second highest mountain in that country. It is an absolutely magnificent mountain, with very difficult routes.

Yeti (Also Abominable Snowman; in the northwestern United States, a similar creature is known as Bigfoot or Sasquatch; indeed, a diverse nomenclature exists, depending on geographical location.) A moot, humanlike creature said to inhabit the upper regions in the **Himalayas**. No example has ever been taken back to civilization, but some remarkable eyewitness accounts exist. Most convincing are Rawicz's comments in *The Long Walk*. Recent diverse scientific analyses of sasquatch sightings and physical castings have convinced some scientific researchers that the sasquatch is not a hoax. Even George Schaller, the noted zoologist, is open-minded. For more information see, **Messner**'s *My Quest for the Yeti*. (See also **yetis in movies**.)

Yetis in movies In 1951, *Time* published the photograph of a huge footprint found in the Himalayan snow. As might be expected, films quickly followed. Yetis were fresh and new, without scary legends or crimes attached to them—except, perhaps, the strange deaths of mountain goats. Yetis are often pictured in movies as overgrown beings with no evil intentions, facing curiosity and invasion. The calm surroundings of high snow enhances the vision of man as an intruder, while yetis seem to fit into their natural though hostile surroundings. However, yeti movies are generally not very good: *Snow Creature* (1954), for instance, has the beast played by an actor wearing a Halloween suit, and the story—written by the director's 19-year-old son—has the animal brought back to Los Angeles, where he is released into the sewers to meet a gruesome fate. *Man Beast* appeared in 1956; this is one of the very few films in which the yeti is the villain. The plot deals with fearless explorers climbing in the Himalayas. In the group is a traitor scouting for women to give to the beast. The 1977 film *Yeti, il Gigante del 20.*

Secolo is also rather poorly made: after the yeti is found stuck in the ice at the North Pole and brought to town, villains falsely accuse him in order to have him shot. Back in 1955, Japanese director Inoshiro "Gojira" Honda shot *Jû Jin Yuki Otoko*, which describes a big animal worshipped by villagers, caught by a circus troop. Once again, man is seen as the danger while the animal fights to protect itself. This approach fits the usual naive handling by the director, and the Japanese version of the movie is quite effective. The more available American version (*Half Human*) drops much of the original footage and, to avoid dubbing, adds John Carradine and a party stuck in a 10-square-foot studio, summing things up in horrific dialogue. Considered the best possible approach to yetis on screen is the 1957 British film *The Abominable Snowman*, starring Peter Cushing (*Dracula, Frankenstein*). People climb in the Himalayas in order to locate yetis, and the beasts are depicted as positive, if frightening, fellows. Director Val Guest conceals his lack of money by cautiously hiding the yetis—one hardly sees them—and switches from location (French **Pyrénées**) to the stage. The main problem here is that since outdoor filming was out of the question, the characters spend a lot of time seated in tents talking. (M-A. H.)

Yosemite Decimal System See **rating systems**.

Yosemite National Park Located in central **California**, Yosemite is home to **Half Dome**, **El Capitan**, and many other extraordinary and beautiful granitic formations and configurations that offer some of the best and most challenging **rock climbing** in the world.

Young, Geoffrey Winthrop (1876–1958) Born: near Cookham, England. An important British mountaineer who holds the **first ascent** of the northeast ridge route on the Nesthorn. He continued to climb after losing a leg in World War I (Unsworth, *Encyclopaedia*). Bibliography: *Wall and Roof Climbing* (1905), *Wind and Hill* (1909), *Freedom* (1914), *Mountain Craft* (1920), *April and Rain* (1923), *On High Hills* (1927), *Collected Poems* (1936), *In Praise of Mountains* (1948), with Eleanor Young, *Mountains with a Difference* (1951), *The Grace of Forgetting* (1953), *Influence of Mountains upon the Development of Human Intelligence* (1957), *Snowdon Biography* (1957), with Geoffrey Sutton and Wilfrid Noyce, *Geoffrey Winthrop Young* (1995), by Alan Hankinson (biography).

Younghusband, Sir Francis Edward (1863–1942) Born: England. He was one of the earliest explorers of the **Karakoram**. Bibliography: *The Heart of a Continent* (1896), *Kashmir* (1909), *Wonders of the Himalaya* (1924), *The Epic of Mount Everest* (1926), *Everest the Challenge* (1936), *Francis Younghusband, Explorer and Mystic* (1952) by George Seaver (biography)

Yukon Lowest point, Gulf of Alaska 0 m; highest point, **Mt. Logan** 5,959 m, 19,551 ft. This is where the highest mountains of **Canada** are, the **Saint Elias Mountains** being the most impressive and heavily glaciated. Major peaks include **Mt. Saint Elias** (on the **Alaska**–Yukon boundary) 5,489 m, 18,009 ft; **Mt. Lucania** 5,226 m, 17,146 ft; **King Peak** 5,173 m, 16,973 ft; **Mt. Steele** 5,037 m, 16,645 ft; **Mt. Wood** 4,838 m, 15,873 ft; **Mt. Vancouver** (on Alaska-Yukon boundary) 4,812 m, 15,788 ft, **Macaulay Peak** 4,690 m, 15,388 ft; **Mt. Slaggard** 4,742 m, 15,559 ft; and **Hubbard Peak** (on the Alaska–Yukon boundary) 4,577 m, 15,017 ft. This immense land of remote mountains and rich wildlife offers wonderful climbing opportunities; ski planes or helicopters provide the fastest approaches to these distant glaciated peaks. (See also color photos.)

Z

Zagros A range in **Iran**.

Zaire The former name of the **Democratic Republic of the Congo**.

Zambia Lowest point, Zambezi River 329 m, 1,079 ft; highest point, unnamed location in Mafinga Hills 2,301 m, 7,549 ft.

Zermatt The Swiss village at the foot of the **Matterhorn**, a mecca for Alpinists and mountaineers from all over the world, and a challenging ski area in winter.

Zimbabwe Lowest point, junction of the Runde and Save Rivers 162 m, 531 ft; highest point, Inyangani 2,592 m, 9,685 ft.

Zinalrothorn 4,221 m, 13,848 ft. This is the 24th highest of the 60 major 4,000-meter peaks of the **Alps**. It was first ascended in 1864 by Leslie Stephen, F. Crawford Grove, and **Melchior** and Jakob **Anderegg**. The Zinalrothorn is located within the **Dent Blanche** group, in the **Valaisan Alps**.

Zmutt Nose The characteristic notch on the Zmutt Ridge of the **Matterhorn**. (See also color photos.)

Zmutt Ridge See **Matterhorn**.

Zug A small canton in **Switzerland**, it lies on the hilly central Swiss **plateau**, rising to the Hohe Rone hills 1,205 m, 3,953 ft to the east, and to the Zugerberg ridge 1,039 m, 3,409 ft of the Rossberg hills in the south.

Zugspitze 2,962 m, 9,718 ft. The highest mountain in Germany; its summit is bedecked with a host of buildings.

Zumstein, Pointe 4,563 m, 14,970 ft. This is the fourth highest peak in the **Alps**, and one of the five main summits of **Monte Rosa**. It was first climbed in 1820 by Joseph Zumstein, Molinatti, Johann Nicklaus, and a number of porters and guides. (See also color photos.)

Zumtaugwald, Johann (1800s) One of the strongest early **guides** in **Switzerland**, he was a member of the different parties who first climbed the **Dufourspitze** (1855), the **Dom** (1858), the **Täschhorn** (1862), and the **Rimpfischhorn** (1859).

Zumwalt, Paul L. (1912–2004) He is the author of the useful book *Fifty State Summits: Guide with Maps to State Highpoints*. He has climbed most of the highpoints, and, at the age of 75, he climbed **Borah Peak**, 3,859 m, 12,662 ft, only a few months after suffering a heart attack!

Zurbriggen, Matthias (1856–1917) Born: Italy. A Swiss **guide** who participated in the first ascents of the **Weissmies** (1855), the **Stecknadelhorn** (1887), and the **Ludwigshöhe** (1898). In 1897, he **soloed** the mighty Cerro **Aconcagua**, thus climbing higher than any man had done before. He was with Conway in the **Karakoram** and Fitzgerald in **New Zealand** and the **Andes**. His adventures are recorded in *From the Alps to the Andes* (1899). (See also the **10 Best Guides** sidebar.)

APPENDIX A: THE WORLD'S 1,000 HIGHEST PEAKS

Authors' note: While there are 14 major peaks above 8,000 meters, the list contains 22 entries above or equal to 8,000 meters; this is because, in addition to the major peaks, there are eight minor or satellite peaks. In the main text, we refer to major peaks: for example, Cho Oyu is the sixth highest 8,000-meter peak in the world. This is indicated in the following table by the note (6/14) at the end of the corresponding entry. The altitudes of the 14 8,000-meter peaks are quoted from *Climbing the World's Highest Mountains*, by Richard Sale and John Cleare, published by the Mountaineers in 2000, except for Everest, whose altitude was recently revised to 8,850 m; Nanga Parbat; and Annapurna I, where the altitudes indicated here are those predominantly used in the literature.

1. Mt. Everest, 8,850 m, 29,035 ft, Himalaya, China & Nepal (1/14)
2. K2, 8,611 m, 28,251 ft, Karakoram, China & Pakistan (2/14)
3. Kanchenjunga, 8,586 m, 28,169 ft, Himalaya, India & Nepal (3/14)
4. Lhotse, 8,516 m, 27,939 ft, Himalaya, China & Nepal (4/14)
5. Kangchenjunga South, 8,476 m, 27,808 ft, Himalaya, India & Nepal
6. Makalu, 8,463 m, 27,766 ft, Himalaya, China & Nepal (5/14)
7. Lhotse Middle, 8,430 m, 27,657 ft, Himalaya, Nepal
8. Kangchenjunga West, 8,420 m, 27,624 ft, Himalaya, Nepal
9. Lhotse Shar, 8,400 m, 27,559 ft, Himalaya, Nepal
10. Cho Oyu, 8,201 m, 26,906 ft, Himalaya, China & Nepal (6/14)
11. Dhaulagiri I, 8,167 m, 26,794 ft, Himalaya, Nepal (7/14)
12. Manaslu, 8,163 m, 26,781 ft, Himalaya, Nepal (8/14)
13. Nanga Parbat, 8,126 m, 26,660 ft, Himalaya, Pakistan (9/14)
14. Annapurna I, 8,091 m, 26,545 ft, Himalaya, Nepal (10/14)
15. Gasherbrum I, 8,068 m, 26,469 ft, Karakoram, China & Pakistan (11/14)
16. Annapurna I Northeast I, 8,051 m, 26,414 ft, Himalaya, Nepal
17. Broad Peak, 8,047 m, 26,400 ft, Karakoram, China & Pakistan (12/14)
18. Shisha Pangma (Xixabangma), 8,046 m, 26,398 ft, Himalaya, China (13/14)
19. Gasherbrum II, 8,035 m, 26,361 ft, Karakoram, China & Pakistan (14/14)
20. Broad Peak North 1, 8,011 m, 26,282 ft, Karakoram, China & Pakistan
21. Manaslu Southeast, 8,010 m, 26,279 ft, Himalaya, Nepal
22. Annapurna I Northeast II, 8,000 m, 26,246 ft, Himalaya, Nepal
23. Xixabangma Northwest, 7,999 m, 26,243 ft, Himalaya, China
24. Manaslu East, 7,992 m, 26,220 ft, Himalaya, Nepal
25. Gyachung Kang, 7,952 m, 26,089 ft, Himalaya, China & Nepal
26. Gasherbrum III, 7,946 m, 26,069 ft, Karakoram, Pakistan
27. Annapurna II, 7,937 m, 26,040 ft, Himalaya, Nepal
28. Gasherbrum IV, 7,932 m, 26,023 ft, Karakoram, Pakistan

29. Ngojumba Kang, 7,916 m, 25,971 ft, Himalaya, China & Nepal
30. Bei Tip, 7,912 m, 25,958 ft, Karakoram, Pakistan
31. Kambachen, 7,902 m, 25,925 ft, Himalaya, Nepal
32. Manaslu East Pinnacle, 7,895 m, 25,902 ft, Himalaya, Nepal
33. Himal Chuli, 7,893 m, 25,895 ft, Himalaya, Nepal
34. Disteghil Sar I, 7,885 m, 25,869 ft, Karakoram, Pakistan
35. Nuptse, 7,879 m, 25,849 ft, Himalaya, Nepal
36. Makalu North I, 7,876 m, 25,839 ft, Himalaya, China & Nepal
37. Ngadi Chuli, 7,871 m, 25,823 ft, Himalaya, Nepal
38. Khunyang Chhish I, 7,852 m, 25,761 ft, Karakoram, Pakistan
39. Masherbrum, 7,821 m, 25,659 ft, Karakoram, Pakistan
40. Gasherbrum I Southeast, 7,817 m, 25,646 ft, Karakoram, China & Pakistan
41. Nanda Devi, 7,816 m, 25,643 ft, Himalaya, India
42. Gasherbrum III West, 7,810 m, 25,623 ft, Karakoram, Pakistan
43. Masherbrum South, 7,806 m, 25,610 ft, Karakoram, Pakistan
44. Xixabangma South I, 7,795 m, 25,574 ft, Himalaya, China
45. Rakaposhi I, 7,788 m, 25,551 ft, Karakoram, Pakistan
46. Makalu South, 7,786 m, 25,544 ft, Himalaya, China & Nepal
47. Batura Muztagh I, 7,785 m, 25,541 ft, Karakoram, Pakistan
48. Namjagbarwa, 7,782 m, 25,531 ft, Himalaya, China
49. Batura Muztagh II, 7,762 m, 25,465 ft, Karakoram, Pakistan
50. Disteghil Sar II, 7,760 m, 25,459 ft, Karakoram, Pakistan
51. Kanjut Sar I, 7,760 m, 25,459 ft, Karakoram, Pakistan
52. Kamet, 7,756 m, 25,446 ft, Himalaya, India
53. Makalu Southeast, 7,753 m, 25,436 ft, Himalaya, China & Nepal
54. Dhaulagiri II, 7,751 m, 25,429 ft, Himalaya, Nepal
55. Masherbrum West, 7,750 m, 25,426 ft, Karakoram, Pakistan
56. Ngojumba Kang II, 7,743 m, 25,403 ft, Himalaya, China
57. Saltoro Kangri, 7,742 m, 25,400 ft, Karakoram, Pakistan
58. Annapurna II East, 7,739 m, 25,390 ft, Himalaya, Nepal
59. Batura Muztagh III, 7,729 m, 25,357 ft, Karakoram, Pakistan
60. Naimona Nyi, 7,728 m, 25,354 ft, Himalaya, China
61. Trivor, 7,728 m, 25,354 ft, Karakoram, Pakistan
62. Kongur Tagh, 7,719 m, 25,324 ft, Kunlun, China
63. Dhaulagiri III, 7,715 m, 25,311 ft, Himalaya, Nepal
64. Jannu, 7,710 m, 25,295 ft, Himalaya, Nepal
65. Tirich Mir, 7,708 m, 25,288 ft, Hindu Kush, Pakistan
66. Saltoro Kangri North, 7,705 m, 25,278 ft, Karakoram, Pakistan
67. Molamengjin Peak, 7,703 m, 25,272 ft, Himalaya, China
68. Gasherbrum II Northwest II, 7,702 m, 25,269 ft, Karakoram, China & Pakistan
69. Disteghil Sar III, 7,700 m, 25,262 ft, Karakoram, Pakistan
70. Ngojumba Kang III, 7,681 m, 25,200 ft, Himalaya, China & Nepal
71. Chomolonzo North., 7,677 m, 25,187 ft, Himalaya, China
72. Saser Kangri I, 7,672 m, 25,170 ft, Karakoram, India
73. Chogolisa Southwest, 7,668 m, 25,157 ft, Karakoram, Pakistan
74. Phola Gangchen, 7,661 m, 25,134 ft, Himalaya, China
75. Dhaulagiri IV, 7,661 m, 25,134 ft, Himalaya, Nepal
76. Chogolisa Northeast, 7,654 m, 25,111 ft, Karakoram, Pakistan
77. Varaha Shikhar, 7,647 m, 25,088 ft, Himalaya, Nepal
78. Dongbei, 7,625 m, 25,016 ft, Kunlun, China
79. Khunyang Chhish II, 7,620 m, 25,000 ft, Karakoram, Pakistan
80. Dhaulagiri V, 7,618 m, 24,993 ft, Himalaya, Nepal

81. Shispar, 7,611 m, 24,970 ft, Karakoram, Pakistan
82. Batura Muztagh I East 1, 7,600 m, 24,934 ft, Karakoram, Pakistan
83. Batura Muztagh III Northeast, 7,600 m, 24,934 ft, Karakoram, Pakistan
84. Gasherbrum II Northwest 1, 7,591 m, 24,904 ft, Karakoram, China & Pakistan
85. Gongga, 7,590 m, 24,901 ft, Hengduan, China
86. Peak 38, 7,590 m, 24,901 ft, Himalaya, China & Nepal
87. Gasherbrum II East 2, 7,588 m, 24,895 ft, Karakoram, China & Pakistan
88. Changtse, 7,583 m, 24,878 ft, Himalaya, China
89. Makalu North II, 7,582 m, 24,875 ft, Himalaya, China & Nepal
90. Bei Peak West, 7,560 m, 24,803 ft, Himalaya, China
91. Annapurna III, 7,555 m, 24,786 ft, Himalaya, Nepal
92. Kulha Kangri, 7,554 m, 24,783 ft, Himalaya, China
93. Nangpai Gossum I, 7,552 m, 24,776 ft, Himalaya, Nepal
94. Broad Peak North Peak, 7,550 m, 24,770 ft, Karakoram, China & Pakistan
95. Talung, 7,549 m, 24,767 ft, Himalaya, India & Nepal
96. Muztagata, 7,546 m, 24,757 ft, Kunlun, China
97. Skyang Kangri, 7,544 m, 24,750 ft, Karakoram, China
98. Gangkar Puesum, 7,541 m, 24,740 ft, Himalaya, Bhutan & China
99. Chomolonzo Northwest, 7,540 m, 24,737 ft, Himalaya, China
100. Gangkar Puesum II, 7,532 m, 24,711 ft, Himalaya, China
101. Kongur Debe, 7,530 m, 24,704 ft, Kunlun, China
102. Noshaq, 7,530 m, 24,704 ft, Hindu Kush, Afghanistan & Pakistan
103. Yushkin Gardan Sar, 7,530 m, 24,704 ft, Karakoram, Pakistan
104. Annapurna IV, 7,525 m, 24,688 ft, Himalaya, Nepal
105. Gangkar Puesum III, 7,516 m, 24,658 ft, Himalaya, China
106. Mamostong Kangri I, 7,516 m, 24,658 ft, Karakoram, India
107. Peak 29 South, 7,514 m, 24,652 ft, Himalaya, Nepal
108. Saser Kangri II East, 7,513 m, 24,648 ft, Karakoram, India
109. Pasu West, 7,500 m, 24,606 ft, Karakoram, Pakistan
110. Saser Kangri II West, 7,500 m, 24,606 ft, Karakoram, India
111. Skyang Kangri Southwest, 7,500 m, 24,606 ft, Karakoram, China
112. Pik Ismail Samani, 7,495 m, 24,589 ft, Pamir, Tajikistan
113. Saser Kangri III, 7,495 m, 24,589 ft, Karakoram, India
114. Pumari Chhish I, 7,492 m, 24,580 ft, Karakoram, Pakistan
115. Broad Peak Northeast 1, 7,490 m, 24,573 ft, Karakoram, China & Pakistan
116. Haramosh, 7,490 m, 24,573 ft, Karakoram, Pakistan
117. Xixabangma South II, 7,486 m, 24,560 ft, Himalaya, China
118. Kangsar Kang, 7,485 m, 24,557 ft, Himalaya, Nepal
119. Jongsong Peak, 7,483 m, 24,550 ft, Himalaya, China
120. Janak Chuli, 7,481 m, 24,543 ft, Himalaya, China & Nepal
121. Gasherbrum II Northwest 4, 7,476 m, 24,527 ft, Karakoram, China & Pakistan
122. Teram Kangri, 7,462 m, 24,481 ft, Karakoram, China & Pakistan
123. Malubiting, 7,458 m, 24,468 ft, Karakoram, Pakistan
124. Gangapurna, 7,455 m, 24,458 ft, Himalaya, Nepal
125. Janak Himal, 7,451 m, 24,445 ft, Himalaya, China
126. Batura Muztagh I East 2, 7,450 m, 24,442 ft, Karakoram, Pakistan
127. Pungpa Ri, 7,446 m, 24,429 ft, Himalaya, China
128. Peak 38 East I, 7,444 m, 24,422 ft, Himalaya, China & Nepal
129. Dome Kang, 7,442 m, 24,416 ft, Himalaya, China
130. Yazghil Dome South, 7,440 m, 24,409 ft, Karakoram, Pakistan
131. Pik Podeba, 7,439 m, 24,406 ft, Tien Shan, China & Kyrgyzstan

132. Nanda Devi East, 7,434 m, 24,389 ft, Himalaya, India
133. Gasherbrum II Northwest 5, 7,430 m, 24,376 ft, Karakoram, China & Pakistan
134. Yangla Kang, 7,429 m, 24,373 ft, Himalaya, China
135. Yangra, 7,429 m, 24,373 ft, Himalaya, China & Nepal
136. Yangran Kangri, 7,429 m, 24,373 ft, Himalaya, China
137. K12, 7,428 m, 24,370 ft, Karakoram, Pakistan
138. Chomolonzo South, 7,427 m, 24,366 ft, Himalaya, China & Nepal
139. Muztagata North Peak, 7,427 m, 24,366 ft, Kunlun, China
140. Urdok I, 7,426 m, 24,363 ft, Karakoram, China & Pakistan
141. Sia Kangri, 7,422 m, 24,350 ft, Karakoram, China & Pakistan
142. Gang Benchnen North, 7,416 m, 24,330 ft, Himalaya, China
143. Xixabangma South III, 7,415 m, 24,327 ft, Himalaya, China
144. Churen Himal Central, 7,412 m, 24,317 ft, Himalaya, Nepal
145. Savoia I, 7,410 m, 24,311 ft, Karakoram, Pakistan
146. Teram Kangri II, 7,406 m, 24,297 ft, Karakoram, China & India
147. Mt. Ghent South, 7,401 m, 24,281 ft, Karakoram, Pakistan
148. Khunyang Chhish III, 7,400 m, 24,278 ft, Karakoram, Pakistan
149. Khunyang Chhish IV, 7,400 m, 24,278 ft, Karakoram, Pakistan
150. Yazghil Dome North, 7,400 m, 24,278 ft, Karakoram, Pakistan
151. Gasherbrum II East 3, 7,388 m, 24,238 ft, Karakoram, China
152. Ultar Sar, 7,388 m, 24,238 ft, Karakoram, Pakistan
153. Rimo I, 7,385 m, 24,229 ft, Karakoram, India
154. Teram Kangri III, 7,382 m, 24,219 ft, Karakoram, China & India
155. Sherpi Kangri I, 7,380 m, 24,212 ft, Karakoram, Pakistan
156. Churen Himal West, 7,372 m, 24,186 ft, Himalaya, Nepal
157. Churen Himal East, 7,371 m, 24,183 ft, Himalaya, Nepal
158. Chongtar, 7,370 m, 24,179 ft, Karakoram, China & Pakistan
159. Labgekung, 7,367 m, 24,169 ft, Himalaya, China
160. Beifeng Peak, 7,365 m, 24,163 ft, Himalaya, China
161. Kirat Chuli, 7,365 m, 24,163 ft, Himalaya, Nepal & India
162. Abi Gamin, 7,355 m, 24,130 ft, Himalaya, China & Nepal
163. Nyainqentangla I, 7,353 m, 24,124 ft, Tanggula, China
164. Peak IV, 7,353 m, 24,124 ft, Himalaya, India & Nepal
165. Jasamba, 7,351 m, 24,117 ft, Himalaya, China
166. Cho Aui, 7,350 m, 24,114 ft, Himalaya, China
167. Chongtar North, 7,350 m, 24,114 ft, Karakoram, China
168. Khunyang Chhish V, 7,350 m, 24,114 ft, Karakoram, Pakistan
169. Pumeri Chhish II, 7,350 m, 24,114 ft, Karakoram, Pakistan
170. Gimmigela Chuli, 7,350 m, 24,114 ft, Himalaya, Nepal & India
171. Talung, 7,349 m, 24,110 ft, Himalaya, Nepal & India
172. Urgend I, 7,349 m, 24,110 ft, Hindu Kush, Pakistan
173. Noshaq Southeast, 7,348 m, 24,107 ft, Hindu Kush, Pakistan
174. Namjagbarwa II, 7,344 m, 24,094 ft, Himalaya, China
175. Momil Sar, 7,343 m, 24,091 ft, Karakoram, Pakistan
176. Mt. Ghent North, 7,342 m, 24,087 ft, Karakoram, Pakistan
177. Peak III, 7,341 m, 24,084 ft, Himalaya, India & Nepal
178. Broad Peak North 2, 7,338 m, 24,074 ft, Karakoram, China
179. Kabru, 7,338 m, 24,074 ft, Himalaya, Nepal & India
180. Beifeng North, 7,332 m, 24,055 ft, Himalaya, China
181. Yutomar Sar South, 7,330 m, 24,048 ft, Karakoram, Pakistan

182. Bojohagur Duanasir, 7,329 m, 24,045 ft, Karakoram, Pakistan
183. Gasherbrum II Northwest 3, 7,328 m, 24,041 ft, Karakoram, China & Pakistan
184. Malangutti Sar I, 7,320 m, 24,015 ft, Karakoram, Pakistan
185. Kabru South Peak, 7,317 m, 24,005 ft, Himalaya, Nepal
186. Dhaulagiri IV East, 7,316 m, 24,002 ft, Himalaya, Nepal
187. Chomolhari, 7,315 m, 23,999 ft, Himalaya, China
188. Zhonghujiang, 7,315 m, 23,999 ft, Karakoram, China & Pakistan
189. Yaleb, 7,312 m, 23,989 ft, Himalaya, China
190. Broad Peak Northeast 2, 7,311 m, 23,986 ft, Karakoram, Pakistan
191. Saser Kangri IV, 7,310 m, 23,982 ft, Karakoram, India
192. Seg Wang, 7,308 m, 23,976 ft, Himalaya, China
193. Yangra South I, 7,305 m, 23,966 ft, Himalaya, China & Nepal
194. Savoia II, 7,302 m, 23,956 ft, Karakoram, Pakistan
195. Baltoro Kangri, 7,300 m, 23,950 ft, Karakoram, Pakistan
196. Chongtar Northeast, 7,300 m, 23,950 ft, Karakoram, China & Pakistan
197. Gasherbrum II Northwest 6, 7,300 m, 23,950 ft, Karakoram, China & Pakistan
198. Jeje Kangphu, 7,300 m, 23,950 ft, Himalaya, China
199. Malubiting Northwest, 7,300 m, 23,950 ft, Karakoram, Pakistan
200. Saser Kangri V, 7,300 m, 23,950 ft, Karakoram, India
201. Saser Kangri VI, 7,300 m, 23,950 ft, Karakoram, India
202. Teram Kangri III West, 7,300 m, 23,950 ft, Karakoram, China & India
203. Teri Nang, 7,300 m, 23,950 ft, Himalaya, Bhutan
204. Broad Peak North 3, 7,298 m, 23,943 ft, Karakoram, China
205. Gyalha Bairl, 7,294 m, 23,930 ft, Himalaya, China
206. Xifeng Peak, 7,292 m, 23,923 ft, Himalaya, China
207. Ranaposhi II, 7,290 m, 23,917 ft, Karakoram, Pakistan
208. Chamlang I, 7,287 m, 23,907 ft, Himalaya, Nepal
209. Ogre I, 7,285 m, 23,900 ft, Karakoram, Pakistan
210. Pasu Peak, 7,284 m, 23,897 ft, Karakoram, Pakistan
211. Porong Ri, 7,284 m, 23,897 ft, Himalaya, China
212. Khartapu, 7,283 m, 23,894 ft, Himalaya, China
213. K6, 7,281 m, 23,887 ft, Karakoram, Pakistan
214. Kangboqen, 7,281 m, 23,887 ft, Himalaya, China
215. Broad Peak Northeast 3, 7,278 m, 23,877 ft, Karakoram, China & Pakistan
216. Kalaxong Peak, 7,277 m, 23,874 ft, Kunlun, China
217. Muztagh Tower, 7,276 m, 23,871 ft, Karakoram, Pakistan
218. Baltoro Kangri Southeast, 7,275 m, 23,868 ft, Karakoram, Pakistan
219. Baltoro Kangri Northwest, 7,274 m, 23,864 ft, Karakoram, Pakistan
220. Taple Himal, 7,273 m, 23,861 ft, Himalaya, Nepal
221. Mana Peak, 7,272 m, 23,858 ft, Himalaya, India
222. Dhaulagiri VI, 7,268 m, 23,845 ft, Himalaya, Nepal
223. Baltoro Kangri South, 7,265 m, 23,835 ft, Karakoram, Pakistan
224. Huangguan, 7,265 m, 23,835 ft, Karakoram, China
225. Summa Ri, 7,263 m, 23,828 ft, Karakoram, China
226. Mulubiting East, 7,260 m, 23,818 ft, Karakoram, Pakistan
227. Wuhujiang I, 7,258 m, 23,812 ft, Karakoram, China
228. Diran, 7,257 m, 23,809 ft, Karakoram, Pakistan
229. Urdok II, 7,250 m, 23,786 ft, Karakoram, China & Pakistan
230. Dhaulagiri V Northeast, 7,249 m, 23,782 ft, Himalaya, Nepal
231. Putha Hiunchuli, 7,246 m, 23,772 ft, Himalaya, Nepal
232. Apsarasas I, 7,245 m, 23,769 ft, Karakoram, China & Nepal

233. Karayalak I, 7,245 m, 23,769 ft, Kunlun, China
234. Mukut Parbat I, 7,242 m, 23,759 ft, Himalaya, China & Nepal
235. Apsarasas II, 7,239 m, 23,750 ft, Karakoram, China & India
236. Chamlang II, 7,239 m, 23,750 ft, Himalaya, Nepal
237. Point 7239, 7,239 m, 23,750 ft, Himalaya, China
238. Apsarasas III, 7,236 m, 23,740 ft, Karakoram, China & India
239. Langtang Lirung, 7,234 m, 23,733 ft, Himalaya, Nepal
240. Rimo III, 7,233 m, 23,730 ft, Karakoram, India
241. Kangbu I, 7,230 m, 23,720 ft, Himalaya, China
242. Hamurjayilak I, 7,229 m, 23,717 ft, Kunlun, China
243. Zhonghujiang South, 7,228 m, 23,713 ft, Karakoram, Pakistan
244. Apsarasas III East 1, 7,226 m, 23,707 ft, Karakoram, China & India
245. Noijinkangsang, 7,223 m, 23,697 ft, Himalaya, China
246. Chamlang III, 7,222 m, 23,694 ft, Himalaya, Nepal
247. Xinan, 7,222 m, 23,694 ft, Kunlun, China
248. Karjiang, 7,221 m, 23,690 ft, Himalaya, China
249. Savoia III, 7,221 m, 23,690 ft, Karakoram, Pakistan
250. Baltoro Kangri Northeast, 7,220 m, 23,687 ft, Karakoram, Pakistan
251. Wuhujiang II, 7,220 m, 23,687 ft, Karakoram, China & Pakistan
252. Annapurna Dakshin, 7,219 m, 23,684 ft, Himalaya, Nepal
253. Karjiang Central Peak, 7,216 m, 23,674 ft, Himalaya, China
254. Kangpenqing, 7,212 m, 23,661 ft, Himalaya, China
255. Kokodak, 7,210 m, 23,654 ft, Kunlun, China
256. Singhi Kangri, 7,207 m, 23,645 ft, Karakoram, China & India
257. Langtang Ri, 7,205 m, 23,638 ft, Himalaya, China
258. Qimgan, 7,204 m, 23,635 ft, Kunlun, China
259. Balarung Sar, 7,200 m, 23,622 ft, Karakoram, Pakistan
260. Gang Chen, 7,200 m, 23,622 ft, Himalaya, China
261. Gieu Gang, 7,200 m, 23,622 ft, Himalaya, China
262. K12 East 1, 7,200 m, 23,622 ft, Karakoram, Pakistan
263. Kangpu Gang, 7,200 m, 23,622 ft, Himalaya, China
264. Khunyang Chhish North, 7,200 m, 23,622 ft, Karakoram, Pakistan
265. Lupghar Sar Central, 7,200 m, 23,622 ft, Karakoram, Pakistan
266. Lupghar Sar East, 7,200 m, 23,622 ft, Karakoram, Pakistan
267. Masang Nang, 7,200 m, 23,622 ft, Himalaya, Bhutan & China
268. Tsenda Nang, 7,200 m, 23,622 ft, Himalaya, Bhutan
269. Lupghar Sar West, 7,199 m, 23,618 ft, Karakoram, Pakistan
270. Tarke Kang, 7,193 m, 23,599 ft, Himalaya, Nepal
271. Gurja Himal, 7,193 m, 23,599 ft, Himalaya, Nepal
272. Doje'ezhong, 7,192 m, 23,595 ft, Himalaya, China
273. Savoia IV, 7,192 m, 23,595 ft, Karakoram, Pakistan
274. Skyang Kangri Southeast, 7,192 m, 23,595 ft, Karakoram, China & Pakistan
275. Shanjian I, 7,187 m, 23,579 ft, Karakoram, China & Pakistan
276. Apsarasas III East 2, 7,184 m, 23,569 ft, Karakoram, China & India
277. Kuksay Peak, 7,184 m, 23,569 ft, Kunlun, China
278. Apsarasas III West, 7,181 m, 23,559 ft, Karakoram, China & India
279. Jobo Garu, 7,181 m, 23,559 ft, Himalaya, China
280. Chongtar South Peak, 7,180 m, 23,556 ft, Karakoram, Pakistan
281. Beifeng Peak, 7,174 m, 23,536 ft, Karakoram, China & Pakistan
282. Ihakora South, 7,170 m, 23,523 ft, Karakoram, Pakistan
283. Rimo IV, 7,169 m, 23,520 ft, Karakoram, India
284. Baruntse, 7,168 m, 23,517 ft, Himalaya, Nepal

285. Aksai Chin, 7,167 m, 23,513 ft, Kunlun, China
286. Pumori, 7,165 m, 23,507 ft, Himalaya, China & Nepal
287. Karun Koh I, 7,164 m, 23,503 ft, Karakoram, Pakistan
288. Hachindar Chhish, 7,163 m, 23,500 ft, Karakoram, Pakistan
289. Yermanedu Kangri, 7,163 m, 23,500 ft, Karakoram, Pakistan
290. Hardeol, 7,161 m, 23,494 ft, Himalaya, India
291. Nyain'a I, 7,161 m, 23,494 ft, Nyain'a, China
292. Manaslu North, 7,154 m, 23,471 ft, Himalaya, Nepal
293. Beifeng South, 7,152 m, 23,464 ft, Karakoram, China & Pakistan
294. Latok I, 7,151 m, 23,461 ft, Karakoram, Pakistan
295. Chomolonzo Northwest 2, 7,150 m, 23,458 ft, Himalaya, China
296. False Junction Peak, 7,150 m, 23,458 ft, Himalaya, Nepal
297. Jialabiali, 7,150 m, 23,458 ft, Himalaya, China
298. Lapsang Karubo, 7,150 m, 23,458 ft, Himalaya, Nepal
299. Mt. Depak, 7,150 m, 23,458 ft, Karakoram, Pakistan
300. Snowdome, 7,150 m, 23,458 ft, Karakoram, Pakistan
301. Peak 38 East II, 7,149 m, 23,454 ft, Himalaya, China & Nepal
302. Bei Peak North, 7,148 m, 23,451 ft, Himalaya, China
303. Gasherbrum V, 7,147 m, 23,448 ft, Karakoram, Pakistan
304. Najagbarwa III, 7,146 m, 23,444 ft, Himalaya, China
305. Gaurisankar, 7,146 m, 23,444 ft, Himalaya, China & Nepal
306. Wuhujiang I Northeast 1, 7,145 m, 23,441 ft, Karakoram, China
307. Kampire Dior, 7,143 m, 23,435 ft, Karakoram, Pakistan
308. Pamri, 7,141 m, 23,428 ft, Karakoram, Pakistan
309. Nemjung, 7,140 m, 23,425 ft, Himalaya, Nepal
310. Chaukhamba I, 7,138 m, 23,418 ft, Himalaya, India
311. Point 7138, 7,138 m, 23,418 ft, Himalaya, Nepal
312. Urdok II South, 7,136 m, 23,412 ft, Karakoram, Pakistan
313. Nunser, 7,135 m, 23,408 ft, Himalaya, India
314. Pik Lenin, 7,134 m, 23,405 ft, Pamir, Kyrgyzstan & Tajikistan
315. Savoia V, 7,134 m, 23,405 ft, Karakoram, Pakistan
316. Tilicho, 7,134 m, 23,405 ft, Himalaya, Nepal
317. Pengqar I, 7,132 m, 23,398 ft, Tanggula, China
318. Savoia VI, 7,132 m, 23,398 ft, Karakoram, Pakistan
319. Mukut Parbat II, 7,130 m, 23,392 ft, Himalaya, China & Nepal
320. Kokoser I, 7,129 m, 23,389 ft, Kunlun, China
321. Pauhinri, 7,128 m, 23,385 ft, Himalaya, Bhutan & China
322. Mandu Peak, 7,127 m, 23,382 ft, Karakoram, Pakistan
323. Himlun Himal, 7,126 m, 23,379 ft, Himalaya, China & Nepal
324. Point 7126, 7,126 m, 23,379 ft, Kunlun, China
325. Pathi Bhara Himal, 7,123 m, 23,369 ft, Himalaya, Nepal & Sikkim
326. Trisul I, 7,120 m, 23,359 ft, Himalaya, India
327. Nanfeng Peak, 7,119 m, 23,356 ft, Himalaya, China
328. Apsarasas I South, 7,117 m, 23,349 ft, Karakoram, India
329. Nyain'a II, 7,117 m, 23,349 ft, Nyain'a, China
330. Koh-e-Shakhawr I, 7,113 m, 23,336 ft, Hindu Kush, Pakistan
331. Lixin Peak, 7,113 m, 23,336 ft, Himalaya, China
332. Nyain'a III, 7,111 m, 23,330 ft, Nyain'a, China
333. Ganesh III, 7,110 m, 23,326 ft, Himalaya, Nepal
334. Nangpai Gossum III, 7,110 m, 23,326 ft, Himalaya, Nepal
335. Latok II, 7,108 m, 23,320 ft, Karakoram, Pakistan
336. Shey Shikhar, 7,108 m, 23,320 ft, Himalaya, Nepal
337. Korzhinievskoi, 7,105 m, 23,310 ft, Pamir, Tajikistan

338. Pabil, 7,104 m, 23,307 ft, Himalaya, Nepal
339. Chomolonzo Northwest I, 7,103 m, 23,303 ft, Himalaya, China & Nepal
340. Gasherbrum II Southeast, 7,103 m, 23,303 ft, Karakoram, China & Pakistan
341. Yulin I, 7,101 m, 23,297 ft, Karakoram, Pakistan
342. K12 East 2, 7,100 m, 23,293 ft, Karakoram, Pakistan
343. Sherpi Kangri II, 7,100 m, 23,293 ft, Karakoram, Pakistan
344. Taqilang, 7,100 m, 23,293 ft, Himalaya, China
345. Tsenda, 7,100 m, 23,293 ft, Himalaya, China
346. Yutomar Sar North, 7,100 m, 23,293 ft, Karakoram, Pakistan
347. Himlung Himal South, 7,098 m, 23,287 ft, Himalaya, Nepal
348. Kuksay East Peak, 7,096 m, 23,280 ft, Kunlun, China
349. Savoia VII, 7,096 m, 23,280 ft, Karakoram, Pakistan
350. Namjagbarwa East Peak, 7,095 m, 23,277 ft, Himalaya, China
351. Kardachangri Peak, 7,093 m, 23,270 ft, Himalaya, China
352. Loinbo Kangri, 7,093 m, 23,270 ft, Gangdisê, China
353. Mt. Hardinge, 7,093 m, 23,270 ft, Karakoram, Pakistan
354. Point 7092, 7,092 m, 23,267 ft, Himalaya, India
355. Ehenta Peak, 7,090 m, 23,261 ft, Karakoram, Pakistan
356. Kangto, 7,090 m, 23,261 ft, Himalaya, China
357. Ansai Chin II, 7,081 m, 23,231 ft, Kunlun, China
358. Mandu II, 7,081 m, 23,231 ft, Karakoram, Pakistan
359. Kunmer, 7,077 m, 23,218 ft, Himalaya, India
360. Kardapu West I, 7,075 m, 23,211 ft, Himalaya, China
361. Satopanth, 7,075 m, 23,211 ft, Himalaya, India
362. Trisuli, 7,074 m, 23,208 ft, Himalaya, India
363. Annapurna South II, 7,071 m, 23,198 ft, Himalaya, Nepal
364. Chong Kumdan Kangri I, 7,071 m, 23,198 ft, Karakoram, India
365. Nyanang Ri, 7,071 m, 23,198 ft, Himalaya, China
366. Sharphu I, 7,070 m, 23,195 ft, Himalaya, Nepal
367. Gasherbrum I South Peak, 7,069 m, 23,192 ft, Karakoram, China & Pakistan
368. Kardapu West II, 7,069 m, 23,192 ft, Himalaya, China
369. Tarke Kang East, 7,069 m, 23,192 ft, Himalaya, Nepal
370. Chaukhamba II, 7,068 m, 23,188 ft, Himalaya, India
371. Yebokangjial Peak, 7,068 m, 23,188 ft, Himalaya, China
372. Dunagiri, 7,066 m, 23,182 ft, Himalaya, India
373. Jangmanjar, 7,063 m, 23,172 ft, Kunlun, China
374. Kardapu North, 7,062 m, 23,169 ft, Himalaya, China
375. Kube Kangri, 7,062 m, 23,169 ft, Himalaya, China & Nepal
376. Urdow Kangri II, 7,062 m, 23,169 ft, Karakoram, China & Pakistan
377. Nilgiri North, 7,061 m, 23,166 ft, Himalaya, Nepal
378. Kanggardo Riz, 7,060 m, 23,162 ft, Himalaya, China
379. Summa Ri North, 7,060 m, 23,162 ft, Karakoram, China
380. Urgend II, 7,060 m, 23,162 ft, Hindu Kush, Afghanistan & Pakistan
381. Kharta Changri, 7,056 m, 23,149 ft, Himalaya, China
382. Kanggado, 7,055 m, 23,146 ft, Himalaya, China
383. Chaglasumgo Peak, 7,052 m, 23,136 ft, Himalaya, China & Nepal
384. Broad Peak Southeast 2, 7,050 m, 23,129 ft, Karakoram, China & Pakistan
385. Fuqu Peak, 7,050 m, 23,129 ft, Himalaya, China
386. Nandali Peak East I, 7,050 m, 23,129 ft, Himalaya, China & Nepal
387. Risum, 7,050 m, 23,129 ft, Himalaya, China
388. Qungmogangze, 7,048 m, 23,123 ft, Nyain'a, China
389. Nyegi Kangsang, 7,047 m, 23,120 ft, Himalaya, China
390. Nyain'a IV, 7,046 m, 23,116 ft, Nyain'a, China

391. Lhagba Peak, 7,045 m, 23,113 ft, Himalaya, China
392. Kangbu II, 7,044 m, 23,110 ft, Himalaya, China
393. Namu Shin Kang I, 7,044 m, 23,110 ft, Tanggula, China
394. Naipeng, 7,043 m, 23,106 ft, Himalaya, China
395. Napung Peak, 7,043 m, 23,106 ft, Himalaya, China
396. Salasungo, 7,043 m, 23,106 ft, Himalaya, China & Nepal
397. Link Sar, 7,041 m, 23,100 ft, Karakoram, Pakistan
398. K6 West, 7,040 m, 23,097 ft, Karakoram, Pakistan
399. Gyanj Kang, 7,038 m, 23,090 ft, Himalaya, Nepal
400. Kezhen Peak, 7,038 m, 23,090 ft, Karakoram, China & Pakistan
401. Skyang Kangri West, 7,038 m, 23,090 ft, Karakoram, China & Pakistan
402. Kanggado North Peak, 7,037 m, 23,087 ft, Himalaya, China
403. Thulagi, 7,036 m, 23,083 ft, Himalaya, Nepal
404. Urgend III, 7,036 m, 23,083 ft, Hindu Kush, Afghanistan & Pakistan
405. Janak, 7,035 m, 23,080 ft, Himalaya, China
406. Tirsuli West, 7,035 m, 23,080 ft, Himalaya, India
407. Saipal, 7,034 m, 23,077 ft, Himalaya, Nepal
408. Pauhunri South, 7,032 m, 23,070 ft, Himalaya, Bhutan & China
409. Shudu Tsenpa, 7,032 m, 23,070 ft, Himalaya, China
410. Kokoser II, 7,031 m, 23,067 ft, Kunlun, China
411. Koskulak Peak, 7,028 m, 23,057 ft, Kunlun, China
412. Nubchu, 7,028 m, 23,057 ft, Himalaya, China & Nepal
413. Spantik, 7,027 m, 23,054 ft, Karakoram, Pakistan
414. Shanjian II, 7,026 m, 23,051 ft, Karakoram, China & Pakistan
415. Chowusha, 7,023 m, 23,041 ft, Himalaya, China
416. Jobo Garu II, 7,023 m, 23,041 ft, Himalaya, China
417. Melungtse II, 7,023 m, 23,041 ft, Himalaya, China
418. Skyang Kangri East, 7,021 m, 23,034 ft, Karakoram, China
419. Point 7018, 7,018 m, 23,024 ft, Himalaya, China
420. Mamostong Kangri II, 7,016 m, 23,018 ft, Karakoram, India
421. Chong Kumdan Kangri II, 7,014 m, 23,011 ft, Karakoram, India
422. Palung Ri, 7,013 m, 23,008 ft, Himalaya, China
423. Point 7013, 7,013 m, 23,008 ft, Himalaya, China
424. Xifeng Southwest, 7,013 m, 23,008 ft, Himalaya, China
425. Mayr Kangri, 7,011 m, 23,001 ft, Kunlun, China
426. Point 7011, 7,011 m, 23,001 ft, Himalaya, China
427. Annapurna IV South I, 7,010 m, 22,998 ft, Himalaya, Nepal
428. Annapurna South III, 7,010 m, 22,998 ft, Himalaya, Nepal
429. Chamlang IV, 7,010 m, 22,998 ft, Himalaya, Nepal
430. Gaurishankar South, 7,010 m, 22,998 ft, Himalaya, China & Nepal
431. Kang Guru, 7,010 m, 22,998 ft, Himalaya, Nepal
432. Lolonaq South, 7,010 m, 22,998 ft, Himalaya, China
433. Rakaposhi III, 7,010 m, 22,998 ft, Karakoram, Pakistan
434. Lap Tshe, 7,009 m, 22,995 ft, Tanggula, China
435. Gasherbrum V East, 7,006 m, 22,985 ft, Karakoram, Pakistan
436. Melunghi Nang, 7,006 m, 22,985 ft, Himalaya, Bhutan
437. Khantengri, 7,005 m, 22,982 ft, Tien Shan, China & Kazakhstan & Kyrgyzstan
438. Dongfang Peak, 7,003 m, 22,975 ft, Himalaya, China
439. Chomolhari II, 7,000 m, 22,965 ft, Himalaya, China
440. Chumhar Gang, 7,000 m, 22,965 ft, Himalaya, China
441. Chura Gang, 7,000 m, 22,965 ft, Himalaya, China
442. Gangchen Tag, 7,000 m, 22,965 ft, Himalaya, China

443. K12 East 3, 7,000 m, 22,965 ft, Karakoram, Pakistan
444. Kang Guru, 7,000 m, 22,965 ft, Himalaya, Nepal
445. Melunghi Kang, 7,000 m, 22,965 ft, Himalaya, China
446. Trivor Southwest, 7,000 m, 22,965 ft, Karakoram, Pakistan
447. Zongophu Gang, 7,000 m, 22,965 ft, Himalaya, China
448. Churen Himal North I, 6,998 m, 22,959 ft, Himalaya, Nepal
449. Machflapuchare, 6,997 m, 22,956 ft, Himalaya, Nepal
450. Chaukhamba III, 6,995 m, 22,949 ft, Himalaya, India
451. North Shawsgam I, 6,994 m, 22,946 ft, Karakoram, China
452. Rhishi Pahar, 6,992 m, 22,939 ft, Himalaya, India
453. High Pyramid, 6,990 m, 22,933 ft, Karakoram, India
454. Dongfang East, 6,988 m, 22,926 ft, Himalaya, China
455. Ganesh V, 6,986 m, 22,919 ft, Himalaya, China & Nepal
456. Teram Kangri II East, 6,986 m, 22,919 ft, Karakoram, China & India
457. Laila, 6,985 m, 22,916 ft, Karakoram, Pakistan
458. Thalaysagar, 6,984 m, 22,913 ft, Himalaya, India
459. Lamjung Himal, 6,983 m, 22,910 ft, Himalaya, Nepal
460. Mt. Lakshmi, 6,983 m, 22,910 ft, Karakoram, India
461. Point 6982, 6,982 m, 22,906 ft, Kunlun, China
462. Bangdag I, 6,979 m, 22,896 ft, Kunlun, China
463. Longpo Gang, 6,979 m, 22,896 ft, Himalaya, China & Nepal
464. Aklangm I, 6,978 m, 22,893 ft, Kunlun, China
465. Gasherbrum VI Southeast, 6,978 m, 22,893 ft, Karakoram, Pakistan
466. Changzheng Peak, 6,977 m, 22,890 ft, Himalaya, China
467. Karun Koh II, 6,977 m, 22,890 ft, Karakoram, Pakistan
468. Mana East, 6,977 m, 22,890 ft, Himalaya, India
469. Barun Glacier Southwest I, 6,975 m, 22,883 ft, Himalaya, Nepal
470. Tongqiang Northwest I, 6,975 m, 22,883 ft, Himalaya, China
471. Ansai Chin North, 6,973 m, 22,877 ft, Kunlun, China
472. Ulugh Muztagh, 6,973 m, 22,877 ft, Kunlun, China
473. Kezhen Northwest 1, 6,972 m, 22,874 ft, Karakoram, China
474. Drohma East, 6,970 m, 22,867 ft, Himalaya, Nepal
475. Malubiting Southeast, 6,970 m, 22,867 ft, Karakoram, Pakistan
476. Kedarnath Peak, 6,968 m, 22,860 ft, Himalaya, India
477. Dorje Lakpa, 6,966 m, 22,854 ft, Himalaya, Nepal
478. Lhagba North, 6,966 m, 22,854 ft, Himalaya, China
479. Point 6966, 6,966 m, 22,854 ft, Himalaya, China
480. Point 6962, 6,962 m, 22,841 ft, Karakoram, China
481. Qong Muztagh, 6,962 m, 22,841 ft, Kunlun, China
482. Galwan I, 6,961 m, 22,837 ft, Karakoram, China
483. Chabuk, 6,960 m, 22,834 ft, Himalaya, China & Nepal
484. Ogre II, 6,960 m, 22,834 ft, Karakoram, Pakistan
485. White Wave, 6,960 m, 22,834 ft, Himalaya, Nepal
486. Aconcagua, 6,959 m, 22,831 ft, Andes, Argentina
487. Mera, 6,958 m, 22,828 ft, Himalaya, Nepal
488. Numbur, 6,957 m, 22,824 ft, Himalaya, Nepal
489. Koskulak East, 6,956 m, 22,821 ft, Kunlun, China
490. Maidan, 6,956 m, 22,821 ft, Karakoram, Pakistan
491. Point 6956, 6,956 m, 22,821 ft, Karakoram, China
492. Tongqiang Peak, 6,956 m, 22,821 ft, Himalaya, China
493. Muzat I, 6,955 m, 22,818 ft, Tien Shan, China

494. Lang Po Peak, 6,954 m, 22,814 ft, Himalaya, China & India & Nepal
495. Longpo, 6,954 m, 22,814 ft, Himalaya, India
496. Baskai I, 6,953 m, 22,811 ft, Karakoram, Pakistan
497. Sani Parkush, 6,952 m, 22,808 ft, Karakoram, Pakistan
498. Dushanbe, 6,950 m, 22,801 ft, Pamir, Tajikistan
499. Kaberi Peak, 6,950 m, 22,801 ft, Karakoram, Pakistan
500. Urdok Kangri III, 6,950 m, 22,801 ft, Karakoram, China & Pakistan
501. Latok III, 6,949 m, 22,798 ft, Karakoram, Pakistan
502. Qiutalut I, 6,949 m, 22,798 ft, Kunlun, China
503. Qomey, 6,949 m, 22,798 ft, Himalaya, China
504. Sangemar Sar, 6,949 m, 22,798 ft, Karakoram, Pakistan
505. Revolutsii, 6,948 m, 22,795 ft, Pamir, Tajikistan
506. Chêm North, 6,947 m, 22,791 ft, Gangdisê, China
507. Sakang Peak, 6,943 m, 22,778 ft, Karakoram, India
508. Tenghi, 6,943 m, 22,778 ft, Himalaya, Nepal
509. Point 6942, 6,942 m, 22,775 ft, Karakoram, China & Pakistan
510. Nilgiri Middle, 6,940 m, 22,769 ft, Himalaya, Nepal
511. Schlagintweit Peak, 6,940 m, 22,769 ft, Himalaya, China
512. Yamit, 6,940 m, 22,769 ft, Hindu Kush, Afghanistan
513. Gyanj Kang South I, 6,939 m, 22,765 ft, Himalaya, Nepal
514. Langjapu, 6,936 m, 22,755 ft, Himalaya, China
515. Kuk Sar I, 6,935 m, 22,752 ft, Karakoram, Pakistan
516. Tserim Kang, 6,935 m, 22,752 ft, Himalaya, China
517. Hill Urdok I, 6,934 m, 22,749 ft, Karakoram, China
518. K7, 6,934 m, 22,749 ft, Karakoram, Pakistan
519. Point 6932, 6,932 m, 22,742 ft, Kunlun, China
520. Sri Kailash, 6,932 m, 22,742 ft, Himalaya, India
521. Annapurna II Southeast, 6,931 m, 22,739 ft, Himalaya, Nepal
522. Gomo I, 6,931 m, 22,739 ft, Kunlun, China
523. Kalanka, 6,931 m, 22,739 ft, Himalaya, India
524. Peak 23, 6,931 m, 22,739 ft, Karakoram, Pakistan
525. Khumbu Himal, 6,930 m, 22,736 ft, Himalaya, China
526. Lamjung Himal West I, 6,930 m, 22,736 ft, Himalaya, Nepal
527. Mukut Parbat III, 6,930 m, 22,736 ft, Himalaya, China
528. Pinnacle Peak, 6,930 m, 22,736 ft, Himalaya, India
529. Trivor South, 6,930 m, 22,736 ft, Karakoram, Pakistan
530. Kyungka Ri, 6,929 m, 22,732 ft, Himalaya, Nepal
531. Purog Kangri, 6,929 m, 22,732 ft, Tanggula, China
532. Kra Bass, 6,928 m, 22,729 ft, Karakoram, China & Pakistan
533. Chorten Nyima, 6,927 m, 22,726 ft, Himalaya, Sikkim
534. Kuk Sar II, 6,926 m, 22,723 ft, Karakoram, Pakistan
535. Pengqar II, 6,926 m, 22,723 ft, Tanggula, China
536. Broad Peak East 1, 6,920 m, 22,703 ft, Karakoram, China
537. Broad Peak Southwest, 6,920 m, 22,703 ft, Karakoram, Pakistan
538. Tukche Peak, 6,920 m, 22,703 ft, Himalaya, Nepal
539. Byasrikh, 6,919 m, 22,700 ft, Himalaya, Nepal
540. Dongfang Southeast I, 6,919 m, 22,700 ft, Himalaya, China
541. Pshavela, 6,918 m, 22,696 ft, Tien Shan, China & Kyrgyzstan
542. Shalbachum, 6,918 m, 22,696 ft, Himalaya, Nepal
543. Kardapu South II, 6,916 m, 22,690 ft, Himalaya, China
544. Khumbu Himal II, 6,916 m, 22,690 ft, Himalaya, China
545. Baruntse West I, 6,913 m, 22,680 ft, Himalaya, Nepal
546. Lixin East, 6,911 m, 22,673 ft, Himalaya, China

547. Satminal, 6,911 m, 22,673 ft, Himalaya, India
548. Chamraogal I, 6,910 m, 22,670 ft, Himalaya, China & Nepal
549. Changzheng South I, 6,910 m, 22,670 ft, Himalaya, China
550. Nepali Peak, 6,910 m, 22,670 ft, Himalaya, Nepal & India
551. Ganesh VI, 6,908 m, 22,664 ft, Himalaya, Nepal
552. Burog, 6,907 m, 22,660 ft, Kunlun, Chin
553. Aksai Chin II, 6,903 m, 22,647 ft, Kunlun, China
554. Point 6901, 6,901 m, 22,641 ft, Himalaya, China
555. Puns Ri, 6,901 m, 22,641 ft, Tanggula, China
556. K6 Northwest, 6,900 m, 22,637 ft, Karakoram, Pakistan
557. Sia Kangri II, 6,900 m, 22,637 ft, Karakoram, China & Pakistan
558. Nanda Devi North, 6,895 m, 22,621 ft, Himalaya, India
559. Chago, 6,893 m, 22,614 ft, Himalaya, China & Nepal
560. Gurkarpo Ri, 6,892 m, 22,611 ft, Himalaya, Nepal
561. Lamjung Himal Northwest I, 6,892 m, 22,611 ft, Himalaya, Nepal
562. Yulin II, 6,892 m, 22,611 ft, Karakoram, Pakistan
563. Khang Cheng Yao, 6,891 m, 22,608 ft, Himalaya, India
564. Reqiang I, 6,891 m, 22,608 ft, Himalaya, China
565. Siniolchu, 6,891 m, 22,608 ft, Himalaya, Sikkim
566. Kezhen West 1, 6,890 m, 22,604 ft, Karakoram, China & Pakistan
567. Phurephu Ri, 6,888 m, 22,598 ft, Himalaya, China
568. Panbari Himal, 6,887 m, 22,595 ft, Himalaya, Nepal
569. Dongfang West, 6,886 m, 22,591 ft, Himalaya, China
570. Zhongshan, 6,886 m, 22,591 ft, Sichuan, China
571. Kanjiroba, 6,883 m, 22,582 ft, Himalaya, Nepal
572. Gasherbrum V Northwest, 6,882 m, 22,578 ft, Karakoram, Pakistan
573. Hill Yulin I, 6,880 m, 22,572 ft, Karakoram, China & Pakistan
574. Ojos del Salado, 6,880 m, 22,572 ft, Andes, Chile
575. Peak 48, 6,880 m, 22,572 ft, Karakoram, Pakistan
576. Kmatolja, 6,875 m, 22,555 ft, Kunlun, China
577. Rossia, 6,875 m, 22,555 ft, Pamir, Tajikistan
578. Jenang I, 6,873 m, 22,549 ft, Tanggula, China
579. Topografov, 6,873 m, 22,549 ft, Tien Shan, China & Kyrgyzstan
580. Darkot, 6,872 m, 22,545 ft, Hindu Kush, Pakistan
581. Salasungo Northwest I, 6,872 m, 22,545 ft, Himalaya, China & Nepal
582. Point 6870, 6,870 m, 22,539 ft, Nyain'a, China
583. Apsarasas I West, 6,867 m, 22,529 ft, Karakoram, China & India
584. Prupuo Burakha, 6,867 m, 22,529 ft, Karakoram, Pakistan
585. Yulin III, 6,866 m, 22,526 ft, Karakoram, Pakistan
586. Changabang, 6,866 m, 22,526 ft, Himalaya, India
587. Mamostong Kangri I East 1, 6,864 m, 22,519 ft, Karakoram, India
588. Jenang II, 6,863 m, 22,516 ft, Tanggula, China
589. Salasungo Northwest II, 6,863 m, 22,516 ft, Himalaya, China & Nepal
590. Teram Sherh I, 6,863 m, 22,516 ft, Karakoram, India
591. Lhagba South, 6,862 m, 22,513 ft, Himalaya, China
592. Nanda Kot, 6,861 m, 22,509 ft, Himalaya, India
593. Buka Daban, 6,860 m, 22,506 ft, Kunlun, China
594. Patrasi, 6,860 m, 22,506 ft, Himalaya, Nepal
595. Sisne I, 6,860 m, 22,506 ft, Himalaya, Nepal
596. Gori Chen, 6,858 m, 22,500 ft, Himalaya, China
597. K7 North, 6,858 m, 22,500 ft, Karakoram, Pakistan
598. Lupghar Sar North, 6,858 m, 22,500 ft, Karakoram, Pakistan
599. Xinquing I, 6,858 m, 22,500 ft, Xinquing, China

600. Bhagirathi I, 6,856 m, 22,493 ft, Himalaya, India
601. Deoban, 6,855 m, 22,490 ft, Himalaya, India
602. Mazeno Peak, 6,855 m, 22,490 ft, Himalaya, Pakistan
603. Mrigthuni, 6,855 m, 22,490 ft, Himalaya, India
604. Pazan I, 6,855 m, 22,490 ft, Tanggula, China
605. Chaukhamba IV, 6,854 m, 22,486 ft, Himalaya, India
606. Savoia VIII, 6,854 m, 22,486 ft, Karakoram, Pakistan
607. Dezhi Peak, 6,853 m, 22,483 ft, Karakoram, China
608. Khatang, 6,853 m, 22,483 ft, Himalaya, Nepal
609. Tuja, 6,852 m, 22,480 ft, Himalaya, China & Nepal
610. Upper Rimo I, 6,852 m, 22,480 ft, Karakoram, India
611. Alan To South, 6,851 m, 22,477 ft, Tanggula, China
612. Kanjiroba North I, 6,851 m, 22,477 ft, Himalaya, Nepal
613. Vigne I, 6,851 m, 22,477 ft, Karakoram, Pakistan
614. Wuhujiang I Northeast 2, 6,851 m, 22,477 ft, Karakoram, China
615. Chogrun Kangri, 6,850 m, 22,473 ft, Karakoram, Pakistan
616. Drohma West, 6,850 m, 22,473 ft, Himalaya, Nepal
617. Pandra, 6,850 m, 22,473 ft, Himalaya, Nepal
618. Pumeri Chhish III, 6,850 m, 22,473 ft, Karakoram, Pakistan
619. Sumgya, 6,850 m, 22,473 ft, Himalaya, China
620. Koktak I, 6,849 m, 22,470 ft, Kunlun, China
621. Daqu Peak, 6,846 m, 22,460 ft, Himalaya, China
622. Gongto, 6,846 m, 22,460 ft, Himalaya, China
623. Batura Muztagh I North 1, 6,845 m, 22,457 ft, Karakoram, Pakistan
624. Xiaofong Tip, 6,845 m, 22,457 ft, Karakoram, China & Pakistan
625. Malubiting North, 6,843 m, 22,450 ft, Karakoram, Pakistan
626. Tirgaran, 6,843 m, 22,450 ft, Hindu Kush, Afghanistan
627. Marshal Zhukov, 6,842 m, 22,447 ft, Pamir, Tajikistan
628. Pasu East, 6,842 m, 22,447 ft, Karakoram, Pakistan
629. Point 6842, 6,842 m, 22,447 ft, Nyain'a, China
630. Point 6842, 6,842 m, 22,447 ft, Karakoram, China
631. Api Nampa II, 6,841 m, 22,444 ft, Himalaya, Nepal
632. Izvestia, 6,841 m, 22,444 ft, Pamir, Tajikistan
633. Koktak II, 6,841 m, 22,444 ft, Kunlun, China
634. Chonbo, 6,840 m, 22,440 ft, Himalaya, China
635. Rimo IV North, 6,840 m, 22,440 ft, Karakoram, India
636. Gasherbrum VI, 6,839 m, 22,437 ft, Karakoram, Pakistan
637. Nilgiri South, 6,839 m, 22,437 ft, Himalaya, Nepal
638. Nanfeng North I, 6,838 m, 22,434 ft, Himalaya, China
639. Phurepu Ri I, 6,837 m, 22,431 ft, Himalaya, China
640. Kommisarov, 6,834 m, 22,421 ft, Pamir, Tajikistan
641. Chonhku Chuli, 6,833 m, 22,417 ft, Himalaya, India & Nepal
642. Khangri Shar II, 6,833 m, 22,417 ft, Himalaya, China & Nepal
643. Tsjeja Kang, 6,833 m, 22,417 ft, Himalaya, China
644. Kanjut Sar II, 6,831 m, 22,411 ft, Karakoram, Pakistan
645. Kedar Dome, 6,830 m, 22,408 ft, Himalaya, India
646. Phamtang Karpo Ri, 6,830 m, 22,408 ft, Himalaya, China & Nepal
647. Yushkin Gardan Sar West 1, 6,830 m, 22,408 ft, Karakoram, Pakistan
648. Xixbangma South IV, 6,829 m, 22,404 ft, Himalaya, China
649. Rakhiot Peak, 6,828 m, 22,401 ft, Himalaya, Pakistan
650. Point 6827, 6,827 m, 22,398 ft, Kunlun, China
651. Pengqar North, 6,826 m, 22,395 ft, Tanggula, China
652. Akal I, 6,824 m, 22,388 ft, Karakoram, China
653. Miar, 6,824 m, 22,388 ft, Karakoram, Pakistan
654. Pathibhara East, 6,824 m, 22,388 ft, Himalaya, India & Nepal

655. Sella Peak North, 6,824 m, 22,388 ft, Karakoram, China & Pakistan
656. Beifeng North, 6,822 m, 22,381 ft, Himalaya, China
657. Gangpu Ri Shar, 6,821 m, 22,378 ft, Himalaya, China
658. Upper Rimo II, 6,821 m, 22,378 ft, Karakoram, India
659. Cheo Himal, 6,820 m, 22,375 ft, Himalaya, Nepal
660. Teram Sherh II, 6,820 m, 22,375 ft, Karakoram, India
661. Yushkin Gardan Sar West 2, 6,820 m, 22,375 ft, Karakoram, Pakistan
662. Chaglasumgo East I, 6,816 m, 22,362 ft, Himalaya, China & Nepal
663. Singhi Kangri West, 6,815 m, 22,358 ft, Karakoram, China & India
664. Zongga South, 6,815 m, 22,358 ft, Himalaya, China
665. Nyainqentanghla I East, 6,814 m, 22,355 ft, Tanggula, China
666. Rapasova, 6,814 m, 22,355 ft, Tien Shan, China & Kyrgyzstan
667. Ama Dablam, 6,812 m, 22,349 ft, Himalaya, Nepal
668. Gyirong, 6,812 m, 22,349 ft, Himalaya, China
669. Sedung Peak, 6,812 m, 22,349 ft, Himalaya, China
670. Baruntse West II, 6,811 m, 22,345 ft, Himalaya, Nepal
671. Khangri Shar III, 6,811 m, 22,345 ft, Himalaya, China & Nepal
672. Simvo, 6,811 m, 22,345 ft, Himalaya, Sikkim
673. Ghondokhoro I, 6,810 m, 22,342 ft, Karakoram, Pakistan
674. Kangbu III, 6,809 m, 22,339 ft, Himalaya, China
675. Maiandi South, 6,808 m, 22,335 ft, Himalaya, India
676. Galwan II, 6,806 m, 22,329 ft, Karakoram, China
677. Langmon Zhabaran, 6,806 m, 22,329 ft, Himalaya, China
678. Lambigad Parbat I, 6,803 m, 22,319 ft, Himalaya, India
679. Maiktoli, 6,803 m, 22,319 ft, Himalaya, India
680. Angelus Peak, 6,802 m, 22,316 ft, Karakoram, Pakistan
681. Drangnag-ri, 6,801 m, 22,312 ft, Himalaya, Nepal
682. Point 6801, 6,801 m, 22,312 ft, Himalaya, Nepal
683. Central Singhi, 6,800 m, 22,309 ft, Karakoram, China
684. Druzhby, 6,800 m, 22,309 ft, Tien Shan, China & Kyrgyzstan
685. Kangcheda, 6,800 m, 22,309 ft, Himalaya, Bhutan & China
686. Shispare Northwest, 6,800 m, 22,309 ft, Karakoram, Pakistan
687. East Singhi, 6,797 m, 22,299 ft, Karakoram, China
688. Kang Guru East, 6,797 m, 22,299 ft, Himalaya, Nepal
689. Kardapu South I, 6,797 m, 22,299 ft, Himalaya, China
690. Sondhi South, 6,797 m, 22,299 ft, Karakoram, India
691. Demo I, 6,796 m, 22,296 ft, Himalaya, China
692. Pilapani, 6,796 m, 22,296 ft, Himalaya, India
693. Mana Parbat I, 6,794 m, 22,290 ft, Himalaya, India
694. Dragkar-go, 6,793 m, 22,286 ft, Himalaya, Nepal
695. Koktak III, 6,793 m, 22,286 ft, Kunlun, China
696. Kongphu, 6,793 m, 22,286 ft, Himalaya, China
697. Satopanth Northwest 1, 6,792 m, 22,283 ft, Himalaya, India
698. Pali, 6,791 m, 22,280 ft, Gangdisê, China
699. Point 6789, 6,789 m, 22,273 ft, Himalaya, China
700. South Shukpa Kunchang I, 6,789 m, 22,273 ft, Karakoram, India
701. Devtoli, 6,788 m, 22,270 ft, Himalaya, India
702. Yangra North, 6,787 m, 22,267 ft, Himalaya, China & Nepal
703. Lungme, 6,786 m, 22,263 ft, Tanggula, China
704. Uzuntal I, 6,786 m, 22,263 ft, Kunlun, China
705. Kra Bass North, 6,785 m, 22,260 ft, Karakoram, China & Pakistan
706. Moskva, 6,785 m, 22,260 ft, Pamir, Tajikistan
707. Phuparash I, 6,785 m, 22,260 ft, Karakoram, Pakistan
708. Polan, 6,785 m, 22,260 ft, Karakoram, Pakistan

709. Jagdula, 6,782 m, 22,250 ft, Himalaya, Nepal
710. Biarchedi I, 6,781 m, 22,247 ft, Karakoram, Pakistan
711. Baridornush, 6,780 m, 22,244 ft, Karakoram, Pakistan
712. Oktiabrski, 6,780 m, 22,244 ft, Pamir, Tajikistan
713. Central Rimo I, 6,779 m, 22,240 ft, Karakoram, India
714. Pissis, 6,779 m, 22,240 ft, Andes, Argentina
715. Bhrikuti, 6,778 m, 22,237 ft, Himalaya, Nepal
716. Tarlha Ri, 6,777 m, 22,234 ft, Himalaya, China
717. Changla I, 6,776 m, 22,230 ft, Himalaya, China
718. Tongqiang Northwest II, 6,776 m, 22,230 ft, Himalaya, China
719. Point 6775, 6,775 m, 22,227 ft, Himalaya, China
720. Khangri Shar IV, 6,773 m, 22,221 ft, Himalaya, China & Nepal
721. Purepu, 6,773 m, 22,221 ft, Himalaya, China
722. Bhrigupanth, 6,772 m, 22,217 ft, Himalaya, India
723. Biale I, 6,772 m, 22,217 ft, Karakoram, Pakistan
724. Gangphu Ri Nup, 6,772 m, 22,217 ft, Himalaya, China
725. Seiri Parkush, 6,772 m, 22,217 ft, Karakoram, Pakistan
726. Mana Parbat II, 6,771 m, 22,214 ft, Himalaya, India
727. Laila West, 6,770 m, 22,211 ft, Karakoram, Pakistan
728. Mercedario, 6,770 m, 22,211 ft, Andes, Argentina
729. Pure Peak, 6,769 m, 22,208 ft, Himalaya, China
730. Sabai, 6,769 m, 22,208 ft, Himalaya, Nepal
731. Uli Biaho I, 6,769 m, 22,208 ft, Karakoram, Pakistan
732. Chago II, 6,768 m, 22,204 ft, Himalaya, Nepal
733. Huascarán, 6,768 m, 22,204 ft, Andes, Peru
734. Chago Peak, 6,767 m, 22,201 ft, Himalaya, China
735. Langchung Khang, 6,766 m, 22,198 ft, Himalaya, India
736. Nilgiri Southeast, 6,765 m, 22,194 ft, Himalaya, Nepal
737. Kartamak, 6,764 m, 22,191 ft, Kunlun, China
738. Pazan II, 6,764 m, 22,191 ft, Tanggula, China
739. Podeba East, 6,762 m, 22,185 ft, Tien Shan, China & Kyrgyzstan
740. Reqiang II, 6,761 m, 22,181 ft, Himalaya, China
741. Chamraogal II, 6,760 m, 22,178 ft, Himalaya, China & Nepal
742. Chago Glacier West I, 6,758 m, 22,171 ft, Himalaya, Nepal
743. Fuqu South I, 6,758 m, 22,171 ft, Himalaya, China & Nepal
744. Dragkar-go South peak, 6,756 m, 22,165 ft, Himalaya, Nepal
745. Kondus Peak, 6,756 m, 22,165 ft, Karakoram, Pakistan
746. Akal II, 6,755 m, 22,162 ft, Karakoram, China
747. Koh-e Keshnikhan, 6,755 m, 22,162 ft, Hindu Kush, Afghanistan
748. M2, 6,755 m, 22,162 ft, Hindu Kush, Afghanistan
749. North Rimo I, 6,755 m, 22,162 ft, Karakoram, India
750. Chumik, 6,754 m, 22,158 ft, Karakoram, Pakistan
751. Hawk, 6,754 m, 22,158 ft, Karakoram, Pakistan
752. Phurepu Ri II, 6,753 m, 22,155 ft, Himalaya, China
753. Shukpa Kunchang I, 6,753 m, 22,155 ft, Karakoram, India
754. Central Rimo II, 6,752 m, 22,152 ft, Karakoram, India
755. Keha I, 6,752 m, 22,152 ft, Himalaya, Nepal
756. Mandaltang I, 6,751 m, 22,148 ft, Karakoram, India
757. Mamostong Kangri I East 2, 6,750 m, 22,145 ft, Karakoram, India
758. Shukpa Kunchang II, 6,750 m, 22,145 ft, Karakoram, India
759. Wengde Peak, 6,750 m, 22,145 ft, Himalaya, Nepal
760. Lingtren, 6,749 m, 22,142 ft, Himalaya, China & Nepal
761. Churen Himal North II, 6,748 m, 22,139 ft, Himalaya, Nepal
762. Dahong Liutan I, 6,748 m, 22,139 ft, Kunlun, China

763. Mamostong Kangri II Southeast 1, 6,746 m, 22,132 ft, Karakoram, India
764. Baruntse Southeast I, 6,745 m, 22,129 ft, Himalaya, Nepal
765. Muztagh II, 6,745 m, 22,129 ft, Karakoram, Pakistan
766. Tsangbu Ri, 6,745 m, 22,129 ft, Himalaya, Nepal
767. Dahong Liutan II, 6,744 m, 22,125 ft, Kunlun, China
768. Hongde, 6,742 m, 22,119 ft, Himalaya, Nepal
769. Lixin West, 6,742 m, 22,119 ft, Himalaya, China
770. Neru, 6,742 m, 22,119 ft, Tien Shan, China & Kyrgyzstan
771. South Shukpa Kunchang II, 6,742 m, 22,119 ft, Karakoram, India
772. Koktak IV, 6,740 m, 22,112 ft, Kunlun, China
773. Moirigkawagarbo, 6,740 m, 22,112 ft, Hengduan, China
774. Chandra Parbat I, 6,739 m, 22,109 ft, Himalaya, India
775. Lekhuwa, 6,739 m, 22,109 ft, Himalaya, Nepal
776. Mamostong Kangri II East, 6,739 m, 22,109 ft, Karakoram, India
777. Pethangtse, 6,738 m, 22,106 ft, Himalaya, China & Nepal
778. Makalu Barun I, 6,736 m, 22,099 ft, Himalaya, Nepal
779. Yurungkax I, 6,736 m, 22,099 ft, Kunlun, China
780. Chekigo, 6,735 m, 22,096 ft, Himalaya, China & Nepal
781. Kang Nachugo, 6,735 m, 22,096 ft, Himalaya, China & Nepal
782. Tsung Suwet, 6,735 m, 22,096 ft, Karakoram, China
783. Bigphera-go Shar, 6,730 m, 22,080 ft, Himalaya, Nepal
784. Mana Parbat III, 6,730 m, 22,080 ft, Himalaya, India
785. Pauhunri South, 6,730 m, 22,080 ft, Himalaya, Bhutan & India
786. Bigphera-go Shar South Peak, 6,729 m, 22,076 ft, Himalaya, Nepal
787. Chago Glacier West II, 6,728 m, 22,073 ft, Himalaya, Nepal
788. Chandra Parbat II, 6,728 m, 22,073 ft, Himalaya, India

789. Chako, 6,727 m, 22,070 ft, Himalaya, Nepal
790. Gyong, 6,727 m, 22,070 ft, Karakoram, Pakistan
791. Hathi Parbat, 6,727 m, 22,070 ft, Himalaya, India
792. Black Tooth, 6,726 m, 22,066 ft, Karakoram, Pakistan
793. Kezhen Northwest 2, 6,726 m, 22,066 ft, Karakoram, China
794. Chagragil, 6,725 m, 22,063 ft, Kunlun, China
795. Chomolonzo Northwest II, 6,723 m, 22,057 ft, Himalaya, China & Nepal
796. Karl Marx, 6,723 m, 22,057 ft, Pamir, Tajikistan
797. Llullaillaco, 6,723 m, 22,057 ft, Andes, Argentina & Chile
798. Shakhdarinski, 6,723 m, 22,057 ft, Pamir, Unknown
799. Achirh, 6,721 m, 22,050 ft, Karakoram, China
800. Annapurna South IV, 6,721 m, 22,050 ft, Himalaya, Nepal
801. Maiandi North, 6,721 m, 22,050 ft, Himalaya, India
802. Matri, 6,721 m, 22,050 ft, Himalaya, India
803. Fikker, 6,718 m, 22,040 ft, Pamir, Tajikistan
804. Mamostong Kangri I Northwest, 6,718 m, 22,040 ft, Karakoram, India
805. Dzerzhinskovo, 6,717 m, 22,037 ft, Pamir, Kyrgyzstan & Tajikistan
806. Kabang Peak, 6,717 m, 22,037 ft, Himalaya, China
807. Pangbug Ri, 6,716 m, 22,034 ft, Himalaya, China & Nepal
808. Vigne II, 6,716 m, 22,034 ft, Karakoram, Pakistan
809. Gurudongmar Sanglapu, 6,715 m, 22,030 ft, Himalaya, India
810. Kuk Sel, 6,715 m, 22,030 ft, Kunlun, China
811. Lambigad Parbat II, 6,715 m, 22,030 ft, Himalaya, India
812. Phrul Rangtshan Ri I, 6,715 m, 22,030 ft, Himalaya, Nepal
813. Tunqatang, 6,715 m, 22,030 ft, Himalaya, China
814. Dokpan, 6,714 m, 22,027 ft, Tanggula, China
815. Yulin IV, 6,714 m, 22,027 ft, Karakoram, Pakistan
816. Chamlang V, 6,712 m, 22,020 ft, Himalaya, Nepal

817. Point 6712, 6,712 m, 22,020 ft, Himalaya, China & Nepal
818. Qatang I, 6,711 m, 22,017 ft, Tanggula, China
819. Donkung, 6,710 m, 22,014 ft, Tanggula, China & India
820. Dzanye, 6,710 m, 22,014 ft, Himalaya, China & Nepal
821. Khumbu Himal III, 6,710 m, 22,014 ft, Himalaya, China
822. Mudztagh, 6,710 m, 22,014 ft, Kunlun, China
823. Pangbug Ri North I, 6,710 m, 22,014 ft, Himalaya, China & Nepal
824. Qogir Northwest, 6,710 m, 22,014 ft, Karakoram, China & Pakistan
825. Serac Peak North 1, 6,710 m, 22,014 ft, Karakoram, Pakistan
826. South of Amphu Gl. I, 6,710 m, 22,014 ft, Himalaya, Nepal
827. Thulagi North I, 6,710 m, 22,014 ft, Himalaya, Nepal
828. Sabai North I, 6,709 m, 22,011 ft, Himalaya, Nepal
829. Ghan Parbat, 6,708 m, 22,007 ft, Himalaya, India
830. Raikana I, 6,708 m, 22,007 ft, Himalaya, Nepal
831. Changzheng South II, 6,706 m, 22,001 ft, Himalaya, China
832. Maquilqo, 6,706 m, 22,001 ft, Kunlun, China
833. Tilicho West I, 6,706 m, 22,001 ft, Himalaya, Nepal
834. Namu Shin Kang II, 6,705 m, 21,998 ft, Tanggula, China
835. Ripimo, 6,705 m, 21,998 ft, Himalaya, China & Nepal
836. Qangring Southwest, 6,704 m, 21,994 ft, Tanggula, China
837. Sabai North II, 6,704 m, 21,994 ft, Himalaya, Nepal
838. Karalax South 1, 6,703 m, 21,991 ft, Kunlun, China
839. Satopanth Northwest 2, 6,702 m, 21,988 ft, Himalaya, India
840. Biantha Brakk, 6,700 m, 21,981 ft, Karakoram, Pakistan
841. Dhaulagiri IV Northwest, 6,700 m, 21,981 ft, Himalaya, Nepal
842. Falchan I, 6,700 m, 21,981 ft, Karakoram, Pakistan
843. Junction Peak, 6,700 m, 21,981 ft, Karakoram, India
844. Kaxtax I, 6,700 m, 21,981 ft, Kunlun, China
845. Malangutti Sar II, 6,700 m, 21,981 ft, Karakoram, Pakistan
846. Malangutti Sar III, 6,700 m, 21,981 ft, Karakoram, Pakistan
847. Momil Sar South 1, 6,700 m, 21,981 ft, Karakoram, Pakistan
848. Momil Sar South 2, 6,700 m, 21,981 ft, Karakoram, Pakistan
849. Point 6700, 6,700 m, 21,981 ft, Karakoram, India
850. Prupuo Barakha Southwest, 6,700 m, 21,981 ft, Karakoram, Pakistan
851. Ramtang Peak, 6,700 m, 21,981 ft, Himalaya, Nepal
852. Sharphu II, 6,700 m, 21,981 ft, Himalaya, Nepal
853. Shukpa Kunchang III, 6,700 m, 21,981 ft, Karakoram, India
854. Tasa Peak, 6,700 m, 21,981 ft, Karakoram, Pakistan
855. Teram Kangri I South, 6,700 m, 21,981 ft, Karakoram, India
856. Thulagi South, 6,700 m, 21,981 ft, Himalaya, Nepal
857. Khamjung Himal, 6,699 m, 21,978 ft, Himalaya, Nepal
858. Xatang Peak, 6,698 m, 21,975 ft, Himalaya, China
859. Xifeng North I, 6,698 m, 21,975 ft, Himalaya, China
860. Koshi Toshi, 6,697 m, 21,971 ft, Kunlun, China
861. Sondhi Northeast, 6,697 m, 21,971 ft, Karakoram, India
862. Panayo Tippa, 6,696 m, 21,968 ft, Himalaya, Nepal
863. Biale II, 6,695 m, 21,965 ft, Karakoram, Pakistan
864. Cho Polu I, 6,695 m, 21,965 ft, Himalaya, Nepal
865. Nyain'a Northeast 1, 6,695 m, 21,965 ft, Nyain'a, China
866. Sabai North III, 6,695 m, 21,965 ft, Himalaya, Nepal
867. Himal Chuli Northeast, 6,693 m, 21,958 ft, Himalaya, Nepal

868. Pandim, 6,691 m, 21,952 ft, Himalaya, India
869. Broad Peak East 2, 6,690 m, 21,948 ft, Karakoram, China
870. Ghondokhoro II, 6,690 m, 21,948 ft, Karakoram, Pakistan
871. Nupchu, 6,690 m, 21,948 ft, Himalaya, Nepal
872. Tukuche Southwest, 6,690 m, 21,948 ft, Himalaya, Nepal
873. Tsoboje, 6,689 m, 21,945 ft, Himalaya, Nepal
874. Garkyagdêugang, 6,688 m, 21,942 ft, Tanggula, China
875. Mangnang I, 6,688 m, 21,942 ft, Himalaya, China
876. Point 6687, 6,687 m, 21,938 ft, Himalaya, Nepal
877. Kang Taiga Northwest I, 6,685 m, 21,932 ft, Himalaya, Nepal
878. Kang Tiaga, 6,685 m, 21,932 ft, Himalaya, Nepal
879. Mani Peak, 6,684 m, 21,929 ft, Karakoram, Pakistan
880. Kyzylagyn, 6,683 m, 21,925 ft, Pamir, Kyrgyzstan & Tajikistan
881. Peak 6682, 6,682 m, 21,922 ft, Himalaya, China & Nepal
882. Reqiang III, 6,681 m, 21,919 ft, Himalaya, China
883. Sultan Chhushko, 6,681 m, 21,919 ft, Karakoram, India
884. Xatang South I, 6,681 m, 21,919 ft, Himalaya, China
885. Trisuli II, 6,680 m, 21,916 ft, Himalaya, India
886. Xiaofong North, 6,679 m, 21,912 ft, Karakoram, China & Pakistan
887. Devistan I, 6,678 m, 21,909 ft, Himalaya, India
888. North Rimo II, 6,678 m, 21,909 ft, Karakoram, India
889. Rathong, 6,678 m, 21,909 ft, Himalaya, Nepal & India
890. Koz Sar, 6,677 m, 21,906 ft, Karakoram, Pakistan
891. Gyirong, 6,676 m, 21,902 ft, Himalaya, China
892. Vigne III, 6,674 m, 21,896 ft, Karakoram, Pakistan
893. Edinstva, 6,673 m, 21,893 ft, Pamir, Kyrgyzstan & Tajikistan
894. Peak 6673, 6,673 m, 21,893 ft, Himalaya, China & Nepal
895. Baudha, 6,672 m, 21,889 ft, Himalaya, Nepal
896. Gangotri I, 6,672 m, 21,889 ft, Himalaya, India
897. Phagmogoldo, 6,672 m, 21,889 ft, Himalaya, Nepal
898. Gobarung Peak, 6,671 m, 21,886 ft, Himalaya, China
899. Amadirne, 6,670 m, 21,883 ft, Himalaya, China
900. Chong Kumdan Kangri III, 6,670 m, 21,883 ft, Karakoram, India
901. Dongfang North, 6,670 m, 21,883 ft, Himalaya, China
902. Tamdyn I, 6,670 m, 21,883 ft, Tien Shan, China
903. Sobithongie, 6,669 m, 21,879 ft, Himalaya, Nepal
904. Langbe Kangri, 6,668 m, 21,876 ft, Himalaya, China
905. Point 6668, 6,668 m, 21,876 ft, Himalaya, China
906. Bigphera-go Nup, 6,666 m, 21,870 ft, Himalaya, Nepal
907. Dansam, 6,666 m, 21,870 ft, Karakoram, Pakistan
908. Kolakir, 6,666 m, 21,870 ft, Kunlun, China
909. Lalaga Ri, 6,666 m, 21,870 ft, Himalaya, China
910. Point 6666, 6,666 m, 21,870 ft, Gangdisê, China
911. Khumbutse, 6,665 m, 21,866 ft, Himalaya, China & Nepal
912. North Rimo III, 6,665 m, 21,866 ft, Karakoram, India
913. Monco Bünnyi South, 6,664 m, 21,863 ft, Tanggula, China
914. Junction Peak II, 6,663 m, 21,860 ft, Karakoram, India
915. Panwali Dwar, 6,663 m, 21,860 ft, Himalaya, India
916. Yapu, 6,663 m, 21,860 ft, Gangdisê, China
917. Drolambao Glacier West I, 6,662 m, 21,856 ft, Himalaya, Nepal
918. Makalu Barun II, 6,662 m, 21,856 ft, Himalaya, Nepal
919. Uzuntal II, 6,662 m, 21,856 ft, Kunlun, China
920. Xatang South II, 6,662 m, 21,856 ft, Himalaya, China

921. Darkot West, 6,661 m, 21,853 ft, Hindu Kush, Pakistan
922. Tughmo Zarpo North 1, 6,661 m, 21,853 ft, Karakoram, India
923. Meru, 6,660 m, 21,850 ft, Himalaya, India
924. Shuqsuna I, 6,660 m, 21,850 ft, Karakoram, China
925. South Kailas, 6,659 m, 21,847 ft, Karakoram, India
926. Noshaq Southeast, 6,658 m, 21,843 ft, Hindu Kush, Pakistan
927. Phurbi Chyachu, 6,658 m, 21,843 ft, Himalaya, China
928. Chêm Northwest, 6,657 m, 21,840 ft, Gangdisê, China
929. Falchan II, 6,657 m, 21,840 ft, Karakoram, Pakistan
930. Ganesh V East I, 6,657 m, 21,840 ft, Himalaya, Nepal
931. Janak Himal, 6,657 m, 21,840 ft, Himalaya, China
932. Jomsang Himal South, 6,656 m, 21,837 ft, Himalaya, Nepal
933. Kangrinboq, 6,656 m, 21,837 ft, Gangdisê, China
934. Lumding I, 6,656 m, 21,837 ft, Himalaya, Nepal
935. Numbur North I, 6,656 m, 21,837 ft, Himalaya, Nepal
936. Hill Yengisogat I, 6,654 m, 21,830 ft, Karakoram, China
937. Matri Southeast, 6,654 m, 21,830 ft, Himalaya, India
938. Mera Peak, 6,654 m, 21,830 ft, Himalaya, Nepal
939. Miyar I, 6,654 m, 21,830 ft, Himalaya, India
940. Nandali Peak East II, 6,653 m, 21,827 ft, Himalaya, China & Nepal
941. Tengi Ragi Tau East Peak, 6,652 m, 21,824 ft, Himalaya, Nepal
942. Abi Gamin East Peak, 6,651 m, 21,820 ft, Himalaya, China & Nepal
943. Kichik Kumdan I, 6,651 m, 21,820 ft, Karakoram, India
944. Kury Kangri, 6,650 m, 21,817 ft, Karakoram, Pakistan
945. Skirish Sar, 6,650 m, 21,817 ft, Karakoram, Pakistan
946. Panayo Shar, 6,649 m, 21,814 ft, Himalaya, Nepal
947. Panayo Tippa South I, 6,649 m, 21,814 ft, Himalaya, Nepal
948. Devi Mukut, 6,648 m, 21,811 ft, Himalaya, India
949. Point 6648, 6,648 m, 21,811 ft, Karakoram, China
950. Qumgan II, 6,648 m, 21,811 ft, Kunlun, China
951. Savoia IX, 6,648 m, 21,811 ft, Karakoram, Pakistan
952. Tilcho East, 6,648 m, 21,811 ft, Himalaya, Nepal
953. Khangsar Kang North, 6,646 m, 21,804 ft, Himalaya, Nepal
954. Pangbug Ri North II, 6,646 m, 21,804 ft, Himalaya, China & Nepal
955. Qianjing Peak, 6,646 m, 21,804 ft, Himalaya, China
956. Yanglang Peak, 6,646 m, 21,804 ft, Himalaya, China
957. Donisha, 6,645 m, 21,801 ft, Pamir, Tajikistan
958. Drolambao Glacier West II, 6,645 m, 21,801 ft, Himalaya, Nepal
959. Phole, 6,645 m, 21,801 ft, Himalaya, Nepal
960. Pindu, 6,645 m, 21,801 ft, Himalaya, China & Nepal
961. Singhu Chuli, 6,645 m, 21,801 ft, Himalaya, Nepal
962. Dongfang Southeast II, 6,644 m, 21,797 ft, Himalaya, China
963. Tuanjie, 6,644 m, 21,797 ft, Kunlun, China
964. Pukpoche, 6,643 m, 21,794 ft, Karakoram, India
965. Xatang North, 6,643 m, 21,794 ft, Himalaya, China
966. Puyung East I, 6,642 m, 21,791 ft, Himalaya, China
967. Yalungang, 6,642 m, 21,791 ft, Tanggula, China
968. Baruntse North I, 6,641 m, 21,788 ft, Himalaya, Nepal
969. East Chamshen, 6,641 m, 21,788 ft, Karakoram, India
970. Gomba, 6,641 m, 21,788 ft, Himalaya, China & Nepal
971. Zetkin, 6,641 m, 21,788 ft, Pamir, Tajikistan
972. Saser Kangri IV Northeast, 6,640 m, 21,784 ft, Karakoram, India
973. Dhaulagiri II Northeast, 6,639 m, 21,781 ft, Himalaya, Nepal

974. Mukut Himal I, 6,639 m, 21,781 ft, Himalaya, Nepal
975. Qatang II, 6,639 m, 21,781 ft, Tanggula, China
976. Spang I, 6,639 m, 21,781 ft, Karakoram, India
977. Chaukhamba V, 6,638 m, 21,778 ft, Himalaya, India
978. Muztag, 6,638 m, 21,778 ft, Kunlun, China
979. Cerro Sin Nombre, 6,637 m, 21,774 ft, Andes, Argentina & Chile
980. Kezhen West 2, 6,637 m, 21,774 ft, Karakoram, China & Pakistan
981. Kyagar Peak, 6,637 m, 21,774 ft, Karakoram, China
982. Shatior East, 6,637 m, 21,774 ft, Tien Shan, Kazakhstan & Kyrgyzstan
983. Xatang South III, 6,637 m, 21,774 ft, Himalaya, China
984. Lhatse Gompa South, 6,636 m, 21,771 ft, Tanggula, China
985. Lhatse Gompa West, 6,636 m, 21,771 ft, Tanggula, China
986. Kyagar II, 6,635 m, 21,768 ft, Karakoram, China
987. Tirsuli West 2, 6,635 m, 21,768 ft, Himalaya, India

988. Yerupajá, 6,634 m, 21,765 ft, Andes, Peru
989. Godong Kangri I, 6,633 m, 21,761 ft, Gangdisê, China
990. Point 6633, 6,633 m, 21,761 ft, Kunlun, China
991. Joanli, 6,632 m, 21,758 ft, Himalaya, India
992. Kharcha Kund, 6,632 m, 21,758 ft, Himalaya, India
993. Kubi Gangri I, 6,631 m, 21,755 ft, Himalaya, China & Nepal
994. Dong Qogir I, 6,630 m, 21,751 ft, Karakoram, China
995. Point 6630, 6,630 m, 21,751 ft, Nyain'a, China
996. Qingnian, 6,630 m, 21,751 ft, Karakoram, China
997. Shukpa Kunchang IV, 6,630 m, 21,751 ft, Karakoram, India
998. Garanphu, 6,629 m, 21,748 ft, Himalaya, Nepal
999. Hathi Parbat North, 6,629 m, 21,748 ft, Himalaya, India
1000. Mukudas, 6,629 m, 21,748 ft, Karakoram, Pakistan

Compiled from: www.highalpex.com/Peaklist/

APPENDIX B:
4,000-METER PEAKS IN THE ALPS

Authors' note: While there are 60 major peaks above 4,000 meters in the Alps, the list contains 70 entries above or equal to 4,000 meters; this is because, in addition to the major peaks, there are 10 minor or satellite peaks. Typically, minor peaks are rarely the goal of a climb; rather, they are noteworthy geographical features: for example the Dôme du Goûter, in the Mont Blanc Range. However, there are important exceptions, including all the secondary summits on the Grandes Jorasses' mile-wide summit ridge, and the Dôme de Neige des Écrins. In the main text, we refer to major peaks: for example, the Dom is the sixth highest major peak in the Alps, which is indicated in the following table by the note (6/60) at the end of the corresponding entry, although it is listed as number seven below because Mont Blanc's minor satellite, the Mont Blanc de Courmayeur, also appears in the table. This example is particularly striking because, as Mont Blanc de Courmayeur is the physical highest point in Italy, it is listed as such in the encyclopedia, although it is almost always climbed on the way to Mont Blanc and not as a stand-alone peak. We also note that the altitudes indicated here are those predominantly used in the literature. The year first ascent is indicated if known.

1. Mt. Blanc, 4,807 m, 15,770 ft, Mt. Blanc, France (1786) (1/60)
2. Mt. Blanc de Courmayeur, 4,748 m, 15,577 ft, Mt. Blanc, Italy
3. Monte Rosa, Dufourspitze, 4,634 m, 15,203 ft, Pennine Alps, Switzerland/Italy (1855) (2/60)
4. Monte Rosa, Nordend, 4,609 m, 15,121 ft, Pennine Alps, Switzerland/Italy (1861) (3/60)
5. Monte Rosa, Zumstein, 4,563 m, 14,970 ft, Pennine Alps, Switzerland/Italy (1820) (4/60)

6. Signalkuppe, 4,556 m, 14,947 ft, Pennine Alps, Switzerland (1842) (5/60)
7. Dom, 4,545 m, 14,911 ft, Pennine Alps, Switzerland (1858) (6/60)
8. Lyskamm, 4,527 m, 14,852 ft, Pennine Alps, Switzerland (1861) (7/60)
9. Weisshorn, 4,505 m, 14,780 ft, Pennine Alps, Switzerland (1861) (8/60)
10. Taschhörn, 4,490 m, 14,730 ft, Pennine Alps, Switzerland (1862) (9/60)
11. Matterhorn, 4,478 m, 14,691 ft, Pennine Alps, Switzerland (1865) (10/60)
12. Mt. Maudit, 4,465 m, 14,648 ft, Mt. Blanc, France (1878) (11/60)
13. Monte Rosa, Pointe Parrot, 4,436 m, 14,553 ft, Pennine Alps, Switzerland/Italy (1863) (12/60)
14. Dent Blanche, 4,356 m, 14,291 ft, Pennine Alps, Switzerland (1862) (13/60)
15. Ludwigshöhe, 4,341 m, 14,242 ft, Pennine Alps, Switzerland (1898) (14/60)
16. Nadelhorn, 4,327 m, 14,196 ft, Pennine Alps, Switzerland (1853) (15/60)
17. Pointe Giordani, 4,322 m, 14,179 ft, Pennine Alps, Switzerland (1872) (16/60)
18. Schwarzhorn, 4,322 m, 14,179 ft, Pennine Alps, Switzerland (1873) (17/60)
19. Grand Combin, 4,314 m, 14,153 ft, Pennine Alps, Switzerland (1857) (18/60)
20. Dôme du Goûter, 4,304 m, 14,120 ft, Mt. Blanc, France
21. Lenzspitze, 4,294 m, 14,087 ft, Pennine Alps, Switzerland (1870) (19/60)
22. Finsteraarhorn, 4,274 m, 14,022 ft, Bernese Alps, Switzerland (1812) (20/60)
23. Mt. Blanc du Tacul, 4,248 m, 13,937 ft, Mt. Blanc, France (1851) (21/60)

24. Stecknadelhorn, 4,242 m, 13,917 ft, Pennine Alps, Switzerland (1887) (22/60)
25. Castor, 4,226 m, 13,864 ft, Pennine Alps, Switzerland (1861) (23/60)
26. Zinalrothorn, 4,221 m, 13,848 ft, Pennine Alps, Switzerland (1864) (24/60)
27. Hohberghorn, 4,219 m, 13,841 ft, Pennine Alps, Switzerland (1869) (25/60)
28. Pyramide Vincent, 4,215 m, 13,828 ft, Pennine Alps, Switzerland (1851) (26/60)
29. Grandes Jorasses, Pointe Walker, 4,208 m, 13,805 ft, Mt. Blanc, France/Italy (1868) (27/60)
30. Alphubel, 4,206 m, 13,799 ft, Pennine Alps, Switzerland (1860) (28/60)
31. Rimpfischhorn, 4,198 m, 13,772 ft, Pennine Alps, Switzerland (1859) (29/60)
32. Aletschhorn, 4,195 m, 13,763 ft, Bernese Alps, Switzerland (1859) (30/60)
33. Strahlhorn, 4,190 m, 13,746 ft, Pennine Alps, Switzerland (1854) (31/60)
34. Dent d'Hérens, 4,171 m, 13,684 ft, Pennine Alps, Switzerland (1863) (32/60)
35. Breithorn, 4,165 m, 13,664 ft, Pennine Alps, Switzerland (1813) (33/60)
36. Bishorn, 4,159 m, 13,645 ft, Pennine Alps, Switzerland (1884) (34/60)
37. Jungfrau, 4,158 m, 13,641 ft, Bernese Alps, Switzerland (1811) (35/60)
38. Grandes Jorasses, Pointe Whymper, 4,148 m, 13,608 ft, Mt. Blanc, France/Italy (1864)
39. Aig. Verte, 4,122 m, 13,523 ft, Mt. Blanc, France (1865) (36/60)
40. Aig. du Diable, 4,114 m, 13,497 ft, Mt. Blanc, France
41. Aig. Blanche de Peuterey, 4,112 m, 13,490 ft, Mt. Blanc, Italy (1885) (37/60)
42. Grandes Jorasses, Pointe Croz, 4,110 m, 13,484 ft, Mt. Blanc, France/Italy (1864)
43. Pointe de l'Androsace, 4,107 m, 13,474 ft, Mt. Blanc, France
44. Barre des Écrins, 4,102 m, 13,458 ft, Oisans, France (1864) (38/60)
45. La Grande Rocheuse, 4,102 m, 13,458 ft, Mt. Blanc, France (1865) (39/60)
46. Mönch, 4,099 m, 13,448 ft, Bernese Alps, Switzerland (1857) (40/60)
47. Pollux, 4,091 m, 13,421 ft, Pennine Alps, Switzerland (1864) (41/60)
48. Pic Lory, 4,086 m, 13,405 ft, Oisans, France
49. Schreckhorn, 4,078 m, 13,379 ft, Bernese Alps, Switzerland (1861) (42/60)
50. Mont Brouillard, 4,069 m, 13,349 ft, Mt. Blanc, Italy (1906) (43/60)
51. Grandes Jorasses, Pointe Marguerite, 4,065 m, 13,336 ft, Mt. Blanc, France/Italy
52. Obergabelhorn, 4,063 m, 13,330 ft, Pennine Alps (1865) (44/60)
53. Gran Paradiso, 4,061 m, 13,323 ft, Graian Alps, Italy (1860) (45/60)
54. Aig. de Bionassay, 4,052 m, 13,293 ft, Mt. Blanc, France/Italy (1865) (46/60)
55. Piz Bernina, 4,049 m, 13,284 ft, Rhaetian Alps, Switzerland/Italy (1850) (47/60)
56. Grand-Fiescherhorn, 4,049 m, 13,284 ft, Bernese Alps, Switzerland (1862) (48/60)
57. Grandes Jorasses, Pointe Hélène, 4,045 m, 13,270 ft, Mt. Blanc, France/Italy
58. Gross-Grünhorn, 4,044 m, 13,267 ft, Bernese Alps, Switzerland (1865) (49/60)
59. Lauteraarhorn, 4,042 m, 13,261 ft, Bernese Alps, Switzerland (1842) (50/60)
60. Aig. du Jardin, 4,035 m, 13,238 ft, Mt. Blanc, France (1904) (51/60)
61. Durrenhorn, 4,034 m, 13,234 ft, Pennine Alps, Switzerland (1879) (52/60)
62. Allalinhorn, 4,027 m, 13,211 ft, Pennine Alps, Switzerland (1856) (53/60)
63. Hinter-Fiescherhorn, 4,025 m, 13,205 ft, Bernese Alps, Switzerland (1864) (54/60)
64. Weissmies, 4,023 m, 13,198 ft, Pennine Alps, Switzerland (1855) (55/60)
65. Dôme de Rochefort, 4,015 m, 13,172 ft, Mt. Blanc, France/Italy (1881) (56/60)
66. Dôme de Neige des Écrins, 4,015 m, 13,172 ft, Oisans, France
67. Dent du Géant, 4,013 m, 13,166 ft, Mt. Blanc, France/Italy (1882) (57/60)
68. Lagginhorn, 4,010 m, 13,156 ft, Pennine Alps, Switzerland (1856) (58/60)
69. Aig. de Rochefort, 4,001 m, 13,126 ft, Mt. Blanc, France/Italy (1873) (59/60)
70. Les Droites, 4,000 m, 13,123 ft, Mt. Blanc, France (1876) (60/60)

APPENDIX C: 6,000-METER PEAKS IN THE ANDES

Authors' note: While the encyclopedia text lists 20 premier peaks in the Andes, this list contains 84 entries above 6,000 meters; this is because, in addition to the major peaks, there are minor or satellite peaks. Typically, minor peaks are rarely the goal of a climb; rather, they are noteworthy geographical features. We also note that the altitudes indicated here are those predominantly used in the literature.

1. Aconcagua 6,959 m, 22,831 ft, Andes, Argentina (1/20)
2. Ojos del Salado 6,880 m, 22,572 ft, Andes, Chile (2/20)
3. Pissis 6,779 m, 22,240 ft, Andes, Argentina (3/20)
4. Mercedario 6,770 m, 22,211 ft, Andes, Argentina (4/20)
5. Huascarán 6,768 m, 22,204 ft, Andes, Peru (5/20)
6. Llullaillaco 6,723 m, 22,057 ft, Andes, Argentina & Chile (6/20)
7. Cerro Sin Nombre 6,637 m, 21,774 ft, Andes, Argentina & Chile
8. Yerupajá 6,634 m, 21,765 ft, Andes, Peru (7/20)
9. Tres Cruces 6,620 m, 21,719 ft, Andes, Argentina & Chile
10. Coropuna 6,613 m, 21,696 ft, Andes, Peru (8/20)
11. Cerro de Incahuasi 6,601 m, 21,656 ft, Andes, Argentina & Chile
12. Cerro Tupungato 6,550 m, 21,489 ft, Andes, Argentina & Chile (9/20)
13. Sajama 6,520 m, 21,423 ft, Andes, Bolivia (10/20)
14. Cerro Puntas Negras 6,500 m, 21,325 ft, Andes, Argentina & Chile
15. Cerro del Nacimento 6,493 m, 21,302 ft, Andes, Argentina & Chile
16. El Muerto 6,476 m, 21,246 ft, Andes, Argentina & Chile
17. Illimani 6,462 m, 21,200 ft, Andes, Bolivia (11/20)
18. Cerro Bonete 6,410 m, 21,020 ft, Andes, Argentina & Chile
19. Cerro Ramada 6,410 m, 21,020 ft, Andes, Argentina & Chile
20. Boneto Chico 6,400 m, 20,997 ft, Andes, Argentina & Chile
21. Huandoy 6,395 m, 20,980 ft, Andes, Peru (12/20)
22. Huantsan 6,395 m, 20,980 ft, Andes, Peru (12/20)
23. Ancohuma 6,388 m, 20,958 ft, Andes, Bolivia (14/20)
24. Ausangate 6,384 m, 20,944 ft, Andes, Peru (15/20)
25. Illampu 6,362 m, 20,872 ft, Andes, Bolivia (16/20)
26. Chopicalqui 6,354 m, 20,846 ft, Andes, Peru (17/20)
27. Siulá 6,352 m, 20,839 ft, Andes, Peru
28. Nevado Parinacota 6,330 m, 20,767 ft, Andes, Bolivia & Chile
29. Cerro las Tortolas 6,323 m, 20,744 ft, Andes, Argentina & Chile
30. Cerro Veladero 6,320 m, 20,734 ft, Andes, Argentina & Chile
31. Cachi 6,310 m, 20,702 ft, Andes, Argentina & Chile

32. Chimborazo 6,310 m, 20,702 ft, Andes, Ecuador (18/20)
33. Cerro Alma Negra 6,290 m, 20,636 ft, Andes, Argentina & Chile
34. Palkaraju 6,274 m, 20,583 ft, Andes, Peru
35. Salcantay 6,271 m, 20,574 ft, Andes, Peru (19/20)
36. Veintimilla 6,270 m, 20,570 ft, Andes, Ecuador
37. Siulá Chico 6,265 m, 20,554 ft, Andes, Peru
38. Santa Cruz 6,259 m, 20,534 ft, Andes, Peru
39. Cerro del Olivares 6,252 m, 20,511 ft, Andes, Argentina & Chile
40. Huakaña 6,249 m, 20,501 ft, Andes, Bolivia
41. Nevado Pomerape 6,240 m, 20,472 ft, Andes, Bolivia & Chile
42. Cerro Pular 6,225 m, 20,423 ft, Andes, Argentina & Chile
43. Chinchey 6,222 m, 20,413 ft, Andes, Peru
44. Cerro Solo 6,190 m, 20,308 ft, Andes, Argentina & Chile
45. Copa 6,188 m, 20,301 ft, Andes, Peru
46. El Ermitaño 6,187 m, 20,298 ft, Andes, Argentina & Chile
47. Cerro Aucanquilcha 6,180 m, 20,275 ft, Andes, Bolivia & Chile
48. Ranrapalka 6,162 m, 20,216 ft, Andes, Peru
49. Quehuar 6,160 m, 20,209 ft, Andes, Argentina & Chile
50. Pastos Grandes, 6,157 m, 20,200 ft, Andes, Argentina & Chile
51. Cerro Pabellón 6,152 m, 20,183 ft, Andes, Argentina & Chile
52. Pukaranra 6,147 m, 20,167 ft, Andes, Peru
53. Sarapo 6,143 m, 20,154 ft, Andes, Peru
54. Chearoco 6,127 m, 20,101 ft, Andes, Bolivia
55. Jirishanca 6,126 m, 20,098 ft, Andes, Peru (20/20)
56. Hualcán 6,125 m, 20,095 ft, Andes, Peru
57. Yerupajá Chico 6,121 m, 20,082 ft, Andes, Peru
58. San Pablo 6,118 m, 20,072 ft, Andes, Bolivia & Chile
59. Chacraraju 6,113 m, 20,055 ft, Andes, Peru
60. Juncal 6,110 m, 20,045 ft, Andes, Argentina & Chile
61. Cerro El Condor 6,103 m, 20,022 ft, Andes, Argentina & Chile
62. Antofalla 6,100 m, 20,013 ft, Andes, Argentina & Chile
63. Chaupi Orco 6,100 m, 20,013 ft, Andes, Bolivia & Peru
64. Chaupi Orco 6,100 m, 20,013 ft, Andes, Peru
65. Marmolejo 6,100 m, 20,013 ft, Andes, Argentina & Chile
66. Solimana 6,100 m, 20,013 ft, Andes, Peru
67. Huayna Potosi 6,094 m, 19,993 ft, Andes, Bolivia
68. Jatunhuma 6,094 m, 19,993 ft, Andes, Peru
69. Huallatiri 6,087 m, 19,970 ft, Andes, Bolivia & Chile
70. Chachani 6,084 m, 19,960 ft, Andes, Peru
71. Colquecruz 6,075 m, 19,931 ft, Andes, Peru
72. Chachacomani 6,074 m, 19,927 ft, Andes, Bolivia
73. Pumasillo 6,070 m, 19,914 ft, Andes, Peru
74. Jatunriti 6,067 m, 19,904 ft, Andes, Peru
75. Nevado del Plomo 6,050 m, 19,849 ft, Andes, Argentina & Chile
76. Cerro Ralplana 6,045 m, 19,832 ft, Andes, Bolivia & Chile
77. Rassac 6,040 m, 19,816 ft, Andes, Peru
78. Pico del Norte 6,030 m, 19,783 ft, Andes, Bolivia
79. Ampato 6,025 m, 19,767 ft, Andes, Peru
80. Cerro San Francisco 6,020 m, 19,750 ft, Andes, Argentina & Chile
81. Colquepunco 6,020 m, 19,750 ft, Andes, Peru
82. Nuevo Mundo 6,020 m, 19,750 ft, Andes, Bolivia & Chile
83. Los Piuquenes 6,012 m, 19,724 ft, Andes, Argentina & Chile
84. Cayangate 6,001 m, 19,688 ft, Andes, Peru

Appendix D:
North America's
14,000-Footers

1. Denali (Mt. McKinley) 6,193 m, 20,320 ft, Alaska Range, Alaska, U.S.
2. Mt. Logan, 5,959 m, 19,551 ft, Saint Elias Range, Yukon, Canada
3. Denali (Mt. McKinley) North Peak, 5,934 m, 19,470 ft, Alaska Range, Alaska, U.S.
4. Orizaba, 5,700 m, 18,700 ft, Sierra Madre Oriental, Puebla & Veracruz, Mexico
5. Mt. Saint Elias, 5,489 m, 18,009 ft, Saint Elias Range, Alaska & Yukon, U.S. & Canada
6. Popocatépetl, 5,451 m, 17,887 ft, Puebla Range, Puebla & Mexico, Mexico
7. Mt. Foraker, 5,303 m, 17,400 ft, Alaska Range, Alaska, U.S.
8. Iztaccíhuatl, 5,286 m, 17,343 ft, Puebla Range, Puebla & Mexico, Mexico
9. Mt. Lucania, 5,226 m, 17,147 ft, Saint Elias Range, Yukon, Canada
10. Mt. King, 5,173 m, 16,973 ft, Saint Elias Range, Yukon, Canada
11. Mt. Steele, 5,073 m, 16,645 ft, Saint Elias Range, Yukon, Canada
12. Mt. Bona, 5,029 m, 16,500 ft, Wrangell Range, Alaska, U.S.
13. Mt. Blackburn, 4,995 m, 16,390 ft, Wrangell Range, Alaska, U.S.
14. Mt. Sanford, 4,949 m, 16,237 ft, Wrangell Range, Alaska, U.S.
15. Atlantic Peak, 4,879 m, 16,008 ft, Saint Elias Range, Yukon, Canada
16. Wood Peak, 4,842 m, 15,887 ft, Saint Elias Range, Yukon, Canada
17. South Buttress, 4,841 m, 15,885 ft, Alaska Range, Alaska, U.S.
18. Mt. Vancouver, 4,812 m, 15,788 ft, Saint Elias Range, Alaska & Yukon, U.S. & Canada
19. Wood, NW Peak, 4,798 m, 15,742 ft, Saint Elias Range, Yukon, Canada
20. Mt. Churchill, 4,766 m, 15,638 ft, Saint Elias Range, Alaska, U.S.
21. Mt. Slaggard, 4,742 m, 15,559 ft, Saint Elias Range, Yukon, Canada
22. MacAulay Peak, 4,690 m, 15,388 ft, Saint Elias Range, Yukon, Canada
23. Mt. Fairweather, 4,663 m, 15,299 ft, Saint Elias Range, Alaska & British Columbia, U.S. & Canada
24. Teyotl, 4,660 m, 15,289 ft, Puebla Range, Puebla, Mexico
25. Nevado de Toluca, 4,632 m, 15,197 ft, Sierra Madre Occidental Range, Mexico, Mexico
26. Hubbard Peak, 4,577 m, 15,017 ft, Saint Elias Range, Alaska & British Columbia, U.S. & Canada
27. Mt. Bear, 4,520 m, 14,831 ft, Saint Elias Range, Alaska, U.S.
28. Mt. Walsh, 4,507 m, 14,787 ft, Saint Elias Range, Yukon, Canada
29. East Buttress, 4,489 m, 14,730 ft, Alaska Range, Alaska, U.S.
30. La Malinche, 4,462 m, 14,640 ft, Sierra Madre Oriental, Puebla, Mexico
31. Nevado de Colima, 4,450 m, 14,600 ft, Sierra Madre, Jalisco, Mexico
32. Mt. Hunter, 4,441 m, 14,573 ft, Alaska Range, Alaska, U.S.
33. Mt. Alverstone, 4,439 m, 14,564 ft, Saint Elias Range, Alaska & Yukon, U.S. & Canada
34. Browne Tower, 4,428 m, 14,530 ft, Alaska Range, Alaska, U.S.
35. MacAulay, SE Peak, 4,420 m, 14,502 ft, Saint Elias Range, Yukon, Canada
36. Mt. Whitney, 4,417 m, 14,494 ft, Sierra Nevada, California, U.S.

37. University Peak, 4,410 m, 14,470 ft, Saint Elias Range, Alaska, U.S.
38. Aello Peak, 4,402 m, 14,445 ft, Saint Elias Range, Alaska, U.S.
39. Mt. Elbert, 4,399 m, 14,433 ft, Sawatch Range, Colorado, U.S.
40. Mt. Massive, 4,395 m, 14,421 ft, Sawatch Range, Colorado, U.S.
41. Mt. Harvard, 4,395 m, 14,420 ft, Sawatch Range, Colorado, U.S.
42. Mt. Rainier, 4,392 m, 14,411 ft, Cascade Range, Washington, U.S.
43. Mt. Williamson, 4,381 m, 14,375 ft, Sierra Nevada, California, U.S.
44. Blanca Peak, 4,372 m, 14,345 ft, Sangre de Cristo Range, Colorado, U.S.
45. Mt. Slaggard, S Peak, 4,370 m, 14,338 ft, Saint Elias Range, Yukon, Canada
46. La Plata Peak, 4,369 m, 14,336 ft, Sawatch Range, Colorado, U.S.
47. Uncompahgre Peak, 4,361 m, 14,309 ft, San Juan Range, Colorado, U.S.
48. Crestone Peak, 4,356 m, 14,294 ft, Sangre de Cristo Range, Colorado, U.S.
49. Mt. Lincoln, 4,354 m, 14,286 ft, Mosquito Range, Colorado, U.S.
50. Grays Peak, 4,349 m, 14,270 ft, Front Range, Colorado, U.S.
51. Mt. Antero, 4,349 m, 14,269 ft, Sawatch Range, Colorado, U.S.
52. Torreys Peak, 4,348 m, 14,267 ft, Front Range, Colorado, U.S.
53. Castle Peak, 4,347 m, 14,265 ft, Elk Range, Colorado, U.S.
54. Quandary Peak, 4,347 m, 14,265 ft, Mosquito Range, Colorado, U.S.
55. Mt. Evans, 4,347 m, 14,264 ft, Front Range, Colorado, U.S.
56. Longs Peak, 4,344 m, 14,255 ft, Front Range, Colorado, U.S.
57. Mt. McArthur, 4,344 m, 14,253 ft, Saint Elias Range, Yukon, Canada
58. Mt. Wilson, 4,342 m, 14,246 ft, San Juan Range, Colorado, U.S.
59. White Mountain Peak, 4,342 m, 14,246 ft, White Mountain Range, California, U.S.
60. North Palisade, 4,340 m, 14,242 ft, Sierra Range, California, U.S.
61. Shavano Peak, 4,336 m, 14,229 ft, Sawatch Range, Colorado, U.S.
62. Crestone Needle, 4,327 m, 14,197 ft, Sangre de Cristo Range, Colorado, U.S.
63. Mt. Belford, 4,327 m, 14,197 ft, Sawatch Range, Colorado, U.S.
64. Mt. Princeton, 4,327 m, 14,197 ft, Sawatch Range, Colorado, U.S.
65. Mt. Yale, 4,326 m, 14,196 ft, Sawatch Range, Colorado, U.S.
66. Mt. Bross, 4,319 m, 14,172 ft, Mosquito Range, Colorado, U.S.
67. Kit Carson Peak, 4,317 m, 14,165 ft, Sangre de Cristo Range, Colorado, U.S.
68. Mt. Wrangell, 4,316 m, 14,163 ft, Wrangell Range, Alaska, U.S.
69. Mt. Shasta, 4,316 m, 14,162 ft, Cascade Range, California, U.S.
70. Mt. Sill, 4,316 m, 14,162 ft, Sierra Nevada, California, U.S.
71. El Diente Peak, 4,315 m, 14,159 ft, San Juan Range, Colorado, U.S.
72. Maroon Peak, 4,314 m, 14,156 ft, Elk Range, Colorado, U.S.
73. Tabeguache Peak, 4,314 m, 14,155 ft, Sawatch Range, Colorado, U.S.
74. Mt. Oxford, 4,313 m, 14,153 ft, Sawatch Range, Colorado, U.S.
75. Mt. Sneffels, 4,312 m, 14,150 ft, San Juan Range, Colorado, U.S.
76. Mt. Democrat, 4,312 m, 14,148 ft, Mosquito Range, Colorado, U.S.
77. Mt. McArthur, E Peak, 4,308 m, 14,135 ft, Saint Elias Range, Yukon, Canada
78. Capitol Peak, 4,306 m, 14,130 ft, Elk Range, Colorado, U.S.
79. Pikes Peak, 4,300 m, 14,110 ft, Front Range, Colorado, U.S.
80. Mt. Steele, SE Peak, 4,300 m, 14,108 ft, Saint Elias Range, Yukon, Canada
81. Snowmass Mountain, 4,295 m, 14,092 ft, Elk Range, Colorado, U.S.
82. Windom Peak, 4,293 m, 14,087 ft, San Juan Range, Colorado, U.S.
83. Mt. Russell, 4,293 m, 14,086 ft, Sierra Nevada, California, U.S.
84. Mt. Eolus, 4,292 m, 14,084 ft, San Juan Range, Colorado, U.S.

85. Starlight Peak, 4,291 m, 14,080 ft, Sierra Nevada, California, U.S.
86. Mt. Slaggard, W1 Peak, 4,290 m, 14,075 ft, Saint Elias Range, Yukon, Canada
87. Mt. Columbia, 4,289 m, 14,073 ft, Sawatch Range, Colorado, U.S.
88. Mt. Augusta, 4,288 m, 14,069 ft, Saint Elias Range, Alaska & Yukon, U.S. & Canada
89. Missouri Mountain, 4,287 m, 14,067 ft, Sawatch Range, Colorado, U.S.
90. Humboldt Peak, 4,286 m, 14,064 ft, Sangre de Cristo Range, Colorado, U.S.
91. Mt. Bierstadt, 4,285 m, 14,060 ft, Front Range, Colorado, U.S.
92. Sunlight Peak, 4,285 m, 14,059 ft, San Juan Range, Colorado, U.S.
93. Split Mountain, 4,284 m, 14,058 ft, Sierra Nevada, California, U.S.
94. Handies Peak, 4,281 m, 14,048 ft, San Juan Range, Colorado, U.S.
95. Culebra Peak, 4,281 m, 14,047 ft, Culebra Range, Colorado, U.S.
96. Ellingwood Point, 4,280 m, 14,042 ft, Sangre de Cristo Range, Colorado, U.S.
97. Mt. Lindsey, 4,280 m, 14,042 ft, Sangre de Cristo Range, Colorado, U.S.
98. Middle Palisade, 4,279 m, 14,040 ft, Sierra Nevada, California, U.S.
99. Little Bear Peak, 4,278 m, 14,037 ft, Sangre de Cristo Range, Colorado, U.S.
100. Mt. Sherman, 4,278 m, 14,036 ft, Mosquito Range, Colorado, U.S.
101. Redcloud Peak, 4,277 m, 14,034 ft, San Juan Range, Colorado, U.S.
102. Mt. Langley, 4,275 m, 14,028 ft, Sierra Nevada, California, U.S.
103. Pyramid Peak, 4,272 m, 14,018 ft, Elk Range, Colorado, U.S.
104. Mt. Tyndall, 4,272 m, 14,018 ft, Sierra Nevada, California, U.S.
105. Wilson Peak, 4,272 m, 14,017 ft, San Juan Range, Colorado, U.S.
106. Wetterhorn Peak, 4,271 m, 14,015 ft, San Juan Range, Colorado, U.S.
107. Mt. Muir, 4,271 m, 14,015 ft, Sierra Nevada, California, U.S.
108. North Maroon Peak, 4,271 m, 14,014 ft, Elk Range, Colorado, U.S.
109. San Luis Peak, 4,271 m, 14,014 ft, San Juan Range, Colorado, U.S.
110. Huron Peak, 4,268 m, 14,005 ft, Sawatch Range, Colorado, U.S.
111. Mt. of the Holy Cross, 4,268 m, 14,005 ft, Sawatch Range, Colorado, U.S.
112. Sunshine Peak, 4,267 m, 14,001 ft, San Juan Range, Colorado, U.S.
113. Polemonium Peak, 4,292 m, 14,080 ft, Sierra Nevada, California, U.S.
114. Thunderbolt Peak, 4,268 m, 14,003 ft, Sierra Nevada, California, U.S.

APPENDIX E:
THE WORLD'S HIGHEST VOLCANOES

Africa

1. Kilimanjaro (Kibo) 19,340 ft, 5,895 m, Tanzania
2. Mt. Kenya 17,058 ft, 5,199 m, Kenya
3. Kilimanjaro (Mawenzi) 16,893 ft, 5,149 m, Tanzania
4. Mt. Meru 14,978 ft, 4,565 m, Tanzania
5. Karisimbi 14,787 ft, 4,507 m, Congo & Rwanda
6. Mikeno 14,557 ft, 4,437 m, Congo
7. Mt. Elgon 14,178 ft, 4,321 m, Kenya & Uganda
8. Muhavura 13,540 ft, 4,127 m, Uganda & Rwanda
9. Mt. Cameroon 13,435 ft, 4,095 m, Cameroon
10. Pico del Teide 12,198 ft, 3,718 m, Canary Islands, Spain
11. Visoke 12,175 ft, 3,711 m, Congo & Rwanda
12. Sabinyo 11,923 ft, 3,634 m, Congo & Uganda & Rwanda

Antarctica

1. Mt. Sidley 13,717 ft, 4,181 m, Marie Byrd Land, Antarctica
2. Mt. Erebus 12,447 ft, 3,794 m, Ross Island, Antarctica
3. Mt. Frakes 11,988 ft, 3,654 m, Marie Byrd Land, Antarctica
4. Toney Mountain 11,795 ft, 3,595 m, Marie Byrd Land, Antarctica
5. Mt. Steere 11,673 ft, 3,558 m, Marie Byrd Land, Antarctica
6. Mt. Berlin 11,411 ft, 3,478 m, Marie Byrd Land, Antarctica
7. Mt. Takahe 11,352 ft, 3,460 m, Marie Byrd Land, Antarctica
8. Mt. Overlord 11,142 ft, 3,396 m, Victoria Land, Antarctica
9. Mt. Waesche 10,801 ft, 3,292 m, Marie Byrd Land, Antarctica
10. Mt. Hampton 10,902 ft, 3,323 m, Marie Byrd Land, Antarctica
11. Mt. Terror 10,597 ft, 3,230 m, Ross Island, Antarctica
12. Mt. Siple 10,203 ft, 3,110 m, Marie Byrd Land, Antarctica
13. Mt. Moulton 10,098 ft, 3,078 m, Marie Byrd Land, Antarctica

Asia

1. Damavand 18,603 ft, 5,670 m, Iran
2. Ararat (Agri Dagi) 16,945 ft, 5,165 m, Turkey
3. Kazbek 16,558 ft, 5,047 m, Georgia
4. Sabalan 15,817 ft, 4,821 m, Iran
5. Klyuchevskoy 15,584 ft, 4,750 m, Kamchatka, Russia
6. Kamen 15,148 ft, 4,617 m, Kamchatka, Russia
7. Krestovsky 13,478 ft, 4,108 m, Kamchatka, Russia
8. Aragats (Alagez) 13,419 ft, 4,090 m, Armenia
9. Suphan Dagi 13,314 ft, 4,058 m, Turkey
10. Taftan 13,262 ft, 4,042 m, Iran
11. Ushkovsky 12,936 ft, 3,943 m, Kamchatka, Russia
12. Little Ararat 12,877 ft, 3,925 m, Turkey
13. Erciyes Dagi 12,851 ft, 3,917 m, Turkey
14. Kerinci 12,497 ft, 3,809 m, Sumatra, Indonesia
15. Fuji-san 12,388 ft, 3,776 m, Honshu, Japan
16. Rinjani 12,224 ft, 3,726 m, Lombok, Indonesia
17. Sahand 12,105 ft, 3,690 m, Iran
18. Tolbachik 12,080 ft, 3,682 m, Kamchatka, Russia
19. Semeru 12,060 ft, 3,676 m, Java, Indonesia

20. Ichinsky 11,880 ft, 3,621 m, Kamchatka, Russia
21. Tendurek Dagi 11,759 ft, 3,584 m, Turkey
22. Kronotsky 11,575 ft, 3,528 m, Kamchatka, Russia

Australasia and Oceania

1. Mauna Kea 13,796 ft, 4,205 m, Hawaii, U.S.
2. Mauna Loa 13,680 ft, 4,170 m, Hawaii, U.S.
3. Mt. Cook 12,349 ft, 3,764 m, South Island, New Zealand
4. Doma Peaks 11,706 ft, 3,568 m, New Guinea, Papua New Guinea
5. Mt. Yelia 11,102 ft, 3,384 m, New Guinea, Papua New Guinea
6. Crater Mountain 10,607 ft, 3,233 m, New Guinea, Papua New Guinea
7. Haleakala 10,023 ft, 3,055 m, Maui, Hawaii, U.S.
8. Ruapehu 9,175 ft, 2,797 m, North Island, New Zealand
9. Balbi 8,907 ft, 2,715 m, Bougainville, Papua New Guinea
10. Hualalai 8,278 ft, 2,523 m, Hawaii, U.S.
11. Taranaki (Mt. Egmont) 8,260 ft, 2,518 m, North Island, New Zealand
12. Ulawun 7,658 ft, 2,334 m, New Britain, Papua New Guinea
13. Ngauruhoe 7,516 ft, 2,291 m, North Island, New Zealand

Europe

1. Elbrus 18,510 ft, 5,642 m, Russia
2. Mt. Etna 10,990 ft, 3,350 m, Sicily, Italy
3. Pico 7,713 ft, 2,351 m, Azores, Portugal
4. Beerenberg 7,472 ft, 2,277 m, Jan Mayen, Norway
5. Oraefajokull 6,952 ft, 2,119 m, Iceland
6. Bardarbunga 6,595 ft, 2,010 m, Iceland
7. Kverkfjoll 6,300 ft, 1,920 m, Iceland
8. Puy de Sancy 6,184 ft, 1,885 m, France
9. Plomb du Cantal 6,086 ft, 1,855 m, France
10. Snaefell 6,014 ft, 1,833 m, Iceland
11. Hofsjokull 5,846 ft, 1,782 m, Iceland
12. Esjufjoll 5,774 ft, 1,760 m, Iceland
13. Grimsvotn 5,660 ft, 1,725 m, Iceland
14. Herdubreid 5,518 ft, 1,682 m, Iceland
15. Eiriksjokull 5,495 ft, 1,675 m, Iceland
16. Eyjafjallajokull 5,466 ft, 1,666 m, Iceland

North America

1. Pico de Orizaba 18,700 ft, 5,700 m, Mexico
2. Popocatépetl 17,930 ft, 5,465 m, Mexico
3. Iztaccíhuatl 17,343 ft, 5,286 m, Mexico
4. Mt. Bona 16,421 ft, 5,005 m, Alaska, U.S.
5. Mt. Blackburn 16,390 ft, 4,996 m, Alaska, U.S.
6. Mt. Sanford 16,237 ft, 4,949 m, Alaska, U.S.
7. Mt. Churchill 15,638 ft, 4,766 m, Alaska, U.S.
8. Nevado de Toluca 15,197 ft, 4,632 m, Mexico
9. Sierra Negra 15,030 ft, 4,580 m, Mexico
10. La Malinche 14,636 ft, 4,461 m, Mexico
11. Mt. Rainier 14,411 ft, 4,392 m, Washington, U.S.
12. Nevado de Colima 14,600 ft, 4,450 m, Mexico
13. Mt. Wrangell 14,163 ft, 4,317 m, Alaska, U.S.
14. Mt. Shasta 14,162 ft, 4,316 m, California, U.S.
15. Cofre de Perote 14,048 ft, 4,282 m, Mexico
16. Atna Peaks 13,860 ft, 4,225 m, Alaska, U.S.
17. Volcan Tajumulco 13,846 ft, 4,220 m, Guatemala
18. Regal Mountain 13,845 ft, 4,220 m, Alaska, U.S.
19. Cerro el Mirador 13,520 ft, 4,120 m, Mexico
20. Volcan Tacana 13,484 ft, 4,110 m, Mexico & Guatemala
21. Mt. Jarvis 13,421 ft, 4,091 m, Alaska, U.S.
22. Cerro Telapon 13,390 ft, 4,080 m, Mexico
23. Volcan Acatenango 13,045 ft, 3,976 m, Guatemala
24. Mt. Zanetti 13,009 ft, 3,965 m, Alaska, U.S.
25. Jocotitlan 12,960 ft, 3,950 m, Mexico
26. Ajusco 12,894 ft, 3,930 m, Mexico
27. Tancitaro 12,664 ft, 3,860 m, Mexico
28. Volcan de Colima 12,631 ft, 3,850 m, Mexico
29. Humphreys Peak 12,633 ft, 3,851 m, Arizona, U.S.
30. Volcan Santa Maria 12,375 ft, 3,772 m, Guatemala
31. Volcan Fuego 12,346 ft, 3,763 m, Guatemala
32. Volcan Agua 12,336 ft, 3,760 m, Guatemala
33. Mt. Adams 12,276 ft, 3,742 m, Washington, U.S.

South America

1. Nevado Ojos del Salado 22,572 ft, 6,880 m, Chile & Argentina
2. Monte Pissis 22,240 ft, 6,779 m, Argentina
3. Cerro Mercedario 22,211 ft, 6,770 m, Chile & Argentina
4. Volcan Llullaillaco 22,057 ft, 6,723 m, Chile & Argentina

5. Cerro Cazadero 21,844 ft, 6,658 m, Chile & Argentina
6. Nevados Tres Cruces 21,719 ft, 6,620 m, Chile & Argentina
7. Nevado Coropuna 21,696 ft, 6,613 m, Peru
8. Cerro de Incahuasi 21,656 ft, 6,601 m, Chile & Argentina
9. Cerro Tupungato 21,489 ft, 6,550 m, Chile & Argentina
10. Nevado Sajama 21,423 ft, 6,520 m, Bolivia
11. Cerro Nacimento 21,302 ft, 6,493 m, Argentina
12. Nevado el Muerto 21,246 ft, 6,476 m, Chile & Argentina
13. Volcan Antofalla 21,027 ft, 6,409 m, Argentina
14. Cerro Bonete 21,020 ft, 6,410 m, Argentina
15. Cerro el Condor 20,909 ft, 6,373 m, Argentina
16. Reclus 20,784 ft, 6,335 m, Argentina
17. Volcan Parinacota 20,767 ft, 6,320 m, Chile & Bolivia
18. Cerro Veladero 20,734 ft, 6,320 m, Argentina
19. Nevado de Cachi 20,702 ft, 6,310 m, Argentina
20. Chimborazo 20,702 ft, 6,310 m, Ecuador
21. Nevado Ampato 20,630 ft, 6,288 m, Peru
22. Volcan Pomerape 20,472 ft, 6,240 m, Chile & Bolivia

Source: www.skimountaineer.com/ROF/VolcanicSeven.html

APPENDIX F:
MAJOR UNCLIMBED
PEAKS ABOVE 7,000 METERS

1. Lhotse Middle 8,430 m, 27,657 ft, Khumbu Himal, Nepal [NOW CLIMBED]
2. Makalu SE 8,010 m, 26,279 ft, 20 km SE of Everest, Nepal
3. Manaslu E 7,992 m, 26,220 ft, Gurka Himal, Nepal
4. Nuptse E1 7,804 m, 25,603 ft, Khumbu Himal, SE of Everest Nepal
5. P7780 7,780 m, 25,524 ft, Khumbu Himal, S of Everest, Nepal
6. Zemu Peak 7,780 m, 25,524 ft, Kangchenjunga group, Sikkim, India
7. Disteghil Sar C 7,760 m, 25,459 ft, Hispar Mustag, near Bularung Sar, Pakistan
8. P7745 7,745 m, 25,410 ft
9. P7739 7,739 m, 25,390 ft, Annapurna II, Nepal
10. Nuptse E2 7,726 m, 25,347 ft, Khumbu Himal, SE of Everest, Nepal
11. Broad Peak S 7,721 m, 25,331 ft, Baltoro, S of K2, Pakistan
12. Saltoro Kangri II 7,705 m, 25,278 ft, Pakistan
13. P7700 7,700 m, 25,262 ft
14. Pc7700 7,700 m, 25,262 ft, Batura Mustag, Pakistan
15. Nuptse E3 7,695 m, 25,246 ft, Khumbu Himal, SE of Everest, Nepal
16. Ngojumba Kang III 7,681 m, 25,200 ft, Khumbu Himal, SE of Cho Oyu, Nepal
17. P25354ft 7,670 m, 25,164 ft
18. Khinyang Chhish S 7,620 m, 25,000 ft, Pakistan
19. Silver Crag 7,597 m, 24,924 ft, Nanga Parbat, 6 km from main summit, Pakistan
20. Gangkar Puensum 7,541 m, 24,740 ft, Bhutan
21. Kangbachen SW 7,532 m, 24,711 ft, Eastern Nepal, W of Kangchenjunga, Nepal
22. P7514 7,514 m, 24,652 ft
23. Saser Kangri II E 7,511 m, 24,642 ft, East Karakoram, India
24. P7500 7,500 m, 24,606 ft
25. Skyang Kangri SW 7,500 m, 24,606 ft, Pakistan
26. P7470 7,470 m, 24,507 ft
27. Kumbhakarna E 7,468 m, 24,501 ft, Eastern Nepal, Nepal
28. Mucho Chhish 7,453 m, 24,452 ft, Batura Mustag, Pakistan
29. P7451 7,451 m, 24,445 ft
30. Batura VI 7,400 m, 24,278 ft, Baltoro, W of Gasherbrum, Pakistan
31. Khinyang Chhish E 7,400 m, 24,278 ft, Pakistan
32. Kabru IV 7,394 m, 24,258 ft, Sikkim, India
33. Kangbachen W 7,385 m, 24,229 ft, Eastern Nepal, W of Kangchenjunga, Nepal
34. Pc7373 7,373 m, 24,189 ft
35. Skyang Kangri II 7,357 m, 24,137 ft, Pakistan
36. P7353 7,353 m, 24,124 ft, 300 km N of Lhasa, Tibet
37. Chongtar N 7,350 m, 24,114 ft, Panmah & Baltoro, Pakistan
38. Khinyang Chhish W 7,350 m, 24,114 ft, Pakistan
39. Pumari Chhish S 7,350 m, 24,114 ft, Pakistan
40. Chongtar S 7,330 m, 24,048 ft, Panmah & Baltoro, Pakistan
41. Saraghrar C 7,330 m, 24,048 ft, Pakistan
42. Chamlang S 7,316 m, 24,002 ft, Khumbu Himal, S of Lhotse, Nepal
43. P7316 7,316 m, 24,002 ft
44. P7310 7,310 m, 23,982 ft
45. Plateau Peak 7,310 m, 23,982 ft, East Karakoram, Saser group, India

46. P7308 7,308 m, 23,976 ft, or Segwang 7,508m (?), Nepal & Tibet
47. Chongtar NE 7,300 m, 23,950 ft, Panmah & Baltoro, Pakistan
48. Malubiting NW 7,300 m, 23,950 ft, Pakistan
49. Pc7300 7,300 m, 23,950 ft
50. Saraghrar NW 7,300 m, 23,950 ft, Pakistan
51. Teri Kang 7,300 m, 23,950 ft, Bhutan
52. P7291 7,291 m, 23,920 ft
53. P7290 7,290 m, 23,917 ft
54. Rakaposhi NE 7,290 m, 23,917 ft, Pakistan
55. Summa Ri 7,286 m, 23,904 ft, Baltoro & Panmah, Pakistan
56. Mucho Chhish E 7,280 m, 23,884 ft, Pakistan
57. Istor-o-Nal NE 7,276 m, 23,871 ft, Hindu Kush, Pakistan
58. Baltoro Kangri IV 7,265 m, 23,835 ft, Baltoro, W of Gasherbrum, Pakistan
59. P7249 7,249 m, 23,782 ft
60. P7239 7,239 m, 23,750 ft
61. Apsarasas II 7,238 m, 23,746 ft, Saltoro & Siachen, NE of Saltoro Kangri, India
62. Apsarasas III 7,235 m, 23,736 ft, Saltoro & Siachen, NE of Saltoro Kangri, India
63. Apsarasas IV 7,221 m, 23,690 ft, Saltoro & Siachen, NE of Saltoro Kangri, India
64. Karjiang S 7,221 m, 23,690 ft
65. Kangphu Kang 7,212 m, 23,661 ft, Bhutan
66. Saraghrar SE 7,208 m, 23,648 ft, Pakistan
67. Gang Chhen 7,200 m, 23,622 ft, Bhutan
68. Gieu Gang 7,200 m, 23,622 ft, near Bhutan, Tibet
69. Kangcheta lll 7,200 m, 23,622 ft, Bhutan
70. Lupghar Sar E 7,200 m, 23,622 ft, Pakistan
71. P7199 7,199 m, 23,618 ft
72. P7200 7,199 m, 23,618 ft
73. Tsogaka 7,193 m, 23,599 ft, Langtang Himal, E of Shisha Pangma, Tibet
74. Apsarasas V 7,186 m, 23,576 ft, Saltoro & Siachen, NE of Saltoro Kangri, India
75. P7186 7,186 m, 23,576 ft
76. P7184 7,184 m, 23,569 ft
77. Chamar S 7,183 m, 23,566 ft, Gurka Himal, E of Manaslu, Nepal
78. Chongtar S II 7,180 m, 23,556 ft, Panmah & Baltoro, Pakistan
79. Masherbrum E 7,163 m, 23,500 ft, Pakistan
80. Savoia 7,156 m, 23,477 ft, Baltoro & Panmah, Pakistan
81. P7149 7,149 m, 23,454 ft
82. Gasherbrum V C 7,120 m, 23,359 ft, Baltoro, Pakistan
83. Mazeno Peak A 7,120 m, 23,359 ft, Pakistan
84. P7120 7,120 m, 23,359 ft
85. Apsarasas S 7,117 m, 23,349 ft, Saltoro & Siachen, NE of Saltoro Kangri, India
86. Nyainqentanglha III 7,111 m, 23,330 ft, N of Lhasa, Tibet
87. Nangpai Gosum III 7,110 m, 23,326 ft, Khumbu Himal, SE of Cho Oyu, Nepal
88. Savoia II 7,110 m, 23,326 ft, Baltoro & Panmah, Pakistan
89. P7108 7,108 m, 23,320 ft
90. Savoia III 7,102 m, 23,300 ft, Baltoro & Panmah, Pakistan
91. Gasherbrum IV S 7,100 m, 23,293 ft, Baltoro, Pakistan
92. Ghenta Peak 7,100 m, 23,293 ft, Batura Mustag, Pakistan
93. Istor-o-Nal E 7,100 m, 23,293 ft, Hindu Kush, Pakistan
94. Jejekangphu Kang 7,100 m, 23,293 ft
95. P7100A 7,100 m, 23,293 ft
96. P7100B 7,100 m, 23,293 ft
97. Pc7100C 7,100 m, 23,293 ft
98. Pc7100D 7,100 m, 23,293 ft
99. Yutmaru Sar II 7,100 m, 23,293 ft
100. Zorggonhu Kang 7,100 m, 23,293 ft
101. Baltistan Peak W 7,099 m, 23,290 ft, Masherbrum Mustag, SE of Masherbrum, Pakistan
102. P7098 7,098 m, 23,287 ft
103. Nobugangri 7,095 m, 23,277 ft, Nepal
104. Loinbo Kangri 7,093 m, 23,270 ft, Tibet
105. Urdok II 7,082 m, 23,234 ft, Pakistan
106. Mandu II 7,081 m, 23,231 ft
107. P7069 7,069 m, 23,192 ft
108. Langar SE 7,061 m, 23,166 ft
109. Janak 7,035 m, 23,080 ft
110. Trisuli W 7,035 m, 23,080 ft, Kumaon Himal, Nanda Devi group, India
111. P7032 7,032 m, 23,070 ft
112. P7032 7,032 m, 23,070 ft, Sikkim, India
113. P7024 7,024 m, 23,044 ft

114. Chowusha 7,023 m, 23,041 ft, Khumbu Himal, Tibet & Nepal
115. Xiang Dong 7,018 m, 23,024 ft
116. P23020ft 7,016 m, 23,018 ft
117. Pamri Sar 7,016 m, 23,018 ft
118. P7013 7,013 m, 23,008 ft
119. P7013 7,013 m, 23,008 ft
120. Mayer Kangri 7,011 m, 23,001 ft
121. Annapurna Dakshin 7,010 m, 22,998 ft, Nepal
122. Lupghar W II 7,010 m, 22,998 ft, Pakistan
123. P7010 7,010 m, 22,998 ft
124. Rakaposhi E 7,009 m, 22,995 ft, Pakistan
125. Chong Kumdan II 7,004 m, 22,979 ft, East Karakoram, India

126. Chomolhari Gang 7,000 m, 22,965 ft, Tibet
127. Gangchentag 7,000 m, 22,965 ft, Chomolhari group, Sikkim & Bhutan
128. Ghent III 7,000 m, 22,965 ft, Siachen Mustag, India
129. Menlunghi Kang 7,000 m, 22,965 ft
130. Pc7000A 7,000 m, 22,965 ft
131. Pc7000B 7,000 m, 22,965 ft
132. Saraghrar SS 7,000 m, 22,965 ft, Pakistan
133. Trivor SW 7,000 m, 22,965 ft, Pakistan

Compiled from: www.peakware.com/encyclopedia/unclimbed.htm

APPENDIX G:
50 U.S. AND
13 CANADIAN HIGHPOINTS

Alabama 734 m, 2,407 ft Cheaha Mountain
Alaska 6,194 m, 20,320 ft Denali (Mt. McKinley)
Alberta 3747 m, 12,293 ft Mt. Columbia
Arizona 3,851 m, 12,633 ft Humphreys Peak
Arkansas 839 m, 2,753 ft Mt. Magazine (Signal Hill)
British Columbia 4,664 m, 15,302 ft Mt. Fair-weather
California 4,417 m, 14,494 ft Mt. Whitney
Colorado 4,399 m, 14,433 ft Mt. Elbert
Connecticut 725 m, 2,380 ft Mt. Frissell–South Slope
Delaware 135 m, 442 ft Ebright Azimuth
Florida 105 m, 345 ft Lakewood (Britton Hill)
Georgia 1,458 m, 4,784 ft Brasstown Bald
Hawaii 4,205 m, 13,796 ft Mauna Kea
Idaho 3,859 m, 12,662 ft Borah Peak
Illinois 376 m, 1,235 ft Charles Mound
Indiana 383 m, 1,257 ft Hoosier Hill
Iowa 509 m, 1,670 ft Hawkeye Point
Kansas 1,231 m, 4,039 ft Mt. Sunflower
Kentucky 1,263 m, 4,145 ft Black Mountain
Louisiana 163 m, 535 ft Driskill Mountain
Maine 1,605 m, 5,267 ft Mt. Katahdin (Baxter Peak)
Manitoba 832 m, 2,730 ft Baldy Mountain
Maryland 1,024 m, 3,360 ft Backbone Mountain
Massachusetts 1,064 m, 3,491 ft Mt. Greylock
Michigan 603 m, 1,979 ft Mt. Arvon
Minnesota 701 m, 2,301 ft Eagle Mountain
Mississippi 246 m, 806 ft Woodall Mountain
Missouri 540 m, 1,772 ft Taum Sauk
Montana 3,901 m, 12,799 ft Granite Peak
Nebraska 1,653 m, 5,424 ft Panorama Point
Nevada 4,006 m, 13,143 ft Boundary Peak
New Brunswick 820 m, 2,690 ft Mt. Carleton

New Hampshire 1,917 m, 6,288 ft Mt. Washington
New Jersey 550 m, 1,803 ft High Point
New Mexico 4,011 m, 13,161 ft Wheeler Peak
New York 1,629 m, 5,344 ft Mt. Marcy
Newfoundland and Labrador 1,652 m, 5,420 ft Mt. Caubwick
North Carolina 2,037 m, 6,684 ft Mt. Mitchell
North Dakota 1,069 m, 3,506 ft White Butte
Northwest Territories 2,773 m, 9,098 ft Mt. Nirvana
Nova Scotia 532 m, 1,745 ft White Hill
Nunavut 2,616 m, 8,583 ft Barbeau Peak
Ohio 472 m, 1,550 ft Campbell Hill
Oklahoma 1,516 m, 4,973 ft Black Mesa
Ontario 639 m, 2,274 ft Ishpatina Ridge
Oregon 3,426 m, 11,239 ft Mt. Hood
Pennsylvania 979 m, 3,213 ft Mt. Davis
Prince Edward Island 142 m, 466 ft (unnamed)
Québec 1652 m, 5,420 ft Mont d'Iberville
Rhode Island 247 m, 812 ft Jerimoth Hill
Saskatchewan 1,392 m, 4,567 ft Cypress Hill
South Carolina 1,085 m, 3,560 ft Sassafras Mountain
South Dakota 2,207 m, 7,242 ft Harney Peak
Tennessee 2,025 m, 6,643 ft Clingmans Dome
Texas 2,667 m, 8,749 ft Guadalupe Peak
Utah 4,123 m, 13,528 ft Kings Peak
Vermont 1,339 m, 4,393 ft Mt. Mansfield
Virginia 1,746 m, 5,729 ft Mt. Rogers
Washington 4,392 m, 14,411 ft Mt. Rainier
West Virginia 1,482 m, 4,863 ft Spruce Knob
Wisconsin 595 m, 1,951 ft Timms Hill
Wyoming 4,207 m, 13,804 ft Gannett Peak
Yukon Territory 5,959 m, 19,551 ft Mt. Logan

APPENDIX H: WEBSITES

www.ablestock.com/

www.adorama.com

www.alpenbooks.com

www.alpineascents.com/media.asp#vinson2

www.alpinisme.com/fr/histoire

www.americanalpineclub.org

www.americasroof.com/

www.andromeda.com

www.angelfire.com/al/badela/PakImager/Mountains/#K2

www.artcyclopedia.com/artists/bierstadt_albert.html

http://atlas.gc.ca/site/english/index.html

www.avalanche.org

www.avalanchecourse.com

www.banffcentre.ca/mountainculture/festivals/

www.bcadventure.com

www.bielefeldt.de/jorasses.htm

www.bonington.com

www.britishcolumbia.com/BookStore/results.asp?Author=44

www.britishcolumbia.com/RussHeinl//

http://cagle.slate.msn.com/politicalcartoons/PCcartoons/stahler.asp

www.canyoneeringusa.com/utah

www.cdc.gov/travel

www.chamonix.net/english/mountaineering/histofalpinism1.htm

www.chesslerbooks.com

http://classic.mountainzone.com/everest/2000/south/photos.html

www.climb.mountains.com/Photo%20Gallery_files/Continent.htm

http://climbing.about.com/gi/dynamic/offsite.htm?site=http%3A%2F%2Fwww.amga.com%2F

http://climbsearch.port5.com/

www.corbis.com/247/index.html

http://dialspace.dial.pipex.com/town/parade/henryr/earth/plate

www.dia.org/

www.dolomiti.it/eng

http://earth.leeds.ac.uk/dynamicearth

www.edviesturs.com

www.explore-himalaya.com/

www.factmonster.com/encyclopedia.html

www.factmonster.com/index.html

www.factmonster.com/ipka/A0001771.html

www.fedpubs.com/topographic.htm

www.firelookout.com

www.firelookout.org

www.fis-ski.com/index.php

http://freespace.virgin.net/paul.benham/dolo/dolomites.htm

www.funimag.com

www.geobop.com/

www.geocities.com/climbersinfo

www.geology.sdsu.edu/how_volcanoes_work

www.geositu.com

www.heinlaerialphotography.com/

http://highpointers.org/index.html

www.holymtn.com/world.htm

www.huntington.org/ArtDiv/ScottGallery.html

www.huts.org

www.ign.fr/affiche_rubrique.asp?rbr_id=1&lng_id=FR

www.imaging-resource.com/PRODS/DSD/DSDA.HTM

www.ismmed.org

www.istm.org

www.itmb.com/

http://it.stlawu.edu/~cnya/

www.ivbv.info

http://jama.ama-assn.org/

www.jerberyd.com/climbing/climbers/

www.johngill.net

www.jonathandanieladams.com/webpages/
    mebio.htm

www.lagrave-lameije.com/us/summer.htm

www.lib.utexas.edu/maps/map_sites/map_sites
    .html

www.lnt.org

http://mac.usgs.gov

www.mapmaker.com/

www.maps.com/cgi-bin/magellan/Maps

http://maps.nrcan.gc.ca/cmo/rdc.html

www.maxximages.com/index2.html

http://mcmcweb.er.usgs.gov

www.metmuseum.org/collections/view1zoom.asp?
    dep=2&full=1&item=07%2E123&action=OUT&re
    ctX1=0.132&rectX2=0.632&rectY1=0.308922558
    922559&rectY2=0.808922558922559

www.metmuseum.org/copyright.htm#permission

www.mindlesspleasures.com/index.htm

www.mnteverest.com/history.html

www.montagnes.com/

www.montagnes.com/us/climber/default.asp

www.mostweb.cc/Classics/Coleridge/PoemsOf
    SamuelTaylorColeridge/PoemsOfSamuelTaylor
    Chttp://oleridge4.html

www.mountainarea.com/argentiere/aiguille.html

www.mountaineersbooks.org/

www.mountainlight.com

www.mountainmadness.com

www.mountainvoices.org

www.mra.org

http://nabataea.net/ppark.html

www.nationalgeographic.com/

www.nationalgeographic.com/adventure/

www.nationalgeographic.com/explorer/petra/

www.newton.mec.edu/

http://nga.gov/

www.ngs.org

www.nols.edu

www.nols.edu/Publications/FirstAid/AltitudeIllness
    .html

www.nps.gov/

www.nps.gov/hale

www.nps.gov/mora/

www.nps.gov/yell/

www.nps.gov/yose/

www.nsidc.org

www.nsidc.org/glaciers/glossary

http://nssdc.gsfc.nasa.gov/photo_gallery/
    photogallery-mars.html

www.omnimap.com/

www.orchestralibrary.com/specialparts.html

www.outdoors.org

http://outside.away.com/index.html

www.pam.org/index.asp

http://park10.wakwak.com/~wwww/waterfall.html

www.pbs.org/edens/bhutan/

www.pbs.org/wgbh/nova/everest/lost/mystery/

www.pbs.org/wgbh/nova/peru/mummies/high
    1.html

www.pcta.org

www.pcta.org/about_trail/muir/over.asp

www.peakbagger.com

www.peakbagger.com/peak/italyhi.htm

www.peakbagger.com/table/tablindx.htm

http://peakbagger.tripod.com/Climbs/Granite/
    granite_pk.htm

www.peakware.com

www.peakware.com/encyclopedia/peaks/orizaba
    .htm

www.peakware.com/encyclopedia/unclimbed.htm

http://phoenix.about.com/library/weekly/
    aa062600b.htm

http://photojournal.jpl.nasa.gov/

www.pinedaleonline.com/Gannett.HTM

www.pinnaclebooks.net/Mountaineering.asp?
    offset=50

www.proteusworkshop.com/index.html

www.reinhold.messner.de

www.rgs.org/

www.rmna.org/display.php?cat=627

www.sacredsites.com/2nd56/232.html

www.sanjuanhuts.com

www.savethegunks.com/

www.savetibet.org

http://7summits.com/

http://7summits.com/pix/denali/denali_body.html

www.simpkins57.freeserve.co.uk/mountain_lakes_
    books/whoswho/whoswhodetails.html

www.skimountaineer.com/

http://store.spaceimaging.com/

www.spaceimaging.com/

www.summitpost.org

www.taiga.net/yourYukon/col171.html
http://terraserver-usa.com/default.aspx
www.timberlinelodge.com/defaultweb.asp
www.topworldbooks.com
www.unesco.org/mab/IYM.htm
www.unitedmedia.com/
www.uiaa.ch
www.usgs.gov/
www.Vermont-Marble.com
www.virtualcascades.com
http://visibleearth.nasa.gov/

http://volcanoes.usgs.gov/Products/Pglossary/
 pglossary.html
http://web.outsideonline.com/system/subsfaq
 .html
www.webref.org/geology/geology.htm
http://whc.unesco.org/sites/326.htm
www.wms.org
www.worldatlas.com/
www.xs4all.nl/
www.zermatt.ch/
www3.bc.simpatico.ca/lightningsurvivor

Bibliography

Note: Many of the articles, books, and films mentioned in the text and sidebars are included in this listing. Those listed in the individual bibliographies are not.

Above All Else: The Everest Dream (DVD). Seattle, WA: Unapix Home Entertainment, 2000.

Accidents in North American Mountaineering. Golden, CO: American Alpine Club, 1968–.

Across the Great Divide. Videocassette. Media/Heron Communications, 1989.

Adkison, Ron. *Hiking Wyoming's Wind River Range.* Helena, MT: Falcon, 1996.

Aitchison, Stewart, and Bruce Grubbs. *Hiking Arizona.* Helena, MT: Falcon, 1992.

Ali, Salim. *Field Guide to the Birds of the Eastern Himalayas.* Delhi: Oxford University Press, 1986.

Alive. Videocassette. Touchstone Home Video, 1993.

Allaby, Michael. *Encyclopedia of Weather and Climate.* 2 vols. New York: Facts on File, 2002.

Allen, Dan. *Don't Die on the Mountain.* New London, NH: Diapensia, 1998.

The Alps. Washington, DC: National Geographic Society, 1973.

Ament, Pat. *A History of Free Climbing in America: Wizards of Rock.* Berkeley, CA: Wilderness Press, 2002.

———. *How to Be a Master Climber in Six Easy Lessons.* Boulder, CO: Two Lights, 1997.

American Mountain People. Washington, DC: National Geographic Society, 1973.

Anderson, Robert Mads. *Summits: Climbing the Seven Summits Solo.* New York: Clarkson Potter, 1995.

Anker, Conrad, and David Roberts. *The Lost Explorer: Finding Mallory on Mt. Everest.* New York: Simon & Schuster, 1999.

Ardito, Stefano. *History of the Great Mountaineering Adventures.* Trans. A. B. A. Milan. Seattle, WA: The Mountaineers, 2000.

———. *Mont Blanc: Discovery and Conquest of the Giant of the Alps.* Seattle, WA: The Mountaineers, 1996.

Auerbach, Paul S. *Wilderness Medicine.* 4th ed. St. Louis, MO: Mosby, 2001.

Barnes, Bob. *The Complete Encyclopedia of Skiing.* 3rd ed. Sliverthorne, CO: Snowline Press, 1999.

Barry, John. *Alpine Climbing.* Seattle, WA: Cloudcap, 1995.

———, and Roger Mear. *Climbing School: An Illustrated Course in Hill Walking, Rock, Snow, and Ice Climbing.* London: Quantum Books, 2003.

Bass, Dick, and Frank Wells, with Rick Ridgeway. *Seven Summits.* New York: Warner, 1986.

Becky, Fred. *Mount McKinley: Icy Crown of North America.* Seattle, WA: The Mountaineers, 1993.

Bernbaum, Edwin. *Sacred Mountains of the World.* Berkeley: University of California, 1997.

Bernstein, Jeremy. *Mountain Passages.* New York: Simon & Schuster, 1977.

Blessed, Brian. *To the Top of the World.* New York: Smithmark, 1995.

Bliss, Lawrence C. "Tundra." *World Book Encyclopedia,* 1998 ed.

Blodig, Karl. *Die Viertausender der Alpen.* Munich: R. Rother, 1923.

Blum, Arlene. *Annapurna, a Woman's Place.* San Francisco: Sierra Club Books, 1980.

Boga, Steven. *Climbers: Scaling the Heights with the Sport's Elite.* Mechanicsburg, PA: Stackpole Books, 1994.

Bonatti, Walter. *The Mountains of My Life.* Trans. Robert Marshall. New York: Modern Library, 2001.

Bonington, Chris. *Mountaineer*. San Francisco: Sierra Club Books, 1990.

Boukreev, Anatoli, and G. Weston DeWalt. *The Climb: Tragic Ambitions on Everest*. New York: St. Martin's, 1997.

Breashears, David. *High Exposure*. New York: Simon & Schuster, 1999.

Buhl, Hermann. *Lonely Challenge*. Trans. Hugh Merrick. New York: Dutton, 1956.

——. *Nanga Parbat Pilgrimage: The Lonely Challenge*. Seattle, WA: The Mountaineers, 1998.

Burnie, David, and Don E. Wilson, eds. *Animal*. New York: DK Publishing, 2001.

Calhoun, Joshua, et al. "The *Outside* Adventure Atlas." *Outside*, October 2002: 39–42.

Cameron, Ian. *Mountains of the Gods*. New York: Facts on File, 1984.

Casewit, Curtis W. *The Mountain World*. New York: Random House, 1976.

Chamoux, Benoît. *Montagnes de l'Esprit*. Paris: Robert Laffont, 1989.

Child, Greg. *Climbing: The Complete Reference*. New York: Facts on File, 1995.

Chisholm, Craig. *Hawaiian Hiking Trails*. Beaverton, OR: Touchstone, 1975.

Chouinard, Yvon. *Climbing Ice*. San Francisco: Sierra Club Books, 1978.

Clark, Ronald. *The Early Alpine Guides*. New York: Scribner, 1950.

Cleare, John. *Mountains of the World*. San Diego, CA: Thunder Bay Press, 1997.

——. *The World Guide to Mountains and Mountaineering*. New York: Mayflower Books, 1979.

Cliffhanger. Videocassette. TriStar Pictures, 1993.

The Climb. Dir. Donald Shebib. Videocassette. Wacho Productions, 1988.

Collins, Henry Hill, Jr., assembler. *Harper & Row's Complete Field Guide to North American Wildlife: Eastern Edition*. New York: Harper & Row, 1981.

Collomb, R. G. *A Dictionary of Mountaineering*. New York: Philosophical Library, 1958.

Cook, Charles. *The Essential Guide to Cross-Country Skiing and Snowshoeing in the United States*. New York: Henry Holt, 1997.

Corbett, James Edward. *Man-Eaters of Kumaon*. New York: Oxford, 1946.

Costello, David F. *The Mountain World*. New York: Thomas Y. Crowell, 1975.

Cox, Steven M., and Kris Fulsaas. *Mountaineering: The Freedom of the Hills*. 7th ed. Seattle, WA: The Mountaineers, 2003.

Culver, David C. and Willaim B. White, eds. *Encyclopedia of Caves*. Boston: Elsevier, 2005.

Curran, Jim. *K2: Triumph and Tragedy*. Boston: Houghton Mifflin, 1987.

da Silva, Rachel, ed. *Leading Out: Women Climbers Reaching for the Top*. Seattle, WA: Seal Press, 1992.

Darvill, Fred T., Jr. *Mountaineering Medicine: A Wilderness Medical Guide*. Berkeley, CA: Wilderness Press, 1990.

"Devastated by a Glacier." *New York Times*, September 24, 2002: A1.

Edrinn, Roger. *Colorado Fourteeners: The 54 Highest Peaks*. Englewood, CO: Westcliff, 1990.

Egan, Timothy. "Courting Disaster, in Search of a Snowy Rush." *New York Times,* February 14, 2003: A1, A28.

Einstein, Herbert H. "Saint Bernard Passes." *The World Book Encyclopedia*, 1998 ed.

Eisenberg, Anne. "On the Slopes, High-Tech Sensors Probe for an Avalanche." *New York Times,* March 6, 2003: E5.

Ellsworth, Allan J., Eric F. Meyer, and Eric B. Larson. "Acetazolamide or Dexamethasone Use versus Placebo to Prevent Acute Mountain Sickness on Mount Rainier." *Western Journal of Medicine* 154, no. 3 (March 1991): 289ff.

Everest: The Death Zone (DVD). Boston: NOVA Videos, 1999.

Everest: The Death Zone. Dir. David Breashears. Narr. Jodie Foster. Videocassette. Boston: WGBH, 1998.

Fairley, Bruce. *A Guide to Climbing and Hiking in Southwestern British Columbia*. Soules, West Vancouver, BC: Gordon Book Publishers, Ltd., 2000.

Faus, Agustín. *Diccionario de la montaña*. Barcelona: Editorial Juventud, 1963.

First Ascent. Dirs. Robert Carmichael and Greg Lowe. Videocassette. Pyramid Films, 1982.

Fjeldså, Jon, and Niels Krabbe. *Birds of the High Andes*. Copenhagen: Zoological Museum, University of Copenhagen, 1990.

Fleming, Fergus. *Killing Dragons: The Conquest of the Alps*. New York: Grove, 2000.

Forgey, William W. *Wilderness Medicine: Beyond First Aid*. 5th ed. Guilford, CT: Globe Pequot Press, 2000.

Freedman, Lewis. *Dangerous Steps*. Harrisburg, PA: Stackpole, 1990.

Freeman, McGillivary. *Everest* (DVD). Burbank, CA: IMAX Miramax DVD Buena Vista Home Entertainment, 1999.

Frison-Roche, Roger. *First on the Rope*. Trans. Janet Adam Smith. New York: Prentice Hall, 1950.

———. *Les Montagnes de la Terre*. 2 vols. Paris: Flammarion, 1964.

Fyffe, Allen, and Iain Peter. *The Handbook of Climbing*. London: Pelham Books, 1990.

Gammelgaard, Lene. *Climbing High*. New York: HarperCollins, 1996.

Gary, Margaret, et al., eds. *Glossary of Geology*. Washington, DC: American Geological Institute, 1974.

Gautrat, Jacques. *Dictionnaire de la Montagne*. [Paris:] Éditions du Seuil, 1970.

Gerrard, John. *Mountain Environments: An Examination of the Physical Geography of Mountains*. Cambridge, MA: MIT Press, 1990.

Green, Randall, ed. *The Rock Climber's Guide to Montana*. Helena, MT: Falcon, 1995.

Hackett, Peter H. *Mountain Sickness: Prevention, Recognition, and Treatment*. New York: American Alpine Club, 1980.

Hamblin, W. Kenneth, and Eric H. Christiansen. *Earth's Dynamic Systems*. 9th ed. Upper Saddle River, NJ: Prentice Hall, 2001.

Harris, Ann G., et al. *Geology of National Parks*. 5th ed. Dubuque, IA: Kendall/Hunt, 1997.

Hemmleb, Jochen, et al. *Ghosts of Everest: The Search for Mallory and Irvine*. Seattle, WA: The Mountaineers, 1999.

Herrero, Stephen. *Bear Attacks: Their Causes and Avoidance*. New York: Lyons, 1985.

Herzog, Maurice. *Annapurna*. New York: Lyons, 1997.

Hiebeler, Toni. *Himalaya and Karakoram*. Zurich: Editions Silva, 1980.

———. *Les Alpes*. Paris: Bibliothèque des Arts, 1976.

———. *Montagnes de Notre Terre*. Paris: Arthaud, 1974.

Hill, Lynn. *Climbing Free*. New York: Norton, 2002.

Hillary, Edmund. *High Adventure*. New York: Dutton, 1955.

———, and Peter Hillary. *Ascent—Two Lives Explored: The Autobiographies of Sir Edmund and Peter Hillary*. Garden City, NY: Doubleday, 1984.

Holmes, Don W. *Highpoints of the United States: A Guide to the Fifty State Summits*. 2nd ed. Salt Lake City: University of Utah Press, 2000.

home.maine.rr.com/snowbird/lingo.htm.

Houston, Charles. *High Altitude Illness and Wellness*. Merrillville, IN: ICS, 1993.

Houston Charles S., et al. *K2: The Savage Mountain*. New York: Lyons Press, 2000.

Hultgren, Herbert N. *High Altitude Medicine*. Stanford, CA: Hultgren Publications, 1997.

Huxley, Anthony, ed. *Standard Encyclopedia of the World's Mountains*. New York: Putnam, 1962.

Irwin, Bill, et al. *Blind Courage*. Waco, TX: WRS Group, 1992.

*Jag Klarede Det/*I Made It. Prod. Frederick Blomquist. Videocassette. 1996.

Jenkins, McKay. *The White Death: Tragedy and Heroism in an Avalanche Zone*. New York: Anchor, 1993.

Jerome, John. *On Mountains: Thinking about Terrain*. New York: McGraw-Hill, 1978.

Johnsgard, Paul A. *Birds of the Rocky Mountains*. Boulder: Colorado Associated University Press, 1986.

Jouty, Sylvain, and Hubert Odier. *Dictionnaire de la Montagne*. Paris: Arthaud, 1999.

Kasahara, Junzo. "Tides, Earthquakes, and Volcanoes." *Science*, July 19, 2002: 348–49.

Katz, Ephraim. *The Film Encyclopedia*. (13th ed.) New York: HarperCollins, 1998.

Kelsey, Joe. *Climbing and Hiking in the Wind River Mountains*. Guilford, CT: Falcon, 1994.

———. *Wyoming's Wind River Range*. Helena, MT: American Geographic, 1988.

Kelsey, Michael R. *Climbers and Hikers Guide to the World's Mountains*. 4th ed. Provo, UT: Kelsey Publishing, 2001.

Kirk, Ruth. *Snow*. Seattle: University of Washington Press, 1998.

Kocour, Ruth Ann, and Michael Hodgson. *Facing the Extreme*. New York: St. Martin's, 1998.

Körner, Christian. *Alpine Plant Life: Functional Plant Ecology of High Mountain Ecosystems*. Berlin: Springer, 1999.

Krakauer, Jon. *Into Thin Air*. New York: Villard, 1997.

Kropp, Göran. *Ultimate High: My Solo Ascent of Everest*. New York: Discovery Books, 1999.

Kwiatkowski, Gerhard. *"Schlag nach!" für Wanderer und Bergsteiger*. Mannheim: Bibliographisches Institiut, Meyers Lexikonverlag, 1976.

Labande, François. *La Chaîne du Mont Blanc, Guide Vallot*. 2 vols. Paris: Arthaud, 1987.

Lane, Ferdinand C. *The Story of Mountains*. Garden City, NY: Doubleday, 1951.

Lansing, Alfred. *Endurance: Shackleton's Incredible Voyage*. New York: Carroll and Graff, 1959.

Le Grand Livre des Montagnes. d'Aurèlio Garobbio Paris: Fernand Nathan, 1976.

Legends of American Skiing, 1849–1940. Dir. Richard W. Moulton. Videocassette. Killington Video Productions, 1985.

Leopold, Donald J., William C. McComb, and Robert N. Muller. *Trees of the Central Hardwood Forests of North America*. Portland, OR: Timber Press, 1998.

Litsky, Frank. "Dick Durrance, 89, Ski Racer." *New York Times*, June 16, 2004: C15.

Lourcelles, Jacques. *Dictionnaire des Films*. Paris: Laffont, 1992.

Lutz, Thomas E. "Observatory." *World Book Encyclopedia*, 1998 ed.

MacFarlane, Robert. *Mountains of the Mind*. New York: Pantheon, 2003.

Madigan, Nick. "5-Year-Old's Survival Tale of 10 Days Alone, Her Mother Dead." *New York Times*, April 15, 2004: A16.

Mann, Thomas. *The Magic Mountain*. Trans. H. T. Lowe-Porter. New York: Alfred Knopf, 1953.

Matthiessen, Peter. *The Snow Leopard*. New York: Viking, 1978.

McClung, David, and Peter Schaerer. *The Avalanche Handbook*. Seattle, WA: The Mountaineers, 1993.

McNeil, Donald G., Jr. "What Makes a Glacier Go? Scientists Look Inside." *New York Times*, May 28, 2002: D1, D4.

Mergen, Bernard. *Snow in America*. Washington, DC: Smithsonian, 1997.

Messner, Reinhold. *All 14 Eight-Thousanders*. Trans. Audrey Salkeld. Seattle, WA: The Mountaineers, 1999.

———. *Bergvölker: Bilder und Begegnungen*. Munich: BLV, 2001.

———. *Everest: Expedition to the Ultimate*. Trans. Audrey Salkeld. New York: Oxford University Press, 1979.

———. *My Quest for the Yeti*. New York: St. Martin's, 2000.

———, and A Gogna. *K2*. Paris: Arthaud, 1980.

Milne, Lorus J., Margery Milne, et al. *The Mountains*. New York: *Time*, 1962.

Morrison, Tony. *Les Andes*. Amsterdam: Editions Time-Life, 1975.

Morrow, Patrick. *Beyond Everest: Quest for the Seven Summits*. Camden House, 1986.

Mountain Light. Author Galen Rowell. Videocassette. Eastman Kodak, 1988.

The Mountain Rainier. Prod. Al Stetson. Videocassette. King Broadcasting, 1979.

Mummery, A. F. *My Climbs in the Alps and Caucasus*. New York: Scribner, 1895.

Munz, Philip A. *Introduction to California Mountain Flowers*. (Revised ed.) Berkeley: University of California, 2003.

Neate, Jill. *Mountaineering Literature: A Bibliography of Materials Published in English*. Seattle, WA: Mountain Books, 1986.

"New Kind of Dam Rises in Switzerland: To Hold Back the Land." *New York Times*, December 13, 2002: A13.

Newby, Eric. *Great Ascents: A Narrative History of Mountaineering*. New York: Viking, 1977.

———. *A Short Walk in the Hindu Kush*. New York: Penguin, 1986.

Nicholls, Graham. *Alpine Plants of North America*. Portland, OR: Timber Press, 2002.

Norgay, Jamling Tenzing. *Touching My Father's Soul*. San Francisco: HarperSanFrancisco, 2001.

Norgay, Tenzing, and James Ramsey Ullman. *Tiger of the Snows*. New York: Putnam, 1955.

Noyce, Wilfrid, and Ian McMorrin, eds. *World Atlas of Mountaineering*. N.p.: Macmillan, 1970.

Obee, Bruce, Tony Owen, and Russ Heinl. *Over Beautiful British Columbia: An Aerial Adventure*. Vancouver: Beautiful British Columbia, 1999.

Ollier, Cliff, and Colin Pain. *The Origin of Mountains*. London: Routledge, 2000.

Olsen, Jack. *The Climb Up to Hell*. New York: St. Martin's, 1998.

Ortenburger, Leigh, and Reynold Jackson. *A Climber's Guide to the Teton Range*. Seattle, WA: The Mountaineers, 1996.

Ortner, Sherry B. *Life and Death on Mt. Everest: Sherpas and Himalayan Mountaineering*. Princeton, NJ: Princeton University Press, 1999.

Pfetzer, Mark, and Jack Galvin. *Within Reach: My Everest Story*. New York: Puffin, 1998.

Polunin, Oleg, and Adam Stainton. *Concise Flowers of the Himalaya*. Delhi: Oxford University Press, 1987.

Potterfield, Peter. *In the Zone: Epic Survival Stories from the Mountaineering World*. Seattle, WA: The Mountaineers, 1996.

Price, Larry W. *Mountains and Man: A Study of Process and Environment*. Berkeley: University of California Press, 1981.

Pyatt, Edward. *The Guinness Book of Mountains and Mountaineering: Facts and Feats*. Enfield, Middlesex, England: Guinness Superlatives, 1980.

Rand-McNally Universal World Atlas. Chicago: Rand-McNally, 1987.

Randall, Glenn. *Mount McKinley: Climber's Handbook*. Evergreen, CO: Chockstone, 1992.

Rao, Nina. *Himalayan Desert*. New Delhi: Roli Books/Lustre Press, 1999.

Rawicz, Slavomir. *The Long Walk*. Guilford, CT: Globe Pequot Press, 1997. New York: Lyons, 1997.

Rébuffat, Gaston. *Le Massif du Mont Blanc: Les 100 Plus Belles Courses*. Paris: Denoël, 1973.

———. *Les Horizons Gagnés*. Paris: Denoël, 1975.

———. *Starlight and Storm: The Ascent of Six Great North Faces of the Alps*. London: Kay and Ward, 1968.

"Recognition Sought for Sierra Icon Who Made History in '29." *USA Today*, April 13, 2004: 21A.

Reider, Richard G. "Cordillera." *The World Book Encyclopedia*, 1998 ed.

Rhoads, Christopher. "High Drama: 30-Year-Old Mystery Roils Climbing World." *Wall Street Journal*, December 10, 2003: A1, A12.

Richard, Colette. *Climbing Blind*. London: Hodder and Stoughton, 1966.

Ritchie, David, and Alexander E. Gates. *Encyclopedia of Earthquakes and Volcanoes*. New ed. New York: Facts on File, 2001.

Roach, Gerry. *Colorado's Fourteeners: From Hikes to Climbs*. Golden, CO: Fulcrum, 1999.

Robbins, Royal. *Advanced Rockcraft*. [Glendale, CA:] La Siesta Press, 1973.

Roberts, David. *Escape from Lucania: An Epic Story of Survival*. New York: Simon & Schuster, 2002.

———. "Foreword." In Lionel Terray, *Conquistadors of the Useless*. Trans. Geoffrey Sutton. Seattle, WA: The Mountaineers, 2001.

Roskelly, John. *Nanda Devi: The Tragic Expedition*. New York: Avon, 1987.

Roth, Arthur. *Eiger: Wall of Death*. New York: Norton, 1982.

Royal Geographical Society. *Everest: Summit of Achievement*. New York: Simon & Schuster, 2003.

Sachs, Harvey. *Toscanini*. Paris: van den Velde, 1978.

Salkeld, Audrey, ed. *The Climber's Handbook*. San Francisco: Sierra Club Books, 1987.

Schneider, Bill. *The Hiker's Guide to Montana*. Helena, MT: Falcon, 1994.

———. *Hiking the Beartooths*. Helena, MT: Falcon, 1995.

Schneider, Stephen H., ed. *Encyclopedia of Climate and Weather*. 2 vols. New York: Oxford University Press, 1996.

Scofield, Bruce. *High Peaks of the Northeast*. North Amherst, MA: New England Cartographics, 1994.

Secor, R. J. *The High Sierra: Peaks, Passes, and Trails*. Seattle, WA: The Mountaineers, 1992.

———. *Mexico's Volcanoes: A Climbing Guide*. Seattle, WA: The Mountaineers, 1993.

Sedeen, Margaret, ed. *Mountain Worlds*. Washington, DC: National Geographic Society, 1988.

Seigneur, Yannick. *A la Conquête de l'Impossible*. Paris: Flammarion, 1976.

Sella, Vittorio. *Summit*. New York: Aperture, 1999.

Selley, Richard C., L. Robin M. Cocks, and Ian R. Plimer, eds. *Encyclopedia of Geology*. 5 vols. Amsterdam: Elsevier, 2005.

Selters, Andy, and Michael Zanger. *The Mt. Shasta Book*. Berkeley, CA: Wilderness, 1989.

Shelton, Peter. *Climb to Conquer: The Untold Story of World War II's 10th Mountain Division Ski Troops*. New York: Scribner, 2003.

Sigurdsson, Haraldur, ed. *Encyclopedia of Volcanoes*. San Diego, CA: Academic Press, 2000.

Silent Roar: Searching for the Snow Leopard. *(Nature.)* (Videocassette). Executive Prod. Fred Kaufmann. New York: WNET, et al., 2005.

Simkin, Tom, and Lee Siebert. *Volcanoes of the World*. 2nd ed. Tucson, AZ: Geoscience Press; Washington, DC: Smithsonian Institution, 1994.

Simpson, Joe. *Dark Shadows Falling*. Seattle, WA: The Mountaineers, 1997.

———. *Touching the Void*. New York: HarperCollins, 1988.

Smith, Jacqueline, ed. *The Facts on File Dictionary of Weather and Climate*. New York: Facts on File, 2001.

Smithey, William. *American Mountains and Canyons*. New York: Gallery Books, 1990.

Smythe, Frank. *Behold the Mountains: Climbing with a Color Camera*. New York: Chanticleer, 1949.

Sorrell, Charles A. *Minerals of the World*. New York: Golden Press, 1973.

Stephen, Sir Leslie. *The Playground of Europe*. New York: Putnam, 1909.

Sterling, E. M. *Trips and Trails, 1: Family Camps, Short Hikes and View Roads around the North Cascades*. Seattle, WA: The Mountaineers, 1986.

——. *Trips and Trails, 2: Family Camps, Short Hikes and View Roads in the Olympics, Mt. Rainier and South Cascades*. Seattle, WA: The Mountaineers, 1987.

Sullivan, Michael. *The Cave Temples of Maichishan*. Berkeley: University of California Press, 1969.

"Super Seven Special." *Climbing*, 2002–2003, entire issue.

Surviving Everest. Prod. Liesel Clark. Videocassette. WGBH and National Geographic, 2003.

Syme, David. "Position Paper: On-site Treatment of Frostbite for Mountaineers." *High Altitude Medicine & Biology*, no. 3 2002: 297–98.

Terray, Lionel. *Conquistadors of the Useless*. Trans. Geoffrey Sutton. Seattle, WA: The Mountaineers, 2001.

Thapar, Valmik. *Land of the Tiger*. Berkeley: University of California Press, 1997.

Thesiger, Wilfred. *The Last Nomad*. New York: Dutton, 1980.

Thomas, Lowell. *Lowell Thomas's Book of the High Mountains*. New York: Julian Messner, 1964.

Tobias, Michael. "Dialectical Dreaming: The Western Perception of Mountain People." In *Mountain People*, 183–200. Norman: University of Oklahoma, 1986.

Tranchefort, Françoise-René. *Guide de la Musique Symphonique*. Paris: Fayard, 1986.

The Treasure of the Sierra Madre. Videocassette. MGM/UA Home Video, 1992.

Tulard, Jean. *Guide des Films*. Paris: Laffont, 1990.

Udvardy, Miklos D. F., and John Farrand, Jr., revisor. *National Audubon Society Field Guide to North American Birds: Western Region*. 2nd ed. New York: Knopf, 1994.

Ullman, James Ramsey. *The Age of Mountaineering*. Philadelphia: Lippincott, 1954.

——. *Americans on Everest*. Philadelphia: Lippincott, 1964.

——. *The White Tower*. Philadelphia: Lippincott, 1945.

"Ulrich Inderbinen, 103, Guide in the Alps for Seven Decades." *New York Times*, June 17, 2004: A27.

Ultimate Guide: Ice Man Video. Dir. Brandon Quilici. Videocassette. Bethesda, MD: Discovery Communications, 2001.

Ungnade, Herbert E. *Guide to the New Mexico Mountains*. Albuquerque: University of New Mexico, 1965.

Unsworth, Walt. *Hold the Heights: The Foundations of Mountaineering*. Seattle, WA: The Mountaineers, 1994.

——, comp. *Encyclopaedia of Mountaineering*. New York: St. Martin's, 1975.

Vertical Limit. Videocassette. Columbia Pictures, 2000.

Vogel, Carole Garbuny. *Science Explorer: Inside Earth*. Upper Saddle River, NJ: Prentice Hall, 2000.

Washburn, Brad. *Mount McKinley's West Buttress: The First Ascent*. Williston, VT: Top of the World Press, 2003.

Waterman, Jonathan. *In the Shadow of Denali*. New York: Lyons, 1994.

Waterman, Laura, and Guy Waterman. *Wilderness Ethics*. Woodstock, VT: Countryman Press, 1993.

Weathers, Beck, with Stephen Michaud. *Left for Dead: My Journey Home from Everest*. New York: Villard, 2000.

Webster, Ed. *Snow in the Kingdom: My Storm Years on Everest*. Eldorado Springs, CO: Mountain Imagery, 2000.

Weihenmayer, Erik. *Touch the Top of the World*. New York: Dutton, 2001.

Weiss, Rudolf. *Mountaineering Dictionary: English, French, German, Italian*. New York: French & European Publications, 1989.

West, John B. *Everest: The Testing Place*. New York: McGraw-Hill, 1985.

Wharton, Thomas. *Icefields*. New York: Washington Square Press, 1995.

Whiteman, C. David. *Mountain Meteorology: Fundamentals and Applications*. New York: Oxford University Press, 2000.

Whymper, Edward. *Scrambles amongst the Alps in the Years 1860–69*. 1871. Reprint. New York: Dover, 1996.

Wickwire, Jim, and Dorothy Bullitt. *Addicted to Danger*. New York: Pocket Books, 1998.

Wilkerson, James A., ed. *Medicine for Mountaineering and Other Wilderness Activities*. 5th ed. Seattle, WA: The Mountaineers, 2001.

Williams, J. G. *A Field Guide to the Birds of East and Central Africa*. Boston: Houghton Mifflin, 1964.

Willis, Clint, ed. *Epic: Stories of Survival from the World's Highest Peaks*. New York: Thunder's Mouth, 1997.

Winchester, Simon. *Krakatoa: The Day the World Exploded, August 27, 1883*. New York: HarperCollins, 2003.

Winger, Charlie, and Diane Winger. *Highpoint Adventures: The Complete Guide to the 50 State Highpoints*. Golden: The Colorado Mountain Club Press, 2002.

Winnett, Thomas. *High Sierra Hiking Guide: Mt. Whitney*. Berkeley, CA: Wilderness Press,1978.

Zimmermann, George. *The Complete Guide to Cabins and Lodges in America's State and National Parks*. Boston: Little, Brown, 1985.

Zorilla, Juan José. *Enciclopedia de la Montaña*. [Madrid:] Desnivel Ediciones, 2000.

Zumwalt, Paul L. *Fifty State Summits: Guide with Maps to State Highpoints*. 4th ed. Vancouver, WA: Jack Grauer, 1998.

Zurbriggen, Matthias. *From the Alps to the Andes: Being the Autobiography of a Mountain Guide*. London: T. F. Unwin, 1899.

INDEX

ABOUT THE AUTHORS

Frederic V. Hartemann, Ph.D., is a physicist at Lawrence Livermore National Laboratory. He has climbed extensively in the Alps, Rockies, Cascades, and Sierras and summitted on well over 50 peaks between 13,000 and 17,500 feet. He has traveled to the mountains of Mexico, Alaska, Japan, Austria, France, Italy, Switzerland, British Columbia, Alberta, the Yukon, Hawaii, and 43 states.

Robert Hauptman, Ph.D., is a professor at St. Cloud State University, where he works as a reference librarian and teaches undergraduate and graduate courses in a variety of disciplines. He does 20 or more climbs each season. He has reached 44 U.S. highpoints.